# Beyond observation

Manchester University Press

## ANTHROPOLOGY, CREATIVE PRACTICE AND ETHNOGRAPHY (ACE)

SERIES EDITORS: FAYE GINSBURG, PAUL HENLEY, ANDREW IRVING
AND SARAH PINK

Anthropology, Creative Practice and Ethnography provides a forum for authors and practitioners from across the digital humanities and social sciences to explore the rapidly developing opportunities offered by visual, acoustic and textual media for generating ethnographic understandings of social, cultural and political life. It addresses both established and experimental fields of visual anthropology, including film, photography, sensory and acoustic ethnography, ethnomusicology, graphic anthropology, digital media and other creative modes of representation. The series features works that engage in the theoretical and practical interrogation of the possibilities and constraints of audiovisual media in ethnographic research, while simultaneously offering a critical analysis of the cultural, political and historical contexts.

*Previously published*

David MacDougall, *The looking machine: Essays on cinema, anthropology and documentary filmmaking*
Christian Suhr, *Descending with angels: Islamic exorcism and psychiatry – A film monograph*

In association with the Granada Centre for Visual Anthropology

# Beyond observation

## A history of authorship in ethnographic film

PAUL HENLEY

Manchester University Press

Published by Manchester University Press
Altrincham Street, Manchester M1 7JA

www.manchesteruniversitypress.co.uk

British Library Cataloguing-in-Publication Data
A catalogue record for this book is available from the British Library

ISBN    978 1 5261 3134 8    hardback

ISBN    978 1 5261 3136 2    paperback

ISBN    978 1 5261 4729 5    open access

First published 2020

The publisher has no responsibility for the persistence or accuracy of URLs for any external or third-party internet websites referred to in this book, and does not guarantee that any content on such websites is, or will remain, accurate or appropriate.

Typeset
by Toppan Best-set Premedia Limited

To Colin Young and Herb di Gioia, film-maker-makers

# Contents

Contents

# Figures

# Acknowledgements

Tнis book has grown directly out of the thirty years that I have taught on the various postgraduate programmes offered through the Granada Centre for Visual Anthropology at the University of Manchester. Most of the chapters began life as notes for a series of lectures on the history of ethnographic film that I gave over many years and in a variety of guises. Although they have undergone many transformations since, my primary intended audience remains those who are approaching ethnographic film-making for the first time, whether it be as students, as teachers of anthropology or any other academic discipline that involves ethnography, or as film-makers working in other documentary genres who may be interested to discover more about ethnographic film.

While I hope to have been able to impart some elements of wisdom to the many students who have passed through our programmes, I am certain that I have learned a great deal from them, so my first expression of gratitude here is to them. I am also particularly indebted to David Turton, then Senior Lecturer in the Department of Social Anthropology at Manchester who was responsible, together with Marilyn Strathern, head of the Department, and Leslie Woodhead, the distinguished documentary director, then of Granada Television, not only for the conception and crea-tion of the Granada Centre in 1987 but also for appointing me as its first Director. I am also grateful to the many other anthropologist colleagues at Manchester, in the broader department as well as in the Granada Centre itself, who have made the Centre such a stimulating and unusual place to work over the past thirty years.

I would probably never have been invited to teach at Manchester had it not been for the time that I had spent at the National Film and Television School (NFTS) at Beaconsfield, in the years 1984–87, as a beneficiary of the Ethnographic Film Training programme, a project conceived and funded by the Royal Anthropological Institute (RAI) with the aid of a grant from the Leverhulme Trust. Much more recently, during 2014–17, the Trust again provided me with inestimably valuable support in appointing me to a Major

Research Fellowship dedicated to an investigation of early ethnographic film. The early chapters of this book represent the first fruits of that period of research.

The people who made the RAI-Leverhulme programme at the NFTS happen in practice were Colin Young, then the Director of the School, and Herb di Gioia, head of the Documentary department. Colin and Herb, both individually and in unison, have inspired the careers of a great many film-makers, and not just in documentary. Their pedagogical styles were rather similar: an unusual combination of being very laid back and informal at a personal level, with being very stern and disciplined when it came to instructing us in how to make films. Why they should have taken such a particular interest in ethnographic film-making when neither had a background in anthropology, nor in any other social science, remains something of a mystery. But the fact remains that they did so, and with great passion, and through the four of us who went through the RAI-Leverhulme programme their ideas and attitudes towards the making of ethnographic film have been passed on to many hundreds of students of anthropology. In acknowledgement of this great debt, both personal and collective, I dedicate this book jointly to them.

I would also like to acknowledge here how much I have benefitted over the years from the advice of David MacDougall, who also first learned his trade as a film-maker under the watchful eye of Colin Young. David has been most generous in commenting with characteristic care and acuity on many chapters of this book. I would also like to thank the various other friends and colleagues who have read and commented on drafts of chapters that are particularly related to their own work. Here I am especially grateful to Phil Agland, the late Asen Balikci, Hugh Brody, Lucien Castaing-Taylor, Pip Deveson, Ian Dunlop, Lorenzo Ferrarini, Carlos Flores, Faye Ginsburg, Aaron Glass, Paul Hockings, Gary Kildea, Melissa Llewelyn-Davies, Brian Moser, Johannes Sjöberg and Peter Whiteley. I apologize in advance for not always following their suggestions!

A great many others have contributed directly or indirectly to the development of the ideas that I present in this book. It is always invidious to offer a list of names, since it is only too easy to miss someone out, particularly when referring to a period as long as the thirty years that this book has been in gestation. So I shall with great restraint restrict myself to mentioning only Peter Crawford and Paul Stoller who acted as the supposedly anonymous but generously self-revealing readers of the manuscript for Manchester University Press. Their comments were extremely helpful in the preparation of the final manuscript.

This book features almost a hundred figures, the great majority of which are based on 'screen grabs' that are used here on a 'fair dealing' basis. However, I would like to register here my gratitude to a number of people for their generosity in allowing me to use the remaining images. Among individuals, I am particularly indebted to the magnificent cinematographer, Phil Agland, one of whose images adorns the cover of this book, whilst others are to be found in Chapters 12 and 13. Here too David MacDougall, equally accomplished as an image-maker, has made a major contribution to this book, generously providing images scattered through Chapters 5 and 14, while Jocelyne Rouch has shown a similar generosity in allowing me to use a number of her late husband's images in Chapter 8. I am also very grateful to Carlos Flores, my son Richard Henley, Lisa Silcock, Andy Jillings and Éric Brochu for allowing me to use their images in Chapters 7, 10, 12, 13 and 16 respectively.

Among organisations, Documentary Educational Resources (DER) of Cambridge, Massachusetts has been especially generous in providing me with images. I am particularly grateful to Alice Apley, the Executive Director for authorising this use and to Frank Aveni, the Director of Design and Media, for the care and diligence with which he sought out the best quality versions of the images that I requested. I would also like to thank the Ngaanyatjarra and Yolgnu community associations for securing permission from relatives to use the images of Aboriginal people that appear in the relevant figures of Chapters 3 and 6.

Meanwhile, in the later stages of production, Tom Dark, social sciences editor at MUP, has shown Job-like patience with the many missed deadlines and word-length overruns that have characterised the preparation of this manuscript. I am indebted both to him and to his various colleagues at MUP who have worked on the book, including particularly Rob Byron and Dee Devine, as well as to the freelance copyeditor, Doreen Kruger. I thank them all for their very valuable contributions. All translations in this book are my own.

Finally, I would reserve the most heart-felt thanks of all to my wife Olivia who has shown an even greater patience throughout the many years that I have been writing this book as well as bringing her proverbial eye for detail to the revision of the final text.

# General introduction: authorship, praxis, observation, ethnography

THIS book offers a historical account of a genre of cinema that combines two distinct practices: the craft of non-fiction film-making, and ethnography, a particular approach to carrying out and representing social research. It is an account that straddles a period of approximately 120 years, from the middle of last decade of the nineteenth century, when the moving image camera was a primitive instrument that was troublesome and expensive to use, and which was therefore reserved to professional elites, mostly in the global North, to the middle of the second decade of the twenty-first century, by which time digital technology had brought the possibility of film-making within the range of both the technical capabilities and budgets of many millions of people the world over. During this period, there have also been major changes both in the conception of ethnography within academia and in the political constitution of the wider world. All of these factors have impacted on the development and diversification of the genre of ethnographic film, as I seek to show.

This book has grown out of the course on the history of ethnographic film that I taught at the University of Manchester for many years, and it retains a tone of address aimed, if not at students exactly, at least at those who are relatively new both to non-fiction film-making and to ethnography. Although it is a substantial book, I make no claim that it is comprehensive: it is *a* history rather than *the* history of ethnographic film authorship. Indeed, it is only a very partial history in that it is primarily concerned with English-language films, supplemented by a few forays elsewhere, notably into the work of Jean Rouch, the leading French ethnographic film-maker who is a towering figure in the field, and about whose film-making I have already written at length in an earlier book.[1] I am only too aware that many traditions of ethnographic film-making have been developed in other languages, not only within Europe but also in other continents, notably Latin America, China and Japan. Even with regard to English-language films, I have had to be highly selective, and there are many film-makers whose works I would have liked to include, had it not been for the fact

1

that this would have tried the publisher's patience even more than it has already been tested.

In approaching this history, I am particularly concerned with how ethnographic films are actually made, not just in terms of the techniques and technologies involved, but more generally, in terms of the whole process whereby an idea is turned into a finished ethnographic film. Again, the origins of the book in the lecture course that I taught at Manchester are relevant here: that course formed part of a Masters programme in which we instructed students in practical film-making and, as part of this instruction, in time-honoured fashion, we encouraged them to look at the work of the Old Masters of ethnographic film history (and they were mostly 'masters', regrettably), not merely to critique their work as examples of how the West construed its Other (though we encouraged that too), but also in a more pragmatic way, to examine their films as artefacts, to look for the seams, to examine how they achieved their effects, all with a view to assessing these films as models or anti-models for their own work. My hope is that this book could serve a similar purpose for any novice ethnographic film-makers who come to read it.

There is a tendency to write or talk about the history of ethnographic film in terms of visual metaphors, that is, as if it were a succession of 'visions', 'views', 'looks' or 'gazes', even 'glances', emanating from 'eyes' that have been diversely construed as innocent, imperial, Third or, more locally, as Nordic, and varying in accordance with a range of different 'visualisations' or 'ways of seeing'. This is, of course, hardly surprising, given the importance of visual technology in the making of ethnographic films. It is also undoubtedly the case that the visual practice of 'observation', in a range of different modes, has been a crucial component in the making of ethnographic films over the years. Equally certain is the fact that to make an effective and engaging ethnographic film requires both a developed visual sensibility and an informed understanding of film as a medium of visual communication, not to mention considerable visual skills. But, for all this, I would contend that there is much more to ethnographic film-making than matters relating to the visual. Rather than thinking of the history of ethnographic film-making as a succession of 'ways of seeing', I suggest that it is more productive to think of it as a succession of 'ways of doing', in which observation, in a variety of guises, is but one component, even if an important one.

In the course of this book, I shall seek to substantiate this proposition through the detailed consideration of a large number of particular examples. But as a first approximation, one can identify here, in a summary way, a number of key respects in which it is necessary to go beyond observation in the making of ethnographic films. First, and most obviously, an ethnographic film involves sounds as well images, listening as well as looking, or at least it has done so, certainly since the development of portable synchronous sound around 1960, and even before that too, given that ethnographic films have featured soundtracks of voice-over commentary and effects, music, even some isolated examples of synchronous dialogues, since at least as far back as the 1930s. Indeed, sound has been the 'secret sharer' for most of ethnographic film history, and one that has been all the more neglected since its effects are often undetected by 'audiences', who, in unwitting contradiction to the very etymology of the term by which one refers to them, are much more likely to think of themselves – and to be thought of by third parties – as 'viewers' or 'spectators' rather than 'hearers' of ethnographic film.

Second, the making of an ethnographic film requires a range of craft skills that amount to considerably more than the fortuitous mechanical operationalisation of an act of observation. Possibly the most significant of these skills and certainly one of the most difficult to acquire is not, as is commonly supposed, the operation of a moving image camera, but rather the ability to manage one of the most distinctive features of cinema, namely, the linear disclosure of a story or an argument about the world in a manner that is both coherent and engaging for an audience while at the same time remaining within the constraints of a time-based medium. Or, to put it more succinctly, the making of an ethnographic film, certainly one that aims to go beyond the merely descriptive, requires the skilful deployment of a filmic narrative.

A third way in which the making of an ethnographic film requires one to go beyond observation concerns the relationship between the film-maker and their subjects. As the leading ethnographic film-maker David MacDougall once remarked, 'No ethnographic film is merely a record of another society: it is always a record of a meeting between a film-maker and that society.'[2] The manner in which an ethnographic film-maker manages this relationship is a very important part of their 'way of doing' ethnographic film-making, and it is one that has ethical, even political implications, as well as epistemological and stylistic consequences for the films that they make.

Finally, an ethnographic film will normally involve more than observation in the sense that – although it is almost a tautology to say so – in order to be ethnographic in anything more than a descriptive sense, an ethnographic film requires an ethnographic analysis. It is impossible to state succinctly what form this analysis should take since it depends on precisely how one defines the much-debated term 'ethnographic'. This is an issue that I will address at some length below, when I will offer a definition of the term as I propose to use it in the course of this book.

As will become clear, in the course of this review of 120 years of ethnographic film-making, I advocate a very particular form of ethnographic film authorship based on a very particular conception of ethnography. This is a second sense in which this book could be considered no more than a partial historical account. In fact, the whole book should be regarded not as a dispassionate chronicle but rather a sustained argument in favour of a very particular approach to ethnographic film-making.

## AUTHORSHIP, PRAXIS, OBSERVATION

In pursuit of this argument, the book is divided into four parts. In the first, in the course of seven chapters, I offer an overview of (predominantly) English-language ethnographic film-making over the course of its first century, from the end of the nineteenth century to the end of the twentieth. Then, in the second part, I examine in greater detail the approach to ethnographic film-making of three key figures in that history: Jean Rouch, Robert Gardner and Colin Young. The third part also consists of three chapters, in which I discuss the remarkable phenomenon of ethnographic film made for British television that was at its peak between the late 1960s and the mid-1990s. Finally, in the last part, in a further three chapters, I consider a number of examples of English-language ethnographic film-making practice over the first fifteen years of the twenty-first century, and consider what promise these might hold for the future of the genre. The whole book is then rounded off with a brief Epilogue.

In the course of all four parts, I make recurrent use of two key terms, 'authorship' and 'praxis'. By means of the first of these, I intend to refer in a very straightforward way to the agency of an ethnographic film-maker in making their films. However, the exercise of this agency is normally anything but straightforward in the sense that it will invariably draw upon a whole series of ideas and beliefs about the world, a given set of methods and techniques, certain aesthetic preferences, a particular set of intellectual goals and ethical postures, as well as various more or less articulated political positions or epistemological presuppositions. Building upon my previous use of the term in my study of Jean Rouch, I refer to such loose assemblages of attributes typically associated with the exercise of ethnographic film authorship – be it by particular individuals or by identifiable groups of film-makers whose work shares a certain degree of common ground – as a 'praxis'. This could be considered a somewhat pretentious term, but it has the merit of being considerably more abbreviated than the phrase, 'way of doing ethnographic film-making', which I nevertheless use on occasion instead of 'praxis', if only to remind the reader of what I mean by this term. In an adjectival form, I render these two key terms respectively as 'authorial' and 'practical'. In the plural, 'praxis' becomes 'praxes'.

Another key term that is prominent in this book and obviously so as it is even in the title, is 'observation'. In fact, in discussions of ethnographic film, this term tends to be most commonly used in its adjectival form, 'observational'. But in either form, nominal or adjectival, it is a very slippery term, with a chameleon-like tendency to change its exact hue according to the context in which it is used.

On first principles, one could argue that all forms of film-making, even scripted feature film-making, are 'observational' in the sense that they involve looking in some form. But in this book, I use the term in a more restricted sense to refer to modes of film-making praxis in which film-makers do not seek to direct the subjects, but rather content themselves with filming the subjects as they go about their business according to their own agenda or whim. However, even when used in this restricted sense, 'observational cinema' covers a range of different praxes, depending on the nature of the relationship between observer and observed. At one extreme, there is a mode of ethnographic film-making in which the film-maker seeks to remain entirely detached from the subjects, observing them from afar, as if from a watch-tower. At the other, there is a highly embedded form of 'observational cinema', in which the film-maker films the subjects from within a close personal relationship.

The latter is the case, for example, with one of the most influential 'ways of doing' ethnographic film-making, which is identified in this book, with capitals, as 'Observational Cinema'. However, it is important to stress that as I use the terms, Observational Cinema and cinema that is observational are not necessarily the same thing. But in all cases, from the most detached to the most embedded forms of observational cinema, I argue that there is much more to these praxes than observation, so much so indeed in the case of Observational Cinema, that one could even consider it a misnomer. But this last is a matter that I shall leave for further discussion until Chapter 10, where I consider the praxis of Observational Cinema in detail.

One respect in which there is more than observation to all these various forms of observational cinema is that they all entail some degree of authorship. Indeed, it is a fundamental contention of this book that – as with any non-fiction film – authorship is a necessary and inevitable feature of the production of any ethnographic film, regardless of the praxis employed. Moreover, it is a feature that is present at every step along the way. Even the simple decision as to when to turn a camera on or off is an act of authorship. Deciding where to place the camera, how to frame a shot, who or what to film and how to film them, are all acts of authorship. Back in the edit suite, nowadays often over 90 per cent of the material shot – the 'rushes' as they are known – usually ends up, at least metaphorically, 'on the cutting room floor'. With every excision, as with every inclusion, an act of authorship is involved. But the aspect of ethnographic film-making in which authorship is most profoundly exercised, I would argue, is in the structuring of these rushes into a narrative, which is something that takes place whenever a film-maker wants to go beyond the merely descriptive.

In this process, the real world is no longer merely being copied, however incompletely or imperfectly. Rather, it is being actively recreated as the sequence of events recorded on location is carefully reordered, with the aim of imparting a particular meaning to the world represented while at the same time engaging an audience in that meaning.

This narrative structuring is something that in my view, in the ideal case, should take place over the course of the whole process of making an ethnographic film. Those who are unfamiliar with ethnographic film-making have a tendency to think of an ethnographic film as a device for communicating knowledge and understanding that has been arrived at previously, by some other means: in this perspective, an ethnographic researcher – a doctoral student, say – having conducted their fieldwork and written up the results, might then return to the field and make a film in order to be able to communicate those results in teaching or to more general audiences. But this is a very limited way of thinking of the potential of film-making as a means of ethnographic representation. Much more productive, and also more in tune with what generally happens in practice, is to think of the making of an ethnographic film as a process of discovery in itself, generating knowledge and understanding through all the various stages of the production.

Most experienced ethnographic film-makers, even if they do not start with anything so formal as a script, will begin to think about the narrative shaping of their material even before they set foot in the field, if only for the pragmatic reason that this will determine when they go, how long they stay and what particular sequences they will shoot when they get there. They will go on thinking about this narrative structure throughout the shoot, changing their ideas in response to what actually happens when they start to film. Later, in the edit suite, they will continue the process of shaping and reshaping the narrative as they engage with the rushes and discover within them connections and insights that they did not realise were there in the moment of shooting. On this matter, Jean Rouch liked to cite the exhortations contained in the 'Ciné-Eye Manifesto' written by the Polish-Russian Soviet film-maker, Dziga Vertov and first published in 1924: edit when you are preparing to shoot, edit while you are shooting and edit again when you are in the edit suite. I have often, in turn, cited this to my students as a guide to good practice.[3]

The final result of all the authorial processes involved in the making of any ethnographic film is a work that represents no more than a transformed fragment of the original material brought back from the shoot. This final film represents, in turn, no more than what David MacDougall has called the 'phantom traces' of the film-maker's original first-hand experience of the situation, events and people that are the subject matter of the film.[4] For all the beguiling mimetic capabilities of modern cameras, particularly when supplemented by the complex and subtle soundtracks that digital audio technology makes possible, one should never allow oneself to forget that a film is always an authored representation of reality, never a literal account of it.

It might appear to some readers that the fact that an ethnographic film is authored is so entirely self-evident that it hardly needs pointing out. Yet, as I describe in the first few chapters of this book, for most of the history of English-language ethnographic film-making, there has been a curious reluctance to come to terms with the inevitability of authorship in the making of ethnographic films. Indeed, there has been a tendency to see film authorship and ethnographic value as somehow locked into a zero-sum equation whereby the more that authorship is exercised, the less the ethnographic value of the work, and vice versa.

As a result of this suspicion of authorship, a variety of strategies have been adopted in order to try and avoid it, minimise it or even eliminate it. The specific reasons for seeking to avoid authorship have shifted around over time, in accordance with broader academic and extra-academic trends. So too have the strategies for avoiding it: initially, they amounted to little more than ignoring or hiding it; later, they were more likely to involve controlling for it, and later still, consigning it to the subjects of the film. An even more recent tendency has been to put all one's material up on the web and allow the audience to act, in effect, as the author as they navigate their way around it. But for reasons that I elaborate upon at length in the course of this book, I consider all these attempts to avoid authorship in the making of ethnographic films, however well-intentioned, to be misguided. Rather than seeking to avoid, sidestep or consign authorship to others, we should be focusing instead on developing modes of film authorship that are in tune with a conception of ethnographic practice that is appropriate to our time. But this begs the obvious question: what exactly *is* ethnography as it is presently practised?

## Defining ethnography, defining ethnographic film

Over the years, there have been various attempts to define ethnographic film, but these have often seemed to be more about keeping films out of the genre rather than embracing the full potential that the conjunction of ethnography and non-fiction film-making can offer. Some sort of working definition is clearly necessary, however, since otherwise 'ethnographic film' would be reduced to a sort of Humpty-Dumpty phrase that means whatever the speaker or writer wishes it to mean. But this definition, I suggest, should be more about identifying the centre of gravity of the genre rather than setting up some kind of embattled frontier with some films safely ensconced within it, while others are cast out as somehow undeserving. This is what I seek to do in the remainder of this Introduction.

Let us begin with the easy part, that is, the second word in the phrase. 'Film' was originally a reference to the strips of cellulose onto which images were imprinted in the early days of cinema at the end of the nineteenth century. But in this book I use the term to refer, in a generic way, to any ordered sequence of moving images and sounds regardless of the physical medium on which they have been recorded, be it film in its original sense, videotape, DVDs, memory cards, hard discs or mobile telephones. Today, most sequences of moving images and sounds made for ethnographic purposes are shot and edited using digital technology, so it could be argued that 'film' has become an anachronism. But I would argue that the term has manifestly long outgrown the original reference merely to its physical medium and has come to refer instead to the whole process of representation generally. It is in this sense that the term is used throughout this book. The hardware used to shoot films, I refer to as 'moving image cameras' unless, that is, there is some very specific reason for discriminating between cameras that use celluloid film and video cameras. Here I could equally well have referred to 'motion picture' cameras, 'movie' cameras or even 'cine cameras', but to me all these terms now seem rather anachronistic.

This definition of 'film' is hardly controversial. It is a very much more challenging task to define what is meant by first word in the phrase, 'ethnographic film'. This will take us on what might appear, to some readers at least, to be a substantial detour. But to borrow a famous phrase from the Michelin Guide, it is a detour worth taking. For unless one can say what 'ethnography' is, how can one possibly define 'ethnographic film'?

In the literature on ethnographic film, there is a tendency to use 'ethnography' and 'anthropology' as if they were synonyms. There are a number of reasons why this is potentially misleading. In the first place, anthropology and ethnography denote rather different forms of intellectual endeavour. The Greek roots of the two terms provide a clue as to the nature of this difference: whereas 'anthropology' involves a discourse (*-logia*) about humanity (*anthropos*), 'ethnography' involves writing (*graphien*) about a people (*ethnos*). Building on this etymology as a first approximation, one might say that whereas anthropology involves the formulation of general theories about human social and cultural life, ethnography is concerned rather with the description of particular groups of people.

In practice, however, these two forms of intellectual activity overlap to a considerable degree. Just as the formulation of an anthropological theory will usually involve reference to ethnographic particulars, so too will ethnographic description usually be informed – even if only implicitly – by some theoretical agenda. Nevertheless, it remains useful to differentiate between the two terms as representing different points on a spectrum running from the most theoretical to the most descriptive modes of representing social and cultural life. This distinction is particularly pertinent to any discussion of film since, as a communicative medium, film lends itself much more readily to ethnographic description than to the formulation of abstract theoretical propositions.[5]

A second reason for questioning the equation of anthropology and ethnography is that it is historically inaccurate. Although ethnography may first have arisen from within the academic discipline of anthropology and remains very closely identified with it, ethnographic research methods have long been routinely employed by sociologists in a range of different contexts, alongside more quantitative and interview-based methods (just as anthropologists can use the latter alongside ethnography). Ethnographic methods are also now employed in a broad range of other academic disciplines, including cultural geography, education, management studies, town planning, medical studies, science and technology studies, criminology and social psychology, to name quite a few. Ethnographic methods are even used outside academic life by market researchers, advertising agencies and polling organisations: the well-known international agency Ipsos MORI, for example, has an Ethnography Centre of Excellence which even produces 'ethnographic films'. Although I myself am an anthropologist by background and institutional affiliation, I would like to think that this book could be of interest to all those who use film for ethnographic purposes, whatever their own background.

So, if 'ethnography' is not just another word for 'anthropology', what precisely is it? One should start by recognising that it is a term that covers both a process of conducting social research and a process of representing the results of that research. In both aspects, ethnography is characterised by certain norms, but it is also important to note that these have varied considerably over time. In the 1890s, when moving image technology first became available to researchers going into what is still rather quaintly called 'the field' – nowadays it is more likely to be an urban environment – ethnography was defined primarily on the basis of the cultural exoticism of the subject matter. With some reason then, one might argue that an 'ethnographic film' in that era was simply about 'other cultures'. But this is a very outdated view: for at least a century, 'ethnography' has been primarily defined not by reference to the cultural characteristics of the community being studied but rather by reference to the method of research employed.

According to the disciplinary origin myth (though one that is also contested, it should be said), it was the Polish anthropologist, Bronislaw Malinowski, based then in Britain, who first developed the ethnographic method when, as a consequence of the First World War, he was stranded for a number of years on the Trobriand Islands, an archipelago lying just off the southeastern tip of Papua New Guinea. But though Malinowski himself may have worked in a culturally exotic location, before the end of the 1920s the ethnographic method was being employed to conduct research on the streets of Chicago. Today, ethnographic methods are used in a broad variety of contexts, irrespective of cultural considerations. They may still be employed in the study of isolated indigenous groups living in the Amazonian rainforest, but they may also be used to study elite scientists working on the human genome diversity project in a laboratory in California. By analogy, I would argue that there should similarly be no constraint on the cultural subject matter of ethnographic film-making as practised today: it is the method employed that should be considered the most important defining feature of this genre of film-making.

Although there is a range of different takes on what exactly constitutes the 'ethnographic method', central to most definitions is what is known as 'participant-observation' (though this term was not actually used by Malinowksi himself). In practical terms, 'participant-observation' is usually taken to imply total immersion in the daily life of a particular human social group over a prolonged period of time. It typically requires interaction not just with the great and the good, but also with 'ordinary' members of the group in question. This form of total participation influences the mode of observation employed: it should not be the dispassionate, objectifying gaze of the laboratory scientist but rather an embedded observation that depends as much on aural as on visual engagement with the subjects.

The principal focus of this 'participant-observation' will normally be the recurrent and the customary aspects of everyday life: exceptional circumstances are also of interest, of course, but they will be related back to the customary and the everyday. At least in the English-language traditions of ethnography, 'participant-observation' involves learning the language of the subjects, so that it is possible not only to speak with them directly, but also to listen to third-party conversations. It involves not just the recording of what is laid out in official documents and formally codified sets of rules – if there are any – nor merely attending to what the subjects say, but also paying close attention to non-linguistic codes, to the 'things that go without saying', that is, to the non-verbal and the performative aspects of social life. It also involves close attention to the way in which material objects are used to sustain that social life, be it simply through exchange or as a means to achieve such things as political prestige or privileged access to the world of the sacred. Increasingly, it is also necessary to pay close attention to the role played by the use of audiovisual and social media in sustaining that life too.

In its simplest form, the output from the application of the ethnographic method during fieldwork consists merely of a descriptive account of how day-to-day life is lived out in a given community. However, most ethnographers will seek to go beyond this modest descriptive level and offer some form of analysis of what they describe. It is at this point that the initial approximative distinction that I have drawn, between ethnography as a mode of description and anthropology as a mode of theory, begins to break down, since the particular form of the analysis offered by an ethnographer will very much depend on their theoretical inclinations. Even so, underlying the very broad range of theoretical paradigms that might potentially be brought to bear upon an ethnographic analysis, one can still identify certain common and very general principles that apply in the great majority of cases.

As a general rule, ethnographic accounts involve an analysis of the manner in which the social life of the human group being studied is created, maintained and reproduced on a day-to-day basis. In offering these analyses, ethnographic accounts are usually concerned to a greater or lesser extent with the identification of the connections between what, for the purposes of this book, I refer to as practices, ideas and relations. By 'practices', I refer to embodied behaviour of all kinds, from the most routinised and public, such as craft skills, subsistence activities and other relations with the natural environment, to the more intimate or informal, such as body decoration, dress, food preparation, children's games or sexual behaviour. By 'ideas', I refer to the full panoply of mental activities, mostly couched with varying degrees of explicitness in language, including not just intellectual ideas, but also codes, norms, beliefs, attitudes, sentiments, also the products of the imagination, including dreams. By 'relations', I refer to aspects of social organisation, particularly familial, economic or political relations, but embracing many other forms as well, which as often as not involve some degree of social differentiation, if not of hierarchy.

In exploring these connections, ethnographers typically make associations between diverse aspects of social life in a manner that would not necessarily occur, purely on a common-sense basis, to a newly arrived visitor to the community being studied. To give a few entirely random examples, these connections might concern such matters as how linguistic codes are used to maintain political differences, what body postures and table manners have got to do with ideas about gender, what family organisation has to do with ideas about spirits, how modes of subsistence impact upon rules of inheritance, and so on.

In helping to identify what constitutes an ethnographic analysis, it is also useful to consider, briefly, what is generally not included. Among notable absences, at least in contemporary ethnographic analyses, are references to aspects of individual psychology, such as, for example, the subconscious, intelligence or personality (though personality theory did have a strong influence on ethnographers in the 1930s through into the 1940s). Generally absent too are references to biogenetic matters, be it the effects of the 'selfish gene', nutritional requirements or circadian rhythms. Indeed, many ethnographers, myself included, consider that ethnography begins where biological determinism peters out: our interest lies in what human beings have made of the cards that the brute facts of material existence have dealt them rather than in using those brute facts to explain away the social and cultural diversity of human experience.

A hundred schools of thought contend about such matters, and no doubt there will be many objections as to precisely how I have divided up the social world, and even to the fact that I have divided it all. However, I would argue that, in broad outline, the exploration of the connections between practices, ideas and relations in the daily construction and reproduction of the social life of a group of people with whom they have been immersed for a prolonged period is what most ethnographers do, and indeed have done, most of the time. Theoretical enthusiasms may rise and fall, fashions in the particular foci of ethnographic interest may come and go, but in the language of Thomas Kuhn's classic account of scientific revolutions, the exploration of these connections is an integral part of the 'normal' procedures of ethnographic research, regardless of the theoretical 'paradigm'.

In that it is entirely possible to explore these connections through the medium of film on the basis of a prolonged immersion in the daily social life of a particular group of people, I would argue that it is also entirely possible for film-making to be a medium of ethnography, in an analytical as well as in a descriptive sense, albeit one that is both different and complementary to ethnography based on written texts.

## THE EVOLUTION OF ETHNOGRAPHIC FILM

This then will provide us with a sort of generic baseline for considering the ethnographic status of the many different films to be discussed in this book. However, as I seek to substantiate through the course of my historical narrative, the role of film as a medium of ethnography has evolved considerably over time, in part as a consequence of changes in the general intellectual climate of the social sciences in the English-speaking world, and in part on account of technological developments.

For around seventy-five of the 120 years that the moving image camera has been used for ethnographic purposes, the role most commonly assigned to it, at least in English-language anthropology, was that of a humble data-gathering instrument that could record the world with an unblemished objectivity and which, as such, could act as a control on the inevitably subjective and faulty observations possible through the naked human eye alone. But as a result of the impact of postmodernism on the social sciences in the 1970s, coinciding with a great leap forward in technology, the door was opened onto a series of much more imaginative ways of using the moving image camera for ethnographic purposes. These developments can be considered under three headings: the theoretical, the representational and the ethical.

The theoretical impact of postmodernism was particularly profound in English-language anthropology. Prior to the 1970s, the exploration of the connections between practices, ideas and relations that I have identified as the hallmark of 'normal' ethnography was often bundled up with one or another body of theory whereby the observable features of everyday life were primarily understood as some sort of manifestation of underlying 'structures', sometimes defined in terms of social relations, sometimes in terms of cultural concepts or intellectual principles, sometimes in terms of primary biological needs. But all that went out of the window under the impact of postmodernism, one of the key characteristics of which was a profound scepticism about 'meta-narratives', that is, abstract general theories of precisely the kind represented in anthropology by these classical social theories. Yet although English-language ethnographers may have come to reject the notion that social life is no more than the 'reflection' of underlying structures or principles, they have continued to be interested in the connections between practices, ideas and relations and in how these interconnections are constitutive of social life. However, in exploring these interconnections, they have also taken much greater interest in the role of the senses and bodily experience as well as in performance in the most general sense.

These changes in the theoretical landscape have played into the hands, as it were, of film as a medium of ethnography, not least because by the time they began to take hold in the 1970s, the complexity of the account of the world that film could offer had been greatly enhanced by the development of portable lip-synchrononous sound and the emergence of affordable colour 16 mm film stocks. In this technically enhanced form, film is particularly effective in representing the sensorial, the experiential, the embodied and the performative aspects of social life. It is especially effective in treating these aspects of social life through the lens of the experience of particular individuals. It was no coincidence, then, that the great efflorescence of ethnographic film-making in the English-speaking world – from the 1970s into the 1980s – was often constructed around the life experiences of a limited group of subjects.

Postmodernism also opened the door on to a more imaginative use of film as a medium of ethnography owing to its association with the so-called 'literary turn', that is, the *prise de conscience* whereby ethnographers came to think of themselves, not as scientists in the manner of biologists or physicists, but rather as writers who authored their works in accordance with a series of textual conventions, literary devices and narrative tropes aimed at convincing the reader of the plausibility of their account of the world. Although mostly still committed to representing the world in a realist manner and basing their arguments on empirical evidence, they recognised that they were doing so through a process of literary reconstruction. At the same time, a more subjective and reflexive form of ethnographic writing became possible, in which authors could admit both to their presence in the field and to the limits of their knowledge.[6] This in turn opened the way for an acceptance of ethnographic film-making as not merely a simplistic process of data-gathering based on the mimetic capacities of the technology, but rather as a representational process that, in common with ethnographic texts, involved an authored transformation of the world. Like texts, films could be subjective and reflexive without necessarily thereby losing their status as ethnography.

Following an initial period of experimentation in the heyday of post-modernism, ethnographic writing has generally settled back down into its customary low-key aesthetic mode. Although it is now undoubtedly more reflexive than it was prior to the 'literary turn', and certainly embraces a broader range of topics, ethnographers do not, by and large, write in a manner aimed at demonstrating their virtuosity as writers. But the important point is that this is no longer associated with the desire to appear scientifically objective. Rather it is the consequence of a more general and long-standing sense, present even in Malinowski's methodological statements, that it is the ethnographer's role to provide a channel through which the voices of the subjects may be heard. If the ethnographer writes in a self-consciously literary manner, there is a risk that this will overlay the subjects' voices and the focus of the reader's attention will become the ethnographer rather than the subjects. The same risk arises, I would argue, when ethnographic film-makers seek to demonstrate their virtuosity in the use of the medium of film.

A third way in which postmodernism had an important knock-on effect on ethnographic film-making concerns political and ethical matters. Prior to the 1970s, it had long been accepted that ethnographic accounts should be entirely non-judgemental in a moral or aesthetic sense: the aim should be to arrive at an understanding of why people do what they do rather than to establish whether what they do is good or bad, right or wrong, beautiful or ugly. But, as ethnographers became more sensitive to the political implications of their research, this traditional ethical positioning came to be finessed by the recognition that an ethnographer had no inherent right to represent the subjects of their study without their consent. Not coincidentally, it was also around this time that the first professional codes of ethics were formulated in English-language anthropology. Although these codes have subsequently been developed and refined, it remains a core principle that the relationship between ethnographer and subjects should be based on mutual trust and reciprocity, reflecting their close and often long-term association. Also still of central importance is the strong obligation on ethnographers to respect their subjects' rights, interests and privacy, and to protect them from any harm that might arise from the research that they conduct.[7]

This ethical positioning serves to distinguish present-day ethnographers both from their predecessors and from members of other professions who make some claim to represent the world. Although there were no doubt many exceptions, it is probably true to say that, in general, earlier generations of ethnographers, in thinking of themselves as the fellow travellers of natural scientists, felt that their first duty was to give an account of the truth, the whole truth and nothing but the truth, whatever the consequences for the subjects. The ethical positioning of present-day ethnographers is also quite different from that of investigative journalists, for whom the audience's right to know is of over-riding importance, and from the tradition of the amoral artist whose primary and exclusive responsibility is to their own artistic vision.[8]

The distinctive ethical positioning of ethnographic research since the 1970s has had a major impact on 'ways of doing' ethnographic films. I would therefore argue that this ethical positioning should be considered as not just some fortuitous supplementary aspect of ethnographic film-making, but rather as an integral, defining feature of the genre as it is practised at the present time. This impact is discernible in the nature of the topics selected, the stories told, the technical strategies adopted, even to some degree in the aesthetico-stylistic choices. Most of all, it is expressed in the kind of relationship that ethnographic film-makers have sought to develop with their subjects. As I discuss in detail in Chapters 5 and 6, in the first instance, it was associated with the development of more 'participatory' modes of film-making, involving a more collaborative relationship between film-maker and subjects and, to a certain degree, the sharing of authorship. But some film-makers went further and, as we shall discover in Chapter 7, rather than making films themselves, dedicated their energies to enabling the subjects to make their own films.

## THE 'ETHNOGRAPHICNESS' OF ETHNOGRAPHIC FILM

Although readers will undoubtedly be able to point to various exceptions and special cases, I would propose that the aggregation of fieldwork practices, modes of analysis, representational norms and the ethical positioning described constitute a reasonable ideal-typical account of contemporary ethnographic practice. If this is true, then we may posit that a contemporary ethnographic film will be one that has been made in accordance with these same general principles.

Such films will, typically, be primarily concerned with dailiness, with the customary and reiterative, and with the lives of 'ordinary' people; if they are concerned with extraordinary, dramatic events such as elaborate ceremonial occasions or political crises, they will relate these back to the everyday; they will adopt a stance of respect towards the cultural practices of the subjects and seek not to judge them, but rather to understand them through making connections between practices, ideas and relations. In doing so, they will explore the non-verbal, the material and the performative practices that are constitutive of social life as much as the verbal and intellectual; they will manifest an intimacy between subjects and film-maker that arises from their long-term relationship and mutual trust. While they will be ready to acknowledge the presence of the film-maker, to the extent that this is necessary or desirable, they will be aesthetically low-key, not in order to mimic supposedly objective scientific reportage, but so as not to mask the voices of the subjects or smother the sounds, rhythms and general aesthetic qualities of the subjects' world.

Although there is a certain degree of overlap, this attempt at a working definition of ethnographic film is different in a number of important regards to the classical definitions proposed respectively by Jay Ruby and Karl Heider in the 1970s, before the impact of postmodernism had made itself felt.[9] First, rather than being tied to specific features of the filmic text deemed necessary to qualify a given work as an ethnographic film ('an anthropological lexicon', or 'whole bodies, whole people, whole acts'), the definition that I am proposing here is based instead on the broader set of methodological, analytical, representational and ethical norms characterising contemporary ethnographic practice. In this view, the particular features of the filmic text are an entirely secondary matter and a film informed by an ethnographic analysis can be made in a broad range of different forms and styles.

Second, my definition is not exclusively linked to the academic discipline of anthropology. In contrast particularly to Ruby, I would argue that it is not necessary to be an anthropologist to make an ethnographic film. Indeed, it is not necessary to be any kind of academic to make an ethnographic film. Although this might seem like a bold assertion, it is no more than a bald statement of fact since many of the leading works in the established ethnographic film canon were made by film-makers who held neither a relevant academic qualification nor a post in an academic institution. Nor should films be considered ethnographic only if they are directed at academic specialists. On the contrary, if ethnographic films can reach out to wider audiences, then so much the better.

Nor is it necessary, as Ruby would require, for an ethnographic film to expound a theory and conform to the norms of presentation associated with academic texts. It is certainly the case that an ethnographic film can be enriched and given focus by an anthropological theory when the latter acts as a source of inspiration for the film-maker's ethnographic analysis. It is also entirely possible, even desirable, for the final edited version of a film to be imbued with connotative theoretical significance, as my Manchester colleague Angela Torresan has suggested.[10] But in my view, we should be asking what theory can do for film-making rather than vice versa. That is, we should be judging the value of an ethnographic film, not by its theoretical relevance as such, but rather by the richness and complexity of the account of human experience that it provides through a combination of the ethnographic method, theoretical inspiration and film-making skill.

As for the need to conform with the norms of an academic text, I would argue that many of the indices of good practice in ethnographic writing, such as the acknowledgement of sources, the cross-referencing of previous work in the same field, being explicit about one's methodological premises and so on, are simply not amenable to the medium of film. Once one begins to burden a film which such matters – which will usually take the form of extended voice-over commentary or lengthy rolling intertitles – one runs the risk of producing what is, in effect, no more than a poor simulacrum of a written text. Instead, I suggest, one should be seeking to use film for ethnographic purposes in a manner that plays to the particular strengths of film as a communicative medium, that is, a means of representing the embodied, the performative and the affective processes whereby social life is constituted on a day-to-day basis.

In the last analysis, I would contend that all that is necessary for a film to be considered ethnographic is for the praxis through which it has emerged to be broadly consonant with the ideal-typical description of contemporary ethnographic practice proposed here. At the same time, however, it should also be recognised that as one moves from one academic discipline to another, or from one individual practitioner to another, the degree to which their 'way of doing' ethnography conforms to this ideal-typical model diverges. The profundity of the ethnographic analysis, the complexity of the description and the degree of participation of the subjects can vary considerably. The same applies to the depth of immersion considered necessary: anthropologists conventionally require a year of total immersion in a community, but other practitioners of ethnography may expect very much less. The degree of linguistic competence required is also variable. In English-language anthropology, it is an article of faith that ethnographic research should be carried out in the language of the subjects, but in francophone anthropology, at least until relatively recently, it was considered perfectly permissible to work through interpreters.

Even though it may be linguistically a little ungainly, here I find the term 'ethnographicness', first coined by Karl Heider, to be very useful for describing this variation. However, in sharp contrast to Heider, I would not tie the 'ethnographicness' of a film to the degree to which authorial intervention in the making of a film has been minimised, but rather to the degree to which this authoring conforms to the ideal-typical model of the ethnographic practice that I have described above. On this basis, the ethnographic status of any particular film can be considered a matter of degree rather than of kind. The great advantage of this relativistic definition is that rather than setting up some kind of absolute frontier, it allows one to admit a broad range of works into the canon of ethnographic film that may address, with an equally broad degree of ethnographicness, the issues that are of contemporary interest and relevance to ethnographers.

## REAPING 'THE GREATEST REWARD' OF ETHNOGRAPHIC FILM

In the past, academic anthropologists have often been reluctant to acknowledge film-making as an important medium of ethnographic representation. Indeed, ethnographic film-making continues to be relatively undervalued in academic anthropology as evidenced by the fact that professional advancement is much more reliably achieved through the publication of texts than through the making of films. But if film-making continues to suffer from a certain marginality in academic circles, I would argue that this is because many anthropologists do not yet fully understand what film can do for them as a medium of ethnography, nor do they yet have the practical skills to use it to best advantage. Contrary to what has become a routinised claim, I would not attribute any continuing marginality of film-making to some deep-seated 'iconophobia', at least not if this is understood as some irrational fear that film-making will somehow destroy more conventional, text-based anthropology.[11]

In fact, in my experience, most present-day anthropologists appear to be generally well disposed towards film and would like to make more use of it in their work. If they harbour any negative sentiments about film, these are much more likely to take the form of indifference and boredom rather fear. In this regard, it certainly does not help that too often those who tax academic anthropologists for their supposed fear of images then point, as examples of good practice, to works that, to be entirely frank, are really rather long and rather dull, and whose ethnographic significance remains, at best, obscure.

In order to motivate anthropologists and other ethnographers to embrace film-making it would be much more potentially productive to demonstrate, through specific examples, that film has the capacity not merely to copy the world, but rather, when authored in an appropriate manner, to generate insights and understandings of a genuinely ethnographic character, particularly in relation to those more experiential and sensorial aspects of social life that are difficult to access through text alone. This is what I shall be seeking to do in the course of this book.

In this respect, I would argue that film-making has the potential to reconnect with an aspect of ethnographic practice discussed at some length in Malinowski's classical account of the ethnographic method, offered in the Introduction to *Argonauts of the Western Pacific*, first published in 1922.[12] Here, Malinowski suggests that the Ethnographer (always spelt with a capital 'E' in this text) should aim to offer an account of the relationship between three different aspects of the community being studied, employing a series of corporeal metaphors that parallel, more or less, the distinction between practices, ideas and relations that I have proposed. Thus, the observable regularities of social relations, Malinowski refers to as the 'skeleton' of a society, while 'views and opinions and utterances' – in effect, those things that I would classify under the general heading of 'ideas' – he refers to as the 'soul' of a society. But more important than either of these, he argues, is what he calls 'the flesh and blood' of social life, or somewhat more scholastically, its 'imponderabilia'. These correspond to aspects of everyday experience that I would include in the general category of 'practices'. But Malinowski goes further, arguing that these 'imponderabilia' are manifestations of what he refers to as 'the subjective desire of feeling', a concept that is awkwardly expressed in this isolated phrase, but which is not dissimilar to what we would now call, in the language of phenomenology, 'lived experience'.

Among the specific examples of practices manifesting this 'subjective desire of feeling' that Malinowski cites, there are many that would be very effectively evoked through film. These include the routines of working life, the way in which the body is cared for, the preparation and consumption of food, the tone of conversation around a campfire, the ripple of excitement at a ceremonial event, the tenor of friendship or hostility, and the subtle manner in which personal vanities are reflected in behaviour. Malinowski argues that in the last analysis, the evocation of these experiential aspects of social life is even more important than the description of 'institutions, customs or codes'. He goes so far as to claim that if an ethnographic account failed to communicate the 'subjective desire of feeling' embodied in daily experience, it would miss – deploying the less gender-aware terminology of his time – 'the greatest reward which we can hope to obtain from the study of Man'.

For the best part of the six decades that followed this foundational statement of the ethnographic method, the experiential 'flesh-and-blood' dimension of social life was largely neglected in English-language ethnographic accounts in favour of an over-riding concern with 'institutions, customs or codes'. But finally, the shift back to a concern with the embodied, the sensorial and the experiential that first emerged in the ethnographic literature of 1970s and 1980s offered the opportunity to reconnect with the 'subjective desire of feeling' in the authoring of ethnographic accounts. By fortuitous circumstance, the technology had so developed by then that it became possible to use film to represent these aspects of social life in an effective and creative manner. In these pages, I shall be considering the many ways in which ethnographic film-makers have attempted to reap 'the greatest reward' that Malinowski promised.

## Notes

1 Henley (2009).
2 MacDougall (1995a), 125.
3 Rouch (1968), 442.
4 MacDougall (2019), p. 14.
5 The distinction that I seek to draw here between 'anthropology' and 'ethnography' is somewhat blurred by a third term, 'ethnology'. In anglophone countries, this is now regarded as rather anachronistic, denoting an old-fashioned cataloguing of customs, not that different from folklore. In France, however, and also in Germany, 'ethnology' may still be used in a positive fashion to refer to the work of scholars who aim to develop theoretical propositions in relation to one particular cultural region. The distinction between 'anthropology' and 'ethnography' is also complicated by the fact that in the USA, the term 'anthropologist' may be used of a scholar who works on human biology. Although film may also have a role to play in biological anthropology, I do not tackle the subject in this book. Whenever I use the term 'anthropology', my intention is to refer to what is known in Britain as 'social anthropology' and in the USA as 'cultural anthropology'.
6 Among many others, key works that promoted this view of the ethnographic author as writer included Marcus and Cushman (1982), Clifford and Marcus (1986), and Geertz (1988).
7 See, for example, the code of ethics of the American Anthropological Association at www.aaanet.org/issues/policy-advocacy/Code-of-Ethics.cfm, or the ethical guidelines of the Association of Social Anthropologists of the United Kingdom and Commonwealth at www.theasa.org/ethics.shtml.
8 On the tradition of the amoral artist, see Winston (2000), 131. Winston quotes the advice given to a young painter by the celebrated late nineteenth-century artist and critic John Ruskin, 'Does a man die at your feet, your business is not to help him, but to note the colour of his lips.'
9 See, particularly, Ruby (1975) and Heider (1976). A second edition of Heider's book, revised, but still offering essentially the same definition of ethnographic film, was published in 2006.
10 See Torresan (2011).
11 The original usage of 'iconophobia' was in the title of a witty polemical essay by Lucien Castaing-Taylor, first published in 1996, in which he upbraided anthropologists, not without reason, for not taking advantage of film as a representational medium (Taylor 1996). However, since then, the term has come to be used in an entirely hackneyed manner to account for the supposed 'failure' of academic anthropologists to embrace visual media.
12 See Malinowski (1932a), particularly pp. 17–25.

# Part I
# Histories: ethnographic film in the twentieth century

# Introduction

THROUGHOUT most of the twentieth century, ethnographic film-makers, particularly those in the English-speaking world associated with academic institutions, were ill at ease with the idea of authoring their films. From the 1890s, when anthropologists first started to take moving image cameras with them to the field, until as late as the 1970s, cameras were considered primarily to be scientific instruments that in the ideal case would allow researchers to bring back objective visual records of certain aspects of their fieldwork. Any exercise of authorship in making these records was seen as diminishing their value. Therefore, as I describe in Chapters 1, 3 and 4, throughout this period academic ethnographic film-makers adopted a range of strategies aimed at eliminating authorship, or when this was not possible, at least minimising it or making it invisible.

But around the middle of the 1970s, there was something of a change of heart. Authorship in ethnographic film-making came to be recognised as inevitable, but nevertheless as something that should be exercised with restraint. As I describe in Chapters 5 and 6, one response to the new climate was the idea that ethnographic film authorship, while clearly unavoidable, could be controlled by means of a 'reflexive' declaration on the part of the film-maker about the subjective elements that they brought to the making of their film. Another was the development of more 'participatory' praxes that entailed, at least to some degree, the sharing of authorship with the subjects of the film. In the 1980s (see Chapter 7), some ethnographic film-makers took this process one logical step further and either alongside their own films, or even instead of making their own films, dedicated their energies to enabling the indigenous peoples who had been the subjects of so many ethnographic films in the past to become the authors of their own films.

Finally, in the 1990s, taking advantage of the new interactive digital media, some anthropologists sought to assign the authorship of their films, at least the final stages of it, not to the subjects, but rather to the audience. They sought to achieve this by placing their film footage, sometimes partially edited but not usually assembled into a single unitary narrative, first on CD-Roms and later on the Web, where it would be available, along with any photographs or texts that they might have produced on related topics, so that audiences could develop their own narrative pathways through their material. This form of assigned authorship lies beyond the scope of this book, but there is a substantial literature on work of this kind to which interested readers may turn.[1]

These anxieties about the exercise of authorship had the most debilitating effect on the first seventy-five years of ethnographic film-making. The period from the 1890s to the 1960s was one of immense cultural and social change, arguably considerably greater than the changes that have taken place in the almost equivalent period since the 1960s. This was also the period of the great fieldwork-based textual monographs that formed the foundations of the modern academic disciplines of social and cultural anthropology. But owing to the lack of a well-thought-through intellectual rationale for film-making within these disciplines, combined with a lack of resources and technical competence, the filmic accounts produced by anthropologists during this period constitute no more than the palest of pale shadows of their textual accounts.

This is particularly true of the period before the Second World War, when anthropologists, though often first-hand witnesses to the most momentous processes of cultural change, produced very little film material of any consequence. Anyone who has reviewed, as I have done, the archives of ethnographic film held in institutions such as the Smithsonian in Washington, the American Museum of Natural History in New York, or the Bibliothèque nationale de France in Paris would surely share my profound sense of a great historical opportunity almost tragically lost.

It is fortunate, then, that alongside this almost century-long agonising over the implications of authorship on the part of academic film-makers, there were also other film-makers, whose original motivations ranged from the artistic to the commercial, or some combination of the two, who made films of broadly ethnographic interest but who had absolutely no qualms about exercising their authorship. In the early twentieth century, as I describe in Chapter 2, these films emerged from two popular genres in particular, the travel film and the melodrama set in exotic locations. Many of the films made under the umbrella of these genres were at best crass and at worst grotesquely racist. The nature of the authorship was such that it is often difficult to disentangle fact from fiction in the final form of these films. And yet, from a general humanistic perspective, we should be grateful that these genres existed since they generated a filmic legacy that is of far greater ethnographic significance than that left by academic ethnographers. Always provided that it is approached critically – though also without presentist prejudice – this legacy remains of immense value not just to academic researchers, but also to the descendants of the subjects of these films.

A film-maker whose work figures prominently in Chapter 2, since it remains central to the ongoing debate about the nature of ethnographic film, even today, is Robert Flaherty. Although he made a number of influential films in the course of a long career, he is arguably still most remembered as the director of his first major film, *Nanook of the North*, a two-days-in-the-life portrait of an Inuit (Eskimo) man and his family living in the Canadian Arctic. Released in 1922, this film is routinely identified as the *ur*-film of ethnographic cinema and, as its maker, Flaherty is described with similar regularity as the 'father of ethnographic documentary', or even of 'documentary' film generally. But in considering these accolades, one should exercise considerable caution. For, seemingly unnoticed by many authors who write about 'documentary', the meaning of this term has changed so radically since the 1920s that its present-day meaning is almost diametrically opposed to its original meaning.

The first use of the term in the English-language literature, as innumerable text books on the history of documentary film relate, was not actually with reference to *Nanook*, but rather in relation to Flaherty's second major film, *Moana*, released in 1926, which follows the coming-of-age ceremonies of a young man of that name on the island of Samoa. The term was used in a review of this film by John Grierson, a leading non-fiction film-maker in his own right and the leader of the so-called British Documentary Movement. Some years afterwards, in the early 1930s, Grierson would formulate a definition of the genre that has since echoed down the decades: it involved, he suggested, an approach to cinema based on 'the creative treatment of actuality'.

Much ink has been spilt in the debate as to what, exactly, Grierson meant by this phrase. The most plausible of the many explanations offered, at least to my mind, is that Grierson was referring to the dramatisation ('the creative treatment') of footage that purported to be about the real world ('actuality', which in the 1930s was a synonym for newsreel footage). Certainly this would be an accurate description not only of the great majority of Flaherty's films but also of the films made by Grierson and his colleagues in the British Documentary Movement. If films of this kind were to be made today they would be called 'drama-documentaries' or perhaps 'docufictions'. They would certainly not be called 'documentaries' without at least some form of qualification.

Exactly why and when 'documentary' changed its meaning is a matter of academic debate. But it appears to have done so gradually in the period following the Second World War when, owing to the development of lightweight equipment, faster film stocks and portable lip-synchronous sound, it became possible for non-fiction film-makers to work in a different way.

Prior to the development of this technology, it had been necessary for non-fiction film-makers to direct their subjects in a very precise manner just to meet the most basic technical requirements of filming. The camera had to be set up, on a tripod, at a spot where there was sufficient light to film, and the subjects then had to be invited to perform a version of their lives directly in front of it. But once the new technology became available, it became possible for film-makers simply to follow their subjects around, without anything like the same need to intervene in what their subjects were doing in order to be able to film.

This shift in meaning was probably also a consequence of the term 'documentary' being commandeered by film-makers working for television news programmes who had a greater concern for literal factual accuracy than the makers of 'documentaries' of the interwar period who drew their inspiration rather from the 'seventh art' of cinema. Certainly by the 1960s, 'dramatisation', understood as the performance of an imagined reality specifically for the camera by the subjects, and 'documentary' had become so clearly opposed that if any of the former was included in a film that purported to be the latter, it was regarded as a matter of contention unless this was clearly indicated.

And yet, even though 'dramatisation' may have become incompatible with the notion of 'documentary', the making of a film of this kind continues to involve some degree of 'creative treatment', albeit in a more general sense. For even when a 'documentary' is made by the most fact-scrupulous of film-makers, it always involves more than holding up a mirror to the world. For a start, a whole range of factors to do with the apparatus of film-making itself limit its literal objectivity: these include the aspect ratio of the image (that is, the ratio of width to height), the perspective offered by the lenses, the balance of the colours offered by the film stock and the balance of sounds offered by the microphones. All these features of the technology, and many more, may be consciously manipulated by the film-maker in a creative manner.

But the sense in which a modern documentary film-maker most actively exercises their creativity is surely in relation to the development of a narrative. For, just as in a fiction film, most documentaries are structured by a narrative that is intended to propel, guide or merely nudge the audience along as the film proceeds. This will usually entail the substantial manipulation of the rushes in the edit suite in order to present a story or argument that has a beginning, a middle and an end, though not necessarily in that order, as Jean-Luc Godard is famously said to have remarked and if so, with good reason, since there are any number of ways of jumping back and forth in time in the course of the unfolding of a film narrative, be it in documentary or fiction.

On account of the ambiguities associated with the term 'documentary', some practitioners of ethnographic film-making have preferred to describe themselves as makers of 'non-fiction film'. However, on balance, I prefer to use the term 'documentary' for a number of pragmatic reasons, mainly linguistic. Not only is it more succinct, but there is also something inherently unsatisfactory about identifying an activity by its antithesis. There is also the consideration that this genre of cinema, however closely its practitioners may believe that it should be tied to the real world of fact, continues to involve certain features that are akin to those of fiction film-making. By referring to it as 'non-fiction', one appears to be denying that this is the case.

Unless otherwise stated, in this book, I use the term 'documentary' in what I refer to as the 'modern' sense, that is, a film based on images gathered in the real world as opposed to an imaginary world performed specifically for the camera, though this does not preclude authorial creativity having been exercised in its making, be it in terms of its technical realisation or its narrative shaping. To what degree and in what form this exercise of authorial creativity is appropriate to a documentary film that has ethnographic objectives is one of the central threads of discussion throughout the entire course of this book.

## Note

1   A good starting point would be the overview account of the use of interactive digital media for anthropological purposes published by Sarah Pink (2011).

# The long prehistory of
# ethnographic film

HE half-century running from the mid-1890s, when moving image
camera technology was first developed, to the period of the Second
World War in the 1940s constitutes over a third of the total time-span of
ethnographic film-making. This was a period of tentative beginnings, sporadic
activity and blurred genres. Though a large number of films made during
this period could be said to possess a certain degree of 'ethnographicness'
– as defined in the General Introduction to this book – many of these were
not produced by academic film-makers, but by commercial production
companies, government or colonial agencies, even private individuals.
Ethnographic film in the form in which it is most frequently encountered
today barely existed, even though the first seeds of later developments were
evident. Borrowing a phrase from the distinguished Belgian anthropologist
and film-maker, Luc de Heusch, in this chapter I refer to this long period
of gestation as the 'prehistory' of ethnographic film.[1]

Throughout this prehistory, indeed until as late as the 1970s, in the
academic ethnographic film-making literature, the moving image camera
was routinely compared to the hero instruments of the scientific world, the
telescope and the microscope particularly, and its function was seen as being
to provide an entirely objective registration of reality. Academic film-makers
did not aim to produce *documentary* films in the modern sense, that is,
non-fiction films structured around a central narrative, but rather films of
*documentation*. In the ideal case, these documentation films would provide
a detailed visual record of given events and situations, and would be executed
in the most objective manner possible. Although they might later be edited
and reordered in a particular way to support a verbal presentation, sometimes
with the addition of explanatory intertitles, there was typically no attempt
to build a narrative directly out of the visual material itself.

In fact, the primary purpose of documentation film-making was not for
public presentation as such but rather for research, taking advantage of the
previously unparalleled mimetic capabilities of the technology and the
possibility it offered to observe the same event or situation in detail over

and over again. The ultimate goal was to build up great archives of visual records of human behaviour that could be analysed for scientific purposes in perpetuity, either by the film-makers themselves or by third parties.

This documentation film-making was also closely tied up with 'salvage' ethnography objectives, that is, the preservation of a record of cultural phenomena threatened with extinction due to social and political change. As the effects of technological and political modernisation spread ever deeper over the course of this period into previously isolated mountain valleys, tropical rainforests and deserts across the globe, communities living in these regions found themselves undergoing a qualitatively greater degree of social and cultural change than they had experienced in millennia. The effects of this change were often highly negative: many communities were dispersed or decimated, some entirely destroyed. In almost all cases, elaborate and often aesthetically beautiful cultural practices, developed and honed over generations, were abandoned as they lost their meaning or purpose. Ethnographic film-makers were intensely aware of these processes and sought through their work to preserve a record of these vulnerable cultural practices for future generations. But anything that hinted at authorship in this form of film-making was thought to compromise the archival value of the material recorded.

The reluctance within academia over this period to engage in any kind of authorial transformation of the material generated by the moving image camera was in marked contrast to the enthusiasm and inventiveness with which film-makers from the emergent cinema industry embraced all manner of authorial devices as a means of representing the cultural diversity of the world. Although their motives may have been commercial and their primary goal merely to provide entertainment, these extra-academic film-makers generated an account of the great cultural changes taking place during the early twentieth century that far excedes in both quantity and complexity the modest film record left behind by academic ethnographers.

The number of films made prior to the Second World War that might be considered to possess at least some degree of ethnographicness is vast. If one were to adopt a definition of ethnography in accordance with the standard modern-day usage, we would have to admit films made in any part of the world into this prehistory. But that would have made this account even more substantial than it is already is. To keep it within manageable proportions, I therefore consider only films made by Europeans or film-makers of European descent about 'other cultures'. While this is clearly unsatisfactory in many regards, it is a choice that can at least be defended on the grounds that this would have been the primary denotatum of the domain of the 'ethnographic' in the period to which my account refers.

I shall further restrict the ground to be covered in this first chapter by reserving a discussion of the most commercial and popular forms of film-making of ethnographic interest to Chapter 2. Though the distinction between commercial and non-commercial film-making in this period is often hazy, in this chapter I am primarily concerned with films that had, at most, limited commercial objectives, and which fall into three broadly overlapping categories: films that were made for the purposes of academic research, films made for museums and, finally, films made for a range of purposes associated with state-funded empire- and nation-building projects that aimed at inventorising and co-opting the culture of First Nations or other indigenous groups.

Even with these restrictions, I can only consider a very limited number of examples. However, I shall frequently direct readers to *The Silent Time Machine*, a website that I have prepared about early ethnographic film, which not only provides more extensive details about individual films but also links through which many of these films are viewable.[2]

## THE FIRST ETHNOGRAPHIC RESEARCH FILMS: REGNAULT, HADDON, SPENCER

Although the makers of the earliest ethnographic research films might have aspired to use the moving image camera to provide entirely objective accounts of the world, their works invariably involved what one might call 'on-request performances', that is, performances that the subjects put on specifically because the film-makers had asked for them. This was inevitably the case since such were the limitations of the technology of the time that it was impossible for a film to be shot without the active collaboration of the subjects, be it to ensure that filming was taking place at a location where there was adequate lighting, or simply to guarantee that they kept within the field of view of the camera. The notion of filming people going about their business without taking into account the camera's presence was simply not realisable at that time. But in making a request to the subjects to perform a particular action in a particular place, early ethnographic film-makers, despite themselves, were in effect engaged in an act of authorship.

The footage that is often said to represent the very first example of moving images produced specifically for ethnographic research purposes certainly involved a series of 'on-request performances' of this kind. This is the material shot by the French anatomist Félix-Louis Regnault and his assistant, Charles Comte, in the spring of 1895, which consists primarily of short sequences of Africans moving in various ways – walking, sitting, running, jumping and climbing trees – and engaging in certain technical activities. These sequences were not filmed in Africa, however, but in Paris, either at a colonial exhibition beside the Eiffel Tower, or in the laboratory of Étienne-Jules Marey, Regnault's mentor. Marey had not only introduced Regnault to the study of human and animal locomotion but was also the designer of the 'chronophotographic rifle', the cinematographic device used by Regnault and Comte.[3]

At the time that he shot these sequences, Regnault was concerned to explore the relationship between bodily movement and racial identity, since the concept of race remained central to the still-dominant evolutionary theoretical paradigm in anthropology. Within a few years, however, in accordance with changes going on more generally in anthropological theory at that time, Regnault had replaced this physiological notion of race as a determining variable in his theories with that of '*ethnie*', a category defined rather in terms of cultural and linguistic criteria. In this latter form, his work anticipates the ideas of both Marcel Mauss and Franz Boas concerning the way in which cultural tradition may be inscribed in bodily movement.[4]

The sequences shot by Regnault were recorded onto strips of sensitised paper and could not therefore be projected. But his aim was not to make a film to show to an audience, but rather to assemble a series of sequences that could later be minutely inspected by academics interested in modes of locomotion. To improve visibility, the subjects filmed in Marey's laboratory were asked to walk in front of a white sheet, while to one side, in some of the sequences, there is a large chronometer presumably intended to allow the viewer to monitor the speed of the subjects' movements. Regnault would later envisage a magnificent future when a great collection of such supposedly objective filmic 'documents' had been assembled and an anthropologist would have 'in his drawer' a dossier of all the many different forms of human locomotion. This dossier would allow him, whenever he pleased, not merely to observe such banal actions as squatting and climbing trees, but also to 'be present at feasts, at battles, at religious and civil ceremonies, at different ways of trading, eating, relaxing'.[5]

The earliest ethnographic research films to be shot actually in the field similarly involved 'on-request performances'. Here the first example is generally taken to be the four minutes of footage shot by Alfred Haddon on the island of Mer (formerly Murray Island) in the Torres Strait, an archipelago lying between northern Australia and New Guinea. In modern geopolitical terms, the Strait forms part of Australia, but in cultural terms the Mer islanders are Melanesian rather than Aboriginal.

Haddon was a zoologist from the University of Cambridge, and he had come to Mer as the leader of a multidisciplinary anthropological expedition. He used a Newman and Guardia kinematograph, an early hand-cranked camera manufactured in Britain that had been modelled on the *cinématographe* first introduced by the Lumière brothers in France in 1895. The film stock that Haddon used, which cost more to buy than the equipment, was 35 mm, the standard gauge of most early moving image cameras. Haddon's diary indicates that he shot the film material shortly before the expedition was due to leave Mer, in early September 1898.

These four minutes of footage show a series of performances by small groups of three or four men, mostly of dancing, but also including one short sequence of traditional fire-making, all carried out at Haddon's request. The most striking part of this material, and seemingly the very last to be shot, is a 45-second take showing three men re-enacting a dance that had once formed part of a secret male initiation ceremony connected with the Mer culture-hero, Malo-Bomai. Under pressure from missionaries, this ceremony had long been abandoned, certainly as a public spectacle. The masks traditionally worn for this part of the ceremony had been made of finely crafted turtle shell and had been decorated with the jawbones of enemies killed in inter-island warfare. As these masks had all been destroyed at missionary insistence, Haddon had to cut up the expedition's cardboard packing cases in order to supply the performers with the wherewithal to recreate them. But even though the masks were made of cardboard, and the dancing was merely a re-enactment, the performers were very concerned that no woman on the island should even see the masks, let alone the performance (figure 1.1a).[6]

Three years later, acting on Haddon's advice, Baldwin Spencer, a biologist and former art student, originally from Manchester, who had been appointed to a chair at the University of Melbourne, took a moving image camera on his renowned expedition with Frank Gillen across Central Australia in 1901–2. 'You really *must* take a Kinematograph', Haddon had counselled, 'it is an indispensible piece of anthropological apparatus'. In this turn of phrase, Haddon neatly encapsulated the then-current idea of the moving image camera as an instrument of the same kind as one might find in a scientific laboratory.[7] Spencer used a Warwick kinematograph to film some 50 minutes of ritual and ceremonial dancing performed by the Arrernte, an Aboriginal people, then often referred to as the 'Aranda', who live in the region around Alice Springs. This was a considerable advance on Haddon's efforts, not only in terms of sheer duration, but also – possibly due to Spencer's early training as an artist – in terms of both content and technique.

Most of Spencer's material concerned ritual events that the Arrernte consider secret and sacred and which should therefore be witnessed only by initiated adult men. For this reason, the present-day Arrernte have asked that access to this material be restricted, so most of Spencer's footage can no longer be viewed by the general public. However, one part of Spencer's footage shows a ceremony known as the *tjitjingalla*, which was a 'corroboree', that is, a form of ceremonial dancing that is not considered sacred and which is therefore open to everyone, including Aboriginal women and children, as well as all outsiders.

Although the *tjitjingalla* filmed by Spencer was more authentic than the initiation ceremony dance filmed by Haddon, in the sense that it was still being actively practised by the subjects for their own reasons, the particular

(a) Mer Islanders recreate the journeys of the culture-hero Malo in the form of a shark in a dance traditionally performed at a male initiation ceremony. Unnoticed by Haddon, the lead dancer's hands evoke a shark's dorsal fins while all three dancers appear to be wearing imitations of women's skirts.

(b) Though barely visible in this still, the *tjintjingalla* dancers, left, carry dance sticks entwined with human hair. The white feathers sticking out of the brushwood shelter in front of them are attached to large prongs that the dancers subsequently positioned around their necks so that they looked 'like horned cattle'. Spencer could not discover the meaning of these dances, but subsequent research suggests they enact a then-recent massacre of Aborigines by police armed with carbines (the dance sticks) and a millenarian ritual aimed at ridding the country of Europeans and their cattle (the feathered prongs).

1.1 Alfred Haddon and Baldwin Spencer – unwitting witnesses.

performance of the *tjintjingalla* that Spencer filmed, neverthless, involved his direct authorial intervention: normally the *tjitjingalla* dances were performed at night, but having no means of artificial lighting, Spencer had to ask for what he called 'rehearsals' to be performed during the day instead.[8]

Considered as works of objective documentation, the films of Haddon and Spencer are clearly compromised in a number of respects. Not only were the performances put on explicitly at the request of the film-makers, but they were performed outside their normal social contexts and in a very abbreviated and reduced form. Even so, when these films are assessed in the light of the comparative ethnography and the historical accounts that have been published subsequently, they can yield valuable insights into the way of life of the subjects, some aspects of which would not have been available to the film-makers themselves.

Thus, for example, without his being aware of it, Haddon's material appears to show that there was an element of transvestism in the traditional male initiation ceremony on Mer in that the dancers seem to be wearing voluminous skirts that imitate the kind normally then worn only by women. If so, this feature would link the Mer ceremony to the discussion of the mobile and socially constructed nature of gender identity in Melanesia that has held a prominent place in the regional ethnographic literature in recent years. Spencer, for his part, equally unwittingly, in filming the *tjitjingalla* appears to have recorded what some subsequent authors have identified as an Aboriginal millenarian dance whose purpose was to rid the country of European settlers and their cattle by ritual means. If this is indeed the case, Spencer's film offers early visual evidence of the Aboriginal will to resist invasion which has ensured the continuation of their culture and identity to this day, entirely contrary to Spencer's own expectations (figure 1.1b).[9]

The textual publications that arose from these two expeditions had an immense impact on the developing academic discipline of anthropology. In contrast, although they are now considered very significant in the history of ethnographic film, their films had no such immediate impact. Haddon appears to have made only very limited use of his film material, be it for scientific research or for public projection, and while Spencer did later use his footage – in an ethically dubious fashion – in a series of very well attended public lectures, and also alluded to it in his popular writings about his 'wanderings in wild Australia', he never made them the focus of an explicitly academic discussion. There is no evidence that either Haddon or Spencer ever encouraged their academic protegés to follow in their footsteps as film-makers.

For the next six decades, ethnographic film-making by English-speaking anthropologists in the British sphere of academic influence was no more than a sporadic activity. David MacDougall has called this period the 'dark age' of visual anthropology.[10] In large measure, this came about because the cost and logistical difficulties of making films were simply too great relative to the perceived academic benefits. In the 1929 edition of *Notes and Queries*, the fieldwork manual published periodically by the Royal Anthropological Institute in London, the entry relating to film-making runs to no more than two pages – only half the number dedicated to the collection of string figures. Under the by-then anachronistic title, 'Kinematography', the film-making entry begins with the observation that: 'The kinematograph, invaluable as it is for giving a record of the life of native peoples, involves difficulties which make its use not very practicable in most scientific expeditions.' Principal among the 'difficulties' listed were the cost of the camera and film stock. It seems very likely that this entry was written by none other than Alfred Haddon, but whoever the author, the decline in perceived importance is notable: what had once been 'indispensible' had now become 'not very practicable'.[11]

Although the *Notes and Queries* entry alludes only to cost considerations, there was undoubtedly more than mere lack of resources to this decline in interest in ethnographic film-making. For if film-making had been thought to make a significant contribution to the generation of anthropological knowledge, no doubt the resources would have been found to support it. The most widely accepted view is that this decline in interest was primarily a consequence of changing ideas about the goals of anthropology as an academic discipline and, concomitantly, about the kind of fieldwork that was necessary to produce the results that this new conception of the discipline required.

Haddon and Spencer had made their films in an era when anthropological fieldwork still consisted of expeditions modelled on the field trips of natural scientists. In this expeditionary format, researchers typically kept on the move, never remaining long enough in any one place to learn the language of the subjects of study. It was also strongly associated with the collection of material objects, mostly artefacts, but also sometimes human body parts, which could then be taken back and examined in greater detail in university laboratories in the metropoli before eventually being displayed to the general public in museums.

Cinematography, like still photography before it, had initially been welcomed by anthropologists as a means of collecting reliable and transportable visual records of technical processes and ceremonial performances as practised in their original environments. These visual media also first became available at a time when evolutionary theoretical paradigms that laid a particular emphasis on the relationship between race and culture were still influential in academic anthropology. In this context, both photography and cinematography provided a convenient way of documenting the external characteristics of the subjects – be it in relation to physiology or to modes of dress and self-decoration – that served to define the racial and cultural categories that were central to these evolutionary theories.

But from around 1910, the itinerant expeditionary model of fieldwork was gradually displaced in English-language anthropology by the intensive study of one particular community based on an extended period of first-hand participant-observation of day-to-day life and competence in the local language. Meanwhile, race as a category of theoretical analysis also progressively lost its prominence in the early years of the new century: rather than seeking to relate cultural practices to racial identity and evolutionary stages, anthropologists sought instead to explain them in terms of social organisation, more general cultural principles or relationships with the natural environment. This new intellectual orientation and method of carrying out fieldwork was paradigmatically exemplified by the work of Bronislaw Malinowski on the Trobriand Islands at the time of the First World War, as discussed in the General Introduction to this book.[12]

As a result of these changes, it has been argued, the importance of detailed textual accounts of systems of belief and social organisation increased and the collecting of material objects correspondingly diminished. This change in emphasis also coincided with a move towards the establishment of departments of anthropology in universities, where there was typically greater interest in social theory than in material objects. As the interest in collecting declined, so too did the importance of photography and cinematography, both as technologies of fieldwork and as a means of presenting the results. Certainly, neither photography nor cinematography is mentioned in Malinowski's famous discussion of ethnographic fieldwork methods in the Introduction to *Argonauts of the Western Pacific*.[13]

Yet while these arguments may hold good for the practice of ethnographic film-making in university departments in Britain, elsewhere ethnographic film-making often took place in association with museums or similar institutions, for whom the ethos of collecting remained important. Another major motivation for making ethnographic films during this period, and which often overlapped with museum-based film-making, were colonial or nation-building projects of various kinds that aimed at inventorising the culture of First Nations and other indigenous groups. It is to these forms of ethnographic film-making that I now turn.

## ETHNOGRAPHIC FILM-MAKING IN THE EUROPEAN COLONIAL EMPIRES: GERMAN, FRENCH, BRITISH

Among European nations maintaining global colonial empires in the early years of the twentieth century, one of the most active producers of films of ethnographic interest was Germany. In the very first years of the twentieth century, anthropologists in Germany were enthusiastic early adopters of the phonograph for recording music and language in the field and it has even been suggested that their interest in moving image cameras was initially to make films that could accompany their recordings rather than being merely an extension of an interest in photography, as was generally the case elsewhere.[14]

After the First World War, Germany would be deprived of its overseas colonies by the Treaty of Versailles, and German ethnographic film-making outside Europe would decline markedly. But for a ten-year period before the war, film-makers associated with German ethnographic museums and other academic institutions were particularly active in the German colonies in Africa and Melanesia. Like Haddon and Spencer before them, these early German ethnographic film-makers were not aiming to produce documentaries as they would be understood today. Rather their goal was to use the moving image camera to document cultural phenomena in the most objective possible fashion.

One of the first to do so was Karl Weule of the Leipzig Ethnological Museum, who made a series of short films about dance during the course of an expedition in 1906 to Lindi, in what is now southern Tanzania but was then the German colony of Tanganyika. Shortly afterwards, in 1908–10, two different German expeditions to Melanesia also came back with film material: one was the Hamburg Museum expedition to various islands in Micronesia and the then German colony of Neu-Guinea on the northern coast of present-day Papua New Guinea, while the other was the expedition of Richard Neuhauss, supported by the Berlin Society for Anthropology, Ethnology and Prehistory, also to the northern coast of Neu-Guinea. However, none of these researchers had any training or experience as film-makers and the equipment that they were using was very primitive. Not surprisingly therefore, the results were very modest, both in a technical sense and in terms of content: the material consists almost entirely of very brief shots of crafts or ceremonies. In no case did these film-makers produce more than around 40 minutes of footage. Only a fraction of this material has survived or has proved viewable.[15]

Much the same has to be said for the material shot in 1911 by the great German Amazonist anthropologist Theodor Koch-Grünberg in Koimelemong, a mixed Taulipang-Wapishana village in Roraima in northern Brazil, close to the frontier with Venezuela. The subject matter consists of the usual staples of the time: technical processes and a ceremonial dance. These probably constitute the very first moving images of the indigenous peoples of the Amazon Basin but they certainly cannot be described as great works of cinematographic art. Although Koch-Grünberg was a talented photographer, his lack of experience as a film-maker is only too evident: the framing is sometimes so poor that the subjects are only just within the field of vision

**1.2** Though an excellent photographer, Theodor Koch-Grünberg had difficulty mastering the skills of cinematography. The shot of Taulipang boys making a string figure, left, is reasonable, but often his images are poorly framed as in the shot, right, of young Taulipang women grating manioc.

of the camera (figure 1.2). He found the experience of shooting this material highly exasperating because the camera kept breaking down. It certainly did not convince him of the value of the moving image camera as a tool of field research. In total, he appears to have shot around 25 minutes of footage. Though much of this is lost or unviewable, a 10-minute compilation is available on the Web.[16]

But of all the early German-speaking ethnographic film-makers, the best known, and also the most controversial, is the Austrian anthropologist Rudolf Pöch, whose work was supported by both the Berlin Museum for Ethnology and the Imperial Academy of Sciences in Vienna. Just as Spencer had done, Pöch sought the advice of Haddon before taking a moving image camera, first to Papua New Guinea in 1904–06 and then to southern Africa in 1907–09. Less well-known is the film material that he shot in 1915, during the First World War, when he was unable to travel abroad. This consists of a series of sequences of dances and traditional crafts performed by Russian soldiers from Central Asia detained in German or Austrian prisoner-of-war camps. Again, the volume of material involved is relatively small: less than 10 minutes survives of Pöch's Melanesian footage, only 30 minutes of his southern Africa footage, and a mere 13 minutes of his prison-camp footage.[17]

Pöch is celebrated as a pioneer in many standard accounts of ethnographic film history. Although his film work is neither very accomplished nor extensive, it has become particularly well-known on account of a 56-second film that he shot in 1908 in northern Bechuanaland (now Botswana). This showed Kubi, a San 'Bushman' of around 60 years of age telling a story into the horn of a phonograph about the antics of a herd of elephants at a nearby waterhole. In 1984, Dietrich Schüller of the sound archive of the Austrian Academy of Sciences managed to synchronise these images with the audio recording that Pöch had simultaneously made on the phonograph.

1.3 Films of Rudolf Pöch. Left, Kubi, a 60-year-old San man, records a story about elephants at a nearby waterhole in August 1908 at Camel Pan, Ngamiland, in present-day Botswana. The phonograph recording was synchronised with the image in 1984. Right, Russian soldiers, probably Chechens, dance for Pöch's camera in a First World War prison camp.

The synchronisation is only approximate and was no doubt aided by the fact that for much of the film, Kubi's mouth is obscured by the phonograph horn. Nevertheless, despite the shortcomings of the synchronisation and the fact that it was achieved some seventy-five years after the original material was recorded, *Buschmann Spricht in den Phonographen* has been widely hailed as the first ethnographic film featuring synchronous sound. As a result, it is now available in multiple versions on the Web (figure 1.3).[18]

In recent years, however, Pöch's reputation has darkened considerably. He held extreme raciological views, believing that culture was strongly determined by physiology. Although he died at a relatively young age in 1921, a decade before the rise of Adolf Hitler, his ideas were later warmly embraced by the National Socialists. Along with his substantial field collections of artefacts, photographs, sound recordings and films, Pöch had also collected human body parts in the hope of being able to prove his raciological theories. This reached a peak during his expedition to southern Africa, after which he shipped back to Vienna some 80 San skeletons, 150 skulls and even the corpses of a San couple preserved in a barrel of salt. All of this material had been acquired under the most ethically dubious, as well as illegal, circumstances. The increasingly intense criticism of this particular aspect of his activity since the turn of the present century has led to a more general denunciation of Pöch and all his works, while the southern African human remains have been the subject of a still ongoing process of repatriation.[19]

However, this ethnographic film-making activity by German-speaking anthropologists in the early years of the twentieth century, although precocious, was but a pale shadow of the production of films of ethnographic interest in France over this same period. In marked contrast to Germany, the most active producers of this kind of film in France at this time were not museums, but commercial production companies, whose operators were sending back films from all over the French colonial empire and beyond. But given the commercial nature of these films, I defer further consideration of them until Chapter 2.

Although publicly funded museums may not have been involved, another museum-like venture based in Paris was an active producer of short films of ethnographic interest at this time. This was *Les Archives de la Planète*, a private collection of films set up in 1912 by Albert Kahn, a hugely wealthy investment banker. The extraordinarily ambitious aim of this collection was to document as comprehensively as possible, by means of both photography and film, all human customs across the globe. In part, this was a straightforward salvage project, but it was also oriented towards the future in the sense that Kahn held what now seems to be the most unworldly belief that by presenting these visual records to the elite figures whom he invited to his mansion on the eastern outskirts of Paris – intellectuals, leading politicians, religious authorities, military figures – it would be possible to promote international understanding and hence world peace.[20]

Under the direction of the distinguished Sorbonne geographer Jean Brunhes, professional camera operators were sent out by the *Archives*, ideally, though in practice rarely, accompanied by a geographer or other suitably qualified academic, to locations across the world. The customs that they were asked to document included not just the standard subjects of ethnographic film at this time (i.e. technical processes and ceremonies), but also the small, usually unconsidered details of everyday life, such as people walking in the street, a group of women washing clothes, a woman breastfeeding her baby.

The principal task of the Kahn operators was to take photographs, using the recently developed Lumière Autochrome colour process, and of these they took some 72,000 between 1912 and 1933 (when the project came to an end after Albert Kahn lost his fortune in the great stock market crash of 1929). Over this same period, cameramen directly employed by Kahn also shot around 165 hours of silent black and white 35 mm footage. This was later supplemented by a further 15 hours of material purchased from newsreel agencies and other sources. Although the project was supposedly global in its reach, for obvious logistical reasons most of this footage was shot in Europe and North Africa, though there was also a significant quantity of material from the Middle East and Asia, particularly from Japan where Kahn had substantial financial interests. In total, the archive gathered together material from forty-eight different countries.

One of the most interesting and substantial bodies of material within the collection concerns the *vodoun* religious cults of Bénin in West Africa (then still known as Dahomey). This material – the only footage in the Kahn archive from sub-Saharan Africa – was shot over a six-month period

1.4 Aupiais-Gadmer footage from Dahomey (1930). Left, in a rare moment of reflexivity, the leader of the *vodoun* cult of Hèbiôssô, god of Thunder, dances up to the camera. Right, converts discover the moral virtues of labour in the Christian mission.

in 1929–30 by Frédéric Gadmer, one of the most experienced cameramen employed by Kahn. In shooting this material, Gadmer worked under the direction of Père Francis Aupiais, a progressive Catholic missionary with some knowledge of academic anthropology. Aupiais had lived in Dahomey for over twenty years and was deeply committed to reconciling what he considered to be the highly moral quality of *vodoun* ceremonial life with the Christian message. Kahn had met Aupiais on one of the latter's visits to Paris and had offered to pay for Gadmer to work with him on the condition that the material that they produced concerning *vodoun* would be deposited in the *Archives*. As part of the deal, it was agreed that Gadmer would also shoot material on the work of Aupiais's mission in Dahomey, which the mission would then be able to edit and use for its own purposes.[21]

In total, Gadmer shot some six hours of footage in Dahomey, two-thirds of which were dedicated to matters relating to *vodoun*. To Aupiais's particular regret, however, no provision was made for recording sound. Moreover, as with the great majority of the footage in the Kahn archive, this material was intended to document the ceremonies in an objective fashion rather than provide the wherewithal from which later to cut a documentary, as that term would be understood today. Thus, although the images are almost invariably beautifully composed and executed, in general the material has been shot in accordance with the most uncompromising of documentation principles, that is, in long wide-angle or at most mid-shots from a tripod, with relatively few pans, or changes of framing or position, and mostly at a certain distance from the subjects (figure 1.4).

Despite these limitations, today this footage represents an invaluable record of the practice of *vodoun* in its heyday, and since 1996 the Musée Albert-Kahn, which is now the custodian of the *Archives de la Planète* collection, has been working with partners in Bénin to make it available to current generations of Beninois. However, at the time that it was made, this footage landed both the principal parties to the project in serious trouble. In Dahomey, Tôngôdô, a leading priest of the *vodoun* cult, and one of Aupiais's principal collaborators, was removed from office by his peers for having revealed too much. Meanwhile, in France, although the footage was received enthusiastically by Albert Kahn and the Parisian intellectuals to whom he showed it, including the eminent anthropologist, Lucien Lévy-Bruhl, the senior figures of Aupiais's own missionary order felt that it gave far too positive an impression of *vodoun* and thereby undermined their work in Africa. Not only did they prohibit Aupiais from showing the material in public, but for many years, they did not even allow him to return to Dahomey.

A very different kind of film-making in sub-Saharan Africa that generated footage of ethnographic interest in the interwar years in France took the form of expedition films. These were often transcontinental or at least transregional in scope, and although they had a variety of sponsors, routes and objectives, underpinning most of them was an unabashed celebration of the French colonial project. The most well-known of these is *La Croisière noire*, released in 1926 to great acclaim: the première was even attended by the French President, Gaston Doumergue. This film followed eight Citröen half-track vehicles as they proceeded, over the course of eight months, from Colomb-Béchar, a colonial garrison town in Algeria, close to the Moroccan border, south across the Sahara to the Niger river basin, then east through the French colonies of Central Africa and the Belgian Congo, before arriving finally at Antananarivo, the capital of Madagascar, in July 1925. In the final phase of the journey, the expedition divided into four groups at Kampala, one going north to seek out the source of the Nile, the others going south to Mombasa, Dar-es-Salaam and even the Cape, but all eventually reuniting in Madagascar.

Both the expedition and the film were paid for by the Citroën company, and at one level, *La Croisière noire* could be read as no more than a publicity stunt intended to promote Citroën half-track vehicles as a better means of crossing the difficult terrain of the Sahara and Central Africa than railways. But dedicated as it is in an opening title to 'The Young People of France' and supported logistically in various ways by French colonial authorities, this film can also be read as a resounding paën of praise to the 'civilising' French presence in the continent and a triumphalist reassertion of the country's imperial ambitions after the pyrrhic victory of the First World War.[22]

The director, Léon Poirier, and the cinematographer, Georges Specht, were both already distinguished figures in French cinema, and the technical quality of the film was remarkably high for the period: it also involved field sound recordings that were later incorporated into a soundtrack. Over the

1.5 *La Croisière noire* (1926) combined big game hunting with ethnographic reportage, left. The hairstyles of Mangbetu women of the Belgian Congo, right, based on cranial elongation, had a major impact on fashionable coiffure in Paris.

course of the journey, Poirier and Specht filmed a number of interesting sequences of traditional custom, including dances, initiation ceremonies, the disturbing lip-plates of the Sara Kaba women in Chad and an open-air court case about a matter of stolen fish among the Wagenia of the then-Belgian Congo (now the Democratic Republic of Congo). A sequence about the practice of cranial deformation and the resulting remarkable coiffure of Mangbetu women gave rise to the abiding iconic image that appeared on publicity posters for the film and had a major impact on Parisian fashions (figure 1.5). Many years later, Jean Rouch, while acknowledging the imperial tenor of the film, praised the directorial skill of Poirier, describing *La Croisière noire* as 'the first true film' to be made in sub-Saharan Africa.[23]

A very different and highly unusual example among French expedition films shot in Africa in the interwar years is *Voyage au Congo*. This was released in 1927 and was jointly directed by the well-known writer, André Gide and his sometime lover, Marc Allégret, who would later go on to become a distinguished film director in his own right. While Allégret shot and edited the material, Gide formulated the elegant literary intertitles (figure 1.6). Despite the celebrity of the directors, this film remains curiously neglected in the literature of visual anthropology.

In marked contrast to most other French interwar expedition films in Africa, the reference to the journey itself and the French colonial presence is minimal: instead, *Voyage au Congo* proceeds via a series of vignettes of the cultural life of the peoples whom the film-makers meet as they travel through Central Africa, with, unusually for the period, a particular emphasis on the activities of women. It also includes a well-executed fictionalised sequence in the central part of the film which follows the courtship of a young Sara couple and the negotiation of bride-wealth payments. This

1.6 *Voyage au Congo* (1927). On the banks of the Logone river, French
Equatorial Africa. Left, 'When the water is low, the pole is used to
advantage over the paddle'. Right, a Massa village: 'The regular reliefs
that decorate the houses form steps that allow one to forgo scaffolding
during construction.'

sequence involves a sense of relaxed intimacy between film-makers and
subjects that would not be achieved again in African ethnographic film-
making until the works of Jean Rouch in the 1950s.[24]

Yet although *Voyage au Congo* does not directly celebrate the French
presence in Africa, in other senses it remained complicit with the colonial
regime, in that it makes no reference to certain compromising circumstances
that arose during the making of the film, which Gide and Allégret would
later describe in print. These include the exploitation of Africans in the
forest extractive industries run by private companies and also as forced
labour working for the French colonial state. The latter even included
working under duress as porters for Gide and Allégret themselves. Nor does
the film allude to the sexual dalliances that Allégret sustained throughout
the journey with a series of local prepubescent girls: these are described in
his personal diary which was published only in 1987, some fourteen years
after his death.[25]

In addition to these transregional expedition films, the French also made
a large number of films directly linked to particular colonies, at least some
of which are of ethnographic interest. From the 1920s, the French Colonial
Ministry began to support the making of films that could be shown through
established cinema distribution networks around France with a view to
raising both awareness of and support for the French overseas empire. Some
African colonies even had their own film-making programmes, Cameroon
and Madagascar being particularly active in this regard. This activity intensified
towards the end of the decade, as film-makers prepared for the International
Colonial Exposition of 1931 in Paris, where, over the course of six months,
some 300 films on colonial subjects were screened in a cinema of 1,500
seats. While most of these films concerned colonial modernising projects

– roads, ports, forest industries, hospitals, campaigns against sleeping sickness and so on – a considerable number were exclusively or predominantly concerned with social and cultural aspects of indigenous life within particular colonies.[26]

Most of these films provided little more than a descriptive inventory of architecture, subsistence practices, crafts and dances within a given geographical area. One significant exception was *Sso: rite indigène des Etons et Manguisas*, released in 1935. This film concerns an elaborate male initiation ceremony involving two subgroups of the Beti in Cameroon. It is a substantial and well-made film of 56 minutes, featuring a musical soundtrack recorded on location, albeit asynchronously. It was directed by Maurice Bertaut, a senior colonial officer in Cameroon who had previously carried out a doctoral study of the customary law of another Beti subgroup, the Boulou. It was shot and recorded by René Bugniet, a professional cartographer who had also trained as a film-maker and who had made at least a dozen previous films for the Cameroon colonial administration.

Now no longer practised, the *sso* ceremony took its name from a particular species of small antelope admired for its speed through the forest. It required the initiands to undergo a series of physical ordeals over the course of six months, along with periods of seclusion and hunting in the forest, interspersed with ritual battles and dancing in the village plaza. A *sso* ceremony usually had a ritual sponsor, who would guarantee the considerable quantities of food and drink consumed. The sponsor could thereby expiate some past moral infraction while at the same time gaining great personal prestige.[27]

Bertaut and Bugniet's film begins with an interesting fictionalised sequence in which, following the death of his son, a senior man, one Bilimá, attributing this loss to a fight that he had had with his brother, undertakes to expiate this infraction by sponsoring a *sso* ceremony. Thereafter the film follows the unfolding of the ceremony in a largely straightforward descriptive manner (figure 1.7). This *sso* turns out to be an impressive affair, involving at one stage perhaps as many as eighty initiands, and featuring many remarkable ordeals and extraordinary dance performances.

Apart from a few occasional lapses, the voice-over, scripted and performed by Bertaut, is remarkably free – for the period – of colonialist or racist prejudice, while the shooting and sound recording by Bugniet is also generally of a high standard. Somewhat disappointingly, the film concludes with a particularly voyeuristic final shot, of the kind that also features in Bugniet's earlier work, in which he explores the scarified bodies of three young women 'to dispel any unpleasant memory of the ordeals undergone by the initiands'. But otherwise, *Sso* is perhaps the closest pre-war example of the kind of event-based ritual film that would become a staple of ethnographic film-making after the Second World War.[28]

1.7 Scenes of Beti male initiation, Cameroon, as featured in *Sso* (1935). This film anticipates the event-based ritual films of the post-war period.

It was also in the mid-1930s that the first ethnographic films involving French anthropologists *de métier* were made, though there appears to have been only two cases. One of these is the case of Marcel Griaule, a founding figure of modern French anthropology and later the mentor of Jean Rouch. In 1935, on his third expedition to Africa, which was to the territory of the Dogon of the Bandiagara Cliffs in what is today Mali and then was the French Soudan, Griaule took with him a young professional cameraman, Roger Mourlan. Initially, Griaule used the footage shot by Mourlan merely to support his lectures and his research, notably to work out the series of drawings of dance movements that are offered as a supplement to his classic work, *Masques Dogons*, published in 1938. But in 1940, Griaule collaborated with a professional film production company to produce two films from this footage, *Au pays des Dogons* and *Sous les masques noirs*, each of about ten minutes duration. These were made specifically to support an exhibition on French colonial Africa at the Musée de l'Homme in Paris.[29]

This exhibition was due to be opened by the Minister of the Colonies, Georges Mandel, and no doubt for this reason both films open with rolling titles offering a panegyric to the 'colonising genius of the French' and a complimentary allusion to Mandel himself. Whereas *Au pays des Dogons* offers a general overview of Dogon life, *Sous les masques noirs* focuses more specifically on masks, starting with their manufacture and then showing them in use during a funeral ceremony, though curiously, in this second film, the Dogon are not referred to by name. Instead, the commentary merely alludes to 'one of the most mysterious peoples of Black Africa'.

Both films were superbly shot by Mourlan and, taken together, offer a valuable ethnographic account of daily life among the Dogon as well as testifying to the extraordinary beauty of Dogon masks and the vitality of

1.8 Marcel Griaule's films of the Dogon (shot in 1935). Left, three
boys pose in Hare masks; right, a mural ostensibly being painted in a
totemic shrine, though in reality it was on the wall of the Griaule
expedition bungalow.

their ceremonial performances. However, in common with Griaule's textual
accounts of the Dogon, these films present the Dogon largely as if they
were living in an atemporal vacuum, more or less unaffected by the French
colonial presence. Early in the second film, Griaule himself appears with
his leading Dogon informants who are presented anonymously, as if they
had no personal history and no contact with the outside world. But these
informants include Doussu Wologuem, who was not only a Muslim, but
also a First World War veteran, a member of the *Légion d'honneur* and a
holder of the *Croix de guerre*.

In a much-cited interview, Griaule once claimed that everything shown
in these films was entirely authentic and that nothing had been set up since
the Dogon themselves would never have allowed it.[30] However, this was
not true, in a number of different respects. The designs that are shown being
painted on what is said to be the wall of a totemic shrine in *Au pays des
Dogons* were, in fact, being painted on the wall of one of the modern
bungalows built to house the expedition (figure 1.8). In *Sous les masques
noirs*, there is a shot of a slit gong being played, ostensibly as part of the
funeral ceremony, when in fact these instruments are never played on such
occasions and the shot was taken on a completely different occasion at the
request of one of Griaule's expeditionary colleagues, the ethnomusicologist
André Schaeffner. But most significantly of all, the 'funeral' shown in these
films was not an actual funeral, but merely a performance paid for by
Griaule.

The commentary tracks of the two films were scripted by Griaule but
performed by professional voice artists in the mannered style of the time.
While praising certain aspects of traditional Dogon life, these commentaries
are also punctuated by condescendingly ironic comment at the Dogon's

expense. No sound had been recorded in the field, so both films feature a soundtrack of extra-diegetic European music that varies from light classical to jazzy. In both regards, Griaule's films now seem much more anachronistic than the film of the non-anthropologists Bertaut and Bugniet. It has been suggested that the condescending attitudes that are a feature of Griaule's commentary script can be put down to the exigencies of having to work with a professional production company. However, it has to be said that there is a certain continuity between the ironic attitudes expressed in these films and those found in Griaule's influential methodological handbook, *Methode de l'ethnographie*.[31]

Apart from Griaule, the only other academically trained French anthropologist to make a film before the Second World War was Père Patrick O'Reilly, a Catholic priest of Irish descent, who studied under Marcel Mauss at the Institut d'Ethnologie and graduated in 1932. Two years later, supported by Paul Rivet, Director of the Musée d'Ethnologie du Trocadéro, the predecessor institution to the Musée de l'Homme, O'Reilly received a grant to carry out field research on Bougainville, an island in the North Solomons, then part of Australian New Guinea (and today part of the independent republic of Papua New Guinea). It was also a place where the religious order to which O'Reilly belonged, the Marist Fathers, had a well-established missionary presence.[32]

The principal objective of O'Reilly's expedition was to collect objects for the Trocadéro museum (of these, he eventually shipped back around 4,000) and at the same time to make a film showing those objects in use. For this purpose, he took with him a sophisticated professional camera, the Debrie Parvo, with a lightweight Bell & Howell camera as a back-up. Initially, he also had a professional cameraman with him, one Pierre Berkenheim, but from O'Reilly's own account it would seem that he shot a large part of the material himself. If so, given that there is no evidence that he had had any prior training or experience as a cinematographer, the technical quality of the footage is astoundingly high.

The main film that came out of the expedition, *Bougainville*, running to 70 minutes, was silent and offered a general ethnographic account of life on the island. Not surprisingly, given O'Reilly's brief, the manufacture of objects plays an important part in the film. But there is also much more, including some very well executed sequences of fishing, which involves a remarkable system of nets suspended from towers built out to sea, and various ritual events, including a marriage, a funeral, and a male initiation ceremony (figure 1.9). What is particularly notable about these images is the easy and intimate rapport that the film-maker had clearly developed with his subjects.

In commenting later on the making of the film, O'Reilly claimed that he treated the subjects with great respect, never asking them to put on or

1.9 *Bougainville* (1935). Left, fishing is conducted by means of large nets slung from towers built out to sea. Right, a widow paints herself with white clay.

take off any items of clothing, nor asking them to remove any medallions (crucifixes are indeed visible from time to time) or add flowers to their hair (as the tropes of the then highly popular South Seas fiction films required). He also aimed not to intrude with his camera where it was not wanted, which is why only part of the initiation ceremony is shown. This is no doubt at least part of the reason why he was able to establish such a good rapport with the subjects.

However, as well as the main film, a shorter film of 20 minutes was cut from O'Reilly's material for general audiences and released under the egregious title, *Popoko – île sauvage*. O'Reilly had a very low opinion of this film, but consoled himself with the thought that it featured a soundtrack of two songs recorded on location. For many years, only one copy of the main film existed, but in the early 1970s, encouraged by Jean Rouch, the French scientific research agency, Centre national de la recherche scientifique (CNRS), agreed to make a new copy. By then elderly, O'Reilly took the opportunity to shorten the film to 37 minutes and to add a voice-over commentary. This version can now be readily viewed through the CNRS online videotheque.[33]

In comparison with the ethnographic film legacy of the French colonial period, the filmic record that the British left behind of local indigenous social life and custom in their many colonies across the globe in the early twentieth century is extraordinarily meagre. When the British made films in their colonies, they tended to be propaganda films about their own modernising activities. Films that respond specifically and exclusively to the immense social and cultural richness of the South Asian subcontinent during the British Raj are very few while those concerned with local life and custom in the many British colonies in Africa during this period are even more limited in number.[34]

1.10 *Song of Ceylon* (1934). 'The Apparel of a God'. In the last sequence, magnificently costumed dancers are intercut with images of a giant statue of the Buddha, though the ethnographic validity of this association has been questioned.

In the context of this relative absence of films directly concerned with ethnographic subjects from the British colonial period, one film that stands out particularly is Basil Wright's celebrated documentary poem, *The Song of Ceylon*. This film might not be considered an ethnographic film in any conventional sense, but it certainly has ethnographic qualities. Originally commissioned by the Empire Marketing Board (EMB) as a four-part travelogue intended to promote the Ceylon Tea Marketing Board, in the course of post-production it became instead a poetic meditation on the religious texture of traditional life on what is now the island of Sri Lanka. It was released in 1934, after the EMB had been dissolved, by the General Post Office (GPO) film unit which was headed by Basil Wright's mentor, John Grierson.[35]

The film is divided into four parts, presented as if they were movements in a symphonic composition. The first part follows Sinhalese pilgrims to the sacred mountain of Sri Pada (known to Europeans as Adam's Peak), while the second presents everyday subsistence activity on the island – fishing, pottery, house-building, rice cultivation – and shows children being trained as dancers. The calm and measured nature of this traditional way of life is then contrasted with the 'voices of commerce' in the third part. This consists of various scenes of colonial economic activity, including the harvesting of tea, the laborious processing of copra and the dispatch of goods on international freighters, overlain with clipped telephone voices referring to stock prices and logistics. The final part returns to religious themes, juxtaposing some magnificently costumed dancers with images of the giant statues of Buddha carved in granite at Gal Vihara (figure 1.10).

The film was mostly shot by Wright himself in a manner that he would later explain had been much influenced by the advice he received from

Robert Flaherty when the latter was briefly attached to the film unit of the EMB in 1931. However, notwithstanding the excellence of the cinematography and the often-daring visual transitions, arguably the most impressive aspect of the film is the highly elaborate soundtrack entirely recorded at post-production in London. In developing this soundtrack, Wright was assisted by another important figure of early documentary film-making, Alberto Cavalcanti, the Franco-Brazilian film-maker who was then working with the GPO film unit. The avant-garde British composer Walter Leigh was also recruited to work on the soundtrack.

Inspired by the contrapuntal theories of the Soviet film-maker Sergei Eisenstein, this soundtrack combined a broad panoply of sounds, including Sinhalese music performed by musicians brought to London specifically for the purpose, Leigh's avant-garde musical compositions, a range of special effects and a number of disembodied voices, some speaking English, others Sinhalese. In addition, it featured a series of texts offering ethnographic observations about Sinhalese life originally published by the sea captain Robert Knox in 1681 and based on his knowledge of the island as derived from his twenty-three years of captivity there. This text was read in a most entrancing manner by Lionel Wendt, who was a Burgher (a person of mixed Dutch and Sinhalese descent) and by profession a photographer. Wendt had also worked with Basil Wright and his assistant, John Taylor, throughout their lengthy shoot of several months, advising them on all aspects of traditional Sinhalese life.

Although *The Song of Ceylon* is widely acclaimed as one of the finest works of documentary cinema of the interwar years, the film has also been criticised, among other things, for presenting an idealised Orientalist vision of Sinhalese life in the 1930s, and for glossing over the exploitation of workers on the tea plantations and elsewhere. It has also been questioned on more specifically ethnographic grounds, including the implication that the dancers juxtaposed in the final section with the statue of the Buddha are engaged in a religious performance of some kind, when in reality they are secular performers with no specific connection to Buddhism, and who hire themselves out to provide entertainment at weddings.[36]

But whatever the validity or otherwise of these criticisms – and there are certainly counterarguments that might be made against them – *The Song of Ceylon* remains a work of incontestable ethnographicness. Not only was it based on extensive prior research and a relatively lengthy shoot, but it is also informed by Robert Knox's ethnographic insights based on even more extended first-hand experience. In more general terms, *The Song of Ceylon* seeks to use the poetic power of cinema to communicate a sense of everyday customary Sinhalese life in a direct and respectful manner. It is surely for this reason that the film would later become a source of inspiration for two of the most influential ethnographic film-makers of the second half of the twentieth century, Robert Gardner and David MacDougall.[37]

## ETHNOGRAPHIC FILM-MAKING IN EMERGENT SETTLER STATES: AUSTRALIA, BRAZIL, THE SOVIET UNION

While museum- or state-sponsored ethnographic film-makers in Europe in the early twentieth century were seeking to document the cultural diversity of colonial empires around the globe, similar processes were going on within emergent European settler states in Australasia, the Americas and Asia.

In Australia, the most substantial body of film of ethnographic interest of this period was produced by the Board of Anthropological Research (BAR), formally part of the University of Adelaide, but also closely linked to the South Australian Museum. From the mid-1920s until the late 1930s, when its activities were curtailed by the outbreak of war, the BAR supported a series of annual expeditions, first to the northern part of South Australia, then Central Australia and eventually into Western Australia. During the course of these expeditions, some ten hours of footage about the Aboriginal population was shot.[38]

As early as 1930, some of this footage was shot in 16 mm, a film gauge that had been introduced by the Eastman Kodak film company only in 1923 and which was still widely regarded as an amateur format, suitable only for home-movie purposes. It did, however, have the great advantage over 35 mm of being very much cheaper. By 1935, BAR film-makers were shooting exclusively in 16 mm, with even a small proportion in colour. This material was edited into a series of films, which, although partly structured around the logistical travails and the scientific activities of the expeditionaries, particularly in their opening sequences, were primarily organised on a thematic basis. In this latter sense, they anticipate to some degree the *Desert People* films made by Ian Dunlop in Central Australia in the 1960s (see Chapter 3).

Where they are very different is in relation to the intertitles. These are often rather jocose, indicating that these films were primarily intended for popular audiences. This is symptomatic of the fact that at this point in Australian history, there was widespread interest in accounts of Aboriginal life since these fed into an intense debate then going on about the place of Aboriginal people within the settler nation's sense of its own nationhood.

The approach to anthropological fieldwork underlying the BAR expeditions was in the pre-Malinowskian survey mould, already considered old-fashioned by most university-based academic anthropologists by this time. The expeditions typically lasted no more than three weeks and involved multidisciplinary teams of biological anthropologists and medical researchers as well was anthropologists interested in cultural or social phenomena. Once an expedition had arrived at its destination, scouts would be sent out to encourage local groups of Aborigines to approach the expedition camp with the offer of food, steel tools, tobacco and medical attention. All research was then carried out through interpreters. The intellectual agenda of the expeditions was similarly old-fashioned: the interest in filming locomotion, hand gestures and technical activities that is a recurrent feature of the films is strongly reminiscent of Regnault's film project carried out beside the Eiffel Tower in 1895, described at the beginning of this chapter.

None of the cinematographers who shot the BAR footage had had formal professional training. In his day job, the most prominent cameraman, E. O. Stocker, was a Sydney businessman, while Norman Tindale, the principal anthropologist, who also shot a number of the films, had started his professional life as an entomologist. Henry Fry had briefly studied anthropology following medical studies at Oxford, but earned his living as a doctor in Adelaide. Charles Mountford, who was also a talented photographer, was entirely self-taught both as anthropologist and cinematographer, having first become interested in Aboriginal life while working as an electrical engineer at the post office in Darwin, in the north of Australia.

Nevertheless, the footage that these cinematographers produced is of a remarkably high standard for the period. In addition to the general stability of the image and the quality of the framing and camera positioning, the BAR film-makers also shot various slow-motion sequences of actions such as spear-throwing, digging and chopping, as a complement to their interest in locomotion. As well as being technically accomplished, the BAR film-makers appear to have established an easy rapport with their subjects. Not only were they able to film both women and men engaged in the demanding and skilful business of daily subsistence in the Australian desert in the most intimate way, but they were also permitted to film many of the most secret and sacred Aboriginal objects, sites and ceremonies, seemingly without restraint. By the request of the descendants of those who appear in these films, the viewing of this secret-sacred material is now restricted.

Some of this material is unflinchingly intrusive, notably the footage relating to the circumcision and subincision processes that constitute an important part of some Aboriginal male initation ceremonies. If certain ethical questions are raised for present-day audiences about this initiation ceremony material, most would unambigously condemn the sequences of sexual activity that are reported to have originally formed the now entirely censored final part of the film corresponding to the 1932 expedition to Mt Liebig. But these more intrusive sequences represent only a relatively small part of the total body of material produced by the BAR expeditions. Taking this material as a whole, one can readily understand why Ian Dunlop should consider this work as being of the highest quality and sensitivity, revealing,

1.11  South Australia Board of Anthropological Research films (1920s–1930s). '… an extraordinary feeling of immediacy and veracity, the beauty and excitement of desert life'.

he suggests, 'an extraordinary feeling of immediacy and veracity, the beauty and excitement of desert life' (figure 1.11).[39]

Another technically accomplished and particularly early example of ethnographic film-making in an emergent settler nation, but one that is relatively little known in the English-speaking world, is the work of Luiz Thomaz Reis, a junior officer in the Brazilian army and the official cinematographer of a programme to colonise the interior of the country that was rolled out over the first three decades of the twentieth century. Reis's most substantial ethnographic film, *Rituais e Festas Borôro*, released in 1917, with a duration of 30 minutes, concerns the funeral ceremony of the Bororo of Central Brazil, later made famous by the writings of Claude Lévi-Strauss.[40]

The merits of this film are both cinematographic and editorial. The coverage of the elaborate ceremony is impressively varied, involving a judicious mixture of wide and mid-shots. The camera is invariably well placed, allowing the dancers to move through the frame elegantly. The narrative structure of the film is of a kind that is easy to recognise a century later: in the first third of the film, the preparatory activities and certain leading figures who will participate in the ceremony are introduced, then, aided by frequent intertitles, the film simply follows the chronology of the event, culminating in a final burial sequence. A concluding intertitle suggests that this scene is reminiscent of the time before the arrival of Europeans in the New World (figure 1.12).

In terms of its technical and aesthetic quality, *Rituais e Festas Borôro* is undoubtedly one of the masterworks of early ethnographic cinema. However, from a strictly ethnographic point of view, the film is problematic in that it misrepresents the chronology of the Bororo ceremony in a radical fashion. In reality, now as much as then, the Bororo practice secondary burial: immediately after death, the body is buried in the centre of the village

1.12 *Rituais e Festas Borôro* (1917). Left, Buturaguire, *aroetoráre*, 'evoker of the spirits', photographed at the same time as the filming, though in the film his lower body is excluded from shot; right, in the burial scene, placed at the end of the film contrary to ethnographic reality, the corpse is doused with water.

plaza and the ceremonial dancing begins. After about a month, by which time the flesh will normally have decomposed, aided by regular dousing of the grave with water – as shown in Reis's film – the body is exhumed and the skeleton is taken apart. The bones are then decorated with feathers and placed in a small basket before finally being immersed in a nearby lagoon.

Probably due to the propaganda purpose of the film, which was to suggest that Bororo culture could contribute to the formation of a new Brazilian national identity, Reis appears to have decided that there was a limit to the degree of ethnographic accuracy that it was advisable to inflict on his audiences. What is certain is that in editing the film, he reordered the chronology of his original material, placing the ceremonial dancing and the dousing of the grave *before* the first burial, whereas in reality they had come afterwards. The burial was then placed right at the end the film, as if it were the final, concluding event of the ceremony, in a manner that would have seem appropriate and familiar to the eventual non-indigenous audience. The more challenging scenes of exhumation and the secondary burial of the bones do not appear in the film at all.

But perhaps the most systematic use of film-making of an ethnographic character in connection with state-building in a settler nation in the interwar years was in the Soviet Union. Over a relatively brief and specific period, from the mid-1920s until the early 1930s, many film studios in the Soviet Union were involved in the production of *kulturfilms*, a term borrowed from German to denote non-fiction films that had edifying educational, scientific or political messages to communicate. Although these films typically involved more editorial artifice than newsreels, and could even involve re-enactments by the subjects, they were generally not supposed to involve scripts, props or professional actors. Many of these films were of an ethnographic character in the sense that they concerned the customary life of one or more of the many ethnic minorities living within the boundaries of the Soviet political universe.[41]

The typical form of the *kulturfilm* is best understood in the context of Soviet nationality policy at the time. In the most summary terms, this was based, in principle, on respect for local cultural traditions and institutions (thereby supposedly distinguishing itself from the 'colonial' policies of the despised prior Tsarist regime), but at the same time on the assumption that these traditions and institutions would be progressively transformed so as to be compatible with membership of a modern, socialist supracultural polity, namely, the Soviet Union. In a typical *kulturfilm*, therefore, in the early part of the film, local cultural traditions would be presented in a broadly positive, often romantic light, but gradually, as the film unfolded, it would show how these traditions were being transformed for the better through contact with the agents of the Soviet state, resulting in a general improvement in the subjects' well-being.

A somewhat idiosyncratic example of the *kulturfilm* was *A Sixth Part of the World*, released in 1926. This was directed by Dziga Vertov, the Polish-Russian director who would later make the highly acclaimed 'city symphony', *Man with a Movie Camera*, released in 1929. The latter involved what Vertov himself called a 'ciné-race', that is, a rapid helter-skelter tour around a number of Soviet cities held together by a virtuoso array of editorial transitions and special effects, as well as a blizzard of carefully scripted intertitles. Although perhaps not quite as pyrotechnical, *A Sixth Part of the World* is much the same, though in this film, the 'ciné-race' covers the whole of the Soviet Union.

Commissioned with a very generous budget by Gostorg, the state export agency, and based on footage shot by a team of a dozen cameramen dispatched to all corners of the Soviet Union, including the shores of the Arctic, the Far East, Central Asia and the Caucasus, *A Sixth Part of the World* directly addresses the many ethnically diverse peoples within the Soviet Union. Repeatedly asserting their ownership of the Union, it urges them to contribute to collective prosperity by offering their products for export so that machinery that will transform their lives for the better – archetypically tractors – can be imported in exchange. At the same time, in conformity with the general pattern of *kulturfilms*, while signalling the richness of the cultural traditions spread over a vast area – the one sixth of the world referred to in the title – the film also celebrates, towards the end, the fact that some communities are abandoning or modifying their traditions so as to take advantage of the possibilities for prosperity, social justice and equality that are being made possible through their membership of the Soviet Union.[42]

While it is a remarkable film in many respects, the ethnographicness of *A Sixth Part of the World* is at best limited. Many individual shots within the film are both striking and ethnographically interesting, while the accumulation of images from across the Soviet Union communicates a strong sense of its cultural diversity. However, the combination of the adversarial, propagandistic nature of the narrative and the constructivist editorial strategy operates against sustained engagement with any particular social situation, event or group of people.

More conventionally ethnographic and also more typical of the *kulturfilm* format is *Forest People*, released in 1928 and directed by Alexander Litvinov, one of the most prolific Soviet non-fiction film-makers of the interwar period. Beautifully shot by Pavel Mershin, one of the leading Soviet cinematographers of the time, this film concerns a small community of Udege, a group of some 1,300 hunter-gatherers who live in the forests north of Vladivostok, on the extreme far east coast of Russia. In making this film and a companion expedition film, *Through the Ussuri Area*, Litvinov was advised by Vladimir Arsenev, a topographer, former military officer and self-trained ethnographer who had lived in the region for many years and had written a number of semi-fictionalised accounts of Udege life.[43]

*Forest People* employs a sophisticated and mostly realist film language to present a series of scenes of everyday life of the Udege. Among the most memorable scenes are a marriage negotiation, the total quarantining of a mother on her own during the period that she is giving birth, various shamanic performances and a remarkable sequence involving the hunting of a bear. But in some ways the most remarkable of all are the quiet scenes around the village, of mothers cradling their babies, men chatting and smoking their pipes, and children constructing their toys. No doubt based on the long-standing prior relationship developed by Arsenev with the Udege, Litvinov and his crew were clearly able to establish a close rapport with the subjects, which is reflected in their apparent ease in front of the camera. In his memoirs, Litvinov describes how he planned each scene together with the subjects, thereby avoiding the breaking of any cultural taboos and using re-enactment where necessary.

However, the last ten minutes of the 45-minute film have a more propagandistic purpose. After a sequence showing young people learning agricultural skills, a committee of Udege elders agrees to send a messenger, one Suntsai, to Vladivostok to request cattle, horses, a plough, even a school and a hospital from the government. In Vladivostok, Suntsai meets up with Arsenev who helps write out a formal request, which, of course, is duly granted. But before Suntsai returns home, Arsenev takes him to the cinema to see the other film that Litvinov made with the Udege, *Through the Ussuri Area*.

1.13 Scenes from *Forest People* (1928). Above left, a bride listens to her family negotiating the terms of her marriage; above right, a shaman calls upon the spirits to release animals for the hunters; below left, the hunter's wife goes to collect his kill; below right, 'Everything filmed truly!' – Suntsai, left, goes to the cinema with the ethnologist, Vladimir Arsenev.

Suntsai is delighted to see his own image on the screen and, according to Litvinov's memoirs, declared in broken Russian, 'Everything filmed truly!' (figure 1.13).

Litvinov's Udege films were released to international acclaim and he found himself being compared with Robert Flaherty, whose work was very popular in the Soviet Union at that time. Indeed it seems very likely that Litvinov himself had been directly influenced by Flaherty since a number of scenes in *Forest People* are distinctly reminiscent of *Nanook of the North* or at least of Flaherty's methods. As a result of this success, Litvinov was rewarded with generous budgets that enabled him to film a series of further *kulturfilms*, first on the Kamchatka Peninsula in 1929–30, then in the circumpolar regions of Chukotka in 1932–33, and then again in Kamchatka in 1934.

However, from the early 1930s onwards, the makers of *kulturfilms* as well as documentary film-makers more generally, came under fierce attack in the Soviet Union for making films that were not sufficiently 'ideological', that is, for not promoting socialist principles and celebrating the achievements of the Soviet state overtly enough. In response, whereas previously the benefits of contact with the Soviet state had typically been celebrated only towards the end of a *kulturfilm*, this theme began to take them over completely. Moreover, in order to ensure that this message was communicated to greatest effect, *kulturfilm*-makers began to bring in professional actors, who by definition were not from the community being represented. In the early 1930s, the very term *kulturfilm* was abandoned and the potential of the form as a vehicle for film-making that was in any sense authentically ethnographic disappeared also.

All these developments can be discerned in the works that Alexander Litvinov produced in Kamchatka and Chukotka during the 1930s. But by remaining 'on-message', Litvinov was able – unlike some of his *kulturfilm* colleagues – to survive the Stalinist purges of the mid-1930s and lived to become a strong supporter of local documentary production in Siberia in the post-war period.[44]

## Ethnographic film-making in the USA prior to the Second World War

As in other emergent settler nations, various projects in the USA in the early twentieth century were managed by museums and aimed at inventorising the lives of the original indigenous inhabitants of the country on film. In addition, both museums and academic anthropologists also made films of ethnographic interest abroad.

Even before the advent of the moving image camera, the villages of the Pueblo Indians and other native communities of the US Southwest had been a popular destination for large numbers of tourists, journalists, artists and photographers, all of whom were attracted by the beautiful traditional dress, pottery and architecture of these communities, but above all by their elaborate religious ceremonies. In the late 1890s, moving image film-makers joined the throng.[45]

The Pueblo religious celebration that attracted the most outside attention was a ceremony often referred to at that time simply as the 'Snake Dance'. This was practised by the Hopi, then known as the 'Moki' (an outsider's term that modern Hopi reject). In fact, this dance constitutes merely the culminating phase of an extended ritual process which would be more accurately described as the Snake-Antelope ceremony since it involves both Antelope and Snake, two of the nine male secret societies traditionally maintained by the Hopi. Over the course of the ceremony, the two societies perform a series of complementary ritual roles. Traditionally, these ceremonies took place in August on a biennial basis but they were managed independently in the various Hopi villages, with some villages holding the ceremony on even years according to the Gregorian calendar, while in others it was held on odd years. In its fully elaborated form, the Snake-Antelope ceremony lasts for nine days and involves many different phases, as well as a complex series of cosmological and ontological ideas. Taken as a whole, it represents, as do many Hopi ceremonies, a prolonged petition to the ancestral spirits to grant generous rainfall and bountiful crops.[46]

The 'Snake Dance' that was of such interest to outsiders takes place on the ninth and final day of the ceremony. In the course of this dance, a collection of some fifty live snakes, previously gathered in the desert and then ritually cleansed, are briefly held in the mouths of members of the Snake Society as they dance in a circle before a line of members of the Antelope Society. The snakes are then symbolically fed with cornmeal before being returned to the desert so that they can carry the community's prayers for rain back to the ancestral spirits.

Most of the outsiders attending the Snake Dance in the 1890s were not so much interested in the broader social and cultural context of the event as in the sensational sight of dancers in exotic costumes and bodypaint holding rattlesnakes in their mouths. Unsurprisingly, it was this image that the first film-makers sought to capture as well. As early as 1898, the well-known travel lecturer Burton Holmes sent his cameraman Oscar Depue to Orayvi Pueblo on First Mesa to capture 'a spectacle unique in its impressive savagery', as Holmes would later put it. Depue also returned the following year and shot the ceremony in the Walpi Pueblo, also on First Mesa. In 1901, Thomas Edison, the cinema pioneer, sent two of his leading cinematographers, James H. White and Frederick Blechynden, to Walpi where they shot four short films of different phases of the Snake Dance. In 1904, the ceremony was filmed at Orayvi by the celebrated photographer Edward S. Curtis, who even claimed to have returned in 1906 to act as a priest. Some years after that, in 1913, no less an eminence than the former President, Theodore Roosevelt and his sons were filmed watching the Snake Dance at Walpi.[47]

Museum-based ethnographers were also keen to document Pueblo ceremonial events, though they were more concerned about issues of authenticity. In 1912, Pliny Goddard, a curator at the American Museum of Natural History (AMNH) in New York, commissioned the artist and cinematographer, Howard McCormick, to go to the Southwest and shoot some footage of the Snake-Antelope ceremony. However, in a letter to Goddard, McCormick reported that he was encountering only 'fake' performances for tourists. His difficulties were compounded by the fact that the ceremony typically takes place late in the day when lighting is poor. Even more problematic, he found that getting the community's permission to film was very difficult.[48]

However, McCormick did eventually manage to shoot an effective sequence of the Snake Dance and, moreover, from a privileged position, close to the ritual action. This was shot at the village of Supawlavi on Second Mesa and runs for around six minutes, a considerable duration for that time. Unfortunately, it appears to be the only part of McCormick's footage that has survived, so there is no indication that he filmed anything of the broader context of the Snake-Antelope ceremonies. It is also not clear whether what he filmed was a genuine religious celebration, though the fact that the audience in the background appears to consist primarily of indigenous children suggests that it was indeed an authentic enactment.

By the 1920s, many Pueblo communities had become highly reluctant to allow their religious ceremonies to be filmed. This is made evident by another film about the Snake-Antelope ceremonies in the AMNH collection. In the catalogue, this film is dated to 1925 and carries a descriptive title, but on the film itself there is no main title, nor any authorial attribution. Nor does it indicate in which Hopi village the footage was shot, though in fact it appears to be Musangnuvi on Second Mesa. The film runs for about 17 minutes and is clearly a fragment of a longer, more general film about the Hopi, since the first seven minutes shows a man carding wool before it abruptly passes on to the Snake-Antelope ceremony.[49]

What is especially interesting about this film – which is now subject to restricted access conditions – is that it contains some sequences of the phases of the Snake-Antelope ceremonies that occur *prior* to the Snake Dance. Also, through the intertitles, it offers some sense of the broader organisational context and meaning of the various elements of the ceremonies. However, in sharp contrast to McCormick's footage from Supawlavi, this material has all been filmed from a vantage point far from the ritual action, seemingly from the roof of a house overlooking the village plaza. Furthermore, as explained by an intertitle that appears just before the culminating moment when the Snake Dance is supposed to occur, 'due to the meddling of a Hopi from another village the consent of the snake priest was withdrawn and the last dance was not secured'. Instead, the film concludes with the material shot by McCormick in Supawlavi in 1912.

A similar situation appears to have arisen during the production of another film made for the AMNH around the same period, this time about the *shálako* ceremony performed at the Zuni Pueblo. This film was shot by Owen Cattell in 1923, the same year in which he also shot *Land of the Zuñi and Community Work* for the Museum of the American Indian (MAI). This latter film was directed by the eminent ethnologist Frederick W. Hodge, then the assistant director of the MAI, and covers a broad range of topics, including crafts, food processing and daily life, as well as various summer ceremonial sequences.[50] By contrast, *Shalako Ceremonial at Zuni, New Mexico*, which was made at the request of the head of the AMNH Anthropology Department, Clark Wissler, is exclusively concerned with the *shálako* ceremony and does not appear to have been directed by Hodge, though he does seem to have played an important part in arranging for the film to be made.

The *shálako* ceremony, which takes place shortly before the winter solstice, constitutes the climax of the complex ritual calendar of the Zuni. The final phase of the ceremony is initiated by the appearance at dusk, on the occasion of a new moon, of six large masked figures, the eponymous *shálako*. These figures are conical, about 3 m high and 1 m across the base, with sides clothed in Hopi blankets (acquired through trade) and surmounted by masks featuring a diadem of eagle feathers, a turquoise horn on each side, and a mobile jaw operated from inside the figure.[51]

These figures are said to be *kokko*, ancestral beings who have returned to celebrate with their living descendants. The same term is used of the two men who take it in turns – on account of the weight – to inhabit and operate the *shálako*, a role for which they have had to prepare throughout the previous year through various forms of abstinence – dietary, sexual and occupational. The *shálako* are welcomed into the village with dance and song by two other, very contrasting masked groups, also representing spirit beings: the finely attired *sayatasha*, a group of five figures often collectively referred to as 'the council of deities' in the ethnographic literature, and the grotesquely costumed *koyemshi*, clownish trickster figures, of whom there are typically around ten. The role of the latter is both to entertain onlookers and to orchestrate the event itself. Although the *shálako* leave the village after twenty-four hours, the celebration continues for another four nights culminating in the ritual welcoming of ten young girls, the Corn Maidens, into the village plaza.

In *Shalako Ceremonial*, Cattell makes an attempt to follow the various stages of the ceremony, providing contextualising explanations in the form of extensive intertitles. But such is the complexity of the event that even the most experienced film-maker working under ideal conditions would have found it a great challenge to make a readily comprehensible film about the *shálako* ceremony. While Cattell was evidently competent in a technical sense, his repertoire as a cinematographer was seemingly quite limited. More importantly, conditions were far from ideal in that it is very obvious from the film itself that his presence was, at best, accepted with reluctance by the subjects.

Contrary to the assumption of some later commentators on the film, Cattell had been given formal permission to film by leading Zuni authorities, including the village governor Latario Luna, as well as the eminent priest Komosana. Their reason for granting this permission was that they had been persuaded by Hodge that a film about the ceremony would demonstrate its genuinely religious character and would thereby help to convince the government not to suppress Pueblo dances on the grounds that this suppression would be in violation of the constitutional protection of religious

1.14 *Shalako Ceremonial at Zuni* (1923). Ancestral beings, *kokko*, make their appearance at the *shàlako* ceremony. Owen Cattell was permitted to film this ceremony to demonstrate its religious nature and thereby to support the Zuni's right to practise it under the terms of the US Constitution.

freedom. Luna and Komosana therefore agreed to let Cattell film provided that he maintained a respectful distance. Cattell clearly complied with this condition, since his camera is mostly situated far from the ritual action, so far indeed that it is often difficult for the viewer to see what is happening. But notwithstanding Cattell's discretion, some Zuni appear to have found the mere presence of the camera offensive.[52]

When the *shàlako* masks finally do appear on the plain beside the village, about two-thirds of the way through the 29-minute film, Cattell's camera is situated at least 150 metres away. Indeed, one of the six masks does not appear at all because, as explained in an intertitle, its wearer did not wish to be photographed. Later, we are afforded a slightly closer view of the masks and it is indeed a truly magnificent sight to watch them as they run back and forth in pairs, in clouds of swirling snow (figure 1.14). But mostly the camera remains remote: the shots of the other two groups of masked dancers, the *sayatasha* and the *koyemshi*, are never more than oblique and distant, while the Corn Maidens are not seen at all for, as another intertitle explains, permission to film on the final day was withdrawn.

This intertitle states that 'the local representative of the Indian Bureau' was responsible for this withdrawal, though in fact the official in question, one Robert Bauman, had been urged to impose the ban by a political faction within the Zuni Pueblo opposed to the governor. This faction claimed that in giving permission for the film, Luna had violated the trust of the community and should therefore be removed from office. As a result of the ban, the forlorn final image of the film consists of a shot taken from some distance outside the village. This shows the backs of spectators standing on the roofs of the village, looking down into the invisible plaza beyond, where, one presumes, the Corn Maidens are making their entrance.

*Shalako Ceremonial* raises a number of important questions about the power relationships implicit in any ethnographic film-making situation, as well as about control over the subsequent circulation of any culturally sensitive images that such situations might produce. These issues have recently been addressed by A:shiwi A:wan Museum and Heritage Center (AAMHC), a non-profit organisation set up in 1992 by a group of Zuni tribal members. Although this group does not appear to be generally hostile to ethnographic film-making by outsiders, in that they publicise Cattell's other films about the Zuni on their website, they take the view that *Shalako Ceremonial* should never have been made, since it shows certain situations that normally only initiated Zuni men would be allowed to see.[53]

However, the AAMHC also recognises that although the viewing of the film at the AMNH itself is now restricted, digitised copies of the film are already circulating widely beyond their control. Rather than take on the pragmatically impossible task of preventing this circulation, they therefore opted instead to work with the AMNH to produce a new version of the film. This is entitled *The Shalako Film Revisited* and excludes a sequence that should be seen only by initiated Zuni men: this is replaced by an intertitle explaining the reason for this exclusion. At the same time, certain factual and interpretative inaccuracies in the original intertitles were corrected, though the latter were retained to demonstrate the difference between the outsider and insider interpretations. A Zuni voice-over commentary that is much more detailed than the intertitles was also added. This version of the film has subsequently been used to promote cultural awareness among young people in Zuni by providing them with a visual dimension to support the oral accounts of the past that still actively circulate within the community. In order to control the circulation of the new film, the AAMHC has made it a condition of viewing it that there should always be a Zuni presence.[54]

In addition to these film-making projects with Native Indian communities within the USA in the interwar years, the AMNH also supported a large number of expeditions across the globe that generated film footage of some ethnographic interest. These expeditions were often paid for by wealthy private sponsors, and the nature of the AMNH involvement was variable: sometimes its own personnel were directly involved, on other occasions it merely lent its name. The aims of these expeditions also varied: most focused primarily on geographical or zoological matters, only shooting ethnographic material along the way, so to speak, though a few were more directly concerned to engage with local people. Professional cinematographers were often involved, so the technical quality of the footage could therefore be high. However, even in the best cases, the ethnographicness of this material is limited by the fact that the film-makers had little knowledge of the people whom they were filming and rarely remained in one place long enough to establish any kind of rapport, let alone learn anything of the local language.

Much the same applies to the expedition films with which other US academic institutions were associated during the interwar years. One that has attracted some attention was *Explorations in the Amazons Basin*, released in 1930. This was made in 1924–25 in the course of an expedition to discover the source of the Orinoco via the Rio Branco in northern Brazil. The expedition was led and largely paid for by a wealthy amateur geographer, Hamilton Rice, who was associated with the University of Harvard while the film was shot by the celebrated pioneer of Brazilian documentary film-making, Silvino Santos. Although this film is certainly accomplished in a general technical sense, the superficiality of the sequences about the indigenous peoples of the Rio Branco is compounded by the blatant racism inherent in Rice's voice-over commentary.[55]

Less accomplished cinematographically, but somewhat more valuable ethnographically is the footage shot for the joint US-Dutch expedition to western New Guinea of 1926–27, led by the anthropologist Matthew Stirling and associated with the Smithsonian Institution. Some of this material was edited into a film, later destroyed in a flood, that was entitled *By Aeroplane to Pygmyland*, and which Stirling used to support a series of lecture tours after returning from the expedition. But judging by the surviving footage, most of this material was shot at a great distance from the indigenous subjects and does no more than show them trading with the expeditionaries or just hanging about the expedition camp. It has a certain ethnographic value nevertheless, particularly when accompanied by the voice-over commentary recorded by Stirling in the 1960s.[56]

Some of the best footage, both ethnographically and cinematographically, to arise from an expedition associated with a US museum in the interwar years, is the material shot by the Oscar-winning cinematographer Floyd D. Crosby and his assistant Arthur P. Rossi during an expedition to the Matto Grosso of Central Brazil in 1930–31, which was associated with the University of Pennsylvania Museum. This includes some interesting footage of the Bororo and of the Xinguano indigenous group, the Yawalpiti. In what could well be the first example of its kind in ethnographic film history, a few shots in the Bororo footage are in lip-synchronous sound recorded in the field on a then-new system provided by the main financial sponsor of the expedition, the RCA Victor phonogram company (figure 1.15, left).

In *Matto Grosso, the Great Brazilian Wilderness*, the principal film to arise from the expedition, which was released in 1932, this footage was mostly used in a knowingly false and confused manner, though almost despite itself it still contains some material of genuine ethnographic interest (figure 1.15, right). Almost ten years later, the Pennsylvania Museum anthropologist on the expedition, Vincenzo Petrullo, arranged for some of the footage to be

**1.15** Films from the Mato Grosso expedition of 1930–31. Left, in a
supplementary film, a Bororo man explains how to make an arrow,
probably the first example of on-location lip-synchronous sound
recording in ethnographic film history; right, in the main film, *Matto
Grosso, the Great Brazilian Wilderness*, a face in the crowd was identified in
2011 as that of Tiriacu Areguiri Ópogoda, a renowned Bororo shaman.

re-cut into two short films that are much more valuable from an ethnographic
point of view. Along with some equally interesting out-takes from the main
film, these two shorter films are now available on the Penn Museum website.[57]

While the number of ethnographic films produced by museum-based
US anthropologists prior to the Second World War was hardly substantial,
it was still greater than the number produced by anthropologists based in
US university departments. Moreover, whereas film-makers associated with
museums were at least motivated by a concern to produce edited films that
they could then project for visitors to their institutions, university-based
scholars tended to think that the primary reason for taking a camera to the
field was simply as a means to gather visual data for later analysis. They
normally did not set out with any prior intention to shoot material for a
film that would be structured by an expository narrative.

One of the first US university-based anthropologists to use film in the
course a field research project was none other than Franz Boas, widely
regarded as the principal foundational figure of US anthropology and
particularly well-known for his work over forty years with the Kwakwaka'wakw,
an indigenous group living on the northeastern shore of Vancouver Island
and adjacent stretches of the Pacific Coast of Canada. In the winter of 1930,
at the age of 70, Boas decided to try his hand at film-making in the course
of what would prove to be his final field-trip to the Kwakwaka'wakw.[58]

Boas took a simple moving image camera and a wax-cylinder phonograph
to record sound. Technologically, this represented more or less the same
array of equipment that Haddon had taken with him to Mer Island more
than three decades before. Conceptually, Boas's project was also much the
same as that of Haddon and indeed had certain resonances with the even

earlier work of Regnault, as described at the beginning of this chapter. Based at Fort Rupert (known as Tsaxis in Kwagulth, the dialect of the local subgroup of Kwakw<u>aka</u>'wakw), Boas recorded around 45 minutes of material on a range of topics including ceremonial dance, music, chiefly competitive oratory, shamanic activities, games and some craft processes. His purpose was to to make a visual record that could be used later, in conjunction with the phonograph recordings, to explore the relationship between 'motor behavior' (i.e. bodily movement), and culture among the Kwakw<u>aka</u>'wakw.[59]

As in the case of Regnault and Haddon, the performances that Boas filmed were 'on-request performances', that is, they were put on, not in the normal social or ceremonial contexts of the activities concerned, but rather at his request in totally controlled and artificial situations where there was adequate natural lighting for the camera. Some of these performances were filmed in the yard of a European-style house while others were filmed in more open countryside, sometimes with an iconic totem pole in the background, at other times in front of a sort of palisade. The performers, mostly in ones and twos, are dressed in a mixture of traditional and modern dress.

Technically speaking, the footage is very poor, featuring numerous jump cuts and inadequate exposures – unsurprisingly, since Boas appears to have had no training whatsoever in the use of a moving image camera prior to this field-trip. In the end, it seems that Boas never completed the study for which he shot this material, in part because he believed (erroneously) that the wax cylinders had been stolen and in part because of his advancing years. It is dubious, in any case, whether his recordings would have been sufficiently sophisticated from a technical point of view to establish the correlations that he was seeking.

Owing to his great eminence in North American anthropology, Boas's efforts at film-making have attracted considerable attention, despite his evident lack of competence. However, there were a number of other US anthropologists of the interwar period who were also prepared to confront the technical and budgetary hurdles involved in film-making, but whose work is not so well known. One of these was Boas's own student, Melville J. Herskovits, most remembered for his work on the African cultural legacy among the African diaspora in the Americas.

Between 1928 and 1934, Herskovits shot almost three hours of footage in the course of three different field expeditions to Surinam, West Africa and Haiti. All these films are in black and white, and shot on 35 mm film, using an Eyemo, a compact, spring-wound camera produced by Bell and Howell specifically for newsreel cinematography. In addition, Herskovits also made over a thousand audio recordings of music and song on wax cylinder recorders, though this material was not synchronous with the film footage.[60]

Herskovits shared his mentor's interest in exploring the connection between motor behaviour and culture, and this is reflected in the nature of the material that he chose to shoot. In addition to the many sequences of music and dance, there are a considerable number of sequences on craft activities, as well as on subsistence activities, including collective work parties, since he was particularly interested in the possible continuities between motor behaviour in everyday life and the movements encountered in dance within the same society.

Herskovits's film work represents a considerable advance on that of Boas, not only in terms of sheer volume, but also editorially, in that both the variety and complexity of the subject matter are much greater. Although some 'on-request performances' are still included in the material, there are also many sequences of spontaneous behaviour, both in ceremonial contexts and in the form of everyday activities, particularly in the West African and Haitian material. Moreover, in contrast to Boas, Herskovits clearly thought of his material as being more than just research footage, particularly that shot in West Africa, since he later edited this into an informational film structured around a series of intertitles and maps presenting the various different groups of the region that he visited. This appears to have been intended to support his textual publications about these groups.

Yet although Herskovits's film work may represent a considerable advance on the work of Boas in an editorial sense, it has to be said that it remains highly deficient technically. The image is often unstable or underexposed, the positioning of the camera is often poor, and very few processes, technical or performative, are covered in their entirety from beginning to end. It is clear that he did not shoot the material with any sense of later editorial requirements since there is very little variety in the nature of the shots: the great majority of the material is shot in mid-distance wide-angle shots, with very few close-ups of either people or objects.

It has been suggested that Herskovits may have chosen to shoot in this detached, wide-angle manner believing that in this form, his material would provide more objective evidence in support of his arguments about the relationships between motor behaviour and culture. But if so, this merely confirms the fact that his approach still lay firmly within the classical paradigm of documentation film-making, even if, after the fact, he sought at the editorial stage to structure his material about West Africa into an expository pedagogical documentary.

Another of Boas's students to make films in the interwar years, and one whose work is much better known, was Margaret Mead. These films were made in the course of the field research carried out on Bali and in the Sepik region of Papua New Guinea in conjunction with her then husband, Gregory Bateson (who, as it happened, was a former student of Haddon at Cambridge). Over a three-year period, 1936–39, with Bateson doing all the shooting but with Mead apparently playing the lead directorial role, they produced some twenty-four hours of black-and-white footage, two-thirds of it on Bali, one-third in the Sepik region. Although relatively modest by present-day standards, this was an unprecedented quantity of material, representing substantially more than the three hours produced by Herskovits, and completely dwarfing the quantities shot by academic film-makers of the generation of Haddon and Spencer.[61]

Another difference was that whereas Herskovits was still shooting on 35 mm, Bateson shot on 16 mm: as Mead and Bateson intended from the start to shoot a large amount of film, they were obliged to keep their costs to a minimum. The camera that Bateson used was a Zeiss-Ikon Movikon, a model that would later be much favoured by German combat cinematographers during the Second World War. In addition to this film footage, Bateson also took a large number of photographs, only a small fraction of which have ever been published.

Mead and Bateson's primary concern was to record mother–child interactions since they believed that it was in this relationship that they would discover the key to understanding the development of schizophrenia, which was the main goal of their research. Their aim was to use the cameras, both moving image and still, as scientific data-gathering devices, in as objective a manner as possible. In one of their later publications, Bateson was careful to distinguish their way of working from the making of 'documentaries', though in the following passage, it is important to note that he is referring not to 'documentaries' as this term would be understood today, but rather to films such as *Nanook of the North*, which while purporting to be about real life were actually based on dramatised performances:

> We tried to use the still and the moving-picture cameras to get a record of Balinese behavior, and this is a very different matter from the preparation of 'documentary' film or photographs. We tried to shoot what happened normally and spontaneously, rather than to decide upon norms and then get the Balinese to go through these behaviors in suitable lighting. We treated the cameras in the field as recording instruments, not as devices for illustrating our theses.[62]

By the 1930s, camera technology had moved on sufficiently for film-makers to be able to aspire to film their subjects without the latter being aware that they were doing so. Indeed, in an attempt to maximise the objectivity of his footage, Bateson would sometimes use a right-angle lens so that the subjects would not realise that they were being filmed. However, at other other times, Mead and he would do the opposite, intentionally provoking reactions, with Mead appearing in shot offering a child a ball, a doll or a piece of cake to see how they would respond. When looking at this material today, one has the impression that one is watching some kind of open-air experiment in developmental psychology (figure 1.16, left).

1.16 Contrasting aesthetics in the films of Margaret Mead and Gregory Bateson. Left, a child is offered a piece of cake in *Karba's First Years* (1952); right, recovering from deep trance in *Trance and Dance in Bali* (1952).

Rather different from the main body of the footage was the material that Mead and Bateson produced with the assistance of their friend, Jane Belo, a North American artist and self-trained anthropologist who was then living on Bali. This footage concerned the *tjalonarang*, a theatrical play supported by a gamelan orchestra that was performed in the grounds of a temple. This was of particular interest to Mead and Bateson since they believed that it represented the playing out in public of certain crucial features of Balinese mother–child relationships. The narrative of the play turns upon the conflict between Rangda, a terrifying masked female witch, and Barong, a male dragon. It culminates in a scene in which Barong sends a group of his followers, armed with long daggers, to attack Rangda, only for her to repulse her assailants by the sheer power of her personal magic so that they fall to the ground in a deep trance. For Mead and Bateson, this scene represented a metaphorical re-enactment of the daily rejection by Balinese mothers of the emotional climaxes of their children, which, they believed, resulted in the sort of unresponsive personality that, in their view, characterised both the Balinese and schizophrenics in Western society.[63]

Although both Mead and Bateson used some of the rushes to support their teaching in the years immediately following their return to the USA, it was not until the early 1950s that the editing of the material into a series of films began. By this time, Mead and Bateson had gone their separate ways both professionally and personally, so Mead oversaw the editing alone, though in the credits the films are attributed to both of them, with Bateson's name first in deference to alphabetical order. With the aid of the editor Josef Bohmer, Mead initially cut six films from the rushes, all of them relatively short, between 10 and 21 minutes long. These six films were presented as a series under the collective title, 'Character Formation in Different Cultures'. Two of the films are comparative, one of them, *Childhood Rivalry* (1954), comparing mother–child relations in Bali and New Guinea, while the other, *Bathing Babies in Three Cultures* (1954), adds a third dimension by including material shot in the USA as well. Some twenty-five years later, Mead edited a seventh film from the material, though this did not form part of Character Formation series. This was *Learning to Dance in Bali* and as the title suggests, it deals not with mother–child relations, but with dance instruction, and primarily with that given by a professional performer, a certain Mario, rather than by parents.

Although Mead and Bateson may have set out with the explicit intention of producing objective visual documentation rather than 'documentaries', as this term was understood in the 1930s, all seven of the final edited films could be characterised as documentaries in the standard modern sense of term. That is, although they intended to present a factual account of the world as it is in reality, the original footage has clearly been manipulated in the edit suite for the purposes of narrativisation. From a stylistic point of view, however, there is considerable variation between the seven films.

Most of the films consist, in effect, of illustrated lectures by Mead, in which the visual documentation is offered in support of verbal arguments delivered through the soundtrack. Although the material presented in these illustrated lectures sometimes has an intrinsic chronological structure, as for example in *A Balinese Family* (1951) and *Karba's First Years* (1952), this is diffuse and it is primarily Mead's narration that carries the film along. By contrast, in a number of the other films, it is the chronological structure of an intensive event over a limited time period that constitutes the main narrative motor of the film. Although these films also feature a verbal narration by Mead, this is more of a response to the various moments of the evolving event rather than being constitutive of the narrative itself. Such is the case, for example, in *First Days in the Life of a New Guinea Baby* (1952), where at various points, Mead's voice falls completely silent and the dramatic detail of the event itself takes over the reins of the narrative, as it were.

If the illustrated lecture films look back towards towards the documentation films of Haddon and Spencer, these films with event-based narratives look forward to the film-making praxes of the leading ethnographic documentary film-makers of the immediate post-war period. By far the most elaborate example of the event-led narrative structure among the Mead-Bateson films is *Trance and Dance in Bali* (1952), which features the *tjalonarang* theatrical performance. This is the film that departs most from the original documenta-tion footage in that it draws on material shot during two different perfor-mances of the event and presents this as if it all formed part of a single event. The narrative arc of the film is also supported by a soundtrack of gamelan music, probably recorded some ten years beforehand, and 'arranged' (as the credits put it) by the then well-known modernist composer, Colin

McPhee, who was, at the time, married to Jane Belo. The dramatic culminating moments of the *tjalonarang*, shot by Belo because Bateson had run out of film stock, are shown in slow motion. In combination with McPhee's musical arrangement, this slow-motion effect considerably enhances the viewer's sense of the trance state of the dancers (figure 1.16, right).

In all these respects, *Trance and Dance in Bali* represented a clear departure from the principle of using the moving image camera merely as a recording instrument. As such, it was clearly at odds not only with Bateson's methodological statement cited above, but also with Mead's frequent later pronouncements about the use of visual media in ethnographic research. It is somewhat ironic therefore that it is for this film that both she and Bateson are most remembered as film-makers.[64]

While, in later years, Bateson appears to have undergone something of change of heart as to the role of the moving image camera in ethnographic research, Mead continued to insist that its main purpose was to serve as an objective recording instrument. As late as 1975, in the introductory chapter to the landmark volume, *Principles of Visual Anthropology*, edited by Paul Hockings, she was still promoting the idea of the moving image camera as analogous to the telescope or the microscope in its ability to enable observations of the world in an entirely objective manner but with the added advantage that it could also record those observations for posterity. She envisaged a utopian future when a fully automated camera with a 360-degree lens could be set up in a central place within a village to record large batches of material without this in any way affecting the customs and behaviour of those being filmed. This filmic data-gathering, she argued, should not involve any sort of selection, either in shooting or in editing. Nor need it be motivated by any theoretical purpose: the important thing was to get it done before the customs being filmed disappeared for ever.[65]

This idea of the moving image camera as analogous to an objective scientific recording instrument has proved remarkably resilient in the history of English-language ethnographic film-making. It is an idea that continues to surface occasionally, even now. Yet notwithstanding its enduring appeal, it is an analogy that should be firmly resisted since it obscures the fact that the creation of a cinematographic image can never be entirely objective given that even in placing a camera and turning it on and off, a film-maker is engaged in a signficant act of authorship. In fact, Mead's dream of a 360-degree camera has recently been realised and is already being used for ethnographic purposes by film-makers in various different parts of the world. But these cameras still have to be placed in certain selected positions as well as turned on and off at certain points, and for these reasons alone, if not for many others, they are no more capable of producing entirely objective accounts of the world than earlier models with a more restricted range of view.

Rather than thinking of the moving image camera as merely an instrument for recording events in an entirely objective fashion, it is both more appropriate and more productive to think of it as a means for producing an authored representation that ascribes ethnographic significance to those events. For although it might faithfully record what is going on in front of it, a moving image camera cannot by itself determine the significance of what it records, and it is this significance, rather than the mere existence of the phenomena recorded, that is of over-riding importance in any form of ethnographic film-making. What Margaret Mead and many of her generation failed to grasp is that it is the manner in which a film is authored, not the absence of authorship, that ensures its ethnographic qualities.

## Notes

1 de Heusch (2007).

2 www.silenttimemachine.net.

3 A sample of Regnault's material (albeit with the superimposition of a saccharine voice-over in Italian and a Chopin nocturne) is available at www.youtube.com/ embed/IvTRx8UGEV8.

4 See Rony (1996), 21–73 for an extensive discussion of Regnault's work.

5 Rony (1996), 48, quotes from an article that Regnault published in 1923.

6 This film can be viewed at aso.gov.au/titles/historical/torres-strait-islanders/clip1/. Haddon also published an extended textual account of the Malo ceremonies (1901, 42–52). For a more detailed discussion of Haddon's film-making, see Henley (2013b), 386–401.

7 Letter from Haddon to Spencer, 23 October 1900. Spencer Papers H2, Pitt Rivers Museum, University of Oxford. Quoted in Dunlop (1979), 112.

8 See Henley (2013b), 401–21, for a more extended discussion of Spencer's film-making activities, including his later work in Northern Australia. The original material is conserved in the Australian National Film and Sound Archive in Canberra, but the rights are owned by Museum Victoria in Melbourne, to whom Spencer donated his film material in 1916. Three extracts from the *tjintjingalla* material as well as more general information about the ceremony are available at https:// collections.museumvictoria.com.au/articles/6785.

9 The case for interpreting the *tjintjingalla* as an anti-European millenarian dance is made at some length in Henley (2013b), 418–21. For a sceptical view about this interpretation, see Hercus (1980), 7, n.4.

10 MacDougall (2019), p. 131.

11 Anon. (1929). Like most contributions to this edition of the manual, the Kinematography entry is unsigned. But Haddon was on the editorial committee and had written the corresponding entry in the previous edition, published in 1912.

12 See pp. 9–10, 18–20.

13 See, among others, MacDougall (1997) (2019), pp. 134–5; MacFarlane (2010), Kuklick (2013).

14 Fuhrman (2007), 3.

15 For a description of Weule's film work, see Fuhrmann (2015), 133–48. For a discussion of the films produced by the German Melanesian expeditions as well as links to the films online, see www.silenttimemachine.net.

16 See Hempel (2009), Fuhrmann (2013), 45–51, and www.silenttimemachine.net/ film-makers/koch-grunberg-theodor/.

17 For further details about Pöch and his films, including links to those that are available on the Web, see www.silenttimemachine.net/film-makers/poch-rudolf/ .

18 A good example can be found at www.youtube.com/watch?v=a2bdPlcrMX4. See
  Schüller (1987) for a technical account of how the synchronisation of the film was
  achieved.

19 See Morris (1987), 15–16; Berner (2006), Rassool (2015). The Austrian institutions
  that hold San remains are committed to digital repatriation but some physical repatria-
  tions have also taken place.

20 These paragraphs on *Les Archives de la Planète* draw on Castro (2008), Amad (2010)
  and Werner (2015) as well as on my visits to the Musée Albert-Kahn, where the
  archives are now held in a restored and repurposed version of Kahn's elegant suburban
  villa. I am grateful to Mme Valérie Perlès, director of the Museum, for providing
  me with access to its holdings when it was closed to the general public. See also
  the Museum's website at: albert-kahn.hauts-de-seine.fr.

21 In these paragraphs on the Aupiais-Gadmer project, I draw on the work of Martine
  Balard, particularly her book (1999), 187–219, and a more recent article (2007). See
  also Beausoleil (1996).

22 See particularly Marc-Henri Piault (2000), 109–13, and Murray Levine (2005). Despite
  the celebrity of the film, it remains difficult to see because the owners have maintained
  a very tight control over the rights. For a more general overview of interwar French
  expedition films in Africa, see Bloom (2006), also Henley (2017), 39–44.

23 Although it is unsigned, there can be litttle doubt that Rouch wrote the entry for *La
  Croisière noire* that appears in the 1967 UNESCO catalogue of films about sub-Saharan
  Africa which he himself edited (Rouch 1967a), 40–1. He also comments on the film
  in an essay that appears later in the same catalogue (Rouch 1967b), 376–7.

24 For further details see Henley (2017), 42–4.

25 Durosay (1993), 39–40.

26 Bloom (2008), 125–35; Murray Levine (2010), 120–4; Henley (2017), 45–6.

27 Quinn (1980).

28 See Henley (2017), 53–5 and www.silenttimemachine.net.

29 In these paragraphs on Griaule's films, I draw on the work of Éric Jolly (2014, 2017)

30 Griaule's comments are reproduced at length by Pierre Leprohon (1945), 185–6.

31 Griaule (1957). Two years later, in 1942, Griaule supervised the release of two further
  films. These were essentially reversions of the original films, involving some reordering
  and the incorporation of a few additional sequences. *Technique chez les noirs*, 15
  minutes, covers much the same ground as *Au pays des dogons*, whereas *Le Soudain
  mystérieux*, which runs to 13 minutes, is effectively a reversion of *Sous les masques
  noirs*. The voice-over commentaries and musical soundtracks are also different but
  not markedly dissimilar to those of the original films.

32 In these paragraphs, I draw on an article by O'Reilly himself, originally published
  in 1949, and republished in the catalogue of Pacific ethnographic films edited by
  Jean Rouch and Monique Salzmann (1970), 281–7, as well as on an article by Hugh
  Laracy (2013), and some personal communications from Jean Guiart in August 2018
  for which I am very grateful. See also www.silenttimemachine.net.

33 See https://videotheque.cnrs.fr/index.php?urlaction=doc&id_doc=403&rang=1.

34 The films made by the Dutch in their East Indian colonies and by the Belgians in
  the Congo were similarly primarily concerned with their own modernising activities,
  though the Dutch were perhaps marginally more active than the British in also
  making a few films about local indigenous social and cultural life. See the collection
  of films held by the Eye Film Museum in Amsterdam at www.eyefilm.nl. See also
  *Belgisch Congo Belge* the recently released DVD collection of colonial films about
  the Congo released by the Cinematek of the Royal Belgian Film Archive. In their
  colonies in Africa, the Portuguese were also primarily concerned as film-makers
  with their own activities (see De Rosa 2018).

35 In these paragraphs, I draw on Seton (1935/1971), Starr (1975/1996), Guynn (1998),
  Gitlin (2012). See also the notes by Jon Hoare on the Colonial Film website at:
  www.colonialfilm.org.uk/node/486.

36 This was the principal criticism of my former Manchester colleague and specialist in the anthropology of Sri Lanka, Martin Southwold, as expressed to me in a personal communication when we screened the film together on one occasion in 1988. However, according to the cinema critic and Indianist, Marie Seton, a contemporary of Wright, the robes of these dancers are said by local people to have been designed by the Buddha two thousand years ago (Seton 1935/1971, 102).

37 See pp. 173 note 4; 285, 396.

38 These paragraphs draw on Dunlop (1979), Batty (2013) and particularly on the archive pages of the South Australia Museum website at archives.samuseum.sa.gov.au/aa346. See also www.silenttimemachine.net.

39 Dunlop (1979), 115.

40 For a more extended discussion of this film, see Caiuby, da Cunha and Henley (2017). It is viewable at www.youtube.com/watch?v=Ein6eKqMBtE&t=860s.

41 These paragraphs draw extensively on the excellent book by Oksana Sarkisova (2017).

42 See Sarkisova (2017), 40–62.

43 See Sarkisova (2017), 84–90. The film itself can be viewed online in reasonable quality, albeit as part of a Russian television programme at www.youtube.com/watch?v=ADyG_YRvn6A. I am particularly indebted to Alex and Riita Pravda for the translation of the intertitles of this film. See also www.silenttimemachine.net.

44 Sarkisova (2017), 90–5, 108–11, 208.

45 I am particularly indebted to Peter Whiteley, Curator of North American Ethnology at the American Museum of Natural History, New York, for his review of these paragraphs concerning the films made in Pueblo communities.

46 See Sutton (2017).

47 See Griffiths (2002), 176; Jordan (1992), 110–17; Gidley (1982), 73. In *Principles of Visual Anthropology*, the influential volume edited by Paul Hockings (1993), plate 7 shows a photograph of a Hopi 'snake dance' at Orayvi village in 1898. In the background, a man stands over what appears to be a moving image camera. The caption suggests that this is Thomas Edison, but this is impossible, as Edison left it to professional operators to do the actual filming of the films that he produced. Given the date and location, it is more likely to be Oscar Bennet Depue, while the tall man standing beside him could even be Burton Holmes himself. The 1913 film featuring Roosevelt, probably shot by Emery Kolb, is available via the Library of Congress website at www.youtube.com/watch?v=mfmPGcyV7lM.

48 Griffiths (2002), 288–93.

49 This film is no. 192 in the AMNH catalogue and its descriptive title is *Hopi Indians of the Southwest and Snake Dance of the 9th Day*. Peter Whiteley kindly reviewed this film at my request and identified the location as Musangnuvi. He suggests that the film might be an amalgam of footage shot in a number of different Hopi villages since he suspects that the sequence of the man carding wool is Sitsom'ovi village on First Mesa.

50 See de Brigard (1995), 20–1. Hodge is perhaps most remembered today as the principal editor of Edward S. Curtis's photographic encyclopaedia, *The North American Indian*.

51 This necessarily highly summary account of the *shálako* ceremony draws extensively on Tedlock (1983).

52 On the internal Zuni politics surrounding this film, see Wenger (2009), 185–7.

53 See ashiwi-museum.org/collaborations/shalako-film-remade/.

54 I regret that I have been unable to see this film on account of the Zuni presence restriction. The complex issues of copyright and control over the new film have been discussed by Anderson and Montenegro (2017).

55 See Martins (2007, 2012).

56 See the Smithsonian website at www.sil.si.edu/expeditions/1926/browse.cfm; also www.silenttimemachine.net.

57 See King (1993), and, in the listing of filmic references at the end of this book, the two films with the common title *Primitive Peoples of Matto Grosso*, released in 1941. Although this title is offensive to modern sensibilities, the films themselves are generally respectful of Bororo and Yawalpiti culture. See also Cunha and Caiuby Novaes (2019) and the references to all the film material arising from the 1931 Mato Grosso expedition at: www.silenttimemachine.net.

58 For many years, the Kwakwa̲ka'wakw were referred to in the ethnographic literature as the 'Kwakiutl', a term which is an anglicisation of *kwagulth*, the name of the particular local group whom Boas primarily studied. Kwakwa̲ka'wakw is a more comprehensive name that has been adopted since the 1980s, which is applicable to all the various different local groups who speak the Kwak'wala language (Peter Whiteley, personal communication, September 2018).

59 In these paragraphs on Boas, I draw on Ruby (1980); Jacknis (1987); Morris (1994), 55–66; Griffiths (2002), 304–9 as well as on my viewing of the Boas footage held by the National Anthropological Film Collection at the Smithsonian Institution. In 1972, Boas's material was gathered into a 48-minute documentary and released by the University of Washington under the title *The Kwakiutl of British Columbia*, but I have been unable to view this.

60 In these paragraphs on Herskovits, I draw on two articles (1990a, 1990b) and some personal communications by John Homiak (in May 2015) as well as on my viewings of Herskovits's films at the National Anthropological Film Collection at the Smithsonian Institution. Herskovits's audio recordings (which I have not had the opportunity to study) are held by the Archives of Traditional Music at the University of Indiana. See www.indiana.edu/~libarchm/.

61 For a more extended discussion of Mead and Bateson's films, see Henley (2013a).

62 Bateson and Mead (1942), 49.

63 Mead and Bateson's theories on this matter, both in relation to the Balinese and in relation to the causes of schizophrenia more generally, are now entirely discredited. See Jensen and Suryani (1992), also Henley (2013a).

64 *Trance and Dance in Bali* is one of a select group of eight supposedly 'ethnographic' films selected by the National Film Registry for preservation in the US Library of Congress (Durington and Ruby 2011, 205).

65 See Mead and Bateson (1977), Mead (1995), 9–10.

# 2

# Travel films, melodrama and the origins of ethnofiction

COMPARED with the films produced by academic anthropologists, which were modest in both scope and technical complexity, or even with those produced for museums or for empire- and nation-building purposes, the films of ethnographic interest made during the first half of the twentieth century by film-makers working for commercial production companies were generally much more imaginative and technically accomplished. In order to make their films accessible to a popular audience, far from eschewing authorship, as anthropologists of the period sought to do, these commercial film-makers had no hesitation in authoring their films. Ironically, a number of these commercially produced films have been claimed, retrospectively as it were, as masterworks of early ethnographic cinema and are now much more frequently watched and discussed, even in academic contexts, than the films made over the same period according to the self-denying ordinances of more academic ethnographic film-makers.

In this chapter, after a preliminary section discussing the very earliest examples of films concerned with culturally exotic subject matter produced by the Edison and Lumière production companies, I consider how two commercial entertainment genres – the travel film and the melodrama set in an exotic location – constituted the cinematic crucible out of which emerged three films that are often referred to as major milestones in the history of ethnographic film: *Grass*, *In the Land of the Head Hunters* and, most important of all, *Nanook of the North*.

## EDISON AND LUMIÈRE

From the earliest days of cinema in the mid-1890s, commercial film producers were actively turning out films about exotic peoples and places, responding to the same strong public demand that at the turn of the twentieth century was also being met, both in Europe and the USA, by Wild West shows, World's Fairs and travel lectures. Initially, these films consisted of no more than a single fixed-frame and wide-angle shot taken from a camera set up on a static tripod. They typically lasted less than a minute since that was the maximum duration of the standard roll of film carried by early cameras. Indeed, these films were little more than photographs with the addition of movement and when viewed in a sequence, the effect would not have been dissimilar to watching a series of images in the 'magic lantern' slide shows that these film shows replaced.

But during the course of the first decade of the twentieth century, commercial film-makers realised that if they covered a particular place or event with a systematic series of shots, ideally in combination with some variation in framing and duration, as well as in the placing of the camera, they could then order these shots in such a way as to produce a visual narrative with a beginning, middle and end in which the links between the individual shots could be created or enhanced with the aid of textual intertitles. The technology also improved greatly over this period so that by the end of the decade, the most sophisticated cameras were equipped with magazines that carried sufficient film to shoot for up to six minutes. While most non-fiction films about exotic peoples and places continued to be less than 10 minutes long, there were some films that reached 20 minutes or even more.

The first commercial organisation to make a film on a culturally exotic subject appears to have been the company set up by the prolific inventor and entrepreneur Thomas Edison, in order to exploit the Kinetograph moving image camera that he and his associates had developed. This camera was housed in a dedicated studio situated in West Orange, New Jersey, not far from New York. Among the earliest films to be made in this studio were two single-shot films of around 20 seconds featuring a small group of Sioux Indians. One of these films, entitled *Buffalo Dance*, showed three dancers moving in a circle with two drummers seated behind them, while the other, *Sioux Ghost Dance*, involved about ten dancers milling back and forth on the small studio stage (figure 2.1, left).[1]

These films were shot on 24 September 1894. Given that they involved an exotic cultural subject and pre-date by some six months the chrono-photographic images of Africans taken by Félix-Louis Regnault and Charles Comte in Paris, as described in Chapter 1, some authors have suggested that these Edison films should be considered the very first ethnographic films. But if they are in any sense ethnographic, they relate more to the ethnography of the end-of-the-century entertainment industry in the USA than to traditional Native American culture. For, as a large sign in the foreground of the *Sioux Ghost Dance* film makes clear, the dancers were performers from Buffalo Bill Cody's Wild West Show, and, as such, there is no guarantee that all of them were even Sioux. Certainly this Ghost Dance would have had very little to do with the millenarian cult of the same

2.1 Left, *Buffalo Dance*, featuring Sioux Indians, shot in the Edison studio, September 1894; right, opium smokers in the French colony of Annam (today central Vietnam) filmed by Gabriel Veyre in late 1898 or early 1899.

name that had swept through Native American communities in the western states of the USA some five years previously. Buffalo Bill was about to take his show on a European tour and he himself features in two other short films that were shot in the Edison studio on the same day. It seems very likely, then, that all four films were made for promotional purposes related to this imminent tour.

In Europe, the Lumière brothers, Auguste and Louis, after unveiling their *cinématographe* camera in Lyon in March 1895, developed an approach to the taking of 'views' – as single-shot films were then known in France – that was very different from Edison's. The *cinématographe* was based in part on the technology first developed by Edison, but whereas the Kinetograph was a heavy metal apparatus the size and shape of a small desk, the Lumière camera consisted of a much lighter mechanism housed in a portable wooden box. The Kinetograph was driven by an electrical motor, so had to be close to a power source, while the *cinématographe* was designed to be cranked by hand. As a result of these differences in technical design, whereas the subjects of Edison films had to be brought to the studio in New Jersey in order to perform in front of the Kinetograph, the Lumière camera operators could take their *cinématographe* anywhere in the world and film people in their normal everyday surroundings.

By placing an additional light source behind it, the *cinématographe* could also double as a hand-cranked projector so that the films it produced could then be projected onto a screen in any convenient room. By contrast, Edison intended that the material produced by his Kinetograph camera should be viewed by means of a separate dedicated device which he baptised the 'Kinetoscope'. This consisted of a chest-high wooden box, surmounted by a small portal containing a magnifying glass, which the viewers, one by one, looked down into in order to view the films. Edison believed that this single-viewer arrrangement would be the most profitable way to charge for the viewing of films and he set up a series of 'Kinetoscope parlours' across the USA and even in Europe.

However, with the Lumières getting audiences of up to 2,500 people per day for their screenings in Paris by early 1896, Edison was rapidly proved wrong and within a very short period, he too was investing in projector technology and sending out cameramen with portable cameras. But although Edison cameramen did film a few culturally exotic sequences around the turn of the century, including some Mexican women washing clothes in 1898, some sequences of Eskimo, Native American, Japanese and Spanish performers at the Pan-American Exhibition in Buffalo in 1900, and four sequences of different phases of the Snake Dance at the Hopi village of Walpi in 1901, as described in Chapter 1, the great majority of the Edison films around this time were either about culturally mainstream North American subjects, or consisted of real or enacted scenes from the Spanish-American or Boer wars.

The number of films featuring culturally exotic subject matter produced by the Lumière company was far higher. So too was the technical quality of the films: while the Edison films were often blurred and unstable, the Lumière films were generally sharp and clear. Between 1895 and 1905, when the company effectively gave up making films, Lumière produced a total of 1422 views. The vast majority of these views are less than a minute long since this was the maximum duration of the 17-metre rolls of film that the *cinématographe* was designed to take. Just over 800 of the Lumière views were shot in France. Although many of these involve events or self-conscious performances, and include such varied subjects as bull-fights, clown routines, boxing matches, military parades, politicians on walkabout and even some historical and biblical fictions, there are also many views of the routines of everyday life, some of them involving the members of the Lumière family. These everyday subjects include children eating a meal, people boarding a train, a game of cards, women washing clothes in a stream, men repairing a road, horse-drawn carriages passing through a flooded street and, perhaps the most famous Lumière view of all, for being supposedly the very first, the view of the workers leaving the Lumière factory. Taken as a collection, the totality of these views offer a remarkable ethnographic snapshot of France at the turn of the twentieth century.[2]

Most of the remaining Lumière views were shot elsewhere in Europe – Italy and Britain being the principal alternative locations. But around 200 Lumière views featured non-European subjects. At first, Lumière cameramen confined themselves to filming performers at the many exotic fairs then travelling through Europe, including Javanese jugglers in London and an Ashanti village and a group of Sinhalese dancers in Lyon, where the Lumière company was based. But before long, Lumière operators were travelling across the globe. One of most energetic was Gabriel Veyre who, between August 1896 and March 1900, made a series of visits to Mexico, Japan, and the French colonies in Indochina (figure 2.1, right). The Lumière catalogue contains details of around sixty views that Veyre shot in the course of these trips. On his way to Japan, he travelled through Canada and on 2 or 3 September 1898, he shot *Danse indienne*, a view of three men engaged in a dance on the Mohawk reservation at Kahnawake, across the St. Lawrence river from Montreal. This is one of the first moving image sequences taken of a North American First Nations people, preceded possibly only by the now seemingly lost footage shot some ten days before, on 22 August 1898, by Burton Holmes's cameraman, Oscar Depue, in the Hopi village of Orayvi, as described in Chapter 1.[3]

By the end of 1901, the Lumière company had shot at least 1300 views (i.e. over 90 per cent of its total output). Although it continued to make films sporadically over the next few years, the Lumière company had given up all film-making by 1905, at the latest, in order to dedicate itself to the development of colour photographic plates and, over the subsequent years, a diverse series of other inventions, including the 'periphote', a 360-degree photographic camera, membranes for loudspeakers, a prosthetic hand and medical dressings for war wounds. But in any case, by this time, the newsreel agencies Gaumont and Pathé had already taken over from the Lumière company as the most active producers in France of films on culturally exotic subjects.

## EXOTIC REPORTAGE AND TRAVELOGUES

According to the French cinema writer, Pierre Leprohon, the cameramen who worked for Gaumont and Pathé in the early years were mostly freelancers who were provided with equipment by the agencies but had to supply their own film. They were then paid for the exposed film that they sent back to the agencies, though there was a significant difference in the rate of pay depending on where the material had been shot: 7 francs per metre of film shot in France, 10 or even 15 francs per metre shot abroad. Unsuprisingly, many operators went abroad, initially to the French colonies in North Africa, but soon to many other parts of the world. Adapting a usage of Leprohon, I refer to these films shot abroad by French newsreel operators as 'exotic reportage'.[4]

Early twentieth-century French audiences appear to have had a great appetite for material of this kind since a large number of films of exotic reportage were produced during this period. These works were typically considerably longer than the 50-second single-shot views produced by the Lumière operators, though the duration of the great majority was still less

than 10 minutes. They were also very much more sophisticated, both technically and as filmic texts, particularly with regard to their narrative structuring.
Even so, the operators who made these films were generally regarded as
no more than technicians and their works often do not even bear their
names, or if they do, it may be only their family name. And yet the aesthetic
quality of their work in a cinematographic sense was often very high, while
their ethnographic observation, though presumably entirely untutored, could
be remarkably acute.[5]

A review of this vast body of work is far beyond the scope of this chapter.
Instead I consider only one example, which will have to stand in a synecdochic
manner for the whole genre of film that I refer to as 'exotic reportage'.
Not only is this example particularly well made, but it is also readily viewable
on the British Film Institute (BFI) website. It was released in 1909 by Pathé
Frères, but testifying to the international nature of Pathé's distribution
network, the BFI version carries a German title, *Delhi: Die Grosse Stadt in
Vorderindien*. Moreover, a very brief logo at the end of the film suggests that
the film may have been produced by Luca Comerio, a production company
based in Milan. However, nowhere on the film is there an indication of
the name of the operator. But whoever did shoot the film clearly knew
what they were doing.

Notwithstanding the title, which translates as *Delhi: Great Capital of India*,
the film does not offer a general portrait of the city, but rather very specifically
concerns the major Muslim festival of Muharram as celebrated at the Jamia
Masjid, the Great Mosque of the city. This festival is Shiite in origin and
evokes the martyrdom of Hassan and Husayn, the grandsons of the Prophet.
The film is only 4 minutes long, but covers considerable ground in a highly
efficient manner, using a cinematographic language that is readily recognisable
more than a century later and which had clearly been carefully thought
through in advance. The general quality of the film has also been enhanced
by stencil-colouring.

Following a brief establishment shot over the mosque, seemingly taken
from one of its minarets, there is then a cut to a series of shots of street
performers entertaining the crowd attending the festival. Next comes the
parading of models of the tombs of Hassan and Husayn and a river of
worshippers flows past the well-positioned camera. Although they are very
varied in age and dress, we note that all the worshippers are men; on their
shoulders, the models of the tombs take an extraordinary range of different
forms.

The second half of the film consists of a series of shots taken in and
around the mosque. First, there is an establishing wide shot of the courtyard
of the mosque taken from a distant elevated position, with a pool in the
foreground where worshippers are carrying out their ablutions. There is
then a cut to a much closer shot of the pool, indicating that the operator

may have changed the lens at that point (it would be another fifty years before the zoom was invented). A third shot, taken from the edge of the pool, at 45 degrees to the line of the previous two shots, offers an intimate view of the worshippers as they wash they feet and arms, and also their teeth. Next we see the worshippers praying in front of the mosque itself: again this starts with a distant shot from an elevated position before cutting to a closer shot of the same scene. The final image, again from afar but this time from outside the mosque, consists of a ravishing shot of the worshippers descending the stairs in front of the mosque as they leave. This shot has a strongly valedictory feel to it and brings the film to an end in a very effective manner (figure 2.2).

This brief film is particularly interesting not only for its cinematographic sophistication but also as a historical as well as an ethnographic document. For, at the time it was made, despite its Shiite origins, many different groups in Delhi would have participated in the Muharram festival – neighbourhood organisations of various kinds, caste representatives, craft guilds, even associations of prostitutes. This would explain why the models of the tombs being carried by the worshippers take such a variety of forms, with some looking more like Hindu temples than mosques. In fact, it is quite probable that there would have been no Shiite participation at all in this event, since not only is Delhi predominantly a Sunni city, but the Jamia Majsid is its principal Sunni mosque. Certainly, the presence of jugglers and acrobats such as we see in the early part of the film would have been incompatible with the original Shiite conception of the fesival, which is as a symbolic funeral procession for the martyrs Hassan and Husayn and as such, as an event that should be conducted in the most solemn manner. Today, as the division between Shiite and Sunni has become more sharply demarcated in Islam generally, Muharram is no longer celebrated in Delhi since it has come to be seen as a festival that belongs exclusively to Shiites.[6]

After the First World War, both Pathé and Gaumont developed their reportage film repertoire and began to produce more extended educational films, often in collaboration with academic advisers. Pathé also collaborated with scientific expeditions, including with the American Museum of Natural History expeditions to Central Asia in the years 1921–30. Although primarily dedicated to zoological and archaeological matters, the films that arose from this collaboration also included a film about contemporary Mongol life and another about 'Peking' as Beijing was then known. In a similar manner, in 1928–29, Pathé collaborated with the Department of Anthropology at Harvard to make the Pathé Science series, which consisted of three short films: one about life in Java, another about Bedouin herders in the Arabian desert and the third about Mongol herders in the Gobi desert.[7]

While all these Gaumont and Pathé films contain material of an ethnographic character, one of the most accessible forms of exotic reportage is

**2.2** *Delhi, Great Capital of India* (1909). In four minutes, a narrative is economically deployed: above, an establishing overview before passing to the procession in the street; middle, a distant shot of the inner court of the mosque gives way to a midshot of the faithful performing ablutions; below, the faithful are seen praying before they finally leave in a classical closure shot.

the so-called Pathé-Baby series, launched in the 1922. This was distributed on 9.5 mm film and was aimed at the domestic market. The films were typically no more than 1½ minutes long and were usually abridged versions of reportage films that had previously been distributed through cinemas, sometimes many years previously. While some of the films were Pathé's own productions, others were bought in. The series covered every genre and every subject, from films about physics to cartoons, with drama, comedy, religious edification and sports films in between. The 1931 Pathé-Baby catalogue covers a dozen such categories, but the first two – 'Voyages' and

'Usages and Customs' – contain a considerable number of films of potential ethnographic interest, including some unattributed extracts from *Nanook of the North*. Many of these Pathé-Baby films are now readily available on the Web.[8]

In the USA, the most prevalent form of commercial film-making to feature exotic subject matter in the period prior to the Second World War was the genre that came to be known as the 'travelogue'. Although the distinction may often have been blurred in practice, the travelogue may be differentiated from the expedition films of the interwar period such as those discussed in Chapter 1, on the grounds that whereas the latter category consisted of films produced as a by-product of journeys that had some other purpose (exploration, the collection of zoological specimens, archaeological research, sometimes merely big game hunting), in the case of the travelogue, the making of the film was itself the primary purpose of the journey.

The origins of the travelogue lay in the phenomenon of the travel lecture, which by the late nineteenth century was a hugely popular form of public entertainment in the USA, capable of generating large returns at the box office. Originally, travel lecturers illustrated their talks with 'magic lantern' slides of scenes from around the world, but by the end of the 1890s they had already begun to use film as well. These film materials would often be specifically commissioned by the lecturers, who would sometimes accompany the cameramen on their expeditions to direct their activities. By the 1920s, the lecturers had begun to appear in front of the lens on location and the fully fledged travelogue format had emerged.[9]

Although travelogue film-makers would often seek to give their films an aura of academic respectability by seeking the endorsement of leading museums, professional associations or universities, the genre was geared from the start towards providing popular entertainment. Whereas in the French reportage film, the film-maker was often not even named, in the travelogue the travel lecturer, now transformed into celebrity traveller, was often the centrepiece of the show. Prior to the development of soundtracks in the 1930s, the commentary of the traveller-lecturer on the subject matter of the film would be made through the extensive use of intertitles. Whereas in the French reportage film, intertitles typically provided no more than low-key factual information, the travelogue intertitle aimed to entertain the audience by mixing the provision of information with some kind of jocose observation. As the joke was often at the expense of the subjects, at least in the films shot in Africa and Asia, today these intertitles often seem at best ethnocentric, and at worst, crassly racist or sexist (figure 2.3).

If the travelogue differed from the French reportage film, it was even further from the modest descriptive films produced by academic anthropologists prior to the Second World War. Whereas anthropologists were often moved to make their films by a perceived need to record the last vestiges

2.3 *Simba, King of the Beasts* (1928), directed by Martin and Osa Johnson. The jocose intertitle on the left immediately precedes the image on the right, which shows a young Samburu of northern Kenya.

of particular cultural phenomena before they disappeared, the makers of travelogues liked to emphasise rather that their films offered records of 'first contacts' – often in direct contradiction to the evidence offered in the actual films.[10] An even greater point of contrast was that while academic anthropologists sought to avoid any kind of authorship and to use the camera simply as a recording instrument, the makers of travelogues had no reservations about trumpeting their authorship and using every possible cinematographic means to make their films more entertaining.

As well as the jocose intertitles, these means included intervening directly in the lives of the subject to produce comedic effects. This is exemplified by a sequence shot in 1932, which is now readily available on the Web. This shows Osa Johnson, who, with her husband Martin, was one of the leading travelogue film-makers of the era, encouraging a group of Mbuti 'pygmies' of the Ituri rainforest in Central Africa to dance with her to the sound of jazz music playing on a wind-up gramophone. Although the sequence is in many ways grotesque, covered as it is by an execrably racist commentary and laying out the disparity in power between film-maker and subjects in the most cringingly blatant way, it is at the same time intriguing that the Mbuti do instantly know how to swing.[11]

Although the classical US travelogues may be mined for the occasional vein of ethnographic interest such as this, films in this genre are usually so submerged beneath a layer of artifice and colonial racist bluster that they are of little value. Yet, as an exception to the general rule, there is one particular film that emerged directly from the cinematic environment of the self-aggrandising travelogue which has often been identified as an important milestone in the development of English-language ethnographic film. This is *Grass – A Nation's Battle for Life*, released in 1925 and directed by Merian C. Cooper and Ernest B. Schoedsack, who a few years later would again combine forces to achieve fame and fortune in Hollywood as the directors of *King Kong*. Given the prominence of *Grass* in the visual anthropology literature, I shall now consider it at some length.

## THE TRAVELOGUE AS PROTO-ETHNOGRAPHIC FILM: THE CASE OF *GRASS*

Cooper and Schoedsack met in Europe in the aftermath of the First World War, when both were involved in the armed conflict between Poland and the fledgling Soviet Union. Cooper was a pilot with the US Army, while Schoedsack was a combat cinematographer. In making *Grass*, they were accompanied by Marguerite Harrison, the daughter of a wealthy US shipping magnate, who had worked in Germany during the war, and later in Moscow, ostensibly as a journalist, but also as a spy for US military intelligence. While in Moscow, she had smuggled blankets and food into the Red Army camp where Cooper had been imprisoned after being shot down, eventually meeting up with him in Warsaw in 1922. At first, Schoedsack was against her involvement in the film, but he later relented, probably not unrelated to the fact that she put up half the budget. The other half was jointly contributed by Cooper and Schoedsack himself, while Schoedsack also contributed the Debrie camera on which the film was shot.[12]

Initially, the three of them spent some time travelling through Turkey and Iraq in search of a suitable subject, with Schoedsack shooting footage along the way to sell to newsreel agencies. This footage included memorable scenes of a dancing bear in a Kurdish village in Turkey, the hunting of a long-horned wild goat in the Taurus mountains on the border with Syria, and an encounter with an Iraqi desert police detachment mounted on camels. Eventually, however, the trio reached what was then Persia and is now Iran, where they met with Sir Arnold Wilson, chairman of the Anglo-Persian Oil Company, and Gertrude Bell, the celebrated Near East specialist.

It was Wilson who suggested to them that they should film the remarkable annual migration of the Bakhtiari sheep pastoralists to their summer pastures in the Zagros mountains, near Isfahan. Wilson knew about this migration because Bakhtiari territory fell within the drilling concession that his company had been awarded by the Persian government. Wilson also had the influence to get the film-makers the necessary permits, both from local government officials and from the Il-Khani, the Bakhtiari paramount leader. Il-Khani in turn provided them with an introduction to Haidar Kahn, chief of the Baba Ahmadi, the subgroup of Bakhtiari who would actually feature in the film. Accordingly, the film-makers made their way to Haidar Kahn's village and after a brief stopover there, set out, in April 1924, to accompany the Baba Ahmadi on their gruelling 48-day 'battle for life', as the subtitle of the film would later have it.

However, in the editing down of the 14 hours of rushes to the 71-minute final film, there was no reference to the film-makers' initial meanderings, nor the circumstances through which they finally hit on the topic of Bakhtiari migration. Instead, in accordance with a classic travelogue trope, *Grass* is presented as a single unitary journey in search of a 'Forgotten People'. Moreover, in being a journey eastwards, contrary to the direction in which the film-makers own 'forefathers, the Aryans of old' had migrated in 'conquest of the earth', it is also construed as being a journey back in time in search of the film-makers' very own 'brothers still living in the cradle of the race'. The point is reinforced by a dramatic, if stereotypical, opening shot of a long line of camels moving from left to right on the horizon, as if it were from west to east on a conventional map.

The three travellers themselves are then introduced, looking elegant and relaxed in the explorer-chic clothing of the day, a style that would later be imitated in the Indiana Jones movies. Although these portraits are presented with a boulder in the background, as if they had been filmed on location, they were actually shot after the film-makers had returned to the USA, in the Paramount Astoria Studios in New York. Thereafter, the two men are not seen again in the film. Although Marguerite Harrison appears prominently in the sequences prior to the arrival at the Bakhtiari village, providing the 'I-was-there' authority typical of the travelogue genre, during the migration itself, she is only ever seen fleetingly and from afar.[13]

The first third of the film is presented as a record of the film-makers' journey across Turkey and Iraq and into Iran in search of the 'Forgotten People': this allows them to present the disparate material shot during the initial exploratory phase of their project in a coherent and cumulative manner. But following the encounter with the Bahktiari, there is a change of gear, as two new characters are introduced: Haidar Kahn, and his 9-year-old son, Lufta. Haidar is described as the chief of a 'tribe' whose way of life has not changed for 3,000 years. On account of their light-coloured skin, they are identified as 'Aryans', and therefore, by implication, as the ancestors for whom the film-makers have been searching. The Islamic title of Haidar Khan, clearly belying the trope of three millennia of unchanged tradition, is not a matter on which the film chooses to dwell.

Haidar is then shown gathering his lieutenants around him and announcing that it is time for the Baba Ahmadi to pitch their tents and head even further east, up into the mountains in search of fresh pastures. Rather than following the journey of the film-makers, the narrative thread of the film then becomes the journey of Haidar, Lufta and, supposedly, 25,000 of their fellow Bakhtiari, not to mention some 125,000 animals (figure 2.4).[14]

In purely cinematographic terms, some of the sequences of this part of the film are truly remarkable, none more so than the sequence of the

**2.4** *Grass – A Nation's Battle for Life* (1925). The story of Bakhtiari migration is built around the headman Haidar Kahn and his son Lufta, left; but during the epic journey itself, right, they are glimpsed only rarely.

seemingly endless columns of Bakhtiari trudging barefoot through the snow-covered Zardeh Kuh mountain pass, some carrying their animals. Also impressive are the shots of the Bakhtiari crossing the glacial Karun river 'over six days and nights' on rafts consisting of no more than inflated sheepskins. Although there are some brief glimpses of Harrison and a stream of alternately dramatising or self-consciously jocose intertitles of the kind that were typical of the travelogue genre, the authorial presence of the film-makers is muted – it is rather the Bahktiari who are the heroes of this part of the film.[15]

The journey ends with Haidar in his tent, with Lufta at his side, puffing on his pipe and looking contentedly at the grazing sheep. Though the characterisation of Haidar and Lufta in the film has been slight and romantically stereotypical, and we only see rare glimpses of them during the migration; this technique of building a narrative around the experiences of a limited number of principal characters is one that would later be much developed within the genre of ethnographic documentary.[16]

However, the happy scene of Haidar gazing at the sheep is not quite the end of the film. For, in a bizarre coda, the travelogue format returns in full force as we are shown a document, formally witnessed by the American vice-consul in Tehran, who, we are informed, was soon to be murdered in the street. This last detail, although completely irrelevant to the principal narrative of the film, adds an additional aura of mystery and danger to the content of the document witnessed by the unfortunate vice-consul. This purports to be a statement by Haidar Khan and Amir Jang, 'prince of the Bahktiari', to the effect that the three travellers were the first outsiders to accompany the Bahktiari on their perilous migration through the Zardah Kuh pass. By this means, we are reminded that it is not, after all, the Bahktiari, but rather the travellers who, in the classic manner of the travelogue, are the real heroes of this film.

## MELODRAMA AND THE *DOCUMENTAIRE ROMANCÉ*: THE CASE OF *IN THE LAND OF THE HEAD HUNTERS*

It was not only through travelogues and other variants on the travel film format that commercial film producers in the early twentieth century sought to satisfy the great public interest in culturally exotic ways of life: early fiction films would also often be set in exotic locations with a melodramatic Western story grafted onto an idealised interpretation of local cultural realities.

In the USA, prior to the First World War, at least two film versions were made of *The Song of Hiawatha*, Henry Wadsworth Longfellow's poetic paean to Native American life immediately prior to the arrival of the Whites, first published in 1855. The first of these *Hiawatha* films, released in 1908, was made by the Baptist-minister-turned-film-maker, Joseph K. Dixon for the Philadelphia department store magnate, John Rodman Wanamaker, while the second was produced in collaboration with the American Museum of Natural History by Frank E. Moore and released in 1913. In Canada, no fewer than three films about a Hiawatha pageant were made over the same period.[17]

The influential early Hollywood director, D. W. Griffith, was but one of many who around this time cut their directorial teeth making films in culturally exotic settings. One of his very first films was *The Zulu's Heart*, a 10-minute two-reel 'short' made for the Biograph company in 1908 which featured 'blacked up' White actors. This told the supposedly heart-rending story of a Zulu chief who after his own child dies of fever is then moved to spare a little Boer girl captured in a raid. The following year, Griffith made at least three shorts in what were purportedly North American Indian settings, *The Mended Lute*, *Comata the Sioux* and *The Redman's View*, but again with White actors playing the principal indigenous parts and with similarly melodramatic storylines.[18]

A similar series of films was made around the same time by Gaston Méliès, the elder brother of Georges, the well-known early French director of fantasy films. Gaston's films were produced by Star Film, a subsidiary company that Georges had set up in the USA in 1904 to protect the copyright of his films. After managing his brother's business in the USA for a while, Gaston set off in July 1912 to travel around the Pacific and East Asia determined to make a series of his own films in exotic settings. Some of these were descriptive films of documentation, while others were examples of the genre known in France as '*documentaire romancé*', a term that could be literally translated as 'storified documentary'. Among the Méliès *documentaires romancés* were two shot in Tahiti and two in New Zealand. Like the Griffith films, these were all short two-reelers based on melodramatic storylines. All of them involved conflicts connected with affairs of the heart, sometimes in an exclusively indigenous setting, but mostly across a European-indigenous fault line. Sadly, all but one of them, *Loved by a Maori Chieftess*, released in the USA in 1913, appear to be lost.[19]

This genre of melodrama played out in an idealised exotic cultural setting also includes another film from this period which, like *Grass*, has often been claimed in retrospect as a major landmark in the development of English-language ethnographic film – even to the extent of being included in the collection of only eight supposedly 'ethnographic' films in National Film Registry of the US Library of Congress. This is *In the Land of the Head Hunters*, first released in 1914. The director and producer was Edward S. Curtis, already well known in the USA at that time for his romantic photographs of Native Americans in traditional dress from which almost all evidence of their contemporary situation as subjugated peoples had been excluded. In effect, *Head Hunters* represented an attempt to employ essentially the same methods to the production of a moving image film.[20]

*Head Hunters* was mostly shot on Deer Island, which lies a few hundred metres off the northeastern shore of the very much bigger Vancouver Island, on the Pacific coast of Canada. Although they are not specifically named at any point in the film, it was made with the active participation of the people who were known for many years in the anthropological literature as the Kwakiutl, but who are now more generally referred to as the Kwakwa̱ka̱'wakw.[21] Curtis would sometimes claim that the film was based on 'tribal lore', but although the Kwakwa̱ka̱'wakw may have had some input into the storyline, it is primarily constructed around the same 'love triangle' trope found in many of the melodramas in indigenous settings produced in the period immediately prior to the First World War.

In this case, the triangle involves the young warrior Motana, the beautiful young maiden Naida, and the Evil Sorcerer to whom, against her will, Naida has been betrothed. After seeing her in a vision quest, Motana successfully woos Naida and asks her father, Waket, for her hand in marriage. But Waket says that he will only consent if he is brought the head of the Sorcerer as a wedding offering. Motana's father, Kenada, then raids the Sorcerer's village, returns with his head and demands that the wedding feast take place (figure 2.5). However, when Motana and Naida return to Kenada's village after the wedding, it is attacked and burnt to the ground by Yaklus, the fearsome brother of the Sorcerer who is enraged at his beheading. Kenada himself is killed, while Motana is left for dead and Naida is carried off by Yaklus.

There then follows the most elaborate ceremonial sequence in the film as Yaklus celebrates his victory back at his own village. This includes dances of the kind that were traditionally performed during Kwakwa̱ka̱'wakw

**2.5** *In the Land of the Head Hunters* (1914). Left, Motana watches Naida depart after he has given her a token of his love; right, later, Motana's party arrives in style for the wedding feast, with the Thunderbird in the prow of one of three highly decorated canoes.

winter ceremonies and which feature dancers wearing a range of magnificent wooden masks. Naida is obliged to dance before Yaklus, who, entranced by her beauty, decides to spare her life and keep her as his slave. But in the night, Motana, who has been resuscitated by a 'Medicine Man', sneaks into Yaklus's house and carries Naida off in his canoe. He is pursued by Yaklus and his warriors, but as the two canoes pass through a surging gorge, Yaklus's canoe capsizes and he is drowned. The final sequence shows Motana and Naida safe in their canoe, followed by a sunset bringing the film to an end.

This was not the first film-making project that Curtis had undertaken: he had previously shot some footage among the Hopi and also the Navajo in 1904 or 1906. He even appears to have previously shot some footage among the Kwakwaka'wakw in 1910 or 1911.[22] But this was an altogether more ambitious work. Although *Head Hunters* had explicitly commercial objectives – Curtis hoped to raise money to support the continuation of his monumental photographic encyclopaedia, *The North American Indian* – he aimed at the same time to achieve a high degree of cultural authenticity.

To this end, he recruited a self-trained ethnologist and former journalist, William Myers, who had worked as his assistant for many years on his earlier photographic expeditions. More importantly, he also engaged George Hunt, a local man of mixed British and Tlingit descent, who had married into the Kwakwaka'wakw. Hunt had been acting as Franz Boas's principal informant since 1888, some two years after the latter began his research on the Pacific Coast, and he would continue to act as such after *Head Hunters* was completed, until his death in 1933. In the case of *Head Hunters*, however, Hunt was clearly more than just an informant: a well-known photograph of the production shows him standing with megaphone in hand, apparently directing the action, while Curtis busies himself with the camera.[23]

In contrast to the cast of the melodramas of D. W. Griffith, the cast of *Head Hunters* was entirely indigenous, mostly Kwakwa̲ka̲'wakw. The actor who played Motana was George Hunt's son, Stanley. A number of Hunt's other relatives also had named roles in the film. As many of the leading actors were from noble lineages, the process of casting was a particularly delicate matter since the Kwakwa̲ka̲'wakw have strict rules about the behaviour appropriate to particular statuses: three different actresses were required to play the female lead, Naida, in part because of a mismatch between the actions called for by the script (for example, paddling a canoe) and the behaviour deemed appropriate to the individuals of elevated status who were supposed to be playing the role. George Hunt would surely have been of great assistance to Curtis in navigating his way through these sensitivities.

The film was set in some indeterminate period in the past: an early working title was 'In the Days of Vancouver', which would have made the setting the 1790s, the period when the British naval officer, Captain George Vancouver, charted the waters of the North Pacific Coast. In effect then, the actors were supposed to be playing their own ancestors. But by 1914, most Kwakwa̲ka̲'wakw had abandoned traditional forms of dress and hair styling, so Curtis commissioned a number of local people, notably George Hunt's wife, Francine, to manufacture both ceremonial regalia and everyday clothing appropriate to the period. Much of this clothing was manufactured out of raffia, which on film reads much like the traditional cedar bark cloth. The actors were also supplied with long black wigs and nose ornaments, while many of the elaborate painted wooden masks that feature strongly in the film were purchased or carved specially for it. The increasingly obsolete massive dugout canoes that also play an important part in the film were repaired and repainted, and a series of totem poles and facades imitating traditional house frontages were erected on Deer Island, which is directly opposite Tsaxis (Fort Rupert) where the production team was based. The principal action of the film takes place in this reconstructed village set or on the beach nearby.

One of the most significant aspects of this filmic recreation of the past was that it featured certain dances and other practices that had traditionally formed part of the competitive gift-giving ceremonies known as the 'potlatch', for which the peoples of the North Pacific coast are renowned. In these ceremonies, the chief hosting the event would compete with visiting chiefs in demonstrating his wealth and generosity, and hence his power, not merely by giving away large quantities of gifts and prestigious ceremonial titles but also by destroying certain valuable commodities. But at the insistence of government agents, who considered it a highly wasteful custom, and missionaries who suspected it of invoking the devil, the potlatch had been outlawed in Canada since the Indian Act of 1884 (and would continue to be outlawed until 1951).

In *Head Hunters*, the potlatch is not specifically referred to, but the wedding feast is, in effect, more of a potlatch than a wedding in that it consists primarily of a sequence of Motana's father, Kenada, giving away a pile of blankets and bark clothing, which is then followed by another sequence showing the competitive consumption of the much valued candlefish oil. The bride and groom, meanwhile, are nowhere to be seen. Potlatch-related dances feature both in this scene and elsewhere in the film, though they are sometimes interspersed with dances invented specifically for the film. Given the political circumstances, the opportunity to perform these otherwise prohibited dances, even if in a modified form, may have been one of the main reasons why many Kwakwaka'wakw were pleased to be involved in the production.

If some aspects of the film represented a partial compromise on the ethnographic reality of traditional Kwakwaka'wakw society, a few were completely alien. One of the most frequently remarked upon concerns a scene in which Motana goes on a whale hunt, supposedly as an aspect of his initiation into manhood. In fact, the Kwakwaka'wakw never hunted whales: this was a practice confined to the indigenous groups living on the Pacific coast of Vancouver Island, such as the Nuu-chah-nulth (formerly known as the Nootka) and the Ditidaht. In order to shoot this scene, Curtis had to rent a whale carcass from a commercial whaling company. Not surprisingly, the scene is rather underwhelming and mostly consists merely of Motana standing on the carcass, with some static canoes in the background.

There is a certain tendency to assume that because Curtis was a highly gifted photographer, he was also an accomplished film-maker. Certainly no one could fault *Head Hunters* for the time and effort committed to the painstaking recreation of traditional Kwakwaka'wakw practices and artefacts, and it contains some truly wonderful individual sequences of ceremonial performance. Perhaps the most impressive of these is the sequence that shows three great canoes arriving for the wedding feast while on their prows, the extravagantly masked and costumed figures of the the Grizzly Bear, the Thunderbird and the Wasp are seen dancing ecstatically, arms outstretched. There are also a number of sequences where the physical demands of the particular location appear to have required Curtis to come up with some visually dynamic shots – for example, when the camera is mounted within a canoe as a raiding party approaches the shore or when Motana and Naida escape along the beach, running towards and past the camera. But for much of the film, wide shot follows unimaginatively upon wide shot, even if in terms of content and composition the quality of those individual shots is often high.[24]

Also, even when considered entirely on its own terms as a melodrama, *Head Hunters* is somewhat confused from a narratological point of view, with a number of scenes that obstruct rather than advance the story, and which appear be there entirely for their spectacular quality. The weighting of the major ceremonial scenes is particularly strange: Yaklus the villain gets to host the most elaborate ceremony, while the wedding feast, after a big build-up, does not feature any sort of wedding. The general sense of confusion is exacerbated by the fact that Curtis used the same set for both warring villages and also the same canoes. While several actors played a single role, as in the case of Naida, in other cases, a single actor played several roles: for example, the actor who played the 'bad' chief Yaklus, also played the 'good' chief Waket, Naida's father. It is therefore often difficult to work out who is who and where one is at any given moment in the film.[25]

Indeed, Curtis appears to have had only a limited grasp of film grammar. Apart from the series of portraits introducing the leading characters with which the film opens (itself more of a theatrical than a cinematic device), close-ups of individuals are relatively few. There is an intriguing close-up of the dastardly Sorcerer when he first appears, emerging from the undergrowth, peering suspiciously. But there is no equivalent shot of the leading 'good' characters. The closest we get is a shot of Motana mugging for the camera from inside the ethnographically inappropriate whale carcass.[26] In the midst of the marriage-cum-potlatch ceremony is a wide shot of men employing extraordinarily large ladles to serve out the candlefish oil that is followed by a close-up shot of one of the visiting chiefs drinking the oil. This works very well but it is the exception to the general rule: for the most part, the ceremonies are shot as a series of wide-angle tableaux, without being leavened by any engaging shots of detail.

Nor did Curtis appear to have any idea how to use anticipatory intertitles to create dramatic tension or interest (this would later turn out to be one of Robert Flaherty's great skills); on the contrary, his intertitles tell us what we are going to see and then we see it. Long before we see Yaklus floating in the sea, apparently drowned, we have already been told in an intertitle that this is going to happen, so we already know what the outcome of the climactic final canoe chase is going to be. While it is true that the grammar of film-making was still being worked out in 1914, Curtis's visual story-telling skills were certainly not as developed as those of some of his contemporaries, including the anonymous French newsreel cinematographers alluded to above.

These cinematographic weaknesses of *Head Hunters* may have been a factor contributing to the commercial failure of the film, notwithstanding the care lavished on the reconstructions, not to speak of the large budget. At the time of the film's release, in December 1914, some six months after the end of the shoot, it was reported in the press to have cost 75,000 dollars to make, the equivalent of almost 2 million dollars today. Perhaps over-influenced by Curtis's already established reputation as a photographer, most cinema critics gave it highly positive reviews. But the public voted with their feet and stayed away. After short runs at prestigious theatres in Seattle and New York, *Head Hunters* remained in circulation for a couple of years in the USA but its distribution was limited. Owing to the collapse of the film's distributor, it never reached Europe, where it might have done well, particularly in France.

In 1924, in a state of financial embarassment, Curtis offered everything that he still had of the film, including a copy of the negative and his master positive, to the AMNH for 1,500 dollars, at the same time renouncing all his rights. The AMNH curator Pliny Goddard consulted Franz Boas about the offer and the latter advised that while the melodramatic story could be dismissed as entirely inauthentic, the film would be valuable as a record of Kwakwaka'wakw ceremonies. Goddard therefore beat the price down to 1,000 dollars (less than 15,000 dollars today), which Curtis found himself obliged to accept. Sadly, however, the AMNH does not appear to have done anything with this print and there is no record of what happened to it.[27]

After its failure at the box office, *Head Hunters* was lost for many years. Then, in 1947, an eccentric film collector donated a copy of the film, seemingly recovered from a skip behind a cinema in Chicago, to The Field Museum of Natural History in the same city. By this time, only about two-thirds of the film's original 90-minute duration was left, and much of that was damaged due to decomposition of the 35 mm nitrate stock. In order to preserve it from further deterioration, this remnant was transferred to 16 mm safety stock by The Field Museum technicians. This ensured its survival, but resulted in a further degradation of the image quality. As it would have constituted a fire risk, the original 35 mm nitrate stock appears to have been destroyed.

It was on the basis of this 16 mm safety copy that in the late 1960s, Bill Holm, an art historian from the Burke Museum in Seattle with a specialist interest in the North Pacific Coast peoples and George Quimby, then a curator in the Department of Anthropology at The Field Museum, began to collaborate on a first reconstruction of the film. This was a very challenging task given the fragmentary state of the material. However, they did have the advantage that at that time quite a number of Kwakwaka'wakw who had been directly involved in the production were still alive, so it was possible to interview them and get their responses to the material that remained. In the summer of 1968, Holm travelled around various Kwakwaka'wakw villages screening a loosely edited version of the film and was impressed by the way in which audiences often responded to the images with improvised dialogue and song. This encouraged him to think that he should create a new soundtrack for the film, and in 1972, with the assistance of a group of student film-makers from Rice University in Houston, Texas, he arranged for these oral reactions to be recorded in an auditorium in Victoria, in the south of Vancouver Island.[28]

The Holm and Quimby reconstruction was eventually released in 1973 and ran to 44 minutes, around half the original length of the film. The general effect of this reconstruction was to reduce the film's melodramatic character and enhance its informationally ethnographic qualities. Believing that it oversensationalised the role of head-hunting in Kwakwa̲ka̲'wakw life, Holm and Quimby changed the title of the film to *In the Land of the War Canoes*. The original melodramatic intertitles were greatly reduced in number and their extravagant language replaced with more sober informational phrases. The font employed was highly functional and there was no decorative border as there had been in the original film. The chanting and improvised dialogues that the Kwakwa̲ka̲'wakw had produced in response to a preliminary assembly of the film were superimposed on certain passages, although these were not subtitled, so they served, in effect, merely to give a general ethnographic 'feel' to the film rather than to provide dialogue as such. A series of ambiental sound effects were also added to further naturalise the general aesthetic effect of the film – breaking waves, the sound of canoes surging through the water, seagulls screeching.

Holm and Quimby also introduced certain changes to the image track. A scene that was vividly remembered by many participants but which had been entirely lost was refilmed: this involved the throwing of a life-size dummy from a cliff top to simulate the killing of an innocent traveller by Yaklus's war party. On the other hand, they chose to eliminate the mugshot of Motana inside the whale carcass, since they considered this to have no place in the story. Another innovation was the introduction of an opening pre-title 'hook' in the form of the dramatic shot of the approaching canoes with the masked figures dancing in the prows (see figure 2.5).

While this first reconstruction undoubtedly saved the film from total oblivion and was also much appreciated by Kwakwa̲ka̲'wakw audiences, it was subsequently criticised for presenting the film as if it were some flawed attempt to make an academic ethnographic documentary rather than what Curtis had originally intended it to be, namely, a fictional 'motion picture drama' aimed at popular audiences. A second reconstruction, which aimed to be closer to the original aesthetic of the film was subsequently released, under the original title, in 2008. This was initiated and coordinated by Brad Evans, an English literature scholar who first became interested in the film on account of the language of the intertitles, and Aaron Glass, an anthropologist and film-maker who has carried out research with present-day Kwakwa̲ka̲'wakw over many years. This second reconstruction project was kick-started by the chance discovery by Glass, in an archive of Curtis's papers in the Getty Research Institute in Los Angeles, of the original musical score. This had been commissioned by Curtis from John J. Braham, an English musician best known for his work with the US branch of the Gilbert and Sullivan light opera company, and who, the previous year, had composed the score for Frank E. Moore's version of *Hiawatha*, the AMNH-sponsored production.

In carrying out their reconstruction, Evans and Glass had the great advantage that following an approach by Glass, the best part of two further reels of the original film were discovered in the vaults of the UCLA Film and Television Archive. Although they were also extensively damaged, in conjunction with further text-based materials discovered in the Getty Research Institute as well as with several dozen frames clipped from a 35 mm print that had been submitted to the Library of Congress as a means of ensuring the copyright of the original film, Evans and Glass were able to use these additional rolls to establish a clearer idea of the overall structure of the film than had been available to Holm and Quimby.

This newly discovered material allowed Evans and Glass to add a number of scenes to the film with the result that their reconstruction runs to 66 minutes (i.e. half as long again as the Holm and Quimby reconstruction), though still only about three-quarters of the probable length of the original film. As well as restoring the original main title, Evans and Glass restored the melodramatic intertitles with their period font and decorative borders. The war canoes 'hook' and the additional scene filmed for the Holm and Quimby reconstruction were eliminated, and the Motana mugshot was reinserted. Also eliminated were the Kwakwa̱ka'wakw chanting and improvised dialogues, as well as the ambiental sound effects added by Holm and Quimby. These were all replaced by a newly recorded performance of the original Braham score. (This was supposedly based on some phonograph field recordings of Kwakwa̱ka'wakw music that Curtis had made in 1910–11, but in fact, it seems to owe very little, if anything, to these.) As a final touch, various scenes in the film were colour-tinted as it was supposed that they would have been in original film. It is on this version of the film that the analysis offered here has been based.

However, if it is inappropriate to construe *Head Hunters* as an imperfectly realised ethnographic 'documentary' in the modern sense, it would be equally mistaken, Evans and Glass argue, to consider it merely as a romantic outsider's construction imposed on entirely passive indigenous subjects. Instead, they suggest, it should be understood as a collaborative venture between Curtis and the Kwakwa̱ka'wakw. They point out that by the time Curtis arrived to make his film, the Kwakwa̱ka'wakw had long been involved in performing a heritagised version of their culture for external audiences. As early as 1893, through coordination between Franz Boas and George Hunt, some fifteen Kwakwa̱ka'wakw had performed their dances at the Chicago World's Fair. Later, in 1904, two other Kwakwa̱ka'wakw dancers had performed at the Louisiana Purchase Exposition in St Louis, as well as in The Field Museum on their way home. On a more regular basis, the Kwakwa̱ka'wakw were accustomed to performing their culture for visiting dignitaries of various kinds, as well as for tourists who arrived on the cruise ships stopping off on their way to Alaska. Evans and Glass suggest that rather than condemn Curtis for misrepresenting the reality of Kwakwaka'wakw life, be it in 1914 or at some indeterminate pre-contact period, one should ask to what extent this film is the result of decisions by the Kwakwaka'wakw themselves as to how they wished to be represented at that particular historical juncture.[29]

More generally, Evans and Glass propose that instead of thinking of *Head Hunters* as a representation *of* the Kwakwaka'wakw that is either true or false, it would more be profitable to think of it as a representation *in dialogue with* the Kwakwaka'wakw and their evolving relationship with their own tradition. This is certainly the framework through which Evans and Glass approached their reconstruction of the film. Throughout the process, they collaborated closely with the U'mista Cultural Society, a Kwakwaka'wakw organisation dedicated to the preservation of their cultural heritage, based at Alert Bay, which lies further down the eastern coast of Vancouver Island from Tsaxis, on Cormorant Island. They had a particularly close association with the executive director of this organisation, Andrea Sanborn, and on the website that first reported on their reconstruction work, she was listed as a co-author of the project. Sadly, however, she passed away before the project was completed.

The collaboration has nevertheless continued in various forms, notably through the involvement of a semi-professional Kwakwaka'wakw dance troupe, the Gwa'wina (Raven) Dancers. When the new version of the film was taken on a tour of six US and Canadian cities in 2008, the Gwa'wina Dancers would often perform after a screening, including some of the dances seen in the film in their repertoire, answering audience questions not only about the film but also about how they related to the world that it represents.[30]

## THE CREATIVE TREATMENT OF ACTUALITY: *NANOOK OF THE NORTH*

Important though *Grass* and *Head Hunters* may be in the history of ethnographic cinema, by far the most influential work to emerge from the early twentieth-century cinematic crucible of travelogue and melodrama was the work that has been identified by many as the original film of the ethnographic genre – *Nanook of the North*. Released in 1922, almost a decade after *Head Hunters* and two years prior to *Grass*, this film portrays the day-to-day life of an Itivimuit Inuit man living with his family on the eastern shore of Hudson Bay, in the northernmost reaches of the Canadian Province of Quebec. The director, Robert Flaherty, was neither an academic researcher, nor a professional film-maker, but rather a US mineral prospector who had been working in the Canadian North for about ten years by the time he came to make this film.[31]

Although actually shot over the course of more than a year, the main body of the film consists of a chronicle of the subjects' lives over what are ostensibly two days, following them in a range of subsistence practices, mostly hunting and fishing, as well as in some domestic routines, as they seek to wrest a living from the challenging Arctic environment. In doing so, *Nanook* offered a degree of intimacy with the subjects coupled with a technical mastery of the medium that had not been previously achieved in any form of non-fiction film-making.

By a thought-provoking coincidence, *Nanook* was released in the same year that Bronislaw Malinowski published *The Argonauts of the Western Pacific*. Although Flaherty was precisely the kind of explorer figure despised by 'the Ethnographer', as Malinowski styled himself, there was a certain similarity in their methods: *Nanook* and *Argonauts* were both works arising from extended first-hand immersion in the world of the subjects; though both covered certain public moments in their subjects' lives, they also described and celebrated the detail of their more intimate personal experiences. But most significantly of all, the ultimate goal of both author and film-maker was to be able to evoke their subjects' vision of their world, or as Malinowski put it, albeit in the androcentric colonial language of the time, 'to grasp the native's point of view, his relation to life, to realise *his* vision of *his* world' and, above all, 'the hold that life has on him'.[32]

Notwithstanding the frequent references to Flaherty's status as the 'father' of ethnographic documentary, and the various parallels that one might draw between his methods and those of Malinowski, *Nanook* presents such a romanticised vision of Inuit life and involves such a degree of construction and artifice that, if judged by present-day criteria, it is highly doubtful that it would be classed as a 'documentary' at all, ethnographic or otherwise, at least not in the conventional modern sense of the term. However, it is important to understand that Flaherty was not trying to make a documentary in the modern sense. Indeed, to attempt to read *Nanook* as some sort of early and imperfect stab at making an ethnographic documentary in the modern sense leads one into the same sort of interpretative errors that Holm and Quimby made in their very well-intentioned but ultimately misconceived reconstruction of *Head Hunters*. Instead, I would suggest that one should think of *Nanook* as something rather different, namely, as an innovative attempt, drawing on the tropes of the travelogue and the melo-drama, to tell an intimate personal story about everyday life in a culturally exotic setting (figure 2.6).

In considering *Nanook*, one should bear in mind first and foremost that it was made for a popular cinema audience. In the 1920s, there were no art cinemas, nor international ethnographic film festivals. The principal

**2.6** *Nanook of the North* (1922) retained certain features of the travelogue, but offered an unprecedented intimacy with the subjects. Left, Nanook is amused by a gramophone at the trade store; right, Nyla, Nanook's screen wife and Flaherty's real life lover, builds an igloo.

patrons for films of this kind were the commercial cinema chains and their greatest concern was not with ethnographic accuracy but rather with whether their audiences would be entertained.[33] Second, we need to remember that even if Flaherty had been seeking to make an ethnographic documentary in the modern sense, involving minimal interference in the lives of the subjects, there would have been severe technical obstacles to his doing so, particularly in demanding sub-Arctic conditions. Much of what today's documentary film-makers would be able to film without intervening in any way was then only possible through considerable contrivance.

A great deal has been made of the technical contrivances that Flaherty adopted in order to make *Nanook*, as if these somehow undermined his 'documentary' purpose. One that has attracted particular comment is the igloo that Flaherty had specially built for filming: in order to give himself sufficient room and light to film, Flaherty asked the Inuit to build an igloo that was very much larger than normal and with one side missing. The sequences of the family getting up two-thirds of the way through the film and going to bed at the end of the film were then specifically enacted for the camera at Flaherty's request in this one-sided igloo. However, as contrivances go, this is surely not that significant, certainly for the period: it would be many years before documentary film-makers would be able to light the interior of an igloo. Much less commented upon, but in my view much more noteworthy for reasons considered below, is that these two sequences of getting up and going to bed were clearly filmed at the same time but were then used at separate points in the film and in the reverse order.

Other contrivances involved in the making of *Nanook* were not motivated in any way by technical constraints but were simply a consequence of the fact that Flaherty was not aiming to produce a literal account of the world, but rather a dramatisation of it, one that involved, in John Grierson's famous phrase, 'the creative treatment of actuality'. Although they were all local people, the principal subjects were, in effect, actors acting out their own lives, though always under Flaherty's direction. There was no script as such, but every scene was carefully prepared in advance in consultation with the subjects. Flaherty even gave this subjects screen names. The real name of the principal subject was Alakariallak: his screen name was a transliteration of *nanaq*, meaning 'bear' in Inuktitut, the Inuit language. Flaherty gave him this name (which may also have been his local nickname) not only because he realised that 'Alakariallak' would be too long for cinema audiences to get their tongues around, but also because he originally intended that the film should culminate in a scene in which Alakariallak killed a bear. For the same reason, he asked Alakariallak to wear bearskin leggings, despite the fact, at least according to some specialist commentators on the film, these were not traditionally worn in his part of Inuit territory. But although Flaherty and Alakariallak spent several weeks on an expedition to film the hunting of a bear, they came back empty-handed and, according to Flaherty's extended account of the journey, almost died of starvation on the way back home.

Nor was it only screen names that Flaherty devised for his protagonists: he also devised the relationships that they should represent in the film. For, in reality, 'Nyla – the Smiling One', Nanook's screen wife – was not actually Alakariallak's wife, but rather his daughter-in-law, one Maggie Nujarluktuk. She was also Flaherty's lover, and after his departure she bore him a son, Joseph, who took his father's surname, though Flaherty never recognised him and may not even have known about him. There is also a second young woman, Cunayou, who appears in various domestic scenes, including in the igloo-building scene in which she is carrying a baby. She is also shown sleeping with the baby in the getting up and going to bed scenes. How she fits into Nanook's on-screen family is not exactly explained in the film itself. In an early scene, when she emerges from Nanook's kayak with the rest of his on-screen family, she looks like a young adolescent, possibly Nanook's daughter. But in the later scenes, she looks much older, leading the viewer to wonder if it is the same actress in both cases. Is she supposed to be a second wife, to whom Flaherty eventually decided not to draw attention in consideration of the possible prejudices of the audience? It has been claimed that she too was Flaherty's lover. But this may be just another wrinkle in the aura of myth and legend that surrounds the person of Flaherty.[34]

All these fictional features clearly limit the status of *Nanook* both as documentary and as ethnography, at least as these terms are most commonly understood today. However, it is what Flaherty left out of the film rather than what he put in that most casts doubt on its status as an ethnographic documentary in present-day terms. Even Flaherty's contemporaries had doubts about the fact that apart from an anodyne scene at the trading post of Revillon Frères, the French furriers who sponsored the film, the contact of the Inuit with the outside world was rigorously excluded. Not only are there no rifles, no steel hunting traps, nor other technological evidence of contact, but the social effects of contact are omitted too. But Flaherty was very clear in his own mind that he did not want to show what he considered to be the disastrous effects on Inuit life of missionaries, mining camps, schools, alcoholism and prostitution. Rather, he wanted to show the Inuit's 'former majesty and character ... while it is still possible – before the White man has destroyed not only their character, but the people as well'.[35]

Yet even when considered as a historical reconstruction of the pre-contact period, *Nanook* is of limited ethnographic value, at least if one accepts the view of Flaherty's contemporary, the distinguished cultural anthropologist Franz Boas. Although Boas is perhaps best known for his later work among the Kwakwaka'wakw, he carried out his doctoral fieldwork on Baffin Island, to the north of Hudson Bay where Flaherty worked, among an Inuit group of similar cultural characteristics. Boas was also interested in the potential of film-making for academic anthropology. But, in a letter written to a leading cinema industry figure some ten years after the release of *Nanook*, Boas commented that if only 'a man who knows Eskimo life in and out had been at hand to direct a film like *Nanook*, many exceedingly picturesque and interesting features of native life might have been brought in which would not only have improved the quality of the film but would have also made it more attractive to the general audiences'.[36]

In considering this opinion, one should allow for the fact that anthropologists without extensive first-hand film-making experience, now just as much as then, are almost invariably disappointed by the limited amount of information that it is possible to include in a film. Even so, Boas's sense that *Nanook* displayed a lack of familiarity with Inuit life should stand as a corrective to the sometimes too-ready assumption, particularly in the screen studies literature, that Flaherty's relationships with the Inuit as his field assistants on his mineral prospecting trips and later as his film protagonists – not to mention as his lovers – would translate automatically into a genuinely well-founded ethnographic knowledge of their social life and culture.

What is certainly the case is that considered as an ethnographic account of Inuit society, be it in 1920 or at some indeterminate period before the arrival of Europeans, *Nanook* makes almost no reference to social life beyond the nuclear family, nor to economic life beyond subsistence tasks, and there is no allusion to shamanism nor to any other aspect of Inuit religious life, which subsequent ethnographic study has shown to be of great importance to the Inuit. But given that Flaherty's decidedly underwhelming autobiographical account of his decade or more living among his 'Eskimo friends' consists of little more than a series of prolonged anecdotes about the logistical difficulties of travelling and making films in the sub-Arctic, it seems that these social and cultural aspects of Inuit life were not matters to which he paid too much attention anyway.[37]

## THE INNOVATIONS OF *NANOOK OF THE NORTH*: THE NARRATIVISATION OF EVERYDAY LIFE

Yet however limited the ethnographicness of *Nanook* may be in regards to the actual content of the film, in two other respects, which are more methodological, it represents an important precursor for future developments in the authorship of ethnographic films. One of these concerns the way in which it presents Inuit daily life through a narrative structure based upon what might be termed an 'as if chronology', that is, a chronology that has been entirely created in the edit suite but which is modelled on a natural chronology. Whereas the device of the unitary journey could be used in the travelogue format to impose order and direction on diverse footage gathered opportunistically in the course of an expedition, an 'as if chronology' – variously construed as a day, a season or a year, or some other easily recognisable unit of time – can be used to impose order and direction on material shot in a given place or among a given group of people, usually over much longer periods than is suggested by the fictitious chronology itself. As one of the most innovative features of *Nanook* from an authorial point of view, this aspect of the film deserves our closer attention.[38]

In a manner that is suggestively similar to the later case of *Grass*, the first third of the film, that is, the first 25 minutes, acts as a sort of prelude to the main body of the film and has a number of features typical of the travelogue format. It begins with a classic travelogue arrival trope: a point-of-view shot taken from on board a large vessel as it pushes its way through a sea littered with ice floes. This is followed by a series of maps interspersed with rolling explanatory title cards stressing the isolation and precariousness of life in the region: in a sense, the Inuit are, like the Bakhtiari, also a 'Forgotten People'. We are then presented with two striking close-up portraits of 'Nanook, The Bear' and his wife, 'Nyla – The Smiling One'. Next come some rather disconnected vignettes of Inuit technical processes (making a moss fire, building a kayak etc.) before Nanook and his family arrive at the Revillon trading post. Here there are a number of jokey scenes, including one of Nanook listening to a phonograph and testing out a vinyl record with his teeth, which are straight out of the same drawer as similar scenes of 'natives' marvelling at modern technology that frequently crop up in the Martin and Osa Johnson travelogues. The prelude then culminates with two sequences in which Nanook demonstrates his prowess as a hunter, first in fishing for sea trout amid the ice floes, and then the celebrated scene in which he harpoons a walrus and, with the help of three other men, hauls it out of the sea.

Also as in *Grass*, there is then a sudden change of gear, narratologically speaking, as an intertitle announces the arrival of 'Winter ...'. But whereas in *Grass*, the progress of the Bakhtiari journey takes over at this point as the structuring principle of the film, in *Nanook* it is an 'as if' chronology. In effect, the remainder of the film is presented as two days in the life of Nanook and his family. The first day mainly consists of them slowly making their way over the chaotic ridges of snow caused by the ice floes driven inshore by winter gales. After Nanook digs out a white fox caught in one of his traps, there is a lengthy sequence in which, while their children play, he and Nyla build an igloo for the night, assisted by the mysterious 'second woman', Cunayou. Once the igloo is built, there are some charming sequences of Nanook playing with his children before the whole family withdraws into the igloo, and with a single shot of a hearthstone arrayed with seal-oil candles, the first day ends.

The second day begins with a lengthy getting up sequence, as the entire family is shown emerging from beneath its bedding of furs. This is clearly based on the second half of the footage shot in the artificial igloo described earlier. The family's naked torsos are briefly exposed, reminding us simultaneously of the warmth and of the vulnerability of the human body in such an environment. Nyla chews Nanook's frozen boots to soften them, and plays with her baby, rubbing noses in the 'Eskimo kiss', another *chapeau* to the travelogue format.

The main scene of this second day is the longest in the film and shows the harpooning of a seal through its blowhole in the ice. However, using the technique of delayed disclosure that he would employ throughout his film-making career, Flaherty does not at first let the audience know that it is a seal that will emerge from this small hole. Nanook plunges his harpoon through the hole, and as he struggles to pull out whatever it is that lies below, the jocose travelogue style returns once more. He is dragged back and forth, turning somersaults and sliding on his backside in a Chaplinesque manner. In fact, this bit of comedic 'business' was entirely contrived: the other end of the harpoon rope was being pulled, not by a seal, but by an off-screen group of fellow Inuit.[39]

Eventually, with the assistance of the whole family, Nanook manages to land his prey and it turns out to be a very dead-looking seal. Its meat is then shared out around the ravenous dogs. But by now it is getting late, the fighting between the dogs is delaying matters and the wind is starting to get up, so the family takes refuge in an igloo that is supposedly 'abandoned', but which bears an uncanny resemblance to the igloo seen being built earlier in the film. The second day, and the film as a whole, then ends with a sequence of the family bedding down for the night, using the first half of the footage shot in the artificial igloo. In a particularly memorable editorial device, these shots of the family are repeatedly intercut with shots of the dogs outside becoming increasingly covered in snow. The final shot of the film is a close-up of Nanook apparently asleep, gently breathing.

The material for these two days in the life of Alakariallak and his fictional family, we should remember, was, in reality, shot over the course of a year. In terms of its general ontological status therefore, one could argue that the narrative structure underlying *Nanook* is just as fictional as the narrative structure underlying *Head Hunters*. But there is an important difference: whereas *Head Hunters* was based on a series of entirely imaginary, extraordinary events, the structure of *Nanook* is made of up a series of everyday events that may not have happened exactly as shown in the film, nor exactly in that order, but which could have happened in something approximating this manner. If one puts aside certain matters of content, such as the many ethnographic inaccuracies and comedic effects introduced to spice up the story for the popular audience, this form of filmic narrative is not dissimilar in formal terms to the narrative accounts one often encounters in ethnographic texts from *Argonauts of the Western Pacific* onwards, in which a typical routine is described as happening over a given length time, be it over a single day or a longer period.

In effect, what Flaherty discovered in making *Nanook* was that the everyday could be dramatised. 'What biography of any man', he asked rhetorically, 'could be more interesting?'[40] Rather than being built on a series of fanciful dramatic events, as *Head Hunters* had been, Flaherty's narrative strategy consisted simply of following an imaginary but naturalistic 'as if chronology'. This not only provides a cumulative link between otherwise disconnected scenes of everyday life, but also ensures an appropriate sense of closure at the end of the film. The audiences of *Nanook* knew that the film had come to an end and that they could go home satisfied, not because the hero had won the maiden's hand and the Evil Sorcerer and his brother had met a terrible fate, but rather because the hero had settled down to sleep, snug within his igloo, while outside in the gathering gloom his dogs endured the Arctic blasts.

## THE INNOVATIONS OF *NANOOK OF THE NORTH*: PARTICIPATION AND FEEDBACK

The other feature of *Nanook* that has been much admired by ethnographic film-makers of later generations are its participatory methods, that is, the way in which Flaherty actively involved his protagonists in the making of the film. This in itself was not entirely original: as shown in Chapter 1, in the very first example of ethnographic film-making in the field, Alfred Haddon had sought the collaboration of his subjects in filming the Malo-Bomai dances, and it was they who made the cardboard masks used in the film. Similarly, as discussed, the Kwakwaka'wakw appear to have actively participated in the creation of *In the Land of the Head Hunters*. What was distinctive about Flaherty's approach was that this process of consultation also involved what would later become known as 'feedback screenings'.

For, defying the lack of mains electricity in his cabin on the edge of Hudson Bay, Flaherty developed his rushes on the spot and then screened them to his subjects at regular intervals as the filming proceeded. Not only did these screenings allow the subjects to understand the nature of film-making – when Flaherty first arrived, he discovered that many Inuit could not even 'read' a still photograph – but they also inspired the Inuit to work with him as partners. When the Inuit saw the rushes of the first day's shooting (the walrus hunt, as it happened), they were entranced. Thereafter, he reported, they were constantly thinking up new scenes for the film.

It was these collaborative methods that undoubtedly accounted for the unprecedented sense of intimacy between subjects and film-maker that is so striking about *Nanook*. When asked how he had managed to achieve this, Flaherty put it down to the simple fact that the Inuit had allowed him to share their way of life. Far from looking down on his subjects, as the travelogue film-makers of his era invariably did, Flaherty looked up to them. As he would later put it:

> I had been dependent on these people, alone with them for months at a time, travelling with them and living with them … My work had been built up along with them; I couldn't have done anything without them. In the end, it is all a question of human relationships.[41]

We should not, however, allow ourselves to be entirely beguiled by the Flaherty legend. Although his methods were unprecedentedly participatory, he remained in firm control. Whatever the Inuit subjects may have wished to do, the 'aggie', as Alakariallak referred to the film-making process, 'would always come first'.[42] There were also some aspects of Flaherty's relationship with his subjects that many audiences today find difficult to approve. The references in the initial rolling intertitles to 'the happy-go-lucky Eskimo' and the 'simple Eskimo', intended by Flaherty to be positive descriptions, would be considered by most modern audiences, including the Inuit themselves, to be intolerably patronising. There were also clearly some aspects of his relationships with Inuit women that would be severely questioned today.

But we should be wary of being too presentist in our judgements. For the era in which he was working, Flaherty's views were certainly progressive and this was reflected in the intimate and assured way in which he presented

**2.7** *Nanook of the North* (1922). Left, the family makes haste to find shelter before the night closes in; right, Alakariallak and 'the hold that life has'.

his Inuit subjects. Previously the protagonists of films about 'other cultures' had been no more than distant figures, without character or individuality. Nanook is a much more rounded character than any we find, not merely in any previous works, but even in the ethnographic films of Margaret Mead and Gregory Bateson that were shot more than a decade later.

There is surely no more telling instance of this than the moment when Alakariallak, framed in close-up, looks directly down the camera lens as he is first introduced to us as 'Nanook, The Bear'. Maggie Nujarluktuk gets the same treatment as 'Nyla – The Shining One', immediately afterwards, but she is shot in semi-profile, swaying slightly, lips moving in some apparently amused comment, and in soft focus like some Hollywood diva. It is an entirely formulaic framing that gives no sense of her individual being. In contrast, Alakariallak's look is directly at the camera and is far more striking. He averts his eyes momentarily but then looks again with an air of curiosity, but also of confidence, no doubt arising from the secure relationship between himself and the film-maker. Rendered all the more poignant by the knowledge that within two years he had died of starvation on a hunting trip, that single image offers us an almost unbearable sense of the being of Alakariallak, the man in flesh and blood, and – in the words of the Ethnographer – 'the hold that life has on him' (figure 2.7).

## THE LEGACY OF *NANOOK OF THE NORTH*

In the years following *Nanook of the North*, Flaherty went on to make a number of other fictional films set in culturally exotic locations. These included *Moana* (1926), a saccharine story about a young man's coming of age in Samoa; *Man of Aran* (1934), about a family's struggles to make a living on an island off the west coast of Ireland; *Elephant Boy* (1937), a rags-to-riches tale about the ambition of a young Indian elephant driver to become a great hunter, and Flaherty's last film, *Louisiana Story* (1948), another coming of age story, this time rather wistful, which centres on a young boy witnessing the arrival of the oil industry in the waterlogged bayous that are his home.

Although Flaherty generally employed much the same participatory methods in making these films, they were not based on the same degree of long-term engagement with the subjects as *Nanook*. Nor did they reveal any greater interest in social and economic relationships beyond the nuclear family and subsistence activities. If anything, they were generally even more fictionalised than *Nanook* and although it could be argued that some of these later films possessed certain ethnographic qualities, they too could only be considered documentaries by present-day norms with some degree of qualification.

Nor does Flaherty's work appear to have had any influence whatsoever on the film-making of the academic anthropologists of his own time. The great Soviet film-makers of the 1920s were much impressed by *Nanook*: Sergei Eisenstein claimed that they showed their print of the film so many times that they completely wore it out. John Grierson and his acolytes in the British Documentary Movement were similarly inspired and invited Flaherty to the UK to work with them. Yet the impact on Flaherty's anthropologist contemporaries was negligible. Not only Franz Boas, but also his student Margaret Mead, were certainly aware of Flaherty's films and, as late as 1972, Mead even based a diorama of Samoan life that she completed for the AMNH on a scene from *Moana*. But Flaherty's work did not influence Boas and Mead's actual film-making practices, nor did it influence their way of thinking about the role of film in anthropology. On the contrary, Mead regarded Flaherty's 'artistic' approach to film-making as the complete antithesis of the way in which anthropologists should be using film in their work.[43]

Indeed, it was only after the Second World War that ethnographic film-makers would come to find inspiration in Flaherty's work. Perhaps his greatest admirer was Jean Rouch, who liked to claim Flaherty as his 'totemic ancestor'. What Rouch particularly admired about *Nanook* was the degree of intimacy that Flaherty had managed to achieve with his subjects. Moreover, Rouch realised that this was a direct result of Flaherty's collaborative methods, particularly his use of feedback screenings, and he made these methods the cornerstone of his own praxis, an approach that he would dub 'shared anthropology'.[44]

But Rouch followed Flaherty in another way also, that is, in his willingness to work with his subjects to produce fictionalised accounts of their own everyday lives. Rouch produced a dozen feature-length films based on this methodology that third parties have dubbed 'ethnofiction'. In that it involved a prolonged collaboration with Alakariallak and his screen family to produce a dramatised version of their everyday life, I suggest that in making *Nanook of the North*, Robert Flaherty was the author, not of the first 'ethnographic documentary' as we would understand those terms today, but rather of the first 'ethnofiction'.

## Notes

1 These films can be viewed on the Library of Congress website at www.loc.gov/item/00694114 (*Buffalo Dance*) and www.loc.gov/item/00694139/ (*Sioux Ghost Dance*). The latter film is sometimes incorrectly identified as 'Indian War Council'.

2 The Lumière view that is widely shown as supposedly the 'first film' is in fact probably only a re-make, being only one of as many as five different versions of the same view that were shot between March 1895 and February 1897. The very first view appears to have been lost or destroyed. The most authoritative catalogue of Lumière films is the one edited by Michelle Aubert and Jean-Claude Seguin (1996). See pp. 19, 214–15 of this work for a discussion of the difficulties in identifying the very first view.

3 See Chapter 1, p. 60. Veyre's footage also just predates that of Alfred Haddon, which was shot in Melanesia on 5 and 6 September 1898 (also see Chapter 1, pp. 31–2).

4 Pierre Leprohon (1903–93) was a journalist and writer on cinema who is remembered in France for his book *L'Exotisme et le Cinéma*, published in 1945. This work is disfigured by some egregiously racist observations as well as by certain major ethnographic errors. However, it contains a number of interesting ideas and offers a very useful review of early twentieth-century examples of what he terms *cinéma exotique*, that is, both fictional and non-fictional films about 'other cultures'. Leprohon himself proposes that the term *reportage* should be reserved for films by named directors who had some particular message to impart while the work of the early newsreel operators should be referred to simply as 'travel documentaries' or 'open air films' (*scènes de plein air*) as they were known at the time because they were not made in studios (see Leprohon (1945), 163). In contradicting Leprohon and employing 'reportage' to refer to the work of the latter, I would argue that my usage reflects the less elevated connotations of this term in English. On the specific matter of the rates paid to early newsreel operators, see Leprohon (1945), 19–21.

5 Many early Gaumont and Pathé films are available at their joint archive at www.gaumontpathearchives.com/index.php?html=17.

6 I am greatly indebted to Faisal Devji, reader in Indian History at the University of Oxford for these comments on the historical significance of the film.

7 See Bell, Brown and Gordon (2013), 247. Copies of the films arising from both the AMNH and the Harvard collaborations with Pathé are held at the National Anthropological Film Center (until recenty the Human Studies Film Archives) at the Smithsonian Institution.

8 A selection of Baby-Pathé films is available on the Princeton University website at rbsc.princeton.edu/pathebaby/. However, they are also available in rather better quality and with an explanatory introduction on a private website hosted on YouTube: www.youtube.com/user/StephendelRoser.

9 See Ruoff (2002), Altman (2006), Gordon, Brown and Bell (2013) among many possibilities in an extensive literature on the travelogue.

10 See Homiak (2013), vii–xi. A variant of the travelogue format – albeit, one that is now generally reverential towards its subjects' way of life – is with us still in the form of the television travel show featuring celebrity presenters sharing their experience of 'first contact' with cultural Others across the globe.

11 See www.youtube.com/watch?v=60004FZ2bes. The clip comes from *Congorilla*, commonly said to be the first sound film shot entirely in Africa. Specifically on the Johnsons, see Russell (1999), 140–8; Lindstrom (2013).

12 This account of the making of *Grass* draws upon the excellent study by Hamid Naficy (2006). For an interesting discussion of the narrativity of this film, see Crawford (1992). For general historical and ethnographic background, see also Bradburd (2013).

13 David MacDougall reports that at a screening of the film that he attended as a student in Los Angeles in 1968, Merian Cooper explained that the footage of the Bakhtiari migration was initially intended merely to serve as background material for a feature film that was never made (MacDougall 2019, 162, 188, n.6). If so, this might explain why Harrison has such a slight presence in this part of the film.

14 These figures are those of the film-makers, who claim in the intertitles that the migration involved 'fifty thousand feet' and 'half a million hooves'. Although these numbers are very likely to have been exaggerated, it was still clearly a vast migration of people and animals.

15 Naficy reproduces an interesting comment by one of the writers of the intertitles, a certain Terry Ramsey (actually spelt 'Ramsaye' in the opening credits of the film), who claims that it is these intertitles that impart an epic character to an event that the Bakhtiari themselves consider to be no more than a twice-yearly 'chore' (Naficy 2006), 138, n. 5.

16 The image of Haidar Khan, presented in the film as the noble leader of his people, is considerably at odds with the film-makers' characterisation of him in print, which Naficy paraphrases as 'gorilla-like, brutal, a wife-beater, an opium smoker, and a horse thief, who loafed about while his people did the work' (2006), 129–30.

17 Griffiths (2002), 236–7, 276–8. Colin Browne reports that a pre-existing Hiawatha pageant first filmed in Ontario in 1903 involving an Ojibwe cast, was then filmed on two further occasions with a Mohawk cast, in 1908 in Quebec and again, in Montreal, in 1911. Remarkably, this last version is reported to have been in colour (Browne 2014), 175–6.

18 Jordan (1992), 154–7, 176–9, Evans (2014), 205–6. All these early Griffith films are available on YouTube.

19 See O'Reilly (1970), 289–90; Piault (2000), 26–7.

20 My discussion of this film draws on a number of sources, including Curtis (1915), Holm and Quimby (1980), Rony (1996), 90–8, Evans (1998), but above all, on the many contributions to the excellent volume edited by Brad Evans and Aaron Glass (2014), particularly their own Introduction (pp. 3–26). I am also indebted to Aaron Glass for his very valuable personal comments during a meeting in May 2015 and in response to the manuscript of this chapter in December 2018.

21 See Chapter 1, p. 76 note 58.

22 Gidley (1982), 71–2; Gidley (2014), 53.

23 This is reproduced on p. 52 of Evans and Glass (2014), in figure 1.5.

24 My sceptical view regarding Curtis's skills as a film-maker, while unusual, is not unique: Jere Guldin, of the UCLA Film & Television Archive, who restored the latest version of the film and therefore knows it particularly well, has commented that Curtis 'an immaculate still photographer, was not much of a hand with a motion-picture camera' (Guldin 2014, 261).

25 See particularly Glass and Evans (2014), 22–3; Evans (2014), 206–8.

26 Aaron Glass (personal communication, December 2018) has suggested that this may be a self-conscious reference to the well-known biblical story of Jonah that was inserted to round off the whale hunting sequence. There is also an intriguing similarity between this shot and the famous shot of Nanook emerging from his igloo to acknowledge the camera in *Nanook of the North* (see Browne 2014, 171). Whatever the precise reason for it, this shot can be understood as a 'cinema of attractions' moment that interrupts the general flow of the narrative diegesis.

27 Glass and Evans (2014), 26.

28 See Holm (2014).

29 See particularly Glass and Evans (2014), 10–11, 16–19.

30 See Glass (2014).

31 The person and life of Flaherty is hedged around by legend and mystery. He himself liked to put about the apocryphal story that he had learned film-making from a missionary who later hung himself in his darkroom, though the more prosaic reality is that the little training that he did receive actually consisted of a three-week course at the Kodak factory in Rochester, New York. Unless otherwise stated, this and other background details regarding the making of *Nanook* are drawn from Rotha with Wright (1980), Barnouw (1983), 23–45 or Ruby (2000), 67–93.

32 Malinowski (1932a), 25.

33 See the remarkably tacky promotional materials for *Nanook* prepared for cinema managers and reproduced in the journal *Studies in Visual Communication* 6 (2) (1980). The subtitle and promotional strap-line for the film was 'A Story of Life and Love in the Actual Arctic'.

34 See Rony (1996), 123; Marcus (2006), 205, 214–18; Winston (2013a), 11.

35 Cited in Rotha with Wright (1980), 47.

36 Cited in Jacknis (1987), 63.

37 See Flaherty with Flaherty (1924).

38 The argument concerning the narrative structure of *Nanook* in the following paragraphs has been strongly influenced by the ideas of Brian Winston (see particularly Winston 1995, 99–102; also Winston 2013). The film exists in a number of different versions, but the version referred to here is the one featured on the Criterion Collection DVD released in 1998. This version was prepared in collaboration with the Film Preservation Society and is based on a re-mastering of Flaherty's personal print acquired by the BFI in 1939.

39 This scene has been the subject of much discussion in the screen studies literature, though this has often been poorly informed. It seems to have been the celebrated French film theorist André Bazin who started this discussion when he described this scene as 'one of the loveliest in all cinema' on the grounds that it shows 'the actual waiting period' and includes 'hunter, hole and seal all in the same shot', without any recourse to montage. As such, he claims, it shows 'respect for the spatial unity of an event when to split it up would change it from something real to something imaginary' (Bazin 2005), 27, 50–1. In fact, however, over the 20-second waiting period in the film (very much less than the 20-minute interval at which seals typically come up for air), not only are there four different cuts, each from a different angle, but in none of them do we see hunter, blowhole and seal all in the same shot.

40 Cited in Ruby (2000), 75.

41 Flaherty (1996), 43.

42 Cited in Ruby (2000), 67.

43 Ruby (2000), 85.

44 See Rouch (1968), 447–55; (1995a), 82. Also Chapter 8 of this book.

# 3

# The invisible author: films of re-enactment in the post-war period

I N the ethnographic film-making that took place in the twenty years
following the Second World War, the documentation paradigm continued
to predominate, at least in the English-speaking world. The moving image
camera was still primarily thought of, not as a means for making documentary
films, but rather as a recording device that should be used to gather visual
data in the most objective possible fashion. The interest in salvage ethnography
also continued unabated, owing to an intensification of the political and
economic processes responsible for the progressive incorporation of previously
isolated communities into national societies, with the concomitant abandonment of traditional customs and ways of life. Many ethnographic film-makers
of this period had a very keen sense that they were being confronted with
probably the last chance to record for posterity cultural practices that had
been going on, largely unchanged, for millennia, but which would soon
disappear forever from the face of the earth.

As in the case of Alfred Haddon's much earlier filming of the Malo-Bomai
performance described in Chapter 1, this salvage documentation often
involved the re-enactment of cultural practices that had already been
abandoned, sometimes very recently, but in some cases many years beforehand.
However, these re-enactments put film-makers working within the documentation paradigm in a contradictory position: on the one hand, they
were seeking to use the camera as an objective recording instrument, while
on the other, in their concern to capture authentic traditional culture, they
found themselves intervening authorially at every turn – for example, asking
their subjects to take off the European-style clothing that they had picked
up through contact, or transporting them from one place to another in
order to film them in supposedly more authentic surroundings.

In an attempt to sidestep this contradiction, some ethnographic film-makers
developed a mode of praxis whereby their authorship would be acknowledged
in preliminary or end credits, or in accompanying texts, but would then
remain largely invisible in the main body of their films. In this way, the
films could look like works of objective documentation even when the

situations that they portrayed had been entirely set up by the film-makers and the subjects were acting out a life that they no longer lived in reality.

This strategy of invisible authoring took a variety of forms depending on the particular technical or aesthetic choices made by the film-makers with the result that the films produced in this way could look very different from each other, even if the motivations underlying them were fundamentally the same. This can be illustrated by a comparison of two of the best-known re-enactment projects that took place during this period: one was carried out in the mid-1960s with a group of Inuit in northern Canada, while the other was a more or less simultaneous project involving Aboriginal people in Central Australia.

## THE PAST IN THE PRESENT TENSE: THE NETSILIK ESKIMO PROJECT

The filming project carried out in Canada concerned the Netsilik Eskimo, or Netsilingmiut, as they are known today (literally, the Seal People). The Netsilingmiut live at Kugaaruk (formerly known as Pelly Bay), lying on the extreme northwestern lip of Hudson Bay, even further north than the area where Flaherty made *Nanook of the North*. Mostly shot over 13 months in 1962–63 and released between 1967 and 1969, these films were commissioned by the Education Development Center (EDC), an organisation based in Cambridge, Massachusetts and associated with Harvard University. This body was funded by the US National Science Foundation and the Ford Foundation and had a brief to develop the teaching curriculum in US high schools. However, the films were actually produced by the National Film Board of Canada (NFB), with their cameramen acting under the 'supervision' – as the film credits put it – of the anthropologist Asen Balikci, with 'additional assistance' from Guy Mary-Rousselière, a French missionary who had been based in the region for many years. In the NFB catalogue, the direction of the films is attributed to a certain Quentin Brown, but he appears to have been more the local producer than the actual director of the films. In other contexts, final authorial responsibility is often attributed to Balikci though the general form of the films was also greatly influenced by the various NFB cameramen who worked on the project as well as by the requirements of the EDC.

At the time of making these films, Balikci held a post at the Université de Montréal and was given leave of absence in order to carry out the project. He had recently completed an anthropology doctorate at Columbia University in New York, based on field research in Kugaaruk in 1959–60, and as part of his training he had attended Margaret Mead's seminar on ethnographic fieldwork techniques in which she had emphasised the importance of using audiovisual media. Mead had taught him, he later reported, 'that the main purpose of ethnographic film-making was to record in an objective and detached manner, and as comprehensively as possible'.[1]

Shooting entirely in colour, Balikci and his colleagues produced a total of around 115 hours of 16 mm footage. With the exception of the material shot over a very much longer time period by John Marshall with the San (which I shall discuss in Chapter 4), this is probably the greatest quantity of 16 mm film footage ever shot in the course of a single English-language ethnographic film project. Even by today's standards, when ethnographic film-making usually involves the use of digital media and the quantity of material shot is generally very much higher, this is still a very considerable amount. These 115 hours were later edited down into nine films, most of them an hour or more in length, with a total duration of almost eleven hours. Since they were intended for use in US high schools, most of the films were then subdivided into two or more parts of around 30 minutes, so that they could be used within the time constraints of a standard US high school lesson period. All these films are now available on the NFB website in remarkably high quality.[2]

Taken as a series, the films follow the migration of an extended Netsilingmiut family from camp to camp over the course of a year. Inspired by the then fashionable culture ecology theories of Julian Steward, the focus is overwhelmingly on everyday subsistence processes and domestic activities at each camp. With a high school audience in mind, there is also a strong emphasis on the life of children, notably on their play and on their relationship with their parents, particularly with their mothers (figure 3.1). Apart from a relatively brief sequence of drumming in the last 10 minutes of the last film in the series, *At the Winter Sea Ice Camp*, there is no reference to ceremonial life, nor to rites of passage or shamanistic religious practices. Nor is there any reference to social relations beyond the immediate family, such as those entailed in marriage exchanges, for example, or trade. The tenor of the human relations in the film is invariably harmonious – only the occasional bawl of a baby suggests any form of emotional discomfort or anxiety. The general approach suggests that Balikci had certainly taken to heart Mead's injunction about comprehensiveness since most processes and situations are covered in great detail. But whether they can be considered 'objective and detached' in the way that Mead envisaged, is another matter.

The technical standard of these films was extraordinarily high for documentaries of the period. The three cameramen who worked on the series were all highly skilled: the first was Doug Wilkinson, who had already achieved renown for *Land of the Long Day*, a classic of Arctic documentary cinema released in 1952; the next was Kenneth Poste, a highly experienced NFB staff cameraman; the last was Robert Young, a freelancer who had already established a name for himself working for National Geographic.

3.1 Netsilik themes. The series was mainly concerned with ecological adaptation: above left, a seal hunt on the winter sea ice, above right, building a kayak. Aimed at high school pupils, there was also a strong emphasis on parent–child relationships: below left, a woman cleans an ice window in her igloo; below right, a father shows his son how to manage a string figure.

Using a vibrant colour stock, these cameramen managed to capture the extraordinary beauty of the Arctic landscape and its animal life in the various seasons of the year. Their filming of the human subjects is also remarkable: discreet and intimate around the camp, it is often technically very skilful in other contexts, such as in the handheld shots of the subjects tramping through deep snow, or in one sequence showing two men harpooning caribou from their kayaks which has clearly been shot from a camera in its own moving watercraft. There are also many well-executed igloo interior shots that are artificially lit but in a manner that does not overly draw attention to itself.[3]

One should also not underestimate the quality of the soundtrack, which is remarkably crisp, a great achievement given the windy conditions in which the film-making took place. Acting under the instruction of the cameramen, Balikci himself recorded most of the 'wild' ambient sounds on location. But particularly impressive is the quality of the subjects' speech, which although limited, usually appears very well synchronised. However, it was only for the last film, *At the Winter Sea Ice Camp*, that synchronous sound was actually recorded on location by a sound recordist. For all the other films, remarkably, the speech was post-synchronised: that is, it was recorded with the subjects later, with the assistance of the French missionary alluded to in the credits, Guy Mary-Rousselière, who was fluent in the local language. Much further work was done on the sound post-production, as indicated by the final credits, which always feature a long list of names related to sound editing. This took place, along with the picture editing, not at the NFB but in Cambridge, Massachusetts, where the EDC was based.[4]

In an aesthetic sense, the films are very low-key: the general style is one of muted observational realism. But this effect has been brought about by very skilful authoring. The framing and exposure is generally immaculate and there are no self-conscious manifestations of cinematographic virtuosity: there are no zooms and only a few, limited pans. There is no voice-over narration, no music and although there is some post-synchronised speech, it is not subtitled.[5] With only some very fleeting exceptions, the subjects do not acknowledge the camera and there are no interviews of any kind. The narrative structure of the films is provided by a chronological sequence of days and nights, or by the intrinsic structure of the subsistence practices or social processes that are the principal foci of the films. Each film begins with a subtitle indicating the month and the mean temperature, followed by a series of establishment shots of the environment and the animals that are in evidence at that time of the year. These are often accompanied by bird cries or the hum of insects, which serve to evoke the general atmosphere and a sense of place. Many films end with the fall of night or some other metaphorical 'farewell' shot, such as a family group disappearing into the distance.

Within this overall framework there is abundant use of feature film continuity codes. There are many matched cuts from wide shots to mid-shots or close-ups, and vice versa. There are many motivated cuts: from one speaker to another; from a shot of a subject turning their head to a shot of an animal at which they are supposedly looking; there is even one motivated cut that moves from a shot of a caribou in the distance looking up, to a shot of a series of cairns erected to give the impression that there are a group of hunters lying in wait in that direction. There are also many examples of intercut sequences clearly intended to suggest simultaneity but which would certainly have been shot at different times. These intercut sequences often contrast men engaged in some exterior form of labour out on the river, or on the ice floes, while women are at work at home in the camp. Alternatively, they contrast the parents at work, while children play, sometimes in an entirely carefree manner, at other times in a form that imitates parental subsistence roles.

This effect of muted realism is well achieved, creating the impression that one is watching descriptive research footage of life as it is lived among

**3.2** Netsilik characters. Itimanguerk, left, a headman of around 50 who remembered the old ways well, was the principal 'actor'. With his wife, right, and their children, he provides a thread of continuity through the 11-hour series.

the Netsilingmiut today. But, in fact, these films are all reconstructions of Inuit life as it was supposedly lived in the early 1920s, before the shotgun, metal traps and other items of modern technology – not to speak of the Catholic mission – had radically transformed Netsilingmiut life. The reconstructed nature of the life being shown in the films is clearly stated in rolling titles at the beginning of each film, but the low-key observational aesthetic and the apparently spontaneous behaviour of the subjects are both so absolute that it is only too easy to forget this as the films unfold.

The seductive reality-effect of the films can in part be put down to very successful 'casting' by Balikci. Consciously following Robert Flaherty's example in casting Alakariallak as the eponymous central figure of *Nanook of the North*, Balikci decided to build the films around a principal 'actor', as Balikci himself describes the leading man. This was a certain Itimanguerk, then aged around 50, who retained a clear memory of traditional subsistence practices from his youth. Being a camp headman, he could co-opt his own family and some other younger people to join him in the venture (figure 3.2). Balikci gave Itimanguerk a free hand to select which traditional practices were to be reconstructed, which animals were to be hunted and where the camps were to be set up as the family migrated from one spot to another over the course of the year.

After initially being perplexed as to what was required, Itimanguerk and his fellow Netsilingmiut soon lent themselves enthusiastically to recreating the old ways of life and quite spontaneously went about clearing their camp of such recently imported items as rifles, teapots, canvas tents and cigarettes, though not metal cutting tools since these had been introduced well before the 1920s, probably as long ago as the eighteenth century when European whaling ships first started to penetrate the Hudson Bay area. Balikci acted as an intermediary between the subjects and the film crew, and it was he who decided, often on the spot, which of the many reconstructed processes would actually be filmed. But as he was very concerned to preserve the spontaneity of their behaviour, he never told the Netsilingmiut how to act, nor did he interfere in any other way with the flow of social action. In this last respect, Balikci's approach was very different from that of Flaherty who, as described in Chapter 2, took a very much more active role in directing his protagonists.

Moreover, although the Netsilingmiut films might look like research footage, their intended audience was not researchers, nor even university students, but rather US high school students. In commissioning the films, the EDC, led by the distinguished Harvard cognitive psychologist Jerome S. Bruner, was aiming to combat the then highly ethnocentric quality of the teaching of social sciences in US high schools. The EDC also had a more general pedagogical objective, which was to use film as means whereby high school students could engage directly with the world and learn about it through first-hand empirical observation. Ideally, the high school students would all have been transported to the Canadian Arctic and encouraged to make their observations there. As this was clearly impossible, a series of films was considered the next best thing.

It was this that accounted for the absence of any guiding commentary track or subtitling of speech. The idea was that without the support of an authoritative explanatory framework, students would ask themselves questions, which they could then pursue with the teacher after the screening, aided by dedicated accompanying textual materials prepared by the EDC. The combined package of films and texts, in those less gender-aware days, was entitled *Man: A Course of Study*, known as MACOS for short. In addition to encouraging autonomous reasoning based on empirical evidence, MACOS was also intended to promote an awareness of the role of culture in accounting for what is specifically human about human beings. It was hoped that this would encourage students to adopt an attitude of tolerance towards 'other cultures' and that this, in turn, would make them better citizens not just of the multicultural USA, but also of the world as a whole.[6]

The anthropological aspects of project were overseen by a committee chaired by Margaret Mead. Her belief that the moving image camera should be used as a means of gathering 'objective and detached' visual data that could later be analysed by third parties would no doubt have harmonised well with the EDC's concern that the films should provide the high school audience with direct access to a different cultural world. But although Mead and the EDC were both reportedly very satisfied with the results, the account of the Netsilingmiut world that the films provided was in no sense 'objective and detached'. In fact, what the films offered was merely a *sense* of direct access to a world that no longer existed – if indeed it ever had existed in quite such an anodyne, conflict-free form.

In the original funding proposal, it was envisaged that the Netsilingmiut films would be the first in a series of projects enabling high school students to discover a broad variety of different ways of life, each based on a particular mode of ecological adaptation. The Inuit were chosen as the subjects of the first project because they were hunter-gatherers, and as such were considered representatives of the 'simplest' mode of ecological adaptation. Of the many possible hunter-gatherer societies that might have been selected, the Inuit were thought to be a particularly good choice because their way of life was already a well-known point of reference in US popular culture – in large measure, Balikci has argued, as a result of *Nanook*. Although still a relatively junior member of the anthropological profession in North America, Balikci was asked to supervise the project, not because he knew anything about film-making – which he readily confessed that he did not – but rather because he had only recently carried out fieldwork among a group of Inuit who were still living in a relatively traditional manner, at least from an ecological point of view.[7] In due course, it was anticipated that similar projects would be carried out among a pastoralist people, and then in an agriculture-based society.

On the surface, the MACOS programme is redolent of the optimism of the Kennedy years in the USA, which was based on the belief that a combination of technological development and a liberal worldview was the most effective means to overcome prejudice and solve societal problems. Pedagogically, MACOS was undoubtedly very progressive for the period. Today, the use of audiovisual media in teaching has become so routinised that it is difficult to appreciate just how original a proposal it was at that time to use film in the classroom. The student-centered learning strategies and humanistic objectives underlying the project were also very radical for the time, and might even be considered to be so today, if perhaps somewhat naive.[8]

However, remarkably, notwithstanding its liberal, humanistic objectives, the MACOS project was an indirect product of Cold War politics. For, in fact, the EDC was but one of several projects initiated by the US government that were aimed at regaining the technological initiative after the Soviet Union had successfully launched Sputnik, the first human satellite to orbit the earth, in 1957. The fact that the USA had fallen behind in the 'space race' was put down by some politicians to the failings of the educational system – hence the perceived need to improve teaching in US high schools and the setting up of the EDC. Initially, the EDC had focused only on curriculum development in mathematics and physics, but Bruner considered this too narrow, so the EDC's remit was extended to include the social sciences. But the same conservative political impulse that lay behind the creation of the EDC would later turn round and destroy it, and the MACOS programme along with it.

The initial reaction to MACOS was very positive. Some 3,000 schools across the USA acquired the programme, and at its peak, in 1972, it is estimated that it was reaching 400,000 high school students. But gradually, critical voices began to emerge from within the most politically and culturally conservative circles across the USA. Certain right-wing politicians were appalled by the cultural relativism implicit in the programme, particularly as it was being funded by public money. The first to raise a formal objection was a Republican member of the House of Representatives from Arizona. Soon more influential figures, including the future President, Ronald Reagan, 'added their voices to the choir', as Balikci would later put it.

These politicians' complaints were echoed by parents' groups who were disturbed by the fact that their children, some as young as 9 or 10, were being asked to watch sequences of animals being unsentimentally killed and butchered, particularly caribou, a species that the children had come to love through such cartoon characters as Bambi and Santa's Reindeer. The films made almost no reference to religious life, but even so, the programme was widely construed as being an attack, not merely on traditional American values, but also on 'Judaeo-Christian' religion. As a result of the outcry, funding for the EDC was withdrawn in 1976. Margaret Mead went before a committee of the House of Representatives to defend the MACOS programme on two separate occasions, but to no avail. Plans to develop a second project, this time about a group of pastoralists in Afghanistan, in which Balikci was also involved and which was already underway, were summarily cancelled.[9]

However, the outcry about the use of Netsilingmiut films in high schools did not prevent them from being used in university contexts and they continue to be used so today, particularly since they are now readily available online. They have also found their way back into school curricula, even if indirectly; owing to the films, the Netsilingmuit are the subject of a chapter in the most commonly used high school textbook on Native American peoples.[10] The films have also been re-edited and used in many different formats by television companies all over the world. In 1970, Balikci collaborated with Robert Young to produce a television documentary for the Canadian Broadcasting Corporation, *The Eskimo: Fight for Life*. In effect, this film was an abbreviated version of *At the Winter Sea Ice Camp* with the addition of an extended voice-over commentary written and performed by Balikci. It received high audience ratings and was later awarded an Emmy. Many other television stations have broadcast the material subsequently. The series has been shown in its entirety on Dutch, German and Russian television, albeit with locally scripted voice-over commentaries. In 2003, Balikci estimated that in one form or another, the films had already had more than 200 television bookings across the world, and no doubt they have had many more since.

Among the current audiences for the films are also the Netsilingmiut themselves. Initially, some younger Netsilingmiut rejected the films because by the late 1960s when the films were first released, the Netsilingmiut were living in prefabricated houses, wearing mini-skirts and riding motorbikes, and many did not want to be associated with what they then considered to be the primitive conditions shown in the films. But today, following the great social and material changes that have taken place in the interim, many Netsilingmiut have come to regard the films as an invaluable record of their history. But if it is a record, it is not the 'objective and detached' record recommended by Margaret Mead, but one that was most profoundly and skilfully authored.

## ABORIGINAL ELEGY: THE *PEOPLE OF THE AUSTRALIAN WESTERN DESERT* PROJECT

In contrast to the Netsilingmiut project, which originated with a US government initiative, the Central Australian project was very much the personal initiative of Ian Dunlop, a British-born film-maker who had had some exposure to anthropology as a student at Sydney University. In 1957, while working on a film about a remote weather station in Central Australia for the Australian Commonwealth Film Unit (CFU), Dunlop came across a number of nomadic Aboriginal families who were living in the region. Overwhelmed by a 'a desire to portray that way of life', combined with a 'terrible sense of tragedy' that such Aboriginal groups were giving up their traditional nomadic life style in the desert and settling down in squalid conditions next to religious missions and cattle stations, he felt that he had to make a film to preserve a record of this way of life before it was too late.[11]

It was eight years before Dunlop was able to persuade the CFU to fund the project, but they finally agreed to do so in collaboration with the Australian Institute of Aboriginal Studies (AIAS). While the CFU would provide the logistical support, the AIAS would cover all the other costs. Dunlop then returned to Central Australia in 1965 accompanied by a profes-sional cameraman, Richard Howe Tucker, and Robert Tonkinson, a young anthropology postgraduate with some knowledge of local Aboriginal dialects. This team was assisted by a number of Aboriginal guides from a nearby mission station who also acted as interpreters. Although similar to the Netsilingmiut project in terms of its salvage objectives and its use of re-enactment, this project was of a very different order regarding both its duration and the volume of material it produced. Over the course of three weeks, Dunlop and Tucker shot around five hours of material with two Aboriginal families, one from the Mandjintjadara linguistic group, the other from the Ngadjadjadjara group. Two years later, they returned to another area of the desert in Central Australia where a patrol officer from the Woomera Rocket Range had located three related Mandjintjadara families still living a nomadic life. Over the course of a further three weeks, Dunlop and Tucker shot another seven hours of material with this third group.

The footage from both expeditions was then edited, at a remarkably low cutting ratio of only slightly more than 2:1, to produce the 19-part series, *People of the Australian Western Desert*.[12] This was released in 1969 and has a total duration of around five hours. Most of the films in the series concern the making of artefacts, the gathering of food such as nuts and witchetty grubs, and the hunting of various species of lizard, bandicoot, emu and kangaroo. There are also a number of films on therapeutic activities, such as preparing medicines, curing headaches and chasing out evil spirits that cause illness. In three of the films the subjects show places or objects that are considered secret-sacred by Aboriginal people and these are not now available for viewing without special permission from Aboriginal custodians. Unfortunately, however, there are no films concerning collective religious or ceremonial activities. This is simply because, in their traditional form, such events required the coming together of large numbers of people and by the time the films came to be made, the Aboriginal population still living in the Western Desert was too small for the celebration of these events to be viable.[13]

In discussing this work, Dunlop himself distinguishes between 'record' films and 'interpretive' films. The former, which constitute the great majority of the films in the series, mostly follow a particular technical process, event or situation in a more or less chronologically faithful manner. The 'interpretive' films, on the other hand, are structured by 'as if' chronologies, that is, they present material filmed over a period of several days or weeks, as if it were occurring within a more restricted time frame.[14]

There are only two major 'interpretive' films in this body of work, the first, *Desert People*, was released independently of the general series in 1966, the year after the first period of filming had taken place. *Desert People* has a running time of 49 minutes and is framed by a classical narrative trope, begining in the morning with the Mandjintjadara family setting out on the day's subsistence tasks and ending with the Ngadjadjadjara family settling down by their fires at night. In the main body of the film, material shot in reality over two or three weeks is presented as if it were taking place over the course of three or four days. The second 'interpretive' film, *At Patantja Claypan*, is 53 minutes long and is based on material shot during the second expedition in 1967. Released in 1969 as part of the main 19-part series, this presents material shot over two weeks as if it were two consecutive days in the life of the Mandjintjadara group who are the subjects of this second period of filming (figure 3.3).

**3.3** *At Patantja Claypan* (1967). Left, a Mandjintjadara girl takes refuge under a shade bush from intense midday sun; right, Djungurai, a senior Mandjintjadara man, skirts the pan as he sets out to hunt emu early one morning.

Although this second 'interpretive' film is much less well known than *Desert People*, in many ways it is the richer of the two ethnographically, both in terms of the primary content of the material itself and in terms of the range of references in the voice-over commentary. It deals with a more complex social situation in that three different family groups are involved, while the subsistence activities, which include a dramatic emu hunt, are more varied and elaborate as well. Whereas both the action and the voice-over narration of *Desert People* remain very closely tied to subsistence or technical activities, in *At Patantja Claypan*, there are allusions to such diverse matters as bodily self-decoration, affinal avoidance and Dreamtime legends, as well as to the imminent abandonment of the desert way of life by Aboriginal people generally. It also begins and ends with some vigorous passages of Aboriginal song on the soundtrack, recounting the deeds of the first Dreamtime beings, the Two Watersnake Men. As such, it anticipates Dunlop's later work in Arnhem Land, on the northeast coast of Australia, which I shall discuss in Chapter 6.[15]

In the two 'interpretive' films, the authorial role of the film-maker is very evident, certainly to any viewer with a knowledge of practical film-making. But as Dunlop candidly describes in the accompanying texts, the 'record' films involved extensive authorial intervention as well. In reality, of the two families portrayed in the 1965 films, only the Mandjintjadara family, consisting of a senior man, Djugamarra, his three wives and their seven children, was still living the nomadic way of life shown in the films. But the film-makers had only been with them for three or four days when, quite unexpectedly, they disappeared into the desert and were not seen by the film crew again. (Robert Tonkinson, the anthropologist advising Dunlop, believed that the crew's Aboriginal guides wanted to return to their families in the mission, so they had encouraged Djugamara's family to leave.) The remaining two weeks of filming in 1965 was therefore spent with the Ngadjadjadjara family, consisting of a senior man, Minmarra Djuburula, his two wives and three junior members. However, this family group had been living on a mission station for nine months by the time that filming commenced, so in order for them to participate in the shoot they had to be taken back to the desert in the film-makers' Land Rovers. Similarly, although the nine members of the Mandjintjadara group filmed two years later were indeed all living in the desert at the time of filming, some of them had also previously lived on the mission station. Moreover, all members of group returned to the mission station after the filming was completed.

Although this history of contact is duly acknowledged in intertitles and occasionally even in voice-over commentary, it is entirely absent from the films' visual images. As Dunlop comments ironically in one of the accompanying texts, prior to filming he had to 'dress the set and undress the actors'. That is, before filming began, the subjects' camps were cleared of blankets, tins, paper and any other rubbish that they might have acquired through contact with the outside world. The subjects were also asked to take off the clothes that they had acquired in the mission. Many of the processes that one sees in the films were then enacted specifically at Dunlop's request.

Dunlop and his crew would sometimes go to considerable lengths to make these enactments possible. Thus for a film showing the spinning of string from human hair, the actual hair was from Dunlop's son; for the final film showing the butchering and cooking of a kangaroo (the only film shot in colour), the unfortunate animal had been shot with a rifle equipped with a telescopic sight by one of Dunlop's Aboriginal assistants, Paul Porter Djarurru. More generally, Djarurru played a highly active role in explaining to the subjects what Dunlop wanted them to do, so much so that in Dunlop's own words, at some points, he 'almost became the film's director'.[16] Djarurru would also sometimes assist the subjects with traditional tasks, but as he was dressed in a 'modern' Australian manner, he would be careful to withdraw before the actual filming began. Dunlop describes an amusing instance in which Djarurru helped a young boy to make fire by rubbing a stick in dried kangaroo dung, but once the stick had begun to smoulder, he then stepped back and, off camera, lit a cigarette with a match.

The nature and status of these films as records of the Aboriginal peoples of the Western Desert was also influenced by a decision that Dunlop took even before the filming began. Being very conscious that this might be the last possible opportunity to film traditional Aboriginal nomadic life, Dunlop wanted to produce a film record of the highest possible technical quality. As 35 mm colour film was out of the question on grounds of cost, he chose to shoot on 35 mm black and white stock instead. When asked, many years later, why he chose not to use 16 mm colour film, which would have been cheaper still, Dunlop said that back in 1965, he was not confident that

16 mm colour stock would stand up to the extreme temperatures of the Central Australian desert. He was also doubtful that it could cope with the contrast in light between the very dark skins of the subjects and the shimmering, reflective landscape.[17]

In terms of its aesthetic impact on the films, however, it could be argued that the most significant consequence of this decision was not in relation to the colour of the image. Rather it was that by opting for 35 mm, Dunlop also ruled out the possibility of using the portable synchronous sound-recording systems that had been developed, relatively recently, for use in conjunction with 16 mm cameras. If he had chosen to record synchronous sound with a 35 mm camera, it would have been necessary to bring along a large amount of sound-recording equipment and at least one sound engineer. As Dunlop was keen to keep the size of his crew down to a minimum in order to reduce its impact on his Aboriginal subjects, he chose instead to do without sound completely.

Dunlop was also disinclined to enhance the soundtrack at the post-production phase by means of wild sound or sound library effects. This was a very common practice in documentary film-making at that time and central to the production of the Netsilingmiut films. Similarly, Jean Rouch had no reservations about post-synchronising the films that he made in Africa in the era prior to the development of on-location synchronous sound. But Dunlop considered post-synchronisation artificial and certainly did not want to 'pollute' the visual images with sounds taken from an effects library. As a result, the soundtrack of these films consists almost exclusively of his voice-over commentary, which is, moreover, very sparse and limited to contextualising factual information. The only exception is some passages of non-synchronous singing recorded on location during the second expedition in 1967. For general atmospheric effect, these are laid over the opening or closing sequences of a number of the second expedition films.[18]

The technical constraints under which Dunlop was working did not prevent his films from receiving highly positive reviews when they were released, both in specialised anthropological journals and in the art cinema press, particularly in France. For many cinema critics, the lack of sound and the sparse factual commentary, far from being seen as imperfections, were interpreted as an inspired aesthetic choice that complemented perfectly the similarly stark and uncompromising desert scenery.[19]

Many critics also commented on the quality of Richard Tucker's camerawork, which is indeed truly remarkable and which, as Dunlop readily acknowledges, played a large part in the success of the films. Although this camerawork is rather formal, it is also very discreet: the subjects often move into the visual field of the camera in a manner that seems to have been very carefully prepared, but if so, they show not the slightest trace of self-consciousness. Throughout the material, Tucker plays very subtly with effects of light and shadow, frequently framing his subjects in interesting ways, using found aspects of the environment, such as trees or grasses. Technical processes are followed in a very clear and informative manner, with a judicious mix of close-ups and reverse shots, while the quality of the night time scenes of bodies, hands and faces in the flickering firelight is magnificent. Despite the fact that there are some extremely tight close-ups on the faces of the subjects, which must have been taken from a position that was physically very close to them, they appear at all times to be entirely at ease with the cameraman's presence.

In effect then, although it might have been Dunlop's general ambition to produce an entirely objective record of the traditional Aboriginal nomadic life before it disappeared, the account that he produced – with Tucker's assistance – was not only very carefully constructed but also has a pronounced authorial signature in a visual sense. In its poignant romanticism, it also carries a strong, if implicit, value judgement. This is particularly well exemplified by a shot from *At Patantja Claypan*, a still from which is reproduced in figure 3.3. This shows Djungurai, a senior Mandjintjadara man skirting the edge of the claypan, on his way to hunt emu in the early morning light. The shot has been taken from a studiedly low angle in such a way that Djungurai first walks into the foreground of the frame and then, as he moves into the middle distance, he is reflected in the water. This is no neutral objective registration, but rather a very carefully constructed image intended to evoke the essential nobility of the way of life that Djungurai represents. No one who sees this shot could doubt for a moment that the threatened disappearance of this way of life is anything other than the 'tragedy' that Dunlop considered it to be when he first came across nomadic Aboriginal groups some ten years earlier.

The record that Ian Dunlop produced of traditional Aboriginal life in the Western Desert is thus no more 'objective and detached', in the manner called for by Margaret Mead, than the record of Netsilingmiut life offered by Asen Balikci's films. In reality, both bodies of work were profoundly authored but in such a way as to render that authorship invisible. That is, they were both based on a series of performances by the subjects that were in large part set up, and which were directed and edited by the film-makers to exclude any reference to the impact of the outside world, including the film-makers' own presence. Although both film-makers were scrupulous in acknowledging in preliminary titles or accompanying literature that their films were based on re-enactment, they nevertheless invite the viewer to witness the human behaviour shown on the screen as if it were spontaneous and unmediated.

However, notwithstanding these similarities in motivation and praxis, not only do the Netsilingmiut and Western Desert films look very different in a stylistic sense, but these differences suggest a difference in the ontological status of the subject matter. Though the aesthetic qualities of the Western Desert films have been widely praised and with just cause, arguably thereby vindicating Dunlop's choice of 35 mm black and white stock, the effect of the monochrome image and the absence of any ambient sound, let alone of subjects' speech, is to make these films appear to refer to the past, not only in terms of style – as the high point of a film-making tradition running back to Spencer and Gillen, as Howard Morphy has put it[20] – but also in terms of content. Looking at them now, despite the engaging tone of Dunlop's commentary voice and his concern to humanise the subjects by giving them personal names, the films read as an elegy to a nomadic way of life that was already irretrievably lost, even at the time of filming.

By contrast, on account of the brilliant colour and skilfully constructed soundtrack of the Netsilingmiut films, one can be lulled into believing that Netsilingmiut life continues in this way even today. Ironically, at the time the Western Desert films were made, the Aboriginal subjects were still living the way of life represented, or had only recently abandoned it, whereas the Netsilingmiut films present a form of life that had undergone radical change some forty years prior to the film-making and now lies almost a century into the past.

There was a period, particularly in the 1970s and 1980s, when more participatory and reflexive ways of doing ethnographic film-making became an almost universal orthodoxy (as I shall discuss in Chapters 5–7) and re-enactment projects such as these came in for a considerable degree of criticism. The invisible authoring that they entailed was rejected not merely as false and artificial in a scientific or stylistic sense, but even as unethical in that it objectified the subjects and denied them a voice. In evoking a world that no longer existed, it was claimed, the film-makers were 'othering' the subjects by suggesting that they were living in a different time to their own. Even Balikci and Dunlop abandoned this way of doing ethnographic films and in their later work adopted more reflexive and participatory strategies.

However, in more recent years, as it has become clear that participation and reflexivity provide no guarantees of either truth or ethical probity, and as the inevitably constructed nature of all ethnographic films has become more widely recognised, these films of re-enactment have begun to receive a more favourable reception. This is true not only of audiences of anthropologists and film-makers, but also of the descendants of those appearing in the films, who have come to appreciate these works as highly valuable, irreplaceable accounts of their collective history.[21]

What is certain is that both projects were executed to the highest technical, aesthetic and ethical standards, and though some commentators might contest the accuracy of the reconstructions, rather than criticising the fact that they were made, present-day viewers are more likely to express regret that those reconstructions did not cover a wider range of topics, particularly collective religious and ceremonial activities. In that they took advantage of a particular historical moment to recreate life as it was experienced in the extreme environments of the Arctic tundra and the Australian desert before extensive contact with the outside world, with subjects for whom the memory of that mode of living was still fresh, both projects deserve to be acknowledged as works of great importance in the canon of ethnographic film.

## Notes

1 Balikci (1989), 4. This section draws from this source in combination with Balikci (1988; 1995) and a filmed interview with Balikci conducted by Mark Turin in January 2003 which is available at www.sms.cam.ac.uk/media/1111527.

2 See www.nfb.ca/subjects/indigenous-peoples-in-canada-inuit/netsilik/.

3 In the filmed interview with Mark Turin (2003), Balikci explains that he worked with Doug Wilkinson for only two months, while shooting the first film in the series, *Fishing at the Stone Weir*. During this time, Balikci confesses that they 'almost killed one another' because, imbued with Margaret Mead's ideas, he tried to teach Wilkinson his job. Most of the remaining films were shot by Kenneth Poste, but the film's executive producer did not consider him sufficiently skilled to shoot the ceremonial scenes that were due to be part of the final film, *At the Winter Sea Ice Camp*. Among those who were approached to work on this last film were Michel Brault, the NFB cameraman who worked on *Chronicle of a Summer* with Jean Rouch, and the Direct Cinema pioneer, Ricky Leacock. After they both declined the invitation, Robert Young was recruited, though Poste remained as his assistant. Balikci greatly appreciated the work that Poste had done previously, but Young was in a different league: 'Within minutes, I understood that I was in the presence of a great artist – he was not shooting with a camera, he was painting!'

4 Asen Balikci (personal communication, March 2014). The team of sound editors included Michel Chalufour who would later play a leading role in the sound editing of Robert Gardner's films (see Chapter 9).

5 A limited number of the films are now available in subtitled versions, but these were a later addition and not part of the original conception of the films.

6 See Lutkehaus (2004). In addition to the sources already cited, these paragraphs draw on *Through These Eyes* (2004), an excellent NFB documentary directed by Charles Laird. See www.nfb.ca/film/through_these_eyes/.

7 The EDC first approached Edmund Carpenter to take on the role of anthropological supervisor. He was an established Arctic specialist and also a pioneer in the use of audiovisual media in anthropology. But he declined the invitation as the EDC would not guarantee him full editorial control (Prins and Bishop 2001–2, 119).

8 Ian Dunlop reports that a modified version of the MACOS programme was developed for use in Australian schools and for which his films about Australian Aborigines of Central Australia (discussed later in this chapter) were used instead of the Netsilik films (personal communication, March 2019).

9 The project in Afghanistan continued, but with different sponsors and objectives. The result was *Sons of Haji Omar*, directed by Balikci in collaboration with Timothy Asch and Patsy Asch, and released in 1978.

10 See Oswalt (2008).

11 See Morphy (2007), 325. I have also drawn on various accounts by Dunlop himself of his work in Central Australia. His notes on the Australian National Film and Sound Archive (NFSA) website, the body that now distributes his films, have been especially useful (Dunlop 2003). More recently, he has advised Philippa Deveson on a comprehensive review of his work (Deveson with Dunlop 2012). I have also drawn on Ian Bryson's history of film-making at the Australian Institute for Aboriginal Studies

(AIAS) (2002, 28–32). I regret that for reasons of space it has not been possible to include here an account of the films of Roger Sandall, who was appointed as the first full-time film-maker at the AIAS in 1965. Sandall made a number of highly valuable films of Aboriginal ceremonial life in the following years, but many of which are now restricted because they contain secret-sacred material. See Sandall (1975); Loizos (1993), 31, 34–5; Bryson (2002), 32–54 (2007), 300–1 and especially Mortimer (2019).

12 As Dunlop explains (2003, 2), the term 'Western Desert' in this context denotes a cultural and linguistic region rather than a topographical one. This region covers an area of about 1.3 million square kilometres in Central Australia, embracing adjacent parts of the states of Western Australia, the Northern Territory and South Australia. The Aboriginal people of this region share certain cultural and linguistic characteristics, though local dialectical variations are very important in defining group boundaries.

13 However, Ian Dunlop reports (personal communication, March 2019) that a rich ceremonial life is still maintained by Western Desert Aboriginals now living a more sedentary life on mission stations and other settlements.

14 See the discussion of 'as if' chronologies in Chapter 2, pp. 104–6.

15 See pp. 179–84.

16 Personal communication, March 2019.

17 At the time of his first expedition, Dunlop had not met Jean Rouch, nor seen his films and was not aware that he had been successfully using 16 mm colour film in similarly harsh desert conditions on the edge of the Sahel in West Africa since the early 1950s.

18 There is also some limited Aboriginal chanting over opening titles and final credits of *Desert People,* but I have not been able to establish where this comes from. Ian Dunlop himself does not remember the exact origin of this music: while he is certain that it is Western Desert singing, he thinks that it was probably recorded at entirely different time and place, and with a group of people other than those shown in the film (personal communication, March 2019).

19 The reaction to the lack of sound was not universally positive. While noting that the films were a 'testament to human dignity and endurance', Roger Sandall, who was also experienced as a film-maker with Aboriginal people, commented in a review that the lack of voice or ambient sounds gives one the impression, contrary to some of the pictorial evidence that 'not only the desert but its inhabitants are bleak, emotionless, and austere' (Sandall 1972), 193.

20 Morphy (2007), 323.

21 As recently as 2009, Sue Davenport, an anthropologist now working in the region where the Western Desert films were made, told Dunlop that before taking young boys out to the bush to teach them about the old ways, Aboriginal elders sit down and watch his films in order to remind themselves about how they used to live (see Deveson with Dunlop 2012), 73.

# 4

# Records, not movies: the early films of John Marshall and Timothy Asch

NOT all post-war documentation projects involved such wholesale re-enactment as the Netsilik and Australian Western Desert films considered in Chapter 3. Others were carried out among peoples who were still largely living in an autonomous way, with only intermittent contact with the 'outside world'. Such was the case with the projects of John Marshall among the Ju/'hoansi of the Kalahari desert in southern Africa, and Timothy Asch among the rainforest-dwelling Yanomami of the northern reaches of Amazonia in South America.

Yet even these projects contained some degree of re-enactment, undermining the goal implicit in all documentation projects to provide the 'objective and detached' account called for by Margaret Mead. In their different ways, both Marshall and Asch also struggled with another issue, namely, the tension between the ambition to provide a scientifically valuable record and the temptation to tell stories, structured by a narrative, about the often remarkable lives of the people with whom they were living.

## THE HUNTERS AND THE GREAT KALAHARI DEBATE

Of all the English-language ethnographic film documentation projects initiated in the period after the Second World War, by far the most prolonged was the one developed by John Marshall, which he began when he was barely 18 years old. Marshall would later become one of the most acclaimed ethnographic film-makers of the latter part of the twentieth century, but at the beginning, he appears to have taken up the moving image camera more on account of the influence of his father, Laurence, than through his own spontaneous choice.

Laurence Marshall was a wealthy and recently retired electronics engineer who, in 1950, asked his son to accompany him on what was to be the first of eight Marshall family expeditions to southern Africa. Continuing until 1961, these were organised in association, primarily, with the Peabody Museum of Archaeology and Ethnology at Harvard University. Their principal aim was to study the linguistically diverse hunting and gathering groups of the Kalahari desert. Known collectively by the derogatory term 'Bushmen' in colonial discourses, these groups are now referred to in the regional ethnographic literature by a variety of other terms, depending on the degree of inclusion involved. Thus 'San' or 'Khoisan' is more or less directly equivalent to the colonial term in its range of reference and embraces all groups, whether they are living in South Africa, Namibia or Botswana. The term '!Kung' or '!Xun', meanwhile, refers to the most northerly group of San whose territory extends through Namibia as far north as the area around the border with Angola. The term 'Ju/'hoansi', also rendered as 'Zhu', refers to the !Kung subgroup with whom the Marshalls mostly worked and whose traditional territory is known as Nyae Nyae. This lies in the northeastern corner of what is now Namibia but which was still known as South West Africa when the Marshalls first arrived, and was a colony controlled by the South African government. Only in 1990 would it become the independent republic of Namibia. Some easterly groups of Ju/'hoansi live just on the other side of the international frontier in what is now Botswana and formerly the British protectorate of Bechuanaland.

Initially, Laurence Marshall tried to recruit an anthropologist to accompany his family expeditions. But at that time, some fifteen years before the 'Man the Hunter' symposium in Chicago and Marshall Sahlins's theory of the Original Affluent Society placed hunting and gathering societies at the centre of anthropological attention, he could not find a single US anthropologist who was prepared to join his family expeditions, not even a graduate student, despite the fact that he offered to pay all their expenses. The few anthropologists who did have an established interest in hunting and gathering societies were wary of contributing to a project that they considered amateurish and redolent of the adventure-exploration projects of the interwar period.[1]

Marshall therefore turned instead to archaeologists, who were much more responsive, particularly J. O. Brew, then the director of the Peabody Museum. At that time, many archaeologists had a particular interest in hunting and gathering groups in Africa because they believed that these groups could provide ethnographic evidence that would help to illuminate the exciting early hominid discoveries then being made across the continent. Underlying this belief was the assumption – one that would come to be strongly challenged – that present-day hunting and gathering groups represented the last untouched vestige of the earliest forms of human society. As such, they offered the possibility, as one archaeologist would later put it, to look through 'a kind of narrow and opaque window to the Pleistocene'.[2]

Being unable to recruit any professional academic anthropologists, Laurence Marshall turned instead to his wife Lorna and daughter Elizabeth and asked them to act as the ethnographers of the expeditions. It was in order to provide supposedly objective data that could be set alongside their descriptive accounts and act as a control against any possible biases of his mother and sister that John was asked by Laurence to make films about those same subjects that they were writing about. To this end, John was given a large quantity of film stock and a simple spring-wound 16 mm camera, a Bell & Howell Filmo 70, with a maximum shot length of around 30 seconds. Laurence had met Margaret Mead socially and was familiar with the films that she and Gregory Bateson had made about Bali and New Guinea. Inspired by her example, he instructed John not to direct or try to be artistic, but simply to film 'what you see people doing naturally'. What he wanted, he said, was 'a record, not a movie'.[3]

Many years later, John would claim that this 'instruction' had had a lasting influence on the way in which he shot, edited and thought about documentary films. But in the years immediately following the giving of this instruction, he made what was, in effect, a truly spectacular 'movie' – one that would become a landmark work in the history of ethnographic film. This was *The Hunters*, mostly shot in 1952–53, though not edited and released until 1957. In colour and 72 minutes in duration, this film follows a group of Ju/'hoansi hunters as they track a giraffe through the thorny scrub of the Kalahari desert until, after five days of hunger and thirst, and many frustrations along the way, they eventually corner their prey and dispatch her with their spears. They then return home to their camp and, to the delight of their families, distribute the meat and tell tales of their heroic adventure.[4]

This film proved that Marshall was a film-maker of great ability, though still very young and without any formal training: he had taught himself to shoot simply by following the instructions in a booklet produced by Eastman Kodak, the manufacturers of the film stock that he was using. He also edited the film himself, albeit with some assistance from another young film-maker associated with Harvard, Robert Gardner, though the degree of this collaboration remains a matter of controversy. In later years, Marshall himself would criticise his cinematography for not being sufficiently responsive to the internal geography of the events and relationships within the film. Moreover, this was in the time before the development of synchronous sound, so the soundtrack of the film is relatively thin. Marshall would also cast doubt on the highly romantic presentation of the four central characters, inspired, he confessed, by the way in which characters were introduced by Herman Melville in *Moby-Dick* (figure 4.1, left). The inspiration for the literary language of the narration, which he described as 'leafy', was the Nobel laureate novelist, William Faulkner. Third parties have criticised this narration for imputing interior thoughts and motivations not only to the hunters, but even to the giraffe. But all these features, which are mostly merely stylistic, do not prevent one from admiring, even today, the quality

4.1 *The Hunters* (1957). Left, the hunters are introduced with romantic profiles inspired by *Moby-Dick*: '/Qui was a simple, kindly man and an optimist, who tended to remember only the better times of his life'; right, the giraffe has come to a halt, but still she will not fall. Filmed in August 1952, this image was intercut with shots of the hunters hurling their spears filmed three years later.

of the cinematography, the coherence of the narrative and, most importantly, the sense of engagement with the principal subjects.[5]

When it was released, *The Hunters* was initially received with great enthusiasm both within academic circles and beyond. Over the next twenty years, it would become one of the most frequently screened ethnographic films in the English-speaking world. But gradually, various details about the making of the film began to emerge, and it became apparent just how constructed it had been. It transpired that the hunt shown in the film as a single event had actually been made up of a number of different hunts, involving several different giraffes and even several unidentified hunters in addition to the four main protagonists. Instead of tramping through the scorching desert for five days, in reality the hunters had travelled around in Marshall's Jeep with access to food and water, and they had all gone back to the expedition camp most nights.

Although the principal giraffe had indeed been finished off by the hunters with their spears, as shown in the film, she had already been wounded by a poisoned arrow shot from Marshall's moving Jeep some time beforehand, and it was this wounding that had slowed her down and allowed the hunters to catch her. Perhaps most remarkable of all, in the sequence showing the final kill, the wide shots of the hunters standing around the giraffe, filmed in August 1952, had been intercut with close-up reverse shots of them hurling their spears filmed three years later, specifically for the purposes of the edit (figure 4.1, right).[6]

It took a long time, but by the 1990s, Marshall himself was ready to acknowledge that *The Hunters* was 'energetically artistic', though he pointed out in mitigation that it was, after all, only the work of 'an American kid'. However, while admitting to many other authorial interventions, he continued to reject very firmly the allegation that the entire hunt had been set up just for the camera. This was also confirmed by ≠Oma, leader of the Ju/'hoansi hunters, in an interview conducted in 1984, which features in one of Marshall's later films. Although giraffe belonged to a protected species and the Ju/'hoansi could be imprisoned for hunting them – making them understandably reluctant to talk about giraffe kills with outsiders, including the Marshall family – John claimed that the Ju/'hoansi continued to hunt giraffe throughout the 1950s and that one of the leading hunters in the Ju/'hoansi group with whom he worked had killed about twenty. If so, then even though the particular episode of giraffe-hunting in *The Hunters* may have been extensively enabled by Marshall, it can be still be considered an essentially authentic account, certainly more so than the re-enacted walrus-hunting scene in *Nanook of the North*, with which it is sometimes compared.[7]

Within a theoretical paradigm in which an ethnographic film was supposed to provide an objective record of the world, the various forms of authorial enablement involved in the making of *The Hunters* were widely regarded as a matter of shame and scandal. Yet any experienced documentary film-maker would have been able to deduce these interventions simply by looking at the filmic text itself. They would certainly not have been either surprised or offended by them since such strategies are commonplace among documentarists, even to this day. They were particularly so at the time that *The Hunters* was shot since technical constraints made it very difficult to film social behaviour, even in much less demanding environments than the Kalahari desert, without some sort of intervention on the part of the film-maker.

The problem with the film was not so much the inexperience of the film-maker, but rather the naivety of some of its critics about the representational nature of the medium. Did they really imagine that Marshall would have followed the hunters on foot under such adverse conditions, filming all the while, or that he would have refused the hunters food and drink, if he had had such supplies himself? In terms of showing what Ju/'hoansi hunting was like in a general way, did it really matter that he sometimes used understudies for both the giraffe and the hunters? Or that because he was there alone with a single camera and could not therefore simultaneously film the wide shot of the kill and a close-up of the hunters hurling their spears that he mocked up the latter some time later? Clearly the wounding of the giraffe by an arrow shot from the Jeep hastened the end of the hunt on that particular occasion, but in other circumstances, it is entirely conceivable that the Ju/'hoansi could have scored a more direct hit earlier in the chase which would have brought the hunt to an end more quickly.

When pushed to identify in what ways *The Hunters* misrepresented the generality of Ju/'hoansi hunting expeditions, Marshall acknowledged that without the reassurance of the supplies in his Jeep, the Ju/'hoansi might not have been prepared to pursue the giraffe for as long as five days since they could have died of thirst out in the middle of the Kalahari. He also regretted that, for want of synchronous sound at that time, he was unable to record the anxious discussion about the distribution of the meat after the kill, since making sure that the distribution of game was equitable was always a delicate matter among the Ju/'hoansi. Further, he thought that he should have included more scenes showing hunters returning empty-handed in order to underscore the point that for all the prestige associated with hunting, the Ju/'hoansi were dependent for much of their day-to-day sustenance on the gathering of 'bush foods', largely carried out by women. But from a descriptive ethnography point of view, these elements of misrepresentation, though not insignificant, surely constitute misrepresentations of degree and emphasis, rather than anything that approaches an outright falsehood.[8]

By the time that Marshall was prepared to admit to these authorial interventions, criticisms of a very different kind were also being made of *The Hunters*, which were not directly related to technical film-making matters as such. For the film had also become centrally embroiled in a wide-ranging argument, with political as well as academic ramifications, often referred to as the 'Great Kalahari Debate'. Even if not exactly ongoing, this is a debate that remains largely unresolved. On one side are the so-called 'traditionalists', who believe that the Ju/'hoansi, and other similarly traditional groups of San, represent one of the last remaining vestiges of Palaeolithic human social organisation, based on hunting and gathering, and a particular 'foraging mentality'. On the other side are the 'revisionists', who argue rather that the Ju/'hoansi and other such groups are the devolved remnants of populations who, over the course of several centuries, have been pushed into the most marginal desert environments by groups of cattle-herding pastoralists, such as the Ju/'hoansi's neighbours, the Herero.

The 'revisionists' insist that far from representing the original condition of humanity, with a way of life based exclusively on hunting and gathering, groups such as the Ju/'hoansi, however remote their isolation within the Kalahari, have long been dependent upon patron–client exchange relationships with local pastoralist groups. These are often based on the exchange of food for San labour, usually on highly disadvantageous terms for the San. Since the relatively recent arrival of European settlers in the Kalahari in the late nineteenth century, this relationship of dependency and extreme exploitation has been reproduced between the San and these new settlers as well. In the view of the 'revisionists', there is more than a purely academic issue at stake here since they maintain that by focusing exclusively on the hunting and gathering activities of the San in order to make the connection with Palaeolithic humanity, and thereby excluding external relationships with other groups from their accounts, the 'traditionalists' are creating a dangerously romantic 'myth' that distracts attention from the exploitation, land-encroachment and racism from which the San suffer as an everyday reality.[9]

The Marshall family as a whole was strongly committed to the 'traditionalist' position, as were most of the archaeologists who provided the principal intellectual justification for their expeditions.[10] Because it presents the Ju/'hoansi as if they were living in some ahistorical idyll without any outside contact, *The Hunters* has been subject to some strong criticism by the 'revisionists'. In response, John has made the counterclaim that when his family first met the Ju/'hoansi in the early 1950s, they were living in almost total isolation and as such, he suggested that his film provided a faithful portrayal of their way of life at that particular time. But a detailed examination of John's film rushes, including those specifically related to *The Hunters*, provides evidence of a considerable degree of contact with the outside world, even then, all of which was omitted from the final version of the film. In a similar vein, the biography that John's sister Elizabeth wrote about ≠Oma, referred to above as the leader of the Ju/'hoansi hunters featured in the film, indicates that he had not only had personal experience of working as a cattle herder for Herero pastoralists, but he had even been born at a pastoralists' settlement since his parents were, as she puts it, 'serfs' of the Herero.[11]

The 'Great Kalahari Debate' is a minefield of controversy into which a non-specialist fears to tread. Clearly, the broader situation in the central Kalahari in the 1950s as highlighted by this debate should frame our understanding of Ju/'hoansi life as a whole at the time that *The Hunters* was made. However, I would argue that this broader historical context does not in itself necessarily invalidate the film in terms of its specific central remit, namely, an account of Ju/'hoansi hunting practices. For the practices shown in the film could indeed have been their practices at that time, even if at other moments of their lives, they worked on Herero cattle farms. There may be San specialists who would question the film's accuracy or validity even in these more restricted terms, but for those of us who have no specialist knowledge, we have to accept, as with any ethnographic account, filmic or textual, that in the absence of evidence to the contrary, the film-maker is not intentionally misleading us. What one should not do is dismiss the film simply because evidence has emerged that the literal film record has been actively manipulated, since this is necessarily the case in any form of ethnographic film-making, for all the reasons discussed at length in the General Introduction to this book.

With these qualifications then, I would claim that notwithstanding the many criticisms of the film that have emerged in recent years, *The Hunters* can still be considered an ethnographic film masterpiece, communicating, with an unprecedented intimacy and sympathy for the principal characters, a powerful understanding of the range of skills that Ju/'hoansi hunters must have possessed at that time and of the difficulties that they must have had to overcome in hunting large game animals with their minimal technology, in such a challenging natural environment.

## A RECORD THAT IS ALSO A MOVIE: THE EVENT-SEQUENCE METHOD

Whatever its merits or deficiencies, in making *The Hunters*, John had clearly strayed a long way from his father's Mead-inspired 'instruction'. Despite its acclamation around the world, the film did not satisfy the critic who mattered most to John. For Laurence was 'uneasy' about the film: he felt that John should have 'made more of an effort with the record'. John concluded that Laurence was right, and in the years immediately afterwards, as if in expiation, he went on to make a large number of shorter films that conformed more closely to his father's idea of what an enthnographic film should be. He would not make another feature-length documentary among the Ju/'hoansi for twenty years, and this would be of a very different kind, charting the destructive effects of contact with the outside world. Those who admire Marshall's skills as a narrative documentary film-maker will surely regret that his plan to follow up *The Hunters* with a feature-length biographical film about the life of a young girl betrothed to be married at the age of 8 was abandoned at an advanced rough-cut stage.[12]

In turning his hand to shorter films, Marshall sought to work out a method that would allow him to make films that were more in the nature of a record, as his father required, but at the same also retained certain movie-like characteristics. The essence of this method was to make films about discrete events and then to use the implicit narrative intrinsic to those events as the narrative of the film. Marshall developed this method in conjunction with Timothy Asch who was then working as his editorial assistant but who would later become a leading ethnographic film-maker in his own right. Over the years, Marshall and Asch used various terms to describe this method, sometimes referring to it as 'event' filming, or more commonly as 'sequence' filming and sometimes 'sequential' filming. In a much-cited paper that they wrote with Peter Spier, they used the rather misleading term 'reportage'.[13] Here I refer to it as the 'event-sequence' method.

The principles underlying this method were very simple. It was presumed that on the basis of prior ethnographic knowledge, it should be possible for the film-maker to identify certain events with a clear beginning and a clear end that could be used to define the parameters of films made about those events. Given that an event with an end and a beginning must also have a middle, a film that followed such an event would have, as it were by default, a classical 'beginning–middle–end' narrative structure without any manipulations of the original chronological sequence being necessary. The event-sequence method did not entail making an entirely literal copy of an event since it did allow cuts in the action to eliminate redundancies or moments of irrelevance. Moreover, in practice, it is evident from closely observing the actual films made by Marshall and Asch that they sometimes involved minor chronological inversions. But apart from this, the event-sequence method can be seen as an attempt to have the best of both worlds, that is, to develop a way of making films that featured a structured narrative of the kind that one would expect to find in a 'movie', while at the same time offering a minimally authored 'record' of the event in question.

Admittedly, neither Marshall nor Asch explained the rationale of the event-sequence methodology in quite these terms, though Marshall did make the tantalisingly brief comment that he thought shooting merely for a record 'artificial and insensitive'. Being a 'would-be artist filming people', he explained, 'my sequences were a kind of compromise'.[14] For his part, Asch thought that the principal purpose of making ethnographic films was for teaching, and his primary ambition at this stage of his career was to produce an extended series of short, free-standing event-based films that taken together would provide a comprehensive film record of a given society that could then be used in an undergraduate curriculum. He believed that through cumulative exposure to these films, appropriately supported by textual materials and presentations by a teacher, students would be able to gain a direct insight into the society in question. He wanted them to feel as if they themselves had been in the field, rather than relying on an understanding filtered through the subjective sensibility of a film-maker, as had been the case, excessively in his view, with *The Hunters*.

Various different influences appear to have come together to shape Asch's ideas about ethnographic film-making. Early in his career, he had taken Margaret Mead's field methods course at Columbia (the same course taken some years earlier by Asen Balikci), and he had also worked for a period as her research assistant. If the notion of using film to build up an archive of objective records is traceable to her influence, then the idea of using those records to offer students the opportunity to do ersatz fieldwork can be attributed to the period that Asch later spent working on the MACOS project. But the specific strategy of making particular discrete events the focus of this filmic record-making was traced by Asch himself to another source, namely, to what he referred to as the 'case-study method' developed by the Manchester anthropologist Max Gluckman, in which particular social events are analysed as microcosms of wider social and cultural realities.[15]

Today /Qui will die with
an erection

**4.2** *An Argument About A Marriage.* /Tikay, left, threatens /Qui for having had a child by his daughter, but /Qui does not allow himself to be provoked. (Compare with figure 4.1).

A well-known early example of the use of the event-sequence method is to be found in *An Argument about a Marriage*, which is a mere 18 minutes long. Although this film was not released until 1969, it was shot only about a year after the release of *The Hunters* and involves many of the same central protagonists. But this film could hardly be more different, in terms of content as well as technique. Whereas in the earlier film, the Ju/'hoansi had been presented in a highly romantic light, as noble beings, epitomising the best in human values, here they are shown to be just as subject to base and violent passions as any other human group. The argument referred to in the title concerns a relationship that developed between Baou, a young married woman and /Qui, a man who was not her husband, when both were being held, more or less as slave labourers, on a White farmer's estate. This relationship had resulted in the birth of a child. When they return to their own camp after being released through the intervention of the Marshall family, the child provides incontrovertible evidence of the extra-marital relationship and this precipitates a crisis. The argument culminates with the Baou's father /Tikay boiling over with rage and threatening to kill her lover: 'Today, /Qui will die with an erection ...', he declares angrily (figure 4.2). Although ≠Oma, the headman, manages to defuse the tension temporarily, the argument remains unresolved at the end of the film.

The many differences between *The Hunters* and *An Argument* were sympomatic of an important change that had taken place in Marshall's general attitude towards authorial intervention. 'In 1955,' he would write later, 'I was still cleaning tin cans out of shot to make the Ju/'hoansi … look real. By 1958, I was filming the people being themselves.'[16] In *An Argument*, far from suggesting that this Ju/'hoansi group lived in isolation, as *The Hunters* had done, the relationship to the wider world is central to the action of the film. Indeed, many of the protagonists are wearing Western-style clothes that they had acquired while working on the White farm (compare the portraits of /Qui in figures 4.1 and 4.2). Even the presence of the Marshalls is directly acknowledged when /Tikay curses them roundly. Such demonstrations of what would later become known as 'reflexivity' were highly unusual in ethnographic film at the time that *An Argument* was released in 1969, let alone when it was shot in 1958.

*An Argument* also features a number of more technical and editorial innovations. Although the sound was not synchronously recorded, it has been so well edited that it almost appears to be so. There are also subtitles: these too were still a relative rarity in ethnographic film.[17] However, the most important authorial innovation in *An Argument* concerns the narrative structure. An introductory sequence showing the arrival by truck of the Ju/'hoansi liberated from the White farm, is followed by a series of still images anticipating the most significant moments of the argument that one is about to see. These images are covered by voice-over narration in which the complex social background to the dispute is outlined. It is explained that the reason that Baou's father /Tikay is so enraged is because she already has a husband, Tsamgao, who has performed several years of bride-service for /Tikay and there is now a risk that /Tikay will lose him. Baou protests that after she had been enslaved, she thought she would never see her husband again and was threatened with starvation until /Qui provided for her. But /Tikay is not placated and continues to threaten /Qui.

With contextualisation thus provided, the argument is then allowed to play itself out with any further voice-over narration. It has to be said, though, that in the case of this particular film, the technique does not work that well. The network of social relationships described in the narration over the stills is so complicated that it is very difficult to follow in the first place and even more difficult to remember later when watching the argument unfold. But it is a technique that both Marshall and Asch would elaborate and use more effectively later in their careers.

From 1958, for a period of twenty years, Marshall was unable to continue his film-making with the Ju/'hoansi as he could not get a visa to return to South West Africa. Initially, he appears to have done very little with his Ju/'hoansi material other than cut two very short films, *A Group of Women* (1961) and *A Joking Relationship* (1962), though both of these are minor masterpieces, each an excellently crafted account of a small event laden with ethnographic significance. It was only after the best part of a further decade that Marshall returned to his Ju/'hoansi material in a sustained way, and it was then that he cut not only *An Argument*, but also a series of around ten further event-sequence films. These are mostly between 5 and 15 minutes in duration, but one, probably the best known, is longer at 20 minutes. This is *N/um Chai: The Ceremonial Dance of the !Kung Bushmen*, released in 1969, the same year as *An Argument*.

More or less simultaneously, in the late 1960s and early 1970s, Marshall also employed the event-sequence method in making of a series of films, some twenty in all, again mostly very short, about a very different kind of event, namely, the cases handled by the Pittsburgh police when out on patrol. But when Marshall did eventually return to southern Africa in 1978, it would be to make a very different kind of film, as I shall describe in Chapter 6.[18]

## THE DEATH OF THE INVISIBLE AUTHOR: TIMOTHY ASCH AND THE YANOMAMɨ SERIES

While Marshall was applying the event-sequence method in Pittsburgh, Asch was in Venezuelan Amazonia, making a series of films about the Yanomamɨ in collaboration with the anthropologist Napoleon Chagnon. These films were shot over the course of two expeditions, one in 1968, the other in 1971. Asch conceived of these expeditions as an excellent opportunity to make what he called a 'film record' of the Yanomamɨ. The great majority of the films that he and Chagnon made were based on the event-sequence method, though in applying it to more complex events than in his previous work with John Marshall, he would eventually come up against its limitations.[19]

Since starting his fieldwork among the Yanomamɨ in 1964, Chagnon had been filming various activities on his own but had come to believe that a more thorough film-making effort was required. Acting on Asen Balikci's recommendation, he therefore invited Asch to work with him. On their first expedition, in 1968, they shot slightly more than five hours of 16 mm colour footage from which they later cut two films. One of these was *The Feast*, which, as the title suggests, is on a conventional ethnographic topic, namely, a large ceremonial event. The other film consisted of a heavily narrated description of the fieldwork of the multidisciplinary research team from the University of Michigan of which Chagnon was then a member. This was headed by James Neel, a medical geneticist whose grant from the US Atomic Energy Commission (AEC) was largely funding the expedition, including the film work. One of the principal aims of this research was to study the population genetics of the Yanomamɨ so that they could be used as a control group against which to measure the effects of nuclear radiation on the genetic profile of the Japanese survivors of the Hiroshima and Nagasaki bombs. The AEC is duly acknowledged in the opening credits of both films shot on this first expedition and is even identified as one of the holders of the copyright, along with Asch and Chagnon.

In the immediately following years, Chagnon returned on an annual basis and shot some additional material on his own. But in 1971, Asch again accompanied him and they collaborated on a second phase of shooting, assisted by sound recordist Craig Johnson (Chagnon himself had taken the sound on the first expedition). This time the project was funded by the National Science Foundation and was based at the euphoniously named village of Mishimishimabiweitheri, which had by then become the principal location of Chagnon's research. Here they shot a further thirty-five hours of material, from which a remarkable thirty-five further films, albeit many very short, would eventually be produced.[20]

Of the thirty-seven films that Asch and Chagnon produced in total over the two expeditions, only twenty-nine are currently in distribution – the others exist only as workprints that have not been finalised. Of those in distribution, there are five films of around 30 minutes or more in duration. In addition to the two films from the first expedition, there are two films from the second expedition that fall into this category: *A Man Called Bee*, which offers a portrait of Chagnon in the field, and *The Ax Fight*, a particularly significant work that I consider later in this chapter. The only other longer film in the Asch-Chagnon Yanomami canon is *Magical Death*, a solo work shot in 1970 by Chagnon, showing a group of shamans taking mind-altering drugs to enable them to enter the world of the spirits.[21]

Apart from two short films about the impact of Christian missions, one Catholic, the other Evangelical Protestant, all the other films, around twenty in number, are short event-based films. These are between 5 and 22 minutes in duration and deal with a variety of topics: in four films senior men relate myths; a number of films relate to subsistence practices, such as working in the gardens, collecting palm fruits or firewood, and include a particularly interesting film about the distribution of meat after a successful tapir hunt. There are also a number of films about mundane, everyday activities such as a father taking his children to the river for a wash, and a man weaving a hammock while engaging in light-hearted banter with his wife, and quite a number of films are about children engaged in various forms of play. In shooting these everyday activities showing the gentler and more light-hearted side of Yanomami life, Asch was actively seeking to counterbalance the image of 'the fierce people' that Chagnon had presented in his best-selling though increasingly contested textual accounts of this group.[22]

It has to be said, though, that while Asch certainly produced a large number of films about the Yanomami, the quality of the cinematography is not outstanding. Like John Marshall, Asch was an autodidact cinematographer, but particularly compared to his friend and contemporary, Asch was no more than a journeyman camera operator. Moreover, although he may have sought to present the Yanomami in a gentler light, he appears to have been rather afraid of them. He frequently begins his shots very far away from his subjects, and when he wants to get closer, he does so by zooming in with his lens rather than by physically moving in closer. In a more technical sense, his positioning, framing and angle of view are often less than ideal and his camera movements uncertain. The contrast with the

4.3 In *Magical Death* (1973), shamans call upon *hekura* spirits to help them with their healing performances: 'The *hekura*, being beautiful, are likewise attracted to beauty'; right, in *The Feast* (1970), the headman calculates the distribution of food while being deloused by one of his wives. 'His hunters have done so poorly that he must make the meat go further than it should.'

assured intimacy and inspired framing and positioning in Marshall's event films is very noticeable.

Of all the films in the Asch–Chagnon canon, arguably the most accomplished, from a purely cinematographic point of view, is *Magical Death*, but this was shot and directed by Chagnon working alone (figure 4.3, left). He clearly had the great advantage of being much more at ease with the subjects than Asch, due to his long-term engagement with them. Also, his many excellent still photographs indicate that whatever one might think of his view of the Yanomami as 'the fierce people', Chagnon has an undeniably strong visual sense. But with this exception, all the other Asch–Chagnon films appear to have been shot primarily by Asch and if the Yanomami films deserve particular attention in the history of ethnographic film, it is more on account of what they represent in terms of methodology than on account of their strictly cinematographic qualities.[23]

Considered in methodological terms, there are two films that are particularly significant and I shall therefore consider them in some detail. One of these is the principal ethnographic film from the first expedition, *The Feast*, which, in effect, is a bold attempt to apply the event-sequence method to a complex event involving a large number of people. The purpose underlying the eponymous feast was the celebration of an alliance between two Yanomami villages that until recently had been at war. The anthropological agenda behind the making of this film, agreed upon by Asch and Chagnon even before they left the USA, was to demonstrate the importance in Yanomami life of the principle of exchange, as formulated theoretically by the French anthropologist Marcel Mauss in his influential essay *The Gift*, originally published in 1925.

In the case of the Yanomami feast represented in the film, this principle is exemplified by the sealing of an alliance between two villages through a series of exchanges in different registers – first of food, then of ritual performances, and finally by the exchange of trade goods. As with *An Argument about a Marriage*, the film begins with a lengthy series of stills in which the context of the event is explained. Given that it is a complex event, this explanation is very lengthy, but is still just about tolerable. Then, again as in the earlier film, the event is allowed to play itself out without any further narration.

*The Feast* has a great number of merits and is considered by many to be a classic of anthropological filmic pedagogy. However, it also suffers from certain limitations. In the first place, it is clear from the very honest memoir that Asch published some years later that he was barely able to keep abreast of what was going on. The social complexities of the shoot were further exacerbated by serious technical problems. As a result, there are certain very significant omissions. For example, the ethnographic literature on the Yanomami indicates that an important phase of alliance feasts takes place at night. But Asch did not have the technical facilities to shoot at night and, moreover, confesses in his memoir to being too tired to film anyway.[24]

These limitations of *The Feast* are the result of contingencies that any documentary film-maker has to confront. But there are other shortcomings that can be attributed more directly to the application of the event-sequence method. Most notably, by summarising the event in advance, the preliminary sequence serves to dispel any sense of the tension that is an important feature of such events, as is indicated near the beginning of the narration and elaborated in greater detail in Chagnon's written works. This tension arises from a fear among the visitors that their hosts will turn upon them and murder them, as is said to have happened notoriously a number of times in the past.[25] But by revealing the outcome of the feast even before the film begins, the preliminary sequence undermines the possibility of creating a strong dramatic sense of this tension.

But conceived specifically as an objective 'film record' of an aspect of Yanomami life, undoubtedly the greatest shortcoming of *The Feast* is the omission of any reference, within the film itself, to the unusual circumstances under which it was made. Asch's memoir reports that the village site where filming took place, located close to a navigable river, had actually been abandoned some time beforehand and its inhabitants, the Patanowatheri, had taken refuge from their many enemies at a new site, several days' walk away in the mountains. However, for the purposes of the film, they were persuaded by Chagnon to come back down to the more accessible riverside location and to hold the feast of alliance with their newfound friends from Mahekodotheri village there.

Down by the river, not only would the filming be easier, but the members of both villages would be more readily available for the collection of blood samples by the geneticists in the multidisciplinary team from the University of Michigan whose AEC grant was, after all, paying for the whole venture. In a controversial account of this programme of research, the journalist Patrick Tierney makes the plausible claim that the Patanowatheri would only have been prepared to move back to their old village site because they knew that Chagnon and his associates, with their firearms and their influence with local Venezuelan authorities, would provide them with protection from their enemies. They also knew that the researchers would provide them with considerable quantities of trade goods. Tierney further alleges that Chagnon actually brokered the alliance that is sealed in the film, though this has been vigorously denied by Chagnon.[26]

But even if it was entirely the Patanowatheri's own idea to hold a feast for the Mahekodotheri, the members of the expedition then played a major part in enabling it. At one point in the preliminary sequence of stills, the narrator (who is Chagnon) comments that in distributing meat to his visitors, the headman is embarrassed because 'his hunters have done so poorly that he must make the meat go further than it should' (figure 4.3, right). But according to Tierney, the hunters who had done so poorly included Charles Brewer Carías, one of Chagnon's Venezuelan associates, who was equipped with a powerful hunting rifle. Chagnon's own ability to contribute to the meat supply was inhibited by the fact that he was too busy hauling in plantains from the gardens in his motorised canoe so that the host women could make beer for the visitors.

The fact of this enablement obviously qualifies in a serious way the status of *The Feast* as an objective record of the event in question. However, the value of this film as an ethnographic account of a particular aspect of Yanomami life is no more necessarily undermined as a consequence of this evidence of enablement than the value of *The Hunters* as an ethnographic account of Ju/'hoansi hunting practices is necessarily undermined by the emergence of details about how certain scenes in that film were enabled by John Marshall. Whatever its shortcomings as an objective record, *The Feast* nevertheless succeeds in providing a rich and ethnographically informed sense, not only of the general importance of the principle of exchange in Yanomami life, but of how this is played out in the course of a feast – as was the film-makers' objective. What the evidence of this enablement does do, however, is completely shatter the epistemologically naive hope that the event-sequence method might somehow make it possible to eliminate authorship from the making of ethnographic films.

As the 1970s progressed, Timothy Asch appears to have become increasingly troubled by the limitations of the event-sequence method. These would become particularly apparent in the *The Ax Fight*, a film released in 1975, four years after *The Feast*. The subject matter is a violent dispute between the permanent residents of Mishimishimabïweitheri and a group of visitors from another village who have overstayed their welcome. The action of the film is relatively straightforward. It begins with a shot of a woman crying in her hammock for reasons that are not immediately clear, though they are clearly related to angry verbal exchanges being shouted across the plaza by a number of other women. A skirmish then breaks out in the central plaza of the village between a small group of men armed with long clubs. This appears to be petering out when suddenly two other men run across the plaza, one carrying an axe. A general scuffle ensues, culminating in one man striking another with the blunt side of the axe-head and felling him to ground. There is then a general stand-off, but after a few moments some senior men, unarmed, intervene to prevent any further fighting, and the victim gets up and staggers groggily away while the crowd gradually disperses.

In common with previous event-sequence films, *The Ax Fight* features a sequence of shots summarising the event accompanied by an explanatory narration, which is then followed by an edited version of the event. This explanatory sequence, narrated by Chagnon, is rather more elaborate than those in previous event-sequence films and is divided into two parts, the first involving stills and slow-motion shots with a voice-over explaining who is who and the significance of their actions, while the second consists of diagrams indicating the kinship relationships between the participants in the event. Chagnon uses this second part of the explanatory sequence to expound his then-current theory – which he was soon to abandon – that tensions in Yanomami villages could be explained in terms of structural relations between lineages, that is kinship groupings based on genealogical descent. An edited version of the event then follows, with subtitles, but without commentary.[27]

But what makes *The Ax Fight* unique as an event-sequence film is that these two sequences are *preceded* by the original rushes in their totality, thereby allowing one to see what has been excluded from the other two versions of the event presented in the film. These out-takes include a shot of Chagnon observing the event from nearby, with what appears to be a certain nonchalance (figure 4.4, left). The sound recordist, Craig Johnson, also appears briefly. We learn from the soundtrack of the rushes that Chagnon's first understanding of the immediate reasons for the dispute was that it had arisen because one of the visitors had forced a Mishimishimabïweitheri woman to have incestuous sexual relations with him in a nearby garden. Later, when Chagnon discovered that in fact the visitor had 'only' beaten the woman when she refused to give him some plantains, he incorporated this into his explanatory narration.

We also discover by inspecting the rushes that in addition to a general abbreviation of the event, the smoothness of the edited version has been

It's the ugly mothers that
made them that way!

4.4 *The Ax Fight* (1975). In the rushes, left, Napoleon Chagnon appears
briefly, apparently unconcerned by the threat of violence; right, a
sequence of a woman shouting insults across the village plaza, originally
near the end of the rushes, opens the edited version of the film.

achieved by some modest manipulations of the chronology. This mainly
consists of moving two shots from close to the end of the rushes and placing
them near the beginning where they serve to cover certain deficiencies in
the original camerawork. As these two shots feature women shouting insults
across the village plaza, this also has the effect of giving greater emphasis
to the role of women in the dispute – though whether this was ethnographically appropriate has been the subject of some subsequent discussion (figure
4.4, right).[28]

There is a tendency in the literature of visual anthropology to hail *The
Ax Fight* as a landmark work. Although this is perhaps to overstate the case,
what is certainly interesting about this film is that by the simple device of
allowing one to compare the rushes with the two edited versions, it reveals
the processes whereby authorship has come into play in its construction.
Significantly, however, these authorial processes are not revealed in their
entirety within the film itself. For it is only from the text prepared to
accompany the film – which most viewers of the film never see – that we
discover that although the rushes presented in the film run for 11 minutes
(the duration of a single 400 ft 16 mm magazine), the event actually took
place over a period of about thirty minutes.[29] The first question one might
therefore ask is what authorial decisions resulted in most of the event *not*
being filmed?

There were also other ways in which the material presented in *The Ax
Fight* was compromised as an objective record of the event. What was also
revealed, some time later, was that since the all-important blow that the
brought the axe fight to an end was hardly audible on the field recording,
Asch enhanced it, using a studio recording of the sound of a watermelon
being hit with a hammer. But this is a mere technical detail. Much more
significant, at least in terms of its influence on the action of the film, but
not mentioned at all in the film itself, is the fact that one reason why the

unwanted guests were hanging on, overstaying their welcome and thereby leading to tensions with their hosts, was that they were hoping to get a share of the trade goods that Chagnon and Asch had brought with them. In this context, one of the most revealing moments captured in the rushes, but eliminated in the edited version, may be Chagnon's seemingly trivial comment that he had just been approached for the tenth time that day by a man asking for a bar of soap.

However, all these various examples of authorial influence on the event itself or on the way in which it was presented would only be disturbing to those still holding on to the illusion that an ethnographic film has the potential to deliver some entirely objective account of the world. Some years later, Asch would comment that as he was cutting this film, he had the feeling that the whole field of ethnographic film, if not the whole of anthropology, was beginning to fall apart before his eyes. We should perhaps allow him a little poetic licence here, since there were other ethnographic film-makers at that time who had already long abandoned any hope that film could rescue fieldworkers from the subjectivity of their fieldnotes, as one astute commentator put it.[30]

But what *The Ax Fight* certainly did do was signal the end of the road for a whole tradition of documentation film-making that reached right back – through the films of Mead and Bateson and others in the interwar years – to the pioneer works of Haddon and Spencer at the turn of the century.

## Notes

1 Gordon, Brown and Bell (2013), 2–3.
2 Yellen (1984), 54, cited in Wilmsen (1999), 233. See also Wilmsen, ibid., 220–2, 232–41 for general background on the Marshall family's relationship to academia.
3 Marshall (1993), 19.
4 Along with most of John Marshall's other films, *The Hunters* is distributed by Documentary Educational Resources (DER), the non-profit distribution agency that in collaboration with Timothy Asch, he himself founded in 1968. Since Marshall's death in 2005, a large number of his works have been restored and can now be seen in their magnificent original colours, with their soundtracks enhanced through digital sound technology.
5 Marshall (1993), 36. See Weinberger (1994), 8, for a light-hearted critique of the narrational style.
6 Marshall (1993), 36–7.
7 See Marshall (1993), 37–9. Also Nancie Gonzalez (1993), 186–90 who suggests, based on the diaries of Lorna Marshall and J. O. Brew, that due to the great hunger among the Ju/'hoansi around the Marshall camp, the hunting of meat, rather than filming, was the primary purpose of John's sorties in the family Jeep with the hunters. The interview with ≠Oma is close to the beginning of *The Far Country*, the first in a five-part series of films, *A Kalahari Family*, released in 2002 (see Chapter 6, pp. 188–93).
8 For details about the possible misrepresentations, see Marshall's 1996 letter reproduced in Tomaselli and Homiak (1999), 173–4. David MacDougall (1995b), 234 has proposed

that *The Hunters* should be read as a Ju/'hoansi hunting story, in which case, the elements of fictionalisation involved become less significant. As he points out, there are certain stylistic parallels with *The Lion Hunters*, a film that Jean Rouch made between 1957 and 1965, which is specifically framed as if it were a hunting story (see Henley 2009, 201–8).

9 The literature on the 'Great Kalahari Debate' is vast; even that which concerns the relevance of *The Hunters* to this debate is considerable. For a very brief summary of the debate, see Schrire (2003), 160–1. For its relevance to *The Hunters*, see the various contributions to the special edition of the journal *Visual Anthropology*, 12 (2–3), dedicated to visual representations of the Kalahari. In writing these paragraphs, I have drawn especially on Tomaselli and Homiak (1999), Homiak and Tomaselli (1999) and Wilmsen (1999).

10 Wilmsen (1999) makes the claim that Laurence Marshall was particularly attracted to the idea that the San represented the original condition of humanity, not just because it legitimated his family expeditions in paleoarcheological terms, but also because it assuaged a personal moral malaise. This, Wilmsen claims, derived from fact that as a liberal-minded individual with a hatred of war due to his experiences in the trenches during the First World War, Marshall felt uneasy at having been a leading figure in the electronics company that designed the trigger for the atomic bombs dropped on Japan at the end of the Second World War. Wilmsen suggests that in the 1950s, at the height of the Cold War, the idea that in its original form, humanity was not inherently violent and was, moreover, capable of finding peaceful means of resolving its conflicts, as supposedly demonstrated by the Marshall family's films and books about the Ju/'hoansi, provided Laurence with some sort of reassurance that it was not the inevitable fate of humanity to annihilate itself through a nuclear exchange. Wilmsen's argument is clearly speculative and not seemingly supported by any direct statement from Laurence himself. However, John's account of his father's motivations, even if much less elaborate, is not that dissimilar (see Marshall 1993), 23–4.

11 See Homiak and Tomaselli (1999), particularly p. 314, for a description of the content of John's film rushes. See also Elizabeth Marshall's biography of ≠Oma (Marshall Thomas 1959), 178 and Wilmsen (2003), 117.

12 See Marshall (1993), 39; Harper (2004), 44–5.

13 Asch, Marshall and Spier (1973).

14 Marshall (1993), 26.

15 On Asch's ideas about pedagogical uses of ethnographic film, see Acciaioli (2004) and Lutkehaus (2004). On the influence of the Manchester School on Asch, see Harper (2004), 50. For the classic description of the method of social situation analysis by Gluckman himself, see Gluckman (1958) while for an overview of the Manchester School, see Werbner (1984).

16 Marshall (1993), 32.

17 The very first example of the use of subtitles in English-language ethnographic film-making appears to have been in Marshall's own film, *A Joking Relationship*. This was shot around the same time as *An Argument* but was released much earlier, in 1962.

18 On the Pittsburgh films, see Marshall (1993), 110–22. The films that he made after his return to Africa are discussed on pp. 188–93.

19 Unless otherwise stated, the account offered here is primarily based on Asch (1979) and Asch (1988). As with many matters to do with this indigenous group, there is considerable dispute about the transliteration of its name into English. Here I follow the lead of a recent authoritative dictionary (Mattei Muller 2007). A further complication is that the Yanomami are only one of four distinct subgroups, each with its own autonym (the others are Sanima, Ninam and Yanomam).

20 These estimates are based on the figures given in Asch (1988), 7–9 regarding the first expedition, and in Chagnon (1997), 270–2 regarding the second. However, the

website of the DER, who distribute the films, reports that in total Asch and Chagnon shot around fifty hours, though this may include footage that Chagnon shot on other occasions. The edited films have recently been digitally restored to a very high quality. See https://store.der.org/yanomam-series-p970.aspx.

21 Asch gives a generally positive account of the collaboration between himself and Chagnon: for an altogether more negative view, see Chagnon's testy account on the CD-Rom of *The Ax Fight*, published some time after Asch's sadly premature death in 1994 (Biella, Chagnon and Seaman 1997).

22 Chagnon has peremptorily dismissed the criticisms of his work as being either the product of political correctness, or of an unwillingness on the part of humanities-oriented anthropologists to accept his quantitative scientific methods. Extra-academic critics, meanwhile, have claimed that the representation of the Yanomami as 'the fierce people' has served as an alibi for those who wish to take their lands or convert them to Christianity. The various sides of the argument are presented in *Secrets of the Tribe*, a feature documentary directed by José Padilha (2010).

23 Curiously, the photographs that Asch took early in his adult life, before he took up film-making, suggest that he too possessed a strong visual sense (see Harper 1994). Unfortunately, it seems that he was not able to translate this talent into the rather different demands of cinematography.

24 See Asch (1979). Important night-time events include formal chanting exchanges and ritualised chest-pounding duels. See Chagnon (1997), 170–83 *passim*.

25 See Chagnon (1997), 3.

26 Tierney (2000), 83–106; Ruby (1995a), 24. Tierney's most serious allegation against the Neel-Chagnon-Asch expedition is that it was responsible for a measles epidemic, which in the months following the filming of *The Feast* led to the deaths of many Yanomami. However, an investigation by the American Anthropological Association (AAA) found that there was no foundation to this allegation (Gregor and Gross 2004), 691. Independently of this exoneration regarding the measles epidemic, there continues to be criticism of certain biomedical aspects of the research conducted during the expedition, in particular the collection of Yanomami blood samples that were taken away and stored in various US research institutions without the subjects' informed consent. Some of these samples have been returned, though others remain in the USA. See www.socioambiental.org/pt-br/noticias-socioambientais/, particularly the reports of 13 April and 25 September 2015.

27 Even though I am familiar with the general principles of Yanomami kinship, I find Chagnon's exposition of the kinship relationships underlying the dispute difficult to follow, even after many viewings of the film. It was precisely around the time of editing of this film that Chagnon was on the cusp of abandoning such structural-functional explanations of Yanomami population dynamics in favour of explanations of a more sociobiological character.

28 Nichols (2004), 231–2 suggests that this narrative reordering 'flirts' with the ethnocentric suggestion that women are the cause of all trouble, but see also Connor and Asch (2004), 176–7, who argue that the film neglects the role of women in provoking the dispute.

29 See Bugos, Carter and Asch (1975).

30 See Ruby (1995a), 28. The 'astute commentator' was Colin Young (1995), 100.

# 5

# Reflexivity and participation: the films of David and Judith MacDougall in Africa and Australia

B Y the time that *The Ax Fight* was released in 1975, a major change was already underway in ethnographic film-making in the English-speaking world. As a result of the general impact of postmodernism on academic anthropology generally, and the associated sense that the conduct of social research involved relationships of power just as much as the disinterested pursuit of knowledge, many ethnographic film-makers came to believe that a mode of film authorship based on detached observation was at best insensitive and at worst, politically suspect. At the same time, communities that had previously been the subjects of ethnographic film began to demand greater control over the way in which they were being represented.

In response to these changing attitudes, over the course of the 1970s and 1980s, ethnographic film-makers developed a range of different practical strategies to share the authorship of their films with their subjects to some degree. These new 'ways of doing' ethnographic film involved setting aside the positivist scientific inheritance represented paradigmatically in the English-speaking world by Margaret Mead, with its emphasis on detachment and objectivity, and engaging the subjects more directly in the process of shooting and even, in some cases, in the process of editing a film. However, in this respect, even the most progressive film-makers in the English-speaking world lagged well behind developments elsewhere, notably in France, where, as described in Part II, Jean Rouch had begun to place such collaborative strategies at the heart of his work as early as the 1950s.

This more collaborative approach was greatly facilitated by a number of technological innovations that had gradually been taking place over the course of the previous two decades. A number of ethnographic film-makers, including once again Jean Rouch, but also John Marshall and others, had made an important contribution to these innovations. Undoubtedly the most significant was the development of portable synchronous sound technology. Although ethnographic film-makers had been making films with synchronous sound in remote locations as far back as the 1930s, it was not until the 1950s that the technology became fully portable, and not until as late as the latter part of the 1960s that 'lip-synch' (i.e. synchronous speech), the most difficult form of synchronicity to achieve, became possible over the full 11-minute duration of a standard 16 mm magazine.

The impact of this new technology on the form and style of documentary film-making was profound. Most obviously, the possibility of representing people talking synchronously greatly increased the mimetic reality-effect of documentary film images, particularly when coupled with the use of colour film stock which also became increasingly common as the 1960s progressed and its cost declined. But much more important than the reality-effect as such was the impact of 'lip-synch' on the narrative devices that documentary film-makers could use to structure their films. For now it became possible to build the narrative of a film around the everyday language-based interactions of the subjects, as in a fictional feature film. It also became possible for the subjects to engage in conversations with the film-makers while the camera was turning.

These effects made possible, in turn, a much more subtle characterisation of the subjects. Previously, ethnographic film subjects had often been presented as representatives of some stereotypical social or cultural type, such as the 'happy-go-lucky Eskimo' referred to in the initial rolling titles of *Nanook of the North*. Although the best ethnographic film-makers had sought to individualise their subjects through intimate cinematography or by giving them personal names in voice-over narration, they remained relatively one-dimensional characters, existing within a limited emotional and intellectual register. But with the development of synchronous speech, it became possible to represent them in all their normal contradictory human ambiguity, no longer as archetypical representatives of a culture, but rather as idiosyncratic individuals who were able to reflect upon and even question their own cultural traditions.

Today, in an era when documentaries can be shot on mobile telephones, portable synchronous sound is so completely taken for granted that it is difficult to appreciate just how transformative this innovation was for documentary film-making. But in my view, the step-change that portable synchronous sound enabled in ethnographic film-making was considerably greater than the much-vaunted advent of digital technology a generation later. Certainly it is difficult to imagine the more collaborative approaches of the 1970s and 1980s taking place without it.

## Reflexivity and participation

In the course of the 1970s, two new terms became commonplace in the English-language literature on ethnographic film-making. Implicit in both was an acknowledgement that the aspiration to use film for detached observation, as envisaged by Margaret Mead, was misguided, and that an ethnographic film should instead be understood as the product of the film-maker's relationship with the subjects of the film.

One of these new terms was 'reflexivity'. In practice, this term was primarily used in two quite different ways, one referring to the subjectivity of the film-maker, the other to their relationship to the subjects. In relation to the subjectivity of the film-maker, 'reflexivity' was used to refer to a process whereby the film-maker would make clear, within the body of the film, how their personal subjectivity had come into play in the making of the film, be it on account of their personal biography, their intellectual or political interests, the technical strategies that they had adopted and so on. Almost paradoxically, the goal of achieving this kind of reflexivity represented a desire to hold on to the status of film as a means of objective documentation. For although it gave due recognition to the fact that a film-maker's subjectivity would inevitably enter into the making of a film, it was based on the supposition that if an audience were made aware of this, it could somehow make allowance for this subjectivity and be left with some residual kernel of objective truth.

However, there are serious grounds for doubting that reflexivity of this kind could ever be fully realised. Even if a film-maker were capable of supplying all the necessary information about all the subjective elements that went into the making of their film – which would be difficult since they would probably be unconscious of many of the most significant – it seems unlikely that the audience would then be able to calculate the significance of this information as they watched the film and even more unlikely, given the constraints of duration that apply to any film, that there would even be sufficient time to deliver it.[1]

The other sense in which the term 'reflexivity' often came to be used around this time was much easier to achieve. This use of the term referred to the direct acknowledgement, again within the body of a film, that the work had arisen from a relationship with the subjects. Whereas in the era of supposedly objective scientific film-making, any acknowledgement of the presence of the camera was regarded as a blemish, it now came to be considered as a badge of authencity if a subject addressed the camera, held open a door, or offered the film-maker a drink. Equally appreciated was the appearance of members of a film-making crew in shot, or a cameraperson's reflection in a mirror. But this kind of 'reflexivity' represented more of a statement about the ethical or political probity of a film rather than any sort of guarantee of its truth status.

In addition to the widespread recognition given to these two very obvious forms of reflexivity, there was also an acknowledgement, though less prominent, of a third form that did not pertain to the relationship between the subjects and the film-maker as such, at least not exclusively or directly, but rather to the authorial signature of the film-maker as it is worked out in the very construction of the work. This 'deep reflexivity', as it has been termed by David MacDougall, is made manifest not only in the nature of the film-maker's relationship to the subjects, including particularly its emotional tone, but also in such practical matters as camera positioning and choice of visual imagery, and in the formal attributes of the narrative developed in the edit suite. However, in contrast to the first sense of reflexivity defined above, which MacDougall describes as merely 'external', even the film-maker may not be fully aware of these reflexive qualities owing to their often unconscious, intuitive nature: in many cases, it will be up to the audience to identify this deep reflexivity inscribed in their work.[2]

The other term that came into common use around this time in English-language visual anthropology literature was 'participatory' film-making. This referred to a mode of film-making in which the subjects collaborated directly with the film-maker in the making of a film. At the simplest level, this could consist merely of the subjects actively cooperating with the film-maker in the practical realisation of the film. In fact, this was nothing new since most ethnographic film-making has been participatory in this sense since the very earliest days of the genre: even Haddon's filming had depended on the collaboration of his subjects, while for Flaherty, the active collaboration of Alakariallak and his fellow Inuit had been the cornerstone of his authorial praxis. Similarly, none of the great documentation projects of the 1950s and 1960s described in the last two chapters could have been carried out without the collaboration of the subjects, though the Netsilingmiut undoubtedly 'participated' rather more actively than the Yanomami. What was new about participation in the 1970s was that it became acceptable, indeed almost a requirement, for the fact of this participation to be revealed in a 'reflexive' manner in the filmic text itself.

Some ethnographic film-makers in this period began to take the idea of participation much further than token 'reflexive' references in their films. Not only did they engage in discussions with the subjects beforehand as to what the topic of the film should be, and how this should be developed during shooting, but in some cases they also arranged for the principal subjects to join them later in the edit suite and advise on the cutting of the film. For film-makers working in a participatory manner, it also became axiomatic that once a film had been completed, it was essential to return to the community where the film had been shot and screen it there. There was both a moral and a pragmatic dimension to this return of the work: not only would the community see the outcome of the work but they could also comment on its validity. In the ideal case, this could then lead on to the development of future collaborative projects.

## MODES OF REFLEXIVITY: THE MACDOUGALLS IN EAST AFRICA

Among the English-speaking ethnographic film-makers who were most active in developing collaborative modes of authorship over the course of 1970s and 1980s were David and Judith MacDougall. Although David had taken some introductory anthropology courses when he was a student of literature at Harvard, otherwise neither he nor Judith had any formal qualifications as anthropologists. On the other hand, they had received an important part of their training as film-makers through the Ethnographic Film Program at the University of California Los Angeles (UCLA) in the late 1960s. It was through this programme that the MacDougalls had encountered the work of Jean Rouch and were inspired by his example to develop a mode of ethnographic film-making praxis that was more participatory than that which underpinned the work of John Marshall and Timothy Asch. This synthesis by the MacDougalls (along with various other film-makers connected with the Ethnographic Film Program) of the long-standing interest of English-speaking ethnographic film-makers in observation with the more participatory Rouchian praxis would give rise to 'Observational Cinema' a distinctive approach to ethnographic film-making that I consider at length in Chapter 10.

As they were among the first students to go through the Ethnographic Film Program, it fell to the MacDougalls to produce a number of the most important early examples of films based on the principles of Observational Cinema. In 1968, the same year as Timothy Asch and Napoleon Chagnon made their first joint expedition to film with the Yanomami, the MacDougalls began working on what would eventually become two distinct series of films about pastoralist groups in East Africa. Initially, however, they went to Africa to work on a film about male initiation among a sedentary agriculturalist group, the Gisu of southeastern Uganda. This was directed by one of the teachers on the UCLA programme, Richard Hawkins, and was based on the doctoral fieldwork of the British anthropologist, Suzette Heald. The MacDougalls were still only students at the time, but they were equipped with what was then the *dernier cri* in 16 mm technology, the Éclair NPR camera, specifically designed for hand-held shooting, and a Nagra III reel-to-reel tape-recorder. Although they were supposed to be acting merely as the crew, in practice, given the constraints of the production, David ended up making most of the decisions as to how the various component scenes of the film should be shot.[3]

Once the Gisu shoot was over, the MacDougalls were permitted by UCLA to keep hold of this equipment and also some of the left-over film stock, and they headed off to the Karamoja District in northeastern corner of Uganda where, over several months, they shot the material for what would eventually become three films about the Jie pastoralists. Two of these films are relatively short, *Nawi*, which is in colour and 20 minutes long, follows a family moving from its homestead to the camps where their cattle are grazing, while *Under the Men's Tree*, 15 minutes long, is in black and white, and as suggested by the title, presents the conversation of a group of men beneath a shade tree, interspersed with short sequences in which they are shown preparing leather straps cut from cowhide.

These two shorter Jie films are not dissimilar to John Marshall's event films. As with the latter, they are shot in an intimate manner, covering relatively circumscribed situations and structured primarily by the internal development of the event itself rather than by a superimposed narrative. The subjects' speech is subtitled, as in Marshall's films too, but then still a relative novelty in ethnographic film. In terms of general form, *Under the Men's Tree* is particularly reminiscent of Marshall's films – for example, *A Group of Women*, in which San women chat as they lie in the shade of a baobab, dandling their children, or *Men Bathing*, in which San men chat as they wash in a pool. There is, however, a significant difference in content in the sense that whereas the San talk about personal matters entirely internal to their world, the Jie in *Under the Men's Tree* are mostly making observations about the habits of motor vehicle drivers, a theme that is strikingly at odds with their very traditional dress and appearance.

The MacDougalls' third Jie film, *To Live with Herds*, is not only much longer, at 70 minutes, but is an altogether more complex work dealing with the problems faced by the Jie as a result of government plans to sedentarise them. This film demonstrated, perhaps for the first time in English-language ethnographic film-making, how the combination of the new synchronous sound technology and a participatory and reflexive authorial strategy could be used to portray the people of another culture in an intimate, personal manner. As such, it would have a major impact on ethnographic film-making, not only in the English-language world but also beyond, and for this reason we should consider it at some length here.

As with the MacDougalls' shorter Jie films, *To Live with Herds* features a number of circumscribed events and situations, but these are linked together as a series of scenes within an overarching narrative structure subdivided into five thematically defined parts, reminiscent of the acts in a play. The first and fifth parts represent pastoralist life in its traditional form. The first part, entitled 'The Balance', is set in and around a Jie homestead, while in the last part, 'News from Home', one of the principal subjects, Logoth, leaves for the cattle camps where Jie herds are customarily taken when the grass immediately around the homestead is exhausted. These scenes of traditional life are in marked contrast with the subject matter of the three central parts, which concern the plans of the newly independent state of Uganda to sedentarise the Jie, ostensibly to

**5.1** *To Live with Herds* (1972). Left, Logoth and his wife Losike reluctantly say goodbye as he leaves for the cattle camps. Right, severely affected by drought, the Jie must sell their animals at knockdown prices in order to buy food.

provide them with schooling and medical services, but also to control and tax them.

We learn that for the Jie, sedentarisation means hunger and the devastation of their herds of cattle, schooling represents the loss of their children to another way of life, while hospitals are seen as places where children are more likely to die than be cured. The fourth part of the film is particularly powerful as first we see the Jie forced to sell their cattle to stave off hunger and then we see them jostling with their gourds to receive famine relief flour at a government station. When we finally return to the traditional way of life in the last part of the film, we realise that its title is ironic. The harsh truth is that there is no 'news from home', except the no longer newsworthy fact that people are hungry (figure 5.1). As Logoth washes in a pool, the soundtrack echoes with a traditional salutation of well-being which, given what we now know about the present situation of the Jie, is particularly poignant, 'May you live with herds, may you live with herds.'[4]

Although the device was applied in *To Live with Herds* in a skilled manner that was unusual in an ethnographic film, cyclical narrative structures of this kind were already a well-established staple of documentary film-making more generally. What was innovative about the film was rather the way in which everyday life was presented, particularly in part 1 in the Jie homestead. Here people talk casually about their way of life and the values that hold it together. They gossip and play with children. The pacing of the film is slow and measured, and, as in everyday life, there is repetition and hesitation, which then – as now – was often cut out by documentary film editors. The camera discreetly observes, but it is no 'fly-on-the-wall'. The subjects not only frequently acknowledge its presence, but actively engage the film-makers in conversation. In one of the most celebrated sequences of the film, Logoth offers the film-makers a 'guided tour' of his homestead, and points out on the horizon the various directions in which other pastoralist peoples live. Although there are a few brief commentary points voiced by David MacDougall, these are personalised rather than didactic: broader contexts are provided rather through intertitle cards. Mostly, however, the film proceeds through the informal subtitled dialogues of the subjects, primarily with one another, but also with the film-makers.

Following its release in 1972, the innovative contribution of *To Live with Herds* to ethnographic film-making praxis was acknowledged in the award of a major prize at the Venice Film Festival. Two years later, the MacDougalls returned to East Africa, and over eighteen months they made a series of three further films about pastoralists that would develop their distinctive mode of ethnographic film authorship. By this time, political unrest meant that it was no longer safe to work in Uganda, so they moved their base across the border to northwestern Kenya. Here they began to film with the Turkana, who are culturally and socially very similar to the Jie, and speak essentially the same language.[5]

The material that the MacDougalls shot in Kenya would, in due course, become the three-part series, *Turkana Conversations*. In terms of purely technical quality, these films demonstrate a mastery of the 16 mm technological 'package' based on a hand-held camera, portable synchronous sound and subtitled speech. The general standard of both shooting and audio recording in these films is remarkably high, certainly for the period, while the subtitling, a very important element, is well composed and the rhythm very fluent. In contrast to *To Live with Herds*, these films are in colour which, when viewed today, gives them a more contemporary feel.

A pronounced feature of the *Turkana Conversations* films is what David MacDougall would later characterise as the 'unprivileged camera style'. That is, any scene based on human interaction is shot from the perspective of a participant witness rather than from some external vantage point that would only be available to someone positioned outside the group. Wide shots predominate and the takes are long, with action being allowed to develop within the frame. Pans are few and zooms even rarer. Although well-established conventions to ensure continuity between shots are respected in the cutting of these films, they are generally very discreetly applied.

These various attributes of technique and style are brought together in some remarkable hand-held tracking shots in the films, none more so than during the 'guided tour' that Lorang, one of the leading characters, leads around his homestead, picking out the houses of his wives and the kraals of his animals as he goes. There are also numerous linguistic exchanges between the film-makers and the subjects, but these are presented not as one-way interrogational interviews, but more as conversations between film-maker and subject, albeit usually through an interpreter, and sometimes using intertitle cards to pose the questions. In addition, outside these

It was just misinformed
gossip . . .

**5.2** *The Wedding Camels* (1977). The formal blessing of the marriage, left, is only a brief interlude in the incessant haggling about bridewealth between the bride's father Lorang and the groom's family, right.

conversational situations, the subjects make frequent references to the presence of the film-makers.[6]

Perhaps the best known of the three films is *The Wedding Camels*, the first to be released, in 1976, but classified as the third in the series. This film explores a classical topic in the ethnography of East African pastoralist societies, namely, the wheeling and dealing that takes place in connection with the payment and the subsequent distribution of 'bridewealth'. This is the technical anthropological term for goods given at marriage by the groom to the family of the bride (and in this sense, the reverse of the European tradition of dowry payments from the bride's family to the groom). In East Africa, bridewealth consists primarily of cattle, including goats, camels and oxen as well as cows and bulls. Prior to a wedding, the negotiation of the terms of the bridewealth is typically a complex matter of much greater collective attention than whether or not the bride wishes to enter the marriage.

In the case of the marriage represented in *The Wedding Camels*, the negotiations are so fraught that at various points, it seems as if the marriage will not happen, and when it finally does, about two-thirds of the way through the 103-minute film, the blessing formalising the union consists of no more than a brief interlude in the incessant haggling over animals. This continues even after the bride has left her homestead to go and live permanently with her husband, as is the Turkana custom (figure 5.2).

As in many ethnographic films about ceremonial events, the structure of the event itself provides the narrative structure of the film. However, what distinguishes *The Wedding Camels* from most ethnographic films about ceremonies, including particularly the event-sequence films discussed in Chapter 4, is that the outcome of the event remains in doubt until the last moment and this serves to charge the narrative structure with a certain degree of dramaturgical tension. In fact, in this sense, *The Wedding Camels* could be regarded as an example, even if a rather diffuse one, of the so-called 'crisis structure' that was typical of the work of the so-called Direct Cinema film-makers who, around this same time, were also using the new portable sound-synchronous technology to shoot observational documentaries, though with journalistic rather than ethnographic objectives and mostly on North American topics.[7]

As the central event in *The Wedding Camels* is extraordinarily complex, with many overlapping threads as well as a large number of participants, in order to aid comprehension the film is subdivided into a number of act-like parts, as in *To Live with Herds*, though in this case, there are only four. It has to be said, though, that this overarching quadripartite division readily gets lost in the veritable flurry of intertitle cards that are used throughout the film to provide the contexts necessary to clarify what is going on and who is who. These cards may seem excessive to some viewers, but presumably the film-makers concluded that this was a price that they were prepared to pay in order to avoid a didactic voice-over commentary.

They were fortunate, however, that they did not need to use even more intertitle cards since the Turkana, both women and men, turn out to be the most eloquent auto-ethnographers, explaining succinctly in their conversations with the film-makers how their way of life as pastoralists makes the payment of bridewealth so vitally important ('Boys are born to herd animals … girls are born to marry. We Turkana are not farmers, so children are our gardens') as well as providing insightful analyses of the events leading up to the wedding as they unfold.

Doubt and uncertainty are also features of the other two films in the *Turkana Conversations* series, albeit in rather different ways. From a narrative perspective, one of these films, *A Wife Among Wives* represents a mirror image of *The Wedding Camels*. If in the latter film the MacDougalls' enquiries into the nature of marriage among the Turkana were located within the overarching framework of the events connected with one particular marriage, in this film their enquiries provide the framework and a particular marriage is located within it. In common with *The Wedding Camels*, this film too has a defuse 'crisis structure', and indeed doubly so, as the subjects' doubts about whether the marriage will take place are skilfully interwoven through the film with the MacDougalls' own doubts about whether they will ever get a marriage to film. Although classified as second in the *Turkana Conversations* series, *A Wife Among Wives* was the last to be edited, and it was not released until 1981. Of all the films that the MacDougalls made in East Africa, it is the most *overtly* reflexive in the sense of revealing the process of film-making within the film itself.[8]

The early part of the film features a series of stills of the MacDougalls with their subjects as well as lists and maps from their notebooks, while on the soundtrack David and Judith alternately read extracts from their field diaries either describing the direction of their enquiries or chronicling their quest to find a marriage. Today, these devices have become commonplace, and might even be considered too contrived, but at that time they were highly arresting when encountered in an ethnographic film. Initially, the MacDougalls' enquiries are directed towards discovering how polygyny is perceived by Turkana women.[9] It transpires that Turkana women are greatly in favour of this system of marriage because, as the MacDougalls' female interlocutors patiently explain, it is the best way within Turkana society of securing their future prosperity and for sharing out the labour that women have to do. They point out that a woman will often encourage her husband to take another wife, and will even contribute her own animals to pay the necessary bridewealth. They then mildly rebuke the film-makers for probing for examples of fighting or jealousy among co-wives, saying that these are European preoccupations, which Europeans can only afford to have because European women have so little work to do.

The film-makers also ask the women what *they* think should be in the film. While one woman says that she has no idea, as she is not a film-maker, others say that what they would most like to film has nothing to do with polygyny, but rather the film-makers' possessions. So the film then cuts to a scene in which one of the older women is shown using a Super-8 film camera to film the MacDougalls' house, their books and, eventually, David himself filming her while she films him.

The doubts concerning the marriage that is negotiated in the course of this film relate not only to the usual disagreements over bridewealth payments but also to the fact that the young girl who is supposedly to be married – to a much older man, as his fifth wife – is absent. Her relatives, both male and female, are anxious that she return, since once the marriage is concluded, they will receive a large number of animals as a bridewealth payment. She, however, is seemingly much more interested in consorting with the young men in the cattle camps. The situation therefore lends itself readily to another well-established narrative device, the 'waiting-for' trope, much used in documentary films generally as well as in ethnographic film, whereby dramatic tension is built around the much anticipated but uncertain arrival of a key protagonist who will transform the lives of the other subjects of the film.[10]

The narrative develops with a series of scenes of senior men haggling over the bridewealth and deploring the attitudes of the young. As the rainy season begins, women are shown working in the millet fields and gathering in the crop that will be needed to provide food for the wedding guests – should there ever be a marriage. Eventually, these various ethnographic threads are woven together with the thread of reflexive enquiry to produce what is, finally, a happy ending: the bride-to-be, a figure of glistening youth and beauty, finally returns from the cattle camps and agrees to the marriage,

5.3 Left, in *A Wife among Wives* (1981), the prospective bride finally appears. Right, 'I've travelled everywhere': in *Lorang's Way* (1979), the subject is revealed to be an idiosyncratic individual rather than a 'typical' Turkana elder.

so the senior men have their marriage, her relatives get their cattle and the film-makers have an event to film (figure 5.3, left).

If *A Wife Among Wives* is overtly reflexive in so far as the presence of the film-makers is concerned and to a degree that was unprecedented in ethnographic film-making until that point, the other film in the *Turkana Conversations* trilogy, *Lorang's Way*, is reflexive in a more subtle, but ultimately more significant way. This film, which the MacDougalls classify as the first of the *Turkana Conversations*, was actually the second to be released, in 1979. It offers a biographical account of the life and worldview of the eponymous Turkana elder, Lorang, and is arranged, as are the other films, as a series of scenes, divided into a number of thematically defined 'parts'.

In sharp contrast to previous hero-figures in the genre of ethnographic film, Lorang is no black-and-white archetype: he is much more ambiguous. He is both curmudgeonly and generous, expansive and calculating in a meanly self-interested way. He is a worrier rather than a visionary, a pragmatist, but also something of an intellectual, capable of great lucidity on occasion about his own culture. But nor is he merely a simple mouthpiece for this culture. Although in some ways he is the bastion of tradition, in his youth, as he explains in the film, he spent some time living in the colonial world after he was forcibly recruited into a British colonial regiment, the King's African Rifles. On his return, he used the skills and knowledge that he had learned in this external world to build up his wealth in traditional terms, that is, by acquiring large herds of animals, five wives and numerous children. And yet, he seems to remain sceptical about these achievements. When pressed to comment on the importance of traditional forms of wealth, he demurs and asserts that life itself is far more important.

In the final sequence in the film, the portrait of Lorang inclines powerfully towards the romantic: it is late afternoon, the cattle are streaming back to the homestead under the watchful eye of Lorang's handsome son. Lorang himself looks on, the master of all he surveys, silhouetted against the gorgeous colours of the evening sky. But just as one is about to succumb to the powerful narrative effect of closure and to the trope of this wise old Turkana Prospero discovering final contentment, Lorang's rasping, doubting tones return in the form of voice-over to leave an unanswered question: 'What then is life? Is it animals or what?'

If *A Wife Among Wives* is reflexive in relation to the film-makers, raising questions about their relationship to the world of the film, *Lorang's Way* is reflexive in relation to the subject, raising questions about his relationship to the world in which he lives.

## MODES OF PARTICIPATION: THE MACDOUGALLS IN AUSTRALIA

Even before they had completed the editing of *Turkana Conversations*, the MacDougalls had moved to Australia to take up positions as film-makers working at the Australian Institute for Aboriginal Studies (AIAS).[11] Here they encountered film-making conditions that were very different from those that they had known in East Africa, and they found themselves obliged to adapt their method of working accordingly.

One important difference was what David MacDougall would later describe as a difference in cultural 'style'. The Turkana had proved themselves to be the most eloquent auto-ethnographers, very ready to provide verbal explanations for their customary behaviour. They also had no reservations about displaying their disagreements and conflicts in public. On the contrary, particularly among men, great store was set on the ability to speak well in public and, as necessary, overcome others through oratorical skills. Both these characteristics lent themselves well to the mode of documentary film-making that the MacDougalls were developing in Turkana: the subjects' own explanations obviated the need for didactic voice-over commentary, while the public performance of disagreement lent itself well to a 'crisis structure' narrative.

By contrast, in Aboriginal communities, the MacDougalls found that there was an unwillingness to engage in public demonstrations of disagreement while the explanations offered for their customary behaviour were more allusive and metaphorical. While for the Turkana the ability to speak well was much admired, for Aboriginal people, reticence was a virtue. Rather than make claims in a verbal manner to promote their personal interests, they found that Aboriginal people had what David MacDougall later referred to as a 'heraldic culture', whereby claims were made through a process of symbolic, often performative displays of art or ritual, the precise significance of which was often difficult for an outsider to grasp. This posed a serious practical problem of cross-cultural translation for the MacDougalls, namely, how could they provide the interpretative context necessary for audiences to understand what they were seeing without recourse to an awkward and alienating didactic voice-over commentary?[12]

The MacDougalls also encountered a much greater sensitivity about the control of knowledge in Aboriginal society. In Turkana, the control of knowledge had certainly been an issue; indeed, one could think of *The Wedding Camels* as representing a prolonged struggle to control knowledge, or more exactly, to determine how many animals were being given and to whom. But in the last analysis, in Turkana it was recognised that everyone could in principle have access to that knowledge – the problem resided rather in getting hold of it. By contrast, in Australian Aboriginal society, the right to hold certain forms of knowledge can be restricted on the basis of gender, age and clan affiliation.

As the leading Australianist anthropologist Fred Myers puts it in a review of a number of the MacDougalls' Australian films, among Aboriginal people 'the authority to tell a story or provide an account is a matter of political concern'. Events taking place in public are constrained, in that participation is not equally open to all members of the community. Rather, as Myers explains, 'the right to represent and the meaning of what is said are linked to specific social relations'. The control of the films being made about them was thus very important for the Aboriginal subjects for reasons that were internal to their own world: more precisely, the MacDougalls' films came to be seen as a means whereby Aboriginal people could supplement the intensely political process of memorialising the dead as well as of asserting land claims vis-à-vis one another.[13]

Control over filmic representations was also important to Aboriginal people in relation to the outside world. Even in the 1970s, Aboriginal people were much more aware than the Turkana of the way in which, in a mediatised world, the manner in which they were represented could impact on their political interests in a national context. Ironic though it was, as Myers points out, Aboriginal people were very alert to the fact that in order to assert their traditional rights, they had to do so through the technology of the world that threatened to deny them those rights. Moreover, although the Turkana often railed against the government, they did not carry the profound sense of historical injury that Aboriginal people felt after two hundred years of colonial subjugation. In these circumstances, the MacDougalls found that 'there had to be a wholly different kind of unwritten contract between ourselves and Aboriginal people which determined why a film should be made at all, and, if it was to be made, what each of us expected to get out of it'.[14]

In order to adapt to this particular conjunction of political and cultural circumstances, the MacDougalls continued to make films that were reflexive

**5.4** Editing *Good-bye Old Man* (1977). David MacDougall is advised by
Thomas Woody Minipini.

in that they made no attempt to suppress any reference to the film-making
process in the filmic text. At the same time, their films became much more
participatory, involving the Aboriginal subjects much more directly in the
process of making the films than had been the case with the Turkana. Even
before the MacDougalls began to work for the AIAS, it was a general rule
of the organisation that all films made under the AIAS banner should
originate as a request from the Aboriginal community where the film-making
would take place. In practice, the MacDougalls would only a make a film
if they could identify some common ground of interest with the subjects,
even if the reasons for this interest were different. But once they had
identified this common ground, the subjects would then be continuously
involved in discussions as to what should or, equally importantly, what
should not be filmed.

Compared to the Turkana, Aboriginal people often had very clear views
regarding what a film should be about and how it should be made. In order
to give them the opportunity to contribute these views, the MacDougalls
would not only consult with their subjects while shooting but, inspired by
Jean Rouch's example in Africa back in the 1950s, they would also invite
their subjects to join them in the edit suite (figure 5.4). Also in line with
Rouch's authorial praxis, it was a fundamental matter of principle for the
MacDougalls that they would take the film back to the community where
it had been made and hold a public screening there.

Over a period of twelve years, from 1975 to 1987, the MacDougalls made a total of eleven films for the AIAS in this participatory manner. A comprehensive review of all these works lies beyond the scope of this chapter. Instead, I focus on three films that they made with members of the community of Aurukun on Cape York Peninsula, northern Queensland, released between 1980 and 1982, since these three films have attracted a particularly high degree of attention and comment, including by the MacDougalls themselves.[15]

Aurukun is a community whose origins lie in a Christian mission settlement established in the early twentieth century. Over the years, members of various different Aboriginal groups have come to live there, resulting in a community in which there is a considerable degree of social and cultural fragmentation, even to this day. At the time that the MacDougalls were working there, Aurukun numbered some 800 people, who between them spoke seven different Aboriginal languages, some of which were spoken by no more than a handful of people.

Probably the best known of the films that the MacDougalls made in Aurukun is *Takeover*. This is an 88-minute feature-length film, which documents the campaign by the Queensland State government in early 1978 to take over the management of Aurukun from the missionary organisations that had been running it since 1904. People in Aurukun were shocked by the cavalier way in which a decision had been taken to change the management of their community without any reference to them and, moreover, they had no wish to be governed directly by the notoriously right-wing Queensland government. What they mainly feared was that this take-over would put a stop to the then-active outstation movement, whereby members of the community were returning to live in the territories around Aurukun from whence their ancestors had originally come. Whereas the missionaries had supported this process, the people of Aurukun feared that the Queensland government would be strongly opposed because of the potentially vast deposits of bauxite that were already known to be lying under these territories.

Faced with this threat, the Aurukun Council appealed for help to the Ministry for Aboriginal Affairs of the Federal Government of Australia. Initially, the ministry was sympathetic and the minister himself, Ian Viner, was but one of many outsiders who came to Aurukun to give the community their support and assure them that nothing would happen without their consent (figure 5.5, left). In the end, however, far from Aurukun, a political deal was struck between the Federal and State governments whereby the community would be governed by a locally elected council, but one that would be subject to the authority of the Queensland government and then only on the basis of a 50-year lease. This outcome was hugely disappointing to the people of Aurukun, not only because they had come under the

5.5 Left, *Takeover* (1979): the Federal Minister of Aboriginal Affairs assures the Aurukun elders, including Francis Yunkaporta, centre, that nothing will happen without their consent – but this will prove to be untrue. Right, *The House-Opening* (1980): the brother of the deceased man wails formally on the shoulder of his widow, the narrator of the film, signifying that the man's family does not blame her for his death.

control of the Queensland state after all, even if indirectly, but because, once again, they had not been party to the decision, and their rights to the land, which they regarded as ahistorical and inalienable, had only been recognised provisionally rather than in perpetuity. As Myers explains in his review of the film, more than being perceived as merely political blows, for the Aurkun community these latter two aspects of the result represented a profound cultural affront.[16]

The Aurukun community invited the MacDougalls to document this process. When the crisis first broke, they had already been resident in the community for some months, working on other projects. They chose to follow it entirely from within the community, referring to the decisions being taken elsewhere in the way they were made known to Aurukun people themselves, that is, primarily through radio news bulletins, and to a lesser extent the printed press. The main body of the film consists simply of following the twist and turns of events as they unfold, interspersing ongoing discussions within the community with much coming and going of outside media people and political figures, all ending up with the final deflating denouement.

Reinforcing this geographically local perspective, the film is narrated in English by Francis Yunkaporta, a leading member of the Aurukun community (figure 5.5, left). He appears at various points in the film to comment on the progress of events and was also later invited into the edit suite to comment on them retrospectively. In both these respects, *Takeover* is highly participatory in the sense that it adopts an Aboriginal point of view, both geographically and politically, while at the same time both literally and metaphorically representing the Aboriginal 'voice'.

However, though Myers considers this film to be 'an ethnographic construction of a high interpretive order', it does not pose any complex issues of cross-cultural translation. Even if there are certain distinctively Aboriginal nuances to the way in which the events shown in the film are understood at a local level in Aurukun, their more general significance is only too readily understandable for a Western audience. In fact, in terms of the overall narrative shape, *Takeover* represents an even more typical example of the standard Western 'crisis structure' trope than the structures underlying *The Wedding Camels* and *A Wife Among Wives*. It is, moreover, a highly effective example of this trope and it was no doubt precisely for this reason that it was selected for so many international documentary festivals.

The other two films that the MacDougalls made in Aurukun posed more challenging issues of cross-cultural translation, which they sought to resolve in two somewhat different ways. One of these films, directed by Judith, is *The House-Opening* (1980), which concerns the ceremonial events that take place following a death and which are intended to enable the family of the deceased to move back into the family house. This was one of the first topics that people in Aurukun had suggested as a possible film subject to the MacDougalls since they were very proud of the ceremony and it had only very recently been developed. Under traditional circumstances, when Aboriginal people still lived in small structures constructed of tree bark and branches, houses would be burnt to the ground following a death, and the family would move away because it was feared that the spirit of the dead person would linger around the spot and might haunt the family, particularly young children. Now that the people of Aurukun lived in substantial, permanent houses, it had become too great a sacrifice to burn down the house of the deceased, so they had developed a new ceremony to reassure the spirit of the deceased person that they have not been forgotten, but then to drive it away. This new ceremony consisted of a highly syncretic blend of local Aboriginal traditions, Presbyterian Christianity and Torres Strait Islander forms of music and dancing.

The new ceremony also fulfilled another important function related to Aboriginal belief. Under traditional circumstances, deaths were often attributed to witchcraft, and when a man died one of the prime suspects would be his widow. In the ceremony shown in *The House-Opening*, in order to assure the husband's family that she has not been responsible for his death, the widow first has to practise extreme avoidance with the family, not talking to them until she has assembled a generous quantity of food to offer them. In accepting this food, they acknowledge that she is not to blame for her husband's death (figure 5.5, right). The husband's family and the widow's family then join together in a Christian service and perform their respective totemic dances for one another. Finally, the following day, the house of the deceased is reopened and the widow enters, accompanied by her husband's relatives. The latter carry a basket of smouldering ironwood tree leaves in order to drive away the husband's spirit.

So that she could provide explanations for the complex symbolic processes going on in this ceremony, Judith invited the widow, Geraldine Kawangka, to join her in the edit suite and comment on the rushes. This commentary was recorded and then used as a narration on the soundtrack of the final version of the film. It mostly works very well: it serves not only to provide the contexts necessary to understand the many different component parts of the ceremony from a religious or sociological point of view, but also to communicate, through the trembling, hesitant voice of Geraldine, the emotional significance of what is happening. It also provides Geraldine with an opportunity to express her views about the importance of preserving the traditional elements of Aboriginal belief and practice that have been incorporated into the new ceremony.

There are, however, certain absences within her commentary: there is, for example, no explicit reference to the suspicion that falls on a widow following a death and it requires a viewer already very familiar with traditional Aboriginal ideas to pick up on the heavy innuendo in the passages in which, relatively early in the film, Geraldine discusses the tense nature of her relations with her husband's relatives in the immediate post-mortem period. But with this relatively minor qualification, the strategy of inviting a leading protagonist to provide a commentary in the edit suite could be considered a very effective solution to the issues of cross-cultural translation posed by a multifaceted Aboriginal ceremony such as the one shown in this film. While providing the audience with the interpretative context that is necessary to understand what is going on, her voice seems to emerge from the world of the film itself rather than being imposed from outside in the manner of a conventional didactic commentary.[17]

The MacDougalls opted for a somewhat different strategy to solve the problems of cross-cultural translation posed by another of their Aurukun films, *Familiar Places*, also released in 1980. This film concerns a journey, seemingly of only a few days, made by an Aboriginal couple, Angus Namponan and his wife Chrissie, accompanied by their children, to visit their ancestral territories, a beautiful mixed landscape of sea estuaries and salt pans, some sixty miles south of Aurukun itself. The immediate purposes of the trip were twofold: to introduce the children to their ancestral clan territories and the spirits that inhabit them, and to map these territories in European terms as the basis for a claim to the land. This claim would not only keep out potential European intruders in search of bauxite, but would also defy the claims of other Aboriginal clans (figure 5.6).

In the film, Angus and Chrissie are accompanied by a young Australian 'linguist anthropologist', Peter Sutton, who is armed with a range of European devices for making visual records. These include a compass, a magnifying

5.6 *Familiar Places* (1980). Left, anthropologist Peter Sutton discusses mapping with Angus Namponan; right, Jack Spear sings about the Dreamtime sisters who drowned when they angered the Shark guardian spirit of the nearby salt estuary.

glass, a still-camera, a collection of aerial photographs and, finally, a film crew, in the form of the MacDougalls. It transpires that the making of the film is an integral part of the process of mapping and laying a claim to the land by Angus and his family. It is thus entirely appropriate that, close to the beginning of the film, when Chrissie introduces her children to the ancestral spirits by rubbing water on them at the edge of an estuary, she then turns and does the same to Judith MacDougall as she records sound, before moving over and doing the same to David as he operates the camera.

Although the film is ostensibly about the journey of Angus and his family, it relies for its central narrative thread on the presence of Sutton and on his extended verbal commentary on the action of the film. This commentary is delivered in a very low-key manner, partly as informal snatches of conversation with the film-makers on location, partly, it would seem, in reaction to a viewing of the rushes. Sutton's voice not only keeps us abreast of the chronology of the journey, but also provides, almost in passing as it were, an explanation of the significance of what the Aboriginal subjects are saying or doing.

The early part of the narrative is somewhat diffuse but midway through the film, it becomes more focused with the arrival of a new character. This is the dramatically named Jack Spear, Angus's uncle and the oldest living member of their clan. First, Jack Spear tells a story, half-sung, half-spoken about two Dreamtime sisters who sang to one another across the nearby salt estuary, but who angered the Shark ancestor spirit who resided there and drowned as a result. Jack Spear then guides the whole party around the area, pointing out where people camped in his youth and where they drew water, telling a story about how he had to hide from his enemies in a shelter in the forest. Finally, in the climax to the film, he takes us to an old burial ground where many hundreds of his relatives were cremated following an epidemic of whooping cough many years ago. Here he relates a further story about spear fights between rival clans, including the detail that his 'eldest father' was speared as he stoked a cremation pyre.

In his review of the film, Myers suggests that *Familiar Places* is 'the most intellectually complex' of the MacDougalls' Aurukun works.[18] But if this is so, it is surely primarily on account of Sutton's commentary which, notwithstanding its informality, is exegetical as well as informational. In the simplest sense, without Sutton's commentary, it would be often impossible to understand what Jack Spear is saying, even though his speech is clearly subtitled, since his remarks are mostly so fragmentary or elliptical that we rely on Sutton to tell us what he actually means. But more than that, Sutton also offers us generalisations and abstractions on the basis of these comments. Thus, for example, when Jack Spear informs him that a particular waterhole was secret, Sutton then explains to the camera, very casually, that traditionally the people of his group distinguished between three different types of waterhole and that the most secret kind was known only to old men. He then continues to an even more abstract observation to the effect that major waterholes were considered to have been left by the First People and that in Aboriginal thinking, this conception of places and resources being *left* from primeval times is more important than the notion of some original process of creation.

Stylistically speaking, in being so casually and simply delivered, Sutton's commentary is far from the ponderous didactic voice-overs that the Mac-Dougalls were seeking to avoid. Yet, in its own downbeat way, it is fulfilling the same explanatory function as a conventional didactic commentary, or the combination of title cards and auto-ethnographic exegesis in the MacDougalls' Turkana films. Although he is an outsider to Aboriginal society and is often providing an abstract analysis rather than describing his personal sentiments, Sutton's ontological position in relation to the film is not dissimilar to that of Geraldine Kawangka in relation to *The House-Opening*: he is both inside the film and outside it at the same time, both playing a part in it and commenting upon it after the fact. As such, as an authorial strategy, it works very well.

In his own discussion of *Familiar Places*, David MacDougall argues that although Sutton appears 'to be in charge of the story as well as the expedition', there are many other verbal discourses going on in this film, that is, between Sutton and the Aboriginal protagonists, between the Aborigines themselves, between the film-makers and the protagonists, as well as with a series of imagined audiences, both Aboriginal and non-Aboriginal. There is also a more visual discourse going on in the sense that the making of the film itself acts as a vehicle whereby the protagonists can make a direct claim to be the owners of the landscape represented in the film. As such, MacDougall suggests, Sutton's voice is not *the* definitive authoritative voice in the film, but merely one part of 'a complex cultural drama'.[19] But while this might be true, it requires Sutton's voice to draw the threads of the various discourses together and make sense of them.

Many years later, in an interview recorded in 2007, when reflecting on the films that he and Judith had made with Aboriginal people, David MacDougall commented that although they had struggled with the issue for 'over a dozen years and a dozen films', he felt that they had never quite solved the problem of how one made the meanings of the often highly coded statements and actions of Aboriginal people accessible to non-Aboriginal audiences.[20] But in my view, *The House-Opening* and *Familiar Places*, albeit in different ways, demonstrate that even if it does not represent a solution that one would want to use in all circumstances and for all purposes, the strategy of inviting the film subjects themselves to provide an interpretative but low-key commentary, be it on location or in the edit suite, can be a very effective method for making semiologically dense statements and actions understandable to third-party audiences without recourse either to an alienating didactic voice-over, or to formal interviews. For this reason, though they were released more than thirty years ago, the MacDougalls' Aurukun films remain of abiding interest as examples of ethnographic film authorship.

## Notes

1 Probably the most energetic advocate of this form of reflexivity has been Jay Ruby. But as of 2000, he was unable to identify a single example in the century-long history of ethnographic film-making that had entirely satisfied his requirements (Ruby 2000), 156–7.

2 MacDougall (1998b), 88–91.

3 David MacDougall, personal communication, March 2017. Unfortunately, this film, eventually given the title of *Imbalu: Ritual of Manhood of the Gisu of Uganda*, was not edited for twenty years, by which time the original negative had been lost, and it had to be cut from a scratched and faded workprint. Nevertheless, when it was finally released in 1990, it received favourable reviews. See MacDougall (2007), 126.

4 The subdivision of the film into five parts was inspired by Basil Wright's classic 1934 documentary, *The Song of Ceylon* (see pp. 50–2) as well as by the narrative devices that Jean-Luc Godard was using in his fiction films at the time (Grimshaw and Papastergiadis 1995), 29.

5 In the interim between the Jie and Turkana projects, David MacDougall shot *Kenya Boran* (1974), and a number of shorter films about the Boran, a pastoralist people of the Marsabit District of northern Kenya, close to the border with Ethiopia. These were based on the research of the Manchester anthropologist, Paul Baxter and were co-directed by James Blue, a film-maker indirectly associated with the UCLA programme. However, these films were made for the American Universities Field Staff (AUFS) series, *Faces of Change* and as MacDougall was only a 'hired hand', he did not have final editorial control over the films. Although he and Blue did a first cut of *Kenya Boran* that conformed to the principles of Observational Cinema, this was later substantially re-cut by Norman Miller, the AUFS series producer, in the didactic, commentary-led manner that the MacDougalls were seeking to get away from in their own work. See https://store.der.org/blue-james-c752.aspx.

6 On the 'unprivileged' camera style, see MacDougall (1998e) and also the more extended discussion in Chapter 10, pp. 300–3.

7 See Mamber (1974). On the 'crisis structure', see especially pp. 115–40. Based mostly on the East Coast of the USA, the Direct Cinema group first became prominent in the early 1960s. See also Saunders (2007) and Grimshaw and Ravetz (2009), 24–50.

8 I stress the word 'overtly' here since David MacDougall has commented that he himself thinks of *The Wedding Camels* as being more reflexive than *A Wife Among Wives* on the grounds it was 'the film in which we made the greatest effort to try to create a sense of indeterminacy about knowledge, about the situation one finds oneself in the field, trying to make sense of complex events, and not necessarily being able to do it' (Grimshaw and Papastergiadis 1995, 36). However, while one might be aware as a viewer that there is this indeterminacy about the process of enquiry in *The Wedding Camels*, the process of enquiry itself is not so directly and openly referred to as in *A Wife Among Wives*.

9 'Polygyny' is the technical term used by anthropologists to describe one of the two possible kinds of heterosexual polygamy, that is, the one in which a man may marry two or more wives. The other kind, in which a woman may marry two or more men is known as 'polyandry'.

10 An early example of this trope, and perhaps even the first usage, is *Waiting for Fidel* (1974), directed by Michael Rubbo for the National Film Board of Canada, in which three Canadians of differing political persuasions go to Havana in the – unrequited – hope of being granted an audience with Fidel Castro. In an ethnographic context, perhaps the most celebrated example is *Waiting for Harry* (1980), directed by Kim McKenzie. In this case, a group of Anbara Aboriginal people conducting a funeral ceremony await the arrival of the eponymous Harry, a relative of the deceased, without whom the ceremony cannot be concluded. Happily, in this case, the waited-for person does finally arrive.

11 In 1989, after the MacDougalls had left the organisation, the AIAS became the Australian Institute for Aboriginal and Torres Straits Islander Studies (AIATSIS).

12 See MacDougall (1992a).

13 Myers (1988), 207.

14 Grimshaw and Papastergiadis (1995), 40.

15 The MacDougalls also made a fourth film in Aurukun, *Three Horsemen* (1982), about Aboriginal stockmen of three different generations. The other films that they made for the AIAS were: *Good-bye Old Man* (1977), about a Tiwi *pukumani* or bereavement ceremony on Melville Island, off the coast of Arnhem Land, northwest Australia, and *To Get That Country* (1978), an account of two political meetings related to the mining of uranium on Aboriginal land on the Arnhem Land mainland; four films focusing on part-Aboriginal people in rural New South Wales, of which the most substantial is *Sunny and the Dark Horse* (1986); and finally, *Link-Up Diary* (1987), which follows the activities of a Canberra NGO that aims to reunite Aboriginal families broken up under the adoption policies of the New South Wales State government between 1900 and 1969.

16 Myers (1988), 208–10.

17 When the MacDougalls returned to screen the film back to the community, they were surprised to discover that the use of Geraldine's voice raised certain political issues. I return to these in the concluding section of Chapter 6, pp. 193–4.

18 See Myers (1988), 213–16.

19 MacDougall (1998c), 160–3.

20 MacFarlane (2007).

## 6

# Entangled voices: the complexities of collaborative authorship

D AVID and Judith MacDougall were far from alone in developing reflexive and participatory 'ways of doing' ethnographic film-making during the 1970s and 1980s. Many other ethnographic film-makers in the English-speaking world were working in a similar manner during this period, including a number of those who had been active in the 1950s and 1960s, and whose work I describe in Chapters 3 and 4. Abandoning the aspiration to produce objective film records of the kind envisaged by Margaret Mead, they too developed collaborative authorial praxes of various kinds, thereby contributing to a great increase in both the quality and variety of English-language ethnographic film during these years.

As noted at the beginning of Chapter 5, this interest in collaborative film praxes had first arisen as a response to the questioning, from the 1970s onwards, of the right of ethnographers, be it in film or in text, to produce accounts of their subjects' lives. To the extent that a collaborative praxis could be understood as a concern to gain the subjects' consent to make these representations, it could also provide a degree of political and ethical legitimacy to the enterprise. At the same time, many film-makers hoped that by working with the subjects of the film, it would be possible to produce films that would in some sense be beneficial to them, thereby providing additional justification for their presumption of the right to place their subjects' lives in the public domain through their film-making.

However, as described in the course of this chapter, after an initial period of enthusiasm, it soon became apparent that collaborative ethnographic film-making could be a more complex process than some of its advocates had anticipated. Gaining general consent to make a film was one thing, but arriving at agreement on exactly who or what should be in the film and how this should be presented was another. For although a film-maker might well be able to find certain areas of common interest with their subjects, the overlap was rarely total and disagreements could therefore arise. Moreover, it was often the case that in the communities where ethnographic film-makers worked, as with all human communities, there would be a range of different interests, be it on the basis of gender or age, or in terms of political affiliation, economic interest or any number of other factors. Film-makers would sometimes find themselves obliged to navigate their way through entangled networks of relationships, making compromises at every turn and producing films that in the end spoke neither for themselves, nor for any particular group of their subjects. This meant, in effect, that they spoke for nobody.

Another reason for disillusionment was the realisation that there was no guarantee that ethnographic film-making – however participatory and reflexive, however collaborative – could bring about significant beneficial change for the subjects. Therefore to seek to legitimate the activity in ethical or political terms on these grounds was at best optimistic and at worst merely self-deluding. Besides, in historical circumstances in which audiovisual technology was becoming increasingly available to the members of the groups or communities with whom ethnographic film-makers worked, the idea that they needed outsiders to make films to bring about beneficial change for them was becoming, in the view of some, little more than a patronising anachronism.

As these complexities became progressively apparent, some film-makers began to feel that collaborative film-making, at least as a means of side-stepping the political and ethical implications of authorship, was actually a dead-end. Instead, they concluded that they would do better to assume more complete responsibility for the authoring of their films, since at least in that regard, their films would speak for somebody, if only for themselves. Rather than aspiring to do good with their films, they adopted the more modest goal of ensuring that their films did at least do no harm to their subjects.

## PARTICIPATORY FILM-MAKING AND ACADEMIC COLLABORATION: TIMOTHY AND PATSY ASCH IN INDONESIA

One of the film-makers who most radically changed their general approach during the course of the 1970s was Timothy Asch, though he remained committed to working with anthropologists in the field and exploring with them the ways in which film could be of use to academic anthropology, particularly in teaching. In 1976, after completing the editing of the Yanomami films that he had made with Napoleon Chagnon, Asch took up a post at the Department of Anthropology at the Australia National University (ANU) in Canberra. Over the next few years, together with his wife Patsy Asch, he shot a series of films in various locations around Indonesia, each based on collaboration with an anthropologist from the ANU department: with James Fox on the island of Roti, and with two graduate students, E. Douglas Lewis on Flores, and Linda Connor on Bali.[1]

The films that arose from these collaborations were very much more reflexive and participatory than the films that Asch had made with Chagnon. They were originally intended to be part of a broader comparative study of ritual performance in Indonesia, but these plans fell foul of a combination of bureaucratic delays and the Indonesian invasion of Timor, which held up the issuing of research permits even more than usual. While Timothy Asch did the shooting, the editing was carried out by Patsy Asch, who also acted as sound recordist and producer of the films. Regardless of the precise order in which their names might have appeared on the credits of any particular film, Timothy Asch was concerned that he, Patsy Asch and the consultant anthropologist should be seen has having produced the film as a collaborative team and therefore as having equal status as its authors.

Whereas the Yanomami films had been narrated exclusively by Chagnon, the films that the Asches made with Fox and with Lewis are narrated by leading subjects, albeit in a manner that is heavily mediated by the film-makers, and in conjunction with a certain degree of narration by the consultant anthropologists in each case. The principal film that the Asches made with Fox on Roti was *The Water of Words*, shot in 1977, though not released until 1983. This concerns the lontar palm, renowned for its juice, which is turned into various alcoholic beverages. It is primarily narrated by two Rotinese elders, each in a different manner: while one elder provides a commentary on practical aspects of lontar palm exploitation in the form of an intermittent subtitled interview, the other relates the mythical origins of the palm in the form of a voice-over dubbed into Dutch-accented English.[2]

A similar technique is used in *A Celebration of Origins*, the film that the Asches made with Lewis on Flores, shot in 1980, though not released until 1993. This film concerns an elaborate ritual in which the leading clan of Tana Wai Brama – a certain 'ceremonial domain' within the island – asserts its primacy as the original founder of this domain. As in *The Water of Words*, the voice-over narration is shared between the anthropologist and one of the principal protagonists, Pins Wai Brama, son of a leading ritual specialist of the clan. However, in this case, the protagonist developed his commentary in reaction to a viewing of the rushes some years later in Australia. As in the earlier film, the protagonist's voice is dubbed into English and rendered in an accented voice, though with the original testimony just audible underneath. There is also a greater degree of reflexivity in this film in that Pins's visit to Australia is shown in one of the early sequences of the film. Also, right at the end of the film, beneath the credits, there is a rostrum-camera pan over a still image of a Wai Brama community group apparently watching the material on a television, with Lewis at the back of the group.

It is in the films that the Asches made with Linda Connor on Bali that participatory and reflexive authorial strategies are most developed. All but one of these five films concern Jero Tapakan, a traditional healer who seeks

6.1 Left, prior to entering into trance, Jero Tapakan appeals to her guardian deity in *A Balinese Trance Seance* (1979); right, Jero discusses this film with the anthropologist Linda Connor in *Jero on Jero* (1981).

to help her clients through contacting the spirit world to establish whether their illnesses and misfortunes have a spiritual origin or are due to a failure to make appropriate ritual offerings. But she also diagnoses and treats more physical illnesses through massage therapy, and prescribes certain herbal remedies that she herself prepares.

In the first of the films about Jero, *A Balinese Trance Seance*, shot in 1978 and released the following year, she contacts the spirit of a dead boy on behalf of a group of his relatives in order to determine the cause of his death (figure 6.1, left). In the second film, *The Medium is the Masseuse*, also shot in 1978, but not released until 1983, she is shown providing massage and prescribing remedies to a series of clients. In both films, there are frequent reflexive references to the fact that a film is being made. In the first film, there is even a title card explaining that a break in the action is due to the fact that a film magazine is being changed. In the second film, Linda Connor, who acted as sound recordist, often appears in shot, and at one point there is a still image of Timothy Asch operating the camera.[3]

These participatory and reflexive elements are even more pronounced in the short film, *Jero on Jero*, shot in 1980 and released the following year, in which Jero is filmed watching *A Balinese Trance Seance* on a television and discussing this with Connor (figure 6.1, right). There is also a rather fragmented biographical film, *Stories from the Life of a Balinese Healer*, shot on a number of different occasions and released in 1983, in which Jero recounts a series of episodes from her life, explaining that she first became interested in healing because of her own experiences of illness and trauma.

The Asches' final Balinese work, *Releasing the Spirits*, was also shot in 1978 but not released until 1991. In this film, which concerns an elaborate cremation ceremony, the participatory and reflexive elements threaten to overwhelm the film completely as several different channels of exegesis compete for the attention of the audience. There is, on the one hand, commentary by four different Balinese participants, including Jero, sometimes shown in synch talking to Connor at a feedback session, sometimes offered in voice-over. At times, this commentary is so extensive that it is rendered as rolling titles over a black screen. Then there is also a voice-over commentary by Patsy Asch, partly reflexive, partly informative, as well as an intermittent off-screen debate between Timothy Asch and Connor about what actually happened during the course of the event as well as the reasons for making the film in the first place. It has to be said that these verbal and textual devices completely swamp the visual qualities of the film, and although apparently intended to elucidate what is clearly a complex ritual event, in fact they make it even more difficult to understand.

The anthropologists involved in the making of the Asches' Indonesian films have all testified to the benefits for their own research of participating in these projects. There can also be no doubt about the descriptive ethnographic qualities of the films and their value as a teaching resource, particularly when viewed in conjunction with the accompanying textual publications. The need for the latter had been one of Timothy Asch's long-standing concerns, which he was finally able to address in the form of a monograph about the Jero Tapakan films that he authored jointly with Linda Connor and Patsy Asch.[4] However, in strictly filmic terms, as with Timothy Asch's films about the Yanomami, these Indonesian films are arguably more significant for their methodological innovations than for their cinematographic merits. In a filmic sense, there is a certain restless and disjointed quality about these works while the technical standard of the cinematography is often disappointing, as Timothy Asch himself acknowledges in the Jero Tapakan monograph.[5]

However, the authorial strategy of allowing the subjects themselves to narrate the films in which they appear, however mediated this may have been, and however imperfectly realised, was a genuinely original idea, at least in English-language ethnographic film-making. The same is true both of building an ethnographic film around a subject's life history and of incorporating feedback processes directly into a film. These strategies may now seem almost self-evident, but in the 1970s and 1980s, as ethnographic film-makers were still exploring the possibilities that the recent development of portable synchronous sound had thrown up, the Asches' films in Indonesia served to suggest several new 'ways of doing' ethnographic film.

## Participatory film-making as political engagement: Ian Dunlop in Australia

Another leading film-maker to change his 'way of doing' ethnographic films during this period was Ian Dunlop, whose films about Aboriginal

**6.2** The Yirrkala Film Project. Left, *Pain for This Land*, filmed in 1970–71 – the Yolngu wanted to film traditional custom as much as the impact of the bauxite mine; right, 'Like me, Dundiwuy has become a proper old man' – Ian Dunlop with Dundiwuy and his daughter in *Conversations with Dundiwuy* (1995).

people of Central Australia, shot in the years 1965–67, I considered in Chapter 3. In 1970, Dunlop started work on what would be a much lengthier series of films with the Yolngu Aboriginal community living at the former mission township of Yirrkala or on nearby clan homelands in northeast Arnhem Land, Australia.[6]

Dunlop went to Yirrkala commissioned by the Commonwealth Film Unit, the same agency of the Australian Federal Government for which he had been working when he made his films in Central Australia. His brief was to make a film about the social and ecological impact of the vast NABALCO bauxite mine that had recently started operations at Nhulunbuy, about 15 miles north of Yirrkala. He was firmly resolved to do this with the active participation of the Yolngu community but when he first arrived, he had no intention of making films about ritual and ceremonial life. However, he soon discovered that while the Yolngu were certainly very interested in the way in which his films could publicise the negative impact of the mine, they were even more interested in using film to record and preserve their traditional cultural activities so that these could then be transmitted to future generations. In fact, as Dunlop would later realise, the two concerns were merely different sides of the same coin for the Yolngu since their concern to preserve their traditional cultural forms was directly related to their concern to assert their rights over the land, which were threatened by the presence of the bauxite mine (figure 6.2, left).

Between 1970 and 1982, Dunlop visited Yirrkala on eight separate occasions and shot material on a broad variety of topics. The editing of this material was delayed by other commitments, but eventually, between 1979 and 1996, with the extensive assistance of Philippa 'Pip' Deveson, Dunlop cut twenty-two separate films from the footage shot in and around Yirrkala. In its final edited form, the total running time of this corpus of films, collectively dubbed the Yirrkala Film Project, is in excess of 20 hours, though the component films are of highly variable duration: the longest is almost 4 hours in its most extended form, while the shortest runs to a mere 15 minutes. Only a relatively small part of this important body of work is widely known about, though the recent making available of the complete project on DVD may help to remedy this situation.

Howard Morphy, who acted as an anthropological consultant on several of the films, has suggested that one can subdivide the Yirrkala Film Project into three broadly overlapping categories: first, the films directly concerned with the impact of bauxite mining and the Yolngu response to this, as per the original brief; second, the films about everyday life, including sequences of Yolngu engaged in traditional crafts as well as in the artwork that they now produce for outsiders; finally, the films about ritual and ceremonial events. Throughout all three categories of film, even the first, the complex and multifaceted connections between land, clan membership, personal identity and metaphysical belief, and the confirmation of these relation-ships in ceremonial performance and material works of art are a constant, recurrent motif.

In authorial terms, there are certain continuities between Dunlop's Yirrkala films and his earlier work in Central Australia. In contrast to a number of the other leading ethnographic film-makers of this period, Dunlop continued, for the most part, to work with a professional crew. There is also a continuing heavy emphasis on detailed documentation filming supported by extensive voice-over commentary performed by Dunlop himself. But in other respects, there are major differences: the earlier films were silent and, for a mixture of budgetary and aesthetic reasons discussed in Chapter 3, they were shot on 35 mm black and white stock. The Yirrkala films by contrast were shot in 16 mm, mostly in colour, and although still heavily narrated, they also have ambient soundtracks and depend crucially on synchronised subtitled speech by the subjects. In methodological terms, whereas the earlier films were shot and edited in such a way as to make their authorship invisible, these films are participatory and reflexive, with Dunlop himself occasionally appearing in shot. They are still very obviously authored by Dunlop, but this is a much more overtly shared authorship than was the case with his Central Australia films.

It is the films in the second of these categories that are arguably the most innovative within Dunlop's personal oeuvre from an authorial point of view, particularly the filmic biographies of Narritjin Maymuru and Dundiwuy Wanambi, both of whom became artists of national renown over the period that Dunlop was working in Yirrkala. These biographical films include the much praised *Conversations with Dundiwuy Wanambi*, released in 1995, a very personal film that was based on the relationship between

Dunlop and the subject as it developed over the principal twelve-year period of filming. In this film, the individual life-experience of Dundiwuy is used as a sort of gauge against which to measure the great changes that had taken place at Yirrkala more generally in those years (figure 6.2, right).[7]

However, of all the many films that Dunlop made in Yirrkala, it was those about ritual and ceremonial life that were the most significant, both for Dunlop himself and for his Yolngu subjects, even though in terms of general film-making praxis they might be considered the most conservative. The best known of these films is *Madarrpa Funeral at Gurka'wuy*, shot in 1976 and, three years later, the first of Dunlop's Yirrkala films to be released. The location of the film was one of a number 'outstation' settlements then being established by the Yolngu in their traditional clan homelands, at some distance from Yirrkala. This particular settlement was on the edge of Trial Bay, in the homeland of the Marrakulu clan. This was the clan to which Dundiwuy Wanambi belonged and it was he who encouraged Dunlop and his crew to come to Gurka'wuy. Initially, the aim was to film a *djungguwan*, a major ceremony combining the commemoration of the dead and the initiation of a new generation. But shortly after the crew arrived, a young child died unexpectedly, so at the invitation of the child's father and the elders of the Madarrpa clan to which the child's father belonged, Dunlop temporarily put the filming of the *djungguwan* to one side in order to follow the child's funeral instead.

In narrative terms, *Madarrpa Funeral* is very straightforward, following the chronology of the unfolding event. But if the chronology is straightforward, the symbolic dimension of the event is not. In effect, the ceremony, and by extension the film, interweaves two complementary processes, one physical and material, the other metaphysical. The former involves the preparations for the disposal of the body at Gurka'wuy, including the painting of the coffin and the digging of the grave. In parallel with these highly material processes, the child's spirit is guided on a symbolic journey, by means of an extended series of songs and dances, through the homelands of the various clans to which his own is affiliated, including particularly the homeland of his mother's mother's clan. Finally, the spirit arrives at the nest of the Crocodile ancestor of his father's clan, located far to the south in the waters of Blue Mud Bay. When the spirit reaches this metaphysical destination, the two parallel processes are reconnected as the child's body is physically buried in its coffin back at Gurka'wuy, and the film itself then draws to a close.[8]

In many ways, in terms of its authorial praxis, *Madarrpa Funeral* represents a continuation of the classical documentation strategies that Dunlop had been practising a decade earlier in Central Australia. The events of the funeral are mostly covered in long unbroken takes, competently executed on a handheld Éclair NPR by the cinematographer, Dean Semler. The original footage has been subject to minimal reduction through editing:

Morphy reports that around three-quarters of the original material was used in the film, which is a remarkably low cutting ratio for a professional production, even for an ethnographic film. The soundtrack is dominated by Dunlop's extremely detailed narration, which continues throughout the film, further supported by intertitles and graphics. Though the protagonists may have invited Dunlop to make the film and though their speech is subtitled, it is his voice that provides the dominant explanatory framework for the event.[9]

This heavy narration now seems rather 'tired', as Deveson and Dunlop themselves put it when commenting on the film some thirty years later. Though it was generally welcomed at the time for providing symbolic and sociological contexts, at least by some academic reviewers, it poses the dilemma that the Asches also confronted when cutting *Releasing the Spirits*, namely, how to provide sufficient context to make an event adequately meaningful for the viewer without burying the film in an avalanche of words. Notwithstanding the very extensive commentary in *Madarrpa Funeral*, there was still a degree of oversimplification due to the inevitable time constraints of the filmic medium: according to Morphy, there is a tendency for the narration to suggest that the meanings attributed to particular features of the funeral are unambiguous and widely accepted by the Yolngu, whereas, in reality, there was often a range of opinions about these meanings.[10]

At 87 minutes, *Madarrpa Funeral* is a long film, but it is relatively short compared to the epic *Djungguwan at Gurka'wuy*, which was the film project that had brought Dunlop and his colleagues to Trial Bay in the first place. This film, in its original edited version, ran to a very challenging 233 minutes, divided into five parts. Although shot on the same visit to Gurka'wuy as *Madarrpa Funeral*, it was not released until ten years later, in 1989. Owing to its sheer length, it is not as well known as the earlier film, but it is the most complex and sophisticated of Dunlop's Yirrkala films, certainly of those dealing with ritual subjects. In stylistic terms, it is in many ways similar to *Madarrpa Funeral* in that the narrative structure largely follows that of the event itself, the takes are long and the editing is minimal, and it is regularly punctuated by what one reviewer has called an 'essay-like' narration performed by Dunlop, again supported by intertitles and graphics.[11] There is, however, a somewhat stronger sense of the subjects' participation than in *Madarrpa Funeral*. Dundiwuy Wanambi directly addresses the camera at various points in order to explain what is going on, while his paintings of ancestral beings serve as a sort of recurrent illustration of beliefs about these beings which in turn act as a key to understanding the ritual action.

A particularly striking example of this is a scene in which Dundiwuy introduces the camera to a seemingly insignificant cluster of small rocks on the shore of Trial Bay and explains that this is the place where one group of his clan's ancestral beings, the Water Goannas, came ashore. The rocks, he informs us, are the material remnants of the bubbles caused by their breath. He then proceeds to draw with a stick in the sand, showing how he represents this event in his bark paintings. He also stresses how important these traces of ancestral presence are to him and that it is for that reason that he has returned from Yirrkala to aid in the re-establishment of his clan homeland.[12]

*Djungguwan at Gurka'wuy* is at one level merely an ethnographic film about a ceremonial event. But, as with the MacDougalls' film, *Familiar Places*, discussed in Chapter 5, at the same time it acts as the visual embodiment of a claim to the land based on ancestral presences. Moreover, the film and the ceremonial event in combination serve as a means of transmitting this claim across the generations through the simultaneous celebration of the epic journeys of the ancestors over the land, the return to Gurka'wuy for burial of the remains of a clan member who had recently died in Yirrkala, and the initiation of a new generation of young boys. As such, *Djungguwan at Gurka'wuy* stands as a strong counterclaim to the shameful judgement of the Australian courts, delivered in 1971, that prior to the arrival of Europeans, the country was *terra nullius*, without owners, thereby legitimating the invasion of Aboriginal lands by, among many others, the NABALCO bauxite mining enterprise on Yolngu land. In this way, although *Djungguwan at Gurka'wuy* is clearly a film about mortuary practices and beliefs about ancestors in primeval times, it is also an intensely political film of immediate contemporary relevance, thereby fulfilling, in the most powerful, even if in the most unexpected way, the brief that Dunlop was given when he first set out to film in Yirrkala in 1970.[13]

## PARTICIPATORY FILM-MAKING AS POLITICAL ENGAGEMENT: SARAH ELDER AND LEONARD KAMERLING IN ALASKA

At around the same time as Dunlop was shooting his Yirrkala films, a more explicitly theorised form of participatory film-making was taking place in various Yup'ik communities in Alaska under the direction of Sarah Elder and Leonard Kamerling. At that time, Elder was a schoolteacher in the small Yup'ik community of Emmonak, close to the mouth of the Yukon river. She had moved there in 1972, after studying anthropology at Sarah Lawrence College in New York and then working for a period as an intern with John Marshall and Timothy Asch in Boston. Her intention was to use her position in the community to carry out participant-observation field research as a prelude to making films there. Once in Alaska, she met Kamerling, a film-maker from New York, who was engaged in making a film further south in Tununak Bay.[14]

Over the next five years, Elder and Kamerling shot the material for eight films, which are now referred to collectively as the Alaska Native Heritage Film Project. The production of these films was based on a series of explicitly formulated rules that ceded a high degree of control to their Yup'ik subjects. Elder and Kamerling started from the principle the Yup'ik community should choose the topic of a film and also participate in that film. Anyone, at any time, could ask them to stop filming and if a subject changed their mind later about participating, they could ask for their image to be removed from the cut of the film. People were invited to speak in the language with which they were most comfortable, which in many cases was Yup'ik, and this speech was then subtitled on the basis of at least two independent translations.

In cutting the films, Elder and Kamerling had in mind the community as the first audience, themselves as the second audience and only then did they think in terms of other audiences. As the cuts proceeded, preliminary versions were shown to the host community and its approval sought. The final version was screened in the community and then multiple copies on VHS cassettes, a technology that had only recently become available, were distributed around the community. Both copyright and any royalties were shared with the community.

Initially, Elder had imagined that it would be possible to accommodate their film-making practice entirely to Yup'ik norms and dubbed this approach 'community-determined' film-making. However, she later came to realise that this resulted in films that were very 'cumbersome' and lacking in focus, particularly as her Yup'ik subjects were often very reluctant to cut anything out of the edits. She found herself obliged to admit that as film-makers who aimed to show their work, if not immediately, at least eventually to non-Yup'ik audiences, they needed to bring their own criteria to bear on the process of editing, at least to some degree. This led her to re-conceive their practice as 'community-collaborative', that is, as based on negotiation with the subjects to find an overlapping 'creative space' where both parties could realise their respective interests.

As with the Yolngu in their collaboration with Ian Dunlop, this common ground proved to be the Yup'ik's desire to preserve a record of their traditional cultural activities for the future, even for generations unborn. In their lifetimes, the oldest generation had seen a radical transformation of their cultural life as a result of the impact, initially, of missionaries, and later of greater social and economic integration with the outside world. These older people were very keen that the traditional cultural activities that had survived the onslaught of new influences should be preserved on film before they too were lost. Although some middle-aged Yup'ik political leaders initially had reservations about Elder and Kamerling's project, they deferred, in

**6.3** *The Drums of Winter* (1988). The Yup'ik potlatch is the occasion for exchanges not only between the living but also between the living and the dead.

accordance with traditional practice, to the views of their elders, and once the filming began, they too were fully supportive.

As a feminist, Elder had hoped their Yup'ik hosts would ask her to make films about domestic and family life, as this would have provided greater access to the experience of women. But what their hosts proposed instead were mostly films about male subsistence activities. This resulted in two notable films, *At the Time of Whaling* and *On the Spring Ice*, a film about walrus hunting. They also recorded a number of senior men telling traditional stories and legends: these were released as a trilogy of three short films under the direction of Katrina Waters in 1988. Two other films concerned more general aspects of contemporary Yup'ik life.[15]

Elder and Kamerling were able to involve women much more directly, both as performers and as interlocutors, in the most substantial work that they made with the Yup'ik. This was *Uksuum Cauyai – The Drums of Winter*, a highly accomplished 90-minute film constructed around the drumming, chanting and dancing that take place in connection with potlatch exchanges. These events, which feature prominently in the ethnographic literature of the region, involve the competitive giving away of goods to relatives, friends and even rivals, as a way of marking significant moments in an individual's life cycle, from a first dance for a girl and a first hunt for a boy to a memorial for the recently deceased. These exchanges between the living are also conceived as a way of continuing exchanges with the dead since giving gifts to strangers is explicitly equated with giving gifts to one's deceased relatives. Despite vigorous attempts to suppress them by missionaries and colonial authorities, the potlatch continues to be an important feature of indigenous life throughout the region (figure 6.3).[16]

In *The Drums of Winter*, potlatch performances are intercut with general shots of the Arctic environment and subsistence activities, as well as with a series of interviews, mostly very informal, in which older participants explain the significance of the potlatch as a form of exchange and how they experience the drumming and dancing, both as individuals and as a crucial aspect of their collective identity. At the other end of the age spectrum, a group of younger women describe their nervousness when they walked out to perform their First Dance. This contemporary material is intercut in a very effective way with archival images from missionary sources, and voiced extracts from missionary letters deploring the potlatch practices of the Yup'ik. These are in marked contrast with the powerful testimony of a contemporary Jesuit missionary who describes his own sense of being spiritually transported when he performed a memorial dance for a Yup'ik friend who had recently died.

The film ends on an uncertain note about the future: while the older people and the Jesuit missionary are confident that the potlatch ceremonies will continue, the younger women fear that they will die out because young men are not interested in performing. An ominous sign is that after the filming was completed, the *kashim*, the modest wood cabin serving as a dance house, steam bathhouse and spiritual centre, where much of the film was shot, was later demolished to make way for a new roadway.

As with all the films in the Alaska Native Heritage Film Project, the style is broadly observational, featuring long takes and a low-key aesthetic, and a complete absence of voice-over narration. Essential contextualising information is supplied through titles superimposed on synch images. The quality of the cinematography is exceptionally high, particularly in the lit scenes inside the *kashim* cabin. So too is the quality of the sound recording. Although the underlying methodology may have been highly participatory, the films themselves are only minimally reflexive: outside the context of interviews, there are only occasional references to the presence of the film-makers. In fact, even the interviews are more like oral testimonies than interviews in the sense that only on one occasion does one hear a question, and even that is posed by a local person rather than by the film-makers.

In her account of making these films, Sarah Elder acknowledges that the way of working that she and Leonard Kamerling developed with the Yup'ik was often difficult. Balancing their own interests with those of the subjects often proved to be 'a real tightrope'. She admits that process could not be described as 'efficient or neat or orderly' – one expression of this being that eleven years elapsed between the shooting of *The Drums of Winter* in 1977 and its final release in 1988. But in compensation, she claims, the films that they made with this methodology have proved to be of interest to a range of different audiences, both internal and external to Yup'ik society. Across Alaska, they have been used in Native communities for a broad variety of purposes in schools, cultural programmes and for political advocacy. But they have also won all manner of awards at international film festivals. The peak of this external recognition came in 2006 when the National

Film Registry nominated *The Drums of Winter* for preservation in the US Library of Congress. Here it joined a collection of the most celebrated Hollywood blockbusters and an extremely select collection of films classed as 'ethnographic', including *In the Land of the Head Hunters, Nanook of the North, Trance and Dance in Bali* and John Marshall's film *The Hunters*.

## REFLEXIVITY AND ADVERSARIAL FILM-MAKING: JOHN MARSHALL AND THE 'BUSHMAN MYTH'

When John Marshall was finally able to return to southern Africa to film with the Ju/'hoansi in 1978, the work that he produced was also far more participatory and reflexive than his earlier films. Although these later films also had a strongly political cast, his objectives differed greatly from those of Ian Dunlop among the Yolngu or those of Sarah Elder and Leonard Kamerling among the Yup'ik. Whereas these latter film-makers had shared a common interest with their subjects in the documentation of traditional culture so that it could be passed on to future generations, Marshall's objective was to work with the Ju/'hoansi to put their former hunting and gathering life behind them, and to establish themselves as farmers and cattle herders instead.

On the basis of his extensive first-hand experience, Marshall considered that the traditional hunting and gathering life of the Ju/'hoansi was extremely hard, or 'thin' as one of his principal subjects had put it. In practice, it was very difficult to make a living by hunting and gathering in the Kalahari and the Ju/'hoansi often went hungry. They were also beset with malaria and other illnesses. As Herero cattle herders encroached on one part of their lands, and another large part was assigned to a game reserve, their tenuous way of life became even less viable and they gravitated en masse to a government centre set up at Tjum!kui, a place where the Marshalls had set up camp in the 1950s. By 1978, when Marshall returned, the Ju'hoansi were living there on food handouts and makework jobs. Drunkenness, violence, hunger and tuberculosis were all common. Desperate to find an income, young Ju/'hoansi men were signing up with the South African Defence Force to fight the SWAPO guerillas who were then still actively engaged in the struggle for Namibian independence.

Marshall chronicled these desperate circumstances in *N!ai, the Story of a !Kung Woman*, co-directed with Adrienne Mesmer and released in 1980. This is constructed around a biographical portrait of a woman whom Marshall had known since she was a child in the 1950s, and he uses this as a vehicle through which to chart the general decline of the Ju/'hoansi. In authorial terms, *N!ai* represented a radical departure from Marshall's earlier work. During the twenty years in which he had been refused a visa by the

**6.4** Left, *N!ai, the Story of a !Kung Woman* (1980) – 'Death is dancing with me'; right, *A Kalahari Family: Death by Myth* (2001) – captured by a night-time camera, an elephant destroys the Ju/hoansi irrigation system.

South African government, Marshall had worked on a number of general documentary productions and had moved far beyond the modest event-sequence films that he had developed with Timothy Asch in the 1960s. Among other projects, he had worked as a combat cinematographer during the civil war on Cyprus in 1964–65, while in 1967 he had collaborated with Fred Wiseman in making *Titicut Follies*, a searingly uncompromising observational portrait of an institution for the criminally insane in Bridgewater, Massachusetts.

*N!ai* was commissioned for US television and it bears the hallmarks of television documentaries of that era. Although it features a number of passages of observational shooting, including some disturbing sequences of Ju/'hoansi people arguing violently with one another, the film as a whole is structured around a series of formal to-camera pieces by the principal protagonist (figure 6.4, left). Partly in speech and partly in song, N!ai laments her difficult circumstances at Tjum!kui, though she attributes these not so much to troubles brought from outside but rather to the jealousy of her fellow Ju/hoansi who resent the fact that she gets paid generously for allowing herself to be photographed by tourists and other outsiders, including Marshall himself. The film is ostensibly (though not very convincingly) narrated by her too, with her commentary voiced by a voice-artist speaking English with an African accent. Although *N!ai* was participatory in the sense that it was clearly based on the close relationship between Marshall and a number of Ju/'hoansi whom he had known over a long period, there is very little evidence that the Ju/'hoansi had played any kind of role in the direction of the film.

Although N!ai herself expresses great regret in the English-voiced commentary for the freedoms of the old way of life – supported visually by extracts from the earlier films with newly enhanced soundtracks – Marshall had concluded by this time that a return to hunting and gathering was simply not sustainable. Not only had the territories available to the Ju/'hoansi been drastically reduced, but many young people who had grown up in Tjum!kui had no idea how to hunt or gather. Very few Ju'/hoansi of any age were interested in returning to a life that had been too 'thin' anyway.

To find a way out of this dilemma, in 1982, together with Claire Ritchie, a British social anthropologist, Marshall set up a foundation to promote agriculture and cattle herding among the Ju/'hoansi. This was initially funded by a donation from Marshall's father, Laurence, but later attracted other major donors who would eventually contribute millions of dollars. But in attempting to achieve this seemingly simple humanitarian solution, Marshall and Ritchie soon came up against a number of obstacles. These included White farmers who wanted to employ the Ju/'hoansi as labourers, Herero cattle herders who wanted the Ju'/hoansi lands and waterholes, and, most intractable of all, a set of ideas about the Ju'/hoansi that Marshall would come to describe as the 'Bushman myth'.

In effect, after returning to the Ju'/hoansi in 1978, Marshall dedicated the rest of his life both as an individual and as a film-maker to combating this 'myth' which, despite its insubstantial foundation, has had very real material consequences for the Ju'/hoansi. In the past, the 'myth' had taken various forms but by the 1970s, it consisted of a highly idealised conception of the Ju'/hoansi as noble hunter-gatherers who lived in perfect harmony with the environment. Poignantly, this iteration of the 'myth' was informed, at least in part, by Marshall's own films from the 1950s. But since then it had been much enhanced and elaborated in popular mass media, as exemplified particularly by the feature film, *The Gods Must Be Crazy*, first released in 1980, which became a huge box-office success around the world.[17]

In the course of the 1980s, Marshall made a number of films that were more in the nature of activist films than ethnographic works. Although he directed these films, he largely handed over the shooting to others and began to appear in front of the lens, playing a leading role in the campaigns to develop Ju'/hoansi farming and herding. Some of these films were shot in video, since this was much cheaper and allowed the extended filming of political meetings. But in the early 1990s, Marshall began working on a major film project that would combine the material shot for these activist films with his earlier work from the 1950s as well as with a large quantity of archival material from other sources. Eventually, this would result in *A Kalahari Family*, a five-part, six-hour series made for television, completed in 2002.[18]

This series charts the experiences of one particular Ju'/hoansi family over fifty years, starting from the time that they first met the Marshalls in 1950. The first film in the series is based on material from the Marshalls' expeditions in the 1950s, but all the remaining films – co-directed by Claire Ritchie – concern Marshall's very personal twenty-year campaign to combat the 'Bushman myth'. As these films describe, it was not only the international development agencies and the SWAPO government that came to power after Namibian independence in 1990 that bought into this myth, but so too did the people who came to control the foundation that he and Ritchie had set up to promote Ju/'hoansi agriculture and cattle-herding. All these third parties, in their different ways, believed that the Ju/'hoansi should continue to live a 'traditional' hunting and gathering life within government-sponsored game conservancies, where they would supposedly derive an income from providing services of various kinds to visiting big game hunters, as well as from tourists and film-makers who would be charged for photographing the Ju/'hoansi themselves.

According to the evidence presented in *A Kalahari Family*, the income that the Ju/'hoansi derive from these sources has never been more than pitiful. Meanwhile, little or no money has been invested in Ju/'hoansi farming and herding activities, which in any case have been blighted by attacks from elephants and lions, both protected on game conservation principles (figure 6.4, right). At the same time, however, large sums have been spent on outside development consultants, managers and scientific experts who have been flown in from far and wide to produce large numbers of reports. The final part of the series, entitled *Death by Myth*, offers a truly devastating critique of the pieties of 'sustainable development', showing very powerfully how degrading it is for the Ju/'hoansi to live in squalor, dependent on handouts, only to be obliged to dress up from time to time in traditional costume and pretend that they still spend their time hunting and gathering for the edification of European tourists and film-makers. The six-hour series ends on a sombre note: after more than two decades and the investment of large amounts of money, the circumstances of the family who are the centre of the film remain extremely precarious. If anything, they seem to be worse off than they were in 1978 when Marshall first returned to the Ju/'hoansi.[19]

*A Kalahari Family* is undoubtedly a masterpiece of television documentary. It succeeds in drawing together a vast body of material, very diverse in nature, and welds it together into a powerful, engaging narrative that amounts to a damning indictment of the way in which the Ju/'hoansi have been treated by agencies supposedly concerned with their welfare. Technically, it is of the highest standard: particularly impressive is the colour grading and post-synching of the sound that gives Marshall's 1950s footage a new lease of life in the first part of the series. But in authorial terms, *A Kalahari Family* is, generally speaking, even further from the norms of ethnographic film-making as I have defined these for the purposes of this book than was *N!ai*. Stylistically, it is heavily narrated, in part by a professional voice, in part by Marshall himself and, as in *N!ai*, in part, but not at all convincingly, by voice artists supposedly speaking the words of the Ju/'hoansi subjects in African-accented English. There are some powerful observational scenes, but interviews, formal and informal, predominate. The camera rarely lingers, the average length of shots is short. To the practised eye, there are innumerable shots that have been set up to ensure continuity or provide editorial 'cover': all manner of Jeeps putatively driven by Marshall speed past waiting cameras in clouds of dust. Specially composed string ensemble music, artfully based on Ju/'hoansi melodies, stir the audience's emotions at appropriate points.

Indeed, as a television documentary, *A Kalahari Family* often seems closer to investigative journalism than to a documentary dedicated to social or cultural matters: indeed, there is even a scene in which Marshall 'doorsteps' a White farmer, only to discover that he is not at home. There is also a marked polemical quality to the films. One cannot help but suspect that the failure of the Ju/'hoansi to be productive farmers is not entirely due to the depredations of elephants and the delusions of development administrators, as the films imply, and that it may also have something to do with the difficulties of changing from hunting and gathering to a farming economy within a matter of a few years. But other than the occasional brief comment to this effect by the various administrators of the Ju/'hoansi foundation, this aspect of the problem is not examined, or certainly not in any depth.

*A Kalahari Family* is abundantly reflexive in that Marshall's presence predominates, either on the screen or on the soundtrack. But, as in *N!ai*, although the Ju/'hoansi are Marshall's (almost) constant companions and therefore clearly participated in the making of the film in that sense, there is no evidence that they played a significant role in actually directing it. Indeed, by the last film of the series, as Jake Homiak has observed, it is not exactly clear for whom Marshall is speaking, if anyone, other than for himself.[20] In the first four films of the series, Marshall is engaged in a recurrent dialogue with the group of Ju/'hoansi whom he has known since the 1950s, though it is evident that there are other Ju/'hoansi with very different views about how to deal with the new circumstances of life. But in the last film, it seems that even some of his closest Ju/'hoansi associates are no longer prepared to go along with his ideas, a fact which, to his great credit, Marshall does not attempt to hide.

None of this should necessarily be considered a criticism of the series as a film-making concept: clearly Marshall felt that the interests of the Ju/'hoansi were best served at the turn of the millennium by a series of campaigning films that would be seen by millions rather than by more narrowly ethnographic works that could never reach such wide audiences. He had a strong and critical view to impart, sincerely held and based on vast experience. Moreover, he was prepared to articulate this view even if he could not carry all his Ju/'hoansi collaborators with him and even if it involved criticising the very foundation that he and Claire Ritchie had set up. Surely no one could deny that *A Kalahari Family* is a most powerful example of sustained adversarial film-making on behalf of an indigenous people. But there is equally little doubt that it is primarily Marshall's voice that is speaking through these films.

## THE LIMITS OF PARTICIPATION AND REFLEXIVITY

The sharing of authorship through the adoption of participatory and reflexive praxes from the 1970s onwards greatly enriched the genre of ethnographic film. Facilitated by the development of portable synchronous sound and subtitled speech, these 'ways of doing' ethnographic film resulted in a large number of films which, in a broad variety of ways, afforded a much stronger voice to the subjects, in both a metaphorical and literal sense. However, the experience of the MacDougalls in making *Takeover* and of John Marshall in his long struggle to secure a viable economic future for his Ju/'hoansi subjects serve as a salutary reminder of the very limited power of documentary film – of any kind, not just ethnographic documentary – to combat powerful vested interests, however admirably participatory, or however conscientiously reflexive that film-making might be.

Moreover, a commitment to a collaborative praxis does not necessarily avoid conflicts of interest with members of the group or community with whom the film is made. John Marshall's gradual falling-out with even his closest Ju/hoansi collaborators offers one sobering example of this. Another is provided by the reaction of the Aurukun Aboriginal community to Judith MacDougall's film, *The House-Opening*. As described in Chapter 5, this film concerns a ceremony to cleanse a recently deceased man's house of the pollution of death and was narrated by his widow, Geraldine Kawanka. But when the MacDougalls screened the film back in Aurukun, they discovered to their surprise that not everyone in the community appreciated it. For Aurukun, now as much as then, is a highly divided community, riven by political factions. At the time the film was made, Geraldine was a leading member of one of these factions, and as chair of the community council she was also personally very powerful. The making of the film was therefore seen by her opponents as reinforcing her position. But given the nature of their relationship with the community as a whole, it was simply not possible for the MacDougalls to allow these conflicts to emerge in their films, nor to position themselves in relation to them.

In an interview given in 1994, David MacDougall commented that he felt, in retrospect, that the participatory mode of film-making that he and Judith had developed in Australia had been merely a transitional strategy, appropriate to a particular historical moment, but no longer valid once Aboriginal film-makers had begun producing their own material.

> in a sense it was a kind of idealisation, perhaps, of a notion of solidarity between Aboriginal people and sympathetic Whites. My view of it now is that it was a kind of film-making that rather confused the issues. In those films one never really knows quite who's speaking for whom, and whose interests are being expressed. It is not clear what in the film is coming from us and what is coming from them … it's a slightly uncomfortable marriage of interests that masks a lot of issues.[21]

In the late 1980s, after more than a decade working as film-makers for the Australian Institute of Aboriginal Studies, the MacDougalls resigned and set themselves up as freelance film-makers. As I describe in Chapter 14, they then began to make films that in authorial terms represented in some respects a reversion to the 'way of doing' ethnographic film that they had practised in Africa in the 1970s.

Under certain historical circumstances, such as those in which Ian Dunlop was working in Australia in the 1970s and 1980s, and Sarah Elder and Leonard Kamerling in Alaska at around the same time, it may well be possible to identify a common 'creative space', in Elder's phrase, where the interests of film-makers and subjects meet, which, in both these particular cases, was a common interest in making a cultural record for future generations. However, even in these cases, in which the film-makers thought of themselves, in good faith, as making the films not only *with* the subjects but also *for* the subjects, they also intended to address audiences beyond the communities in which they were made. In order to do so, it was necessary both to shoot and cut the films in ways that made communication with those audiences not merely possible but also effective, or, to put it another way, to author the films in accordance with the conventions of documentary cinema which, by definition, were alien to the communities with whom the films were made. Hence Elder realised that she and Kamerling were engaged not in 'community-determined' but rather 'community-collaborative' film-making.

The general conclusion that one can draw from the varied experiences of collaborative film-making by English-language ethnographic film-makers from the 1970s to the 1990s that we have considered in this chapter is that, ultimately, it is necessary to come to terms with what Clifford Geertz, in relation to ethnographic writing, called 'the un-get-roundable fact' that all ethnographic accounts, be they in form of films or texts, involve 'the representation of one sort of life in the categories of another'.[22] The 'un-get-roundable' fact in the case of ethnographic documentary film-making is that films have to be authored in such a way as to make them accessible to audiences beyond the community in which they were made. This applies not only in situations where the cultural differences between the subjects and the audiences are great, but even in situations where they are small or non-existent. This authorship may be tempered by the participation of the subjects in the conception and realisation of a film, and there may be a way in which a film based on such participation can be 'for them' in a real and genuine way. But in the last analysis, there is no getting around the simple if banal proposition that any ethnographic documentary is aimed, eventually if not immediately, at broader audiences, and that to communicate with those audiences, films need to be authored in such a way that those audiences will understand and appreciate them.

## *Notes*

1 This section draws on the contributions by James Fox and E. Douglas Lewis to the *festschrift* dedicated to Timothy Asch's work, which was edited by Lewis and published ten years after Asch's tragically premature death in 1994 (see Fox 2004; Lewis 2004a, 2004b, 2004c). There is some inconsistency in the sources about the exact release dates of Asch's films: here I have followed those given in the Appendix of the *festschrift*, on pp. 286–7.

2 Lewis (2004c), 280, n. 1 reports that the dubbing voice belongs to E. M. Pono, listed in the film's credits as the 'transcriber' of the Rotinese narration. In addition to this film, Fox made another, shorter film on Roti with the Asches, *The Spear and the Sword*, released in 1988, which concerns the bridewealth negotiations between two Rotinese families.

3 The title of the second film is clearly a play on the famous catch-phrase 'the medium is the message', first coined by the media theorist, Marshall McLuhan, in the early 1960s, and later reworked in the title of *The Medium is the Massage*, the book that he wrote with the graphic designer Quentin Fiore (McLuhan and Fiore 1967).

4 See Connor, Asch and Asch (1986). Neither Fox nor Lewis has published dedicated accompanying texts, but they have both produced publications that are complementary to the films (Fox 1977, Lewis 1988). Both Fox and Lewis also collaborated with the Asches in shooting material on other topics, but this footage remains unedited.

5 Asch (1986), 49–53.

6 This account of Dunlop's work in Yirrkala draws primarily on Deveson with Dunlop (2012), Morphy (2007), 330–7, and Morphy (2012). I am also very grateful to Pip Deveson for reviewing and commenting upon this section. Shortly before he began work at Yirrkala, Dunlop also directed *Towards Baruya Manhood*, a series of nine films made in collaboration with the French anthropologist, Maurice Godelier. Shot in 1969 and released in 1972, and with a total running time of 465 minutes, these films concern the male initiation ceremony of the Baruya of the eastern Highlands of Papua New Guinea. In terms of general praxis, these films are in much the same vein as his earlier documentation films in Central Australia in that they offer a heavily narrated descriptive account of the ceremony. Although they were shot on 16 mm colour film and have synchronous sound, Dunlop found, to his great disappointment, that neither Godelier's command of the language, nor that of the consultant linguist was sufficiently precise for him to be able to subtitle the films (see Deveson with Dunlop 2012), 57. A shorter version of the film in French, a mere 202 minutes, was released in 1976 under the title *Planète Baruya*.

7 *Conversations with Dundiwuy Wanambi* was awarded the Royal Anthropological Institute Film Prize in 1996. The judges commended particularly the editing by Pip Deveson.

8 Howard Morphy has published a companion text that offers a detailed exegesis of the complex symbolism of the songs, dances and paintings that feature in this film,

as well as an account of the general process of making the film (Morphy 1984). Some years later, he also published a more general theoretical reflection on the interpretation of ritual symbolism that is primarily based on this film (Morphy 1994).

9 See Morphy (1994), 142. Dean Semler later went on to win an Oscar for Best Cinematography for his work on Kevin Costner's *Dances with Wolves* (1990).

10 See Deveson with Dunlop (2012), 73; Morphy (1994).

11 See Myers (1993) for a detailed review.

12 This scene is reproduced as a video extract in Deveson with Dunlop (2012), 68.

13 In 2006, Film Australia re-released the film in a slightly shorter 199-minute version on a 2-disc DVD, accompanied by two other films about the *djungguwan*, one of which was shot in 1966 by Roger Sandall, the other in 2002 by Trevor Graham. See filmaustraliaceremony.com.au/s2.htm.

14 This account of the work of Elder and Kamerling is drawn from two main sources, Elder (1995) and Miller (2007).

15 For a comprehensive listing of the films made by Elder, Kamerling and Waters with the Yu'pik, see https://store.der.org/elder-sarah-c685.aspx.

16 See Chapter 2, pp. 93–4 for a discussion of potlatch ceremonies in connection with Edward Curtis's film, *In the Land of the Head Hunters* (1914).

17 In *N!ai* there is a farcical sequence following the multiple takes required to shoot just one scene of *The Gods Must Be Crazy*. On the 'Bushman myth', the definitive work is by Robert Gordon and Stuart Douglas (2000), the first edition of which directly influenced John Marshall (see 1993), 4. See also Gordon (2003), Van Vuuren (2013).

18 Among the film-makers who worked with Marshall during this period were Ross McElwee and John Bishop (Bishop 2007). Marshall shared much of the editing of *A Kalahari Family* with Sandeep Bhusan Ray, and was advised and assisted by a number of anthropologists, including Megan Biesele, Robert Gordon and Marjorie Shostak. See https://store.der.org/marshall-john-c331.aspx.

19 Wiessner (2003) provides detailed data that support Marshall's general conclusions while a film shot in 2007 and released in 2010, *Bitter Roots*, directed by Adrian Strong, who worked as an agronomist with Marshall in the 1980s, and also featuring Claire Ritchie, shows that seven years after filming for *A Kalahari Family* had been completed, both the vulnerable situation of the Ju/'hoansi family at the centre of the film and the tension between wildlife conservation and the promotion of Ju/'hoansi farming remained entirely unchanged.

20 See Homiak (2003), 132.

21 Grimshaw and Papastergiadis (1995), 44–5.

22 Geertz (1988), 144.

# 7

# The subject as author: indigenous media and the *Video nas Aldeias* project

## THE DEFINITION OF 'INDIGENOUS MEDIA'

If the emergence of portable sychronous sound in the 1960s was fundamental to the emergence of more overtly participatory modes of ethnographic film authorship over the following decade, a further technological development in the 1970s facilitated a film-making praxis in which those who had traditionally been only the subjects of ethnographic films could become the authors of their own films about their lives. This technological development took the form of portable, easy-to-use and, above all, cheap analog video camcorders.[1]

The widespread availability of this new technology from the late 1970s led to a great efflorescence of projects across the globe aimed at empowering 'subaltern' groups – that is, those who are in in some sense politically disadvantaged – by teaching them to make films that could serve to raise awareness of common problems and interests within the group, and which could then communicate these issues to outsiders, including, most importantly, other groups in a similar situation to their own. In the global North, these projects have involved such diverse groups as ethnic minorities, senior citizens and unemployed young people while in the global South, video has been a tool of 'development communication' for similarly diverse groups, including peasant farmers, women's credit cooperatives and street children. In the Americas and Australasia particularly, a number of anthropologists and others took advantage of this new technology to encourage the development of film-making projects among communities – variously described as indigenous, First Nations or Aboriginal – who had previously featured strongly in the canon of ethnographic film as subjects.

In the 1980s, Faye Ginsburg coined the term 'indigenous media' to refer very specifically to these self-representational film-making projects among culturally distinctive minorities living within the 'settler states' that arose as result of European colonial expansion. In her original usage, the 'media' part of the term referred not merely to the films themselves as physical artefacts but also to the fact that these films serve to 'mediate', that is, both to represent and impact upon social relations, both within the groups that produced them and between those groups and outsiders. Typically, she argued, 'indigenous media' productions are concerned with healing the 'ruptures in time and history' brought about by contact with the settler states. As such, they can be both 'assertive and conservative' of local identities, on the one hand documenting injustices and demanding reparations, while on the other seeking to conserve a record of traditional subsistence, religious or ceremonial practices.[2]

Subsequently, other authors have sought to apply the term 'indigenous media' to community film-making projects taking place within polities that are not 'settler states', at least not in the classic European colonial mould, such as, for example, the People's Republic of China, Taiwan and Russia. The term has also been applied within Europe, including to projects among the Saami in northern Scandinavia, and even to Welsh-language programming on television in the UK. This broadening of usage has been accompanied by some scholarly debate as to whether it is appropriate to use the term 'indigenous' in relation to these further instances of community-based film-making, given the diversity of meanings that this term has across the world.[3]

Even when used in the restricted sense originally envisaged by Ginsburg (i.e. in relation to film-making by members of communities in the Americas and Australasia), 'indigenous media' is a term that has come to be applied to a very wide range of productions – technically, editorially and budgetarily – from major feature-length fiction films with substantial budgets that have been screened at the Sundance and Cannes film festivals to ultra low-budget videos about such practical matters as the use of pesticides, forest management and the sinking of water boreholes. In between lie many other forms, including, activist films of various kinds, melodramas and music videos, the latter being a form that is increasingly used by younger members of indigenous communities not merely as a vehicle for musical performance as such but also as a means of expressing social and political ideas through the lyrics. All these various forms of 'indigenous media' production have intensified and diversified considerably over the last two decades as the Web has made it increasingly easy to distribute such media productions at minimal cost.

A comprehensive treatment of the vast range of different activities going on across the world that have been, or could be, classed under the umbrella of 'indigenous media' lies far beyond the possibilities of this chapter. Ginsburg herself has published a relatively recent review of this proliferating field, paying particular attention to the emergence of indigenous television stations in Australia, Canada, New Zealand, Taiwan and in certain countries in Latin America (notably Mexico and Bolivia), as well as to the emergence of 'Fourth Cinema', that is, internationally distributed fictional feature films that not only treat indigenous themes, but are produced according to indigenous ideas about collaborative authorship. While outsiders, including in some cases anthropologists and ethnographic film-makers, might have contributed in the early days to the emergence of a few of the more high-profile contributions to the indigenous mediascape, it is clear that the relative importance of these outsider contributions has long been superseded in most instances by that of the indigenous media producers themselves.[4]

In this chapter, I confine myself to a very limited arena within the general field of indigenous media, namely, an overview historical account of projects in which ethnographers and other outsiders have played a leading role as enablers of film-making by indigenous communities, with a particular emphasis on projects in Amazonia, as this is where my own regional expertise as an anthropologist lies. In the latter part of the chapter, I give more detailed consideration to the *Video nas Aldeias* project in Brazil, one of the most successful and long-running of indigenous media projects in the world, but still strangely under-appreciated in the English-language literature.

In considering these examples, I am particularly concerned to assess what the existence of these indigenous media projects implies for the other modes of ethnographic film authorship discussed here. Do indigenous media complement or add to these other modes of film-making, or do they, in fact, simply make them obsolete? At the very least, as Ginsburg has commented, the emergence of indigenous media means that external ethnographic film-makers no longer have a monopoly on the visual representation of cultural difference, thus providing the opportunity for a 'salutary dialogue' between practitioners of the two forms. But some authors have gone further, arguing that indigenous media render all ethnographic film-making by outsiders no longer necessary. If the ultimate goal of ethnography, as formulated by Malinowski himself, is 'to grasp the native's point of view ... to realise his vision of his world', then surely, these authors contend, this function is now fulfilled by indigenous media. As Jay Ruby has asked, in his characteristically forthright way, 'If anthropologists want to see the world through native eyes, why don't they simply watch their videos?'[5]

## FILM-MAKING AND CULTURE

When projects to introduce video technology to culturally distinctive minority communities, such as indigenous groups in Amazonia or Aboriginal communities in Australia, were first developed in the 1980s, certain authors argued that given that the whole apparatus of film-making is so burdened with hegemonic Western cultural values, far from empowering these communities, as the initiators of these projects liked to claim, the new technology in fact undermined those communities' own distinctive values and thereby served to subjugate them even further.[6]

That film-making, be it for fictional or non-fictional purposes, embodies certain specific values is surely beyond doubt. In the sense that these values are not given in nature, but are the product of human invention, one must necessarily describe them as 'cultural' in the broadest sense. There are certain values of this kind embedded in the very technology itself, in relation, for example, to the aspect ratio of framing, the rendering of colour and the perspective offered by standard camera lenses. There is also a whole series of conventions associated with the 'language' of film, be it to do with matters of detail such as the use of close-ups, or more generally, in relation to issues of characterisation and narrative structure. Film-making also poses a raft of culturally variable issues to do with what it is appropriate to see, by whom and under what circumstances, as well as with questions of ownership over images and the right to make the representations in the first place. It also entails certain fundamental philosophical or epistemological assumptions, which also cannot be taken as natural givens, about the relationship between the visible exterior of the human body and interior psychology, about the hierarchy of importance between sound and vision, and perhaps most fundamentally, about the relationship between representational realism and objective reality.[7]

As film-making technology was first invented and developed in the West, there is a tendency to assume that all the cultural values associated with its use are therefore 'Western'. From there, it is a short step to conclude that the diffusion of film-making technology propagates Western values and serves therefore to reinforce Western political power. However, this conclusion begs many intermediate questions. In the first place, although the technology and the conventions associated with its use may indeed have first been developed in the West, this does not necessarily mean that the values associated with this technology are exclusive to the West: they may also be shared by other cultural traditions, at least to some degree. The fact that this technology has been adopted so enthusiastically in the geographical East, and that it is in Asia that most of this technology is now manufactured, certainly suggests that these values are not exclusively Western.

But even if one were to accept the argument that the values associated with this technology were exclusively Western, at least in origin, this would not necessarily entail that they serve to propagate Western political power: these values may be neutral in their effects, they may be adopted so enthusiastically that they become an integral part of a given non-Western culture, or they may even be turned around so that they can be used against Western political power. As Ginsburg has argued, the view that the effect of the new technology will be necessarily destructive of non-Western values depends in great measure upon an anachronistic conception of culture as static and unchanging so that, by definition, any innovation is necessarily negative in its consequences. She argues rather for a more dynamic conception of culture and cultural identities as processes that are in a state of constant construction and transformation, within which new signifying practices such as media production may be accommodated in a positive fashion without any necessary loss of cultural identity.[8]

SOME EARLY CASE STUDIES

Ultimately, one might think, the question of the degree to which, or the form in which, the values associated with film-making technology can be reconciled with ideas about visual representation in non-Western societies is a matter that could be resolved by a series of empirical case studies. But isolating the various factors involved is easier said than done. In practice, in the relatively few systematic studies that have been carried out of self-representational film-making by non-Western groups, it has generally proved very difficult to disentangle the effects that arise from simple lack of experience in the use of the medium from those that could be attributed to local cultural norms.

The first and most celebrated study of this kind took place even before the development of cheap video technology. This was the project directed by John Adair and Sol Worth in the Navajo community at Pine Springs, Arizona, in 1966. Whereas later video-based self-representational projects have usually been motivated by an intention to empower the film-makers' communities politically, this was more in the nature of a social scientific field experiment. Lasting a total of two months, its aim was to explore how cultural factors might influence the way that individuals use film as a medium of communication. With the assistance of the now-eminent anthropologist Richard Chalfen, then a graduate student, Worth and Adair gave seven Navajo a minimal, non-prescriptive training in basic film-making techniques, based on spring-wound 16 mm cameras. They used black and white film, and there was no provision for the recording of sound. The participants were then invited to make films about whatever was important to them.

Most of them chose straightforward local themes: traditional crafts (weaving and silversmithing), healing practices, the construction of a new well. However, one film-maker, Alfred Clah, who was an art student in Santa Fe, New Mexico at the time, made a more abstract film, entitled *Intrepid Shadows*. This explored movements, shapes and shadows in the natural environment and features an anonymous intruder, apparently identified with the film-maker himself since this intruder is wearing a traditional Yeibechai mask modified by the addition of a vertical film-strip on the face and a 'nose' resembling

7.1 *Navajo Film Themselves* (1966). *Intrepid Shadows*, left, featured a character in a traditional mask modified by a vertical strip resembling film stock and a 'nose' suggesting a camera lens. Right, in *The Navajo Silversmith*, the main character walks a great deal, associated by Worth and Adair with the 'long journey' trope of Navajo story-telling.

a camera lens (figure 7.1, left). These films were subsequently distributed as a collective compilation work entitled *Navajo Film Themselves*.[9]

Worth and Adair concluded that the films produced by the Navajo featured certain narrative codes that distinguished them quite clearly from the first films made by Anglo-Americans. As a particularly significant example, they noted that there was a marked tendency to include a great deal of walking through the natural environment, not just as a bridge between two places or activities, but as a focus of interest in itself (figure 7.1, right). This they associated with the strong emphasis on travel and the 'long journey' in the narratives of traditional Navajo myths and stories. However, some subsequent commentators have asked whether this preoccupation with walking was not merely a sign of the film-makers' lack of expertise.[10]

Another complication arises from the fact that by the time that non-Western novice film-makers gain access to the technology, they have usually been exposed to Western media as viewers, through television or feature films, and therefore are likely to have already been influenced by Western media values. This was certainly the case with the Navajo, and it has also generally been the case with the more recent self-representational video projects involving non-Western film-makers in the Americas and Australasia. Even in instances where this prior exposure has been minimal or non-existent, as in certain cases in Amazonia, it is arguable that the very process of instructing the indigenous people in the use of the technology already serves to inhibit them from using it in their own culturally idiosyncratic manner.

Yet notwithstanding the difficulty of carrying out any kind of strictly controlled test, there is certainly some evidence to suggest that the values embedded in the technology are not so overwhelming as to make it impossible for film-makers from non-Western backgrounds to make non-fiction films that represent, in some degree, a response to their own cultural norms of representation. This may be in relation not just to the aesthetic characteristics of the films themselves, but also in relation to the way in which the production of the films is organised.

In a pioneering study of video production in the Warlpiri Aboriginal community of Yuendumu in the 1980s, Eric Michaels identified various ways in which the films produced by the Warlpiri film-makers reflected distinctively Aboriginal cultural values. Mostly this concerned the impact of prior kinship relationships on the control of the equipment and on who appeared in the films, but Michaels also discerned some more aesthetic effects. For example, in a film in which an old man related a well-known story about a notorious massacre of Aboriginal people by police in the 1920s, the man walked into the field of the camera from a considerable distance. Michaels associates this with 'bringing in the Dreaming' at the beginning of a traditional ceremony, whereby the performers dance into the ceremonial ground from the particular direction from which the ancestral story underlying their performance is deemed to have come. The same film also featured many long pans over the landscape, punctuated by zooms in and out, which, as the cameraman explained in a later interview, was a conscious reference to ancestral Dreamtime tracks.[11]

Similarly, in his analysis of films produced by Kayapo film-makers involved in the Kayapo Video Project that he enabled in Central Brazil in the early 1990s, Terence Turner identified various ways in which these films reflected certain key Kayapo ideas about social relations and aesthetics (figure 7.2). In Turner's earliest ethnographic writings about the Kayapo, which predate their use of video, a recurrent theme is the way in which social and political relations are actively created and maintained through public political dialogues and by ceremonial performances. These social and political relations are also sustained through the elaborate forms of body decoration and ceremonial regalia for which the Kayapo are justly famous. Turner argued that for the Kayapo, the camcorder represented a highly effective means for recording these socially generative forms of public performance and corporeal expression. He also stressed that from the Kayapo point of view, the motivation for making these recordings was not merely to contribute to the video archive that he had set up as an integral part of the Kayapo Video Project; equally significant, indeed perhaps more so, these video recordings were also a way of increasing the publicly perceived importance of the performances being recorded, while at the same time conferring prestige on the person actually doing the recording.

Turner also discerned distinctively Kayapo qualities in the aesthetic characteristics of the films themselves. He noted that the Kayapo spontaneously tended to shoot long shots, alternating pans and midshots while avoiding extreme close-ups of the face. Once in the edit suite, they showed little

7.2 Left, Mokuka, of the Kayapo Video Project, at a rally in 1989 to protect against the Altamira dam on the Xingu River. Right, the Kayapo also use camcorders to record traditional ceremonies.

interest in cutting this material down, which Turner attributed to fact that the elimination of material would clash with one of the central principles of Kayapo thought, whereby social and cultural life is conceived of as a constant, repetitive but also cumulative reiteration of certain foundational schemas laid down at the dawn of time. In collective ceremonies, these principles of replication and reiteration are played out in successive repetitions of the same dance patterns, with each performance increasing in social value as it integrates additional elements. For the Kayapo, this represents the pinnacle of beauty, both as an aesthetic ideal and as a moral and social principle. Thus, Turner proposed, in preserving every repetition of every performance, each with its successive increment of regalia and participants, the Kayapo editor, far from proving himself to be merely inexperienced, as the sceptic might suppose, was in fact replicating the reiterative structure of the ceremony itself and thereby producing a visual representation that in Kayapo terms is supremely beautiful.[12]

This concern to identify enduring non-Western attributes in the films produced by non-Western film-makers is, of course, an entirely valid goal of ethnographic enquiry. However, there is a risk that in pursuing this goal too intently, one can come to endorse the same static view of culture as those who presume that the effects of the new technology will necessarily be destructive. In the absence of any firm ethnographic evidence one way or another as to the precise cultural effects of film-making technology, I would argue on first principles that it is surely inevitable that the Kayapo, in common with other non-Western film-makers, take on board certain new values when they use film-making technology, particularly if they seek to address Western audiences. Yet this need not necessarily be a negative matter, nor need it necessarily undermine their distinctive non-Western identity more generally. As Mokuka, one of the leading contributors to the

Kayapo Video Project, famously asked during a visit to a film festival that we organised in Manchester in 1992, does the fact that he is holding a camera mean that he is no longer a Kayapo? The answer to this must surely be a resounding 'no'.

But more fundamental in my view than any of these questions about the cultural freight of non-fiction film-making processes, and certainly of greater significance for the general arguments of this book, is the more ethical and political question posed by indigenous media projects, namely, how should these insider accounts be assessed relative to those produced by outsiders with ethnographic objectives? For, however good, or however poor, the fit between the values embedded in film-making technology and the pre-existing values of the community engaged in a self-representational project, the films that emerge from those projects are, by definition, insider accounts and are therefore bound to be different from those produced by outsiders. From an ethnographic point of view, are they merely different, or is one form of representation in some sense more valuable than the other?

## INSIDER VERSUS OUTSIDER PERSPECTIVES

At first sight, indigenous media projects might seem to offer an effective solution to the sometimes seemingly intractable political or ethical issues raised by ethnographic film-making when this is in the hands of outsiders. In some situations, local communities may have become so deeply suspicious of films made by outsiders that self-representation might be the only form of film authorship that they will accept. However, this is far from being universally the case. According to Turner, the Kayapo positively welcome films made by outsiders, and do not see them in any way as being at odds with, or in contradiction to, their own self-representational productions.[13]

On looking at the proposition more closely, the limitations of the idea that all ethnographic film-making can now simply be consigned to the subjects soon become apparent. There is, first of all, the general methodological point that, notwithstanding the Malinowskian rhetoric, ethnography does not consist merely of reproducing, in a literal manner, the 'native's point of view'. Certainly, a descriptive account of the social life of a given community by a member of that community can be of great ethnographic value. But for the reasons discussed at some length in the General Introduction to this book, in order to produce an ethnographic account that goes beyond the merely descriptive, it is also necessary to engage in some form of ethnographic analysis. This applies whether or not there is any major cultural difference between the observer and the observed. That is, it is as true of an account of life in a Californian research laboratory as it is of an account of life in a remote Amazonian village. Insiders can also certainly engage in such analyses and often do, but these analyses are certainly likely to be very different from those of outsiders.

This point also applies regardless of the specific medium of ethnographic representation. There is no more reason for assuming that self-representation using video technology can replace ethnographic film-making by outsiders than there is for suggesting that ethnographic literature has become redundant now that most subjects studied by present-day ethnographers can write, and could therefore produce their own written accounts of their lives, or if they are not literate, could at least speak their thoughts into an audio recorder.

The differences between a self-representational indigenous media account of the life of a given community and the representation that might be produced by an outside ethnographer can be compared to the differences between autobiography and biography in relation to the life of an individual: both offer perspectives that are simultaneously privileged and partial, each in its own particular way.

The fact that film-making is undertaken by insiders is no guarantee that it will not give rise to political or ethical problems since it is rare, whatever the nature of the community, for there to be complete unanimity about how social life should be understood, let alone about how it should be represented. In practice, indigenous media film-making usually falls into the hands of young people, mostly young men, because only they have the interest and, even more importantly, the lack of social commitments that allows them the time necessary to acquire the skills. As in any community, these young people will often view their society in a manner that is quite unlike those of their parents and therefore they will have very different ideas about what should be filmed.

This was the case, for example, with the project in which my then-student Carlos Flores became involved when carrying out his doctoral research in Esperanza Chilatz, a Q'eqchi' Maya community in Alta Verapaz, Guatemala, in the mid-1990s. This project was first developed by a group of young people who were receiving funding that came from various international agencies but which had been channelled through the local Catholic church and the central Guatemalan government (figure 7.3, left). When Carlos arrived, the group was engaged in making films about development-related topics, such as community health issues or the activities of work cooperatives. Carlos then suggested that they should also make films about traditional Mayan religious ceremonies connected with the planting of crops or life-cycle rituals. This idea was warmly welcomed by older members of the community but to his surprise the film-makers themselves were initially reluctant to tackle such topics. It was only later that he realised that this reluctance was due to the fact that in suggesting this change of focus, he

My mother always stresses the importance of our marriage laws

7.3 Modes of collaboration. Left, a Q'echqi' Maya crew enquire about the planting of maize in the community of Esperanza Chilatz, Guatemala, April–May 1995; right, *In Search of a Bororo Mr. Right* (2019) – a romantic comedy with an ethnographic subtext.

was undermining the position of the young film-makers as 'brokers of modernity' and re-empowering the older generation, whose authority had recently been greatly weakened by the civil war that had recently afflicted the region.[14]

Clearly, in communities split by political factions or other social divisions, it is even less likely that the films produced through indigenous media projects will be approved or welcomed by everyone. This may not be anything to do with the actual content of the films; it may simply be on account of the prestige that the act of film-making itself or even the mere possession of the equipment confers. Among the Warlpiri, Michaels found that film-making skills, like many other forms of specialist knowledge in Aboriginal society, became a kind of private property with the result that those who possessed it were reluctant to pass it on to others unless they stood in a particular kinship relationship to themselves. Similarly, in the case of the Kayapo Video Project, Turner discovered, to his chagrin, that guardianship of the cameras that he had introduced became the subject of intense political rivalry, not because they allowed those who held the cameras to control the content of the representations made about the community, but simply on account of the status of the cameras themselves as prestige items.[15]

There are also a series of very pragmatic reasons why it is simply not realistic to rely exclusively on self-representational indigenous media projects as a means of audiovisual ethnography. In the first place, it would be optimistic to presume that large numbers of indigenous groups around the world are anxiously waiting for the opportunity to make films about themselves for the edification of ethnographers. The recent experience of another of my doctoral students, Flavia Kremer, is instructive in this regard. During the fieldwork that she carried out in a Bororo community of Central Brazil in 2011–12, she sought to interest a group of young women to work with her to develop video film-making skills. Her hope was that in doing so she would be able 'to give something back' to the community for allowing her to carry out her research there. But, to her great disappointment, the response was poor. Some young women did express an interest in learning how to take photographs and envisaged using these new skills to put up images on their Facebook pages. But there was little interest in dedicating time and effort to making a film about the remarkable endurance of traditional marriage patterns among the Bororo, which was the topic that particularly interested Flavia herself. In the end, rather than develop a self-representational project, Flavia opted instead to work with two young women on making a collaborative ethnofiction, which she herself shot, and in which these two women visit a distant village in search of a potential husband of the traditionally correct social category. The result was a sort of romantic comedy with an underlying ethnographic subtext. This proved to be a much more effective way of engaging in a collaborative project around a topic of common interest than going through the lengthy procedure of training her subjects to make films themselves. Although the situation that the film created was fictional in the sense that it had been entirely set up by Flavia, the two young women did in fact encounter a young man of the 'right' kinship category whom they both found so attractive that at first they were barely able to speak to him (figure 7.3, right).[16]

Another pragmatic consideration is that even when self-representational projects have taken off well, they have often proved difficult to sustain once the initial impetus and funding provided by outsiders comes to an end. Almost twenty-five years after its foundation, in 2014, the Kayapo Video Project was still in operation, but only fitfully, and was still dependent on inputs from outsiders.[17] But the self-representational video-making project among the Venezuelan Yanomami that Timothy Asch announced in the early 1990s has disappeared without trace, seemingly without producing any films, certainly none that is easily accessible.[18]

The reasons for this vulnerability are not surprising: maintaining the cameras, editing and storing the films, distributing them afterwards, all involve a commitment of resources that the members of such communities typically do not have. But the most significant issue is usually motivation: once the outside enablers of these projects have left, who are the indigenous film-makers making their films for? If they are making them at all, it will be for local people rather than for outsiders. As such, there is no guarantee that they will tackle ethnographic topics of interest to outsiders, nor even that the films that they produce will be comprehensible to outsiders since they could well depend on taken-for-granted knowledge that will be obvious to any insider but completely opaque to an external audience.

Yet another pragmatic issue concerns technical film-making skills. Learning to operate a modern digital camera is not difficult: they are generally very user-friendly and can function in a wide range of lighting conditions. Today, many young indigenous film-makers, like young people generally, can quickly master the basic functions. Conceptually, meanwhile, the idea of using the camera to make a copy of the world is not a complex notion to take on board. Although there is obviously a great deal more to skilled camerawork than simply pressing the 'on' button and copying the world as seen through viewfinder, the functional operation of a moving image camera is not the obstacle that it once was.

However, operating an edit suite is not only technically more complex than operating a camera, but conceptually more complex too. With the arrival of digital technology, editing systems may have become cheaper, easier to operate and portable, but this has done nothing to diminish the conceptual complexities associated with the transformation of the copy of the world produced by a camera into a film with some sort of narrative structure or argument. It is on account of these complexities that editing remains not only the film-making skill that takes the longest time to acquire but is also the point in the film-making process at which culturally variable values about the relationship of representation to reality are most likely – literally – to enter the frame.

In my experience, Western ethnographic film students often have difficulty in mastering the process of editing and what little evidence there is suggests that non-Western novice film-makers not only also find it difficult, but may not even regard it as significant. Eric Michaels found the Warlpiri reluctant to dedicate time to editing and even when they did do so, they were reluctant to cut anything out. For his part, Terence Turner observed that even when the Kayapo Video Project was at its most active, the difference between a fully edited and an unedited video appeared not to be culturally significant for the Kayapo in the sense that they were just as willing to watch unexpurgated rushes as a film edited in a polished manner.

Similarly, in his collaborative work with Q'eqchi' Maya film-makers, Carlos Flores noted that the film-makers' lack of interest in the editorial process contrasted markedly with their enthusiasm for shooting. He attributed this to the fact that the shooting of the film was a very prestigious activity, partly because it was a very visible way of offering a service to the community and partly because it demonstrated the film-makers' connection with the powerful external sponsors of the project. By contrast, the editing of the film was an activity that, for technical reasons, had to take place in a nearby city and, as such, was invisible to the community. The city was also more his environment than theirs and he also had a better technical command of the editing system. All these factors contributed to the indigenous film-makers' feeling that they should leave the editing to him.[19]

In short, although the quality of films produced through indigenous media projects can be remarkably high given the limited amount of training and experience of their makers, for quite understandable reasons they are often of only a moderate standard in a technical sense. When circulated within the community within which they were made, this may well be of no importance, while for external consumption, indigenous media films can still be of ethnographic interest, whatever the technical quality. This interest may derive simply from their status as descriptive accounts of the communities in which they were produced, but additionally, they may also be ethnographically revealing in some way, be it in relation to the topics chosen for filming, the film-making approach adopted, the relationship between film-makers and fellow community members during filming, or the way in which the films are used afterwards. In a series of publications, Turner has shown, for example, how the display of their use of cameras has become an integral part of the Kayapo strategy of performing their 'culture' in an objectified way for external audiences so as to achieve their political objectives on a national and even international stage (figure 7.2, left).[20] However, as a means of ethnographic representation rather than as an object of analysis, indigenous media films can also be very limited, not rising above the purely descriptive documentation of social life.

For all these reasons, it is unrealistic to assume that self-representational indigenous media can act as a direct substitute for ethnographic film-making by outsiders. Rather than thinking of one potentially replacing the other, Faye Ginsburg has suggested that it is more productive to think of the two forms of authorship as operating in the manner of the 'parallax effect': in the same way that the slightly different positioning of the two human eyes allows one to see in three dimensions, Ginsburg suggests that the different perspectives offered by indigenous media and ethnographic film-making by outsiders offer the possibility of a more rounded and comprehensive account of the cultural encounters that are taking place in the highly mediatised arenas of the contemporary world.[21]

Yet although it might be unrealistic to assume that indigenous media can act as a direct substitute for ethnographic film-making by outsiders, it would also be a mistake to consider them as entirely different enterprises. Both may involve an attempt to communicate across a social or cultural boundary, and to do so successfully requires some sort of accommodation with those lying on the other side of that boundary. Moreover, in practical production terms, neither form of authorship is likely to be entirely autonomous. Outside ethnographic film-makers have generally required the collaboration of their subjects to make their films, while indigenous media film-makers typically depend not only on the technology but often, at least to some extent, on skills and ideas introduced by outsiders. In the same way that in the past, there was a tendency for ethnographic film-makers to minimise the contribution of the subjects to the realisation of their films, so too has there been a tendency to minimise the dependence of indigenous media projects on outside support.[22]

In fact, as several contributors to the debate about indigenous media have suggested, one can identify a continuum of productions, ranging from films made by outsiders in the supposedly objective and detached manner recommended by Margaret Mead at one extreme, through the various permutations on collaborative authorship described in Chapters 5 and 6, to self-representational indigenous productions at the other extreme, which themselves range from those that are outward-facing to those that are aimed only at the community in which they were made. In effect then, though their points of departure and underlying objectives may be very different, at the midpoint on this continuum, where productions based on principles of collaborative authorship and outward-facing indigenous media productions meet, the films that emerge from these supposedly radically different processes can be remarkably similar.

## THE *VIDEO NAS ALDEIAS* PROJECT

An important example of this blurring of boundaries between insider and outsider productions is provided by one of the longest-running indigenous media projects in the world, namely, the *Video nas Aldeias* (VnA) project in Brazil. This was launched in 1987 by a Brazilian film-maker, Vincent Carelli, with the support of his wife Virgínia Valadão, an anthropologist, as a unit within an activist NGO concerned with indigenous rights, the Conselho do Trabalho Indigenista (CTI). The project is still ongoing, though since 2000 it has been an autonomous NGO in its own right rather than a dependency of the CTI. It has also moved its base from the city of São Paulo to Olinda in Pernambuco State, on the Atlantic Coast.

Although it has been the subject of relatively little attention in the English-language literature of visual anthropology, VnA has been extraordinarily productive: over more than thirty years, it has produced almost 100 films with forty indigenous communities all over the country, on a broad variety of topics and in a broad variety of formats. In doing so, it has provided training to around forty indigenous film-makers. Any profits arising from the distribution of the films are divided on an equitable basis: 35 per cent to the community where a film was made, 35 per cent to the film-makers and 30 per cent to the programme for reinvestment so as to enable further work by or with indigenous film-makers. Though Valadão died unexpectedly at a young age in 1998, Carelli remains one of the directors of the project.[23]

In the early years particularly, an important principle for the directors of the VnA project was to maintain their independence from the Brazilian government, especially from FUNAI, the government agency responsible for administering indigenous affairs. In order to finance its activities, VnA has sought funding instead from a broad assortment of international donors. Notable contributors have included the Norwegian government aid agency Norad, UNESCO and the Ford, Volkswagen, Guggenheim, Rockefeller and MacArthur foundations. Only recently, and generally in connection with particular projects, has VnA received funding from the Brazilian government through the ministries of Education, Health and the Environment as well as through various academic research funding bodies, while its website suggests that it also receives funding from the state oil producer, Petrobras. Following the withdrawal of support after twenty-five years by the Norwegian government in 2016, VnA has suffered from funding difficulties, but nevertheless continues to operate.

Since it was first launched, the nature of the films produced by VnA has diversified greatly. Initially, it focused very directly on activist objectives: the immediate aim was to use video to support the political claims of indigenous people to fundamental rights, including rights to land and even rights to life, and to counteract the many negative stereotypes held by non-indigenous Brazilians and reproduced in Brazilian mass media. Another recurrent theme of the films produced by VnA, now as much as then, has been the denunciation of the environmental destruction wrought by logging, ranching, mining and the building of dams in or around indigenous areas. But VnA also wanted to make indigenous people more knowledgeable about audiovisual media and of its potential to do good as well as harm. A very important aspect of this aspect of the project therefore was to use video to make Brazilian indigenous groups aware of one another's existence and in this way build a pan-indigenous consciousness that could be channelled towards the achievement of political objectives.

The goal of building up a pan-indigenous consciousness depended in part on the circulation of films but also on creating the conditions for members of different indigenous communities to get to know one another personally through mutual visiting. A relatively early film that is emblematic of this aspect of the work is *Meeting the Ancestors* (*A Arca dos Zo'é*), released in 1993 and directed by Vincent Carelli. This concerns a journey made by a number of Wayampi, an indigenous group who live in the extreme north of Brazil, close to the border with Guyane, and who have been in intermittent contact with the outside world for many years. The purpose of this journey, which was by light aeroplane paid for by VnA, was to visit the Zo'é, a fellow Tupi-speaking group, then only recently contacted, who live hundreds

**7.4** *Video nas Aldeas* cinematographers. Left, Kasiripinã Waiãpi, who shot additional footage for *Meeting the Ancestors* (1993); right, Divino Tserewahú, the highly accomplished Xavante cameraman.

of miles further south, on the other side of the Amazon river. The aim of the visit was for the Wayampi to warn the Zo'é of the dangers arising from contact with the non-indigenous population. The film not only follows the visit itself, but also covers the reactions of the travellers' fellow Wayampi when the travellers return home and screen footage of the Zo'é on a television supplied by VnA.

When he started the VnA project, Carelli intended merely to put his own film-making skills at the service of indigenous communities. But very soon, his indigenous collaborators began to ask to become directly involved as film-makers themselves. At first, indigenous film-makers were instructed informally and merely shot alongside Carelli and his colleagues; their footage might then be included in the final edited version of the film. This was the case, for example, with *Meeting the Ancestors*, for which a Wayampi cameraman, Kasiripiña Waiãpi, shot some of the footage (figure 7.4, left). But since 1997, the running of formal film training workshops has been a central part of VnA's work, taking place either in the indigenous communities themselves, or back at the VnA headquarters in São Paulo, and later in Olinda. The workshops in the communities, which typically last up to a month, have become the vehicle not just for training, but also for the making of films while the workshops are going on. As the training programme has been in place for so long, and will often return a number of times to a given indigenous community over a matter of years, several indigenous film-makers have been able to achieve a very high level of skill, both as directors and as camera operators. Perhaps the most accomplished of all is Divino Tserewahú, a Xavante film-maker, who has now been making films through VnA for around twenty years, not only about his own village, but also about other indigenous groups (figure 7.4, right).

However, for all their many merits, both technical and editorial, the degree to which the films produced by the VnA project can be said to represent the views and interests of the indigenous communities where they are made should be finessed in a number of important respects. First of all, those who have gone through the film-making training are predominantly young men: of the thirty-eight indigenous film-makers currently listed on the website, only three are women, also all young. Second, many of them appear to be the offspring of politically important people in their communities, or to hold a government-funded post as a schoolteacher, medical auxiliary, forest ranger or the like. This would appear to confirm a pattern also noted by Turner among the Kayapo, namely, that film-making technology tends to be monopolised by up-and-coming political leaders, predominantly male. So while the VnA films are undoubtedly examples of self-representational indigenous media, they would appear to be representations that are mostly produced by a very particular group defined by gender, age and political prominence.

But the most important qualification on the self-representational nature of the VnA films concerns the editing. Although training in editing has certainly been offered to indigenous people, the great majority of the films listed in the VnA catalogue have involved non-indigenous editors, sometimes working in collaboration with indigenous editors, but often on their own. Nor is the non-indigenous contribution confined merely to the technical process of editing. While many of the films have been directed and shot entirely by indigenous film-makers, the logistical coordination of the productions, and the distribution of the films that arise from these productions, are also predominantly in the hands of non-indigenous members of the VnA organisation. The same would appear to apply to the funding of these projects.

Probably for these reasons, in aesthetic terms the films produced by VnA mostly conform to standard cosmopolitan documentary film-making codes, though within the broad range of works produced by VnA, the precise style of the films has varied considerably in light of the subject matter and the audience at which the films are aimed. Some films are activist documentaries, held together by voice-over narration. In others, a series of indigenous subjects speak directly to camera, denouncing the invasion of their lands and environmental degradation. Some consist of descriptively ethnographic accounts of ceremonial events, intercut with interviews with participants who provide some sort of exegesis. Other films are more historical, and involve extensive use of archival materials. Yet others are about the work of the VnA itself, particularly the training workshops. There are also a number of portrait films of individual indigenous film-makers, including two of Divino Tserewahú. A number of VnA films are straightforward television programmes, aimed at educating the non-indigenous Brazilian public and featuring the usual panoply of television devices such as talking-head interviews, voice-over, a presenter and jolly extra-diegetic music.

Yet this broad variety of formats includes some recurrent aesthetic characteristics. A particularly important one is the commitment to use indigenous languages, usually subtitled into Portuguese and often into other European languages as well. Unless the subject matter warrants a serious tone, there is, in general, a certain playfulness about the way in which indigenous culture is presented in VnA films that contrasts markedly with the often rather sombre tone of much ethnographic film-making by outsiders. This is something that Carelli and his associates have been particularly pleased to encourage since they see it as capturing the great sense of humour that they have encountered among indigenous people. Again in marked contrast to the works of some external film-makers, far from seeking to minimise the presence of the outside world, the VnA film-makers seemingly go out of their way to stress the juxtaposition of traditional indigenous culture with symbols of modernity, for example, by framing indigenous dancers in traditional dress so that the large satellite dish that brings television to their community is very visible behind them. The underlying message here is very clear: indigenous groups can preserve their distinctive cultural identity while also being part of modern Brazil.

Another recurrent feature is the relating of mythological narratives. In the early films particularly, these narratives are sometimes told with the aid of video special effects (which now look rather dated) or, less frequently, animated cartoons. Alternatively, they may be told through re-enactments by members of the community where the filming is taking place, not in any enclosed theatrical space but in the locations of their everyday life – in their collective houses, on the central plaza of the village, or out in the forest. These re-enactments, which are particularly common in the recent films made in the Upper Xingu region, clearly reflect the centrality of mythological narratives to indigenous life, as well as indigenous ideas about performance and its relationship to historical reality. Even so, in formal terms, these re-enactments are shot and edited in a manner that follows standard cosmopolitan film conventions very closely.

Both the form and subject matter of the films produced by VnA underwent a decisive change when the film-maker Mari Corrêa joined the programme in 1998, following the death of Virgínia Valadão. Although she is Brazilian, Corrêa had trained at VARAN, the centre set up in Paris by Jean Rouch and his associates. Through her influence, the films produced by the project began to pay much greater attention to everyday life. Corrêa's concern was to convince indigenous film-makers that their culture inhered not just in dramatic ceremonial display and mythological narratives, but also in how they lived out their lives on a daily basis.

A particularly striking example of this new work was *From Ikpeng Children to the World*, a video 'letter to the world' from children living in the Xingu Park in Central Brazil. This was released in 2001 and featured a group of four Ikpeng children introducing everyday aspects of their life (including even their latrines) as well as certain traditional subsistence techniques of their grandparents. This film was shot and directed by three adult Ikpeng film-makers, including one woman, though it was edited by Corrêa. Later the same team combined again, though this time with Corrêa in a directorial role, to produce a conventional feature-length documentary for adults, *Pirinop*, released in 2007 and aimed at international audiences. This film combined present-day footage with archival materials and re-enactment to reconstruct the traumatic period following the Ikpeng's first contact with Brazilians and their enforced transfer to the Xingu Park in the 1960s.[24]

In recent years, the films produced by VnA have involved various different combinations of insider and outsider contributions. At one extreme are investigative documentaries, mostly shot, directed and edited by Carelli himself. These films include *Iauaretê – Waterfall of the Jaguars*, released in 2006, about the official demarcation of indigenous sacred sites in the Upper Rio Negro; the harrowing *Corumbiara*, released in 2009, a remarkable first-hand witness account of the contact between isolated indigenous groups and an expanding front of loggers and landowners in Rondônia shot over a twenty-year period; and, most recently of all, the even more disturbing *Martírio*, released in 2016, which traces the long history of land invasion and violence against the Kaiowa Guarani people who live in the extreme south of Brazil. One could debate the extent to which these films should be described as ethnographic films, but they are certainly of great ethnographic interest, and are clearly based on a close collaborative relationship with the indigenous subjects over an extended period. However, in contrast to many other VnA productions, they do not involve indigenous people in any prominent technical roles.

At the other extreme, VnA has continued to produce works that have been shot and directed entirely by indigenous film-makers, even if they have also involved non-indigenous editors. Some of these films are unambiguously ethnographic. Particularly good examples of this latter kind of work are the films made by two brothers who live in the Xingu Park, Takumã and Maricá Kuikuro. These films include *Nguné Elü* (*The Day the Moon Menstruated*), released in 2004, which concerns Kuikuro ideas regarding the link between the moon and menstruation, and *Imbé Gikegü* (*Scent of the Pequi Fruit*), released in 2006, which explores the association between the fruit of the pequi tree and fertility. These films combine actuality footage of collective ceremonial dancing and some scenes of everyday life with interviews and the re-enactment of scenes from origin myths. Although a severe critic might point to certain loose ends, particularly in *Imbé Gikegü*, both films compare well with the work of most outside ethnographic film-makers. One major difference is that as the two brothers are filming their family and friends, a wonderful degree of intimacy with the subjects emanates from the films that no external film-maker could ever hope to match.

In this particular case then, if an anthropologist wanted to know how the Kuikuro view the world, or at least the particular questions of how they view the relationship between the moon and menstruation, or between the pequi fruit and fertility, they would indeed do well to follow Jay Ruby's advice and simply watch their videos. But accomplished though they may be as ethnographic films, they could not in any sense be considered the result of the efforts of Takumã and Maricá alone. As indicated in the credits – entirely openly – these films were made during the course of various VnA training workshops in the film-makers' community and were edited by Leonardo Sette, a non-indigenous Brazilian contributor to VnA, trained in Cuba and France. Two distinguished non-indigenous anthropologists, Carlos Fausto and Bruna Franchetto, are credited with being 'advisers', while Carelli and Corrêa are credited with being 'co-ordinators'.

More recently, the same team worked together again, with some reshuffling of roles, to make *The Hyperwomen*, a feature-length documentary, released in 2011. This concerns the Janurikumalu, a Kuikuru women's festival, variants of which were once performed throughout the Upper Xingu region, which has a certain renown in the literature of Amazonist anthropology on account of the overt teasing of male sexual prowess that it involves. *The Hyperwomen* was jointly directed by Sette and Fausto, co-directed and shot by Takumã and two other Kuikuro cameramen, and produced by Carelli. It is an ethnographic film of the highest technical and editorial quality, and has been screened at a number of major documentary film festivals (figure 7.5).

However, as is clear from *Eu já virei espirito* (*I Have Already Become A Spirit*), released in 2013, which describes the making of *The Hyperwomen*, jointly directed by Fausto and Takumã and shot by Carelli, the ceremony was in danger of disappearing and was only performed on this occasion for the purpose of recording it on film for posterity. (These circumstances explain perhaps why one of the recurrent themes of *The Hyperwomen* is the passing on of songs from one generation of women to the next). More broadly, this film formed part of a more general accord between the director-anthropologist Fausto and Afukaká, the chief of the Kuikuru, to make a series of films in order to preserve traditional Kuikuru culture for future generations. As Fausto has described, this was an agreement that they had arrived at over a cup of coffee early one morning when they happened

**7.5** *The Hyperwomen* (2011). This film about the Janurikumalu ceremony was shot and co-directed by the indigenous cinematographer Takumã Kuikuru.

to coincide – in New York. In short, when considered simply as a filmic text, *The Hyperwomen* may appear to be a very 'classical' ethnographic film, but it is one that has emerged from a far from 'classical' set of circumstances.[25]

These films made with the Kuikuru represent not so much a replacement for ethnographic films made by outsiders as a different way of combining contributions by insiders and outsiders. In that they are based on the identification of a common interest between insiders and outsiders in using film to preserve a record of traditional custom, they are not that different from the collaborative film projects described in Chapter 6, notably those of Ian Dunlop in Australia and of Sarah Elder and Leonard Kamerling in Alaska. What is different is that in the VnA films, the indigenous subjects have been able to play much greater technical and directorial roles, greatly enriching the films in the process.

The VnA project has afforded these indigenous film-makers the opportunity to acquire the necessary skills, not just in providing techni-cal training in the first place, but equally importantly, in providing them with a framework within which to develop their skills over a prolonged period of time. However, VnA is a highly unusual project and one that is not easily replicated. In order to achieve their objectives elsewhere, under different social and historical circumstances, ethnographic film-makers may well need to develop other ways of managing their relationship with their subjects – other 'ways of doing' ethnographic film-making – so that not only will they and their subjects feel that the results are valuable, but also their audiences.

## Notes

1 I am grateful both to Faye Ginsburg (in 2015) and to Carlos Flores (in 2017) for their comments on preliminary drafts of this chapter, but its deficiencies are entirely my own responsibility. Both these scholars have a far more in-depth grasp of this topic than I do, and I can only hope that the limitations of this chapter will spur each of them on to write a synthesising monographic treatment of the kind that the field of visual anthropology desperately requires.

2 See, for example, Ginsburg (1991; 1994 and 1995a).

3 For more recent applications of the term 'indigenous media', see Wilson and Stewart (2008) and Wortham (2013). Also Zhang (n.d.), for an account of film-making by Chinese villagers. In a specifically South American context, important recent publications include Schiwy (2009), Zamorano Villareal (2017) and Muenala (2018), while for a Central American example of indigenous media see https://realizadorestzikin.org/.

4 See Ginsburg (2011). More recently, Ginsburg has proposed a more comprehensive term, 'relational documentary', that would embrace all forms of film-making, including 'indigenous media', that are posited upon respectful – though sometimes off-screen – relationships between film-makers and subjects, the recognition of the accountability of the former to the latter, and the observance of appropriate cultural protocols in the production of such films (Ginsburg 2018).

5 See Ginsburg (1994), 64; Ruby (1995b), 77; also Malinowski (1932), 25.

6 For a particularly direct expression of this argument, see Faris (1992), 170–1.

7 A vigorous discussion of the cultural issues raised by film-making by non-Western groups was prompted by an article by James Weiner published in *Current Anthropology* in 1997. This in turn provoked a series of counter-comments by other scholars, including by Faye Ginsburg, Marilyn Strathern and Terence Turner (all 1997).

8 See Ginsburg (1995a), 259–60.

9 The films were later analysed by Worth and Adair in a joint monograph, *Through Navajo Eyes* (1972). See also Chalfen (1992; 2007) while for a re-reading of the films following their repatriation to Pine Springs in 2011, see Peterson (2013). See also the Penn Museum website at www.penn.museum/sites/navajofilmthemselves/.

10 The sceptics include Heider (1976), 43, and Winston (1995) 179–80.

11 See Michaels (1986), 61–8. For a more recent and sophisticated treatment of the way in which local cultural norms may influence both the mode of production and the content of films made in Aboriginal communities, see the work of Jennifer Deger among the Yolngu of Arnhem Land, northern Australia, particularly her book (Deger 2006) and her website, https://research.jcu.edu.au/portfolio/jennifer.deger.

12 See Turner (1992a), 8–11. The anthropologist and film-maker Glenn Shepard has identified similar principles underlying the work of a new generation of Kayapo film-makers. See his blog entry, dated April 2012, at http://ethnoground.blogspot.com/2012/04/miss-kayapo-filming-through-mebengokre.html (accessed 11 February 2019).

13 See Turner (1995), 105.

14 See Flores (2007), 213–14, 222, n. 6.

15 Michaels (1986), 55–6; Turner (1991b), 75–6.

16 The final version of the film was entitled *In Search of the Bororo Mr Right* and has since been widely shown at festivals and other venues.

17 This was the situation as reported to me in 2014 by Terry Turner in a personal communication. However, very sadly, Terry himself died the following year, and since then I have no further information.

18 Asch et al. (1991).

19 See Michaels (1986), 60; Turner (1992a), 7–8; Flores (2007), 215–16.

20 See Turner (1990; 1991a; 2002).

21 See Ginsburg (2011), 237–8, also her earlier and more developed formulation of these arguments in texts such as Ginsburg (1994 and 1995b).

22 This is the essence of the critique by Melinda Hinkson of Eric Michaels' pioneering work with the Warlpiri (Hinkson 2008).

23 Some fifty of the films produced by *Video nas Aldeias* (translated as 'Video in the Villages') are now distributed with English subtitles by DER: see https://store.der.org/video-in-the-villages-series-p973.aspx. Further films, sometimes also subtitled in English are available via the programme's website at www.videonasaldeias.org.br from whence they are distributed through YouTube or the digital platform provided by the Canadian Inuit organisation, IsumaTV. In this chapter, background information about the project is drawn from this website or from two articles by the documentary film scholar Patricia Aufderheide (1995; 2008).

24 In the anthropological literature, the Ikpeng are often referred to as the Txikão, though this was originally a name used by other indigenous groups rather than an autonym.

25 See Fausto (2011).

# Part II
# Authors: three key figures

# Introduction

IN *Works and Lives*, his well-known study of the anthropologist as the author of texts, Clifford Geertz draws upon a concept of authorship that was originally formulated by Roland Barthes. This is based upon a distinction between those who not merely write, but who in writing establish a distinctive model for doing so, and those who come later and write within the model established by the former. Barthes reserved the term 'author' to the originators of models of writing, distinguishing them from the mere 'writers' who come afterwards and write within the 'praxis' established by the 'authors'. Geertz argues that one can identify a number of key, praxis-originating 'authors' in the Barthesian sense in the history of anthropological writing. However, he then goes on to suggest that those who came later and adopted their praxes did not always do so slavishly, nor were they necessarily inferior. Thus, for Geertz, Raymond Firth was 'probably our best Malinowskian' while 'Kroeber did what Boas but promised'.[1]

I suggest that a similar argument can be made with regard to the three key ethnographic film authors whose praxes I consider in this part of the book – Jean Rouch, Robert Gardner and Colin Young. In each case, they were responsible for establishing a particular ethnographic film-making praxis that other film-makers have since followed, though rarely so systematically that any clearly defined 'schools' have emerged.

In Rouch's case, as his producer Pierre Braunberger once said of him, he had no direct predecessors, nor any direct successors, but rather 'a profound influence'.[2] Similarly, Robert Gardner's work was, for most of his life, more of a beacon than a guiding light, though as I describe in Part IV of this book, in recent years his influence is certainly discernible in the works currently being produced by the Sensory Ethnography Lab at Harvard. Of the three, perhaps Colin Young has had the most direct disciples and in a sense ironically so, because he himself has never, in any serious way, been an active maker of ethnographic films himself. He has been, as he himself once put it, not so much a film-maker as a 'film-maker-maker'. Or to put it in Barthesian terms: Colin Young may be an Author, but he is an Author who has never written anything. There are, however, many ethnographic film-makers who have come afterwards and who have given body and shape to the praxis that he first conceived.

As we shall see, although there is some degree of overlap, not least because all three Authors knew one another well, there are also some fundamental differences between their respective praxes, both in terms of practical matters of cinematography, sound recording and editing, as well as regarding more abstract issues of an epistemological or aesthetic nature, their ultimate intentions and, importantly, their ethical posture regarding the subjects.

*Notes*

1  Geertz (1988), 17–19.
2  Serceau (1996), 171.

# 8

# Jean Rouch:
# sharing anthropology

THE very nature of ethnographic cinema – how it is practised, how it is talked about, where its limits are deemed to lie – has been profoundly shaped by the work of Jean Rouch. Through his personal example, he established the *métier* of ethnographic film-making as a creative activity of potentially broad horizons whose practitioners could engage in a lively exchange of ideas and methods with film-makers from many other backgrounds and with very different agendas. Moreover, he showed that it was not necessary for anthropologists to rely on professional technicians to help them make films. Rather, they themselves could use a camera, not as some sort of scientific instrument for gathering data in an objective fashion, as had previously been the orthodox view, but rather as a means of representation that could go far beyond the mere recording of social and cultural life, and could even embrace fiction (figure 8.1).

Most important of all, Rouch established that an ethnographic film-making praxis based on a collaborative relationship between film-maker and subjects could afford a much more profound understanding of the subjects' world than one posited, in the name of science, on a radical separation between observer and observed. This idea of a 'shared anthropology', realised through all the different stages of making an ethnographic film, was the ethical cornerstone of his own practice and has since been widely adopted by ethnographic film-makers all over the world.[1]

## An ocean to be discovered

In the period prior to the Second World War, as described in Chapter 1, a number of leading anthropologists had made films, including Jean Rouch's own doctoral supervisor, Marcel Griaule.[2] However, these films were not only very limited both in number and quality, but were peripheral to their makers' principal identities as anthropologists. Meanwhile, among Rouch's contemporaries, there were a number of ethnographic film-makers, such

**8.1** Jean Rouch in 1954 on the Gold Coast (now Ghana), aged 36. He is using the Bell & Howell Filmo 70 that he bought in the Paris Flea Market in 1946.

as John Marshall and Robert Gardner, who had some engagement with academic anthropology but who then developed their careers largely outside academic life. Rouch was unique in that, having studied anthropology to the doctoral level, he then held an academic post throughout his career and made film-making central to his professional identity. This was something that no leading anthropologist had done before, nor, for that matter, have many been able to do since, either in France or in the English-speaking world, at least not to anything like the same degree.

Rouch was a person of great energy and imagination, but his ability to dedicate so much of his time to film-making was made possible by a particular set of institutional circumstances. Early on in his career, in 1948, when he was 30 and still a doctoral student, he was appointed to a position at the principal academic research institute in France, the CNRS. By this time, he was already closely associated with the Musée de l'Homme, which, in 1952, became the seat of the newly created Comité du film ethnographique. Rouch was appointed its general secretary, a position that he would retain for the rest of his life: the Comité would become the principal vehicle through which he would conduct his professional affairs, including the production of most of his films. Apart from a brief interlude in 1951–53, when he was temporarily expelled for failing to complete his doctoral thesis on time, largely due to the call of competing film-making activities, Rouch's position at the CNRS gave him the freedom, throughout his career, to pursue his film-making interests more or less as he saw fit. This enabled him to spend part of every year on a film-making expedition, mostly to West Africa, untroubled by any major teaching obligations.

But even given these advantageous circumstances, the sheer volume of Rouch's oeuvre is truly remarkable. In the course of a film-making career that spanned more than fifty years, beginning with *Au pays des mages noir* (In the Country of the Black Wizards), a short expedition film that he made with some war-time comrades as they travelled down the Niger river by canoe in 1946, and ending with his last film, poignantly entitled *Le Rêve plus fort que la mort* (The Dream more Powerful than Death), and released in 2002, Rouch completed just over a hundred films. In addition, at the time of his death in 2004, aged 86, in a road accident in rural Niger where he had shot most of his films, he left perhaps as many as seventy further films unfinished. This vast corpus of work contains within it an invaluable and irreplaceable record not only of traditional customs and practices in West Africa, many of which have now been all but abandoned, but also of the period of transition from the European colonial regime to the era of independence.

An excellent catalogue of Rouch's films has recently been produced by the CNC, the French national film institute.[3] As this catalogue makes clear, not all Rouch's films were ethnographic films. A considerable proportion were of limited ethnographicness and some were not ethnographic at all. These other films were on a wide variety of subjects and were mostly relatively short. They included films about economic or social development projects, films on a broad variety of political and cultural events, even three promotional films for a West African car dealer. In the latter part of his career, he also made a dozen short interview-based portrait films, mostly of close friends or associates, and produced a number of 'ciné-poems' and '*promenades inspirées*' about Paris and elsewhere. More substantial were his seventeen fiction films, mostly of feature length, which he began to make in the early 1950s. Although dealing in many cases with the same themes as his ethnographic films, only about half were linked to his ethnographic research.

When all these other films are subtracted from the Rouchian filmography, one is left with a corpus of around a hundred films that could be described as substantially ethnographic. Of these, about half remain incomplete: while some have been subject to a certain degree of editing, others consist of little more than titles given to a set of synchronised rushes. Yet even if all these incomplete works are also removed from the list, one still remains with a final tally of around fifty completed ethnographic films, making Rouch by far the most productive of all ethnographic film-makers, past or present.[4]

Rouch's textual publications also numbered around a hundred and were just as eclectic as his films. His most substantial publication was his doctoral thesis, which concerned religion and magic among the Songhay, an ethnic group distributed widely across West Africa, but particularly in Niger, where Rouch conducted his doctoral fieldwork. This thesis, which he defended in 1952, was first published in 1960 and then republished in an extensively annotated second edition in 1989. Also based on his doctoral research among the Songhay were a historical memoir of about hundred pages published in a French colonial journal in 1953, and a more general monograph of a similar length published in 1954.

Otherwise, Rouch's most significant published work was a detailed report on his post-doctoral research into migration from the edge of Sahel to the cities on the coast of West Africa. This ran to almost two hundred pages and appeared in 1956 in a French academic journal, directly complementing the films that he was making at the same time. But he also published a considerable number of other articles and reports on migration, and an even greater quantity of articles about ethnographic film-making and cinema more generally. At the same time, as an editor, he oversaw the production of two catalogues of ethnographic film for UNESCO, one about films made in sub-Saharan Africa, the other, co-edited with Monique Salzmann, about films made in the Pacific region. In addition to all these texts that he himself authored, he gave a great many interviews to journals, magazines and newspapers, particularly in the latter phase of his life, and was himself the subject of over twenty films. He also made regular appearances on television.[5]

While a small part of this oeuvre has been widely distributed and has had an influence far beyond the confines of academic anthropology, the vast majority remains – to borrow a phrase from the CNC catalogue – 'an ocean to be discovered'.[6]

### A SHOOTING STAR WITH A LONG TRAIL

Jean Rouch was, famously, an entirely autodidact film-maker. As he himself put it, he learned to operate '*le cinématographe à la Cinemathèque*', that is, by simply watching films at the cinema.[7] He shot the great majority of his ethnographic films himself, usually with a non-professional local person acting as the sound recordist. With the exception of one or two fiction films, which were shot on 35 mm film, all his films were shot on 16 mm. While initially welcoming the democratisation made possible by the appearance of cheap portable video cameras in the 1970s, he later rejected video completely, in part on grounds of its suspect longevity, but more importantly because, in his view, it encouraged sloppy film-making habits.

Rouch first taught himself to shoot using a US Army newsreel camera, a spring-wound Bell & Howell Filmo 70 (shown in figure 8.1), which he came across in the Paris flea market in 1946. Shortly afterwards, on the plane to West Africa to begin his expedition down the Niger with his war-time friends, Edmond Séchan, a professional cameraman who happened to be on the same plane, showed him how to load the magazine. As Rouch liked to relate, he then lost his tripod, supposedly as the expedition went over some rapids, and contrary to accepted wisdom, he learned that it was perfectly possible, indeed preferable, to shoot handheld. He would go on using the Filmo 70 for the next ten years, by which time he had already become one of the leading film-makers in France.

The films that Rouch made in the early part of his career, especially those made between the early 1950s and the early 1960s, established a new benchmark in ethnographic film-making. Among many others, these films include the classically ethnographic works *Bataille sur le grand fleuve* (Battle on the Great River) and *Yenendi: les hommes qui font la pluie* (Yenendi: the Men who Make the Rain), both shot in 1951 and released in 1952. These were concerned respectively with hippopotamus hunting on the river Niger, and with rain-making and spirit possession in Simiri, a drought-afflicted village on the edge of the Sahelian desert. Both hunting and spirit-possession would be recurrent topics of his work.

These early films were followed by a further series that he made while carrying out his migration research. The first to be released, in 1955, was *Les Maîtres fous* (The Mad Masters) which concerned spirit possession among Nigerien migrants to Accra, in what was then the British colony of the Gold Coast and today is Ghana. This was the film that first brought Rouch widespread international recognition, though it also caused a scandal since some of the spirits by whom the subjects become possessed take the form of colonial authority figures who, in this guise, slaughter and eat a dog. The film had the dubious distinction of being banned by the colonial authorities in Ghana while also being simultaneously denounced by anti-colonial African intellectuals in Paris and by Rouch's former doctoral supervisor, Marcel Griaule, for showing Africans behaving in a 'savage' way.

Two other well-known films arising from Rouch's research into migration would later come to be known as 'ethnofictions', that is, films that were fictional in the sense that the subjects were asked by Rouch to act out – on an improvisational basis, without a script – a series of scenes based either on their own lives or the lives of people very like them. One of these was *Jaguar*, shot on the Gold Coast around the same time as *Les Maîtres fous* in 1954–55, but not completed in its definitive form for budgetary reasons until 1968. The other was *Moi, un Noir* (Me, a Black Man), which was shot in Abidjan, capital of the Ivory Coast in 1957, though not released in its definitive form until 1960 (figure 8.2).

**8.2** Experiences of migration. In *Les Maîtres fous* (1955), left, in the bush near Accra, a Nigerien migrant is possessed by the 'Lieutenant from the Red Sea'; right, *Moi un Noir* (1960) is based on the real life experiences of Oumarou Ganda, a Nigerien migrant to the Ivory Coast.

This highly productive period culminated with the release in 1961 of another ethnofiction, *La Pyramide humaine* (The Human Pyramid), this time about the relationships between African and European pupils at an elite high school in Abidjan, and then Rouch's first film in France, *Chronicle of a Summer*, which he co-directed with the sociologist-philosopher Edgar Morin. This latter film, ground-breaking both in form and in technique, and without doubt Rouch's best-known film, particularly outside anthropology, offered a portrait of Paris in the summer of 1960, at the height of Algerian war, as mediated through the experiences in work and at leisure of a small group of young people.

It was around this time that Rouch's reputation as a film-maker was at its peak in France. In 1959, he was awarded the Prix Louis-Delluc, arguably the most presitigious of all French film prizes for *Moi, un Noir*. Writing in the fashionable film journal, *Cahiers du Cinéma*, Jean-Luc Godard wrote a eulogistic review, praising this film for simultaneously revolutionising French cinema and giving a voice to Africa for the first time. Godard was but one of the tyros of the emergent New Wave who admired Rouch's work. In the early 1960s, Rouch himself made a number of short fiction films in Paris that were in similar in both style and subject matter to those of the New Wave directors. By contrast, his work was virtually unknown at this time in what the French like to call the 'Anglo-Saxon' world. Although *Chronicle of a Summer* attracted the attention of reviewers from the world of documentary film-making, it had no impact whatsoever on English-language ethnographic film-making at the time of its release.

Through the 1960s, Rouch's film work underwent a sort of bifurcation. On the one hand, he continued to make fiction films, some set in Paris, others in West Africa, all highly authored, and increasingly imaginary and detached from his ethnographic field research. On the other hand, he continued to return annually to West Africa to make highly observational films of ethnographic documentation. Many of these films were straightforwardly descriptive accounts of religious ceremonies, mostly among the Songhay in Niger and mostly involving spirit possession. He would shoot several such films in a given year: in the later 1960s and early 1970s, he was shooting five or more a year. In 1967, he shot a remarkable eleven films. As one might expect, given the sheer volume of production, not every one of these films was a masterpiece. A considerable number, perhaps as many as a third, remained unfinished.

From the mid-1960s through the early 1970s, Rouch also dedicated a couple of months every year to shooting a series of films about the Sigui, a world renewal ceremonial cycle that every sixty years is celebrated by the Dogon of eastern Mali over the course of seven consecutive years. These films were made in collaboration with Germaine Dieterlen, the long-term partner – in both life and work – of Rouch's mentor, Marcel Griaule, from the 1930s until the latter's death in 1956. Eventually, in 1981, Rouch gathered all these Sigui films together into a single major compilation, *Sigui synthèse (1967–1973) – L'invention de la parole et de la mort* (Sigui Synthesis, 1967–73 – The Invention of Language and Death).

As if this were not enough, during this same period, Rouch and Dieterlen also collaborated on a number of films about Dogon funerals as well as on a film about the *dama*, an elaborate ceremony that the Dogon hold a number of years later to bid a final farewell to the deceased and to bring the period of mourning to an end. Shot in 1974 but not edited until 1980, *Le Dama d'Ambara* concerns the *dama* held for Ambara, who had been one of Griaule and Dieterlen's main informants since the 1930s. Arguably the most accomplished of all Rouch's films about the Dogon, this film can be read not only as a *dama* for Ambara, but also as an *hommage* on Rouch's part to Griaule, whose texts he performs verbatim and at some length in the voice-over commentary on the soundtrack (figure 8.3).

Despite this continuing productivity, Rouch's star was gradually waning in France over this period, though leaving behind it a very long trail. His name, once ubiquitous in *Cahiers du Cinéma*, became scarce. The Dogon films appear to have been too specialised to have the same impact on the general public as his earlier work. Although he would continue to shoot minor ethnographic films in West Africa over the coming years, many were left unedited. Never again would he take on a major ethnographic film project. Instead, he threw his energies into other genres, such as portrait films, ciné-poems in Paris and elsewhere, and fiction films, some with only a tangential relationship to his ethnographic research. But with only a few exceptions, these did not feature prominently in the pages of *Cahiers du Cinéma* either.

8.3 *Le Dama d'Ambara* (1980). The *kanaga* masks, left, evoke the Pale Fox, a trickster demiurge, while the longer *serige* masks, right, represent vertical snakes, creatures associated with immortality because they can change their skins.

Ironically, it was precisely around this time, at the end of the 1970s and beginning of the 1980s, that Rouch was 'discovered' by English-language visual anthropologists, since his views about anthropology and cinema, particularly his reflexive, participatory methods, struck a chord with the postmodernist tendencies that were then sweeping through English-language anthropology, particularly on the US side of the Atlantic. Yet although Rouch may have been hailed as a prophet of postmodernism in English-language anthropology – very much to his surprise and amusement – his particular mode of ethnographic film authorship was deeply rooted in a number of intellectual and artistic traditions that were arguably more modernist than postmodernist, and certainly very distinctively French.[8]

## THE SURREAL ENCOUNTER

One of the most important of these traditions was Surrealism, which was very much in vogue in Paris in the 1930s when Rouch was still a teenager. Indeed, it was through a prior interest in Surrealism that Rouch first encountered anthropology.

Rouch liked to tell the story of that first encounter, which took place one spring afternoon in 1934, when, as a 17-year-old, he stopped in front of a bookshop in the Montparnasse quartier of Paris, close to his parental home. There in the window, in a pool of light cast by the setting sun, was a display of double-paged spreads from two different volumes of *Minotaure*, a recently founded journal which featured an eclectic mix of articles by Surrealist poets and artists, along with more conventional contributions by art historians, archaeologists and anthropologists.

One of those spreads, from the second volume, showed some photographs of masked dancers performing at a Dogon funeral in front of some tower-like adobe structures, the typical houses and granaries of the Dogon. These images formed part of the main feature of that volume, which was a special report on the Dakar-Djibouti expedition of 1931–33, written by its leader, Marcel Griaule. The other two-page spread showed the frontispiece of the most recent volume of *Minotaure*, which consisted of a colour reproduction of a painting by Giorgio de Chirico, an artist much admired by the Surrealists. This painting was *The Duo*, which features two masked mannequins standing in a dream-like landscape, with a pink tower and other structures in the background, not dissimilar to the structures in the Dogon funeral images.

In the mind of the young Rouch, as a *coup de foudre*, these images suddenly became inextricably entangled. The masked characters common to both sets of images seemed to him to offer a privileged means of access to the innermost recesses of the unconscious. The West African landscape took on the character of a fabulous terrain to which Rouch felt the urgent need to travel. In due course of time, not only would he seek out the photographer, Marcel Griaule, to be his teacher, but he would indeed travel to West Africa and would spend most of his life working there as both film-maker and anthropologist.[9]

The many connections in 1930s Paris between ethnology (as the study of social or cultural anthropology was then known in France), Surrealism and *l'art nègre* – the latter embracing everything from traditional African masks to African-American jazz, the exotic dancer Josephine Baker and even professional boxers – have been extensively commented upon, including by Rouch himself.[10] The distinguished historian of anthropology in France, Jean Jamin, has suggested that the association between ethnology and Surrealism at this time was more a question of two activities occupying adjacent intellectual spaces rather than being involved in a genuine exchange: while the ethnologists were committed to detached observation and rigorous analysis, the Surrealists sought a subjective immersion in other cultural realities, hoping to tap into the creative life forces that they imagined to be inherent in such cultures, particularly those of Africa. According to Jamin, although there may have been certain 'complicities and affinities' between ethnology and Surrealism, there was no long-term or systematic transfer of methods and concepts.[11] But while this may have been generally true, it certainly does not apply to Jean Rouch, whose work continued to be influenced by Surrealist methods and concepts throughout his career, long after they had fallen out of fashion in the visual arts and poetry.

Rouch was particularly attracted to the Surrealist notion of the *rencontre*, the chance encounter between strangers or between disparate objects that produces unexpected manifestations of beauty or sources of inspiration. The account of Rouch's own *rencontre* with the juxtaposed images of Dogon masks and the dreamscape of the de Chirico painting – a sort of *rencontre* with a *rencontre* – was but one of many stories that Rouch liked to tell about his own life in which an unexpected encounter had produced a positive outcome. These stories also included his discovery of a camera in the Paris flea market (a place much frequented by the Surrealists also) and the serendipitous subsequent meeting with Edmond Séchan on the flight to West Africa. The moral of these stories was invariably the importance of responding spontaneously to such opportunities.

However, the impact of Surrealism on Rouch's work is only occasionally evident in so far as the specific visual content of his films is concerned. Although Rouch liked to allude to René Magritte and Salvador Dalí in interviews, and he remained an admirer of de Chirico throughout his life, for the most part the visual style of his films remained resolutely realist and naturalistic. There are few flights of visual fantasy in Rouch's films, even in the dream sequences that occur in his ethnofictions. Indeed, Surrealist poetry had arguably a somewhat greater impact on the content of his films than did Surrealist visual art: Rouch often referred in interviews to Surrealist poets, particularly André Breton and Paul Eluard, and across his total film oeuvre, there are many different references to, and even direct citations of, the works of Surrealist poets or of their precursors, Arthur Rimbaud and Charles Baudelaire.

But the influence of Surrealism on Rouch's film authorship is most marked in relation to the actual practical processes of film-making. Although Rouch would sometimes stress the importance of being well-prepared through careful prior research, inspired by the example of the Surrealists he considered that spontaneity and the ability to improvise in the actual moment of shooting were what counted above all in making a film. In this way, in the manner of the Surrealist technique of automatic writing, a film-maker could draw upon the creativity hidden within their unconscious. It was for this reason that Rouch would never ask his documentary subjects to repeat any actions, and even in his fictions, he tried to restrict himself and the actors to a single take. If any action had to be rehearsed or repeated, he believed that the quality of both the performance of the subject and the performance of the film-maker would suffer.

For a shot to turn out really well, Rouch believed that there should be improvised performances on both sides of the lens, in harmony with one another. Over the years, Rouch used many different analogies to describe this ideal situation. Sometimes he compared it to a ballet, at other times to a matador improvising his passes before the bull. But in an interview published in 1981, he proposed that these totally harmonised performances are so rare and so exquisite that they can only be compared to 'those exceptional moments of a jam session between the piano of Duke Ellington and the trumpet of Louis Armstrong, or the electrifying encounters between strangers as described for us on occasion by André Breton'.[12]

As this remark shows, even some fifty years after they had been at the height of intellectual fashion in Paris, the associations between *l'art nègre*, Surrealist poetry and ethnography continued to be of central importance to way in which Rouch conceived of his film-making practice.

## THE JOKING RELATIONSHIP

Although Rouch may have been entirely self-taught as a film-maker, he did receive a formal anthropological training. In the academic year 1940–41, still inspired by his *rencontre* with the Dogon images in the Montparnasse bookshop window, Rouch enrolled on an extramural course at the Musée de l'Homme given by the creator of those images, Marcel Griaule. These were supported by 'magic lantern' slide shows managed by Germaine Dieterlen. At the time, Rouch was in his final year as an engineering student at the elite *grande école*, Ponts et Chausées, and had no formal connection with either anthropology or film-making. But with Paris already under the German occupation, he considered these lectures in the darkened basement of the Musée as one of the few available windows on to the outside world. The relationships that he formed with Griaule and Dieterlen through this extramural course would be of crucial importance in shaping his future career.

Shortly afterwards, to fulfil his dream of travelling to West Africa as well as to escape from wartime France, Rouch took a job as a road-building engineer in Niamey, capital of the then French colony of Niger. Here he came across spirit possession among his labourers at first hand and began his first ethnographic researches of the phenomenon. Later, in 1944–45, after a couple of years combining engineering work with private study in the Institut français d'Afrique noire (IFAN) in Dakar, the capital of Senegal, he joined the Free French forces in Africa and participated in the liberation of France and the invasion of Germany. But immediately after the war, even before he had been formally demobilised, he returned to France and enrolled at the Sorbonne to study for a doctorate in anthropology under the supervision of Marcel Griaule.

In the immediate post-war period, Griaule was under something of a cloud. Unlike many leading anthropologists, he had not taken refuge abroad during the war. Instead he had chosen to remain behind and collaborate with the Vichy government, even accepting a chair at the Sorbonne during this period. But despite his deep personal aversion to everything associated with the Vichy regime, Rouch elected to study under Griaule because, he claimed, Griaule and his group simply 'had more fun' than the other leading Africanists with whom he might have worked. There were probably some more pragmatic considerations too: Griaule was the leading French authority on the middle Niger where Rouch wanted to work and, with Dieterlen, he had supported Rouch's first amateur ethnographic research during the war years.[13]

Yet for all that he chose Griaule to be his teacher, there remained a certain ambiguity in Rouch's attitudes towards his mentor, involving a curious mixture of disdain and respect. Rouch liked to present this as an extrapolation of the traditional joking relationship between the cliff-dwelling Dogon, whom Griaule had studied, and the Songhay and the other peoples of the lowland fluvial plains of the Niger with whom he himself mostly worked. This seems to have proved an effective way of both masking and managing the differences in their political views, not only in relation to collaboration with the Vichy government during the war years, but also with regard to the French colonial presence in Africa.

In contrast to the ambiguity in his relationship with Griaule, Rouch always retained the highest regard for Germaine Dieterlen. Not only did they collaborate on a large number of Dogon film projects in the 1960s and 1970s, but in the latter part of his career Rouch made no less than four 'ciné-portraits' of Dieterlen. When they were both in Paris, they spent a great deal of time in one another's company, particularly after Rouch's first wife, Jane, died in 1987. When Dieterlen herself died in 1999 at the age of 95, Rouch's closest associates report that he was cast into a deep depression and never quite recaptured his celebrated *joie de vivre* again.

Griaule passed on to Rouch his particular take on the intellectual inheritance that he had received from his own mentor, Marcel Mauss. From a methodological point of view, this involved a clear differentiation between the process of ethnographic description and the process of theoretical explanation. The first stage of a research project should consist of the systematic accumulation of large numbers of 'documents', that is particular bodies of ethnographic data, equivalent to what today might be called 'files'. Only once these have been assembled and rigorously analysed should one aspire to draw any theoretical conclusions.

Although some of the theoretical conclusions that Mauss drew from the detailed analysis of ethnographic 'documents' have been the source of great inspiration to subsequent generations of anthropologists – notably his theory of the gift and its relationship to other forms of exchange – contemporary accounts of his lectures suggest that Mauss often got so immersed in the ethnographic detail that he never quite arrived at the theoretical conclusions. Rouch's recollection of Griaule's lectures as a series of disaggregated eth- nographic titbits suggests that they may have suffered from the same shortcoming.[14] One can also discern something of this tendency to accumulate the data first and ask questions later in a certain strand of Rouch's film- making praxis too, notably in his accumulation of large quantities of observational rushes about spirit-possession ceremonies, the great majority of which remained unedited when he died.

If Rouch's general intellectual formation can be traced ultimately to Mauss, his ideas about fieldwork were more directly influenced by Marcel Griaule. For although Mauss actively advocated fieldwork, his own investigations were entirely bibliographic. Griaule, by contrast, was highly committed to fieldwork in practice as well as in principle and his ideas about how to conduct fieldwork are laid out very explicitly in a slim handbook, *Méthode de l'ethnographie*. This was not published until 1957, the year after his death, but it drew upon his experience of working with the Dogon since the 1930s.

The approach to fieldwork advocated by Griaule in this book is quite unlike the one developed around the same time by English-language anthropologists. In the ideal 'Anglo-Saxon' model, the fieldworker, working alone, would take up residence in the community being studied, learn the language and aim to become a discreet observer of day-to-day life. Griaule, by contrast, advocated the formation of teams of fieldworkers, organised along quasi-military lines. The advantage of these teams, he argued, was that they would not only maximise the collection of data within any given time period, but they could also triangulate their results. Griaule's methods were also highly proactive in the sense that they involved intensive interviews based on systematic questionnaires. Far from discreetly observing the subjects interacting among themselves, Griaule preferred to work with a select group of elite informants, using bilingual intermediaries rather than the indigenous language.[15]

In certain regards, the fieldwork methods adopted by Jean Rouch were similar to those of his mentor. Like Griaule, he returned faithfully to the same field sites in West Africa year after year: he was fond of quoting Griaule and Dieterlen's view that one needed at least twenty years of first-hand experience of a given society before one could begin to achieve a 'deep knowledge' of its systems of thought.[16] However, this 'deep knowledge' did not presuppose a profound competence in the subjects' language for, like Griaule, Rouch tended to rely on a key group of informants with whom he worked through the medium of French. Also like Griaule, Rouch tended to focus his attention on the public as opposed to the domestic domain. The great majority of his films are about public ceremonial performances of one kind or another, and there is very little emphasis on domestic life and the routines of the everyday. As a result, his films mainly concern the world of men while the more domestic world of women remains relatively neglected.[17]

In his camera-less fieldwork in West Africa, like his mentor, Rouch often conducted interviews using formal questionnaires. Although he very rarely used interviews of any kind in his African ethnographic films, one may also detect, as James Clifford has done, a certain continuity between Griaule's method of using an interrogatory schedule of questions to provoke his subjects into revealing answers and Rouch's use of the camera to provoke his subjects into revelatory performances.[18] Indeed, one could take the analogy further and say that in the same way that Griaule's proactive fieldwork methods contrasted with the more passive methods of his English-language contemporaries in anthropology, so too did Rouch's proactive cinematographic methods contrast with the more low-key methods of Direct Cinema and Observational Cinema as practised by his English-language film-making contemporaries.[19]

## SHARED ANTHROPOLOGY

If Rouch's film-making praxis was based on a methodology that was in some ways similar to that of his mentor, in other respects it was radically different. This applies particularly to the key Rouchian concept of 'shared anthropology'.

Griaule's fieldwork method may have involved a form of dialogue with his subjects, but it was essentially antagonistic, being based on the assumption, stated repeatedly in *Méthode de l'ethnographie*, that his informants were lying. In an extended legal analogy, Griaule suggests that an informant should be considered the equivalent to the 'guilty party' in a court of law, while the remainder of the society should be considered his 'accomplices'. In order to combat an informant's congenital tendency to mislead, Griaule recommended that the researcher – compared variously to a prosecution lawyer, judge and even a bloodhound – should use whatever trick or stratagem was necessary to circumvent the informant's defences. Although Griaule may have developed a profound respect for African culture, coming to regard Dogon cosmology as the equal of that of Ancient Greece, his methodological recommendations suggest that he had no respect for the Africans themselves as individuals.[20]

Griaule's unscrupulous attitudes, self-evidently the product of a colonial mentality, could not be further from those of Rouch. Whereas Griaule turned to the police sniffer dog as a metaphor for the process whereby anthropological knowledge is to be achieved, Rouch thought of the

8.4 Sharing anthropology over the long term. Left, Damouré, Lam and fellow Nigerien migrant Douma Besso (in shadow) at their stall in Kumasi Market, in 1954, at the time of filming *Jaguar*; right, with Moussa Hamidou recording sound, extreme left, and guided by a Dutch assistant, Jean Rouch shoots Damouré, Tallou Mouzourane and Lam while making *Madame l'eau* in Amsterdam in 1992.

relationship between researcher and subjects as being, in the ideal case, like the improvised harmonisation of performances between jazz musicians.

Shortly after his arrival in Niger in December 1941, and in defiance of the Vichy governor's disapproval of familiarity with Africans, Rouch became friendly with a young local man, Damouré Zika, and appointed him as his assistant. Damouré was a member of the Sorko subgroup of the Songhay, known for their expertise in fishing the waters of the Niger. It was he who first introduced Rouch to spirit possession cults through his grandmother, Kalia, a priestess of one of the local cults. Damouré was the first and most important of a group of Nigeriens whom Rouch subsequently gathered around him and who accompanied him whenever he went to Africa. Later additions to this group included Lam Ibrahim Dia, a Fulani cattle-herder, Illo Gaoudel, also a Sorko fisherman, and Tallou Mouzourane, a Bella orphan without a family to support him. Somewhat later, Moussa Hamidou, who belonged to the Zerma ethnic group, also joined this inner circle of Rouch's confidants (figure 8.4).

These men helped Rouch in a variety of different ways: they conducted surveys for his migration studies, crewed on his documentaries and took a leading part as actors in his ethnofictions. They also drove his Land Rover, carried his equipment and generally acted as his local fixers. In return, Rouch not only paid them salaries while they worked for him, but shared the profits of his films on a 50/50 basis. He also supported them in many other ways too: he arranged for Damouré to be trained as a medical auxiliary and later as a pharmacist, which allowed him, in local terms, to achieve great wealth and status; Lam learned to drive with Rouch and became a professional driver, using his income from the films to buy vehicles; through his cinema work with Rouch, Moussa was able to pay for all his sons to be educated as professionals; when Rouch met Tallou, he was suffering from leprosy, so Rouch arranged for him to be cured and then took him under his wing, supporting him for the rest of his life. When Rouch died in the tragic road accident in February 2004, travelling in the same car with him, though fortunately not seriously hurt, was Damouré, still accompanying Rouch more than sixty years after they had first met.[21]

These attitudes of respect for his subjects were made manifest in a variety of ways in Rouch's film-making praxis. One of the most important was his practice of screening back his films to the subjects. Rouch liked to trace this practice back to the example set by Robert Flaherty, who, during the making of *Nanook of the North* in the early 1920s, had screened his rushes to his subjects in order to decide what they should film the next day.[22] But Rouch went very much further than this, giving his African collaborators a much greater role in contributing to his films than Flaherty ever gave to the Inuit. Flaherty asked the Inuit to adjust their house constructions, subsistence activities, their costumes and even their personal identities to the requirements of his film. In contrast, Rouch was reluctant to ask his subjects to dress up or behave in any special way. Instead he would simply ask them to improvise along whatever lines they themselves thought fit. Rouch's feedback procedures were also very much more elaborate. He did not merely screen his rushes to his subjects in order to plan the next day's shooting: often he would return, months or years later, not with the rushes, but with the completed film and screen that to his subjects.

Rouch readily acknowledged that there were certain pragmatic advantages to be derived from such feedback screenings. At first, he had tried giving his written works to the Songhay, but had quickly discovered that they had no use for them. On the other hand, when he started screening his films, not only did the Songhay understand his objectives more clearly, they became his active collaborators. At the simplest level, this consisted of merely commenting on the ethnographic content of the films. But this was only the start of a longer-term process. More important than the feedback per se was the collaboration that followed thereafter. For Rouch discovered that at the end of a feedback screening, members of the audience would often come up to him and suggest an idea for a new film. These could be people who had been directly involved in the first film, or other members of the audience who had concluded that a film about their activities would be even more interesting than the film that Rouch had just shown. In this way, the screening of one film could lead to the making of another in which the subjects who proposed the idea were not merely protagonists, but stakeholders in the making of a new film.

But Rouch thought of feedback screenings primarily in ethical terms, describing them as a form of 'audiovisual countergift' – a very Maussian term – offered in exchange for the support he had received from the subjects during the production process. By this means, the making of an ethnographic film could form the basis for promoting mutual understanding and respect between observer and observed:

> This is the start of what some of us are already calling 'shared anthropology.' The observer is finally coming down from his ivory tower; his camera, tape recorder, and his projector have led him – by way of a strange initiation path – to the very heart of knowledge and, for the first time, his work is not being judged by a thesis committee but by the very people whom he came to observe.[23]

## POSTCARDS AT THE SERVICE OF THE IMAGINARY

This commitment to the idea of a shared anthropology which Rouch formulated as far back as the early 1950s (even if he did not give it precisely this name until the early 1970s) anticipated by more than two decades the 'dialogical anthropology' that, under the influence of postmodernism, became fashionable in English-language anthropology from the late 1970s onwards. This was one of the aspects of Rouch's authorial praxis that led to his work being warmly embraced by English-speaking ethnographic film-makers at that time. But although Rouch's methodology was certainly marked by this and a number of other apparently postmodern traits – including his rejection of the great twentieth-century metanarratives of Marxism and psychoanalysis – he had arrived at these positions, not through antipathy to modernism as such, but by a series of quite different routes.[24]

As far as the technology of film-making was concerned, Rouch was certainly very modernist in his ideas, believing enthusiastically in the potential of technological advance to transform human experience for the better. In the early 1960s, drawing on his engineering background, Rouch collaborated actively with camera and sound-recording engineers in the development of a system of portable lip-synchronous sound. Experiments with this new technology were taking place on both sides of the Atlantic at this time, and there was considerable exchange of technical ideas and equipment between Rouch's group in France and both the Direct Cinema group on the east coast of the USA and a group of mostly francophone film-makers working for the Canadian National Film Board. One of the latter, Michel Brault, came across to Paris at Rouch's invitation and played a major role as a camera operator in the making of *Chronicle of a Summer*.

However, although there might have been a considerable degree of transatlantic cross-fertilisation in a technical sense, it soon became clear that there were major differences in ideas about how this new technology should be used. In North America, the Direct Cinema group sought to use the new portable technology to maximise their own effacement while shooting, interfering as little as possible in the behaviour of their subjects. In this way, they hoped that they would be able to film their subjects going about their lives just as they would have done had the camera not been there. Rouch's attitude to the new technology was very different: he believed that the presence of the camera would inevitably affect the performance of the subjects, however discreetly it was operated. But far from devaluing the quality of the material that was filmed, he thought that this provocation of extraordinary behaviour *increased* its value. This was because, in putting on a special performance for the camera, the subjects would reveal more about themselves, and particularly about their inner thoughts, dreams and fantasies. 'What has always seemed very strange to me', he commented in an interview in 1964, 'is that contrary to what one might think, when people are being recorded, the reactions that they have are always infinitely more sincere than those they have when they are not being recorded.'[25]

Although the new technological advances greatly increased the fidelity of the copy of the world rendered by the cinematographic apparatus, it was rather its enhanced capacity to bring to the surface that which was normally hidden that was most appreciated by Rouch. This, for him, was the ultimate objective of film-making. As he put it in a 1967 interview:

> For me, cinema, making a film, is like Surrealist painting: the use of the most real processes of reproduction, the most photographic, but at the service of the unreal, of the bringing into being of elements of the irrational (as in Magritte, Dalí). The postcard at the service of the Imaginary.[26]

The greater capacity of the new technology to provoke revelatory performances on the part of the subjects derived in large part from its portability, which allowed much greater immersion on the part of the film-maker in the subjects' world. In this connection, Rouch enthusiastically endorsed the analogy drawn by the co-director of *Chronicle of a Summer*, Edgar Morin, who proposed that with the aid of the new technology, Rouch could become a sort of 'film-maker-diver' who, unencumbered by equipment, could 'plunge into real-life situations'.[27] But for Rouch, this immersion in the world of the subjects entailed more than just a pragmatic technical strategy: in the ideal case, it also enabled the film-maker to enter a particular state of mind, one that he referred to as the 'ciné-trance'.

## THE CINÉ-TRANCE AND '*LA BARBARIE DE L'INVENTION*'

Rouch's most systematic discussion in print of the notion of the ciné-trance is in an article that he wrote shortly after completing one of his most frequently cited films, *Les Tambours d'avant: Tourou et Bitti*. This is a very short film, consisting almost entirely of a single sequence-shot, that is, an unbroken take lasting approximately 11 minutes, which is the full duration of a 16 mm film magazine of 400 feet. The subject of this film is a spirit possession ceremony in Simiri, the Zerma village in northwest Niger where he made many of his films on this subject. On this occasion, the villagers were asking the spirits to prevent locusts from destroying their millet crop. A number of different strands of Rouch's authorial praxis come together in this film, so I shall describe it here in some detail.[28]

After a couple of preliminary shots outside the village, Rouch begins the sequence-shot on the sun and then pans down to enter the village with a tracking shot, passing a herd of tethered sacrificial goats on the left and, on the right, a disconsolate male medium, Sambou Albeybu, still awaiting inspiration. He then crosses the small plaza and approaches the orchestra composed of two or three drummers and a monochord violinist. The musicians redouble their efforts as the camera glides over them, revealing their various instruments one by one. At this point, the music begins to peter out and the camera starts to withdraw, when suddenly there is a cry of 'Meat!' and Sambou goes into trance as he is possessed by the spirit of Kure the Hyena. The priests of the cult, the *zima*, then engage Sambou-Kure in a bantering dialogue, offering him 'meat', in the form of sacrificial animals, in exchange for 'grass', a good harvest. At this point, with the camera still turning, an old woman, Tusinye Wazi, hops across the plaza, shivering all over because she has been possessed by the spirit of Hadyo the Fulani Slave. The *zima* continue their negotiations with Kure, who is now threatening to leave unless he gets 'blood'. But as Rouch could tell from the rattle of the film in the magazine that he was nearing the end of the roll, he withdraws at this point to the edge of the plaza. From here, he ends on a wide shot showing the young people looking on, before finally panning up to the now-setting sun.

Rouch would frequently refer to this film as a prime example of the way in which the presence of a camera can provoke a revelatory change in reality. For, he claimed, it was his shooting that led the mediums to go into a trance state, at least indirectly: in the middle of the shot, as the drum music began to peter out, the violinist noticed that Rouch was still shooting and presuming that this must be because he could see the spirits with his camera, the violinist began to play more energetically, which encouraged the drummers to start again, which in turn sent the mediums into trance (figure 8.5).

This film also exemplifies Rouch's understanding of the play between subjectivity and objectivity that is involved in making a film. Over an opening pre-title shot, Rouch comments that the film is 'an attempt to practise ethnographic cinema in the first person'. This is then followed by a cut to black with the title and '*un film de Jean Rouch*', discreetly displayed

8.5 The ciné-trance in *Les Tambours d'avant* (1972). When the musicians, left, saw that Rouch was still shooting, they started to play with renewed vigour, sending the spirit medium, right, into trance.

in one corner. Then the sequence-shot begins, with Rouch commenting over it, 'To enter into a film is to plunge into reality, and to be, at once, both present and invisible'. Thus the film is presented as a direct 'plunge into reality' (possibly a reference to the metaphor of the 'film-maker-diver') but at the same time as a view of this reality that is both subjective ('ethnographic cinema in the first person') and authored ('*un film de Jean Rouch*').

This authorship is evident also in the narrative structure of the film, which conforms to a series of highly conventional tropes, exemplified particularly by the framing of the entire sequence-shot by a shot panning down from the sun at the beginning and another panning up to the sun at the end. The tracking movement entering the village is balanced by a similar tracking movement towards the end of the sequence-shot as the camera withdraws to the edge of the circle where the action is taking place. Before the final pan back up to the sun, there is a shot of the children metaphorically looking into the future, a very common trope of narrative closure. It is not clear quite how conscious Rouch was of this process of narrativisation, but his observation on the commentary track, as the camera is withdrawing, that he would have liked to have continued amidst the dancers but wanted 'to return to the beginning of my story' suggests that at some level of consciousness, it was entirely intentional.

However, for Rouch, the most important feature of this film was the example that it offered of the ciné-trance. He later described how, when he and the sound recordist, Moussa Hamidou, put down their equipment at the end of the sequence-shot, they were both trembling. Rouch attributed this to the fact that the insistent rhythm of the music had not merely sent the two mediums into trance, but the two film-makers as well. This trance he characterised as a sort of 'enthusiasm' that was 'essential to poetic creativity'

244

and comparable to the German concept of *Stimmung*, a term which literally means 'a frame of mind' or 'a tuning', as of a musical instrument, but which, in Rouch's view, defies translation in this more poetic sense. Rouch claimed that when he entered this state, he felt liberated from the weight of anthropological and cinematographic theory and became free to rediscover what he called '*la barbarie de l'invention*' – a phrase that also defies a simple translation but which one might render as 'raw creativity'.[29]

## CINÉMA-VÉRITÉ

There was also another, very different ingredient to Rouch's notion of the ciné-trance. The fact that he refers to this trance-like state not just as a trance, but as a *ciné*-trance is a sign of the influence of the Polish-Russian Soviet film-maker, Dziga Vertov. Along with Flaherty, Rouch considered Vertov as his filmic 'totemic ancestor', claiming that everything that he himself had tried to do as a film-maker could be traced to these two predecessors.[30] Best known for his 1929 film *The Man with the Movie Camera*, Vertov's work was an enthusiasm that Rouch first took up around the time that he was making *Chronicle of a Summer* in 1960–61. Though Vertov had died – relatively young – only in 1954, by the 1960s he was a largely forgotten figure in the Soviet Union. However, the promotion of his ideas in France by the Marxist cinema historian Georges Sadoul, and also by Edgar Morin, Rouch's co-director on *Chronicle of a Summer*, had served to maintain an interest in his work among French film-makers.

Rouch found in Vertov's work an endorsement of his own very modernist view that the cinematographic apparatus offered a new and privileged way of representing the world:

> Dziga Vertov ... understood that the cinematographic way of looking was highly distinctive, employing a new organ of perception, the camera, which bore little relation to the human eye, and which he called the 'ciné-eye.' Later, with the appearance of sound, he identified a 'radio-ear' in the same way, as an organ specific to recorded sound ... Taken as a whole, he called this discipline *cinéma-vérité* (cinema-truth), which is an ambiguous expression since, fundamentally, cinema cuts up, speeds up, slows down, thereby distorting the truth. For me, however, 'cinema-truth' has a specific meaning in the same way that 'ciné-eye' does, designating not pure truth, but the truth particular to recorded images and sounds: 'ciné-truth'.[31]

The term *cinéma-vérité* – a direct translation into French of Vertov's original compound Russian term *kino-pravda* – has had a chequered history in non-fiction film-making. For a period, in North America particularly, it was understood to denote a documentary-making practice that aimed to reveal an entirely objective truth about the world. As such, it came to be used to refer to the work of the Direct Cinema film-makers, who, as described earlier, aspired to use the new portable synchronous sound technology to maximise their self-effacement and thereby provide an account of the world that was as objective as possible. For Rouch, on the other hand, as the passage quoted above makes clear, *cinéma-vérité* did not denote some chimerical objective truth, but rather a distinctive form of truth that was particular to the cinema.

Yet while Rouch and Vertov may have shared this general view about the nature of cinematographic reality, at the level of actual practice they shared little in common. Whereas the visual aesthetic of Rouch's films was generally realist and, once the technology allowed, was based as much as possible on the extended sequence-shot, Vertov's praxis involved the extensive use of montage and special effects, and a complete disregard for any naturalistic conception of realism.

Another fundamental difference concerned the circumstances of shooting. Both Rouch and Vertov laid great emphasis on recording life *sur le vif*, that is, not in a studio but directly as it is lived, out on the streets or in the countryside. But as Edgar Morin pointed out, there is a certain voyeuristic quality to Vertov's work, with the camera often intruding clandestinely on the privacy of its subjects.[32] By contrast, in Rouch's work, the process of filming normally took place within a well-established prior relationship with the subjects. In order to realise his shots, Rouch did not place himself in extraordinary physical situations, as Vertov's cameraman is shown doing in *The Man with the Movie Camera*, but sought instead to harmonise his performance as a cameraperson with the performance of his subjects.

But perhaps the most fundamental difference of all concerned the precise nature of the truth that Vertov and Rouch respectively believed was made possible by cinema. For Vertov, the term *cinéma-vérité* referred to the process of perceiving the world: the ciné-eye could go anywhere and see anything. It could fly in the air with aeroplanes, watch from beneath as a train thundered overhead, pry into a woman's boudoir. The images captured by this roving ciné-eye could then be transformed in all manner of ways in the edit suite: they could be cut up, speeded up or slowed down. In this way, humanity's vision of the world was transformed. By this means, as Vertov put it, 'life-facts' were turned into 'film-facts'.[33]

For Rouch, on the other hand, *cinéma-vérité* was achieved not by the transformation of *the perception of the world* by means of the camera but rather by the transformation of *the world itself*, as the camera, by its mere presence, provoked film subjects into performances that were different from their everyday behaviour, and which could thereby reveal their innermost thoughts and dreams. Once back in the edit suite, in total contrast to Vertov, Rouch sought to keep the further transformation of these revelatory epiphanies to a minimum. In fact, for him, the ideal was to make the process of editing in the edit suite completely unnecessary by shooting the entire film in a single unbroken sequence-shot, as in *Les Tambours d'avant*. But Rouch seems never to have acknowledged these fundamental differences between his own authorial praxes and those of Vertov, and he continued to invoke him as a 'totemic ancestor' until the end of his life.

In attempting to theorise his concept of the ciné-trance, Rouch draws directly on the ideas of his 'totemic ancestor' in proposing an analogy between the condition of Songhay mediums and film-makers immersed in the ciné-trance. Whereas the medium's body is taken over by a spirit, the film-maker is taken over by *Stimmung*, poetic creativity. In the same way that the Songhay mediums possessed by a spirit imagine themselves to be entering a world that differs from everyday experience, so too do 'possessed' film-makers cross the threshold of a different reality when turning on the camera and entering the ciné-trance. This different reality is the world where truths particular to the cinema hold sway, the world of *cinéma-vérité*.[34]

When film-makers are in the ciné-trance, Rouch suggests that everything they do is determined by this condition. In describing his own actions while in a state of ciné-trance, Rouch attaches Vertovian prefixes to all the verbs. Thus when he films, he 'ciné-looks', when he records sound, he 'ciné-listens', and while editing, he 'ciné-thinks' as he 'ciné-cuts'. In fact, he becomes totally identified with this ciné-persona:

> With a ciné-eye and a ciné-ear, I am ciné-Rouch in a state of ciné-trance engaged in ciné-filming … That then is ciné-pleasure, the joy of filming.[35]

Moreover, as this ideal state can only be achieved if there are effective performances on both sides of the lens, his film subjects too should become involved in this world. Rouch claimed that since they understood perfectly well what he was doing as a result of his many feedback screenings, his subjects reacted to his film-making as they would do to those who are possessed by spirits, namely by lending themselves to the performance on its own terms. Thus as he 'ciné-observes', they allow themselves to be 'ciné-observed'.[36] And in the most extreme case – as he suggests may have happened in the filming of *Les Tambours d'avant* – in response to the film-makers' ciné-trance, the subjects may go into their own kind of trance.

This attempt by Rouch to theorise the ciné-trance as a means of gaining access to the domain of *cinéma-vérité* through the yoking together of Songhay and Vertovian ideas has attracted much comment. Whether it is convincing is another matter. For the fact that one can draw certain analogies between the conditions of the immersed film-maker and the possessed medium does not mean that these conditions are, in any genuinely meaningful sense, the same.

The film-maker immersed in a ciné-trance may come to see and under-stand the world in a distinctive manner, which, moreover, might seem to them to emanate from outside their conscious mind. While in this state, they may be able to produce a representation of the world that could be considered an example of *cinéma-vérité* in that it communicates a truth about the world in a way that only cinema can do. But even in Rouch's most enthusiastic formulation of the concept of the ciné-trance, there is no sense that in the course of generating this *cinéma-vérité* representation, the film-maker has been invaded by a foreign being. By contrast, for the Songhay mediums, the spirits by whom they become possessed and whose known typical behaviours they enact when under their influence, are understood to be an extraneous form of being that has taken up residence inside their bodies. In view of this fundamental ontological difference, rather than burden the concept of the ciné-trance with the notion that it represents a portal to *cinéma-vérité* construed as some privileged domain of reality that is equivalent to the world of Songhay spirits, it would be more appropriate, I suggest, to regard it simply as an instructive metaphor based on certain functional parallels between the state of mind of a cinematographer totally immersed in their work, and that of a spirit medium.

One of the most interesting of these parallels, though one that Rouch himself does not seem to have been aware of, is the fact that although the immersed cinematographer and the possessed medium may both be drawing on the unconscious mind, their performances remain structured by culturally specific codes. Thus, just as Songhay mediums possessed by spirits in *Les Tambours d'avant* reveal the identity of those spirits to onlookers by acting in particular conventional ways, so too Rouch, the film-maker-diver, even though immersed within the ciné-trance, still shoots his sequence-shot according to the most conventional of narrative tropes. Even Rouch, it seems, for all his virtuosity and despite his sense of being in contact with *la barbarie de l'invention* when in the ciné-trance, could not entirely escape from the 'prison-house of language'.

## THE MASTER'S VOICE

One of the most distinctive features of Rouch's authorial praxis concerns the role of language, though his pronouncements on this matter could be rather contradictory. Although he played a leading part in the technical development of lip-synchronous portable sound technology in the early 1960s, he could be very dismissive of films that relied on conversational exchanges between the subjects, once observing that the films of the Direct Cinema group were 'spoiled by incredible regard for the chatting of the people filmed, as if oral testimony were more sacred than the visual sort'.

He confidently predicted that this 'archaic habit', which he believed had derived from radio, would 'disappear quite soon'.[37]

However, Rouch himself made abundant use of language in his films, and in a variety of ways, depending on the genre in which he was working. But whatever the genre, the language employed was almost invariably French (or very occasionally English). The sharing of anthropology may have been the cornerstone of his authorial praxis, but it was a sharing that almost always took place in Rouch's own language rather than that of his subjects.

In addition to all his other skills, Rouch was a very able verbal performer, as he demonstrates in his African documentaries, in which his voice predominates in the form of a voice-over commentary that typically runs from beginning to end. He not only speaks about the subjects, but he also speaks for them, paraphrasing what they are saying in a variety of tones of voice, speeds, and styles of delivery, according to the subject matter and circumstances. But while his declamatory and poetic commentary style worked well enough when it came to paraphrasing speech that was itself declamatory and poetic, as in the chanting that might take place during a ritual event, it was less successful stylistically when it came to paraphrasing everyday conversation, and more or less unworkable in situations in which several different voices were involved.

Rouch could have overcome this problem if he had been prepared to use subtitles when these first became technically possible in the 1960s. But Rouch consistently refused to take advantage of this possibility, offering a whole range of arguments against them. He would claim that they 'mutilate' the visual images of a film and to no avail, because they give only a very poor translation of what is being said. He argued that subtitles could slow up a film too much, since one often found oneself waiting for a statement to be completed before one could cut. Yet another reason was that he wanted his films to be watched in West Africa, and for these audiences, he claimed, voice-over was preferable to subtitling because literacy rates were very low.[38] But whether these various practical problems were the most fundamental reason why Rouch was unwilling to employ subtitles is debatable. At least equally important, one suspects, is that the technique of poetically paraphrasing his African subjects' speech had become such an integral part of his cinematographic *écriture* in the pre-synchronous sound era that he was unwilling to give it up in favour of the more puritanical disciplines of subtitling.

What is certainly the case is that when the language employed by the subjects is French, the role that language plays in Rouch's films is very different. Among the various genres of Rouch's film-making in which the subjects speak French are his ethnofictions, even though the subjects of these ethnofictions are mostly African. The language component of his earliest ethnofictions (*Jaguar* and *Moi, un Noir*) consists primarily of a voice-over improvised by the subjects in response to a projection of an assembly of the film rushes. In sharp contrast to his conventional ethnographic documentaries, Rouch's voice is heard only briefly and intermittently. In the later ethnofictions, starting with *La Pyramide humaine*, released in 1961, by which time lip-synchronous sound had become possible, these improvised voice-overs are displaced as the principal linguistic device by interactive dialogues between the subjects, though these too were mostly improvised rather than scripted. These dialogues are entirely in French, though in the case of *La Pyramide humaine*, it is less artificial than in the earlier ethnofictions in the sense that many of the subjects are the children of colonial personnel, whose first language would have been French. But even when the Africans are speaking to one another in this film, they also always speak in French.

Of all Rouch's films, the one demonstrating the greatest elaboration of linguistic devices is *Chronicle of a Summer*. As it is set in Paris and the south of France, this film is, of course, also in French. But in other respects, this film is very different in its use of language both from Rouch's African documentaries and from his ethnofictional works. Although there is a very limited amount of voice-over spoken by Rouch at the beginning of the film and a certain amount of informal dialogue between the subjects that they themselves have apparently initiated, the predominant linguistic mode of *Chronicle of a Summer* consists of dialogues between the subjects and the film-makers, or alternatively, dialogues between the subjects that have been set up by the film-makers.

These exchanges between film-makers and subjects, direct or indirect, take a variety of forms. They include highly formal, interrogational interviews conducted by Morin, who often appears in shot, and proxy interviews of one subject by another. They also include vox pops conducted by two of the subjects around the streets of Paris and also various examples of what one might now call 'focus groups'. The latter involve not only the subjects, but also both Rouch and Morin and even the production crew, and are often disguised in a charmingly French way as postprandial discussions around tables laden with evidence of a good meal and many bottles of wine recently consumed. Towards the end of the film, there is another type of focus group scene in which most of the principal subjects are gathered together in a small cinema and asked for their feedback on a preliminary assembly of the film. This is then followed by a sequence of Rouch and Morin walking up and down among the display cases of the Musée de l'Homme in which they engage in a reflexive conversation about what the feedback from the subjects has revealed about the nature of the truth that can be achieved through film (figure 8.6).

There is also a soliloquy in *Chronicle*, one that is often commented upon and which has Surrealist improvisational resonances, though to the best of

**8.6** Language in *Chronicle of a Summer* (1961). Top left, the interrogational interview of Marilou; centre left, mutual proxy interview between Angelo and Landry; bottom left, vox pop interviews by Nadine and Marceline. Top right, a focus group in the form of a meal at *Le Totem* restaurant; centre right, the film-makers in reflexive conversation at the Musée de l'Homme; bottom right, Marceline's soliloquy on the Place de la Concorde.

my knowledge, it is the only time in the whole of his oeuvre that Rouch used this device. It is performed by one of the leading subjects, the late Marceline Loridan, who was given a microphone linked to a tape-recorder hidden in a shoulder bag and invited to walk through Paris saying whatever came into her head. Yet although the soliloquy was spontaneous in this sense, the circumstances were set up by the film-makers – by agreement with Marceline, who seems to have had the idea in the first place – so that she would have a very particular kind of thought, namely, a reflection on her experiences of deportation to a Nazi concentration camp during the Second World War. To this end, the film-makers took Marceline to the Place de la Concorde in the centre of Paris, which had recently been the location for the making of a feature film about the German occupation. By the time they arrived, all the German army signs had been taken down, and the uniformed extras were no longer to be seen, but the location had the desired effect anyway. Later in the same sequence, they transferred her to the old Les Halles market where the architecture reminded her of the railway station at which she had boarded the train to Germany, provoking further reflections on her heart-rending experiences.

Although *Chronicle of a Summer* may be Rouch's best-known film, there are many ways in which, in terms of its praxis, it is atypical of his work as whole, the use of language being one of the most salient. However, what is distinctive about the use of language in the making of this film is not so much the fact of the dialogues between film-makers and subjects, as the fact that these dialogues are presented on screen. Interviews, informal conversation and focus groups had all been a regular part of Rouch's participatory methodology earlier in his career in Africa, as had the screening back of rushes to the subjects. But with the exception of some brief passages in *La Pyramide humaine*, Rouch had not previously shown himself in his films actually using these methods. What we are offered in *Chronicle of a Summer* then, in an almost uniquely reflexive way within Rouch's oeuvre as a whole, is the opportunity to see some of the practical principles underlying his concept of shared anthropology being played out in front of us.

## Jean Rouch as author: the legacy of shared anthropology

Feedback screenings and the ciné-trance represent two poles of sharing anthropology as Rouch conceived it, the ciné-trance constituting the most active, performative form, with feedback screenings being more passive. While there was some common ground between the more passive forms of Rouchian shared anthropology and the collaborative 'dialogical' approaches to anthropology that English-language anthropologists began to advocate in the 1970s, there was an extra, performative dimension to the Rouchian conception of shared anthropology. Whereas English-language dialogical anthropology typically consisted of a merely verbal exchange between researcher and subjects, in the most active form of Rouchian shared anthropology, the parties to the exchange are conceived as undergoing a radical transformation as each puts on an almost theatrical performance for the other, thereby jointly creating a form of knowledge that is a direct result of the encounter itself. In Rouch's view, this knowledge, far from being dismissed as false because it is an artifice of the encounter, should be considered, if anything, more valuable than any form of objective, detached observation that reveals only the surface of things.

Whatever reservations one might have about some of the more ambitious theoretical ramifications of Rouch's concept of the ciné-trance, one can still recognise the value of the proposition that is inherent to it, namely that the production of knowledge about the world cinematographically involves a process of exchange and mutual accommodation between film-maker and subjects. This was an idea that carried both methodological and ethical implications and Rouch deserves particular credit for having had the originality and independence of mind to develop such an idea, particularly since he spent his formative years working under the restrictive conditions of colonial West Africa.

However, some African film-makers and scholars have been critical of Rouch's work, considering it irredeemably colonialist, even if in a largely benign paternalist manner. These critical voices should be understood within the complex entanglements of the late colonial and postcolonial period and in particular, of the effects of the Laval Decree which, in place since the 1930s, prevented any form of film-making by Africans in French colonial Africa until after independence. In the circumstances, it cannot have been anything other than profoundly galling for Africans to see Rouch fêted, by the likes of Jean-Luc Godard and others, for having given a voice to Africa.[39]

These critical voices should make one cautious about laying too great a burden of expectation on the Rouchian notion of shared anthropology. In the last analysis, although his subjects and his local collaborators may have played a highly active part in creating his films, Rouch remained the overall author: they may have received screen credits and also considerable material benefits, but the films still bore the legend '*un film de Jean Rouch*'. As Jean-Paul Colleyn commented in his obituary for Rouch, within the inequalities of North–South relationships, the idea of an entirely shared anthropology, based on a genuinely collective authorship of equals, was always going to be something of a fiction and it continues to be so, even under present circumstances, some fifty years after the end of European colonialism in West Africa.[40]

But even while we should recognise all this in more sober moments, we should not be too 'presentist' in our assessment of Jean Rouch's work. We should not underestimate the hurdles of both a cultural and political nature that Rouch had to vault in order to make collaborative films with Africans of socially and politically marginal status in the still-colonial era of the 1940s and 1950s. Nor should we forget that the idea of surrendering any degree of authorship to the subjects of study was far in advance of the practice of the great majority of even the most progressive of his contemporaries, in both French- and English-language anthropology. Even if Rouch's ability to practise a fully shared anthropology was limited by the particular conjuncture of historical conditions under which he himself was working, this does not diminish the challenge and inspiration that his participatory authorial praxis continues to offer to ethnographic film-makers working today.

## Notes

1 This chapter draws extensively on my previous monograph on Jean Rouch, which has recently been republished in French in a substantially revised form (Henley 2009; 2020). Essential reading in any serious study of the films of Jean Rouch is the earlier monograph by Paul Stoller, *The Cinematic Griot* (1992). Two valuable additions to the literature on Jean Rouch's film-making have recently been published under the editorship of Luc Pequet (2017) and Rina Sherman (2018).

2 See the discussion of Griaule's work, pp. 46–8.

3 de Pastre (2017).

4 Rouch was also a prolific photographer, particularly in the early stages of his career. Very few of his photographs have been published, but in 2000 the Comité du film ethnographique put on an exhibition which led the distinguished photojournalist and film-maker Raymond Depardon to place Rouch, as a photographer, on a par with Pierre Verger and Cartier-Bresson (Gauthier and Pellé 2000, 4). A selection of Rouch's photographs is discussed at www.comitedufilmethnographique.com/jean-rouch/phototheque/.

5 For the film catalogues, see Rouch (1967a) and Rouch and Salzmann (1970). More generally regarding Rouch's publications, see Henley (2009), 465–7, while for the films about Rouch, see ibid., pp. 431–2. See also www.comitedufilmethnographique.com/jean-rouch/bibliographie/.

6 de Pastre (2017), 187. In recent years, the process of discovery has been greatly aided by Éditions Montparnasse who have made a considerable number of Rouch's films available in a series of DVD box sets: *Jean Rouch* (2004), *Jean Rouch: Cocorico! Monsieur Poulet* (2007), *Jean Rouch: une aventure africaine* (2010) and *Jean Rouch: un cinéma leger!* (2017).

7 Rouch (1955), 147.

8 Michael Eaton's edited collection of articles (1979) played an important role in introducing Rouch to English-speaking audiences as did the special editions of the journals *Studies in Visual Communication* vol. 11, no. 1 (1985) and of *Visual Anthropology* vol. 2, nos 3–4 (1989), edited by Steven Feld and Jay Ruby respectively.

9 Rouch (1995c), 410. See also Henley (2009), 19–23.

10 See, among many others, Clifford (1988b, 1991), Thompson (1995), Douglas (1995), also Rouch (1995c).

11 Jamin (1991), 84.

12 See Rouch (1995a), 89–90; Fulchignoni (2003), 185–6.

13 Rouch (1989), 10; (2003b), 110.

14 Clifford (1988b), 123–5; Rouch (2003b), 103–4.

15 See Mary Douglas (1975), who contrasts the Griaulian approach with the Malinowski-inspired approach of British social anthropologists of the same period.

16 Rouch (2003b), 111.

17 When challenged about the relative absence of women in his African films, Rouch explained that he had found it quite impossible as a European man to film African women, since this would not have been permitted by local people (Georgakas et al. 2003, 217). While this may have been true to a certain extent, it is not an entirely

convincing explanation as he did, on occasion, manage to film women's lives, as did Griaule also. Later in his career, Rouch encouraged anthropologist-film-maker Nadine Wanono to work with the Dogon with the explicit objective of presenting a female perspective on Dogon society (Wanono 1987; 2006).

18 Clifford (1988a), 77.
19 On Observational Cinema, see Chapter 10.
20 See particularly Griaule (1957), 59.
21 Rouch also supported the careers of many of his other African associates, including Oumarou Ganda, Moustapha Allasane and Safi Faye, all of whom became significant figures in West African cinema.
22 See Chapter 2, p. 106.
23 Rouch (1995a), 96.
24 Rouch disdained both Marx and Freud on the grounds that they were thinkers who exploited other peoples' dreams rather than being dreamers themselves (Taylor 2003), 132.
25 Blue (1996), 268–9.
26 Fieschi and Téchiné (1967), 19.
27 Morin (2003), 230–1, 264, n. 3.
28 The article inspired by *Les Tambours d'avant* has been republished several times, most recently in a collection of Rouch's articles edited by Jean-Paul Colleyn (Rouch 2009). It has also been translated into English by Steven Feld (Rouch 2003a).
29 See Rouch (1989), 186n; Rouch (2003a), 100. I suspect that Rouch borrowed the phrase '*la barbarie de l'invention*' from one of his Surrealist poet-heroes, but I have not been able to identify the precise source.
30 Rouch (1968), (1995a), 82; (1995b), 217.
31 Rouch (2009), 151.
32 Morin (2003), 230.
33 Petric (1987), 3–4.
34 See particularly Fulchignoni (2003), 185.
35 Fulchignoni (2003), 150.
36 Rouch (2009), 152. See also Rouch (2003), 99.
37 See Rouch (1995a), 94.
38 Colette Piault (2007a and 2007b).
39 For critical voices, see Cervoni (1982), Gabriel (1982), 74–7, Haffner (1996). But see also Jamie Berthe's recent finessing of these criticisms (2018).
40 Colleyn (2005).

# 9

# Robert Gardner: beyond the burden of the real

As an Author of ethnographic films, Robert Gardner developed a praxis that was not only very different from that of Jean Rouch but also one that was at odds with some of the central tenets of contemporary anthropology as an academic discipline. The ultimate purpose of his film-making was not so much to discover what other ways of life might mean to those who lived them but rather to explore what those ways of life signified for him personally in existential or aesthetic terms. In sharp contrast to Rouch who returned faithfully to West Africa every year, Gardner travelled all over the world to make his films, rarely lingering long enough in any one location to develop profound personal relationships with the subjects, to learn their language or engage in any extended ethnographic research. Even so, there is much that ethnographic film-makers can learn from the detailed study of his works, in particular with regard to way in which he seeks to communicate both meaning and experience, not through verbal language nor by means of the mimetic reproduction of the world in a direct observational manner, but rather through the carefully wrought juxtaposition of visual symbols.

Over the course of a lengthy film-making career that began in 1951 and which continued until shortly before his death in 2014 (thereby rivalling even that of Rouch in duration, if not in productivity), Gardner shot, directed and edited five major feature-length documentaries on ethnographic topics. The first of these was *Dead Birds* (shot in 1961, released in 1964), which concerned traditional warfare in highland Papua New Guinea. There then followed two films set in Africa, dealing broadly with issues of gender: *Rivers of Sand* (mostly shot in 1971, released in 1974), an exploration of relations between women and men among the Hamar of southern Ethiopia, and *Deep Hearts* (shot in 1978, released in 1981), which concerns a ceremonial display of beauty by the young men of a Nigerien group of Fulani, in West Africa. Gardner's more recent major films dealt with religious topics: *Ika Hands* (shot in 1981, though not released until 1988), which presents the life of the priestly figures known as *mama* among the Ika, an Amerindian

**9.1** Robert Gardner, aged 58, in Varanasi in 1984, during the shooting of *Forest of Bliss* (1986).

indigenous people of the Sierra Nevada de Santa Marta, northeastern Colombia, and, finally, *Forest of Bliss* (shot in 1984, released in 1986), an extended meditation on mortality in the form of a day-in-the-life account, from one sunrise to the next, of the funeral practices in and around the cremation pyres on the ghāts, the stepped embankments of the Ganges as it passes through the Hindu holy city of Varanasi (Benares) (figure 9.1).

Gardner also directed four shorter ethnographic documentaries in collaboration with others. Early in his career, in collaboration with William Heick, he made *Blunden Harbour* and *Dances of the Kwakiutl* (both released in 1951) in a Kwakwaka'wakw community on Vancouver Island.[1] Somewhat later, in mid-career, he made two collaborative films in India: *Altar of Fire* (released in 1976), produced in collaboration with the Sankritist J. F. Staal, which presents the re-enactment of an ancient Vedic ritual in Kerala; while *Sons of Shiva* (released in 1985), produced in collaboration with anthropologist Ákos Östör, follows a contemporary four-day ritual celebration in West Bengal. Gardner also collaborated in a less central way – as producer, cinematographer or editor – on half-a-dozen further documentaries on a broad variety of ethnographic topics.

Another important strand of Gardner's film work, though not ethnographic in intention, was a series of short portrait films, around ten in total, about North American or European visual artists. This strand began in the earliest period of his career but became increasingly prevalent in later years. He also worked on a number of other films of various kinds, including one feature-length work of fiction, which he produced for the Hungarian director, Miklos Jancso (also the subject of one of his portrait films). In the last decade or so of his life, he dedicated his energies to marshalling his cinemato-graphic legacy, producing two compilation films based on a reworking of what he referred to as 'forsaken fragments' drawn from various different points in his sixty years of film-making. He also published two limited edition collections of photographs and three largely autobiographical books related to his film work. During this period, he actively supported the activities of a number of independent film artists through his production company, Studio7Arts.[2]

## ROBERT GARDNER AS ETHNOGRAPHIC FILM-MAKER

Gardner would often assert that he thought of himself primarily as a poet or an artist rather than as an ethnographic film-maker. At the beginning of his career, while studying anthropology at the University of Washington in Seattle in the early 1950s (a degree that he never completed), he came across the experimental film-maker Sidney Peterson, the painter Mark Tobey and the poet Theodore Roethke, and quickly realised that the poet's view of the world was the one that he wanted to emulate. He found himself drawn to what he called 'lyrical' forms of documentary film-making, as represented by such diverse figures as Maya Deren, Stan Brakhage and Leni Riefenstahl, and the kind of truth that they could communicate. By the same token, he was not attracted to 'the hard-edged *cinéma-vérité* style of truth every 24th of a second'. He concluded that there was probably no truth in the films produced by this approach and even if there was, he was more interested in the truths that lay beyond those delivered by 'conventional storytelling or straight observational documentary'.

As a corollary of this self-identification as an artist or poet, Gardner was often ambiguous about the anthropological status of his work. Sometimes he would rather grandly declare an interest in 'a higher anthropology' while at others he would deny that his work had any anthropological import or intention. David MacDougall has suggested that we should take this disavowal with a pinch of salt, as analogous to the disavowal of symbolic intent by the poet Robert Frost. But if we consider Gardner's film-making career as a whole, it is clear that there was a marked shift in his relationship to anthropology, at least in its most academic manifestations.[3]

In the mid-1950s, Gardner returned to Harvard where he had studied for his first degree and enrolled on a Masters programme in anthropology. It was at this time that Gardner began working with John Marshall on the editing of the latter's Ju/'hoansi material, including the most celebrated of Marshall's films, *The Hunters*, though his precise role in this process remains a matter of controversy. Later, he also participated in the Marshall expedition to the Kalahari in 1958.[4] At this stage of his career, Gardner was actively involved in promoting the use of film in anthropology, in both teaching and research, and played a leading role in setting up the Film Study Center in the Peabody Museum of Archaeology and Ethnology at Harvard in 1956. Gardner became the first director of the Center and remained so in its various institutional guises over the next forty years.

In the early 1960s, when preparing to shoot *Dead Birds* (1964), the film that marks the beginning of his most productive period as a documentarist, Gardner continued to feel, as he would later put it, 'bound by anthropological scruples'. But gradually, 'bewildered by such dismal notions as functionalism and structuralism' which 'in some miraculous way overlooked people entirely', he progressively moved away from academic anthropology. By the 1980s, he claimed that all he needed to prepare himself for shooting *Forest of Bliss* was some literature that he had read in his student days, in combination with what he had gleaned more recently from a random selection of Indian novels. Under his direction, the interests and activities of the Film Study Center suggest a similar move away from a formal connection with academic anthropology over this period.[5]

Whether or not Gardner's work can be considered 'anthropological' very much depends, of course, on how one defines anthropology, a famously contentious task. But it is certainly very different from the 'shared anthropology' of Jean Rouch. The longest that Gardner remained in any one location appears to have been the six months that he spent, when making *Dead Birds* in 1961, in the Baliem Valley in the highlands of West Papua, in what is now the Indonesian Province of Papua. For his later productions, as his recently published field journals make clear, he would often be on the move. As one would expect under these circumstances, he was not able to learn any local languages, nor develop extensive personal relationships. The journals reveal that he was often unsure of the significance for his subjects of what he was filming, even though he might have his own ideas about its potential meaning within his eventual film. They also reveal a sometimes disturbing detachment, even disdain for his subjects, as well as a number of examples of what many anthropologists would surely consider an unacceptable indifference to the subjects' objections to the intrusion of his camera.[6]

In order to overcome difficulties of comprehension or access in the field, Gardner usually worked with collaborators, often anthropologists, who had a more long-standing engagement with the subjects of the film. These collaborators would act as his interpreters and provide him with ethnographic contextualisation. Some of these collaborations appear to have been mutually richly rewarding: this appears to have been the case, for example, in Gardner's collaborations with Karl Heider on *Dead Birds*, with J. F. Staal on *Altar of Fire* and with Ákos Östör on *Sons of Shiva* and *Forest of Bliss*. All of these collaborators have testified eloquently to the manner in which working with Gardner opened their eyes to certain aspects of the ethnography of the people whom they were studying.[7]

But in other instances, including his early work with John Marshall, Gardner's collaborations were decidedly fraught. Although personality issues appear also to have intervened, it seems that these tensions would often arise because the collaborators felt that Gardner was too ready to allow his personal vision to blind him to what they considered to be the ethnographic reality. One cause of tension with Marshall, for example, concerned Gardner's proposal to follow up *The Hunters* with a general film about Ju/'hoansi women, to be entitled 'The Gatherers'. Marshall was adamantly opposed to this project, believing that Gardner's conception of this film 'would bend reality too far out of shape'.[8] Some years later the anthropologists Jean Lydall and Ivo Strecker, who worked with Gardner on *Rivers of Sand*, would claim that it presented Hamar life in such a fragmented and inaccurate way that it was no better than 'an ethnographic farce'.[9]

Whatever the rights and wrongs surrounding the disagreements about the ethnographic probity of these particular films – and Gardner has certainly had his champions[10] – the general circumstances of filming remain inscribed in the films themselves. From simply looking at the films, it is immediately clear that Gardner's praxis was minimally dialogical, minimally participatory and minimally reflexive. With one or two exceptions, the language of the subjects is almost entirely absent or, if it is present at all, it is not subtitled. Unsurprisingly, since he did not speak their languages, there is little or no engagement between subjects and camera. But not only do they not speak to it, they rarely even look at it: the invisible fourth wall of classical theatre mostly remains firmly in place. The relationship between film-maker and subjects remains completely unacknowledged.

The exceptions to these generalisations are notable, but also only partial. One of these is to be found in *Rivers of Sand*, which involves some degree of participation in the sense that it features an extended oral testimony by a married woman, whom Gardner names as Omali Inda, in which she describes the manner in which women are controlled and disciplined by men in Hamar society. This is also an unusual film in Gardner's oeuvre in terms of content since whereas most of his ethnographic films are primarily concerned with ritual and ceremonial life, or if not, with warfare, all typically male domains of experience, this film accords greater attention to everyday life and also to women's experience. Made in the immediate aftermath of the collapse of Gardner's first marriage, it offers a particularly bleak vision of the possibility for harmonious relationships between women and men, not just among the Hamar, but anywhere. Indeed, Omali Inda's testimony is intertwined with Gardner's own more personal ruminations on the subject both at the beginning and at the end of the film, in the first case in the

9.2 *Rivers of Sand* (1974). Left, the beating of women by men is part of
Hamar tradition, 'so how can it be bad'?, asks Omali Inda. Right,
according to Gardner, 'Men are also afflicted, through their own tyranny,
with wasted energies, idle spirits and self-doubt'.

form of a rolling title, in the second, as a voice-over comment. However,
their two statements remain quite separate: Omali Inda's testimony is delivered
as a monologue rather than as part of some form of dialogical exchange
with the film-maker (figure 9.2).[11]

Another partial exception is *Ika Hands* (1988). This film is unusual within
Gardner's oeuvre in that it is structured around a discussion between Gardner
and the eminent Colombian anthropologist Gerardo Reichel-Dolmatoff
as they watch a preliminary edited version of the film, several years after
the filming had been completed. This conversation is reflexive in the sense
that it is initially shown in synch on screen and later heard in voice-over,
providing not only some ethnographic contextualisation but also reflection
on the film-making process. When Reichel-Dolmatoff observes that there
are no shots showing social relations in the film, evoking a great sense of
loneliness, Gardner wonders, interestingly, whether this says more about
him than about the Ika subjects.

These exceptions merely prove the more general rule that Gardner's
films arose primarily from a detached and subjective vision rather than from
his interactions with the film subjects. But if this limits the ethnographicness
of his films, at least as I have defined this concept for the purposes of this
book, the most significant divergence concerns the general objectives of
his film-making. Over the course of his whole career, very candidly and
entirely consistently, Gardner made no bones about the fact that he was
more interested in what culturally exotic ways of life meant for him as a
film-maker concerned with issues of what he on occasion identified as
moral philosophy than he was in what those ways of life meant for those
who actually lived them. Thus, early in his career, he observed that while
his first responsibility in making *Dead Birds*, both to himself and to the
Dani, had been 'to document with as much discernment as possible the

most telling and important aspects of their life', what the film represented for him was 'the opportunity of speaking to certain fundamental issues in human life'. The Dani, he frankly acknowledged, 'were less important to me than those issues'.[12]

In this particular case, these 'issues' concerned the existential question of how it is possible for human beings to preserve a sense of meaning and value in the face of an awareness of their inevitable physical extinction, or as Gardner puts it, rather more resonantly, 'how we all, as humans meet our animal fate'. This philosophical concern was a recurrent feature of Gardner's work and also animated the making *Forest of Bliss* some twenty years later. And as in the film about the Dani, Gardner approached the issue on his own terms, even when these ran against the grain of local attitudes. In the journal recording his initial reactions to the rushes of his material from Varanasi, we find him reminding himself that even though for him, the city is a place of pain and abandonment, for Hindus it is 'a place of and an opportunity for exultation'.[13] Nevertheless, what we are offered in the final film is an unrelenting portrait of pain and abandonment leavened only by the most evanescent prospect of redemption. In this sense, as so often in his films, in *Forest of Bliss*, ethnographic understanding derived from engagement with the point of view of the subjects has been displaced or submerged by Gardner's more personal subjective vision.

## ROBERT GARDNER AS CINEMATOGRAPHER

Whatever reservations one might have about the ethnographic status of his films, Gardner was undeniably a highly accomplished cinematographer. His camera style was predominantly realist, though within this stylistic register he mixed a great variety of shots, from hand-held wide-angle tracking shots to tripod-based shots on the end of a long lens, all executed with consummate skill. Intermediate midshots or close-ups exploring intimate details of human bodies or material objects are a particularly important element within this repertoire. All his feature-length documentaries were shot in a richly saturated 16 mm colour stock, seemingly Kodachrome. This serves to give his films a suffused, poetic aura, though in considering his rushes from Varanasi, Gardner himself worries that this stock can also have the effect of aestheticising rubbish and decay in an overly saccharine manner.[14]

Somewhat at odds with the predominantly realist tenor of his camerawork, Gardner had a tendency, particularly in his later films, to insert special effects, such as slow motion, time-lapses, unusual camera angles or distortions arising from the use of extreme lenses. The significance of these special effects is often either obscure or rather self-consciously artistic: as the screen studies scholar Scott MacDonald has put it, they are 'little more than affectations – "arty" rather than artful'. MacDonald suggests, plausibly, that they can be put down to Gardner's 'decades-long wrestle with the idea of being both documentarian and poetic film-maker'.[15]

These special effects are most evident in the third of Gardner's feature-length documentaries, *Deep Hearts* (1981). This is a film about the *geerewol*, a ceremony involving the competitive display of song, dance and beauty by the men of a particular subgroup of the Fulani pastoralists of West Africa. Most commonly referred to in the English-language literature as the Wodaabe, this subgroup is also known as the Bororo or Borroro, which is the term preferred by Gardner.[16] The prevalence of unusual camera angles and other effects in this film is due to the fact that, owing to technical problems with Gardner's own camera, some of the cinematography was performed by his long-term friend and collaborator Robert Fulton, a specialist in using the Bolex, a non-synchronous 16 mm camera that allows one to achieve a range of special effects while still on location. At one point in his field journal, Gardner remarks that he is hoping to persuade Fulton 'to look for the meaning in gestures and not be content with optical allure alone'. The final film suggests that he had only limited success in this matter.[17]

Not only in this respect but in others too, *Deep Hearts* is certainly the weakest of Gardner's feature-length documentaries. In terms of substantive content, there really is not a great deal to this film other than a description of one part of the performance of the *geerewol* itself (figure 9.3). Although this is indeed a truly remarkable event, there is little exploration of the social or cultural complexities associated with it, other than some portentous and rather vacuous generalisations delivered through the narration. Rather than suggesting some further level of analysis or insight, the special effects appear to be merely making up for the shortcomings of content that one might expect in a film shot in just under four weeks, in what were clearly very difficult circumstances. Gardner's witnessing of the climactic events of the *geerewol* itself was confined to no more than a few days, and his various attempts to settle down with a group of Bororo to film everyday life met with repeated rejections. Although he did have an anthropological adviser with him on this trip, one Patrick Paris, introduced to him by Jean Rouch, Gardner frequently expresses concern in his field journal about Paris's shortcomings and his name does not appear in the credits to the film.[18]

In both the variety and complexity of the shots employed, as well as in the occasional use of special effects, Gardner's cinematographic signature was quite unlike that of Jean Rouch. In general, Rouch's camerawork was much more rough and ready, not necessarily because he had a lesser cinemato-graphic 'eye' than Gardner (though this may indeed have been true), but also because, through his engagement with this subjects and his stress on spontaneity, Rouch did not have the time and detachment in the moment of shooting to achieve the disciplined cinematographic effects that Gardner

**9.3** *Deep Hearts* (1981). Left, a young man prepares for the *geerewol* ceremony; right, a young woman selects her favourite from amongst the line of male dancers.

was able to do. This difference relates to their respective attitudes regarding the direction of the subjects of their films. Neither Gardner nor Rouch worked with anything resembling a formal script, but whereas Rouch might have actively sought to provoke his subjects into performances for his camera, he was reluctant – at least in principle, not always honoured in practice – to instruct them specifically in what they should then do. Gardner, by contrast, was prepared to direct his subjects, particularly in the early period of his career.

But surely the greatest difference between Gardner and Rouch in terms of cinematographic practice concerns their respective attitudes to sound synchronicity. Throughout the early part of his career, Rouch was actively seeking to overcome the technical difficulties of achieving synchronous sound on location. By contrast, even when the technical means to shoot in synchronous sound were readily available, which would certainly have been the case by the time that he shot *Rivers of Sand* in 1971, Gardner continued to shoot and record sound separately, and he went on doing so until at least as late as 1984 when he made *Forest of Bliss*.[19] This technical choice was symptomatic of a belief, shared by many film-makers who learned their craft in the era prior to the development of lip-synchronous sound, that the introduction of synchronous speech threatened to reduce non-fiction film-making from a form of cinematographic art to no more than a banal form of current affairs journalism.

## ROBERT GARDNER IN THE EDIT SUITE

Although Robert Gardner's skills as a cinematographer were undoubtedly remarkable, his skills as an editor were, arguably, even greater. Indeed, it was in the edit suite that his authorship as a film-maker took on its most distinctive form, considerably exceeding in sophistication the editorial praxis of Jean

Rouch. It is for this reason that I shall give preponderant attention to this aspect of his work in the remainder of this chapter.

A privileged insight into Gardner's editorial praxis is afforded by the release on DVD of two of his major films, *Forest of Bliss*, in 2001, and *Dead Birds*, in 2004. In both cases, the films are accompanied by commentaries by Gardner on the postproduction process, delivered in informal conversation with colleagues. The conversation about *Dead Birds* is available as additional material on the DVD itself, and took place some forty years after the film was released. In the case of *Forest of Bliss*, it takes the form of a free-standing book with the DVD inserted into the back sleeve. The book reproduces a conversation between Gardner and the anthropologist with whom he worked on this film, Ákos Östör. Although this text was not published until 2001, the conversation took place as they watched the film together in 1987, when the memory of shooting the film was still fresh in their minds.[20]

In effect, Gardner began editing his films as he was shooting them, not only, as many documentarists do, at the level of the sequence or the scene, but even at the level of the individual shot. As his field journals make clear, while still on location, Gardner was always on the look-out for iconic shots that, through metaphorical association, would point to some domain of meaning lying beyond mere surface appearances. Contrasting his approach with that of anthropologists who are interested in social change, he comments in his Hamar field diary that, 'My own interests are to look for that which is an apt symbol or sign and, at the same time, is distinctive in and of itself.'[21] This was also the key to his praxis once he was back in the edit suite. Rather than take Gardner's images at face value as descriptive registrations of the world as it is, one should be constantly reading them as signifiers of some more transcendent meaning, even while bearing in mind that these images may be burdened with a phenomenal surface meaning that acts as an obstacle to grasping their true ulterior significance.

In order to help his audiences to get past surface meanings, Gardner often makes use of montage, though not in the most common present-day sense of the term, that is, a rapid sequence of images intended merely to truncate time or to summarise an event. It is a form of montage more akin to the so-called 'intellectual montage' developed by Soviet directors in the 1920s in which the aim was to generate, from the juxtaposition of two or more shots, a meaning that goes beyond the sum of the parts. But whereas Soviet montage was typically based on a sequence of brief shots, often self-consciously non-realist in character (in order to produce *ostranenie*, to defamiliarise), in Gardner's films these montages are typically composed of stylistically realist shots, often of relatively long duration.

This montage technique may also be applied to whole sequences based on a progressive, normal chronology that are intercut in the manner of parallel editing. But whereas conventional parallel editing is normally intended

9.4 *Dead Birds* (1964). Left, a Dani man injured by an enemy arrow; right, a warrior holding a feather head-dress looks over the battleground.

only to suggest temporal simultaneity, in Gardner's use of the device it often also carries some additional symbolic significance. Precisely because of the cinematographic realism and the often-normal chronology, a viewer who is not alert to Gardner's semiotic purposes may be lulled into interpreting these juxtapositionings as being merely descriptive. This is one of the reasons, I suspect, why some critics have been unable to read the carefully thought out analyses that are embedded in Gardner's films.

In the course of his career, Gardner's use of symbolic association in his editorial juxtapositionings became increasingly sophisticated and correspondingly more difficult to read. In the opening sequence of *Dead Birds*, his semiotic intentions are almost too obvious. Over the opening image of a gliding hawk shot from above, a sonorous voice-over, delivered by Gardner himself, relates a Dani legend that the Bird, on winning a race with the Snake in mythological times, became destined thereafter to die. This is immediately followed by a shot of a dead young man being taken down from a funeral chair prior to his cremation. This direct association of humans and birds as sharing the common condition of mortality is heavily reinforced by the title graphics. These come up in two stages, in reverse order, with 'BIRDS' over the end of the outgoing shot of the hawk, with 'DEAD' only coming in with the cut to the human corpse. Throughout the remainder of *Dead Birds*, there are recurrent juxtapositions of images of men with images of birds or sounds of birds. There are also many shots of men with feathers in their hair or with the elaborate feather head-dresses which they wear when engaged in warfare (figure 9.4).

Somewhat more difficult to read is the intertwining at certain points of the symbolic interplay between birds and humans with the contrast between men and women. For example, in an early sequence, Gardner intercuts between Weyak, the principal male subject, looking out for enemies from a watchtower silhouetted against the sky and Lakha, his wife working in the gardens nearby, apparently in the same late afternoon. But as Gardner explains in his discussion with fellow film-maker Ross McElwee on the DVD, the intercutting of their activities was intended to indicate more than mere simultaneity. What he also wants us to understand from this juxtaposition is not merely the contrast between men's work (seemingly light) and women's work (seemingly heavy), but between men's symbolic identification with the sky (and hence with birds) and women's identification with the earth. This association of humans and birds is also invoked in the contrast between Weyak and Pua, a young 'swineherd' who anxiously anticipates his own manhood. Towards the end of the film, these contrasts are elided as the women too become symbolic birds when they dance to celebrate the revenge killing of an enemy, while Pua kills and eats a bird and, as sign of his developing maturity, puts the feathers in his hair.

In *Forest of Bliss*, released some twenty years later, the symbolic elements are not only more numerous, but their juxtapositions are more complex and varied. Nor does Gardner provide any helpful keys to interpretation through voice-over narration. In *Dead Birds*, there is very substantial narration, written and delivered in a somewhat literary style. In addition to alerting the audience to the significance of what is happening on the screen, it is also used for retailing ethnographic information. Looking back at the film forty years later, Gardner regrets this, saying that it resulted from a 'weird' sense of the need to be a responsible witness. After *Dead Birds*, voice-over narration progressively diminishes in Gardner's work so that by the time of *Forest of Bliss*, it has disappeared entirely. Instead, Gardner seeks to communicate both significance and context by a series of non-verbal means, some of which involve metaphorical association, while others rely rather on formal properties of the filmic text, notably the transitions between sequences and the overall narrative structure.

## MATERIAL METAPHORS

In his conversation with Östör about *Forest of Bliss*, Gardner gives a number of different examples of how he sought to use non-verbal means to impose some order on the 'endless possibilities for confusion' that Varanasi represented for him. In the first instance, he did so by approaching the reality of the city through a number of particular elements which, although very simple and very material, he saw as being laden with potentially illuminating metaphorical meanings: wood, marigolds, dogs, birds, children's kites. Rather than using doctrinal exposition by local ritual specialists or voice-over narration, Gardner takes on the extraordinarily bold challenge of evoking the principles of Hindu eschatology through the images and sounds of these simple material features of the world within which the disposal of the dead takes place in Varanasi.

Central to this eschatology, as described by the Indian sociologist Radihka Chopra in her review of the film, is the idea that life is to death as creation is to destruction, but that even while being opposed, these binary oppositions are connected to one another cyclically. Far from being kept apart in everyday life, they exist side by side, in a state of constant interpenetration with one another.[22] In *Forest of Bliss*, this philosophical dialectic is played out by the recurrent juxtaposition of opposites that are simultaneously both solidly material and highly symbolic. Thus the snarling dogs, scavengers of filth and gnawers of human corpses and, as such, symbols of extreme pollution as well as of the boundaries between human and animal, and beyond that, between life and death, are recurrently opposed in the film to the beautiful and bright marigolds, gathered in the peaceful countryside. Marigolds are also used as ritual markers of transition in a variety of contexts: adorning images of deities at the threshold of the human and the divine, garlanding a newly blessed boat about to be launched, as well as newly dead corpses, newly born babies and even the neck of a young puppy.

Similarly, heavy piles of wood destined for the funeral pyres are associated with dead bodies, while both are juxtaposed and contrasted, on the one hand with the healthy bodies of those who load the wood onto barges and row it downstream to the cremation grounds and, on the other, with the kites that are children's playthings and whose progress across the sky, dancing on the uplifting thermals from the cremation fires, evokes lightness, vitality and vulnerability all at the same time. In the striking montage of shots with which the film begins, it is suggested, by editorial juxtaposition, that a young boy, in seeking to launch his kite, is also somehow pulling up the sun. Much later in the film, shortly before dusk, two of these kites happen to fall down into the river in the background of a shot just at the moment that a child's corpse is being committed to the river. At this moment, the dialectical connection between the symbolically opposed values of sky and river, of spirit and body, of life and death is rendered in a form that is, as Gardner puts it, 'powerfully actual'.[23]

This last shot is one of the many ways in which the spatial relationship between the sky and the river are exploited symbolically in the film. There are frequent cuts from dogs or corpses, in the river or on its banks, to shots of birds flocking noisily in an azure sky. Sometimes the two come together, as when we hear the sound of carrion birds cawing in the background while dogs gnaw on something, perhaps a corpse, or as the birds flock around the boat bearing wood for the funeral pyres upstream. Some of these birds are kites, others vultures, others sparrows, but all of them, although symbolic of the vitality of life in the moment, are also, for Gardner, harbingers of mortality, just as birds of other species had been for him in New Guinea.[24]

Nor is this vertical connection between sky and river the only form of movement through space that is used to symbolic effect. Equally important

9.5 *Forest of Bliss* (1986), material metaphors. Feral dogs eating carrion
left, evoke Cerberus, the guardian of the Underworld in Greek
mythology, while the wood transported upriver for the cremation pyres,
right, suggests the presence of death.

is the horizontal relationship between upstream and downstream, as manifest
in the movement of boats through the frame of the film: at the very
beginning of the film – as noted by Michael Oppitz in a perceptive early
review – they move from left to right, while at the very end, they move
in the opposite direction. At the beginning, the boats come out of a haze
and gradually take shape, while the boat in the final scene gets wrapped
up again in this haze before it disappears into the void. Oppitz concludes
that 'the former may be taken as movements into life and the later ones as
movements out of life'.[25] Gardner's comments, although not published until
some fifteen years later, indicate that this change of direction was certainly
intended and although he does not quite confirm the interpretation offered
by Oppitz, it seems very likely that this is what he had in mind.[26]

On the other hand, Gardner is entirely explicit in identifying the symbolic
significance for him of the diagonal movements in space from one side of
the river to the other – that is, from the active western bank, site of the
city and the cremation ghāts, to the sandy and unpopulated eastern bank.
Even before he began filming, Gardner formed an analogy in his mind
between the Ganges and the Styx, with the eastern bank being that 'far
shore' from which, proverbially, no traveller returns, while the feral dogs
that ranged there were, for him, none other than real-world embodiments
of Cerberus, the hellhound who guarded the entrance to the Underworld
of Greek mythology (figure 9.5). Although the people of Varanasi might
consider the eastern bank no more than a place of recreation, and while
Östör thought of it as a peaceful refuge from the confusion of the city, for
Gardner it was a place of 'quite forbidding mystery', representing the world
of death as opposed to the world of life on the more populated shore.[27]

In this spatial distinction, Gardner saw yet another way to organise the
'chaos' of Varanasi. Thus the film opens with a series of shots from the 'far

shore', with 'spectral galleons' passing through the mist and Cerberus-like dogs on patrol, before crossing to the inhabited shore with all its confusion and vitality, for the main body of the film. There the action remains, apart from one or two interpolated shots from the 'far shore' that act as a sort of memento mori, before seemingly returning there in the final shot in which a rowing boat disappears slowly and inexorably into the mist once again.

## AURAL METAPHORS

Throughout his career, Gardner generally acted as his own picture editor but, as a sign of the importance that he attributed to the soundtrack of his films, he often worked hand in hand with highly skilled sound editors. In his first film, *Blunden Harbour* (1951), Gardner used asynchronous drumming and shamanic chanting to suggest transcendent significance. In his later ethnographic films, the sound editing becomes progressively more sophisticated. In *Dead Birds*, the soundtrack is greatly enriched but largely in a straightforward realist manner. In *Rivers of Sand* (1974), however, it begins to take on a more metaphorical function. Early in the film, the sound from a shot of a donkey braying in synch is carried over to cover the next shot, which shows a young man whipping a woman, a ritual practice that forms part of the Hamar male initiation ceremony. The clear implication of this sound overlay is that in Hamar society, men treat women as if they were no more than beasts of burden. Though this view of gender relations in Hamar society has been vigorously disputed by Jean Lydall and Ivo Strecker, the anthropologists who advised Gardner during the shooting of this film, the editorial technique itself nevertheless remains very interesting.[28]

The principal sound editor on *Rivers of Sand* was Michel Chalufour who would later work on a number of Gardner's other films, including *Forest of Bliss*.[29] In the latter, the manipulation of sounds takes a variety of forms but one of its primary metaphorical purposes is to provide an aural complement to the many visual memento mori. The combined effect is to suggest that even in life one is surrounded, if not by death itself, then at least by potentially fatal suffering or menace. In some instances, the manipulation of sound consists merely of enhancing the diegetic synchronous sound. A simple example occurs when a carpenter takes a break from constructing the ladder-like bamboo biers that are used to transport corpses around the city. He lights up a cigarette and then exhales very loudly. This exhalation has been much augmented, Gardner explains, in order to suggest the final expiration of a dying person.[30]

There are many similar examples of sound augmentation in the film, some of which are intradiegetic, that is, they come from within the world of the film, while others appear to be entirely extradiegetic, that is, they come from outside the material recorded on location. The latter appears to be the case, for example, with the sharp, staccato footsteps of a dog trotting along a sandy riverbank that feature in the opening shot of the film. The crisp, almost percussive effect of the footsteps adds a pronounced sense of menace to the image, anticipating the violence of the snarling dog-fight that follows immediately afterwards.

The mere augmentation of sounds can be distinguished from a more elaborate intradiegetic use of aural metaphors. A recurrent example in *Forest of Bliss* involves the sound of chopping of wood. Throughout the film, this functions as a memento mori on account of its association with the preparation of wood for the funeral pyres. Often we see this in synch, but at other points the sound is featured in scenes in which the wood chopping itself is not visible. The first example occurs under the main title of the film, where one hears the sounds of trees being felled. Gardner was influenced here by a comment made by Baidyanath Saraswati, an Indian ethnographer who, along with Östör, worked as an anthropological adviser on the film. Saraswati said that as a child growing up in a rural village, whenever he heard the sound of mango trees being chopped down, he knew that a death had occurred. In their discussion, Gardner and Östör reflect on how they went to a great deal of trouble to film tree felling at some distance from the city. However, in the end, Gardner decided that the visual image of the woodsmen actually doing the felling would be 'too puny' to carry such a weighty metaphorical charge.[31] Yet without the aid of the contextualising comment from Saraswati, it is surely optimistic to think that any viewer will be able to understand this metaphorical reference, especially as it occurs quite so early in the film.

Another acoustic effect used in this way is the sound of bells tolling. Although tolling bells do occur in synch in the sequences set in temples and shrines, they are also used in an intradiegetic way, with ambiguous effects since, as Östör suggests with regard to a usage very early in the film, one is not quite sure whether they are tolling to announce a death or are simply liturgical bells marking the time of day. Gardner confirms that he wanted this ambiguous effect to encourage the audience to ask questions:

> The bells are both merry and not so merry. They are meant to be full of the possibility of delight and, equally, the possibility of sorrow ... Ambiguity plays such a prominent part in creating an atmosphere. It is this mood that I hope continues through the whole film until there is real clarity and the mysteries get solved.[32]

Throughout the film, a number of sounds are used recurrently to emphasise and reinforce the juxtaposition of the symbolic opposites of life and death, of sky and water, purity and pollution. These include funeral chanting (*rama nama satya he* – 'God's Name is Truth'), the swishing of water, the barking of dogs and the squawking of birds. But of all the aural metaphors used in the film, undoubtedly the most striking is one that we hear for the first time about seven minutes into the film. Here it features over a shot of the prow of a boat which, together with a brief and difficult-to-discern shot of a dog gnawing at a half-submerged corpse, is inserted non-sequentially into the middle of an otherwise largely observational sequence of one of the main characters taking an early-morning bathe in the river. It is a strange, creaking, and somehow ominous sound, which, like the sound of the tolling bells, is clearly intended to provoke a question in the mind of the viewer.

This sound occurs on two further occasions over shots of a boatload of wood being rowed upstream for the funeral pyres, but it is not until some 37 minutes into the film that we finally discover what it is. It turns out to be the sound produced by the grating of bamboo oars in the small rope lassos that serve as rowlocks on these boats. Oppitz describes this acoustic device as a '*coup de maître*' and suggests that it acts as 'the musical *leitmotiv* of the entire film, a sound metaphor for terrestrial suffering, pain, labour, and disharmony'. The most dramatic use of all is saved for the long final shot of the film in which a rowing boat slowly disappears into the mist on its way to 'the far shore'. With this usage, Oppitz remarks, 'Gardner strikes his best transcendental string'.[33]

## Subjects as metaphors

One of the most distinctive features of Gardner's ethnographic film-making praxis is the absence of subjects of rounded, idiosyncratic character. As he said of the Dani early in his career, the subjects themselves are not of interest to him as actual, embodied individuals: what is of interest is what they signify. Some twenty years later, in his conversation with Östör, he goes further, arguing that the idea that one could capture the sense of an individual human being on film is a complete illusion.[34] Certainly, the subjects of Gardner's films are not characters of the kind that one discovers in the films of Jean Rouch or David and Judith MacDougall, that is, individuals full of ideas and opinions, and a range of moods and humours, often mutually contradictory, as in human experience generally.

The closest that Gardner comes to such characters are Weyak and his wife Lakha, and most of all, the young swineherd Pua in *Dead Birds*, but even they come across more as archetypes rather than rounded individuals. More usually, Gardner's characters are primarily vehicles through which he can explore particular issues or aspects of the human condition that he perceives as being played out within the cultural arena in which those subjects happen to live. By taking away the particularising detail of their

9.6 *Forest of Bliss* (1986), subjects as metaphors. Left, the holy Ragul Pandit performs prayers at dawn; right, Dom Raja, the Untouchable cremation businessman, a character of 'utter balefulness'.

lives, Gardner seems to be encouraging us, rather in manner of the hagiographers of Christian saints, to attend more directly to what his subjects' lives might signify transcendentally.

In *Forest of Bliss*, the three principal subjects each represent different aspects of life in and around the funeral ghāts, like so many characters in a morality play, and there is no sustained attempt to establish the idiosyncratic person behind or beyond the role that each plays in the film. Even the device of personalising the subjects through naming them, as in *Dead Birds*, is not employed here. As with the manipulation of material symbols described above, the three subjects are used instead to present a series of fundamental symbolic contrasts. At one extreme is a priestly figure whom Östör identifies as Ragul Pandit, a 'ritualist'. He represents a series of positive values: wisdom, serenity, purity. His ritual incantations at dawn, reminiscent for Gardner of Gregorian chant, are intended to provide some redemption for the audience at the end of the film, after they have been taken through the valley of the shadow of death. At the other extreme stands the Untouchable, the Dom Raja, a character of 'utter balefulness', as Gardner describes him. His ugly and sick body, his broken voice and manner of arrogant contempt accord perfectly with his very worldly business as supervisor of the funeral pyres, an enterprise that he appears to pursues with a ruthless indifference to the bereavement of his clients (figure 9.6).

If the Pandit represents the spiritual life and the possibility of renewal, the Dom Raja represents the utter ineluctability and meaninglessness of the material world. Between these two poles, as a sort of trickster, lies a healer and diviner, identified by Östör by name as Mithai Lal, who like the Pandit engages in ritual activity, but who like the Dom can also be vulgar and materialistic. Whereas the other two characters both represent their station in life unambiguously and with utter seriousness, the healer seems

273

to be a joker, capable of both good and evil, banality and religious inspiration, whose mental state verges at some points on insanity.[35]

## TRANSITIONS

As Oppitz astutely pointed out in his review, Gardner employs a range of different types of editorial transition to suggest symbolic significance in *Forest of Bliss*.[36] Sometimes this significance is achieved through the juxtaposition in a sequence of shots that are reiterative of the same point. One of the most striking examples here is a sequence in which a number of dead animals are shown being dragged down the steps of a ghāt, without ceremony, in order to be disposed of in the river: first a donkey and a cat, and then a dog, are hauled down, their bodies twisting awkwardly and their skulls resounding hollowly, probably with the aid of some acoustic enhancement. But this series of images is preceded and made meaningful by a shot of an elderly blind man also making his way, carefully and elegantly, down the steps of a ghāt. In his rushes log, Gardner records that he had decided long before going to Varanasi that 'steps would be important indicators of transition: between life and death as much as between river and city'. The implication of this sequence then is that for all their dignity, human beings share the 'animal fate' of other creatures, that is, we too, actually or metaphorically, will one day be taken down the steps of a ghāt and disposed of in a river somewhere.[37]

These serial montages may be contrasted with a technique whereby semiotically significant juxtapositions are incorporated within a sequence that is ostensibly a real-time event but which has actually been constructed in the edit suite. An example in a relatively early sequence shows a boat being rowed upstream, heavily laden with wood. As it progresses, there are two shots, presented as if they were taken from the point of view of someone in the boat, first of vultures whirling in the sky, then of a corpse floating face-downwards in the shallows, anus towards the camera. In commenting on this sequence, Gardner is quite candid in admitting that these two shots were 'connected by editing, not at all by actuality'. His intention, he explains, was to intimate that this consignment of wood, the purpose of which has not yet been made clear, has 'some death-related meaning, that it is not just for keeping people warm at night'.[38] Only later do we discover that this is the wood for the funeral pyres.

In this case, the shots of the vultures and the corpse, although only connected to the boat in the edit suite, have been carefully woven into the narrative of the film: not only do they fit very smoothly into the chronological progression of the boat upriver, but they also appear to be representing the point of view of somebody in the boat. But in other cases, Gardner inserts into the middle of a sequence one or more shots that are heavily charged with metaphorical meanings, yet are quite clearly from another place or another time.

A good example here is the lengthy opening sequence in which the healer-diviner Mithai Lal makes his way down the ghāt steps to bathe. Once he has immersed himself in the river, the generally observational quality of the sequence is suddenly interrupted by an abrupt cut to a tightly framed long shot taken from the 'far shore' showing a sail going by, with a funeral pyre burning in the background. Then, after returning for another couple of shots of the healer frolicking in the water, there is a cut to two people launching an offering of marigolds laid out upon a large leaf. Shortly afterwards, the bath time routine is again interrupted, this time in an even more startling fashion, by two further shots, one of a dog gnawing at what seems to be a corpse and the other, the prow of a boat shot from above that is accompanied by the grating sound of the unseen rope rowlocks. The exact import of these interpolated shots is not clear at this stage, but Gardner comments that he wants the viewers to become aware right away that the river has many meanings beyond that of simply being a good place to bathe.[39]

In all these cases, the juxapositioning for semiotic purposes involves the insertion of one or more metaphorically significant shots *within* a sequence. But in other cases, it is complete sequences that are associated semiotically by being intercut with one another, in the manner of conventional parallel editing. This occurs in one of the most important scenes midway through the film, in which a sequence of a new boat being launched into the river, garlanded with marigolds, is intercut with a sequence in which a corpse, similarly garlanded, is shown being brought down on a bier and immersed in the river. The meaning of this conjunction was immediately clear to Radhika Chopra, as she describes in her review:

> We see body and boat launched into the River Ganga in what are almost physically similar movements. In the absence of a commentary, the visuals leave it to us to realize that the 'inaugural' and the 'end' partake of a shared meaning where death is clearly not an end but an inaugural into another journey.[40]

Gardner insists that these events were *not* brought together in the edit suite but in reality did actually happen simultaneously at the same ghāt. All documentarists live in the hope of being blessed with such epiphanies, but Gardner is only too aware of how such simultaneities can be editorially manufactured. He therefore now worries that despite 'this sanction of reality', the conjunction of the two events in *Forest of Bliss* might be considered just too contrived. He also worries that the two events might be considered not only metaphorically linked, but metonymically, that is, the audience might presume that the deceased once owned the boat, or that the boat is being launched for the purposes of carrying the corpse. But he concludes, 'that may be part of the price you pay in order to get the effect you want'.[41]

But if all these editorial juxtapositionings refer to contexts of metaphorical meaning that pertain to Varanasi in particular, there are other instances in which they appear to be reaching out to meanings of more general significance. For Gardner's ultimate objective is not just to treat the subject of death in Varanasi but also, as he puts it, euphemistically, 'journeys to any far shore'. This, as he remarks with good reason, is not easy, given the very literal and specific nature of film as a medium.[42]

An example of how Gardner attempts a generalising reference of this kind occurs in a key scene almost halfway through the film. This is set in what we learn, albeit from sources outside the film, is a hospice for the dying.[43] We have been introduced to this hospice before and now return to it for a second time. On this occasion, from a respectful distance, we observe the corpse of a recently deceased person as it is carried down from an upstairs room, wrapped in a white shroud, to the sound of chanting by the attendants. On the ground floor, it is placed on a simple bamboo bier and decorated with a single garland of marigolds, before being carried out to the cremation ghāts. Although we have encountered all the elements of this scene before – even, one supposes, the deceased person, since in the previous scene in the hospice we saw some old women *in extremis* – this is the first time that they are presented to us in a single, consecutive strand.

However, what distinguishes this from a conventional example of chronologically progressive editing is that towards the beginning of the sequence, just before the corpse is brought down by the attendants, there is a highly subjective point-of-view shot, perhaps even slightly in slow motion, that descends the empty staircase on its own, as it were. As it is strikingly out of character stylistically with the rest of the sequence, this is clearly intended to remind the viewer that death is not just something that happens to people in 'other cultures'.

## STRUCTURES

All Gardner's major films are organised around relatively conventional cyclical narrative structures. These typically commence with the posing of some initial issue, problem or mystery and then progressively carry the audience forward to some final culmination, before returning literally or metaphorically to the beginning.

In *Dead Birds*, the return to the beginning is essentially metaphorical, though the link between beginning and end is also made through an ingenious narrative device, itself also metaphorical. After proposing the common mortality of humans and birds in the opening sequence, as described above, the narrative is thereafter both framed and advanced by the weaving of a band by one of the principal characters, Weyak. This functions as a sort of 'clock', as Gardner has put it.[44] Weyak starts to weave the band at the beginning of the film, is shown working on it at various points during the film and finally completes it at the end. As such, the progression of the band parallels the temporal progression of the film through a series of events related to the ongoing ritual warfare between Weyak's group and their enemies. These culminate in a revenge killing and a celebratory dance. However, the band also represents the progression of time in a more sinister metaphorical sense since, as we discover about ten minutes into the film, it is a funeral band. As Weyak completes his task following the celebratory dance and disappears over a slight rise, the narration brings the film to an end by returning to the theme of the common mortality of men and birds announced in the opening sequence.

In *Rivers of Sand*, the link between beginning and end is somewhat more obvious. In this case, the film ends with a return to the opening oral testimony of Omali Inda as well to Gardner's initial pessimistic ruminations about the inevitable 'painful' differences that separate women and men. This thematic return to the beginning is reinforced by a very literal visual device. In the opening montage, we are offered a shot, taken from a low angle, of a Hamar man walking towards the camera across one of the eponymous rivers of sand that feature in this film, his sandals scrunching loudly on the gravel. The final shot of the film is of the same man, taken from the same position and angle, and presumably taken at the same time as the first shot, but this time the subject is walking away from the camera, his sandals still scrunching loudly.

The narrative structure of *Forest of Bliss* is also cyclical, though in the absence of an orientating voice-over to provide signposts along the way, the progress from beginning to end is advanced instead through another classical structural device, the 'as if' chronology that we have identified a number of times already this book. In this case, it is based on a 24-hour cycle, running from one sunrise to the next. As the material for this film was shot over a period of some ten weeks, we can be sure that this 24-hour cycle would have been entirely constructed in the edit suite, involving a wholesale rearrangement of chronology.[45] This constructed diurnal format fulfils, very effectively, the basic function of all narrative structures, that is, it carries the audience forward, with the aid of subliminal sign-postings afforded by the progression of the day, towards an ending anticipated in advance. Moreover, in this particular instance, the use of this structure is particularly appropriate since it offers yet another echo of the cyclical principle underlying Hindu eschatology as the film moves from daybreak to night and back again, ending with the 'rebirth' of the new day.

It is also more than an inert formal pattern for ordering the material. Deploying yet another classical narrative strategy, Gardner animates this structure by posing a series of enigmas that he hopes the viewers will be intrigued by and will therefore allow themselves to be carried forward to the next stage of the film. In effect, *Forest of Bliss* develops by a process of slow disclosure, with each material component of the funeral procedures being introduced independently with, as it were, a question mark attached. Most of these are finally brought together in the scene in the hospice described above, which occurs shortly before the midpoint of the film. Only one major component is still missing, namely the wood, but then there is an immediate cut back to the athletic young boatman whom we have already seen a number of times before, working his way upstream with a large load of logs destined for the funeral pyres.

Thereafter, the pace of the film picks up and corpses on stretchers appear to converge on the Manikarnika cremation ground from all directions to the recurrent chant of 'rama nama satya he', sung in a variety of speeds and styles. However, there is still a considerable delay before we finally see a cremation, even though we see everything associated with it: we see wood being stacked, weighed and thrown down to the cremation ground; we see smoking pyres; we see women, a young boy and a dog picking among charred embers, we see stretchers of corpses being washed in the river and then lined up on the ghāt, we see lamenting mourners from a distance and a close-up of the doleful expression of a water buffalo whose symbolic role in this film appears to be to epitomise melancholy.

Even when the chief mourner takes a smouldering straw torch from the Dom Raja's hearth and walks down towards the cremation ground, we are not immediately vouchsafed a clear view of the cremation itself. Instead, there is a very long shot, taken from a boat of the kind used for hauling the firewood, now empty and almost imperceptibly pitching off shore. The empty boat itself takes up most of the image while the chief mourner is barely visible among a knot of other mourners at the top right of frame. Here he circumambulates a pyre with the now-flaming torch and then finally sets light to it. The soundtrack is rather muted compared to the previous tumult of chanting, but there is a low howling of dogs, the ever-present acoustic markers of the frontier between life and death (figure 9.7, left).

Gardner explains that throughout the editing, he was dubious about whether he would use this shot but finally decided to do so because it pulls together a number of threads:

> Now, I don't know whether this really works, but it certainly contains all the elements I was looking for: namely, the boat, the river, the fire, and a soul being dispatched. The boat seems to be waiting on the shore for the crossing. It's a kind of summary shot which, if inspected at all carefully, contains a tremendous amount of information.[46]

**9.7** *Forest of Bliss* (1986), metaphors of transition to the 'far shore'. Left, while a cremation takes place in the far distance, an empty wooden barge stands offshore, as if waiting to carry the soul of the deceased across the river. Right, in the final shot, a rowing boat disappears into the mist to the sound of grating rowlocks.

Even then, remarkably, we still do not cut back straight to the pyre. In-between there are two shots, first of a water pipe emptying into the river and then of a boy drinking from it. These shots, Östör points out, are there to remind the viewer that in Varanasi the ordinary is combined with the extraordinary. But the sound of the splashing water runs into the crackling of a fire and finally, we at last see a close-up of a shrouded head licked by flames, at what is almost exactly the three-quarters point of the 89-minute film.

Gardner says that he found this part of the film more difficult to cut than any other. Even while shooting, it had occurred to him repeatedly that he should avoid 'simply documenting cremation'. He felt that he had an obligation to preserve the dignity of the corpses while at the same time making the subject of death itself interesting. He was convinced that simply showing a long shot of a burning body would be 'pretty tedious'.[47] So now, having finally arrived at the culmination of the event towards which the whole film has been moving up until that moment, he quickly withdraws. After a single shot of the burning corpse, he returns briefly to the mourners lamenting and to the Dom Raja counting his money as the pathetic material goods left by one of his clients are kicked into the dust. Then he wraps up the whole sequence with a montage of the later stages of the cremation, moving very quickly over some of the more challenging moments, such as when the skull is smashed to release the spirit and the brains fall out.

In their conversation, Östör expresses surprise that Gardner should deal so briefly with this stage of the process, particularly since he had been so uncompromising in showing corpses in the river earlier in the film.[48] But there is a clear similarity here with the way in which Gardner treated the cremation of the boy killed in *Dead Birds* some twenty years previously:

there too, though Gardner had been totally uncompromising in the build-up to the climax of the funeral, we do not actually see the final consummation of the corpse by flames. Once it has been enclosed within the funeral pyre, the scene is elegantly and swiftly brought to an end by means of a pan off that follows the first wisps of smoke arising from the pyre as they disperse into the sky.

It is also highly characteristic of Gardner that he should not be interested in faithfully documenting the ritual processing of a dead body per se, but rather in interpreting its significance. As he puts it:

> The whole Manikarnika (cremation ground) episode in the film had to end in a way that resulted in some understanding and that also created some useful mystery. I worked a long time to get it to satisfy these two requirements.[49]

If I understand Gardner's intentions correctly, these requirements are not met by the documentation of the cremation itself but rather by its juxtaposition with the shots immediately before and after: that is, by the conjunction beforehand with, first, the shot from afar in the boat of the circumambulating mourner, suggesting tranquility and the imminent dispatch of a soul, then with the shot of the boy drinking water indicating the everyday nature of the event, next by the conjunction with the shots underlining the insignificance of the material possessions left behind, and finally and perhaps most importantly, with the serial montage of shots which follows the cremation ground sequence. This consists of a veritable flurry of metaphors of transition – birds descending to the river and alighting on driftwood, dogs circling one another, various boats now moving downstream from right to left and, on the soundtrack, the ever-ambiguous tolling of bells and the cawing of birds.

The final quarter of the film, covering the period from sunset to sunrise, is largely 'redemptive', as Gardner terms it, intimating that life goes on, not despite death but in association with death since the two are connected cyclically. The continuation of life is represented by the children flying their kites, by a brief return to the marigold gardens, by the devotional ritual in a temple and eventually by a return to Ragul Pandit chanting at dawn. But in the midst of this predominantly life-affirming final quarter, there is a disturbing and ambiguous sequence in which Mithai Lal, the healer-trickster, apparently in trance, is shown chanting over a flaming pit. The section is also regularly punctuated by memento mori: by the burial of a child in the river, by the burning funeral pyres and the tolling of bells at night, by dogs on the shore at dawn and further boatloads of wood for the funeral pyres. Finally, the film returns to where it began, both visually and aurally, on the river, with the boat disappearing into the mists to the sound of the grating rowlocks (figure 9.7, right).

## EXPERIENCE, SUBJECTIVITY AND ETHNOGRAPHICNESS

Through the gradual, unrelenting, almost overwhelming accumulation and superimposition of symbolic juxtapositions, Gardner moves the audience of *Forest of Bliss*, in a manner analogous to the participants in a religious ritual, that is, without consciously understanding all of the connections, towards the master tropes of Hindu eschatology: if opposites are necessarily connected, as dogs are to marigolds, as birds in the sky are to wood on the river, and as day is to night, if bliss can exist amid squalor, if the river Ganges is both a place of pollution and of purification, if the fire of the funeral pyre both consumes and releases, if in life we are in death, then in death we are necessarily also in life, and the committing of the body or its ashes to the waters of the holy river is not just the end of a cycle, but also a beginning.

It seems that Gardner intends this to be not so much a film *about* a rite of passage but *to be* a rite of passage. Through the narrative of the film, he aims to engage and carry the audience down to the cremation ground to confront their own mortality. But then, having forced them to look into the void, he offers the possibility of redemption in the form of Ragul Pandit:

> He will give the final benediction here at the end of the film, not just to the people who are in the shrine but, if it isn't too presumptuous, to everyone who is watching the film. People in the audience have been through a relatively unsparing account of some of life's fundamental issues, and they deserve it.[50]

Gardner is aiming, above all, to communicate an experience. However, the meaning of this experience is highly mediated through his own subjectivity rather than of the subjects. It is here that both he and his critics consider that his work may be in conflict with the some of the central tenets of academic anthropology. Reflecting on the report that certain world-renouncing saddhus would go to the cremation grounds to lie down on the pyres in anticipation of their own immolation, even engaging in cannibalism to transgress beyond all social convention, he comments:

> I think that everybody who goes there is something of an apprentice saddhu, insofar as there is any living through these preoccupations. I don't see how you can escape it. And then the question is what happens to a film that is connected with or even driven by that concern ... I suppose I'm asking the usual question of how the non-fiction film can survive the presumed conflict between personal issues and informational or anthropological ones.[51]

In this passage, if somewhat contortedly, Gardner poses an important question: is there, in fact, a *necessary* conflict between an anthropological approach and the exploration of existential issues of personal importance to a film-maker? Or is it merely, as he suggests here, merely a *presumed* conflict?

My own view is that while there is no necessary conflict between the pursuit of personal existential enquiry through film and anthropological objectives more generally, what anthropology as an intellectual discipline teaches, surely above all else, is that this personal existential enquiry should always be channelled and tempered by sensitivity to local ethnographic contexts.

When *Forest of Bliss* was first released, it was the subject of a number of excoriating reviews by anthropologists in the pages of the visual anthropology newsletter of the American Anthropological Assocation. These provoked a series of equally robust responses by Gardner, Östör and various other supporters. The controversy soon began generating more heat than light and quickly became unnecessarily personalised. What was clear, though, was that at least some of the anthropologist reviewers had entirely failed to recognise the film as a complex and finely crafted work that sought to explore funeral practices in Varanasi through cinematic means, using non-verbal metaphor and montage rather than didactic explanatory exposition of the kind that one might expect in a written text. However, at the same time, the critics also raised a number of legitimate points about the ethnographic status of the work that are worthy of closer attention.

First, there are a number of points in the film where ethnographic reality appears to have been subordinated to Gardner's metaphorical purposes, a criticism that has been made about his previous work too, as described earlier in this chapter. In his review of the film, Jonathan Parry, an anthropologist who has carried out extensive fieldwork in Varanasi, points out a number of examples, but here one will suffice: Parry explains that Mithai Lal, the trickster-healer character, has no direct connection with the funeral industry while the temple in which we see him at work is at some distance from the cremation ghāts. In reality, he is a spirit-medium of the Goddess Kali or Durga, and his ministrations are concerned with petty marital squabbles, troubles in business and minor illnesses rather than with major eschatological issues of life and death, as is suggested by his metaphorical function in the film.[52]

A second matter of concern relates to the fact there is a complete absence of the indigenous voice in the film. I refer here not just to the literal voice of the subjects, but also more metaphorically to their general views and understandings. But here too *Forest of Bliss* is entirely consistent with Gardner's praxis in his earlier works. Just as he was only secondarily interested in what the Dani might think about their warfare and its connection to mortality, he is only secondarily concerned with local eschatological understandings in Varanasi. Instead, he approaches these matters through the clues provided by the classical Greek mythology that he encountered in his childhood: thus the Ganges becomes the Styx, the scavenger dogs on its shores become transformations of Cerberus and the eastern bank that 'far shore' from which no traveller returns.

A particular example relates to the title of the film. Although it is poetically evocative in some indeterminate way, we do not learn from within the film what this phrase means for Hindus. It could be argued that we are the poorer for this as it could have enriched our viewing if we did. As Chopra helpfully explains in her review, this is the name given to Varanasi in certain classical Sanskrit texts and refers to the supposed abundance of lingas, the phallic symbols connoting Lord Shiva and associated with *ananda*, the sheer bliss of creation. (It is presumably some of these lingas that we see Mithai Lal assiduously anointing with water from the Ganges in one of the early sequences). However, this blissful aspect of Shiva as Creator exists in necessary assocation with his complementary aspect as Destroyer, as represented in Varanasi by the cremation grounds.[53] Armed with this understanding, one would surely have viewed the film in a very different way.

There is, admittedly, an oblique reference to the interdependence of creation and destruction in Hindu thought in the card immediately adjacent to the main title of the film, which offers a sombre verse from W. B. Yeats's translation of the Upinashads. But much more striking and immediately apprehensible is the sequence that leads up to the title and which culminates in a particularly vicious dog-fight. This suggests anything but bliss and has led many reviewers to assume that the title is ironic. Whatever Gardner's precise intentions here, it is clear from the entry in his notes about the rushes that he was perfectly well aware that Varanasi is viewed as a place of 'exultation' by Hindus. So one can only assume that he intentionally decided to give priority to his own very much darker personal view of the city as a place where, as with the world in general, nothing lasts for ever and all living beings end up being either burnt or eaten.[54]

Both these points relate to a third, namely, intelligibility. There can be no doubt that *Forest of Bliss* is a challenging film, dense with meaning, which is very difficult to comprehend in its full complexity, particularly on the basis of a single viewing. The detailed interpretations that I have offered here have been made possible not only by repeated viewings, but also with the aid of the conversation between Gardner and Östör which offers a series of vital clues as to the intentions underlying the many diverse elements of the film. As a viewer without any specialist knowledge of Hinduism, my understanding of the film was also greatly aided by the key provided by Chopra in her review of the film, in which she immediately identifies 'a central principle of Hindu thought – the juxtaposition and interpenetration of opposites'. It is surely no coincidence that she was able to do so, being Indian herself and therefore, one assumes, exposed to these ideas since childhood. But without these extra-filmic aids to interpretation, most audiences will inevitably miss a great deal in viewing the film. Certainly, my experience of showing this film year upon year to students of visual anthropology, also without any specialist knowledge of Hinduism, proves that while they are usually entranced by the film, they generally glean only a small fraction of its significance.

Gardner is far from unique in grappling with this problem since it confronts all ethnographic film authors who make a film about a subject that is culturally unfamiliar to their audience. Nor is there an easy solution. While some audiences may be relied on to make connections, others will not; the same applies at the level of the individual too. If one provides insufficient means for understanding the cultural significance of what the film portrays, then it is likely that audiences will fill that vacuum of incomprehension with their own, usually ethnocentric, interpretations. If, on the other hand, one burdens a film with too much explanation, which will usually take a verbal form, one runs the risk of turning it into an illustrated lecture, thereby undermining the distinctive capacity of film to communicate an experience, even if vicarious, of the reality portrayed. Indeed, too much verbal explanation can obscure rather than clarify, as another ethnographic film about Hindu cremation practices, *Releasing the Spirits*, made by Timothy Asch and his colleagues in Bali, around much the same time as *Forest of Bliss*, demonstrates in a particularly cautionary manner.[55]

Given these difficulties, one cannot but respect the sheer boldness of Gardner's attempt in *Forest of Bliss* to provide explanatory frames of reference for abstract religious concepts through a combination of non-verbal symbolism, metaphorical association and montage. Equally, however, one cannot escape the conclusion that Gardner's refusal to provide more explicit devices that would allow the audience – on the basis of viewing the film alone and without the benefit of his after-the-fact exegesis – to connect the practices shown in the film with the ideas and relations that underpin them necessarily means that its value as a specifically ethnographic film is diminished. Even so, it is still possible to admire the praxis that underlies it. Indeed, I see no reason why Gardner's distinctive mode of film authorship, albeit more fully anchored in local ethnographic understanding, should not be a source of inspiration to all those ethnographic film-makers who continue to harbour 'anthropological scruples'.

## ROBERT GARDNER AS A 'MASTERFUL CUTTER'

Peter Loizos once characterised Robert Gardner's work as 'experimental' on the grounds that it goes beyond currently dominant realist orthodoxies.[56] Yet while it may be true that Gardner's work holds promise for the future in this sense, it also represents the continuation of an older tradition of documentary film-making. As both critics and admirers have pointed out, there is an echo in *Forest of Bliss* of the 'city symphonies' of the 1920s and 1930s. However, Gardner himself established the connection between his own approach and that of an earlier generation of film-makers more directly, in the form of a tribute to Basil Wright, a leading figure of the British Documentary Movement of the 1930s, who died in 1987, not long after *Forest of Bliss* had been released.

The account that Gardner offers of Wright's editorial technique in *The Song of Ceylon*, released in 1934, when Wright was only 27, could almost be a description of his own technique in *Forest of Bliss*. This technique, he suggested, consisted of establishing

> relationships through editing that were astonishingly courageous and quite amazing in the way new perceptions emerged from the observed actualities. It did not matter that these were frequently commonplaces. Their humanity drew strength from the fact that that is what they were. I am reminded in this connection of the almost literally transporting spirituality he evoked in the Buddha segment, near the beginning … where stone, birds, air, and water are joined to create an abiding atmosphere of holiness. Such an outcome would not seem likely, if one were to look at the shots singly and silently. Occasionally they are not even particularly well photographed … But when looked at assembled by this masterful cutter … hearing the tintinnabulation of those relentless bells guiding the senses into novel excitations, the effect is transfiguring. We are in his grip and we are changed forever.[57]

So is it with *Forest of Bliss*. For no one who has watched this film with an open mind can fail to be enchanted and transformed by it. By carefully examining the works of the 'masterful cutter' who made it, ethnographic film-makers too may learn how to enchant and transform their audiences.

## Notes

1  Gardner refers to the indigenous people living at Blunden Harbour as 'Kwakiutl', a term that was widely used in the anthropological literature at the time. For the reasons underlying the change of nomenclature in the 1980s to Kwakwa̱ka'wakw, see Chapter 1, endnote 58, p. 76. Although Gardner edited the rushes and composed the voice-overs for these films, they were actually shot by Heick. Gardner did not learn to shoot himself until sometime later and appears not have even been present on location during the shoot (MacDonald 2015), 53–4.

2  See MacDonald (2013), 61–110 for an overview of Gardner's career and MacDonald (2015), 48–77, for an interesting autobiographical interview with Gardner. I draw extensively on both these sources in this chapter. For a complete listing of Gardner's films, see www.robertgardner.net/category/film/.

3  Barbash (2007), 110; MacDougall (1998a), 72.

4  See Gardner's acerbic diaristic account of this expedition, published fifty years after the event, by which time most of the principal protagonists were long dead (Gardner 2010). See also Chapter 4, pp. 133–8 for a discussion of *The Hunters*.

5  Gardner (2006), 279, 333.

6  See, particularly, Gardner (2006), 2. But there are many other examples scattered through the various diaristic accounts of his film projects in this same book.

7  See Staal (1989); Östör (1994), particularly pp. 74–6; Heider (2007), 81–2.

8  See Marshall (1993), 71–2. On the grounds that her circumstances were not typical, nor properly explained, Marshall objected particularly to Gardner's proposal that the

film should culminate in a sequence that Gardner himself had shot of an old woman, whom he calls /Gasa, or sometimes Naowka, who had supposedly been abandoned by her family and left to eat sand. In the years following Marshall's death in 2005, Gardner returned to her case a number of times, publishing two texts about her and several photographs (Gardner 2006), 1–4; (2010), 2, 13–4, 20–1, 27 as well as including his 1958 footage of her in his late compilation film, *Nine Forsaken Fragments* (2009). Notwithstanding Marshall's objections, Gardner remained convinced of the metaphorical resonances of /Gasa as a symbol of mortality, both individual and collective (MacDonald 2013), 102–4.

9 See Lydall and Strecker (1978), Strecker (1988). Both Lydall and Strecker were motivated by the experience of working with Gardner to become film-makers themselves in order to be able to offer an alternative filmic account of Hamar life. See Chapter 16, pp. 470–6.

10 See, particularly, Loizos (1993), 140–68; (1995).

11 How accurate this testimony is regarding the circumstances of women generally in Hamar society, or even those of Omali Inda herself, is strongly contested by Lydall and Strecker (see Strecker 1988), 373. A further possible exception to the general rule that subjects do not speak or look at the camera in Gardner's films is to be found in *The Nuer* (1971). In this case, some individuals do speak briefly and the content of what they say is translated in the voice-over delivered by Gardner. However, although Gardner co-produced this film and is credited with 'additional photography', he did not direct it. There is also a very unGardnerian pre-title montage of portraits of individual Nuer, in which they smile and look directly at the camera.

12 Gardner (1972), 34–5.

13 Gardner (2006), 282.

14 Gardner (2006), 293.

15 MacDonald (2013), 81.

16 Under this name, the Wodaabe should not be confused with the Bororo indigenous people of Central Brazil.

17 Barbash (2007), 97–8; Gardner (2006), 210.

18 Gardner (2006), 182–215, *passim.*

19 Barbash (2007), 97. In the interview with Scott MacDonald, Gardner describes the synchronous sound film-making developed by the Direct Cinema group in the 1960s as 'something of a dead end' and claims to have made only one synch-sound film himself: this was *Marathon* (1965) about the Boston Marathon, which he co-directed with Joyce Chopra (MacDonald 2015), 63–4.

20 Gardner and Östör (2001). Östör kindly provided me with a copy of his own account of the collaboration with Gardner, which I also draw on here (Östör 1994).

21 Gardner (2006), 116.

22 Chopra (1989), 2.

23 Gardner and Östör (2001), 110.

24 Gardner and Östör (2001), 20.

25 Oppitz (1988), 211.

26 Gardner and Östör (2001), 17–18, 20, 116.

27 Gardner and Östör (2001), 16–17, 38. See also Gardner (2006), 281.

28 In his discussion with Östör, Gardner explains that this use of donkey braying was a 'gesture' to Luis Buñuel in whose film *Land Without Bread*, a donkey is shown being stung to death by bees (Gardner and Östör 2001), 75.

29 Earlier in his career, Chalufour had worked on the *Netsilik Eskimo* series, see Chapter 3.

30 Gardner and Östör (2001), 57.

31 Gardner and Östör (2001), 25.

32 Gardner and Östör (2001), 21–2.

33 Oppitz (1988), 212.

34 Gardner and Östör (2001), 99.
35 Gardner and Östör (2001), 102–4, 115.
36 Oppitz (1988), 211.
37 Gardner (2006), 281, 300. See also Gardner and Östör's discussion of this sequence (2001, 68–70). When Östör raises the issue of what the disposal of animals in the river means in terms of sanitation, Gardner acknowledges that this is a serious problem that should be addressed. 'But', he continues, 'that was not what interested me at the time, nor does it today… my feeling is that the metaphysical stairs will always be there, even if dead donkeys are disposed of in the electric crematoria they were talking about getting.'
38 Gardner and Östör (2001), 48.
39 See Gardner and Östör (2001), 27–35, for an extended discussion of this sequence.
40 Chopra (1989), 3. The association was also clearly understood by Oppitz (1988), 211.
41 Gardner and Östör (2001), 87.
42 Gardner and Östör (2001), 89.
43 See Parry (1988), 6; Östör (1994), 91–2.
44 See Gardner's conversation with Ross McElwee in the supplementary material on the *Dead Birds* DVD.
45 This is amply confirmed in the rushes log: for example, the scene of Mithai Lal, the healer, taking his early morning bath, which features early in the film was, in fact, one of the last things that Gardner filmed (2006), 299–300. Interestingly, Gardner reveals that he was initially considering using the reconstruction of the boat launched from the cremation ghāt as the overall structuring device of the film. To this end, he shot a great deal of material of the boat being prepared for the launch, most of which he later discarded when he decided to opt for the diurnal structure instead (Gardner and Östör 2001), 85–6.
46 Gardner and Östör (2001), 106.
47 Gardner and Östör (2001), 95.
48 Gardner and Östör (2001), 107.
49 Gardner and Östör (2001), 106.
50 Gardner and Östör (2001), 115.
51 Gardner and Östör (2001), 97.
52 See Parry (1988), 5–6; also Östör (1994), 85–8.
53 Chopra (1989), 2. See also Parry (1988), 4; Östör (1994), 70.
54 Gardner and Östör (2001), 23.
55 See Chapter 6, pp. 178–9 for a discussion of *Releasing the Spirits*.
56 Loizos (1993), 139–40.
57 Gardner (2006), 310. See Chapter 1, pp. 50–2 for a discussion of *The Song of Ceylon*.

# 10

# Colin Young: the principles of Observational Cinema

THE third Author whose contribution to the praxis of ethnographic film-making we consider in this part of the book is very different from the other two. Colin Young was both the original intellectual architect and also the initial practical enabler of the approach to ethnographic film-making known as Observational Cinema, which since the 1970s has been one of the most influential in the English-speaking world. However, although he may have shot some ethnographic footage now and again, he has not been a practitioner in the active sense of Jean Rouch or Robert Gardner. Although, like them, he may be considered an Author in the sense defined by Roland Barthes, that is, the originator of a praxis that has served as a model to others, he has been an Author who has not produced any major works himself (figure 10.1).

Nor, in contrast to the other two Authors, did Young have any formal training in anthropology or indeed any other social science involving the practice of ethnography. Having studied moral philosophy as an undergraduate in his native Scotland, Young moved to California in the early 1950s where, after taking an MA in Theater Arts and spending a relatively brief period working in various practical capacities in the feature film industry, he became a teacher of screen studies at the University of California Los Angeles (UCLA). By 1965, when he was still only 38, he had risen to the position of full professor. As a result of this background, Young had a sophisticated knowledge of the history, theories and methods of cinema, and it was this, rather than practical experience of film-making or any knowledge of ethnography, that he brought to the original formulation of the principles of Observational Cinema.[1]

The first appearance in print of Young's conception of Observational Cinema took the form of a manifesto-essay in *Principles of Visual Anthropology*, the landmark volume edited by Paul Hockings first published in 1975. Central to this conception was the idea that ethnographic film-makers should refrain from directing their subjects while on location and instead merely follow them as they went about their business. Once back in the

10.1　Colin Young in his 91st year, in conversation with the author,
August 2017.

edit suite, they should eschew excessive manipulation or embellishment of
their material through cinematic devices such as montage, pedagogical
voice-over narration, melodramatic narrative, extra-diegetic music or special
effects. The overall aim should be to offer the audience direct access to the
material presented, to see what the film-maker had seen, so that they could
form their own conclusions about it.

This conception of Observational Cinema was based on a mode of
observation that was in sharp contrast to the 'instrumental observation' that
Margaret Mead had called for in the Introduction to the same landmark
volume. Here Mead proposes that the camera should be considered an
instrument like the telescope or the microscope and that it should be used
in an entirely detached manner, from afar. Mead's hope was that in this
way, one could produce entirely objective accounts of human behaviour.[2]
The form of the observation that Young was proposing could hardly be
more different. Whereas Mead was calling for a completely detached form
of observation, Young was calling for one that that was highly engaged. In
order to work, he claimed, it had to be based 'on an intimate, sympathetic
relationship between the film-maker and the subject – not the eye of the
aloof, detached observer but of someone watching as much as possible from
the inside'. Moreover, he believed that the film-maker should not be afraid

to reveal their presence in their film. 'Trying to conceal our act is defeatist', he argued, since it meant 'throwing away the most important advantage of the non-scripted, observational approach and lending support to the fiction that our work is objective'.[3]

This participatory dimension to Observational Cinema as conceived by Young serves to distinguish it very clearly from the praxis of Robert Gardner while bringing it closer to that of Jean Rouch – but not through mere coincidence. Young had come to know Rouch during the latter's visits to the USA in the 1960s and he was a great admirer of his films, particularly *Chronicle of a Summer*. In the concluding paragraphs of his manifesto-essay, Young identifies this film as a 'watershed' in documentary film-making specifically on account of its participatory praxis.[4] But there were also a number of important differences between Rouch's praxis and that of the practitioners of Observational Cinema, as I shall describe in this chapter.

## THE EMERGENCE OF OBSERVATIONAL CINEMA AS A MODE OF ETHNOGRAPHIC FILM-MAKING

Although Young has never had any formal training as an anthropologist, he has spent a great deal of time and effort collaborating with anthropologists in the promotion of ethnographic film-making. Why he should have done so is something of a mystery – even seemingly to Young himself. But a key factor was his encounter, in the early 1960s, with the charismatic figure of Edmund Carpenter, pioneer visual anthropologist, innovative communications theorist and interlocutor of Marshall McLuhan, also known in anthropological circles for his ethnographic work with the Inuit and in Papua New Guinea.[5] In 1966, Young was invited by Enrico Fulchignoni, a UNESCO functionary in Paris, and an associate of Jean Rouch, to collaborate with Carpenter on the production of a report on North American ethnographic films about the Pacific region. Young was then invited to present this report at a conference in Sydney later that same year. It was there that he became aware just how diverse the inhabitants of the world of ethnographic film-making were. The participants included Jean Rouch and Robert Gardner, both of whom he already knew, but others whom he did not, including Ian Dunlop and Roger Sandall, both then engaged in forms of 'salvage' ethnographic film-making among Australian Aborigines, as described in Chapter 3.[6]

On his return from Australia, in the autumn of 1966, Young launched the Ethnographic Film Program at UCLA. This involved collaboration between a number of different departments, including most importantly Anthropology, but as the Chair of Theater Arts, Young was the main driving force behind it. The praxis of Observational Cinema would be developed in a dialectical fashion over the next few years through the intersection of

Young's ideas about cinema and the practical film-making experiences of the students and members of staff directly involved in the Ethnographic Film Program, or of independent film-makers who came to be associated with it.[7]

Among those whose practical film-making contributed at this very early stage to the working out of the praxis was Paul Hockings, then an associate professor in the Anthropology department. Hockings was involved in teaching the Ethnographic Film Program in its very first year, 1966–67, and in the summer vacation he teamed up with Mark McCarty, a colleague of Young in Theater Arts, to shoot a film on the west coast of Ireland. McCarty acted as the cameraman and Hockings as the sound recordist, with two students from the Ethnographic Film Program, Mike Hall (later a BBC sound recordist) and Alex Prisadsky (later an experimental film-maker), as their assistants. Young himself acted as the producer of the film, though he did not go on location. Originally conceived by McCarty as a film about life in an Irish bar, the project was transformed under Hockings's influence into a general ethnographic account of the small village of Dunquin, on the Dingle Peninsula. The film that eventually arose from this project, *The Village*, was released in 1968 and had a running time of 70 minutes, distilled from fifteen hours of rushes.

In effect, this represented the first sustained attempt to put into practice the principles of Observational Cinema that were being developed through the Ethnographic Film Program. There was no script and Hockings and McCarty made no attempt to direct the subjects by telling them what to do or say, nor did they ask them to repeat an action or a comment in order to do a second take. Although they were happy to include reflexive moments such as when subjects reacted to the camera, or made comments about the film crew, they did not attempt to engage proactively in conversation with them while shooting, let alone conduct anything resembling a formal interview. Nor did they pursue any particular narrative storyline, or seek to build up any particular characters. In the final film, there was no voice-over commentary to explain everything and hold the film together. What there was, however, was an 'as if' chronology constructed in the edit suite. This presented various scenes of village life, in reality filmed over three months, as if they were taking place over a prolonged summer weekend and culminating in a highly conventional manner with the Dunquin village crew winning the canoe race at the annual Dingle Regatta (figure 10.2).[8]

Hockings and McCarty wanted to encourage their audience to become as immersed as possible in the life of the village and to make sense of it from the inside, in the manner of an anthropologist newly arrived in the field. It was precisely because they felt that it would have inhibited this process of first-hand discovery that they decided to do without a voice-over commentary. Yet although specifically intended to evoke the experience of

**10.2** The 'as if' chronology of *The Village* (1968). In reality shot over three months, this film presents scenes of everyday life as if they were happening over a prolonged summer weekend, culminating in the victory of the rowing crew, right, in the Dingle Regatta

ethnographic fieldwork, when the film was first screened to an audience of anthropologists, it was greeted with catcalls and derision. It was only later, once the Observational Cinema approach had become more established, that it came to be recognised as a pioneering example of an approach to ethnographic film-making that required the audience to do its own looking rather than be guided by a narrator.[9]

Two other film-makers whose work was particularly important in contributing to the development of the distinctive praxis of Observational Cinema in its earliest phase were Herb Di Gioia and David Hancock. In his manifesto-essay, Young frequently alludes to their work and quotes extensively from notes that Hancock had written about their film-making experiences. Although Di Gioia and Hancock were not formally enrolled on the Ethnographic Film Program, they were students of Theatre Arts and came into contact with Young and the programme around the time of its third year, 1968–69. Shortly afterwards, in the early 1970s, they made a series of four films in rural Vermont, later distributed under the collective title, *Vermont People*. While Hancock did most of the shooting, and Di Gioia most of the sound recording, they thought of themselves as co-directors and cut the films together.

Three of these films consisted of portraits of single male characters, all of whom were in some sense marginal to mainstream local society, while the fourth followed the experiences of an idealistic young couple of incomers who had abandoned city life and were trying to make a living as smallholders. Neither Di Gioia nor Hancock had any formal qualifications as anthropologists, but their films have a pronounced ethnographic 'feel', no doubt derived from the fact that prior to shooting both had had strong personal connections with Vermont over many years, knew their subjects well and had shared their lives in one form or another. Their films also all explore, albeit in an informal, conversational manner, the connections between their subjects' material practices and their general ideas about the world.

Of the four films, perhaps the most emblematic of the 'way of doing' ethnographic film-making that Di Gioia and Hancock were developing was *Peter Murray* (1975), a 50-minute film which follows a craftsman, the Peter Murray of the title, as he completes the making of one maplewood rocking chair and then begins another. After a preliminary title card indicating the date, September 1974, and the location of Murray's workshop, the film begins in the midst of the action as he works on the woven back of the first chair. There is no voice-over, nor anything approaching a formal interview, but as he proceeds, Murray engages in casual conversation with the film-makers, though this is more of a monologue than a normal conversation in the sense that we never hear the film-makers' voices. He speaks softly and his comments are punctuated by long silences. We learn from his remarks that having been through the Peace and Love experience in California, he has come to Vermont to reconnect with nature, and in particular with woodland, a world that he had loved as a boy. He explains that he sees the output of his labour, the rocking chairs, as almost coincidental to his primary purpose which is to bring out, with the blade of his knife, the 'light' that is inherent in any piece of wood. When he is engaged in this work, he loses all sense of time.

Prompted by these insights, we are then encouraged to share the subject's communication with the pieces of wood that he is fashioning through a beautifully executed series of intimate and discreetly lit sequences that show him carving, planing, drilling, sawing, constructing. The pacing is leisurely, while beyond the sound of this manual labour, a profound sense of silence pervades the workshop. Everything is done by hand since to use power tools, Murray explains, can force the wood to become something that it is not, and as in the treatment of a woman, he suggests, this prevents any kind of exchange or understanding. The film ends with a lengthy shot showing him, roll-up cigarette in hand and framed by the back of the second chair, silently contemplating his creation (figure 10.3).

In that it was based on an intimate relationship between film-makers and subject, and in eschewing commentary and interview in favour of informal conversation, *Peter Murray* exemplified a number of key features of the emergent praxis of Observational Cinema. In other respects, however, it diverged from what would later become the most common orthodoxies. One of these concerns cinematographic technique: that is, Hancock makes extensive use of the zoom, which other film-makers working in this way tended to avoid. The other divergent aspect is more editorial: as I shall discuss in the section 'Restrained narratives' below, notwithstanding normative comments to the contrary in Colin Young's manifesto-essay, in actual practice a recurrent feature of Observational Cinema films are often barely discernible

**10.3** *Peter Murray* (1975). Left, 'the more energy you put into a piece, the brighter its light'. Right, Peter Murray silently contemplates his creation in the long final shot.

narrative topoi that beneath the surface provide shape and direction to the films made in this way. In this sense, *The Village* was very much in line with what would become the most prevalent model in Observational Cinema. *Peter Murray*, by contrast, in that it boldly both begins and ends in the middle of the process of building a chair, could be considered somewhat divergent.[10]

The film-makers whose work would have by far the most substantial impact on the development of the praxis of Observational Cinema were David MacDougall and Judith Henderson, who met during the first year of the Ethnographic Film Program and who later married, with Judith taking David's family name. Apart from some introductory courses that David had taken when he was an undergraduate at Harvard, neither had any prior training as anthropologists. But through the Ethnographic Film Program, they not only encountered the work of the leading ethnographic film-makers of the time, but also met many of them in person when they came to a major 'Colloquium on Ethnographic Film' that took place at UCLA in April 1968. These leading figures included Jean Rouch who showed *Jaguar*, then only recently completed. Later, David would describe his attendance at this Colloquium as a transformative experience, particularly seeing *Jaguar* for the first time. 'From that point on', he has commented, 'I felt ethnographic film could do anything.'[11]

However, it was not only ethnographic film, strictly defined, that the MacDougalls were exposed to during their time at UCLA. They also encountered the work of the Italian Neorealists, the French New Wave, Yasujirō Ozu and Akira Kurosawa among fiction film-makers and, among documentarists, the work of the Direct Cinema group and Frederick Wiseman. In Young's own teaching, he encouraged students to take a particular interest in the possibilities of cross-fertilisation between documentary and fiction film-making, as well as to think about the epistemological status of film.

It was in this context that he would show *Chronicle of a Summer*, both on account of the questions that it posed about the relationship between fact and fiction, and because it shared the film-making process with the audience to an unprecedented degree. Yet as David MacDougall recalls, Young was careful to stress that the principal merit of this display of the film-maker's methods was not that it guaranteed some higher degree of objective truth but rather that it encouraged the audience to engage more critically with the film.[12]

All these influences were brought to bear on the films that the MacDougalls would make during the 1970s and 1980s, first in East Africa among the Jie and Turkana pastoralists, and later in Australia with various Aboriginal communities. As described in Chapter 5, over the course of this period of twenty years, their praxis became progressively more reflexive and participatory, particularly after they moved to Australia, which required the development of a different kind of relationship with their subjects. But taken as a whole, these films are now widely regarded as the epitome of the praxis of Observational Cinema in what might be called its 'classic' phase. By analogy with Clifford Geertz's suggestion, cited in the Introduction to this part of the book, that Raymond Firth's writings represented at that time the best example of the Malinowskian mode of textual authorship, one could say that David and Judith MacDougall's films in East Africa and Australia represent the most comprehensive exposition of the mode of ethnographic film authorship originally conceived by Colin Young.[13]

## ETHNOGRAPHIC FILM-MAKING AS 'CONVERSATION'

The most significant difference between the praxis of Observational Cinema in this 'classic' phase and the praxes of both Jean Rouch and Robert Gardner concerns the role of language. As described in Chapter 9, language was of very little importance within Gardner's praxis: his subjects say little or nothing in his films, while over the course of his career, his own use of language in the form of voice-over commentary gradually diminished until in his last major film, *Forest of Bliss*, it is entirely absent. At no point, in any of his films, does Gardner ever ask his subjects an interview question.

As for Rouch, as we saw in Chapter 8, while he certainly made use of language, this was very much dependent upon the genre in which he was working: in his African documentaries, his own voice predominates, both speaking about and speaking for the subjects, while in his ethnofictional films, the principal mode of language takes the form either of voice-over performed by the subjects, or of linguistic exchanges between them, both of which are always in French. Though it is surely his best-known film, *Chronicle of a Summer* is atypical of Rouch's praxis as a whole in that the dominant linguistic mode takes the form of exchanges between the film-makers and the subjects, or of exchanges between the subjects that have been directly provoked or set up by the film-makers. In Rouch's films more generally, although a great deal of dialogue took place between him and his subjects both before and after a shoot, during the actual process of film-making itself it is typically entirely absent.

By contrast, linguistic exchanges between the subjects, in their own language, were absolutely central to Observational Cinema in its classic form. Voice-over narration, on the other hand, was relatively rare. In these regards, the praxis of Observational Cinema was similar to a certain degree to that of the Direct Cinema group, whose works also served to some extent as a model for the Observational Cinema film-makers. But there was also a major difference: while Direct Cinema film-makers worked to the general principle that they themselves should not speak unless spoken to, in Observational Cinema as it developed at UCLA, linguistic exchanges between the film-makers and subjects could be initiated by either party.

Linguistic exchanges along both these axes – between the subjects, and between the subjects and the film-makers – were subsumed in Observational Cinema discourse under the general notion of 'conversation'. The centrality of this notion to the praxis of Observational Cinema was flagged in *Turkana Conversations*, the name that the MacDougalls gave to the trilogy of films that they made among the Turkana in the late 1970s. It was also flagged in the title, 'MacDougall Conversations', which Colin Young gave to the review of those same films that he published in *RAIN*, the Royal Anthropological Institute Newsletter in 1982. In this same review, Young cites a letter from David MacDougall, in which the latter explains that the name given to the Turkana trilogy had first come to him some years earlier when making a film about the Boran pastoralists of northern Kenya with James Blue, another independent film-maker associated with the UCLA group. Although they had finally settled on a more descriptive title, *Kenya Boran*, MacDougall and Blue had originally thought of calling it 'Boran Conversations'. MacDougall also reports that, quite independently, Herb Di Gioia and David Hancock had originally intended to call their series, not *Vermont People*, but rather 'Vermont Conversations'.[14]

In making 'conversation' a central feature of their praxis, Observational Cinema film-makers were aiming to go beyond the praxis of those ethnographic film-makers of their own era who, while observing their subjects very carefully, and while often having a close relationship with them off-screen, excluded any on-screen reference to this relationship, verbal or non-verbal. This was the central thrust of an article by David MacDougall that immediately followed Colin Young's manifesto-essay in *Principles of Visual Anthropology*. The title of MacDougall's article – 'Beyond Observational Cinema'

– initially caused some confusion since it appeared to suggest that MacDougall was proposing a film-making praxis that sought to go beyond the praxis of Observational Cinema as laid out by Young in the immediately preceding article. In fact, however, MacDougall was not arguing for the need to go beyond the praxis laid out by Young, since this too actively embraced the possibility of revealing the relationship between film-makers and subjects on screen in a reflexive and conversational manner. Rather the praxis to which MacDougall was referring was the one underlying the work of film-makers such as John Marshall and Timothy Asch, and indeed the MacDougalls' own first two films among the Jie, *Nawi* and *Under the Men's Tree*, in which there are certainly some references by the subjects to the presence of the film-makers, but nothing resembling a fully developed conversation between them.[15]

In order to underline the fact that the relationship between subjects and film-makers would be central to the praxis that he was proposing, MacDougall suggested that it should be dubbed 'Participatory Cinema'. But although this would arguably have offered a more accurate description of the praxis of Observational Cinema as it developed over the 1970s and 1980s, this name never caught on. Instead, 'Observational Cinema' came to stand for the participatory, conversational variant of the film-making praxis that both Young and MacDougall were proposing. As Lucien Castaing-Taylor would put it, many years later, what happened, in effect, was that 'an observational approach' came to be understood 'not in con-tradistinction to participatory or "reflexive" propensities, but rather as their consummation'.[16]

Although the 'conversations' between film-makers and subjects in Observational Cinema could certainly entail the asking of questions by the film-makers, they did not take the form of interviews, at least certainly not interviews of the kind that is the standard fare of television current affairs documentaries, that is. a one-way interrogation of the subject by the interviewer shot in a different way to the main body of the film, usually in special conditions of lighting and camera placement, and which stands outside the temporal world of the main action of the film. Rather, the 'conversation' between film-maker and subjects in Observational Cinema could be initiated by either party and, all importantly, would arise – or at least would appear to arise – in the normal ebb and flow of the events being represented in the film. Also, given that these 'conversations' were often taking place in languages other than English, extensive use was made of subtitles. Indeed, the skilful use of subtitles was one of the defining features of Observational Cinema in its classic phase, and another feature that served to distinguish it from the praxis of Jean Rouch.[17]

While both Young and MacDougall allude specifically to *Chronicle of a Summer* as an example of good practice in their contributions to *Principles of*

*Visual Anthropology*, the way in which the relationship between film-makers and subjects is handled in Observational Cinema is very different from the way in which it was handled by Rouch and Morin. In general, in Observational Cinema this relationship is managed in a very much more low-key manner. Although the film-makers may be frequently acknowledged, and may even fleetingly appear, they never take centre stage in quite the way that Rouch and Morin frequently do in *Chronicle*. Also, the questions asked by Observational Cinema film-makers are generally very much more discreet. There is nothing even close to the forensic, almost psychoanalytical questioning of the subjects of the kind in which Morin engages in *Chronicle*. Nor is much use made of all the other direct or indirect interrogatory linguistic devices employed by Rouch and Morin: in Observational Cinema in its classic form there are no postprandial focus groups, no on-screen feedback sessions, no vox pops, no soliloquies.

What there is, however, is the device that one might call the 'proxy conversation', which is used both in *Chronicle* and by Observational Cinema film-makers and which represents a kind of hybrid of the conversation between subjects and the conversation between subjects and film-makers. This form of conversation does not arise of its own accord, but comes about when a particular subject is asked by the film-makers to raise a given topic with another in the hope that this will provoke some sort of revelatory statement. David MacDougall provides a good example of the use of this device during the shooting of *Kenya Boran*. In this case, the film-makers asked one of the subjects to raise the delicate issue of the Kenyan government's promotion of birth control during the course of a typical conversation between Boran men as they drank tea. Just as the film-makers had anticipated, this provoked a very strong reaction on the part of one of the senior men present who, in passionately rejecting the very idea of birth control, laid out with great clarity how the traditional pastoralist life of the Boran depended on men having many wives and a great number of children.[18]

It is important to stress, however, that for all their apparent spontaneity, the conversations of Observational Cinema, of whatever kind – between subjects, between subjects and film-makers, or proxy conversations – remained a device that could be manipulated for narrative purposes. That is, they were not necessarily situated in the final film in exactly the same place where, chronologically speaking, they had occurred in reality in relation to the rest of the action represented in the film. Rather, they would be placed where it best suited the narrative development of the film. But once a conversation had been used in the final edit, in sharp contrast to the television interview, it would typically never be returned to again, certainly not in synch, though very occasionally the soundtrack of the original conversation might be used as voice-over commentary elsewhere in the film.

## FILMING EVERYDAY EXPERIENCE

Another feature of Observational Cinema in its classic form that serves to distinguish it very clearly from the praxes of both Rouch and Gardner is the concern with the experience of everyday life. Central to this engagement with everyday life was the representation of domestic spaces, which de facto tend to be predominantly female. Although still less prominent than the public spaces typically dominated by men, these private domestic spaces are generally given much more attention in Observational Cinema films than in the ethnographic works of either Rouch or Gardner, the majority of which were primarily focused on ritual or ceremonial events, or failing that, on hunting or warfare, all of which tend to be male-dominated activities in the traditional societies where they worked.

In the praxis of Observational Cinema, on the other hand, even when the subject matter is a major ceremonial or political event, the principal focus of attention of the film is not so much on the public performance of the event itself, as on the way in which this event is construed and emplaced within the ideas and relations of the everyday life of both women and men. Thus, for example, in *The Wedding Camels*, the second film in the *Turkana Conversations* trilogy, the actual wedding ceremony takes up no more than three minutes of the 103-minute film: the rest of the film is almost entirely dedicated to the incessant haggling over bridewealth and the implications of these negotiations for both the domestic well-being of women and the public renown of men. As the MacDougalls attempt to follow these negotiations, the public debates of men are recurrently balanced with scenes of the everyday life of women and children in the family compounds.

We might contrast this with, say, *Les Maîtres fous*. Having watched this film, one would be excused for thinking that there were no women present at all at the *hauka* ceremony which constitutes its central subject matter since the action is almost exclusively focused on the male mediums possessed by spirits. It is really only from the production stills that one becomes aware that, in the background, witnessing the event, there are a considerable number of women.

This concern to communicate a sense of everyday life-experience involved a configuration of the relationships between subjects, film-maker and viewer that was significantly different from the typical alignment of these relationships in the films of Rouch and Gardner. For everything that reaches the viewer of the works of Rouch and Gardner has always been heavily filtered through their sensibilities as film-makers. By contrast, an important feature of Observational Cinema praxis in its classic form consisted, in effect, of an invitation to the audience to consider the film-maker's own experience of the life of the subjects as a sort of open channel through which they too could have an experience of that life. As Young once put it, the aim was to achieve an increase in the 'congruency between the subject as experienced by the film-makers and the film as experienced by the audience'. However, there was no pretence that this strategy resulted in an account of the subjects' life that was in any sense objective, or indicative of some definitive truth, nor even descriptively comprehensive: in none of these senses was this strategy 'a recipe for enlightenment', to use David MacDougall's phrase, rather it was merely 'a point of reference for communication'.[19]

This strategy had a number of practical consequences. First, it was necessary for the film-makers to share with the audience a sense of the nature of their relationship with the subjects, which in the ideal case should be close and intimate. An Observational Cinema film should never be based on the conceit of the 'fly-on-the-wall', as if the film had been made by a disembodied recording angel: it should be reflexive, freely incorporating not only conversations, but also any other manifestations of the relationship between subjects and film-makers in the form of look or gesture. It also required the film-makers to share with the audience a sense of the physical experience of participating in the subjects' life. What this meant in practical cinematographic terms was the preservation of what MacDougall would later call the 'distinctive spatial and temporal configurations' of the circumstances of filming. This meant that special lenses, extreme angles, slow- or fast-motion or any other special effects, even zooms and pans, anything that suggested some form of cinematographic manipulation, were all to be avoided. It also meant including the inconsequential, the banal and the reiterative in the final edit as well as the moments of greater or more lasting significance.

The sense of the film-maker's presence as a witness could be particularly well achieved by shooting long takes that allowed events to play themselves out within the take at the speed and in the form in which they had occurred in reality. But it could also be suggested by relatively short takes singling out for close observation particular actions or physical details that had attracted the film-maker's attention. Although the juxtaposition of shots in the final edited film could also be significant, in general, what was more important in the praxis of Observational Cinema in its classic form was the nature of what happened within the course of the individual shot. It is this, MacDougall has argued, rather than the length of the shots per se, that is most critical to communicating the sense of witnessing an event.[20]

## THE UNPRIVILEGED PERSPECTIVE

MacDougall sought to encapsulate these various practical entailments of filming everyday life in what he called an 'unprivileged camera style', a term that he first used in an article published in 1982 in *RAIN*, immediately following Young's review of *Turkana Conversations*.[21] Although he referred to the camera when first giving a name to this 'style', in practice it had as much to do with editing as with cinematography. Indeed, given the way in which MacDougall later developed the notion, rather than call it a 'camera style', it would be more appropriate in my view to refer to it as an 'unprivileged *perspective*'.

As with many aspects of Observational Cinema praxis, the notion of the unprivileged perspective was one that arose not from theoretical first principles, but through practical experimentation. It first came to the MacDougalls as they were editing the material that would eventually become *To Live with Herds*, their much-lauded film about the Jie. As they set about this task, they found themselves confronted with a problem: for reasons that they could not explain, the cut just did not seem to be working. After struggling with it for a while, they eventually realised that there was a conflict between the manner in which they were attempting to structure the material in the edit suite and what they had been trying to achieve while shooting, namely, to communicate a sense of everyday life in a Jie compound. In order to achieve this latter objective, they had mostly covered daily goings-on within the compound from a single static camera position, without using zooms or pans, and had made sure to incorporate both any acknowledgements of their presence and also inconsequential 'low energy level' events such as 'one would witness in ordinary experience [rather] than choose as film subjects'. However, on occasion, in order to get a better view of some technical process, or to show all those involved in a conversation, they had moved their camera position from one side of the compound to another.

But once in the edit suite, they found that cutting back and forth between these two camera positions involved 'a contradiction in premises': on the one hand, they were trying to communicate a sense of 'being there' in the Jie compound, while on the other, in cutting back and forth, they were adopting the perspective of an external observer who could flit magically from one place to another, unconstrained by the social and physical constraints of the situation. They eventually concluded that in editing any one particular event in the Jie compound, they had to commit to either one or the other perspective, even if this meant cutting some material that might be valuable in itself.

In referring to this perspective as 'unprivileged', MacDougall aimed to distinguish it from the 'privileged camera angle', the term used in the screen studies literature on the Hollywood movie to describe a camera position that offers a perspective to the audience that is not available to the subjects. This may be for straightforward physical reasons (for example, the camera is positioned on the other side of a door as the subjects enter a room) or for social reasons (because it implies a knowledge of events or circumstances of which the subjects are not aware). However, in his later writings, MacDougall would develop this notion of the unprivileged perspective in a more editorial sense, going far beyond the limited issue of camera positioning.

MacDougall developed the concept in two directions in particular. The first was in relation to the quality of the knowledge of the world that an Observational Cinema praxis can deliver. On this matter, there is a subtle difference of emphasis in the writings of MacDougall and Young. While it is true that in his manifesto-essay Young extols the virtues of an Observational Cinema praxis as a means of allowing the viewer 'to have a sense of experiencing the event', he also mixes these references to *experience* with references to the superior quality and even quantity of *information* that an Observational Cinema praxis can generate. Thus he rails against 'manipulative classical melodrama and didactic educational films' because they both restrict 'the flow of information' and therefore do not allow the viewer to make their own analysis. The implication is that the Observational Cinema film-maker should aim to lay out the world as comprehensively and as impartially as possible – even while recognising that complete objectivity is a chimera – so that the viewer can then construe its meaning for themselves.

By contrast, in MacDougall's writing the emphasis is not so much on laying out the world in an impartial way, as on sharing with the viewer the experience of *both film-makers and subjects* that their knowledge of the world is partial and incomplete, and in this sense is 'unprivileged'. This sense of uncertainty and doubt is particularly characteristic of the MacDougalls' films about the Turkana, and especially true of *The Wedding Camels*. It was on account of this quality that this film was characterised by Peter Loizos as 'an exercise in sustained ambiguity', while MacDougall himself has described it as a film 'about what one can and cannot know'.[22]

The other direction in which MacDougall developed the concept of an unprivileged perspective was in relation to nature of the story told in an Observational Cinema film. As part of his general argument in favour of a participatory form of cinema, MacDougall proposes, in an article first published in 1991, that Observational Cinema film-makers should acknowledge that 'the subject's story is often more important than the film-maker's'. This 'stance of humility', as he terms it in a memorable phrase, had been prefigured in Young's manifesto-essay when he argued that directors should never ask for an action to be repeated, since this might lead the subjects to start 'acting for him instead of for themselves'. But MacDougall develops this concept further in arguing that Observational Cinema film-makers should, as a matter of course, make a point of being open to categories of meaning that might transcend their own analyses. In practice, what this meant was actively allowing the subjects to take the story of the film off in directions that the film-maker had not anticipated when they first started shooting.[23]

## RESTRAINED NARRATIVES

Even though an unprivileged perspective became both cinematographically and editorially a central principle of the praxis of Observational Cinema in its classic form, this did not mean that the structuring of the material in the editing suite from a privileged, external perspective was entirely abandoned. Observational Cinema films continued to be structured editorially, but very discreetly. In his manifesto-essay, Colin Young cites with approval the practice of the French New Wave feature film directors, who, having studied classic Hollywood cinema in order to identify the conventions whereby it achieved its effects, then used those same conventions themselves but in a more low-key way, leaving much more to the imagination of the audience. 'They were not so much unconventional as restrained', Young comments. 'They left us space to fill and we participated.' In his view, this was the goal towards which Observational Cinema film-makers should also be striving.[24]

As I described in Chapter 5, the narrative structures around which the films that the MacDougalls made in East Africa and Australia are very much like this. Although the narrative tropes on which these films are based are relatively conventional, they are so subtly deployed that one can often be barely aware of them. All their major African films are subdivided into thematically defined 'acts' in the manner of a stage play, a device originally inspired by *Song of Ceylon*, the classic film directed by Basil Wright and released in 1934. While this device is relatively obvious in the first film, *To Live with Herds*, it is more submerged in the others. Although the theatrical act device disappears in the MacDougalls' best-known Australian films, these continue to be structured by highly conventional narrative tropes: a 'crisis structure' in the case of *Takeover*, the unfolding of a ritual event in the case of *The House-Opening*, and a journey in the case of *Familiar Places*. As we shall see when we consider their more recent work in Chapter 14, the films they have made since the early 1990s continue to have these conventional but restrained, almost invisible, narrative structures.

Indeed, such is the degree of restraint in the MacDougalls' films that some viewers do not detect the narrative structures at all. These viewers would appear to have included even Jean Rouch, who on first seeing *To Live with Herds* famously declared, 'This is not a film!' Whether it was the apparent absence of a readily identifiable narrative structure, or rather the focus on the everyday of the life of the Jie that led him to make this remark, or, as is most likely, some combination of the two, is not clear. But whatever the precise reason for it, the remark clearly testifies to a fundamental difference in praxis between the Observational Cinema film-makers and Jean Rouch, despite the great respect that the former had for the work of the latter and vice versa.[25]

## OBSERVATIONAL CINEMA MOVES BEYOND THE USA

In 1970, Colin Young left Los Angeles and returned to Britain to become the first Director of the newly created National Film School at Beaconsfield, about thirty miles west of London. Around the same time, his principal ally in the Anthropology department, Paul Hockings, left to take up a post with the MGM film production company, advising on a major anthropology series about human evolution. Without their involvement, the Ethnographic Film Program back at UCLA died a slow death. The Masters programme towards which they had been working never happened. However, from his new position at what would soon become the National Film and Television School (NFTS), Young continued to promote ethnographic film, and to keep in contact with his former associates in the USA. Shortly after he arrived at the NFTS, David and Judith MacDougall came to seek his advice on the final cut of *To Live with Herds*. Some years later, in 1980, they returned as 'film-makers-in-residence' for six months while they used the NFTS facilities to cut the last of their *Turkana Conversations* trilogy to be edited: *A Wife Among Wives*.

Another means by which Young kept his US links going was by persuading Norman Miller, the producer of the American Universities Field Staff (AUFS) series, *Faces of Change*, to produce it through the NFTS. This series entered production in 1972 and involved a number of people associated with the UCLA Ethnographic Film Program: James Blue and David MacDougall shot a series of four films in Kenya with the Boran pastoralists, advised by the Manchester anthropologist Paul Baxter, while Herb Di Gioia and David Hancock shot a series of four films in Afghanistan with the Harvard anthropologist, Louis Dupree. The best known of the latter is *Naim and Jabar*, released in 1974, which concerns the relationship between two teenage boys as they are growing up in rural Afghanistan in the years before the Russia's invasion in 1979.[26]

It was also during his early years at the NFTS that Young wrote the manifesto-essay on Observational Cinema that appears in *Principles of Visual Anthropology*. This volume was edited by Paul Hockings, and arose from a major international conference held in Chicago in 1973. Young was unable to attend the conference himself, but through the persistence of Hockings, was persuaded to produce his contribution some six months later. Eventually published in 1975, this volume played an important role in the establishment of the academic sub-discipline of Visual Anthropology with the result that both Young's manifesto-essay and David MacDougall's counterpoint contribution, 'Beyond Observational Cinema' became standard reference texts on visual anthropology programmes across the world.

Around the same time, Young started to use NFTS resources to encourage ethnographic film-making in the Observational Cinema manner outside the USA. He became a regular participant in ethnographic film festivals across Europe but also went further afield, taking part in a conference at the Australian Institute of Aboriginal Studies (AIAS) in Canberra in May 1978. This was organised by the MacDougalls, who had recently moved to Australia to take up positions in the AIAS Film Unit.

But Young's most systematic project to promote ethnographic film-making following his return to the UK was the training programme that he developed at the NFTS in conjunction with the Royal Anthropological Institute (RAI). This programme, which was funded by the Leverhulme Trust and which ran from 1984 to 1987, represented a reprise of the UCLA progamme in that it was based on a similar principle of bringing together film students and anthropologists so that they would learn from one another. Ultimately, however, the aim was to train the anthropologists to make their own films, without the need for technical assistance from professional film-makers. Although Young played a major role in enabling this programme, it was actually directed on a day-to-day basis by Herb Di Gioia, whom Young had by then appointed to run the documentary department of the NFTS.

Along with the ethnomusicologist John Baily, I was fortunate enough to be selected for the first round of this progamme myself and over two years, I received a thorough training as a director-cameraman grounded in the Observational Cinema 'way of doing' ethnographic film-making. The programme was very generously funded and even allowed for the making, each year, of an extended 16 mm film in whichever part of the world the participating anthropologists had some previous ethnographic research experience. In my own particular case, this allowed me to make three films in Venezuela in collaboration with Georges Drion, who was attending the NFTS as a conventional film student. In the first year, we made *Reclaiming the Forest*, which concerned indigenous gold-miners on the Gran Sabana in the southeast of the country, while in the second year, we were able to spin out the budget to shoot *Cuyagua*, a two-part film about religious ceremonies in a community of African descent on the Caribbean coast. Although ostensibly Catholic, these ceremonies included powerful elements of African music and dance (figure 10.4).

Although a number of the films produced by the RAI/NFTS programme were later screened at international ethnographic film festivals around the world, undoubtedly the most signficant legacy of the programme was the impact that it had on the teaching of visual anthropology in UK academic

10.4 Left, a 'devil' renders homage to the altar at the church door, as in *Cuyagua – Devil Dancers* (1986); right, the statue of St John the Baptist makes its way around the village, as in *Cuyagua – The Saint with Two Faces* (1987). (Photographs taken in 2006).

institutions. When I was appointed to direct the Granada Centre for Visual Anthropology at the University of Manchester in 1987, shortly after completing the programme at the NFTS, I was able to place training in Observational Cinema methods at the heart of our MA programme. It remains so to this day, more than thirty years later and after more than 400 students have passed through the programme. My colleagues on the RAI/NFTS programme were similarly able to promote the Observational Cinema approach in their own subsequent academic careers.[27]

## THE DIVERSIFICATION OF OBSERVATIONAL CINEMA

As a result of these various initiatives, the general influence of Observational Cinema has spread far beyond the immediate circle of those who had been involved in the Ethnographic Film Program at UCLA and, along with Direct Cinema and various other interpretations of the *cinéma-vérité* approach contributed in a major way to the general zeitgeist in ethnographic film-making in the English-speaking world in the 1980s. Making a particularly important contribution to this general ferment of related approaches was *Celso and Cora*, a film released in 1983. This highly acclaimed account of the everyday lives of a young couple living in an impoverished *barrio* in Manila was directed and shot by the Australian film-maker, Gary Kildea. In many ways, this film exemplifies the praxis of Observational Cinema in its original form with a determination and rigour that even goes beyond the work the Ethnographic Film Program's original participants.

Prior to making *Celso and Cora*, Kildea had spent a year at the NFTS in 1974–75. By this time, he was already an experienced film-maker, having worked since 1970 in Papua New Guinea, where he made a number of films in collaboration with another leading Australian documentarist, Dennis O'Rourke. However, prior to *Celso and Cora*, Kildea was probably most known for *Trobriand Cricket*, released in 1974, which he made in conjunction with Jerry Leach, an anthropologist then at the University of Cambridge. As suggested by the subtitle, *an ingenious response to colonialism*, this film concerns the adaptation of the game of cricket to the norms of Trobriand competitive ceremonial performance. In terms of its praxis, *Trobriand Cricket* had been quite unlike *Celso and Cora*, combining the very different agendas of its two makers: while the first part involves voice-over commentary, interviews, even archival footage, and is a reflection of the pedagogical concerns of Leach, the second part of film reflects Kildea's already developing interest in an observational mode of film-making.

Kildea applied to study at the NFTS because he wanted at that stage in his career to become a fictional feature film-maker. However, while he was there, as he himself has put it, Colin Young 'gently' made sure that he was introduced to 'the best that Observational Cinema of the day could offer', and this prepared the way for his 'eventual return to the fold' of documentary. But of all the influences to which Young introduced Kildea while he was at the NFTS, the one that he himself believes had the most fundamental impact on his career was that of the Japanese feature film director, Yasujirō Ozu. The subtitling of *Celso of Cora* as *A Manila Story*, is a direct *hommage* to Ozu's classic film, *Tòkyo Story*, released in 1953.[28]

*Celso and Cora* shows the eponymous couple struggling over a three-month period to make ends meet as cigarette vendors on the street while trying to support themselves and two small children. As in the works of the MacDougalls, conversation plays a central role in the film, both between the two principal subjects as well as between the film-makers and the subjects. A photograph of the film-makers with the subjects, placed right at the beginning of the film and accompanied by some brief remarks in voice-over by Kildea explaining the circumstances of film-making, serves to give the viewers a sense of to whom the subjects are talking. These conversations were greatly facilitated by the fact that the Filipina sound recordist, Rowena Katalinekasan-Gonzalez, spoke Tagalog, the lingua franca of the Philippines spoken by Celso and Cora, while Kildea himself had some familiarity with it too. This circumstance, coupled with the remarkable loquacity of Celso and Cora, and their total lack of self-consciousness, gives these conversations a fluency and energy that are rare even in the MacDougalls' films.

Also as in the ideal-typical Observational Cinema film, the action of *Celso and Cora* concerns everyday life, including domestic spaces as much as life on the streets, with Cora playing just as prominent a role in the film as Celso, except in the latter part of the film, following a bust-up, when she takes off with one of the children and goes to live with her mother.

10.5 *Celso and Cora* (1983). After one of their recurrent arguments, Celso ends up sleeping rough beside the sea wall with their daughter, right.

There is one ritual event in the film, by the graveside of Cora's late father, but this is passed over rapidly. The camera is radically unprivileged, always adopting the perspective of someone deeply immersed in the action: this was taken to the extent of rejecting a striking shot taken from the driver's cab of a train passing through the *barrio*, because, Kildea reasoned, this was a perspective that was not available to the subjects and as such, it was therefore not appropriate to include it in the film. More generally, there is a strong point-of-view feel to many of the shots, notably those that follow the protagonists as they walk through the narrow alleyways of the *barrio*. Most of the shots in the film are in fact long and well executed sequence-shots. Most strikingly of all, these are separated from one another by short sections of grey leader, as if to reject the artificiality of continuity editing.[29]

Yet, at the same time, despite this refusal to use conventional editorial devices at the level of the individual sequence-shot, there is still a 'restrained' though highly conventional narrative topos underlying the progression of the film. The presence of this narrative structure is signalled in Kildea's opening remarks, albeit in a somewhat coded manner, when he explains: 'this story has been constructed from fragments of [the subjects'] lives, taken over a three-month period'. This allusion to the *construction* of *fragments* refers to the fact that the course of the events shown in the film has been manipulated in such a way as to produce a very familiar narrative arc: that is, the film builds to a climactic argument between Celso and Cora but shortly before the end there is is a reconciliation and the film returns to the situation in which the family had been shown at the beginning of the film. This, in its circularity, and entirely intentionally, provides a sense of narrative closure (figure 10.5).[30] In that it involves this marked contrast between the overt demonstration of the absence of manipulation of the filmic text at the level of the shot or sequence and the more covert presence of an underlying narrative that is restrained but nevertheless constructed, *Celso and Cora* is entirely typical of the praxis of Observational Cinema.

In his subsequent work, Kildea has moved away from the particularly rigorous interpretation of the principles of Observational Cinema that *Celso and Cora* represents.[31] Similarly, as discussed in Chapter 5, the Mac-Dougalls' film-making praxis has also changed over the years, becoming more participatory as they moved the main location of their filming from Africa to Australia. Since then, after they left the AIAS in the late 1980s and began making films elsewhere, mostly in India, the MacDougalls' work has changed again, in some senses moving even further away from the principles of Observational Cinema as they were originally formulated, though in other senses returning to them, as I discuss at some length in Chapter 14.

For our part, at the Granada Centre for Visual Anthropology, we continue to instruct our students in the principles of Observational Cinema at the initial stages of their training, since we believe that it remains a highly effective mode of film authorship for a range of ethnographic purposes, with many points of overlap with ethnographic practice more generally, particularly in its emphasis on everyday experience and the importance of immersive, first-hand fieldwork. But over time, it has become clear to us that Observational Cinema also has its limitations and that some ethnographic topics or situations call out for a different approach. Accordingly, in the later stages of the training offered on our MA programme, we introduce the students to alternative approaches and encourage them to think how these may be combined with the principles of Observational Cinema, or if the circumstances require it, even adopted in preference to the latter.

All this was anticipated by Colin Young who closes his original manifesto-essay with the comment that any intellectual discipline 'will outgrow its early enthusiasms and change its methodologies', adding that it is a 'waste of time' to argue for a single method since there may be any number of different ways to achieve one's goals.[32] By virtue of a powerful imagination and a determination to overcome institutional obstacles, Colin Young created the springboard in 1960s UCLA for a mode of documentary film authorship whose influence has expanded across the world of ethnographic cinema, like ripples across a pond, transforming itself as it goes.

## Notes

1 This chapter draws extensively on a series of conversations that I have had with Colin Young over thirty years. These are presented at greater length in a recent article (Henley 2018).
2 Mead (1995), 10.
3 Young (1995), 110, 112–13.

4 Young (1995), 112.

5 Around the time that Young first met Edmund Carpenter, he was the head of the Anthropology Department at San Fernando Valley State College (later the State University of California at Northridge). Previously he had been at the University of Toronto, which is where he had met Marshall McLuhan. For a good account of Carpenter's extraordinarily diverse intellectual history, see Prins and Bishop (2001–2). Carpenter died in 2011.

6 The UNESCO report presented at Sydney was published as Young with Carpenter (1966). This was later incorporated into a more general catalogue on ethnographic films about the Pacific region edited by Jean Rouch and Monique Salzmann (1970).

7 There is some uncertainty about when the term Observational Cinema first came to be used of the praxis emerging from the Ethnographic Film Program. According to some of those involved, it was already in circulation in the 1960s while the Ethnographic Film Program was active. The first use of the term in print, on the other hand, is often said to be in an article published in 1972 by Roger Sandall. But although Sandall cites the MacDougalls' early work, *To Live with Herds*, as an example of what he considers to be 'observational cinema' (without capitalisation), more generally his conception of this praxis excludes any of the more reflexive and participatory elements that are integral to Colin Young's presentation of Observational Cinema in his manifesto-essay (see Sandall 1972).

8 Both Hockings (1988) and McCarty (1995) have written amusing accounts about the making of this film. For a definition of an 'as if' chronology, see p. 104 of this book.

9 See Hockings (1988), 154–5, for a vivid description of the first public screening, which took place at the American Association of Anthropologists meeting in Seattle in December 1968. For a more extended discussion of *The Village*, see Henley (2018), 203–5.

10 The other three films of the *Vermont People* series were *Duwayne Masure* (1971), *Chester Grimes* (1972), and *Peter and Jane Flint* (1975). Tragically, the partnership between Di Gioia and Hancock was brought to a premature end by Hancock's death at the age of 30 in 1976. See Grimshaw and Ravetz (2009), 53–78 for a more thorough analysis of their work.

11 Personal communication, July 2012. See also MacDougall (2007), 126–7.

12 MacDougall (2007), 128–9.

13 This is not, however, a universal view. In their book *Observational Cinema*, Anna Grimshaw and Amanda Ravetz suggest that on account of their more reflexive and participatory elements, not only the MacDougalls' Australian films, but even their Turkana trilogy might be considered 'a critique of the genre' and for this reason, they do not discuss them in any detail (Grimshaw and Ravetz 2009), 79.

14 See Young (1982a), 5–6.

15 The work of John Marshall and Timothy Asch is described in Chapter 4, while the MacDougalls' early films among the Jie are described in Chapter 5, pp. 156–7. David MacDougall has explained in a personal communication that the unfortunate conjunction of titles in *Principles of Visual Anthropology* arose because at the time that the volume was in press, he himself was away in the field in Africa, Colin Young was in the UK, and Paul Hockings, the editor, was in Chicago. As a result, it was only after the volume had been published that the potential for confusion became apparent.

16 Taylor (1998), 3. Writing more recently about this praxis, David MacDougall has commented, '"Observational" … has always seemed to me a curious word to apply to it. Whatever form documentary takes, it is generally a more interactive process than the word implies … if I was observing, I was also being observed. "Participant-observation", long a watchword of anthropologists in the field, would seem to be the better term. But we are stuck with "observational cinema", so let it stand' (MacDougall 2019), 119.

17  See MacDougall (1998d).

18  MacDougall (1995a), 127.

19  Young (1982b), 63; MacDougall (1998e), 205. See also MacDougall (2019), 2.

20  Young (1995), 101, 110; MacDougall (1998c) (1998f) (2019), 30–7 and 126–7.

21  This article was later republished in a collection of MacDougall's essays. All the quotations in the following paragraphs are from this republication (MacDougall 1998e), *passim.*

22  Young (1995), 102, 104; Loizos (1993), 102; MacDougall (1998e), 208.

23  Young (1995), 102, 105; MacDougall (1998c), 156.

24  Young (1995), 103.

25  Young (1995), 107; Colette Piault (2007b), 48–9.

26  *Naim and Jabar* is distributed by DER, along with the three shorter films that Di Goia and Hancock made in Afghanistan. See www.der.org/films/faces-of-change-afghan.html. See Chapter 5, footnote 5, p. 173 for further details about Blue and MacDougall's film on the Kenya Boran.

27  Later Professor of Ethnomusicology at Goldsmiths, University of London, John Baily went on to make a series of films on Afghan music, his specialist interest and to encourage his doctoral students to do likewise (see Baily 2017). The other participants in the programme were Marcus Banks, who as professor and head of the School of Social Anthropology and Museum Ethnography at Oxford developed a visual anthropology Masters programme there and also wrote an important textbook on visual methods of social research (Banks and Zeitlyn 2015), and Felicia Hughes-Freeland, who set up a practice-based visual anthropology programme at the University of Wales at Swansea and now continues to be actively involved in the field as a research associate of the School of Oriental and African Studies. As a sort of further extension to the RAI scheme, Anna Grimshaw, later Professor of Visual Culture at Emory University, Atlanta and co-author of a major study of Observational Cinema (Grimshaw and Ravetz 2009), but then a newly appointed lecturer at the Granada Centre for Visual Anthropology, attended the NFTS for a period in the academic year 1991–92. However, she was funded by the Granada Centre and the University of Manchester rather than through the RAI scheme.

28  Gary Kildea, personal communication, August 2018. For a more extended account of Kildea's career, see Crawford (2004) and Kildea (2007).

29  See MacDougall (1998e), 205–7.

30  See Kildea's comments in Kildea and Willson (1986), 15–16.

31  A comprehensive review of Kildea's later films is unfortunately not possible here, but in Chapter 16, I consider at some length *Koriam's Law and the Dead Who Govern,* a film that he made in conjunction with Andrea Simon and which was released in 2005, see pp. 466–70.

32  Young (1995), 113.

# Part III
# Television as meta-author: ethnographic film in Britain

# Introduction

Eᴛʜɴᴏɢʀᴀᴘʜɪᴄ film-making, broadly defined, has been supported by television companies in many different countries around the world since as far back as the 1950s. However, in most cases, this support has been intermittent and contingent: the occasional series, an evening of special programming, the one-off major documentary feature. In Britain, by contrast, for a period of around twenty-five years, from the late 1960s until the mid-1990s, the national television network provided sustained and materially very substantial support for ethnographic film-making in a variety of forms. Prior to this period of intense productivity, ethnographic film-making in Britain barely existed. Since the decline of ethnographic film on television in the mid-1990s, all ethnographic film-making in Britain exists in its shadow. If there is such a thing as a distinctively British tradition of eth-nographic film-making, it is one that is profoundly marked by its origins in television.[1]

It is in the nature of television to be transitory: yesterday's programme is quickly forgotten in the constant rush to seek new – or supposedly new – means of improving audience share. But against the grain of this propensity of television to consign its own productions to oblivion, as well as the tendency of academic commentators to attribute greater value to works of cinema, I would contend that among the considerable number of ethnographic films produced for British television, there are many that are as worthy of critical attention as those that I have considered elsewhere in this book. My concern, then, in the following three chapters is to chart the rise and fall of this television-based ethnographic film-making in Britain, to analyse the authorial praxes that developed within it and to consider its legacies.

Putting a precise figure on the quantity of ethnographic films produced for British television during this period clearly depends on how, exactly, one defines ethnographicness in this context. What is comparatively easy to measure is the number of television programmes that were directly based on the ethnographic field research of anthropologists and which also involved them in an active way in the actual production. Programmes of this kind numbered around a hundred over the period from the late 1960s to early 1990s, most of which ran for the length of the television 'hour', that is somewhere between 48 and 58 minutes, depending on the duration of the intervening commercial breaks and programming announcements. I offer a tentative listing of these programmes in the Appendix at the end of this book. In effect, presuming an average budget of around £100,000 per programme at current values, surely a conservative estimate, this means that during this period British television invested the remarkable sum of at least £10 million in films based on academic ethnographic research. It is not for nothing then that this period has sometimes been referred to as the 'golden era' of ethnographic film-making on British television.

In addition to these programmes based directly on academic research, British television during the 'golden era' also regularly supported a form of documentary film-making that could be described as 'para-ethnographic'. Typically, this kind of film-making did not involve academic anthropologists in a direct or active way in the production itself, nor was it necessarily based on prior academic research. However, its underlying production methods were similar to the field research methods typically employed by academic ethnographers in the sense that they were based on a prolonged period of participant-observation by the film-makers of a relatively small group of people or of a specific social institution, often over several months or even years, and they could also involve, even if only implicitly, some form of social or cultural analysis.

An early example of this kind of 'para-ethnographic' film-making is the BBC series, *The Family*, produced by Paul Watson and broadcast over twelve 30-minute parts in 1974. This so-called 'fly-on-the-wall' observational series followed the day-to-day life of the Wilkins, a working-class family from Reading, and was based on two months of pre-production research, followed by three months of filming during which time the film crew spent up to eighteen hours a day with the subjects. These circumstances of production required the development of a high degree of mutual rapport between subjects and film-makers that is evident in the final films. The films were motivated by an explicit agenda on Watson's part, namely to show British working-class life as it really is experienced, with all its ups and downs, rather than in the idealised form in which it had previously been shown, not only on television, but in British documentaries in the Griersonian mould. In all these regards, *The Family* offers what I would argue is an insightful para-ethnographic account of British working-class life in the 1970s.[2]

The ethnographic status of the films made in this way for British television is certainly debatable, but notwithstanding these doubts, quite a number have been screened at international ethnographic film festivals, and some have even been awarded prizes. If these films were also included in the calculation, the figure one could put on the underwriting of ethnographic film-making by British television during the 'golden era' would be very much more substantial, of the order of several times the £10 million invested in films based directly on academic research.

However, the fact that these films, ethnographic or para-ethnographic, were being made for television necessarily entailed certain compromises. Typically, they were shot over a period of no more than four to six weeks, often by television crews who may have been very skilled in their work, but for whom the film was just one more job rather than a passionate commitment. It was also the case that as they started with different agendas, the director and the academic consultant, if there was one, would often find themselves at odds and the resulting film would end up being a compromise between their respective points of view. Moreover, the role and degree of participation of the academic consultant could vary considerably: in some cases, the consultant was almost a co-director, in other cases little more than a purveyor of information and guarantor of access in the field. The 'balance of power' would also typically shift over the course of the production: in the field, for obvious reasons, the academic consultant had considerable influence over the direction of the shoot, but once the rushes were back in the edit suite, the consultant typically had less control. Even if the director and the academic consultant could arrive at complete agreement, they might then find their ideas being over-ridden by series producers and other senior executives higher up the typically very hierarchical television line of management.[3]

Yet despite all these limiting factors, I would argue that in the great majority of the cases listed in the Appendix, the films that emerged from the process featured a high degree of ethnographicness. Although the film crews may have remained in the field only for a limited period by anthropological standards (albeit a very long one by television standards), they would generally have been obliged to work within the parameters set by the knowledge and understandings developed by the academic consultant beforehand over a prolonged period. Equally importantly, they would usually find themselves working within the set of relationships and associated ethical and interpersonal compromises that the academic consultant had built up over that time.

While there may often have been arguments and disagreements between directors and academic consultants, and many instances in which the academic consultants were uncomfortable about the compromises that they had to make in order for the film to work as a television programme aimed at a popular audience numbered in millions, there were also many instances when the perspectives of both parties were enriched by the contribution of the other. As I shall relate in these chapters, many of the leading directors of British ethnographic film in the 'golden era' were themselves anthropology graduates, some with postgraduate degrees. They were therefore predisposed to be sympathetic to the consultants' points of view, even if they might disagree as to the best means to represent those points of view in the films that they were making. Only in very few instances was the disagreement so great that the academic consultant later dissociated themselves entirely from the result. In most cases, I would venture to suggest, the academic consultants came to value the final film highly, even if it took them some time to come round to appreciate that as a film, it was bound to be different in nature to the kind of representation that they might have produced in a textual form.

Moreover, it would be wrong, in my view, to assume that all the com-promises that the anthropologist consultants found themselves obliged to make had negative consequences, as some academic commentators tend to assume: the obligation to address non-specialist audiences did not necessarily result in 'dumbing down', but rather could serve as the catalyst for experienced film directors to identify the essence of an issue or set of circumstances so that it could be presented in a readily accessible manner. This is a skill that, proverbially at least, many academics lack.

At the same time, the technical standards of broadcast television required craft skills that were far greater than anything most academics could manage by themselves. Although academics like to stress that content is more important than technical quality, a proposition which when baldly stated is of course true, the accessibility of the content of any film, or indeed of any text, depends in the last analysis on the mastery of certain technical skills. To oppose technique and content is therefore a false dichotomy: certainly a lack of technique is no guarantee of ethnographic significance, in either a film or a text.

In short, there were benefits as well as costs to collaborating with a televi-sion production company, even when considered from a strictly academic point of view. In the best cases, the film-makers, working together as a team, including here the camera operators, sound recordists and the editors as well as the directors, could bring to the representation of the academic consultants' ethnographic understandings a whole range of imaginative cinematic devices that not only embodied those understandings in a more engaging manner for a popular audience, but could even provide insights into those ethnographic understandings of which the academic consultants themselves had not been previously aware.

From the directors' point of view, the need to reconcile the requirement to address a mass audience with the concerns of an academic consultant was but one of the many challenges that had to be confronted. In comparison with the relative freedom enjoyed by the other leading authors whose work is considered in previous chapters, the directors of the ethnographic films made for British television were obliged to work within a series of editorial and organisational constraints that had a strong impact on their individual authorial signatures: these constraints ranged from programme formats and stylistic conventions to the use of professional crews bound by various agreements between their unions and management.

But as with matters of content, it would be a mistake to assume that the conditions governing the making of ethnographic films for television always had negative effects: in certain regards, they could be very positive. One of the most significant positive examples is the opportunity that British television afforded to women to become leading ethnographic film directors. In this regard, the patronage of British television had a considerably more progressive effect on ethnographic film-making than the film-making supported by museums or academic institutions, not only in the UK, but anywhere else in the English-speaking world.

For good or for ill then, the general circumstances of the production of ethnographic films for British television – technical, editorial or organisational – had a major impact on film-makers working in this medium. There were certainly some directors who managed to produce films of both originality and distinction within the constraints of television over this period, while others pushed those constraints to breaking point. But however accomplished or idiosyncratic their works, the authorship of even these directors was always ultimately shaped by the protocols of the medium in which they were working. In this sense, I would claim that British television itself acted as a sort of meta-author of the works produced during the 'golden era', both stimulating and restraining ethnographic film-making praxes.

### Notes

1   The only comparable example known to me is from Japan, where television support of ethnographic film-making took the form of the series, *Our Wonderful World*. This was produced for a prime-time slot by the now-defunct company Nippon A-V from 1966 until 1990. Its focus was primarily on societies of the Asia-Pacific region, though it also featured films shot in Africa, South America and Europe. Although the films were not generally based on the work of academic anthropologists, they were often shot in an ethnographic manner, with small crews embedded in the host societies for several months. See Ichioka (1995).

2   *The Family* is viewable online in an abbreviated form at www.youtube.com/watch?v=ZArtrC5rpVs. The British series was itself inspired by the US television documentary series, *An American Family*, about the middle-class Loud family of Santa Barbara, California, which had been released in 1973.

3   The best account by an anthropologist consultant about collaborating with British television during the 'golden era' is by the late Terence Turner, a US academic who worked on a range of different programmes (Turner 1992b).

# Ways of doing ethnographic film on British television

## THE ORIGINS OF ETHNOGRAPHIC FILM SPONSORSHIP BY BRITISH TELEVISION

Prior to its sponsorship by television, ethnographic film-making in Britain was almost non-existent. Since the pioneering work of Haddon and Spencer at the turn of the twentieth century, the number of British anthropologists who had taken moving image cameras with them to the field had been very few, and even those that had done so, had generally used them not to make documentaries as such, but rather for documentation purposes. Facilities and support for ethnographic film were extremely limited: in contrast to France and the USA, British museums did not support ethnographic film-making to any great extent, nor did British research councils or universities. Nor were there any leading individual film-makers, such as Jean Rouch in France, or John Marshall and Robert Gardner in the USA, whose personal example might have served as an inspiration to others. Colin Young, who acted as the initial enabler of Observational Cinema, as described in Chapter 10, was still based in UCLA in the late 1960s and it would be some years before he brought his influence to bear on ethnographic film-making back in Britain.[1]

A major reason for the support given to ethnographic films by British television can be traced to the very particular circumstances of British mass media in the post-war period. Since its foundational charter in the 1920s, the British national broadcaster, the British Broadcasting Corporation (BBC), had been under a formal obligation to 'educate and inform' as well as 'entertain'. This is generally referred to as the 'Reithian' tradition of public service broadcasting, on account of the role of the first Director General of the BBC, John Reith, in formulating these principles. When it launched a television service in the early 1950s, the BBC remained bound by these Reithian principles, as were the 'independent' commercial companies that were awarded television broadcasting franchises later in the same decade. These franchises were assigned on a regional basis and as time went on, the various franchise holders operated what was, in effect, an informal division of labour in relation to this obligation to produce educational material: some chose to make films about natural history, others about opera or ballet, others again about the visual arts. The holder of the franchise for the northwest of England, Granada Television, based in Manchester, chose to support the making of ethnographic films.[2]

Why Granada Television should chose ethnographic film-making in fulfilment of its educational remit was due to a set of entirely fortuitous personal circumstances. The chief executive of the company since its formation in 1955, Sir Denis Forman, was a man of broad cultural interests, including an interest in anthropology, which stemmed from his reading of *The Golden Bough* as an adolescent. For the son of a Scottish Presbyterian minister, the encounter with Sir James Frazer's presentation of Christianity as just one more set of religious beliefs, no more securely founded than any other, proved to be a life-changing experience, leading him to reject religion, much to his devout parents' consternation.[3] Later, as director of the British Film Institute (BFI) in the immediate post-war period, Forman came to admire the works of Flaherty, and the Cooper and Schoedsack classic, *Grass*, as well as the early works of Jean Rouch.

As he would later confess, he long harboured a personal desire 'to spend time alone in the company of remote tribal people', though he saw no realistic way of doing so, except vicariously, through the works of ethnographic film-makers. Forman also had a keen sense of the major cultural changes taking place as ethnic minorities across the globe came into closer contact with the outside world and he thought it imperative that these ways of life be documented on film before they disappeared for ever. 'I am sure', he wrote in 1985, 'that one hundred years from now there will be no documentary film material in existence, whether it be of World War Two, or the arrival of the aeroplane, that will surpass in value the record of vanished societies in reaching a better understanding of the human condition as it changes through the centuries.'[4]

It was on account of this idiosyncratic personal interest that Forman's attention was drawn to *Piraparaná*, a short film about the indigenous peoples living in the Vaupés region of Colombian Amazonia that was submitted to Granada Television sometime in 1965. The directors of this film, who had no film-making training whatsoever, were Brian Moser and Donald Tayler. The film had been shot in October–November 1961 in the course of an ethnomusicological expedition to Colombia that Moser and Tayler had organised shortly after they graduated from the University of Cambridge. The cameraman, who shot the material on a spring-wound Bolex, was Niels Halbertsma, a Dutch freelancer whom Moser and Tayler had met by chance at a party in Bogotá, while the editor was David Gladwell, who would later go on to have a distinguished career in the feature film industry. Since shooting this film, Moser had been working as a geologist in Africa but was now looking for a change of direction. Tayler, meanwhile, was pursuing postgraduate studies in anthropology at the University of Oxford.

Forman was impressed by the content and general approach of *Piraparaná*, but considered it too amateurish to be broadcast on television, so he made Moser an offer: Granada would give him a year's training as a professional film-maker, whereafter it would finance the making of a series of films about indigenous peoples of Latin America under his direction. This was an offer that Moser was delighted to accept though, in the event, he then spent three years learning the craft of television film-making, mostly on Granada's *World in Action* current affairs progamme, renowned for its investigative journalism. Eventually, in 1968, as a result of a dispute between Granada management and the technicians' union, Moser found himself marooned in Bogotá with the time to prepare a proposal for the series, which he did with the assistance of his wife, the urban anthropologist Caroline Moser.

Integral to this proposal was the idea that each film would be directly based on the fieldwork of an anthropologist. Although he had never studied anthropology himself, Moser had long been convinced of the need to collaborate with anthropologists in making films about culturally exotic societies, not merely on account of their academic expertise, but also as a means of gaining a more intimate rapport with the subjects of the films. At this time, the standard model of British television programmes about exotic societies was either that of the scientific explorer in the David Attenborough mould, or that of the African safari expedition in the mould of Armand and Michaela Dennis. In both cases, the human subjects would typically be presented merely as one feature of a programme structured around the presenter's journey, which would also include sequences dedicated to natural history or the environment. Although the human subjects might be extensively talked about by the European presenter, they never spoke themselves. Moser was determined to go beyond this model and he saw collaboration with anthropologists as a means to achieve this, building upon the rapport that they had built up over years of fieldwork and their command of the subjects' language.

The proposal that Moser eventually submitted to Granada was entitled 'The Vanishing Tribes of Latin America'. It was readily accepted by Forman, but also had to be approved by the programme controller, David Plowright. Being a veteran of *World in Action* himself, Plowright insisted that the new series should not just be about traditional ways of life, but also about the forces that were threatening to destroy them. At Forman's suggestion, the series was dubbed 'Disappearing World'.[5]

## THE BASIC FORMATS OF BRITISH TELEVISION ETHNOGRAPHIC FILM: THE 'ONE-BY-FOUR' VERSUS THE COMPARATIVE MODEL

The first *Disappearing World* series consisted of three films about indigenous groups in Colombia, directed by Moser, and a fourth, actually the first to broadcast in May 1970, about the Panare of southern Venezuela (among whom, by an entirely unrelated coincidence, I would carry out my own doctoral fieldwork five years later). Based on the field research of the French anthropologist Jean-Paul Dumont, *Clearing in the Jungle* was directed by Charlie Nairn, who, like Moser, had learnt his craft on *World in Action*. This proved to be merely the first of some sixteen *Disappearing World* series, in effect constituting a strand that would continue to be broadcast, albeit with various interruptions and many changes of personnel, until 1993. Over this period, fifty-seven films were produced by the various *Disappearing World* teams (though not always under that series title), in a great many different locations around the world and on a broad variety of topics.[6]

Once it settled down, the ideal-typical format of films in the *Disappearing World* strand conformed to what one might call the 'one-by-four' formula: that is, a series of progammes of *one* television hour, each dealing with *one* social group and structured narratively around *one* central theme or topic as it affected an even smaller subgroup, sometimes no more than one or two principal families, even a single charismatic individual. These films were almost always based on the research of *one* anthropologist, who, typically, played an active part in making the film, both on location and back in the edit suite.

The roster of anthropologists who were involved with the strand was highly international. Many were only at the beginning of their careers when the films that they worked on were produced but they included such leading academic figures as Akbar Ahmed, Caroline Humphrey, Gananath Obeyesekere, Sherry Ortner, Andrew Strathern, Terence Turner and Annette Weiner. The films were also made to the highest technical standards, mostly by experienced and talented television crews. Among the cinematographers were Charles Stewart, Ivan Strasburg and Ernie Vincze. Among the editors were David Gladwell, Oral Norrie Ottey and Ted Roberts. Also involved was Dai Vaughan, who would later cut two films for David MacDougall as well as publish a number of thoughtful essays about documentary film editing.[7]

The *Disappearing World* strand also attracted a number of the leading British television documentary directors of the period. These included Mike Grigsby, much fêted at the time that the strand was launched for his Griersonian documentaries about North Sea trawlermen, and Leslie Woodhead who, like Moser and Nairn, and also Grigsby, was yet another film-maker who had been trained on *World in Action*. Already well-known for his drama-documentaries on Cold War topics, Woodhead only became involved in the strand by chance in 1974 when another distinguished director, Roger Graef, dropped out following Granada management's refusal, on budgetary grounds, to include a doctor in the team sent to make a film among the Mursi pastoralists of southern Ethiopia. Woodhead went on to direct a total of ten films for the strand, five of them about the Mursi in conjunction with the anthropologist David Turton, who from 1986 until it closed in 1993 acted as adviser for the strand as a whole.

The strand also recruited and trained a number of anthropology graduates who in due course would go on to become leading directors of British ethnographic film in their own right, including Chris Curling, Melissa Llewelyn-Davies and André Singer. Moreover, as these directors moved on to other posts within British television, they took the *Disappearing World* format with them and ran similar series for other broadcasting companies. It was no exaggeration then for Turton to observe, in 1992, of British television generally, 'Scratch almost any programme, on any channel, which can be described as anthropological and you are very likely to find a *Disappearing World* connection of one kind or another'.[8]

However, although it may have been the dominant form, the *Disappearing World* one-by-four formula was not the only format based on the fieldwork of academic anthropologists to emerge during the 'golden era' of British television ethnography. There was also a more comparative format, initially favoured particularly by the BBC and also, much later, by the satellite-based television channels that came on stream in the 1990s. In this comparative format, the duration of the programmes was also typically one television hour, but sequences from several culturally diverse societies would be juxtaposed as a series of segments within this hour. The links between these segments would then be made through voice-over commentary, sometimes in conjunction with pieces to camera by an on-screen presenter.

Whereas films in the one-by-four format could aim to communicate some sense of the experience of other ways of life and what this way of life meant to those who lived them, in the comparative format the segments of ethnographic footage were used merely to illustrate the verbal analysis. On the other hand, the comparative format opened up the possibility of using a television programme to make more theoretical anthropological propositions. In effect, the two formats, in their ideal forms, represented a mirror image of one another: while the one-by-four model offered ethnographic accounts of particular societies informed by an anthropological analysis, the comparative model represented an opportunity to present an anthropological analysis supported by ethnographic examples.

## THE DEVELOPMENT OF THE COMPARATIVE FORMAT

The first television series in the comparative format based directly on the fieldwork of academic anthropologists began broadcasting in late 1969, some months before the first *Disappearing World* programme was transmitted. This was *Family of Man*, a seven-part series produced and directed for the BBC by John Percival, a Cambridge social anthropology graduate. This series aimed to show the broad variety of ways in which the different stages of the human life cycle are experienced and managed through family organisation in a range of societies across the world. Each one-hour programme dealt with one particular life stage, from birth through to death, but involved the presentation of material shot in five different social groups. These groups included the Kawelka, a Papuan group living in the forested Hagen area of Highland New Guinea; the Pahari-speaking people of the village of Andheri, perched among the foothills of the Himalayas in northwest India and renowned for its polyandrous marriage practices; and the Hambukushu, Bantu-speaking agriculturalists and cattle-herders living on the savannas of the Okavango Delta region in northwestern Botswana.

The anthropologists on whose work these segments were based were respectively Andrew Strathern and Roger Ballard, both of whom were graduate students at Cambridge at the time, and Thomas J. Larson, an Oxford-trained anthropologist from the USA, recently appointed as a lecturer at the University of Witwatersrand. The programmes also included material shot with two British families, one a middle-class family living in Esher, a wealthy suburb in southwest London, the other a working-class family from Colne in Lancashire, in northwest England. However, in what would turn out to be a recurrent pattern, these British segments were not based on the research of anthropologist consultants.

Although the comparative ethnographic approach offered by the series was innovative and, even now, makes for interesting viewing, the format of *Family of Man* represented no more than an extension of an already well-established model. The various ethnographic segments within each programme were linked together by didactic explanatory pieces to camera by Percival himself, shot in the various different locations around the world and for which he always seemed to be wearing the same clothing, with only minor concessions to local climatological conditions. His voice was also laid over the images as off-screen narration as if it were a continuation of these synch to-camera pieces. This was a model that had long been employed in current affairs programmes on British television as well as in natural history series or 'safari' programmes. (Indeed, it is a model that continues to be widely employed to this day). The series also featured some relatively formal interviews, not only with the two English families in their homes, but also with individuals of the other groups. These interviewees spoke their own language, though their words, still just audible on the soundtrack, were then voiced-over in English. But the consultant anthropologists were neither seen nor heard.

Some years later, the BBC broadcast another series of ethnographic films under the title *Face Values*. This represented a somewhat different twist on the comparative format. The series was proposed to the BBC by a committee of the Royal Anthropological Institute (RAI), chaired by Sir Edmund Leach, though the idea appears to have first originated with Charles, Prince of Wales, who had recently taken over as the royal patron of the RAI and who had been taught by Leach when he was a student of anthropology at Cambridge in the mid-1960s. At a time when Britain was becoming an increasingly multicultural society through the effects of migration, Prince Charles saw the series as an opportunity to disseminate some insights from anthropology into the reasons for cultural difference and thereby help reduce prejudice against immigrant populations.[9]

The series began production in 1976 and was broadcast in seven one-hour instalments in 1978. In contrast to *Family of Man*, which had presented cultural variation as largely a function of differences in family organisation, *Faces Values* was based rather on the idea of culture as a system of symbols that can be organised in a broad variety of ways. Instead of being structured around the major phases of the human life cycle, as *Family of Man* had been, each programme in the *Face Values* series explored cultural variation in ideas relating to one particular aspect of human life: gender, the body, space, ethnic identity, rites of passage and religious experience, also concepts of the past. As such, it reflected the impact on British social anthropology over the previous decade of the Lévi-Straussian structuralist ideas of which Edmund Leach had been a leading proponent.

The series drew on material based on the fieldwork of five anthropologists: Jeremy Boissevain in the parish of Naxxar on Malta, Patricia Caplan on the island of Mafia, off the coast of Tanzania (referred to in the series by the archaic name of 'Chole' on account of the potentially confusing associations of its more modern name), Anthony Forge on Bali, Anne Sutherland among the Gypsies of California and Terence Turner among the Kayapó of Central Brazil. The eminent Africanist anthropologist, Jean La Fontaine, acted as consultant for the series as a whole. As with *Family of Man*, the series also included some sequences shot in Britain, dealing with topics such as the treatment of the body at a health farm, spatial strategies at a campsite and the 'banging out' ceremony of a young printer in Birmingham completing his apprenticeship. However, as with *Family of Man*, although the publicity for the series went to some lengths to stress that anthropological concerns apply as much to 'ourselves' as to exotic Others, these British sequences were not based on systematic anthropological fieldwork.

In terms of general format, this series was also different from *Family of Man* in one major respect, namely that there was no on-location presenter. In order to establish the connections between the ethnographic segments juxtaposed in each programme, a combination of two other devices was used instead. One of these was a conventional BBC commentary performed by a voice artist (who, unusually for the time, was female) while the other, quite different, involved none other than Prince Charles himself. In addition to introducing each programme, Charles appeared in a series of linking sequences, shot in a sumptuous drawing room in Windsor Castle, either speaking directly to camera or interviewing the consultant anthropologists, one by one, asking them a series of supposedly layman's questions. Otherwise, as in *Family of Man*, the anthropologists did not appear in person in these films (except sometimes fleetingly and by accident), though their voices were sometimes heard asking questions during interviews, which were subtitled, probably following the prior example of the *Disappearing World* series.

Although the series received high audience viewing ratings – primarily due to the involvement of Prince Charles – the critical response, both in the national press and among anthropologists, was mixed. The critics generally acknowledged the series to have been well-intentioned and laudably ambitious, and often pointed to one or more of the component ethnographic segments as being both effective and technically accomplished. But the balance of the reviews was generally on the negative side, particularly among those written by anthropologists themselves. There was a certain degree of mutual contradiction in these criticisms: some reviewers thought there was too much commentary, others thought there was too little; while some said the comments were too bland, others regarded them as too specialised. But the general tenor of the criticism was that the argument of the programmes was often either not clear or simply banal, and that the various different segments often did not hang together well, a fault that was not helped, a number of reviewers commented, by the transitions via Prince Charles in his drawing room at Windsor.[10]

It also later emerged that while making the series, there had been certain tensions between the BBC production team and at least some of the consultant anthropologists, both in the field and at the editorial phase. Almost forty years later, one of those involved, Patricia Caplan, was still feeling sufficiently marked by the experience to publish a scathing memoir, in which she commented that the films 'oversimplified to the point of distortion' and that messages that she sought to convey about her fieldwork on Mafia Island were sometimes entirely contradicted.[11]

While it is possible that some of the perceived shortcomings of the series might have been remedied with more effective linking devices or if the series producer, who had no background in anthropology, had been more attuned to the academic consultants' ways of thinking, there was also a more fundamental problem relating to the comparative format itself. It is one of the most basic principles of cross-cultural comparison that in order for such comparisons to be meaningful, it is necessary to provide sufficient context. This is difficult enough to achieve even in a textual form, where there is relatively little time constraint. But to make such comparisons, as *Face Values* sought to do, across three or more culturally diverse societies, based on the work of anthropologists approaching their material from a range of different angles, all in the course of a single television hour and in terms that would be readily accessible to a popular audience, was extremely challenging. It is little wonder then that the series received such mixed notices. Both the RAI and the BBC were chastened by the experience, indeed the latter so much so that when it set up a new ethnographic film series in Bristol in 1979, the year after the broadcast of *Face Values*, it turned instead to the one-by-four format of *Disappearing World*.[12]

## THE *DISAPPEARING WORLD* PROTOTYPE: THE LAST OF THE CUIVA

Although the basic features of the one-by-four format remained more or less fixed throughout the entire existence of the *Disappearing World* strand, in a more stylistic sense the strand changed in a number of significant ways over the years. In being structured around a denunciatory journalistic storyline, the first two series still bore the marks of the prior experience of the directors, Brian Moser and Charlie Nairn, on the current affairs strand, *World in Action*. Thus the first *Disappearing World* series, broadcast in 1970–71, condemned the destructive impact of cattle ranchers, missionaries and road-building on the indigenous peoples of Colombia, while in the second series, broadcast in 1972 and consisting of only two programmes, Moser chronicled the devastating effect of the Vietnam War on the Meo (Hmong) in Laos, while Nairn exposed the negative influences of drought and tourism on the Tuareg of southern Algeria.

These storylines were delivered through a clear narrative structure, supplemented by various editorial devices characteristic of current affairs television: voice-over narration, 'talking head' interviews and explanatory graphics, particularly maps. They also often featured devices that were aimed at keeping the potentially disloyal viewer from switching off or changing channels. In the early films, these included a 'hook' placed at the head of the programme of some particularly dramatic material, sometimes as a pre-title sequence, while later films would also add a 'cliff-hanger', just before the commercial break, in which, typically, some dilemma or crisis is anticipated that will only be resolved after the break. There was also usually some sort of recapitulation of the storyline on the voice-over commentary track after the break, both to remind returning viewers and to orient any new viewers who might have switched on in the interim.

Traces of an earlier television format were also evident in the way in which the consultant anthropologists were presented in these early films. As in the scientific explorer format pioneered by David Attenborough as far back as the 1950s, the anthropologists usually played a prominent on-screen part, often being introduced through establishment shots showing them directly involved in the life of the subjects. The anthropologists then acted as spokespersons for the subjects of the film, explaining through interviews or in voice-over how their societies were organised, what their core values were and how they were being affected by the threats to their traditional way of life. They sometimes also offered very personal subjective comments on the experience of carrying out fieldwork among the subjects of the film, and even about the experience of making the films. Although the subjects of the films did occasionally speak directly to the camera, their words were then voiced over in English, as in the *Family of Man* series.

Although it was actually the second *Disappearing World* film to be broadcast, *The Last of the Cuiva*, first screened in April 1971, served as a sort of baseline from which the series would later evolve. Directed by Brian Moser and based on the research of the French-Canadian anthropologist Bernard Arcand among a small group of hunter-gatherers living on the savannas of eastern Colombia, this film is also a testimony to the skills of the cameraman Ernie Vincze and the editor Dai Vaughan. Owing to its iconic status, I shall consider here in some detail.

The film opens with a highly cinematic pre-title sequence lasting 90 seconds without any music or commentary that it is impossible to imagine being permitted on British television today. This 'hook' starts with a close-up shot focused on a lattice of hammock threads that then pulls back to reveal a young Cuiva man sitting in the hammock looking directly and impassively at the camera. The sequence then cuts back and forth between a series of close-ups of the Cuiva in their forest camp and the cattle, horses, guns and drunkenness that are central to the *llanero* cowboy culture of the settlers invading the Cuiva's territory. On the soundtrack, throughout this pre-title sequence, there is nothing but the acute humming of forest insects (figure 11.1).

After the title card, the film then reverts to a more current affairs authorial mode as Moser explains in voice-over, with the aid of maps, where the film is located and that the Cuiva, of whom very few remain, have been reduced to a fraction of their former territory. The film then returns to synch action and the conventional scientific explorer trope as Moser introduces us via the voice-over to a 'White man', that is, Bernard Arcand, making his way upstream to visit a previously uncontacted group of Cuiva. Arcand

11.1 *The Last of the Cuiva* (1971) opens with a 90-second pre-title sequence intercutting images of the Cuiva and the cowboys threatening their way of life, with only the acute humming of forest insects for a soundtrack.

then takes over the voice-over narration and in a very laid-back way, supported by a series of equally leisurely quasi-observational sequences exquisitely shot by Vincze, he talks about the way in which the Cuiva live, their patterns of exchange, their high degree of nomadism, the division of labour between men and women, their use of hallucinogenic drugs. He frequently underlines the advantages of their 'original affluent society' over that of life in a 'modern' industrial society.

But these idyllic tranquil scenes are constantly intercut with sequences featuring the *llaneros*, which are not only generally much briefer but also more agitated and noisy, thereby evoking the threat to the Cuiva. Moser, off-screen, interviews some of these salt-of-the-earth cowboys and seems to be goading them into confessing that relations with the Cuiva have in the past been violent. However, it is not until two-thirds of the way through the film that we are finally presented with direct evidence of this violence as two Cuiva, a man and then a woman, in tight close-up, offer the most chilling but entirely deadpan first-hand accounts of the murder of their relatives by *llaneros*.

This testimony then segues into various sequences of life in the local *llanero* town where the Cuiva go to work in order to get the money to buy salt, alcohol, soap, clothes. There are sequences of a Catholic parade, cockfighting, cattle wrangling and even girls playing basketball, with the Cuiva looking on, seemingly marginal and disoriented. Arcand explains in an interview that there are two ways to destroy a society: the obvious way, through physical extermination, or through acculturation and the creation of dependence on externally produced goods. The film then ends with a classical reversion to the beginning as we return to the camp of the isolated group of Cuiva with whom the film had begun and observe them setting light to the savanna. Accompanied by a loud crackling sound, the final shots feature a man silhouetted against billowing smoke and the long grass in flames, ending the film on an apocalyptic note.

In a review of the films that had been produced for the strand by 1980, Peter Loizos commented that *Last of the Cuiva* constituted 'a kind of prototype, which once made, could never again be equalled'.[13] Yet while it is true that *Last of the Cuiva* served as a model for the strand as a whole, and also true that in terms of the quality of the film-making, it represents one of the high points of the tally of more than fifty films eventually produced, the strand did, however, undergo a series of gradual changes as it developed over the next two decades.

## THE REFINEMENT OF THE *DISAPPEARING WORLD* FORMAT

While the prospects for the survival of the Cuiva did indeed seem bleak, even at this early stage the general title of the *Disappearing World* strand was threatening to become a misnomer, at least in some cases. The Tuareg, for example, filmed for the second series, were certainly not in any imminent danger of disappearance, even if they were confronting the prospect of radical social change and political turmoil. By the time of the third series, consisting of two films broadcast in late 1973, the strand title had become positively misleading. The first of these films, *Kataragama – A God for All Seasons*, directed by Charlie Nairn, concerned a festival in southeast Sri Lanka dedicated to a local god much admired for its ability to solve practical problems, while the other, *Dervishes of Kurdistan*, directed by Brian Moser, was about the ecstatic Qaderi Dervish cult in a village of refugee Iraqi Kurds living just over the border in Iran. The consultant anthropologist on the first film was the Sri Lankan anthropologist Gananath Obeyesekere, while on the second film, unusually, there were two consultants, André Singer and the Iranian anthropologist Ali Bulookbashi, both of whom had recently completed postgraduate degrees in social anthropology at Oxford.

In neither of these films was the principal storyline about the subjects' relationship with an 'outside world': the existence of neither the Sinhalese, nor the Qaderi Dervishes was then under threat, nor have they subsequently 'disappeared', even though both have been affected by major geopolitical conflicts originating far outside the immediate geographical region in which the films were made. If these two films had a common theme, it was rather about the disposition of religious believers to subject themselves to extreme bodily mortification. As shown very graphically in the films, this included pushing skewers through their cheeks in the case of the dervishes, and by suspending themselves from hooks pushed through the flesh on their backs in the case of the Sinhalese.

This change in the general nature of the storyline became even more marked in the fourth series, which consisted of six films broadcast in late 1974, with a further additional film broadcast in early 1975 as a sort of postscript. Not only was this the most extended series of the whole *Disappearing World* strand, but it could be argued that it represents the strand in its most classical form. However, with one exception, the subject matter of these films did not relate to external forces threatening the existence of the communities where the films were made but rather to internal events and processes. Moreover, in comparison to the films of the second series, the new series involved much stronger characterisation, with greater reliance on the subjects' own voices in both a literal and a metaphorical sense.

In part, these stylistic changes can be attributed to the influence of the anthropology graduates, Chris Curling, Melissa Llewelyn-Davies and André Singer who had by then been recruited to the *Disappearing World* production team, first as researchers and later as directors. This group in particular was greatly influenced by David and Judith MacDougall's film, *To Live with Herds*, which had recently won a prestigious prize at the Venice Film Festival. Moser had been alerted to the existence of this film by Colin Young, who had recently returned from the USA to head up the National Film School at Beaconsfield. Moser then arranged, sometime in 1973, for *To Live with Herds* to be screened to the *Disappearing World* production team. While some members of the team were highly sceptical that such a leisurely paced film could ever be shown on British television, for others it was a revelation, proving that a film could be structured around the subjects' personal testimonies while still remaining highly engaging.[14]

Initially, however, the most immediately practical effect of this screening on the *Disappearing World* format was the adoption of subtitles. Although at first somewhat tentative and partial, it was this technical device, which, in effect, enabled the greater commitment to representing the voice of the subjects in the 1974 series. The stylistic inheritance of *World in Action* still remained dominant in the form of extensive voice-over narration, explanatory graphics and interviews, but now the interviews were with the subjects rather than with the anthropologists. The subjects were also shown speaking to one another, without the intervention of either the anthropologists or the film-makers. Once central to the story, the anthropologists now only appeared in shot briefly, if at all, and although they might still have their say in the voice-over narration, often in a highly didactic fashion, the subjects themselves would typically now also play a leading role in explaining how their social institutions worked and what their key values were.

The opening film of the 1974 series, *The Mursi*, directed by Leslie Woodhead and based on the fieldwork of David Turton exemplified the new approach. Here the the focus is not on the threat of change but on the political oratory of the Mursi cattle pastoralists of the Omo River valley in southern Ethiopia, as they find themselves involved in a war over grazing land with their traditional enemies, the neighbouring Bodi. The film begins with the familiar journalistic trope of the film crew arriving by air, accompanied by animated aerial maps, but this device is quickly left behind and the narrative thread develops instead around a number of key Mursi characters and their participation in a series of public political debates among senior men, mostly subtitled, about how they should react to the Bodi incursions into their territory. On the voice-over commentary track, Woodhead sets the scene and Turton provides contextualising explanations of a more comparative anthropological character, but there is no interview with Turton and he appears on screen only very briefly.

Although the prospect of imminent warfare lends a certain degree of spectacle to the film, as the Mursi warriors chant and brandish aloft their ancient rifles in a series of dramatic scenes, it is actually the form of the debates that constitutes the primary substance of the film. Indeed, around half the total duration of the film is dedicated to following the dynamics of these debates and to showing how, through a series of unspoken oratorical conventions, unanimity and collective solidarity is achieved. At the end of the film, the war with the Bodi remains unresolved, but narratively speaking this does not matter, as the viewer has been offered instead the satisfaction of having gained some understanding of how Mursi political oratory works.[15]

Similarly, *Ongka's Big Moka*, another well-known film from the 1974 series, is not concerned with the threat of externally induced change but is rather focused on an entirely internal process. This was a major gift-giving ceremony, known as a *moka*, as practised by the Kawelka of Highland New Guinea, which, as elsewhere in Melanesia, is the means whereby a local political leader, a 'big-man', can establish his prestige and pre-eminence by outdoing potential rivals with his generosity. This film, directed by Charlie Nairn, was based on the fieldwork of Andrew Strathern, one of the three anthropologists who had previously participated in the *Family of Man* series. The narrative of this film revolves around the person of a particular charismatic 'big-man', Ongka, and it follows him as he goes about the wheeling and dealing necessary to assemble the vast numbers of pigs, cassowaries, cattle and other valuables – including a Toyota pick-up truck and a motorbike – that he plans to give away at a particularly extravagant *moka* (figure 11.2).

Nairn's voice-over commentary is very extensive, while the subtitling is at best intermittent. Even so, Ongka's voice, both literally and metaphorically, is central to the narrative development of the film. Again, the process at the centre of the film remains unresolved at the end of the film since the crew had to leave before the final stage of the ceremony, which Ongka was obliged to postpone when a rival 'big-man', a certain Raima, intentionally circulated malicious rumours that caused social unrest and made the celebration of the *moka* impossible. But although this is somewhat disappointing,

11.2 In *Ongka's Big Moka* (1974), two Melanesian 'big-men', Ongka, left, and Raima, right, compete for prestige in a *moka* gift-giving ceremony.

by the end of the film one feels that through the personal experience of Ongka and his long-suffering wife, Rumbocol, who has to look after all the pigs, one has been given a valuable insight not only into the *moka* itself but also into the values of Kawelka society more generally.[16]

Traditional ceremonial performance, this time relating to gender and fertility, was also central to another film in the series, *The Mehinaku*, which concerns the indigenous group of the same name who live in the Xingu Park in Central Brazil. This film was directed by the Argentinian director Carlos Pasini and was based on the fieldwork of the leading Amazonist anthropologist, Thomas Gregor. Again there is sympathetic characterisation of a number of central protagonists, while the narrative structure intrinsic to the preparation and performance of the ceremony provides the main backbone of the film. However, almost as an afterthought, the film then ends with a virtuoso 360-degree pan around a circle formed by all the living members of the Mehinaku village while a commentary voice laments that this generation will be the last to lead a traditional way of life. But the threat to this way of life is not otherwise referred to in the film and, moreover, it proved to be much less significant than the film-makers anticipated. The Mehinaku, along with a number of other indigenous groups of the Xingu, to this day continue to practise the traditional ceremonies that are the central focus of the film.[17]

Given this change in the focus of the films, the directors on the *Disappearing World* production team made a concerted effort around this time to change the title of the strand. But this was firmly resisted by the senior management of Granada Television: not only had *Disappearing World* by now become firmly established as a commercially valuable brand, but also, Denis Forman, whose personal interest had been responsible for bringing the strand into being in the first place, was adamant that 'salvage ethnography' should remain the series' highest priority since in his view there were still

11.3 New 'ways of doing' ethnographic film for television, 1977. Left, a veiled bride is displayed in *Some Women of Marrakesh*, the first film to be made by an all-woman crew; *Eskimos of Pond Inlet*, right, was innovative in that members of the community were consulted at all stages, including editing.

'whole tracts of the world with societies which should and must be recorded urgently before they go'.[18]

## FURTHER INNOVATIONS IN THE *DISAPPEARING WORLD* FORMAT

Notwithstanding the retention of the anachronistic strand title, a number of further innovations in the *Disappearing World* format took place over the ensuing years. Some of these were stylistic, others more editorial. One of the latter concerned the representation of women – on both sides of the lens. One of the films of the 1974 series, *Masai Women* directed by Chris Curling and based on the field research of Melissa Llewelyn-Davies had broken new ground in British television ethnography – and possibly in anglophone ethnographic film in any medium – in presenting the life of a 'traditional' society from the perspective of the female members of the group. As such, it paralleled a similar tendency then emergent in ethnographic writing.[19]

Three years later, Llewelyn-Davies took this process one step further when she herself directed *Some Women of Marrakech*, broadcast in early 1977. This film focused on the way in which the radical separation of the worlds of women and men required by Islam was experienced by women of various different social backgrounds in Morocco. It was based on the work of the late Elizabeth Fernea, an ethnographer who had written extensively about the seclusion of women in the Islamic world. This was the first documentary film on British television to be shot entirely by an all-women crew. Today, it seems remarkable that there was any resistance to all-women crews, but at that time, resistance there certainly was. Indeed, Llewelyn-Davies was only able to overcome this resistance by arguing that, given its subject matter, the film could only be made with an all-women crew since no man would be permitted to film Muslim women living in seclusion (figure 11.3, left).

One scene that would certainly have been quite impossible to shoot without an all-women crew – a scene that would later cause considerable controversy – was shot in a women's communal bathhouse. Although they are filmed from a highly discreet angle, and no individual is clearly identifiable, it is clear that the subjects are entirely naked. Elizabeth Fernea reports that it was the subjects who suggested the shooting of this scene but on the condition that the all-women crew also remove their clothes. This represented something of a challenge for the film-makers, though Fernea, who was American, claims to have been less 'prudish' than her British colleagues. However, this shared experience proved to be an effective means for developing rapport with the subjects.[20]

The cinematographer on this film, Dianne Tammes, would later work as a member of another all-women *Disappearing World* crew when she shot *Asante Market Women*, broadcast in 1982. The sound recordist was Marilyn Gaunt, a distinguished documentary director-cameraperson in her own right, while the voice-over commentary was performed by the anthropologist Gillian Shepherd. The only man involved in a creative role on *Some Women of Marrakesh* was the editor, Dai Vaughan, who had cut *The Last of the Cuiva* and *Masai Women* and would also work on a number of Llewelyn-Davies's subsequent films.[21]

*Some Women of Marrakech* was also innovative in another way in that by using a qualified title, it sought to avoid the pretension that could be read into the use of the definite article in many earlier *Disappearing World* titles – The *Tuareg*, The *Mursi*, The *Mehinaku* – that is that they concerned the whole society, when in fact they usually only explored the lives of a very few people within those societies. In other respects, *Some Women of Marrakech* conformed in general stylistic terms to the standard *Disappearing World* format, notably in the use of formal interviews and an extensive voice-over commentary. In this last regard, however, the film was distinctive in that in contrast to the *Disappearing World* norm of commentaries that were generally merely contextualising, it offered what one reviewer called a 'feminist-ethnographic' analysis that went far beyond what was directly visible on the screen.

Thus at the end of the wedding that serves as the climax of the film, the commentary offers various observations on the symbolic significance of the event, concluding with the observation that 'every wedding re-enacts the drama of men's control over women's sexuality and fertility'. To reinforce the point, the film then ends with a coda in which a young schoolgirl chants her way uncertainly through a series of verses from the Koran which declare the authority of men over women because God has made them superior.[22]

Another *Disappearing World* film broadcast in early 1977 was *Eskimos of Pond Inlet*. This too was innovative, but in a very different way. Based on the fieldwork of the anthropologist Hugh Brody over two years in a small community on Baffin Island in the far north of Canada, in terms of content this film represented a return to the earliest *Disappearing World* series in that it was centrally concerned with the effects of contact with the 'outside world'. But in terms of film-making praxis, it was very different not only from any *Disappearing World* film that had come before but also from any that would come afterwards.

There is, for a start, no voice-over commentary of any kind; instead intertitle cards provide minimal contextualising information. There are no formal interviews, though the camera eavesdrops, as it were, as mostly elderly subjects talk around a kitchen table about the effects, mostly negative, of contact with the 'Whites'. The camera style is highly observational, with many long unbroken wide shots, including commanding shots of the vast landscape, with no zooms, very few close-ups or cutaways, and only minimal panning. The linear storyline found in so many *Disappearing World* films is also absent: instead the narrative proceeds through a series of loosely connected vignettes, gradually building up an overall impression of life in the community, a more elliptical movement aptly compared by one reviewer to the movement of the knight on a chessboard.[23]

In all these regards, stylistically speaking, *Eskimos of Pond Inlet* is by far the closest of all the *Disappearing World* films to the works of the MacDougalls and other exponents of Observational Cinema. But notwithstanding this similarity, the inspiration lying behind *Eskimos of Pond Inlet* actually came from another source entirely. The director, Mike Grigsby, had worked for many years for Granada Television, including on *World in Action*, but right at the beginning of his career he had been mentored by figures such as Karel Reisz and Lindsay Anderson, who came from the more poetic British documentary tradition originating in the work Humphrey Jennings. In fact, many of the observational stylistic features that distinguish *Eskimos of Pond Inlet* from the other *Disappearing World* films were already evident in Grigsby's earlier film, *A Life Apart* (1973), which concerns the life of the men on board a Fleetwood fishing trawler as it makes its way to Iceland. This film was shot by Ivan Strasburg while the sound was recorded by Mike McDuffie, both of whom then worked on *Eskimos of Pond Inlet*.[24]

As a director, Grigsby aimed to allow his subjects to speak directly to the audience as much as possible, with minimal intervention from the film-maker. In this regard, he found immediate common cause with Hugh Brody, who was keen that the film should provide a vehicle for the Pond Inlet Inuit to express their deep concerns about the threats posed by government measures aimed at limiting their rights over their land and its natural resources, particularly their right to hunt. This theme had been central to Brody's then recently published book, *The People's Land* (1975), whose title serves as a subtitle for the film.

Brody was also insistent that the film should be made with the active participation of the Inuit. Prior to the shoot, he spent two weeks in Pond Inlet seeking permission from the community to make the film and discussing with its members what should be included. He also agreed with them that a senior member of the community should come over to Britain and approve the final cut before the film was transmitted. As described in Chapter 5, participatory praxes were becoming increasingly common among ethnographic film-makers generally in the mid-1970s, but to the best of my knowledge, this was the only *Disappearing World* film in which a member of the host community played a direct role at the postproduction stage.[25]

## The later years of *Disappearing World*: variations in content

Although there were also a number of other innovations in the later years of the strand, these were more to do with issues of content than with transformations in film-making praxis. Two of the later series were shot in Communist states prior to the end of the Cold War, one in Mongolia, broadcast in 1975 and consisting of two films, the other in the People's Republic of China, which was broadcast in 1983 and consisted of three films. To a degree that is difficult to appreciate today, in the years prior to the collapse of the Soviet Union and the rise to power of Deng Xiaoping in China, relatively little was known in the West about the cultural life of even the majority populations of these countries, let alone their ethnic minorities. These films therefore opened up what were, in effect, entirely new worlds for most Western viewers, including many anthropologists. One of the main themes of these series concerned the way in which traditional cultural practices, far from 'disappearing', were being more or less successfully reconciled with the requirements of living in a Communist state. These series were therefore not broadcast under the standard series title, but rather as *Mongolia* and *Inside China* respectively.

The two films that made up the *Mongolia* series, *On the Edge of the Gobi* and *The City on the Steppes* were both directed by Brian Moser in collaboration with the veteran Sinologist and Central Asia specialist, Owen Lattimore, who had first visited the country in the 1920s. The *Disappearing World* crew was the first Western documentary team to be allowed to film in Mongolia and, as Moser explains in a short prelude to each film, in accordance with the general terms of the agreement that gave them access, which had been

11.4 Newly appearing worlds in Communist Asia. Left, *Mongolia: On the Edge of the Gobi* (1975) showed how traditional pastoralism on the steppes was adjusting to collectivisation; right, 'If a girl is born, your roof will lower three feet.' *Inside China: Living with the Revolution* (1983) celebrated the passing of old attitudes.

negotiated by Lattimore on the basis of his long-standing contacts, the crew was accompanied at all points by various minders who were charged with ensuring that the films offered a positive image of their country. These minders controlled the subject matter of what Moser and his crew were able to film, down to the level of the individual shot.

In authorial terms, no doubt at least partially in response to these difficult shooting conditions, *Mongolia* represents something of a return to the format of *The Last of the Cuiva*, with Lattimore playing the role of Arcand in that earlier film in the sense that he is frequently present on screen and acts as the main guide and explicator of Mongolian life, either through informal to-camera pieces or in voice-over. Apart from some very brief exchanges between Lattimore and a Heroine of Socialist Labour, and later with a herder and then a schoolgirl who wants to become a teacher, no Mongolian subject speaks to the camera, and even the exchanges between subjects themselves are no more than sporadically subtitled.

Even so, notwithstanding these constraints, by virtue of Lattimore's obviously relaxed relationship with the subjects, the magnificent cinematography of Ivan Strasburg, the equally magnificent cutting of Jane Wood and Dai Vaughan, not to mention Moser's directorial skill in welding all these components together, the result is two films that manage to present the extraordinary beauty of the landscape, the people and their interaction with their animals alongside an ironic, almost surreal vision of the Mongolian version of Soviet kitsch. At the same time, Lattimore draws on his deep-seated knowledge of the country to offer a series of interesting insights into the many ways in which Mongolian people are seeking to reconcile traditional customs and processes with the organisational structures and attitudes of Socialist modernity (figure 11.4, left).

Similar themes were central to the three films of the *Inside China* series. Permission to make these films was negotiated at the highest levels, involving banqueting in London at the Chinese Embassy and even a Granada Television delegation to Beijing led by Sir Denis Forman. During the shoots, the *Disappearing World* crews were always accompanied by a team of minders from Chinese state television, CCTV, but although this had its frustrations, the constraints on the process of production appear to have been considerably less than they had been with the *Inside Mongolia* films.[26]

Two of the *Inside China* films were directed by Leslie Woodhead and were shot in two different peri-urban Han village communes near the industrial city of Wuxi, located on the north side of Taihu Lake, in the hinterland of Shanghai. The third film concerned the Kazakhs of Xinjiang in northwestern China and was directed by André Singer, by then the *Disappearing World* series producer. This particular Chinese ethnic minority group was selected because Singer thought it would be interesting to make a film about an Islamic pastoralist society in China which could then be paired with an earlier film in the strand about a similar Islamic pastoralist group, *The Kirghiz of Afghanistan*. There was also a plan to make a film about a second ethnic minority, this time in Yunnan province in southwestern China, but this fell foul of a union-management dispute within Granada Television about crewing levels. In order to make up a trilogy, the material filmed in the Wuxi communes by Leslie Woodhead and his team was used to cut two films.

The selection of these communes as a location for filming was a matter over which the *Disappearing World* team had relatively little control. Originally, Singer had wanted the film to be made in Kaixian'gong, a village on the south side of Taihu Lake where the renowned Chinese anthropologist and student of Malinowski, Fei Hsiao-T'ung, had carried out his doctoral fieldwork in the late 1930s. However, the CCTV minders informed the *Disappearing World* team that 'suitable accommodation' was not available in Kaixian'gong, and directed them instead towards shooting in the more prosperous Wuxi communes, which were about 125 miles away by road. This was far from ideal from the *Disappearing World* team's point of view, but it was made clear to them that they would have to film there or not all. The film-makers had to content themselves therefore with a voice-over statement at the beginning of the first film to the effect that the Wuxi area is wealthy by rural standards in China and viewers should therefore not assume that they are representative of China as a whole.

Within these constraints as to location, the directors of the *Inside China* films had a relatively free hand in choosing what and with whom to film, though the presence of the minders would obviously have affected the way in which the subjects reacted to being filmed. The film-makers also remained heavily dependent on the minders to help them identify protagonists and situations in which to film, particularly since contrary to the *Disappearing World* norm, the ethnographic consultants – the anthropologist Barbara Hazard in the case of the Wuxi communes and the ethnolinguist Shirin Akiner in the case of the Kazakhs – were recruited to their respective films after all the decisions about location had been taken and, moreover, were not personally familiar with the specific communities in which the films were to be made.

Despite these limitations, the three films of the *Inside China* series offered Western audiences an intimate view of everyday life in rural China that was still highly unusual for the period. This was particularly true of *The Kazakhs*: the eminent Sinologist anthropologist, Stephan Feuchtwang, commented on reviewing the film that 'we have … never even read, let alone seen, details of a north-western minority nationality of contemporary China'. He then commended the film for showing, albeit more through visual means than through explicit commentary, the many tensions between traditional custom and the encroaching sinicisation associated with political developments.[27]

Although perhaps not quite so unusual, the Wuxi films also impressed critics, at least in the mass media, because they located the well-known facts of recent Chinese history in the experience of two contrasting families. Far from being drab automatons dressed in Mao suits, as Chinese peasants were popularly deemed to be in the West at that time, these two families proved themselves to be as engaging, accessible and as varied in character and temperament as any other group of human beings. The first of the Wuxi films, *Living with the Revolution*, compares life before and after the revolution of 1949, contrasting the bitter experiences of the pre-revolutionary period, including the Japanese invasion, with the experience of life under the Communists. The subjects explain that the Communists were initially feared, but later accepted for the many improvements that they brought to village life, particularly for women, despite certain errors in the policies of collectivisation and the excesses of the Cultural Revolution (figure 11.4, right). However, these political themes, mostly presented through interviews, are skilfully interwoven with the events surrounding a wedding, the conduct of which shows just how much traditional cultural norms survive, despite the political changes.

In the second film, *The Newest Revolution*, attention turns to the way in which the village was by then adjusting to the post-Maoist return to family-centred economic production and the encouragement of a new interest in the acquisition of consumer goods such as televisions and washing machines. The film suggests a tension between the individualism encouraged by this new materialism and responsibilities to the collective interest, particularly of the young towards the old. These political themes are again explored and presented through the personal experiences of the same two families that featured in the first film. Although some critics with specialist knowledge of China complained that the film-makers had not been sufficiently critical of the testimonies offered by the films' protagonists, these two films were certainly successful in giving a strong sense of how Chinese political events of those years were being experienced at a grass-roots level.[28]

Another innovation in the later years of the *Disappearing World* strand, reflecting, even if somewhat belatedly, a concurrent change of emphasis in academic anthropology, was the making of films about European communities. The first of these, *The Basques of Santazi*, broadcast in 1987, concerned a Basque village on the French side of the Pyrenean border with Spain. This too was directed by Leslie Woodhead and was based on the work of the Oxford-based US anthropologist Sandra Ott. These European films were still mostly about rural communities, however, though an exception was *Across the Tracks*, broadcast the following year, which concerned a group of Vlach Gypsies living on the outskirts of a provincial town in the then still-Socialist state of Hungary. Directed by John Blake and based on the research of anthropologist Michael Stewart, this film was somewhat more observational than many films in the strand, though it also featured its fair share of standard television authorial devices. These included an archetypal 'cliff-hanger' at the end of Part 1, whereby the viewer is left to wonder over the commercial break whether a much-loved and economically valuable mare, which had had problems in giving birth, will be saved by the offering of two candles to the Virgin Mary. Happily, in Part 2, after the commercial break, the Virgin accepts the candles and the horse survives.

But perhaps the most significant innovation in terms of content in the latter years of the strand was the practice of returning to a community where a previous *Disappearing World* film had already been made. By far the most elaborate example of this was the cycle of five films about the Mursi pastoralists of southern Ethiopia, all directed by Leslie Woodhead and based on the fieldwork of David Turton, which were made over a period of almost twenty years. Following the film from the 1974 series about political oratory, Woodhead and Turton made a second film, broadcast in 1982, dealing with the Mursi's symbiotic relationship with the Kwegu, a neighbouring population of hunters and settled cultivators. They then made a third film examining the more long-term movements of the Mursi population. Even at the time of the first film, when the subject of the Mursi's political oratory had been the warfare arising from their movement into Bodi territory, Turton had been aware of a long-term pattern whereby the Mursi were moving north from their traditional territory around the lower Omo River up into the Mago valley, in search of what they termed 'cool ground', that

11.5 Films about the Mursi age-set ceremony (1991). Left, 'That's terrible!' – in *The Land is Bad*, the Mursi are incredulous that in the film-makers' society, there is no age set ceremony; right, among the Mursi, as in *Nitha*, an age set has to fight the one above it – symbolically – in order to enter the adult age grade.

is, higher ground, less subject to drought and which could provide better grazing for their cattle. In 1985, this historical process became the focus of *The Migrants*, which was broadcast as part of a trilogy, *In Search of Cool Ground*, along with re-versions of the two earlier films.[29]

*The Migrants* highlighted the various threats that the Mursi's new location in the Mago valley entailed for their traditional way of life. One of these was the presence of the tsetse fly, which threatened to destroy their cattle. This was a very serious matter for, as Turton explains in the film, cattle are not only of great material significance to the Mursi but also the key to their cultural identity. Other threats were implicit in the new proximity of the small Ethiopian town of Berka. Previously the Mursi had had very little contact with the 'outside world', but now they had become regular visitors to the Berka market and, at the same time, were increasingly under the control of the Ethiopian state: several Mursi had been drafted into the Ethiopian army and had been on active service in the Ogaden and Eritrea.

These threats would become the focus of the fourth and fifth films in the cycle, *The Land is Bad* and *Nitha*, broadcast consecutively in 1991 (figure 11.5). The first of these showed that the Mursi were now faced with severe famine and raids by neighbours armed with Kalashnikovs, while the second followed a major ceremony, the *nitha*. This involved the initiation of a new age-set of young men, which the Mursi saw as being essential to guarantee their future, particularly at a time of such crisis as they were then undergoing.

In effect, then, this cycle of Mursi films had brought the *Disappearing World* strand back to the themes of the very first series, that is, the effects of social and cultural change, the relationship with the 'outside world' and

11.6 *We Are All Neighbours* (1993). Left, Nusreta and Nuria, Bosnian Muslims, listen anxiously to the Serb bombardment of distant Sarajevo. But in the end, right, their house was destroyed by their Croatian Catholic neighbours.

the threat that these represented to the very physical existence of the societies concerned.

## THE FINAL *DISAPPEARING WORLD* SERIES: THE RETURN TO THE BEGINNING

This return to the earliest concerns of the strand became even more marked with the very last series, broadcast in 1993 under the executive direction of David Wason. This dealt explicitly with the devastating impact of externally generated warfare on three communities, the Uduk in the Sudan, the Karen on the border of Myanmar with Thailand, and Visnjica, a mixed Catholic and Muslim village in the heart of Bosnia-Herzegovina. While the first two films were shot in refugee camps or villages where the effects of warfare were already all too apparent, when filming began for the third film, *We Are All Neighbours*, the conflict arising from the break-up of Yugoslavia was still something that was happening at a certain distance, though even as the film opens, the soundtrack is punctuated by the dull but disconcerting sound of distant heavy gunfire (figure 11.6, left).

Based on the fieldwork of the Norwegian anthropologist, Tone Bringa and directed by Debbie Christie, the opening scenes of *We Are All Neighbours* show Catholic and Muslim families living peaceably side by side as they had done for generations, symbolised particularly by visits to one another's houses to drink coffee. But as the war approaches, it becomes necessary for all families to take sides, with the result that friendship between neighbours breaks down and the coffee drinking comes to an end. Religious and ethnic identity, previously ignored in everyday life, becomes crucial, so that people who had had friendly and mutually supportive daily contact start avoiding one another and militias from each ethnic-religious group begin to patrol the streets at night. The film concludes with a deeply sombre coda, shot after the village had been over-run by Croatian paramilitary forces. The houses of the Muslim villagers, where earlier in the film scenes of happy family life had taken place, are now shown abandoned and bombed out, while the Catholic houses remain in pristine condition with neatly tended gardens (figure 11.6, right). Most of the Muslims have fled and many have been murdered, not by any invading army, but by the very neighbours with whom they had lived in harmony for so long. The survivors who have taken refuge elsewhere declare that even should peace return, they will never return to Visnjica.

As the anthropologist Patricia Caplan commented in a review, although the strand title might sometimes have aroused negative comment in the past, in this film, 'we watch a world literally disappear before our eyes'. Indeed, this film offers a unique and riveting first-hand participant-observer account of the way in which friendship can be gradually corrupted by hatred, and peace by warfare, in a situation of interethnic tension vitiated by nationalist sentiments. It may have been one of the last to be made, but *We Are All Neighbours* is without doubt one of the most powerfully affecting as well as one of the most ethnographically significant of the entire strand of *Disappearing World* films.[30]

## Notes

1 British anthropologists or those based in Britain who made films prior to the period of television patronage included Beatrice Blackwood (in the 1930s), Ursula Graham Bower (1930s–1940s), Colin Turnbull (1950s–1970s) and James Woodburn (1960s). However, by far the most prolific was Christoph von Fürer-Haimendorf, who between 1940 and 1976, assisted by his wife Betty, shot some 50–60 hours of 16 mm film in India and Nepal. Some of Haimendorf's footage was assembled into television programmes by the BBC and he also made two independent films of his own. But his primary purpose was not to make narrativised documentaries as such but rather to produce visual documentation. He therefore did little to circulate his material around professional circles and some of it he may not even have looked at himself. For further details on these pioneers based in Britain, see my website on early ethnographic film, www.silenttimemachine.com. Specifically on Haimendorf, see Alan Macfarlane (2010) while on Ursula Graham Bower, see the material that MacFarlane has put up at https://upload.sms.cam.ac.uk/collection/1810528.

2 Singer (1992), 269–70.

3 Forman underlined the importance to him of Frazer's classic work during an interview with Jeremy Isaacs for the BBC programme, *Face to Face*, in October 1997.

4 Forman (1985), 3.

5 Moser and Tayler (1963); Forman (1985), 2–3; Moser (1988), 9–10; also Brian Moser (personal communication, October 2014).

6 In referring to *Disappearing World* as a 'strand', I follow the common usage in British television, employing this term to refer to what is, in effect, a series of programme series, each of which may consist typically of between three and twelve individual programmes.

7 Vaughan (1999).

8 Turton (1992a), 284.

9 See Prince Charles's preface to the book that was published to accompany the series (Sutherland 1978).

10 See, for example, the reviews of the series and the accompanying book that appeared in *RAIN*, the RAI newsletter, and the response to these from the series adviser Jean La Fontaine (*RAIN*, no. 27, 1978), 6–10.

11 See Caplan (2013); (2014), 15.

12 The BBC did not, however, entirely abandon its support for the comparative format in that they would later act as one of the co-sponsors, along with a long list of US television production companies, of *Millenium: Tribal Wisdom and the Modern World*, a ten-part series that was broadcast in the USA in 1992 and in Britain the following year. This drew on footage shot among twelve different indigenous peoples from around the world, as well as a number of sequences shot in US cities. It was presented by the eminent Amazonist anthropologist David Maybury-Lewis, who since the 1970s had been an active campaigner for indigenous rights. It was directed by Adrian Malone, who had first made his name producing the celebrated BBC series, *The Ascent of Man* some ten years previously but who had since moved to Los Angeles. However, notwithstanding the great expertise of Maybury-Lewis and Malone in their respective fields, and their shared and entirely laudable intention to encourage respect for the wisdom of indigenous peoples, the series was subjected to some harsh criticism by both anthropologists and television critics, and was screened by the BBC, 'almost surreptitiously', as one commentator put it, in a Sunday afternoon slot (Beidelman 1992: Knight 1993: Benthall 2014).

13 Loizos (1980), 577.

14 Brian Moser (personal communication, October 2014), see also the comments of Melissa Llewelyn-Davies in Grimshaw (1995), 41–2. For a discussion of *To Live with Herds* itself, see Chapter 5, pp. 157–9. The role of Colin Young in promoting ethnographic film in the UK is discussed in Chapter 10, pp. 304–6.

15 However, in an article written many years later, David Turton (1992b), 171–3, laments the fact that as a result of the need to cut down the four debates in the film in order to make them accessible to a British television audience, coupled with the limitations of subtitling at that time, the oratical performances lost much of their 'complexity, richness and therefore meaning … for the participants', or so he felt when he screened the completed film back to the Mursi in 1985. Leslie Woodhead (2006) has also written about the experience of making *The Mursi* from his perspective as the director of the film.

16 Andrew Strathern, the consultant anthropologist, also later wrote an interesting account of the making of this film (Strathern 1977).

17 See Chapter 7, pp. 216–18.

18 Forman (1985), 3.

19 See Grimshaw (2001), 157. I return to *Masai Women* in Chapter 12, pp. 000–000.

20 Fernea (1998), 65–8.

21 See Chapter 12, pp. 357–68 in which I discuss Llewelyn-Davies's films at greater length. Marilyn Gaunt would later work again with both Elizabeth Fernea and Dianne Tammes when she directed *Women of the Middle East*, a series of three films about women in the Islamic world broadcast by Channel 4 in 1982 (See Appendix, p. 494).

22 For a review of the film from a feminist perspective, see Brown (1978). A shorter film cut from the same footage and emphasising the more strictly religious aspects of Moroccan women's lives was released in 1979 under the title, *Saints and Spirits: Religious Expression in Morocco*.

23 Wright (1992), 279.

24 The editor of *Eskimos of Pond Inlet* was David Gladwell, who a decade previously had cut *Piraparaná*, the film directed by Brian Moser and Donald Tayler which had

so impressed Sir Denis Forman and which had thereby led, indirectly, to the creation of *Disappearing World*. In the interim, Gladwell had worked on a number of major feature films with Lindsay Anderson. Some years later, he would cut *1919*, a fictional feature film directed by Hugh Brody about an imagined meeting between two of Sigmund Freud's former patients.

25 For an account of the process of making this film, see Brody (1977).

26 In describing the *Inside China* series, I draw on the account by Alan Jenkins, which was based on interviews with many of those involved, including André Singer, Leslie Woodhead and Denis Forman (Jenkins 1986).

27 Feuchtwang (1983).

28 In common with some of the specialist reviewers in the UK national press, Alan Jenkins claims that the oral testimonies that are a central feature of these films conform to a well-established propaganda genre of 'speaking bitterness' about social conditions prior to accession to power of the Communist Party in 1949 (Jenkins 1986), 12.

29 See Turton (1988) for a more detailed historical discussion of Mursi migration over the long term.

30 See Caplan (1993), 20, also Tone Bringa's book about Visnjica, which describes the background to the conflict and also refers to the film (Bringa 1995). Later, between 1999 and 2001, Bringa collaborated with Peter Loizos in making a follow-up film, *Returning Home*, based on interviews with displaced families from both sides of the ethnic divide.

# 12

# Beyond the 'disappearing world' – and back again

Iɴ a purely technical sense, the quality of the *Disappearing World* films was a match for most of the films considered in previous parts of this book. This can largely be attributed to the fact that many of those who worked on the strand were members of television crews who had honed their skills over many years. But this also had a major downside: television crews at that time were required to belong to a trade union and as a result, whatever their personal commitment and interest might have been, they were bound by a series of agreements between their unions and Granada Television management. These dealt with such matters as crewing numbers, overtime rates and meal breaks and often greatly constrained the way in which the crews could work on location. These production conditions therefore had a direct impact on the collective authorial praxis of the *Disappearing World* strand.

For most of the period that the strand was in production, the management and unions at Granada Television worked to a general agreement whereby a documentary crew would normally consist of a team of at least six people: the director-producer, a researcher, a cameraperson and assistant, and a sound recordist and assistant. If anything other than natural lighting was involved, an electrician and an assistant also had to be added to the crew. Similar norms were applied across all the commercial television channels and to BBC documentary productions also, though the precise conditions of their union agreements were somewhat different. But whatever the production company, the idea that a director could also shoot their own material, as recommended by Jean Rouch, or as much later would become a common occurrence in British television documentary too, was completely out of the question.[1]

For the *Disappearing World* producers, these general agreements about crewing levels represented a major problem: not only would a large crew increase the budget to unsustainable levels on a foreign shoot, but the presence of so many outsiders in many of the small traditional communities in which they aimed to work could be unsettling. For a period, in the early years of the strand, a special agreement was reached whereby the *Disappearing World* films could be shot with a 'short' crew of only four people: director-producer, researcher, cameraperson and sound recordist. But towards the end of the 1970s, these agreements unravelled, *Disappearing World* was discontinued and many of the directors in the *Disappearing World* production team left Granada Television. Although these industrial relations problems would later be resolved and the strand would start up again, by then the film-makers who had left the strand had begun producing films based on a similar format elsewhere in British television.

## BEYOND *DISAPPEARING WORLD*

Those who left Granada Television at the end of the 1970s included the original series producer, Brian Moser, who went to work for another regional broadcaster, ATV, shortly to become Central Television, which was based in Birmingham. With this company, Moser produced a number of films involving collaboration with academic anthropologists. The first was *People of the Barrio* (1980), a film based on the research of his wife, anthropologist Caroline Moser, in a shantytown in Guayaquil, Ecuador. This involved some nine months of pre-production research by Brian Moser himself and generally conformed to the *Disappearing World* one-by-four format. The research phase of the project was actually funded by Granada Television, but when the *Disappearing World* strand closed down, Moser took the project to ATV.

Later in his career, Moser would make a number of further films with academic anthropologists. These included *A Small Family Business*, based on the work of Stephen Hugh-Jones. This was shot in the Colombian Vaupés region, where they had worked together before in making *War of the Gods*, a film about missionary activity that had formed part of the very first series of *Disappearing World* in 1971. This new film was the first in a series about cocaine trafficking that was broadcast in 1985. This series also included *God Gave Us the Leaf*, a film about coca cultivation in the Bolivian Andes, for which Moser was advised by the Bolivian anthropologist, Mauricio Mamani, among others. Later still, in making *Before Columbus*, a series broadcast in 1992 to mark the 500th anniversary of the 'discovery' of the Americas by Europeans, Moser worked closely with the US anthropologist Stephan Schwartzman.

However, the most extensive recycling of the *Disappearing World* format in these years was by Chris Curling and Melissa Llewelyn-Davies, who also left Granada when the strand closed down, and who were appointed as the executive producers of a new strand based at BBC Bristol. Between 1982 and 1985, under the general title, *Worlds Apart*, they oversaw the broadcast of eleven films based on the research of consultant anthropologists. Five of these conformed more or less to the standard one-by-four *Disappearing World* format and included *The Panare: Scenes from the Frontier*, broadcast in 1982, which was directed by Curling and based on my own field research in Venezuelan Amazonia.

The remaining six films were all about the Maasai of the Loita region in southern Kenya, close to the Tanzanian border, and were directed by Llewelyn-Davies, based on her own field research. Although these films still owed a great deal to the stylistic conventions and technical praxes typical of *Disappearing World*, they also broke new ground in the authorship of British television ethnographic film and for this reason, I consider them separately in the latter part of this chapter, in a section dedicated exclusively to Llewelyn-Davies's Maasai films.

The early 1980s also saw the launching of a new terrestrial television channel in Britain, Channel 4, which was set up with a brief to produce innovative forms of programming. One of its first contributions to ethnographic film-making was *People of the Islands*, broadcast in 1982. This was directed by Hugh Brody and concerned various Inuit communities in the Canadian Arctic, on Baffin Island and some other smaller islands north of Hudson Bay. In authorial terms, it built upon the collaborative methodology that Brody had first developed with Mike Grigsby in making *The Eskimos of Pond Inlet* for the *Disappearing World* series, as described in Chapter 11. An additional innovative feature was that the film was part-funded by the Inuit community who were the subjects of the film.

Over the course of the ensuing decade, Channel 4 supported a number of documentary series that were 'para-ethnographic' in the sense defined in the Introduction to this part of the book. That is, although they were not based on academic ethnographic research, they nevertheless possessed a certain degree of ethnographicness as a result of having been made in the course of a prolonged period of immersive cohabitation with the subjects and also because they explored the multiple connections between practices, relations and ideas that underpinned the social worlds of those subjects.[2]

These para-ethnographic series took a variety of different forms. A particularly interesting example was *Caught in a Web*, a series in three parts, each a single television hour in duration, which compared and contrasted life in a traditional village in rural Dorset (or more strictly speaking a cluster of small hamlets) with life in Villes-sur-Auzon, a village of Haute Provence in France. The director was Toni de Bromhead, a film-maker trained at the NFTS where she had been greatly influenced by Colin Young and his ideas about Observational Cinema. Prior to attending the NFTS, de Bromhead had also studied social anthropology at the London School of Economics, where she had encountered the ethnographic literature on the Mediterranean region. By special dispensation from the technicians' union, she was allowed to direct and shoot *Caught in a Web* herself, supported only by a sound recordist, in the manner recommended by proponents of Observational Cinema. The series was commissioned not long after the launch of Channel 4 in 1982, though it was not actually broadcast until 1986.

As de Bromhead has described in an account published in 2014, her explicit concern was to find a means 'to communicate anthropological concepts through film in a non-expository way'. While she appreciated the methods of Observational Cinema as a means of achieving an engagement with the subjects which could then be passed on to the viewer, she had doubts about its effectiveness in communicating more abstract analytical concepts about the principles embedded in social life. At the same time, she wanted to avoid heavy-handed explanatory commentary, so had turned to the idea of comparison between the two villages as a way of making audiences aware of these embedded principles without her having to identify them explicitly by verbal means.[3]

The two villages contrasted in *Caught in a Web* were chosen on entirely contingent pragmatic grounds: it happened that de Bromhead's mother had grown up in Dorset and had later moved to Villes-sur-Auzon, so de Bromhead *fille* had a ready-made entrée to both villages. In cutting the films, de Bromhead wisely avoided the temptation to switch back and forth between the two communities in the course of a single programme. Instead, in the first two films, the first half deals with the Dorset village and the second with Villes. In the third film, each of the two communities is shown watching the material shot in the other and the subjects' comments are then invited, mostly through interviews of varying formality, sometimes as individuals, but often in small groups. In effect, the subjects acted as the consultant ethnographers, reflecting on their own way life at the same time as they comment on the life of the other village.

Although they had been selected on an entirely fortuitous basis, the two villages presented in *Caught in a Web* offered a fascinating ethnographic contrast. The Dorset village is portrayed as being in a quasi-feudal situation: social life is dominated both economically and culturally by the families living in the manor houses while the village church plays an important part in the community, though more for social reasons than on account of personal religious conviction. By contrast, Villes is shown to be a staunchly republican community with a socialist tradition: the *mairie*, the town hall, is the centre of social life and there is a strong ethos of egalitarianism. Although some members of the community are practising Catholics, there is much anti-clerical sentiment, funerals are often entirely secular and the church building itself is in a state of decay.

What the two villages have in common, however, is a passion for hunting, though here too there are major differences. In Dorset, hunting takes various

But the film gave me the impression I was going back to the Middle Ages

12.1 *Caught in a Web* (1986). Left, in Dorset, after the pheasant shoot, Lady Williams comes downstairs to visit the 'beaters', who eat separately from the 'guns' upstairs in her manor. This reminds a councillor from Villes, right, of a world that disappeared long ago in France.

forms that testify to class differences: working people hunt rabbits with the aid of ferrets while the elite engage in the traditional mounted foxhunt, or in pheasant shooting, with working people providing ancillary support in both cases as 'beaters'. In the post-hunt feasting, social differences are reinforced in Dorset, with the elite and the working people eating and drinking separately, and with each group saying that they prefer it that way (figure 12.1). In Provence, by contrast, the principal prey is wild boar and it is an altogether more egalitarian affair, with social differences being actively minimised in the after-hunt feasting. But here too, there are exclusions, though on the basis of gender rather than class. For in Provence, hunting is an entirely masculine activity while in Dorset both men and women participate, albeit with certain restrictions on the use of guns by even the most elite women.

As de Bromhead readily acknowledges, *Caught in a Web* was not based on academic field research. She spent ten weeks in each community, which although very long for a television production, is still relatively short by academic standards and she confesses to doing no literature research prior to the shoot. She also acknowledges that if she had spent more time living in the two villages, particularly in Villes, she might have been able to draw a more fine-grained comparison that included a focus on gender as well as class differentiation. But regardless of these limitations, *Caught in a Web* represents a unique comparative project informed by an undoubted ethnographic sensibility.

Around this same time, Channel 4 also supported another major project that was very different in authorial terms, but which could also be said to possess ethnographic qualities on account of the way in which it was made – despite not involving the direct participation of an academic anthropologist. This was *Baka: People of the Rainforest*, first broadcast in 1987. The ethnographic status of this film is perhaps more debatable than *Caught in a Web*: be that as it may, it was awarded an ethnographic film prize by the Royal Anthropological Institute the following year.

The director of *Baka*, Phil Agland, is a highly skilled and entirely self-taught cameraman whose academic background is in geography rather than anthropology. He first came to prominence in British television through *Korup*, a remarkable documentary about a rainforest on the frontier between Cameroon and Nigeria, which was the first natural history documentary to be screened on Channel 4 in November 1982. Following the critical accolades showered on *Korup*, Agland was then commissioned to make a film about the Baka, a hunting and gathering people who live in the rainforest of southeast Cameroon.

In order to make this film, Agland spent two years living with one small local group, along with the associate producer Lisa Silcock and the sound recordist Mike Harrison. During this time, although she was not a trained anthropologist either, Silcock achieved fluency in the Baka language. Before they began to shoot seriously, the entire team spent six months in preparatory research and in developing relationships of trust with the subjects. A number of anthropologists acted as advisers on the film, though none of them played an active role in the production itself.[4]

*Baka* is a feature-length documentary, with a duration of two television hours, divided into four parts. It approaches Baka life primarily through the experiences of a single nuclear family, consisting of Likano, a man in his 40s and one of the oldest in the local group, his wife Deni, some twenty years his junior, and their two small sons, Yeye and Alime. Most of the film concerns the way in which the Baka make a living from the forest: it shows them hunting, fishing, gathering forest fruits and, very dramatically, extracting wild honey from hives some 40 metres above the forest floor (figure 12.2). There are also brief sequences of them working in their banana grove, said to be 'unusual' among the Baka in the voice-over commentary, and also in the cacao plantation of the Konabembe, a local Bantu group of permanently settled agriculturalists with whom the Baka have a trading relationship.

Various scenes show the preparation and use of medicines made from forest plants, and also a curing ceremony. The film is punctuated with scenes of singing and dancing, which in the final part are related to a visit from a forest spirit, Jengi, who has been called upon to bring calm to the group following the outbreak of an argument between Likano and a younger man, Babu, who wants to marry his daughter by his first marriage. As part of the argument, Likano accuses Babu of using sorcery against him and Babu takes a life-threatening 'truth drug' to prove his innocence. But Jengi has the desired effect, the argument is forgotten and the film concludes with Deni giving birth to a sister for Yeye and Alime.

12.2 *Baka: People of the Rainforest* (1987). Left, shot from a platform above, Mewunga, in search of honey, climbs through the forest canopy on an emergent tree; right, a *nganga* curer uses the heat of a wood fire to cure a baby.

As far as the content is concerned then, *Baka* covers terrain that is very typical of the canon of ethnographic film. But in its technical praxis, *Baka* is quite different from most of the films conventionally considered to be ethnographic. For, in making this film, Agland simply extended the methods that he had developed so successfully in his earlier natural history films and applied them in an ecological setting that also included human beings. Alongside the sequences featuring the Baka themselves, there are also many that could have come straight out of a natural history film, showing, for example, worker bees inside a hive, or animals such as the pangolin, the hyrax and the utterly charming honey bear foraging at night.

The way in which the Baka are filmed has many of the same technical attributes: shots are usually taken from a single static position, with no pans or zooms, often on a long lens or from a 'privileged' perspective, that is one not available to the subjects, such as from the top of a tree. The subjects never acknowledge the camera and there are no interviews, formal or informal. Shots have often clearly been set up, particularly at night, when they are always immaculately lit. Later, in the edit suite, these shots have been constructed according to the norms of fictional cinema to suggest continuity or simultaneity when, to the eye of any experienced film-maker, it is clear that the shots concerned must have been taken at entirely different times or in a different order.

This process of editorial construction is sometimes remarkably elaborate. Thus at one point in the film, there is a sequence that cuts back and forth to suggest simultaneity between a number of sub-sequences, including an obviously set up shot of a forest cat gnawing at the carcass of an antelope, a group of women damming a river to fish and a man climbing a tree to gather honey. The latter process is being followed by a camera that is supposedly simultaneously in the canopy with the honey-gatherer and with the eager children 40 metres below, one of whom looks up, beautifully back-lit, while playing the *ngombi*, a sort of four-stringed harp. In the midst of this construction, there are also cuts to close-ups of a particular species of bird that likes to feed on beeswax. This fictional 'feel' is further enhanced by the use of incidental music that is a subtly augmented version of the Baka's own music, while the voice-over commentary is delivered in a smooth actorly manner by Sir Ian Holm in the UK version, and in the version made for US television by Denzel Washington. This commentary often directly endorses the many constructed simultaneities of the action.

But underlying all this cinematographic construction, the film remains based on a close participant-observation of Baka life carried out, over a prolonged period, within a relationship of trust developed between film-makers and subjects. It was surely this that permitted the intimate style of camerawork through which the audience is invited to get to know the Baka, not as curious small people of the rainforest, as they had so often been presented in the past, but rather as human beings with many of the same preoccupations and characteristics as the audience might have. It was also no doubt this quality to which the jurors of the RAI were responding when they awarded *Baka* the Institute's most prestigious ethnographic film prize in 1988.[5]

In addition to these series concerned with culturally exotic societies, British television in the 1980s regularly supported para-ethnographic series shot in Britain itself that were also based on the close participant-observation of small groups of people, often living in spatially confined institutions, over a relatively prolonged period. These series included *Strangeways*, an eight-part series broadcast in 1980 and directed for the BBC by Rex Bloomstein, which portrayed life in the broodingly ominous Victorian prison of the same name in Manchester. Two years later, the BBC also broadcast *Police*, produced by Roger Graef but shot and directed by Charles Stewart, who had worked as a cameraman on a number of *Disappearing World* films. Over nine 45-minute parts, this series followed the day-to-day activities of a Thames Valley police station in Reading. But these were merely the most celebrated of a large number of extended series that were broadcast around this time on British television, which dealt with everyday life in institutions such as schools, hospitals, naval ships and railway stations.[6]

Towards the end of the 1980s, a somewhat more interactive variant of this para-ethnographic genre of films about institutions emerged, exemplified particularly by the work of Molly Dineen, a documentarist who, like de Bromhead, had been trained in the Observational Cinema approach at the NFTS. In the classical 'fly-on-the-wall' variant, as exemplified by *The Family*, Paul Watson's observational series from 1974, or by Roger Graef's later series on the Reading police, there had been a director, accompanied by a technical crew, who had largely remained silent apart from interviews or voice-over, or in certain exceptional situations, as at the very beginning of *The Family*, when Paul Watson is shown explaining the 'ground rules' of the filming to the assembled Wilkins family.[7] By contrast, in accordance with the authorial strategies typically associated with Observational Cinema, Dineen often speaks in a conversational manner with her subjects from behind the camera that she herself is operating.

An early example of Dineen's approach to filming British institutions was *The Heart of the Angel*, a short film broadcast in 1989, which provided a behind-the-scenes portrait of the staff of the Angel Islington, a station on the notoriously antiquated Northern Line of London's underground railway system. However, Dineen then went on to offer a much more developed example of her approach in *The Ark*, a four-part series about London Zoo. Shot over a period of nine months in 1991, involving more than 100 hours of rushes, and then cut over the course of a year in collaboration with the editor Ted Roberts, it was not until 1993 that *The Ark* was finally broadcast.

At one level, *The Ark* could be construed as an intimately observed para-ethnographic account of human–animal interactions and the ideas about nature that sustain these interactions in an urban zoo. But this is only the background story: as one newspaper reviewer commented at the time, with only a slight degree of exaggeration, *The Ark* is as much about animals in a zoo as George Orwell's novella, *Animal Farm* was about animals on a farm.[8] For tying together all the many scenes of the zoo keepers and visitors maintaining and imagining relationships with animals, the series is underpinned by a storyline that captured the spirit of the times, namely, the reorganisation of London Zoo in accordance with the market-led neoliberal economics introduced into British life by successive Thatcher governments through the 1980s.

Having been set up as a private philanthropic society in the early nineteenth century in order to promote zoological science and educate the public at the same time, by the last decade of the twentieth century the zoo had become heavily dependent on government subsidy. As this was about to be withdrawn, the zoo faced closure unless it radically cut its costs and found new sources of income. The dramatic arc running through all four parts of the *The Ark* is the process whereby the zoo is transformed from being primarily a scientific and educational institution into one that is, in effect, part of the leisure industry, in which the most important criterion is the number of people buying tickets at the gate.

As a result of this process, a third of the animals and a considerable number of keepers are 'let go', as the euphemism of the day had it, and the zoo management re-orients its priorities to ensure that it places primary emphasis on the animals that the public really wants to see and on organising media events. But this leads to a counter-challenge by an alliance of keepers and council members that eventually results in the director of the zoo

12.3 *The Ark* (1993). Left, the Head Keeper bids goodbye to a bird of prey that has been in the zoo for twenty-five years. Right, the management team is advised by a public relations consultant to acknowledge criticisms.

himself being 'let go' (figure 12.3). The intertwining of the many different strands of this story are very skilfully followed by Dineen, who seems to have won the confidence of those on all sides of the argument.

For many commentators, London Zoo as presented in *The Ark* acted as an extended metaphor for many British public institutions of the time, including particularly the BBC and the Reithian tradition of public service broadcasting that went with it. Indeed, at precisely the same time as *The Ark* was being made, British television was undergoing many of the same processes of organisational change as shown in this series. And as I shall discuss in Chapter 13, just like the less popular animals in London Zoo and the supposedly superfluous keepers, one of the casualties of these processes of change would be ethnographic film-making.

## MELISSA LLEWELYN-DAVIES AS ETHNOGRAPHIC FILM AUTHOR: THE MAASAI FILMS

Among the many talented directors who made ethnographic or para-ethnographic films for British television during the 'golden era', one of the most innovative was Melissa Llewelyn-Davies. Although she made films on a broad range of subjects, from polo-playing by the English upper classes through to cultural change in Eastern Europe in the period of *perestroika*, the most distinctively original films within her body of work are those that she made about the Maasai of southern Kenya. These include two early *Disappearing World* films, *Masai Women* and *Masai Manhood*, broadcast in the 1970s, and the films that she made while based at BBC Bristol in the 1980s, *The Women's Olamal* and the five films of *Diary of a Maasai Village*. They also include *Memories and Dreams*, produced right at the end of the 'golden era' and broadcast as part of the BBC series *Fine Cut* in 1993. It is this cycle of nine films about the Maasai that will be my exclusive concern here.[9]

Prior to joining the production team at *Disappearing World*, Llewelyn-Davies had been a student of anthropology, first as an undergraduate at University College London in the late 1960s, when she had developed a particular interest in the newly emergent feminist approaches, and later as a postgraduate student at Harvard in the early 1970s. It was while she was at Harvard that she had begun fieldwork among the Maasai with the intention of producing a doctoral thesis. She later gave up the doctorate in favour of a film-making career, but not before she had immersed herself in Maasai society for a prolonged period and had developed a fluent command of their language. Although she also published a couple of academic articles, in effect it was primarily through her films that she presented the results of her doctoral fieldwork. It was also through her film-making that she developed and extended her understanding of Maasai life over the next twenty years.[10]

Although Llewelyn-Davies's films about the Maasai are strongly marked by the authorial praxes and stylistic conventions typical of ethnographic film on British television, she was continually pushing the boundaries. As far as the one-by-four format is concerned, her most obvious break with the conventional model was when she moved to BBC Bristol in the late 1970s and persuaded the management there to support films that went far beyond the single television hour: two hours in the case of *Olamal*, just over four in the case of the full series of *Diary* films. The latter also represented a break with the convention of pursuing a single theme, since several major themes and a multitude of minor ones are interwoven through the length of the five films. Although her films conformed to the one-by-four model to the degree that they were based on the research of a single anthropologist in a single community, this was her own work, rather than that of a third party. This too was highly unusual in British television.[11]

However, although Llewelyn-Davies may not have been dependent on a consultant anthropologist in making her Maasai films, as a maker of ethnographic films for television she was necessarily dependent on others for their practical realisation. Her first two films about the Maasai, that is, those made for *Disappearing World*, were actually directed by Chris Curling: her role on these films was formally that of researcher and anthropological consultant. Curling is also jointly credited as the series producer of the *Olamal* and *Diary* films. At the time that these films were produced, Curling and Llewelyn-Davies were a married couple and shared much in common professionally as well. Although they subsequently went their separate ways, both professionally and personally, it remains the fact that Curling contributed greatly to the authoring of all these films.

Also, as Llewelyn-Davies herself has often commented, the final shape of her Maasai films was greatly influenced by the contribution of Dai Vaughan, the highly esteemed editor who cut all but the last film, *Memories and Dreams*, while the general look of the films was largely due to the highly skilled cinematographers who worked under her direction: the *Disappearing World* films were shot by Charles Stewart, while the *Olamal* and *Diary* films were shot by Dick Pope and Barry Ackroyd, both of whom went on to become leading feature film cinematographers. Pope also later shot the cinematographically magnificent *Memories and Dreams*.

Moreover, even a film-maker of the originality and determination of Llewelyn-Davies could not escape entirely from the stylistic constraints of making films for British television. In this regard, among the features of her Maasai films that most readily identify them as television productions is the use of voice-over commentary to deliver contextualising information as well as some low-key anthropological analyses. In all her Maasai films, Llewelyn-Davies performed her own voice-overs and although this has the merit of linking up the commentary voice with her voice as we hear it in interviews, the quality of these commentaries, both in scripting and delivery, is variable, as she herself has observed.[12] Interestingly, over the complete cycle of nine films, the nature of her commentary changes significantly: in the later films, there is not only very much less commentary, but it tends to be more subjective and informal.

But the feature that most marks these films out as television productions is the extensive use of 'talking head' interviews. These are typically seeded throughout the length of the films, providing not only information and cultural context but also, due to the intimate way in which they are shot and conducted, a strong emotional texture as well. The interviews in the pre-title sequence of *The Women's Olamal* represent a particularly effective example of Llewelyn-Davies's technique. This sequence involves interviews with two women of different generations who have been beautifully shot, in a particularly intimate manner, in low light and framed in an interior doorway of their houses. Although they appear to be dressed in all their finery, their answers are simple and informal. These interviews establish, very poignantly, the inflexible nexus that connects cattle-ownership, fertility and a woman's well-being in Maasai society.

Among the Maasai, these subjects explain, a woman owns nothing. Her husband will give her some cattle to look after when she moves to his house after marriage, but this herd is merely held in trust to be passed on to her sons; if her husband dies and she has had no sons, she will be chased away by the sons of his other wives. If she has had daughters, she may go and live with them, though she will be dependent on the charity of her daughters' husbands. But if she has no children at all, she will have nowhere to go. A barren woman is therefore 'very bad … like a wilderness', and her

12.4 *The Women's Olamal* (1984). Left, Kisaru explains that if a Maasai woman is childless, she will have no means of support in later life; right, when male elders threaten to withhold the *olamal* fertility blessing, some women become hysterical and have to be restrained.

life is full of suffering: as one of several wives, she will only occasionally see her husband and there is often therefore no one to cook for, no one with whom to share the night.

The establishment of these painful interconnections in the pre-title sequence provides a key to reading the whole film: they not only explain why Maasai women are so keen to hold an *olamal*, which consists primarily of a ceremonial blessing to ensure their fertility, but they also prepare the viewer for the later hysterical behaviour of some of the women when it transpires that the ceremony may not take place after all (figure 12.4).

In part, the interviews in Llewelyn-Davies's films work very well because Maasai women, in common with the women who appear in the MacDougalls' Turkana films, prove themselves to be the most remarkable natural philosophers, capable of combining, in the most eloquent way, such diverse matters as sociological insight into their own society, reflections on the nature of God, and the expression of personal views and sentiments. But equally important are Llewelyn-Davies's long-standing relationship with her subjects, her obvious fluency in their language and her intimate knowledge of their society. This combination of factors enables her not only to frame succinct questions that generate interesting answers, but also to ask more difficult, sometimes even importunate questions, in a manner that seemingly does not offend, nor even surprise her subjects. Almost invariably, they respond to the questions with an air of patience and a concern that Llewelyn-Davies should fully understand the answer. Among these interlocutors, there is none more solicitous and precise in her answers than Nolpeyeiya, who is older than Llewelyn-Davies and talks to her as mother to daughter, and who regularly appears in the films over the full twenty-year period.

Yet although the relationship between Llewelyn-Davies and her principal subjects may have remained constant, the nature of the films themselves changed considerably, particularly with regard to the way in which they are structured narratively.

The early *Disappearing World* films offer what might be described as predominantly normative accounts of Maasai gender relations within highly conventional narrative structures adapted to the requirements of commercial television. Thus *Masai Women* is constructed in accordance with the normal stages of the female life cycle in Maasai society: after setting the general scene of life in a Maasai village, Part One deals with a woman's adolescent life, culminating in the circumcision ritual that will mark her transition into full womanhood and legitimate fertility. In making way for the commercial break, this part is rounded off with some further chanting and dancing. Part Two then opens with a wedding party and the life of young wives becomes the focus of attention. Their subservience to the authority of their husbands – leavened by the possibility of affairs with young unmarried men of the warrior age grade – and the relationships among co-wives are then considered before Part Two also culminates in a ceremonial performance, this time of young men leaving the warrior age grade to become junior elders. However, this dramatic performance is presented as if seen through the eyes of the warriors' mothers, thereby completing, by proxy as it were, the stages of the typical female life cycle.

The other *Disappearing World* film, *Masai Manhood*, which concerns an equally dramatic male age grade ceremony, was not originally conceived as a film but rather was 'cobbled together', in Llewelyn-Davies's phrase, from footage shot opportunistically. It is a less complex film narratively speaking than *Masai Women*, but it too is divided into two parts, each culminating in a ceremonial event.

The *Women's Olamal* is a very different film from the first two, both in the way that it presents Maasai gender relations and in terms of its narrative structure. Although the subject matter of the film is again a ceremonial event, the first two-thirds of the 115-minute film are dedicated not to the *olamal* itself, but rather to the events leading up to it, as suggested by the subtitle to the film: *The organisation of a Maasai fertility ceremony*. Contrary to what one might expect from this rather dry phrase, suggestive of an academic thesis, this 'organisation' primarily consists of an intense argument between women and men about whether the event will take place at all. For although the women are desperate for the *olamal* to happen for the reasons explained in the pre-title interviews, the senior men responsible for dispensing the blessing are reluctant to perform their role because a murder has taken place among a neighbouring group of Maasai. According to customary belief, to perform the *olamal* at such a time would not only be inauspicious, but also ineffective.

Narratively speaking, the first two-thirds of the film take the form of a classic 'crisis structure'. (Given that this film was made for the BBC, there was happily no need for a commercial break halfway through.) As the women marshal their arguments in formal debate, first among themselves – in a manner highly reminiscent of the male orators of Woodhead and Turton's Mursi films – and then in their verbal confrontations with the senior men, they show themselves to be highly accomplished public speakers, with developed rhetorical skills. But when their verbal arguments prove to be of no avail, some of the older women threaten to curse the senior men while some of the younger ones fall to the ground, shouting out and writhing in a disturbing hysterical manner. As a curse is believed by the Maasai to carry a serious threat of death for those to whom it is directed and furthermore, can be issued, even unintentionally, by people in an emotionally disturbed condition, the men capitulate and agree to the hold the *olamal* after all. The final third of the film is then structured around the performance of the ceremony itself. But although this offers a magnificent visual spectacle, in dramatic terms and arguably in ethnographic terms also, it is somewhat anti-climactic after the intense scenes that had come before.

While *The Women's Olamal* is organised around a cumulative series of events, the five films of *Diary of a Maasai Village* are ostensibly structured simply by the passage of time over a given seven-week period in July and August 1983. Rather than focusing on specific events or stories, Llewellyn-Davies intended merely to follow the Maasai of a particular village as they lived out their daily lives in all their multifaceted complexity, covering incidents both great and small, significant and trivial, in a manner that she explicitly conceived of as being like a soap opera. The village in question was the same one in which the all earlier films had been shot, and which, by this time, Llewelyn-Davies had known for more than ten years. This village had been built up around a prophet, or *laibon*, by the name of Simel, a now-elderly man with thirteen living wives and more than sixty children. Eleven of his married sons remained in his village with their respective families and, of course, large herds of cattle (figure 12.5, left). Though these were much reduced compared to former times, largely due to the effects of disease, the villagers remained entirely dependent on them in the traditional Maasai way and did not practice agriculture in any form.

In an opening passage of voice-over commentary in the first film, reiterated somewhat more briefly in the others, Llewelyn-Davies explains her objectives. Her general aim, she says, is simply to describe how the Maasai of Simel's village were living 'at a particular moment in their history'. Among the many scenes of domestic life, this also entails showing how these Maasai were coming to terms, in a matter-of-fact daily sort of way, with social change arising directly or indirectly from their progressive incorporation into the modern nation state of Kenya. This was a new theme in Llewelyn-Davies's work: previously the 'outside world' had barely been mentioned. In another contrast to her earlier work, Llewelyn-Davies explains that she

**12.5** *Diary of a Maasai Village* (1985). Left, Simel, the *laibon* prophet and leader of the village, who has thirteen wives and more than sixty children. Right, Miisia, one of Simel's sons, undergoes the *ibaa* ceremony, promoting him to a more senior level of elderhood.

has made a particular effort to concentrate on the experience of Maasai men. In fact, these two changes of emphasis are related since it is the men who have most contact with the world outside the village.

The opening commentary also explains that in adopting a diaristic narrative structure, Llewelyn-Davies had wanted to avoid the positing of an opposition between supposedly unchanging traditional Maasai culture and what she refers to as 'development'. At face value, this last statement might not seem particularly significant, but there is an important agenda underlying it. Although Llewelyn-Davies does not make this explicit, in East Africa, as any viewer familiar with the MacDougalls' work or the Woodhead-Turton films will surely be aware, 'development' is often merely a euphemism for change imposed on pastoralist societies by national governments. By means of a diaristic narrative, Llewelyn-Davies appears to have been seeking to distance herself from the intense political polemic surrounding pastoralism in the region so that she could focus instead on the reality of everyday experience for the Maasai, or as she puts it 'to give their present, room to breathe'.

Many different themes are interwoven over the course of the five films, some of which are encountered in the earlier films, some of which are new. We hear how men can achieve a sort of immortality through acquiring many wives, many children and many cattle. A group of young warriors gets into trouble because they have illicitly eaten one of the *laibon*'s goats and have to pay a fine, which they try to extort from a local shopkeeper from a different ethnic group. One young woman gives birth and another gets married: as she approaches her husband's village, she is insulted in the customary way, as we saw in *Masai Women*. At one point, in a scene reminiscent of the famous scene in *To Live with Herds*, a uniformed administrator harangues a group of Maasai for not sending their children to school. Also reminiscent of the MacDougalls' film is a particularly interesting sequence when a group of Maasai go to Ngong, a town on the outskirts of Nairobi to sell their cattle. There is much coming and going between villages and many shots of day-to-day livestock management. There is also complex episode of divination involving stones, a great deal of daily gossip, and much else besides.

As in normal life in reality, there are many loose ends, that is, events and situations that are not resolved, at least not within the films. However, running through all five films and holding them together is a recurrent storyline concerning one of the *laibon*'s sons, Rerenko, who has been unjustly imprisoned in Nairobi, supposedly for cattle theft. Here he has been subject to regular beatings and fed such a poor diet that his relatives are seriously worried about his health. Various delegations of male relatives go to the city to secure his release, but in vain. Cattle are sold at Ngong to pay for a lawyer, but the lawyer pockets the money and still Rerenko languishes in prison. It is not until Llewelyn-Davies herself provides a 'loan' to bail him out that Rerenko is finally released, thereby providing a 'happy ending' in the fifth film.

This film also provides a happy ending of a different kind as another of the *laibon*'s sons, Miisia, who has just taken a fourth wife, goes through a ceremony promoting him to a more senior level of elderhood (figure 12.5, right). Notwithstanding the introductory disclaimer of any polemical intent back in the first film, Miisia represents a reassuring figure of the continuity of tradition, holding at bay 'development' which in these films has been represented primarily by the irascible administrator threatening to beat any fathers who refuse to send their sons to school and by Rerenko's terrible experience of imprisonment in Nairobi.

The intervention by Llewelyn-Davies in the release of Rerenko is merely the most instrumental of many reflexive moments in the *Diary* films. From the earliest films in her Maasai cycle, the viewer had been made aware of Llewelyn-Davies's presence through her voice, be it in the commentary or in the interview questions. She even appeared briefly in front of the lens in both *Masai Women* and *Masai Manhood*. But in the *Diary* films, this reflexivity becomes more marked, in line with the general zeitgeist of ethnographic film in the 1980s, as described in Chapter 5. All five films include numerous references by the subjects to the fact that a film is being made, a feature that had been rare in the earlier films.

More significant, given that they are so central to Llewelyn-Davies's authorial praxis, is a subtle change in the balance of the interviews. In the earlier films, these had been very one-sided in the sense that the interlocutors commented only on Maasai life. But now the interviews become more of a conversational exchange. Thus, at one point, a young woman states as a matter of general principle that women are less intelligent than men. When Llewelyn-Davies gently demurs, the woman counters by saying that

Llewelyn-Davies's husband, Chris Curling, who was also present at the shoot, is clearly more than intelligent than she is. When Llewelyn-Davies again demurs, the interlocutor insists that Curling really is the more intelligent.

In this interview, as with a number of others, the interlocutors end with a series of requests for food and fuel. Llewelyn-Davies's relationship with the Maasai was already long-standing by this point and one imagines that many such conversations would have taken place before, both on- and off-camera. What is significant is that now these conversations are retained within the film rather than being consigned to the proverbial 'cutting room floor'.

This more reflexive dimension is further developed in the last work of Llewelyn-Davies's Maasai cycle, *Memories and Dreams*, released in 1993, some eight years after the *Diary* films. Her motivation for making this film was highly personal. Feeling that she was now reaching middle age and having recently been through some testing personal experiences, including separation from her husband, she was in the process of reviewing of her own life trajectory and wanted to compare this with what the Maasai women whom she had known over twenty years thought about the way in which their own lives had turned out.

From a stylistic perspective, a feature that was unprecedented in Llewelyn-Davies's Maasai films are extracts from the earlier films, presented with a vignette-like sepia effect around the edge of the frame to indicate that they refer to the past. In what had by then become a familiar trope in ethnographic film-making, the film opens with a scene in which the Maasai are shown looking at this earlier material on a monitor and commenting on how they looked and behaved in those distant bygone days.

But otherwise, *Memories and Dreams* represents, in many ways, simply a further extension of authorial strategies that Llewelyn-Davies had been developing in her earlier BBC Bristol films. Though it is considerably shorter at 90 minutes, the narrative structure is, if anything, even more diffuse than that of the *Diary* films. There is still some voice-over commentary, but it is limited to some orientating remarks right at the beginning of the film. Rather, the film is built up through a series of scenes of everyday life, punctuated with interviews, which as in the *Diary* films, are more two-sided and conversational than the interviews in her earliest work. In one memorable exchange, a woman asks Llewelyn-Davies about her recent marital separation and whether she will have any further children, or be offered a new husband. When the answer to both is in the negative, the woman compares this with the Maasai way of dealing with marital separation, which is for the woman to leave her children behind and return to her own village, where a man would soon come to seek her as a wife and with whom she would then have further children. But although this general trend towards greater reflexivity is continued, this does not extend to Llewelyn-Davies actually appearing in shot.[13]

In making this film, Llewelyn-Davies made a most interesting ethnographic discovery, but one that she would later regret not making clearer within the film itself, even though it is alluded to in the title. This discovery was that her Maasai interlocutors did not normally think of themselves as the heroic protagonists of their own life history, as Europeans tend to do. Rather they thought of themselves as belonging decisively to their particular age grade and sought to be, as best they could, good representatives of that grade. To think of oneself at an earlier age was therefore regarded as a childish attempt to recapture something that was definitively over.

As a result, Llewelyn-Davies found it difficult to get her interlocutors to recount their memories in a biographical manner. The best way, she discovered, was to ask them to recount a dream, in which case, what she might be offered would be something 'halfway between a memory and a dream'. In the absence of the recounting of substantial memories of the past by the subjects themselves, the footage from the earlier films comes to stand for the past instead. However, as Llewelyn-Davies herself recognises, the status of this archival material remains uncertain, since it is not clear whether it is supposed to represent the subjects' memories directly or to be merely some kind of objective statement about how Maasai life was in earlier times.[14]

Given the Maasai subjects' reluctance to engage in protracted autobiographical reflection, *Memories and Dreams* perforce became less the exploration of individual life histories that Llewelyn-Davies had originally intended and more an account of how life had turned out for the Maasai as a collectivity over the previous twenty years. The balance of this account is at best ambiguous. In the first part of the film, there is a return to themes of female experience that were also explored in the earlier films, central to which is the importance for women of having children, both for sustaining them in life and as a legacy that they will leave behind when they die. There is also much discussion of the challenges of marriage, the solidarity between co-wives and the pleasures of the seemingly almost-universal practice among women of taking lovers.

But in comparison to the earlier work, Llewelyn-Davies is more disposed to confront head-on some of the aspects of traditional Maasai life that are less attractive to European audiences. Her interlocutors recount, for example, how they learn to endure the beatings that they receive from their husbands. The issue of female circumcision is again considered, as it was in *Masai Women*, but at considerably greater length: the interlocutors again insist that it is a truly happy occasion for a young girl as she passes into womanhood. But this time Llewelyn-Davies juxtaposes these statements with the wailing that she recorded in 1974 but did not then dare use.[15]

Yet punctuating this fundamentally celebratory, even if warts-and-all, portrait of traditional Maasai life, there are recurrent references to decline.

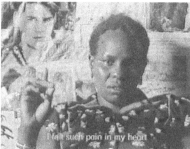

12.6 *Memories and Dreams* (1993). Left, Miisia's senior wife says she misses her co-wife, right, who has run off to town as she could no longer tolerate the beatings from her husband. As a childless woman, her future prospects in Maasai society were very bleak.

The cattle are dying of tick-borne diseases, present-day warriors are puny compared to those of a generation ago, girls are being initiated too young, and people are losing confidence in the old ways. But if traditional Maasai life has its hardships, particularly for women, the alternatives presented by the film of life outside the Maasai world are hardly appealing. About a quarter of the way into the film, there is an abrupt and almost shocking cut to Loise, a young Maasai woman who has run away from her village after her husband – who is none other than Miisia, the junior elder whom we had encountered in a more charming incarnation in earlier films – began beating her with a piece of wood. Loise has abandoned the beads and ear adornments traditionally worn by Maasai women, her head is no longer shaven and her hair is roughly cut in a standard 'modern' way (figure 12.6). Prior to her flight, she had been one of Miisia's five wives and her co-wives say that they miss her and hope that one day she will return. Miisia, meanwhile, threatens angrily to bring her back by force. But Loise was childless, and we know only too well from *The Women's Olamal* what a bleak future would have awaited her if she had remained at home. Instead she has taken up with a poor man, Samwell, also Maasai, but who has no cattle. They have converted to Christianity and together eke out a meagre living on the outskirts of a small town.

*Memories and Dreams* is undoubtedly a masterpiece, not only superbly directed, but also magnificently shot and edited. Looking back at it from a vantage point of more than twenty years, it now seems truly remarkable that British television could once have made possible such a work. But although it represents on the surface a wholehearted paean to the beauty and complexity of traditional Maasai life, it also carries an undertow of melancholy and nostalgia – on the part of both Llewelyn-Davies and her subjects – partly at personal level for people who featured in the earlier films and who have since died, but also, more generally, for a world that is on the wane. The integrity of Maasai life is shown to be fracturing as some Maasai, like Loise and Samwell, reject tradition completely while even those who remain in the countryside find themselves obliged to hoe the land like 'those who wear trousers'.

In effect, by the end of her cycle of Maasai films, which also coincided with the end of the 'golden era' in ethnographic film on British television, Llewelyn-Davies had come round to the theme of externally induced change that had been central to the early series of the *Disappearing World* strand but which had then been displaced by the more internally oriented themes of the films in the 1974 series, including *Masai Women* and *Masai Manhood*. In practical authorial terms, *Memories and Dreams* and *The Last of the Cuiva* may be very different. But both are concerned with the historical process that in the dry language of social science could be termed the profound dislocation caused in traditional societies by rapid social and cultural change. What both these films show, in their different ways, is what this process means in terms of the intimate personal experiences of those caught up in it.

## Notes

1 When agreements struck in relation to working conditions in Britain were applied in the locations where ethnographic films were typically shot, a great many absurdities arose. A single illustrative example will have to suffice here: in 1983, when Leslie Woodhead was shooting a *Disappearing World* film in China, he wanted to film inside a factory, but as there was no electrician on the crew, he had to ask for the lights in the factory to be turned off. Naturally, the factory manager was completely mystified.
2 See p. 316.
3 de Bromhead (2014), 61–121.
4 I am very grateful to Phil Agland for commenting on earlier drafts of this section (personal communications, September 2014 and December 2018). As he informed me, prior to shooting he consulted the Baka specialists Robert Dodd and Serge Bahuchet, and while on location, he and his colleagues were visited by Robert Brisson, a French missionary ethnologist who had worked with the Baka over many decades. Bahuchet also came to look at the material in the edit suite. But none of these consultants had the degree of engagement that was typical of anthropologists working with the *Disappearing World* strand.
5 After an absence of twenty-five years, Agland returned to make another film in the same Baka community, with many of the original protagonists. Released in 2013, *Baka: A Cry from the Rainforest* shows that though this community is living in much the same place in the forest, their circumstances have greatly deteriorated. Their hunting and foraging territories have been circumscribed by conservation reserves while the little game that remains outside these reserves has been frightened off by logging activities. Now dependent on working for the sedentary local Bantu population, many Baka have become addicted to a highly alcoholic liquor distilled from bananas which the Bantu give them in lieu of payment. Shot in the same intimate manner, the ethnographicness of this new film is even greater than the original film. It includes less natural history footage and is narrated by Agland himself in a sensitive

and discreet manner. In June 2015, a jury that I myself chaired had no hesitation in awarding this new film the same prestigious RAI film prize that the first film had won back in 1988. At the time of writing (January 2019), Agland is preparing to make another film with the Baka but this time for cinema release.

6 In addition to these para-ethnographic observational series, in the latter part of the 1980s British television also supported a number of more discursive series based explicitly on anthropological concepts. Although ethnographic material could be used in these series to illustrate these concepts, this was mostly secondary to the analytical purposes of the programmes. The most ethnographically substantial of these series was *Native Land*, a six-part series, directed by Tim Raynor and broadcast by Channel 4 in 1989, in which the anthropologist Nigel Barley travelled around England 'to try to pin down some general idea of the contemporary English identity' (Barley 1989, 1). Somewhat earlier in the decade, in 1986, Central Television broadcast *Strangers Abroad*, which was more historical and biographical than ethnographic and which consisted of six parts, each one dedicated to the work of a leading early anthropologist. This series was directed by André Singer, formerly of *Disappearing World*, and was made shortly after he left Granada Television.

7 *The Family* is described in the Introduction to this part of the book, p. 316.

8 Lawson (1993).

9 In this section, I draw on earlier analyses of Melissa Llewelyn-Davies's work by Peter Loizos (1993), 115–38, 198–205, and Anna Grimshaw (2001), 149–71, as well as on an interview conducted with Llewelyn-Davies by Grimshaw (1995). I am also very grateful to Llewelyn-Davies herself for commenting on an earlier draft of this section.

10 For the academic publications, see Llewelyn-Davies (1978; 1981).

11 The only other cases of which I am aware are those of Hugh Brody, André Singer and Michael Yorke.

12 See Grimshaw (1995), 35, 49.

13 On the subject of her appearance in front of the lens, Llewelyn-Davies comments in her interview with Anna Grimshaw: 'I want people to see what I see; I don't think I really want them to see me seeing it. And once you see a white person in a film about black people … you kind of latch onto the white person, you start thinking about them, I think. We always used to make the attempt, but then it would end up on the cutting room floor' (Grimshaw 1995), 59.

14 Grimshaw (1995) 47, 56–8.

15 Llewelyn-Davies has given various reasons for this change of heart. These include the fact that as a young film-maker, she felt that she should protect the Maasai from all negative criticism, while with greater experience, she came to the view that she should not try to second-guess audience reactions and should put what she saw on the screen as a way of communicating her fascination with the Maasai way of life (Grimshaw 1995), 36–8, 60–1.

# 13

# The decline of ethnographic film on British television

## THE 'LESS-THAN-HAPPY MARRIAGE': THE ACADEMIC RECEPTION OF TELEVISION ETHNOGRAPHY

For a period of some twenty-five years, from the late 1960s until the mid-1990s, the television patronage of ethnographic film-making served to give academic anthropology a public profile in Britain that it had not previously enjoyed and, arguably, has not enjoyed since. Although little more than anecdotal, there is some evidence to support the view that during this period the presentation of the work of anthropologists on television served to encourage students to apply to study anthropology at university, a valuable effect in a country where anthropology is almost entirely absent from the secondary school syllabus.[1] Yet notwithstanding these positive circumstances, the reception of the films by British academic anthropologists during this period was, on the whole, no more than lukewarm.

Throughout the 'golden era', the ethnographic films broadcast on television were regularly reviewed by academic anthropologists in *RAIN*, the newsletter of the Royal Anthropological Institute (RAI), and in its successor publication, *Anthropology Today*, both under the film-sympathetic editorship of the then director of the Institute, Jonathan Benthall. (Significantly, films were only rarely reviewed in the more seriously academic journal of the Institute, which over this period still carried the anachronistic name of *Man*). Typically, these reviews would acknowledge the technical quality of the films and their potential use in teaching, but then go on to lament their deficiencies, be it in terms of content (because some aspect of the society portrayed in the film, that the reviewer deemed of fundamental importance, had not been dealt with in sufficient detail) or in terms of analytical framework (either because there was insufficient allusion to broader historical or political contexts, or because there was no explicit theoretical focus).

In later years, when reflexivity became a fashionable methodological posture in text-based anthropology, ethnographic films on television would be criticised on the grounds that they were insufficiently transparent about the circumstances of their own production and did not confess to the constructed and provisional nature of all representations of Otherness. But many of these reviews would then end with an acknowledgement – drawing to some extent their critical sting – that the film in question had, after all, been made for a mass television audience and therefore certain compromises would inevitably have been necessary in its making.[2]

However, while it is undeniable that the production of ethnographic films for television did require some degree of adjustment to the requirements of addressing a mass audience, underlying this tepid reception there was a more fundamental issue at stake, namely, the place of film of any kind, be it made for television or otherwise, in what Margaret Mead had famously described as a 'discipline of words'. For many academic anthropologists – certainly then, if less so now – would probably have had some sympathy for the views expressed by my late Manchester colleague, Paul Baxter, in the course of a lengthy review in *RAIN* of *The Rendille*, a film about camel-herding pastoralists of northern Kenya that was directed by Chris Curling for the *Disappearing World* strand and broadcast in 1977. Here, early in the review, in a much-cited passage, Paul admits to the sense that there is 'a basic incompatibility between the purposes of anthropology and the aims of film', since 'each seeks quite different aspects of truth and utilises quite different means of stitching scraps of culture together creatively'. In his view, whereas anthropology requires detailed probing of connections in order to arrive at always tentative conclusions, film in its 'bossy one-eyedness' necessarily involves an often seductively beautiful over-simplification.[3]

When he wrote this, Paul knew whereof he spoke in the sense that he had had relatively recent direct personal experience of film-making through working with James Blue and David MacDougall on a film about the Boran, another pastoralist group in the same region of Kenya.[4] But while one might agree with him that films and texts do indeed differ in the way they creatively 'stitch together' accounts of social and cultural realities, this does not necessarily imply that they are 'incompatible', at least not within a more broadly conceived multimedia anthropology. On the contrary, I would argue that the intrinsic differences between films and texts as communication media offer the opportunity for complementary forms of ethnographic representation.

Indeed, the latter part of Paul's review, much less frequently – if ever – cited, suggests precisely this for, in seeming direct contradiction to his earlier strictures on the role of film in anthropology, he then proceeds to praise in generous terms what he sees as the sustained 'aesthetic and intellectual continuity' of *The Rendille*, in particular its 'constant, but unobtrusive, awareness of the physically close relationships and symbiotic interdependence of people and stock'. He comments with approval on the way in which the various different sequences dealing with political leadership, religious belief and the management of animals reinforce one another in an incremental fashion to demonstrate the fundamental rationality of the Rendille way of dealing with the highly uncertain ecological conditions in which they live. Although he notes some minor inaccuracies in the final part of the review, he concludes by expressing the hope that 'this film will persuade some influential people that the pastoral life is useful, productive and dignified so that they will seek to alleviate its hardships, not simply stop it'.

Paul Baxter was far from alone among British academics in holding reservations about ethnographic films made for television. The sceptics included even those who were generally well disposed towards film as a medium of ethnographic representation. In a series of articles published around the turn of the 1990s, the leading British visual anthropologist, Marcus Banks, who had himself trained as a film-maker at the NFTS, questioned the whole project of making ethnographic films for television, suggesting that the involvement of anthropologists in television film-making had 'often' amounted to 'a less-than-happy marriage'. He pointed out that the decisions as to which films came to be made for television were usually taken by media professionals rather than by anthropologists with the result that the films did not necessarily reflect the priorities of the academic discipline: thus his own region of specialisation, India, although of great prominence in English-language academic anthropology, had been largely neglected by television ethnographic film series. Moreover, he argued, television ethnographic films tended to be conservative, not only stylistically but also in terms of their content, over-emphasising the study of the exotic as the defining feature of anthropology and, more generally, projecting an outdated image of the discipline as a whole. Given these circumstances, Banks proposed that anthropologists 'should not be afraid to say a polite "no, thank you"', at least to 'certain productions' and 'to welcome instead those that might be scorned by the media professionals'.[5]

Even David Turton, who as the overall anthropological adviser to *Disappearing World* remained deeply committed to making ethnographic films for television, acknowledged that by the early 1990s, the 'house style' of the strand had become outmoded and required 'radical revision'. He had various suggestions as to the forms that this revision should take, but the most fundamental was that the strand should abandon the 'distanced empiricism' that had characterised both academic anthropology and the strand when it first began in the 1970s, and adopt instead a more reflexive mode of enquiry, so that the films would be presented to the television audience 'more as encounters than as observations, more as dialogue *with* than as dialogues *about* people'. This would mean that both anthropologists and film-makers would have to reveal more about themselves, including their mistakes and misunderstandings, which could be 'uncomfortable'. But, he believed, it would also make the films more interesting for the television audience and hence one could have the best of both worlds: not only would it make for better anthropology, it would also make for better television.[6]

## THE RETREATING TIDE OF ETHNOGRAPHIC FILM ON TELEVISION

But even as Banks and Turton were offering these criticisms and suggestions for rebooting the marriage of academic anthropology and television, the first signs of a separation were already apparent, and these would eventually lead to a full-scale divorce. Over the course of the 1990s, the presence of ethnographic film on British television would be like an ebbtide: although there were temporary resurgences, the overall pattern was one of decline and retreat.

The initiative for this parting of ways came as much from the television as from the academic side of the relationship. For, by the beginning of the decade, the same neoliberal forces that Molly Dineen had shown at work in *The Ark*, described in Chapter 12, were also affecting British television. As a consequence of the Broadcasting Act of 1991, the obligation on franchise holders to produce educational material diminished and the importance attributed to audience viewing figures correspondingly increased. At the same time, with the emergence of television delivered through extra-terrestrial satellites, the number of channels available in Britain increased exponentially. Until 1982, when Channel 4 came on stream, there had only been three channels: two were public service broadcasting channels operated by the BBC, the other was a commercial channel operated on a regional franchise basis. It was on this commercial channel that the *Disappearing World* films were broadcast. But by the end of the 1980s, there were at least forty channels, mostly operating on the basis of exclusively commercial criteria and no longer necessarily tied to regional franchises.[7]

This combination of factors directly conspired against the making of ethnographic films for television. For relative to the numbers of viewers who wanted to watch them, ethnographic films were expensive to make as they typically involved long shoots, usually abroad. In an unmitigated cost–benefit equation of production costs balanced against audience figures, a game show had always been a more commercially attractive proposition than an ethnographic film: only the obligation to produce educational programming had weighted the balance towards ethnographic film. Moreover, in a three- or four-channel environment, if an ethnographic film was showing on one channel, potential viewers did not have many other choices, so they might stay with the ethnographic programme, even if their first preference might not have been to watch a subtitled film about, say, symbiotic relationships between pastoralists and sedentary agriculturalists in East Africa. These circumstances explained why, in 1982, a *Disappearing World* film on just such a topic, *The Kwegu*, could earn viewing figures of several million people when it was broadcast, at prime time, on a weekday evening. But by the early 1990s, the ground rules were very different and viewing figures for ethnographic films began to fall drastically. As a result, in the particular case of *Disappearing World*, the programmes were scheduled at increasingly later times, outside prime time. Predictably, in the implacable Catch-22 logic of television, this merely increased the decline in viewing figures so that eventually, in 1993, the series was finally and definitively axed.

Similar processes were taking place during this period across British television, on the BBC as well as on the commercial channels. The general pattern of temporary resurgences within an overall pattern of decline is well exemplified by the BBC strand *Under the Sun*, which produced around 50 programmes between 1989 and 1999 over the course of ten series. The first executive producer was Chris Curling, who moved to the BBC studios at Elstree on the northwestern outskirts of London, after the *Worlds Apart* strand produced out of the BBC Bristol studios had come to an end. However, the format of *Under the Sun* was significantly different from that of *Worlds Apart*. Although all ten of the programmes in the first series, which straddled 1989 and 1990, were in some sense about 'other cultures' and, as such, of potential ethnographic interest, only one was directly based on the field research of an academic consultant anthropologist. This was *The Shaman and His Apprentice*, based on the work of Graham Townsley among the Yaminahua of Peruvian Amazonia and directed by Howard Reid, who held an anthropology doctorate from Cambridge and had first entered television as a researcher on the *Worlds Apart* strand.[8]

The same overall pattern was repeated in later series of the *Under the Sun* strand, as series producers with no connection to anthropology succeeded Curling. Even so, there continued to be occasional examples of films that were based directly on the ethnographic research of academic anthropologists, and which were of a quality that rivalled the best that *Disappearing World* had been able to achieve in its heyday. One example was an impressive trilogy of films about the Hamar pastoralists of southern Ethiopia produced over the course of several series of *Under the Sun* between 1990 and 1994. These films were directed by Joanna Head, a School of Oriental and African Studies (SOAS) anthropology graduate who had also entered television as a researcher through *Worlds Apart*, and were made in collaboration with Jean Lydall, the anthropologist who, with her husband, Ivo Strecker, had worked on Robert Gardner's *Rivers of Sand*.[9] Meanwhile, another SOAS anthropology alumnus, Jean-Paul Davidson, directed two films about the Mehinacu of the Xingu National Park in Central Brazil based on the work of eminent Amazonist Thomas Gregor, who had been one of the consultants on the celebrated 1974 series of *Disappearing World*. One of these,

*Feathered Arrows*, was broadcast in 1990, and the other, *Dreams from the Forest*, in 1993.[10]

Yet another SOAS alumnus, Michael Yorke, who had completed a doctorate based on his work with the 'tribal' Gond population and acted as both director and academic consultant on the *Worlds Apart* strand, also made a number of films for *Under the Sun*. These included the remarkable *Dust and Ashes*, which featured in the 1989 series, and which concerned the vast Kumbh Mela pilgrimage to the banks of the Ganges near Allahabad. The following year, the strand featured *The Left-handed Man of Madagascar*, a film based on the work of anthropologist John Mack, then of the British Museum, and directed by Jeremy Marre. In the 1994 series, Paul Reddish directed *Guardians of the Flutes*, a film about male initiation, in collaboration with the eminent Melanesianist anthropologist Gilbert Herdt. But these examples were few and far between: the great majority of films made for the *Under the Sun* strand as it continued through the 1990s had little or no connection to academic anthropology.

Films based on the work of academic anthropologists and conforming broadly to the one-by-four format still continued to surface occasionally on Channel 4. In 1991, this channel broadcast a four-part series, *Nomads*, three of which were based on the work of academic anthropologists. From time to time, the ecology-oriented strand, *Fragile Earth* would also include a film of this kind. In 1993, it broadcast *Survivors of the Rainforest*, a film about the Yanomami of Venezuelan Amazonia. This was directed and shot by Andy Jillings, a film-maker trained in the Observational Cinema approach at the NFTS, while the anthropologist-consultant was the French anthropologist, Jacques Lizot, who by that time had been working with the Yanomami for some twenty-five years, more or less consecutively. Though not well known in academic circles, this film represented a considerable advance on the films in the Asch–Chagnon canon: not only is it much better shot, but it is editorially richer in an ethnographic sense too. The central feature of this film, as in the Asch–Chagnon work, *The Feast*, is a collective feast aimed at re-establishing the alliance between two warring villages. But in this case, not only is the feast itself presented, but the background to the tension between the two villages is explored as well (figure 13.1). This film also covers a number of other topics, some of which are also covered in the Asch–Chagnon films (shamanic curing, children playing) but some of which are not, notably an extended sequence on funerary practices.[11]

Another example of a temporary resurgence within the general ebbing away of ethnographic film on British television in the 1990s was the *Fine Cut* strand, for which André Singer acted as the first series producer. Singer's brief on his appointment was to schedule 'auteur' feature documentaries and under this guise, 'almost by subterfuge' as he himself has put it, *Fine Cut* supported either the making, or the broadcasting, of a number of films

**13.1** *Survivors of the Rainforest* (1993). During a three-day feast of reconciliation between warring villages, Hisiwe, left, leader of a Yanomami village on the upper Orinoco, Venezuela, sits with his guests as they watch the dancing.

by leading ethnographic film-makers. These included Robert Gardner's masterwork, *Forest of Bliss* and Jean Rouch's late work, *Madame l'eau*. The strand also broadcast *Titicut Follies*, a portrait of a Massachusetts institution for the 'criminally insane' that was directed by Fred Wiseman and shot (in some accounts co-directed) by John Marshall, which in the USA had languished under a ban for many years. It also produced Melissa Llewelyn-Davies's *Memories and Dreams* (discussed at length in Chapter 12), and contributed to the budget of David MacDougall's film, *Tempus de Baristas*, released in 1993 (to be considered in Chapter 14). But Singer then left the strand and in 1994, it was put in the charge of Nick Fraser, who changed the strand name to *Storyville*, which it retains to this day. Fraser's interests in documentary lay elsewhere and once he took over, the strand no longer supported ethnographic film-making.[12]

## THE PERSISTENCE OF PARA-ETHNOGRAPHIC FILM-MAKING

Although films based explicitly on academic ethnographic research were becoming increasingly rare as the 1990s progressed, British television continued to support documentary series that were 'para-ethnographic' in the sense

376

defined in the Introduction to this part of the book. Paul Watson returned to the form in two series that were very different in terms of their subject matter but which were both based on participant-observation of the subjects over a prolonged period: one of these, *Sylvania Waters*, concerned a nouveau riche middle-class family in a wealthy suburb of Sydney, broadcast by the BBC in 1992, while the other, *The Factory*, produced for Granada Television in 1995, followed the struggles of one of the last remnants of manufacturing in what had once been a highly industrialised part of Liverpool. Both series, in their different ways, confirmed Watson as an acute and critical observer of the cultural attitudes and practices that serve both to demarcate and sustain class differences. This was a seam that had run through all his work since *The Family*, including also his oblique but highly controversial 'fly-on-the-wall' representations of British elites in one-off documentaries such as *The Fishing Party* (1986) and later, *The Dinner Party* (1997).

Other notable examples of para-ethnographic works on British television in the 1990s include two remarkable series that Phil Agland shot in China. The first, *Beyond the Clouds*, in seven parts and broadcast in 1994, was filmed in and around the traditional town of Lijiang in Yunnan province, in the southwest of the People's Republic, while the second, *Shanghai Vice*, also in seven parts and broadcast in 1999, concerned China's so-called 'second city'. Both series were built on the same mix of authorial strategies that Agland had deployed in making *Baka*: two years in production permitting the development of relationships of trust with the protagonists as well as an understanding of their situation and the necessary linguistic competence; an interwoven set of narratives constructed around the experiences of a small group of key characters; observational cinematography of the absolutely highest quality which was then cut according to the continuity codes of fictional cinema, with assistance from an actorly voice-over and passages of extra-diegetic music with a local flavour. There were no interviews: instead the voice-over served as the principal means for providing the necessary social and political contexts.[13]

Whereas *Baka* had been based around a single local group and had focused mostly on one particular nuclear family, the cast of characters of Agland's Chinese films was much broader and they were related to one another primarily by geography rather than through family ties. In *Beyond the Clouds*, these characters come from various different groups within Lijiang and include an acupuncturist doctor, a butcher, a schoolteacher and a carpenter from the local Yi ethnic minority, as well as four elderly 'grannies' who dress in traditional Naxi minority dress and do everything together. In *Shanghai Vice*, they include the daughter of the Lijiang doctor, Teng Shao, who has come to Shanghai to study, thereby linking the two series, as well as a diverse range of other characters, including Teng Shao's landlady, the latter's gentleman companion who is a professor of Japanese, a well-known

**13.2** Film series made in China by Phil Agland. Left, the acupuncturist Dr Teng is a leading character in *Beyond the Clouds* (1994), while his daughter, Teng Shao, and her extrovert landlady, Mrs Feng, right, feature prominently in *Shanghai Vice* (1999).

radio talk-show host, a group of Chinese opera performers, as well as a young boy suffering from a serious heart condition and the surgeon who operates on him (figure 13.2).

While the Chinese films continue to focus on intimate personal experience, and even include sequences in which characters discuss their love life in a relatively uninhibited manner, the underlying themes are social and political rather than ecological, as they had been in *Baka*. One of these themes, which emerges in *Beyond the Clouds* and then becomes central to *Shanghai Vice*, is crime and its (sometimes capital) punishment in contemporary Chinese society. Indeed, the title of the latter series is a reference to the fact that one of the most important characters is Zhu Daren, a leading figure in the Shanghai police force: the work of Zhu and his colleagues in tackling murderers, rapists and particularly drug-dealers serves as one of the principal vehicles through which we are introduced to everyday life in contemporary Shanghai. The access that Agland gained to the most undercover of these police activities was truly extraordinary, particularly in a totalitarian state not known for its concern for transparency. The action cuts back and forth between the lives of the various characters, and through this mosaic offers the audience what is, in effect, a thoroughly engaging ethnographic portrait of the city as it opened up following the reforms promoted by Deng Xiaoping.

Another film-maker working in a para-ethnographic manner and whose work became prominent on British television over the 1990s was Kim Longinotto. Like Toni de Bromhead and Molly Dineen, Longinotto had also trained as a film-maker at the NFTS in the heyday of the observational ethos there and like them, she shoots all her own material, always supported, in her case, by a woman sound recordist. However, Longinotto had attended the school somewhat earlier than de Bromhead and Dineen, that is, in the

**13.3** Films by Kim Longinotto. Left, in *Divorce Iranian Style* (2004), a woman pleads for divorce in an Islamic court in Tehran; right, on the other side of the bench, a Senegalese judge dispenses justice in *Sisters in Law* (2005).

mid-1970s when the dominant influence in the documentary department was more the approach of Direct Cinema than the anthropologically inflected Observational Cinema approach that would become prominent in the school in the 1980s. Perhaps for this reason, Longinotto's authorial signature is less overtly reflexive and certainly less conversational than the authorial signatures of de Bromhead and Dineen.

Throughout a long career, embracing more than twenty films, the recurrent leitmotif of Longinotto's work has been women's struggle to throw off repressive or restrictive gender roles, a theme that she has pursued in a number of different cultural contexts around the world. In the early 1990s, she made a number of films about women contesting conventional gender roles in Japan, two of which were broadcast as part of the BBC's *Under the Sun* strand. But in 1998, she expanded her range, collaborating with the Cambridge-trained Iranian legal anthropologist Ziba Mir-Hosseini to make *Divorce Iranian Style*, a feature-length film produced for Channel 4 that followed the struggles of three women to secure their rights in an Iranian divorce court (figure 13.3, left). In order to make this film, which was shot over a period of a month, the all-women crew and Mir-Hosseini meticulously observed Islamic dress codes whenever they were filming in the court.[14] Three years later, Longinotto and Mir-Hosseini returned to Iran to make *Runaway*, also for Channel 4, which offered a classical observational portrait of an institution, in this case, a refuge for girls who have run away from repressive family environments.

Since these Iranian films, Longinotto has made an impressive series of feature-length television documentaries about women who reject conventional expectations or who campaign against injustice in many different parts of the world. These films, sometimes made in collaboration with a co-director, have featured such diverse subjects as the team of doughty female wrestlers in Japan who are the focus of *Gaea Girls* (2000), the equally redoutable Cameroonian lawyers who are central to *Sisters in Law* (2005) and the extraordinary Tamil women's rights poet and activist who is the eponymous principal character of *Salma* (2013) (figure 13.3, right). Although none of these later films involved collaboration with academic anthropologists, their ethnographic qualities have been recognised in their frequent selection for self-definingly ethnographic film festivals, where they have been awarded prizes and commendations. Another indirect indicator of their ethnographic status is that almost all Longinotto's major films are now distributed by the Royal Anthropological Institute.[15]

Towards the end of the 1990s, a rather different form of para-ethnographic film-making became prominent on British television. This was enabled by developments in lightweight digital video technology which allowed a single person to shoot and at the same time to record sound with the aid of radio microphones, while also maintaining a sufficiently high technical standard for the work to be broadcast on national television. One of the pioneers of this way of working was Chris Terrill, who holds a doctorate from the University of Durham based on anthropological fieldwork in southern Sudan. In interviews, Terrill has explained that participant-observation over an extended period, the attempt to see the world through the subjects' eyes and a non-judgemental ethical positioning – all classical markers of the ethnographic method – are central to his practice as a film-maker. Having already worked with a conventional crew to make *HMS Brilliant*, an observational series broadcast by the BBC in 1995 about life on board a naval ship, Terrill shot and recorded the twelve-part series *Soho Stories* on his own. First broadcast on BBC Two in 1996, this offered a portrait of the well-known red-light and entertainment zone in central London through interweaving the personal stories of a varied collection of its inhabitants. Later, he applied the same methods to a range of institutions, including a cruise ship, a women's prison and various military and naval units on active service.

These developments in lightweight digital technology also underpinned the emergence of a new system for producing documentary series for British television around this time. This involved the commissioning, within the general rubric of a given series, of a number of freelance film-makers to make films for which they would act as camera operator, sound recordist and 'on-location director'. However, the editing of the footage that they produced would then be entirely controlled by the series producer and if the 'on-location directors' entered the edit suite at all, it would be merely to offer suggestions on the cuts produced by the series producer and the editor.

The production company Mosaic Pictures played a leading role in developing this format and produced a number of series in this way, including

13.4 *Royal Watchers* (1997). The Queen, left, meets the 'royalists' outside Lincoln Cathedral in October 1996, while Diana, Princess of Wales, right, meets the same group in London three days later.

series about Russia, the UK and the European Union. Although some of the films produced for these series had certain para-ethnographic qualities, very few were based on anything that one could describe as extended ethnographic research. One exception was *Royal Watchers*, produced by Mosaic Pictures in 1997. I myself shot, took sound and directed this film on location, and it was made in active collaboration with the Manchester anthropologist Anne Rowbottom. Broadcast by BBC Two as part of their series *United Kingdom*, this film was based on Rowbottom's doctoral research into popular perceptions of the British monarchy and, in particular, her fieldwork among a highly dedicated group of self-defining 'royalists' who travel all over the country to attend royal 'walkabouts' (figure 13.4).[16]

Over the same period, lightweight digital technology was also associated with the development of the so-called 'docu-soap' format on British television. In contrast to the para-ethnographic works of Watson or Dineen, Agland or Longinotto, or even the series produced by Mosaic Pictures, it was no longer a central concern for those working in the docu-soap format to make some sort of comment upon social or political matters. Rather, the principal aim was simply to follow the interplay of a select group of per-sonalities, often carefully chosen on account of their eccentricity, with the action cutting repeatedly back and forth between them in a series of very short scenes, in the manner of a fictional soap opera.

While arguably even these series could be said to have had certain minimally descriptive ethnographic qualities, the subject matter was typically very trivial, focusing on the most banal activities of the practitioners of particular occupations, such as driving instructors, traffic wardens, vets and holiday tour 'reps'. Soon, even these modest real-life ethnographic contexts were abandoned as the format morphed again and was reduced merely to the interplay of eccentric personalities in the entirely artificial social environ-ment of the Big Brother house.[17]

# ETHNOGRAPHIC FILM-MAKING ON BRITISH TELEVISION SINCE THE MILLENIUM

By the early years of the new century, film-making based directly on ethnographic research by academic anthropologists in particular communities or with particular groups of people had almost disappeared without trace from British television. In the latter part of the 1990s, a number of series involving co-production deals with US television channels had dealt with such classical anthropological topics as magic, sacrifice, head-hunting and cannibalism, but these were more in the comparative format of earlier BBC series such as *Family of Man* and *Face Values* as described in Chapter 11. That is, the constituent programmes were typically structured around a central argument delivered through voice-over commentary that was then illustrated by footage relating to a range of different societies. This footage was often second-hand or archival rather than being dedicated material shot expressly for the series in question. Over time, these co-productions had a tendency to become increasingly archaeological or historical rather than anthropological, dealing with such topics as mummification, Ancient Egypt or medieval witchcraft.[18]

In 2001, commissioned by the Channel 4 strand, *True Stories*, Leslie Woodhead and David Turton returned to Ethiopia to make a sixth film with the Mursi. This was *Fire Will Eat Us*, which showed how the Mursi had been reduced to performing a simulacrum of their life for tourists. But this was possibly the very last example of a British television film based directly on academic research according to the classic 'one-by-four' model developed on *Disappearing World*. By 2003, a leading British anthropologist could lament in print, only partly in jest, that the only time that anthropology was likely to be referred to on British television was in the form of a particularly difficult quiz show jackpot question, 'What is anthropology?'[19]

The situation has not changed significantly in the years since then: the tide of anthropologically informed ethnographic film on British television remains at a very low ebb. In 2004, a new strand appeared on British television screens, produced by BBC Wales, which was widely dubbed as 'anthropological' in the British press, including in the more 'serious' newspapers. This was *Tribe* (screened on US television as *Going Tribal*), a travel show featuring a supposedly intrepid explorer, a former Royal Marine and physical education instructor, who visited 'tribal' peoples around the world for up to a month at a time, submitting himself to physical ordeals in the process. In each programme, he gave simple to-camera explanations about the way of life of his hosts and usually made something of a fool of himself trying to perform traditional male tasks, much to his hosts' amusement. At the end of each programme, he would routinely declare how honoured he felt to have been received by his hosts and that he would never forget the experience of getting to know them.

This presenter had no anthropological training, did not speak the local languages and his visits were very short, at least by anthropological standards, so not surprisingly his understanding of the societies whose lives he presented to the world was no more than superficial. To do them justice, although the series clearly played into popular perceptions of anthropology, the producers themselves never claimed that the strand was anthropological. The academic anthropologists who reviewed *Tribe* radically disowned it, but in terms of audience viewing figures it was highly successful, and went through three series.[20]

More generally, if anthropologically informed ethnographic film-making has been taking place at all on British television since the millenium, it is because anthropology graduates continue to enter British television taking with them certain anthropological ideas, attitudes and methods that can remain discernible in their work, even if they are heavily overlaid by the stylistic conventions and formats of present-day British television production. A good example here is *Welcome to Lagos*, a three-part series produced by Keo Films for the BBC, which was broadcast in 2010 and won several highly prestigious awards, including from the Royal Television Society and BAFTA, the British Association of Film and Television Arts – the British equivalent of the Academy of Motion Picture Arts. The series was shot in an observational manner over a period of several months by Gavin Searle, and executive produced by Andrew Palmer, both of whom had studied with us at the Granada Centre for Visual Anthropology at the University of Manchester.

This series follows the experiences of a number of different subjects living in the most marginal areas of the most populous urban centre in Africa. Many of those featured in the series had migrated to the Nigerian mega-city from all over West Africa in search of a better life, and rather than bemoaning their poverty and deprivation, *Welcome to Lagos* celebrates their resourcefulness and enterprise (figure 13.5). In both these respects, the series is reminiscent of, and a worthy successor to, *Jaguar*, Jean Rouch's classic film about migrants to Accra and Kumasi shot in the mid-1950s, even if some viewers had reservations about the patronising tone of the voice-over commentary and the Nigerian government detested it because it suggested that the whole of Lagos consisted of shanty towns.

But apart from these almost covert examples of programmes underpinned by an ethnographic sensibility, there is little evidence of a turning of the tide and a return to anything like the vast investment of time and resources in films based directly on academic anthropologists' research that was a defining feature of the 'golden era' of ethnographic film on British television. This is a matter of regret, of course, but this regret about the present state

**13.5** *Welcome to Lagos* (2010). Left, cattle are brought to Lagos market from as far away as Chad and Southern Sudan. Right, Eric Obuh, aka 'Vocal Slender', scavenges in the rubbish tip to pay for his music recording career.

of affairs should not blind us to the value of the legacies left by that immensely productive period.

## The legacies of British television ethnography

As I described at the beginning of Chapter 11, the great commitment to ethnographic film-making on British television during the 'golden era' can be traced to the unique circumstances of commercial television in the post-war period and, more particularly, to Sir Denis Forman's highly personal belief that a series of ethnographic films about groups whose very existence was under threat would result in an archival record that would be of inestimable value in the future. Even in the early 1970s when the *Disappearing World* strand first began, this interest in 'salvage' ethnography was regarded by many anthropologists as highly anachronistic. By the time the strand ceased in 1993, it had become even more out of tune with what were then the cutting-edge concerns of the academic discipline of anthropology as a whole.

Yet even while one might readily acknowledge these intellectual limitations and while it seems that all the groups who featured in the series, even the Cuiva, have survived physically, there can surely be no doubt that in the four decades since *Disappearing World* was first broadcast, the great majority of these groups have undergone major social and cultural changes as they have become progressively incorporated into a more globalised world. Thus, however contestable the original motivations or however inappropriate the series title, the ethnographic films produced for British television, either by the *Disappearing World* strand itself or by its many imitators, offer a now irreplaceable account of the social and cultural diversity of the world as it was in the second half of the twentieth century.

Moreover, although they may have been given only a lukewarm reception by academic anthropologists at the time they were made, the films of the *Disappearing World* strand continue to be widely used in the teaching of anthropology both in Britain and the USA, despite the fact that even the most recent of these films is more than twenty-five years years old.[21] In part, this is because although, in theory, given the greater technical ease and lower cost of making films with digital technology, academic anthropologists could now be making their own ethnographic films, as has often been optimistically proposed by critics of television films in the past, in practice this has simply not happened, certainly not to any major extent. The reasons for this are too complex to consider here, but they include the continuing low status of ethnographic film-making in a 'discipline of words' and the associated difficulty of accruing any professional academic credit from making ethnographic films. This is compounded by the continuing failure on the part of many academic anthropologists to appreciate the potential of visual media for communicating their knowledge and understanding not just to non-specialist audiences, but also to their academic colleagues.

But the films themselves are not the only legacy of the sponsorship of ethnographic film-making by British television. Another of which I am particularly aware, for obvious reasons, is the Granada Centre for Visual Anthropology, which was created as a direct result of the *Disappearing World* strand. In the first instance, it was the product of a joint initiative by David Turton, overall anthropological consultant to the strand, and then a member of staff of the Department of Social Anthropology at the University of Manchester, and Leslie Woodhead, the *Disappearing World* producer-director with whom Turton had collaborated in making a trilogy of films about the Mursi pastoralists of Ethiopia between 1974 and 1985, as described in Chapter 11. In 1987, with the active support of Marilyn Strathern, head of the Department of Social Anthropology, Turton and Woodhead persuaded David Plowright – who with Denis Forman had been one of the original initiators of *Disappearing World* and who was by then the chief executive of Granada Television – to provide some financial backing for the creation of a centre that would offer a Masters programme in visual anthropology.

The sum provided was relatively modest, and was far outweighed by the investment made in the centre by the University of Manchester itself. But it was offered entirely without strings and continued on an annual basis until as late as 2007, long after the closure of *Disappearing World* in 1993. As such, it acted as seed-corn funding that allowed us to develop the centre in a variety of different directions, including the creation of a doctoral programme to supplement the original Masters programme, and more recently, a short course aimed specifically at ethnographic researchers. As a result, several hundred people from all over the world have now been instructed in practical ethnographic film-making as they have passed through these various programmes.[22]

There is, finally, a somewhat more intangible but equally important legacy of the twenty-five years of sponsorship of ethnographic film-making by British television. During that time, many talented film-makers – including here cinematographers, sound recordists and editors as well as producer-directors – became involved in making ethnographic films for television and developed a broad and highly skilled range of ways of doing so within the constraints of the need to address audiences counted in millions. As I have described in earlier chapters of this book, there is a long tradition in ethnographic film-making of drawing upon modes of authorship first developed outside the specialist, mostly academic world in which ethnographic film-making has typically been practised: just as Jean Rouch was inspired by Robert Flaherty, so Robert Gardner was inspired by Basil Wright and Colin Young by the Italian Neorealist cinema. In the same way, rather than looking down on them because they were produced for a mass medium, as is too frequently the tendency, ethnographic film-makers would do well to study the films produced for British television in the 'golden era' and explore the ways in which the authorial praxes that their makers developed for making films in that environment could enrich their own repertoires.

## Notes

1 In 1989, the Royal Anthropological Institute carried out a survey among first-year students of anthropology, receiving 256 responses. Of these, 25 per cent said that they had first come across anthropology through 'seeing films or TV programmes', a proportion exceeded only by 'talking to friends or relatives' (27 per cent) and considerably higher than 'reading books' (18 per cent) or 'advice from schoolteacher' (9 per cent). See Richardson (1990).

2 When the *Disappearing World* series was exported to the USA and shown on television there, reviews also began to appear in *American Anthropologist*. Although these could sometimes be highly dismissive, they tended on balance to be more appreciative than the reviews written by British academics. I suspect that this was a consequence of the fact that at that time, US anthropologists had been using film in teaching for much longer than their British colleagues and were more accustomed to assessing them on their own terms as films rather than as failed texts. It was probably for this same reason that the producers of the *Disappearing World* strand found that there was generally a much greater interest on the part of US academics in acting as consultants on the strand (David Wason, personal communication, September 2014). See also the comments of Terence Turner, a US anthropologist who worked in the UK as a consultant for both the BBC and for the *Disappearing World* strand (Turner 1992b).

3 Baxter (1977).

4 See p. 173 note 5 regarding Baxter's work with Blue and MacDougall on *Kenya Boran*.

5 See Banks (1988); (1992), 116; (1994).

6 Turton (1992a).

7 See Singer (1992), 271; Singer with Seidenberg (1992), 124.

8 See Banks (1994), 25–30 for an overview of the first two series of the *Under the Sun* strand.

9 See Chapter 9, pp. 260–1 and also Chapter 16, pp. 470–6 for an extended discussion of these films as well as of *Duka's Dilemma* (2002), a fourth film about the Hamar directed by Lydall independently of the BBC.

10 Around the same time, Jean-Paul Davidson also directed a film about another Xinguano group, the Waurá, in collaboration with the Yale anthropologist, Emelienne Ireland, for a different BBC strand, *Bookmark*. This charming film, *The Storyteller*, broadcast in 1990, concerns the enactment of mythological events by the Waurá and anticipates the films made by the Video nas Aldeias film-makers Takumã and Maricá Kuikuro, as discussed in Chapter 7, pp. 216–18.

11 For a more detailed review of this film, see Henley (1999). See Chapter 4, for a discussion of the Asch–Chagnon films, pp. 142–9.

12 It was Nick Fraser's rejection of David MacDougall's proposal to make a film about the Doon School in India that in 1997 led MacDougall to begin shooting with very much cheaper digital technology and to adapt his authorial strategies accordingly. See Chapter 14.

13 See Chapter 12, pp. 352–5 for a discussion of *Baka*.

14 Ziba Mir-Hosseini has published an interesting account of the making of *Divorce Iranian Style* and the diverse reactions to the film afterwards, both within Iran and abroad (2002). A sign of the times is the striking contrast between the obligation on Mir-Hosseini, Longinotto and their colleagues to wear the full hijab in order to make their film in Iran in 1997 with the situation twenty years earlier when the all-women crew took off all their clothes to shoot one of the scenes in *Some Women of Marrakesh*, as described in Chapter 11, p. 336.

15 See raifilm.org.uk/films/.

16 See Rowbottom (2002a, 2002b).

17 For a good discussion of docu-soaps, see Bruzzi (2000), 75–98.

18 A number of these thematic series made in collaboration with US channels were executively produced by André Singer. These included *Divine Magic* (1996), a ten-part series for Channel 4 and Discovery Channel, and *Forbidden Rites* (1999), a three-part series co-produced and co-directed with Tom Sheahan for the National Geographic Channel and also screened on Channel 4.

19 Sillitoe (2003), 2.

20 For critical assessments, see Caplan (2005) and Hughes-Freeland (2006). But see also the response of André Singer, who was involved in the production of the series (Singer 2006).

21 In the five year period 2009–14 the RAI, one of the principal distributors of films from the *Disappearing World* strand, sold an average of around 150 copies of the films a year, mostly to educational institutions for teaching purposes (Susanne Hammacher, RAI Film Officer, personal communication, October 2014).

22 Granada Television itself has not merely abandoned ethnographic film-making but all forms of factual film-making, including even its flagship current affairs programmes. In fact, in legal terms, it now exists only as a regional badge for the London-based media corporation, Independent Television (ITV).

# Part IV
# Beyond observation: ethnographic film in the twenty-first century

# Introduction

IN this last part of the book, over the course of three chapters, I consider a number of recent examples of English-language ethnographic film-making. These films have mostly been produced in the first decade and a half of the twenty-first century, though I also discuss a number of films produced in the last decade of the twentieth. As with the whole of the book, it is a partial selection, in both senses of the term. That is, I make no claim that it is either a representative or a comprehensive sample of the English-language ethnographic films that have been produced since the millenium. It is rather a selection of films that seem to me to have had a significant impact or which provide potentially interesting models for the future direction of the genre – given the particular ideas advanced in this book about the nature of contemporary ethnographic practice and the way in which it may be realised through film.

These three chapters correspond, more or less, to the three modes of authorial praxis that I consider in Chapters 8–10, albeit in reverse order. In Chapter 14, I examine how David and Judith MacDougall have developed the practice of Observational Cinema; in Chapter 15, I explore in what ways certain film-makers of the Sensory Ethnography Lab (SEL) at Harvard have taken on the legacy of Robert Gardner, while in the final chapter, Chapter 16, I consider a number of films that draw on the participatory praxis that informed Jean Rouch's concept of shared anthropology

Central to all three chapters is the argument that has been a guiding thread through the book as a whole, namely, that in order to make films that are ethnographic in anything more than a descriptive sense, it is necessary to go beyond observation and to explore the connections between the practices, ideas and relations that underpin and constitute the social worlds represented in those films. This, I have suggested, often requires some recourse to language, be it in a literal sense in the form of verbal discourse or in a more metaphorical cinematographic narrative form.

This argument is somewhat at odds with a set of views that in recent years have become almost an orthodoxy in certain spheres of ethnographic film-making. For if it is true that once upon a time, ethnographic film-makers had to struggle against a certain 'iconophobia' within the academic discipline of anthropology, now the wheel appears to have gone full circle, and it has become necessary to combat a deep-seated 'logophobia' that has taken root instead. The principal reason for the current antipathy to the use of language in ethnographic film-making appears to be the belief that language is inimical to the evocation of sensorial experience, a goal that has recently become a matter of great importance to ethnographers generally. The medium of film offers the possibility of evoking sensorial experience with a density and a corporeality that goes far beyond anything that may be achieved through text. Therefore, it is suggested, to burden a film with language is to undermine its greatest potential contribution to the practice of ethnography.

There is no doubt that when one introduces language into a film, there is a risk that this will undermine its sensorial qualities. A film smothered with voice-over commentary, or dominated by 'talking heads' delivering facts and figures can all-too-readily become 'a radio programme with pictures', as my tutor at the NFTS, Herb di Gioia, used to put it, growling. But if more than a century of ethnographic endeavour has proved anything, it is surely that even the most private, even the most subjective forms of experience are informed and moulded by the social and cultural environments in which they take place. Thus the mere evocation of experience, however exquisitely achieved, is not in itself of any more than descriptive ethnographic significance.

Given that language is often the most effective way to communicate the nature of the social and cultural environments in which experience takes place, it is of vital importance that ethnographic film-makers, rejecting both iconophobia and logophobia, confront the challenge of how to reconcile the analytical and contextualising qualities of language with the distinctive sensorial and experiential qualities of cinematic images. But in doing so, they should always bear in mind Robert Flaherty's remark that 'you can't say as much in a film as you can in writing, but what you can say, you can say with great conviction'.[1] Better then to say only a little, but with great conviction, rather than sink your film under a heavy layer of language in the vain hope of saying everything.

## Note

1  Cited in Ruby (2000), 86. The remark was originally made in 1949 in a talk for BBC radio.

# 14

# The evolution of Observational Cinema: recent films of David and Judith MacDougall

As originally conceived by Colin Young and subsequently worked out in practice by David and Judith MacDougall and various other film-makers, the praxis of Observational Cinema in its classical form involved very much more than observation: not only was it a particular 'way of seeing', it was also a particular 'way of doing' ethnographic film-making. Central to this praxis, as described in earlier chapters, was a collaborative relationship with the subjects, the adoption of an 'unprivileged' perspective in both shooting and editing, and a low-key aesthetic based on the preservation during editing of the original sounds and rhythms of the way of life recorded.[1]

In order to provide context and meaning, this praxis also typically featured the extensive use of conversational exchanges not only between subjects but also between subjects and film-makers. Although the overall aim was to provide the viewer with some sense of the film-makers' original experience of the subjects' world, this was often presented through relatively conventional but often almost invisible 'restrained' narrative tropes, inspired originally by the films of the French New Wave and Italian Neorealists. Taken together, these constituted the principal ingredients of a discreet but nevertheless considered form of participatory and reflexive ethnographic film-making praxis.

The precise balance between these various elements in the praxis of Observational Cinema has varied in accordance with both the subject matter and the social and political circumstances in which the films were made, not to mention the idiosyncratic inclinations and interests of individual film-makers. In the particular case of the MacDougalls, described in Chapter 5, when they moved from filming among the pastoralist peoples of East Africa in the late 1970s in order to take up posts with the Film Unit of the Australian Institute of Aboriginal Studies (AIAS), the participatory element in their films became very much more pronounced as they and their Aboriginal subjects sought to develop more overtly collaborative ways of working with one another.

But after more than a decade making films with Aboriginal communities, the MacDougalls began to feel that this sharing of authorship involved so many compromises that the resulting films spoke neither for the subjects, nor for themselves as film-makers, but rather for some indeterminate third party, which, in effect, meant for nobody. They therefore resigned their posts at the AIAS in the late 1980s and though they remained based in Australia, they set themselves up as freelance ethnographic documentary film-makers.[2]

Since then, the MacDougalls have released a total of fifteen films between them. Apart from one solo film that David made in Sardinia and another that Judith made in China, all these films have been made in India. Moreover, the great majority of these Indian films have concerned the lives of children living in institutions of one kind or another. With one exception, these films about children have all been made by David working alone. When all these post-AIAS works are added together, they amount to almost half the MacDougalls' total oeuvre to date. In terms of the sheer number of films, they come to slightly less than the nineteen films that they made in Africa and Australia. But in terms of running time, they actually exceed the total duration of all the African and Australian films put together: whereas the latter comes to close to twenty hours, the films that the MacDougalls have made since leaving the AIAS total slightly more than twenty-two hours.[3]

This substantial body of later work deserves a far more extended discussion than is possible here. What I offer in this chapter is no more than an outline account of how the MacDougalls' work has evolved sine the early 1990s. While they have continued to draw on key elements of Observational Cinema as it was practised in the 1970s and 1980s, they have reinterpreted and expanded this praxis through a constant process of experimentation and innovation. While some of their films have conformed quite closely to the classical model, others have departed from it to a significant degree.

## CONTINUITIES AND RUPTURES

Although the MacDougalls have stepped back from the explicit sharing of authorship that characterised their work with Aboriginal communities, their general praxis has remained participatory in other, more generic senses. They have continued to make their films from an unprivileged perspective, that is, they have continued to shoot from camera positions that reproduce the perspective of an immersed participant in the social interactions being recorded, without the use of exaggerated camera movements, special effects or cross-cutting montage. Informal conversations with the subjects, in various guises, have remained an important part of their practical repertoire, while formal interviews and voice-over have remained a relative rarity. They have continued to adopt what David MacDougall once called a 'stance of humility' before the world of the subjects, being respectful of its physical rhythms, and allowing the story of the film to be taken off in unanticipated directions. And although they may no longer aim to share the authorship of their films, they have been concerned, at least in the work with Indian school-children, to train their subjects to make films for themselves. These training workshops have often taken place at the same time as they have been making their own films in particular schools.[4]

Another element of continuity has been the editorial structuring of the films in accordance with conventional narrative tropes, particularly 'as if' chronologies. In many of these later films, particular attention has been paid to the cutting of opening sequences, both immediately before and immediately after the main title. These sequences often involve scenes of people getting up or other early morning activities. Many films also conclude with classical valedictory devices: characters saying goodbye and leaving to go elsewhere, or going to bed, or wide shots of the landscape at dusk or after nightfall, and so on. A number of films end by returning visually or metaphorically to the beginning of the film.

However, notwithstanding these many continuities, there are also a number of ruptures with the praxis of MacDougalls' earlier body of work. One of the most signficant is that in all but two of the films of this later period, David and Judith have been working separately: previously, although David had made a number of films with other film-makers, and one alone, most of the MacDougalls' films were shared endeavours. Since the 1990s, although they have actively assisted and advised one another at various stages of their respective productions, particularly at the editing stage, for the most part each has been directing their own films. Moreover, most of the films of this later period have been solo works by David. Judith has made two films of her own, and shared the direction of two others with David, but otherwise she has largely dedicated her professional life in recent years to teaching in many different parts of the world, including China, Singapore, Norway and Italy.

One of the two joint works is *Photo Wallahs*, shot in 1988–89 and released in 1991, and the first film that the MacDougalls made after leaving the AIAS. This film was mostly shot in Mussoorie, a small town in the Himalayas, about 175 miles by road north of New Delhi, which was a so-called 'hill station' at time of the British Raj, where the families of colonial administrators would take refuge from the summer heat. Today it continues to be a holiday destination, but for middle-class Indian families. The subtitle of the film is 'an encounter with photography', but in fact, the subject matter of the film would be more accurately described in the plural, as it consists of a series of encounters exploring the meaning of photography for a diverse range

of both practitioners and consumers in Mussoorie and the nearby town of
Dehra Dun.

Although it was a joint work, this film represents something of a rupture
with the MacDougalls' earlier praxis in a number of more editorial senses.
As in their earlier films, there are frequent conversational exchanges between
the film-makers and subjects, and the general perspective of the film is
unprivileged. But in contrast to most of this earlier work, *Photo Wallahs*
generally eschews the long take and the development of action within a
fixed frame. Instead it is constructed around a series of much shorter takes,
with images juxtaposed through montage in order to make intellectual
connections. The pattern of the characterisation is similar: rather than being
built around a few strong central characters, as in the earlier films, there
are a considerable number of relatively minor characters, whose ideas about
photography are juxtaposed and contrasted one with another. As David
MacDougall has put it, *Photo Wallahs* represents 'a kind of scattering of
images, with a certain kaleidoscopic feeling to it'.[5]

This film also represented a departure from the MacDougalls' prior praxis
in that, for the first time, they invited a third party to edit the film. This
was Dai Vaughan, a highly experienced 16 mm editor who had previously
worked with Brian Moser, Melissa Llewelyn-Davies and a number of other
ethnographic and para-ethnographic film-makers in British television, as
well as being an astute and thoughtful writer about documentary generally.
The MacDougalls had admired his work for many years and invited him
to collaborate with them because they believed that he would be stimulated
by the ideas underlying the film. Vaughan's participation was made possible
by yet another feature that was unusual about this film within the MacDougall
oeuvre, namely that it was first of their films to be financed by television,
in this case, by the French channel, La Sept, though they also received
funding from the Australian Film Commission.[6]

David MacDougall reports that in editing the film, they went through
'at least ten different versions' before they felt that they had worked out
an effective structure. In that it is divided into a number of distinct parts,
as with *To Live With Herds* and *The Wedding Camels*, released some twenty
years earlier, there are certain echoes here too of the structure of *The Song
of Ceylon*, the classic 1934 documentary directed by Basil Wright. Indeed,
the first part of *Photo Wallahs*, in which middle-class tourists are shown
coming up by cable car to a mountain look-out point and then dressing
up and dancing in Bollywood costumes, has been explicitly associated by
MacDougall with 'Apparel of a God', the last part of *The Song of Ceylon*,
which features a performance by elaborately costumed dancers.[7]

The photographers who lie in wait for these fantasy Bollywood stars
are the first of several different kinds of practitioner – the 'photo wallahs'
of the title – who feature in the film. Others include traditional studio

**14.1** *Photo Wallahs* (1991). Left, R. S. Sharma, at the doorway of his studio in Mussoorie, specialises in formal black and white portraits, right.

photographers, who work strictly with black and white, though some then tint their photographs by hand with watercolour paints (figure 14.1). Another group are the largely middle-aged members of an amateur photographers' club who go round taking pictures of the countryside while debating just how artistic it is permissible for a photographer to be. Among the consumers of photography, we are introduced to a former Maharani who takes us through an album of photographs of herself and her family dressed for formal occasions or fancy dress parties as far back as the 1920s. An eminent writer reads a short story about his grandmother's reaction to a photograph of herself as a child. Photographs are also shown being used to provide evidence of missing persons, the beauty of potential marriage partners, and even graves in a local cemetery. The film also considers moving images as represented by soap-opera-ish television religious dramas, and wedding videography. There is even a reflexive shot of David and Judith themselves, standing laden with all their equipment.

Lying behind these many particular cases, the film hints at some more general ethnographic issues. It suggests, for example, that the boundary between photography and religious iconography is much more porous in India than in the West: whereas in the West, great emphasis is laid on the indexical quality of a photographic image, so that any embellishment reduces its authenticity and hence its value, in India there is a tendency to think of a photograph as if it were a religious icon, which it is not merely legitimate but also desirable to embellish. Another issue that emerges from the film is that whereas still portraiture usually involves highly mannered deadpan poses, the shooting of moving images often provokes some kind of performance involving music and dance. But in both cases, in contrast to some parts of the world, being photographed appears to be generally regarded in Mussoorie as an entirely positive experience.

Dai Vaughan also acted as the editor of the next of the MacDougalls' films, *Tempus de Baristas*. This was released in 1993 and was one of the few films that David MacDougall had made without Judith up until that point. This film concerns a group of shepherds living around the town of Urzulei in the mountainous central heartland of Sardinia. MacDougall again had the budget to be able to invite Vaughan to cut this film because, as with *Photo Wallahs*, part of the funding came from television, though this time it came from the *Fine Cut* series of the BBC, then under the direction of André Singer, an anthropologist by training and for some years, the series producer of *Disappearing World*. However, most of the funding as well as the original initiative for the film came from the Istituto Superiore Regionale Etnografico (ISRE), a dependency of the regional government of Sardinia and situated in Nuoro, in the north of the island, where local Sardinian cultural traditions remain strongest. Under the enterprising director at that time, Paolo Piquereddu, the ISRE had been running an ethnographic film festival for many years, and had frequently screened the MacDougalls' films. Piquereddu invited David to make a film based on the research that the ISRE itself had been carrying out among local shepherds (many of whom herd goats rather than sheep). As MacDougall did not speak the regional dialect of the shepherds, he was assisted by a local sound technician, Dante Olianas.

Although shepherds play a prominent part in the collective imaginary of Sardinia, and vie with miners and fishermen as the most heroic male exemplars of regional identity, their traditional way of life has long been under threat for a mixture of economic and cultural reasons. This is particularly true of shepherds who herd goats. There is no longer much demand for goat products, particularly their meat, and few young people want to take up shepherding on account of its extreme physical demands, including the requirement to spend most of the summer months living in isolated *cuile*, primitive shelters consisting of dry stone walls and brushwood roofs, situated high up in the mountains.

This threat to the shepherds' traditional way of life is the central theme of *Tempus de Baristas*, the title of which, in the local dialect, means 'time of barmen'. This is a reference to a phrase used by one of the leading characters in the film, a shepherd by the name of Miminu, who laments that at the present time, if one wants to make a decent living, it is much better to work in a bar than as a shepherd. Like many shepherds, this character, a seemingly popular and attractive man in his 40s, remains unmarried because young women are no more attracted to the traditional shepherding way of life than young men. Miminu is one of three main characters, the other two being Franchiscu, a grizzled shepherd in his 50s, and his lithe and handsome son, Pietro, who is only 17 and about to leave school. The main narrative tension of the film revolves around the question of whether Pietro will follow in his father's footsteps. Although he is clearly attracted to the shepherding way of life in some ways, like other young people Pietro enjoys

14.2 *Tempus de Baristas* (1993). Left, Franchiscu with his goats and right, Miminu and Franchiscu's son, Pietro. But will Pietro continue with the goat-herding life?

the social life of the town. He has also been offered the possibility of going on to further study elsewhere on the island (figure 14.2).

In terms of subject matter, *Tempus de Baristas* is reminiscent in a number ways of the MacDougalls' films about East African pastoralists. As in the earlier films, an important secondary theme concerns the interference of the local state in the subjects' way of life. Whereas in the East African cases, local administrators had been seeking to sedentarise the pastoralists, in Sardinia government agencies are seeking to restrict the activities of traditional shepherds in order to preserve the mountains as a supposedly 'natural' environment that will be attractive to tourists. Another theme reminiscent of the earlier work is scepticism about the benefits of a school education: the shepherds are aware that education can be highly advantageous for the individual but know full well that those who succeed educationally will not continue with the shepherding life. In the case of Pietro, the matter still hangs in the balance at the end of the film.

As far as its cinematographic praxis is concerned, *Tempus de Baristas* is certainly much more in tune with the MacDougalls' East African work than with *Photo Wallahs*. The general perspective is unprivileged, the takes are generally long. Conversation is an important ingredient of the film, though more between the subjects themselves than between the subjects and the film-maker. Elegantly cut by Vaughan, the film proceeds by a series of clearly demarcated scenes, each carrying a weight of ethnographic significance beyond its manifest content. Although there is possibly some redundancy in the last third of the film, there are also many memorable scenes, superbly executed cinematographically by MacDougall. There is none more so than the penultimate scene of the film, which consists of a single long shot of Miminu slowly and laboriously climbing the mountainside. Over his shoulder, there is a large tree trunk with protruding roots, almost like a cross, destined, one supposes, to be used in the

**14.3** Films directed by Judith MacDougall. Left, *Diya* (2001) concerns the Lal family of potters in Dehra Dun, north India, while *The Art of Regret* (2007), right, explores the uses of photography in Kunming, southwest China.

construction of his *cuile*, but at the same time symbolising both the resilience of the shepherds and also the heavy burden that their way of life imposes upon them.

After completing *Tempus de Baristas*, the MacDougalls returned on various occasions to make films in Dehra Dun, the small town close to Mussoorie where they had shot a number of sequences for *Photo Wallahs*. But for these later films, David and Judith each worked on their own. In 1997, David began shooting what would eventually become a series of five films about the Doon School, an elite private boarding school for boys. These films were released at various points between 2000 and 2004, and proved to be merely the first in an extended series of films about Indian children, which I shall discuss separately later in this chapter.

For her part, Judith made *Diya*, released in 2001, a film that explores the 'life cycle' of the humble earthenware oil lamp known as *diya*, which is essential to the celebration of Hindu festivals. Made in accordance with a broadly Observational Cinema praxis, this film focuses initially on the Lal family of potters, of modest circumstances, and follows them as they prepare a large consignment of *diya* to sell in the local market (figure 14.3, left). Although the family is proud of its craft, it is also very demanding work and depends critically upon the labour of the children. The latter part of the film moves to the house of the more prosperous Gaur family and shows them lighting the *diya* in celebration of Diwali, before finally putting them out on the street where they will break down into the earth from whence they came. In a postscript, Judith returns to the Lal household to discover, to her surprise, that the family has decided to give up on pottery and prioritise the children's schooling, thereby bringing to an end an activity that had stretched back over seven generations.

400

Some years later, while she was teaching ethnographic film-making at the University of Yunnan, in Kunming, in southwest China, Judith made another film without David, this time in collaboration with the Chinese visual anthropologist, 'Kathy' Zhang Jinghong. This was *The Art of Regret*, released in 2007, which offers an insight into contemporary China through the way in which photographs are taken and used. This film was not based on extensive ethnographic research, and although it employs the same quadripartite narrative structure as *Photo Wallahs*, in terms of its general praxis it stands at quite a distance from Observational Cinema in its classical form. A combination of personal essay film and road movie, it is structured by a personal voice-over narration and makes abundant use of 'talking heads' of varying degrees of formality, some of which stand outside the temporal horizon of the film. In a more general editorial sense, it is also a somewhat more rough-hewn work than one normally associates with the MacDougalls' films.

In terms of content, however, *The Art of Regret* makes a fascinating companion film to *Photo Wallahs*. In part, this is due to the very different social and historical milieu into which photographs are inserted in post-millennium urban China as compared to that of rural India almost twenty years before. In China, photography is being merged, not with religious iconography, but rather with a distinctively Chinese tradition of heroic imagery in the Soviet Realist style, associated particularly with the Communist Party and the Cultural Revolution, though this is also clearly being strongly challenged by modern cosmopolitan imagery influenced by contemporary Western popular arts. Also, photographs are not apparently used in the process of courtship as they are in India. On the other hand, highly idealised wedding photographs, studio portraits of extended family groups, as well as high-quality black and white photographs for the prospective memorialisation of the elderly are all big business in modern-day Kunming.

But what really differentiates the world represented in *The Art of Regret* from that of *Photo Wallahs* is the fact that in the interim between the two films, the digital revolution in photography had taken place. Whereas in *Photo Wallahs* we see traditional craftsmen assiduously tinting black and white photographs by hand by means of watercolour paints, in *The Art of Regret* all manner of embellishments are achieved in an instant on a computer. However, in many ways, the desired objective is the same, namely, to idealise a perceived inherent essence of the human subject that mere mimesis cannot achieve. Traditionally in China, as one young studio photographer explains, photography was known as 'the art of regret', for however much one tried, one never quite managed to capture the inner essence of the subject. Now, however, with the aid of digital technology, that regret could at least sometimes be assuaged, after the fact, with the aid of an 'app'.

# David MacDougall's films with Indian children: *The Doon School Quintet*

These technological changes were also impacting directly on the MacDougalls' own work as film-makers. For another major rupture between their early film-making praxis in Africa and Australia and their later work in India was the abandonment of 16 mm film in favour of digital video technology. *Tempus de Baristas* would prove to be the last film that they would shoot on 16 mm.

This change initially came about through necessity rather than by design. When David MacDougall was preparing his project at the Doon School in 1996, he again approached the BBC for support. But by then André Singer had been succeeded by a new series editor at *Fine Cut* who was unsympathetic to ethnographic film and turned down MacDougall's proposal. This rebuff turned out to be 'a liberation', as MacDougall would later describe it, since it obliged him to shoot on digital video, as this was much cheaper than film. Using video, he was able to shoot the five films that would eventually make up *The Doon School Quintet* for a total production cost that amounted to no more than a tenth of the production budget of *Tempus de Baristas*.

Not only did this switch of medium permit MacDougall to increase the sheer quantity of films that he made, but it also allowed him to be more experimental, since he no longer needed to be preoccupied about what a commissioning editor might think about the results.[8] Over the course of several visits to Dehra Dun between 1997 and 1999, he shot some 98 hours of material, supplemented by a limited amount of additional footage taken during later visits while the editing was proceeding. When he began shooting, MacDougall did not have a clear idea of how many films would emerge from the rushes: it was only gradually that he determined that they should together make up a quintet which, in total running time, amounts to just over eight hours, a cutting ratio of approximately 12:1.[9]

The original idea for this project arose from a suggestion by the Indian anthropologist Sanjay Srivastava that MacDougall might like to make a film that would complement Srivastava's own text-based ethnographic study of the Doon School in the early 1990s. Often referred to as 'the Eton of India', the Doon School is modelled on the most progressive variants of the British private school system and is renowned for having been attended by leading figures in many different walks of Indian public life: political, military, professional, also academic and literary. Founded in the 1930s, already in anticipation of political independence from Britain, the Doon School was committed to forging an Indian identity that stood above the many social, religious and regional differences within the country. Initially, MacDougall had been attracted to the idea of making a film that would explore the

**14.4** *Doon School Chronicles* (2000). The first film of the quintet focuses on the way in which the environment of the school – physical as well as social – moulds the boys.

school as a 'site of diversity, an intersection of different cultural strands in Indian society', but as the project developed, he began to think of it rather as a study of the way in which the school generated what was, in effect, 'a carefully constructed island of cultural homogeneity in the lives of the diverse students who passed through it'.[10]

As presented by MacDougall across the five films, this cultural homogeneity is only partially brought about through the explicitly verbal passing on of abstract ideas, moral precepts or cultural norms from teachers to pupils in the context of formal instruction. Just as important, perhaps even more so, is what he refers to as the 'social aesthetics' of the school. Here MacDougall is using the term 'aesthetics', not in its most conventional contemporary sense to refer to taste and the evaluation of beauty, but rather in its original eighteenth-century sense to refer to sensory experience conceived as a mode of apprehending the world that is both distinct from, and to some extent opposed to, the apprehension of the world through abstract, language-based ideas. Applied to the Doon School by MacDougall, this concern with 'aesthetics' entailed a close attention to the way in which features of the day-to-day social and physical environment of the school moulded the identities and beings of the pupils (figure 14.4).[11]

Given that *The Doon School Quintet* is concerned with a school, at first sight it seems strange that over the five films there is relatively little material showing teaching taking place in a classroom. But this is entirely consistent with MacDougall's emphasis on sensory 'social aesthetics'. Instead of formal instruction, there is an abundance of material on such matters as the norms concerning the wearing of uniforms: in fact, clothes are a particular focus of interest as they are often directly concerned with issues of status and personal identity and the first film in the quintet begins and ends with a scene in the school laundry. Other subjects include the weighing, measuring and assessing of pupils; the taking of meals in the collective dining room or the sharing of 'tuck' (i.e. sweets and potato crisps); the making of beds, dressing, washing, and generally 'hanging out' in the dormitories, of which there is a great deal; the playing of both informal games and more formal sports, particularly cricket and gymnastics, but also early morning physical exercises and military drills around the field; school morning assemblies in the gymnasium, involving non-denominational prayers, and the Founder's Day celebration at the end of the year attended by parents, alumni and the great-and-the-good (who are often all one and the same).

There are also many shots of the general physical environment – the buildings, the main playing fields, the gardens, the school museum – as well as of everyday material objects, usually rather dog-eared. The latter often consist of stills rather than moving images and present such things as suitcases, lines of coat pegs, metal spoons and plates, ceiling fans, beds. Sound is also a very important ingredient of the films, particularly those that testify to the sheer frenetic energy and activity of teenage boys. MacDougall reports that as he moved about the school, he was constantly aware of noises of all kinds: shouting and calling, the sound of shoes resounding along corridors, a constant scuffling and the incessant tap-tapping of table tennis balls. This lively sonic environment is extensively but discretely reproduced in the films as well. In the exteriors, birdsong is particularly noticeable, also the rumour of traffic, one of the few examples of the outside world intruding upon the hermetic world of the school.

As the project developed, however, MacDougall came increasingly to think of 'social aesthetics', not as something that the school did to its pupils, but rather as something that the boys themselves played an active part in creating and reproducing. He felt that he was observing a kind of theatre in which the boys were both actors and audience. They were not, he realised, mere 'ballast' in an institution for the production of postcolonial subjects but rather active agents in their own transformation from children on the threshold of teenagerhood, each with his own individuality, into boys who, in the metaphor of the founding headmaster, would be like playing cards, all with the blue and grey uniform of the school on their backs, while on the front, on their faces, they would retain their own special individual character (figure 14.5).

In accordance with MacDougall's developing interest in the boys' agency in their own transformation, the focus of the quintet as a whole lies preponderantly with the boys. There are some occasional, relatively informal interviews with members of staff: with the headmaster in the first film and in later films, with the housemaster of Foot House, a 'holding house' for new boys, and particularly with the female Foot House Tutor, Minakshi Basu, who appears in three out of the five films, and whose voice within the quintet MacDougall equates with his own. But otherwise, the teachers are a remote and infrequent presence in the films. Also present are the

14.5 Later films in the Doon School quintet focus more on the boys' own agency. Left, an argument breaks out in *The New Boys* (2003); right, Abhishek Shukla, principal subject of *The Age of Reason* (2004).

various support staff required to maintain the elaborate infrastructure of the school – kitchen workers, laundry staff, handymen, gardeners, sports instructors, a venerable bell-ringer – but they too are mostly merely observed rather than directly engaged.

In terms of overall praxis, the first film, *Doon School Chronicles*, is significantly different from all the others. Despite the chronological reference in the title, of all the films in the quintet, it is the one that narratively speaking is the least structured by chronology. Instead, it is constructed around a series of ten parts, each dealing with a different aspect of life in the institution, introduced by an epigraph featuring some sort of precept about the school's ethos, as originally formulated by A. E. Foot, the school's first headmaster, or some distinguished alumnus.

As in the classical Observational Cinema praxis, informal conversations are of central importance in *Doon School Chronicles*, both between the subjects and between the subjects and film-maker. These conversations reveal the remarkable intellectual sophistication of the boys, many of whom are impressively articulate. There are also some more formal interviews with two particular boys, Rohan and Veer that, contrary to the classical Observational praxis, stand outside the temporal horizon of the film in the sense that the film returns to these interviews on several separate occasions. The 13-year-old Rohan, whom MacDougall describes as 'an amateur sociologist', provides intelligent social analysis of the school and of his fellow pupils recurrently through the film; Veer, who is 16, is equally acute in his social commentary but only appears in the latter part of the film. He is an actor and theatre director, and has found a way of winning respect among his peers even though he is not interested in sports, which is normal way to achieve esteem at the Doon School. Two other boys are also picked out as leading characters, but they feature less prominently.

*Doon School Chronicles* differs from the other films in the quintet in a number of other ways too. MacDougall himself has described it as 'a web in which the other films are suspended'.[12] That is, it offers a general portrait of the school as an institution, thereby providing a contextualising framework for the other films. In the latter, the centre of gravity has shifted: the main focus is no longer on how the institution operates as such but rather on the way in which the boys deal with the experience of living in the school on a day-to-day basis. Furthermore, whereas *Doon School Chronicles* is concerned with the school population as a whole, the four subsequent films are about boys who have only just arrived at the school, typically aged around 12. MacDougall then follows these boys as they try to forge both a personal identity and a sense of community with other boys from all over the Indian subcontinent, all within the physical conditions of the Doon School which are not only quite spartan but also afford almost no personal privacy.[13]

In effect, these four films constitute two similar pairs, with the first film in each pair offering a portrait of a particular cohort of newly arrived boys, followed in the second film by a more focused portrait of an individual boy from within that cohort. Thus, the second film in the quintet, *With Morning Hearts*, shot in 1997–98, follows a cohort of some thirty 12-year-olds as they pass through Foot House while the third film, *Karam in Jaipur*, takes the eponymous Karam Rai Mehra, who had featured centrally in *With Morning Hearts*, and follows him in the early weeks of his life in Jaipur, one of the senior houses, the following year. Similarly, the fourth film, *The New Boys*, follows the 1998–99 Foot House cohort while in the fifth and final film, *The Age of Reason*, the focus is on one particular boy within that cohort, Abhishek Shukla, though not as he moves into a senior house, but in the course of that same year.

In practical film-making terms, this last film is rather different from all MacDougall's previous films. While the relationship between subjects and film-makers had always been readily acknowledged in his earlier work with Judith and had sometimes even been of central importance – as in *Lorang's Way*, for example – this relationship was typically presented in a low-key and discreet manner, and was subordinate to the more general purposes of the film. By contrast, in *The Age of Reason*, the relationship between MacDougall and the principal subject is not merely foregrounded, but defines the parameters of the film. Thus the film begins when the newly arrived Abhishek, a Nepali and therefore something of an outsider to the other boys, just like MacDougall himself, attaches himself to Mac-Dougall, 'a little like my shadow', as MacDougall puts it. The film ends when Abhishek becomes more integrated with the other boys and prefers to spend his time with them rather than with MacDougall. As the film unfolds, the evolution of this relationship is commented upon by MacDougall in voice-over narration at various key points, a device which although not entirely unprecedented, is certainly very unusual within his work as a whole.[14]

As he is represented in *The Age of Reason*, Abhishek epitomises, in a particularly impressive manner, a set of personal and intellectual qualities that MacDougall came to appreciate in the boys passing through Foot House. An important key to reading the film is offered close to the beginning, just after we have been introduced to Abhishek, in the form of an intertitle card with an extended quotation from the late-seventeenth-century philosopher, John Locke. This asserts that children already have a fully formed sense of themselves and are as independent and free in their thinking 'as any of you grown Men'.[15]

As MacDougall came to see it, far from involving the refinement and expansion of the sensibilities established in childhood, the boys' progress through the Doon School involved a paring back and limiting of the 'high point of proficiency and competence' reached in the period immediately prior to adolescence, as exemplified particularly by Abhishek. This was a point of view that was clearly completely at odds with the pious epigraphs that punctuate *Doon School Chronicles*, and even with the views of the boys themselves, at least as expressed in the concluding sequences of *With Morning Hearts*, in which they look forward to expanding their horizons in the senior houses, even if they also express their fears, particularly of being bullied by older boys.

It was also not a point of view that MacDougall had brought with him to the Doon School and it had not been his original intention to pay quite so much attention to 12-year-olds. In fact, he had first come upon Foot House entirely by chance, when sheltering from the rain. He had initially formed the idea that it would be interesting to make a film about the Doon School as perceived by the newcomers in Foot House, thereby paralleling his own discovery of the school and that of his eventual audience as well. But as the filming progressed, what had begun as an exploration of the ethnographic particularity of Foot House within the Doon School opened up into a much wider and more fundamental preoccupation with the way in which childhood is thought of generally, not just in the Doon School but universally, in the literature of the social sciences and psychology as well as in popular culture.

In effect, the experience of working in Foot House led MacDougall to question the conventional models that he himself had previously unthinkingly shared, whereby child development is primarily understood in terms of progress and improvement, and in which children are often perceived as merely the passive recipients of socialisation. MacDougall came to believe instead that adulthood did not necessarily constitute a refinement of childhood, but rather that 'children might actually write the agenda for adults, and that adult society might more properly be regarded as a paring down of children's discoveries'.[16]

It was this 'refractory idea', as he called it, that led MacDougall to dedicate four out of his five Doon School films to the world of the 12-year-old boys of Foot House. It would also be central to all his subsequent film work with Indian children, despite the very great differences in the institutional contexts in which these later films would be made.

## DAVID MACDOUGALL'S FILMS WITH INDIAN CHILDREN: THE RISHI VALLEY FILMS

After seven years dedicated to shooting and editing the Doon School films, David MacDougall returned to India in 2004 to make another series of films about a school, though one that was very different from the Doon School. This was the Rishi Valley School in Andhra Pradesh in South India. Although its pupils are also mainly drawn from the Indian professional classes and it is also a boarding school, Rishi Valley is a progressive, co-educational institution originally founded in 1934 by the twentieth-century Indian philosopher Jiddu Krishnamurti whose ideas still underpin the school ethos and its pedagogy. In the course of five years, from 2004 to 2008, MacDougall shot seven films at this school, though here I consider only the three most substantial works, *Some Alien Creatures*, *Schoolscapes* and *Awareness*.[17]

Although the two schools are very different, the general cinematographic praxis underlying two of these three films is broadly similar to that of the Doon School films, particularly the three central films of the quintet. This is especially true of the first of the Rishi Valley films, *Some Alien Creatures* – shot over three months in 2004 and released the following year – which was made by David MacDougall working alone. It is also true, albeit to a slightly lesser extent, of the third Rishi Valley film, *Awareness*, which was shot over two months in 2006, though not released until 2010. This latter film was jointly made by David and Judith MacDougall, and as such, was the first and, to date, the only film on which they have shared both technical and directorial roles since *Photo Wallahs* was released in 1991. The second film in the Rishi Valley trilogy, *Schoolscapes*, was shot over two months in early 2005 and released in 2007. This was a solo work by David and is very different in practical terms both to the Doon School films and to the other two films in the Rishi Valley trilogy. For this reason, I shall deal with it separately.

As in the later Doon School films, the central focus of *Some Alien Creatures* and *Awareness* is on the pupils and the day-to-day experience of their lives as boarders at the school. Again, there are many extended scenes of mundane everyday activities, such as getting up, washing and dressing or generally messing about and relaxing in the dormitories. The pupils are shown playing football or other more informal games, exploring the grounds, playing music or dancing, eating in the dining hall, sharing their 'illegal grub' (sweets and crisps), attending assemblies, sometimes studying or reading quietly. In both these films, there is some sort of Open Day, attended by parents in *Awareness*, with the same painful emotional awkwardnesses as shown in the Doon School films when the moment for the parents' departure approaches.

Within these broad similarities, there are also some differences. Considered as a whole, the average age of the leading subjects of the Rishi Valley films appears to be slightly older than that of the Doon School subjects, though again the focus is primarily on the younger members of the school population. By far the greatest difference relates to the fact that as Rishi Valley is co-educational, a large proportion of the subjects are girls, particularly in *Awareness*, which was the film made jointly with Judith who, by virtue of her gender, was able to shoot scenes of the girls relaxing in their dormitories that complemented the similar scenes that David was shooting in the boys' dormitories. We discover, however, that although boys and girls may share certain geographical spaces within the school, they lead largely separate lives: not for nothing is the first film of the trilogy called *Some Alien Creatures*, a title based on a comment by one boy regarding the way in which boys are perceived by the girls (figure 14.6, top).

As another boy explains later in the same film, although the school encourages boys to have girls as friends, it does not encourage boys to have girlfriends. The closest the Rishi Valley films come to any emotional engagement between the two genders is the exchange of friendship bands, the making of which is a recurrent leitmotif. Otherwise the co-educational nature of the school is mainly flagged by scenes of formal instruction in the theory of sexual reproduction, either in the form of biology classes or sexual hygiene seminars.

Although there is perhaps a slightly greater preponderance of classroom scenes in the Rishi Valley films than in *The Doon School Quintet*, there are absolutely no interviews with the teachers, or with any other adults. Nor is there any systematic formal exposition of the pedagogical principles derived from the teachings of Krishnamurti on which the school is based. There is certainly nothing akin to the intertitle epigraphs expounding the school philosophy that run through *Doon School Chronicles*. In fact, the only specific mention of Krishnamurti is in a conversation towards the end of *Some Alien Creatures*, when a boy who is one of MacDougall's principal interlocutors briefly remarks on the impact of the philosopher's ideas on the school. He suggests that it is on account of Krishnamurti's influence that pupils are encouraged to be highly independent while at the same time being sensitive to other people's feelings.

**14.6** Films at the Rishi Valley School. *Some Alien Creatures* (2005), above, is similar in praxis to the Doon School films, while *Schoolscapes* (2007), below, is more experimental.

There are, on the other hand, various scenes showing activities around the school, which, one surmises, might owe something to Krishnamurti's ideas, such as, for example, the collective meditation at sunset with which *Awareness* concludes. The same might apply to the prevalence in both films of shots of the natural world in and around the school, and of the pupils' frequent engagement with it. Also, the very title of *Awareness* would appear to be a reference to a key Krishnamurtian concept, one that he used to refer to a state of mind in which one looks at things in the world unencumbered by any prior judgements or knowledge about them. Under these conditions, Krishnamurti proposed, one could achieve a state of 'awareness' in which the distinction between observer and observed disappears, and all that remains is an intense, all-engaging attention. But these connections between Krishnamurti's ideas and what one sees on the screen in these two films in the Rishi Valley trilogy remain oblique and unspecified.[18]

By contrast, there is a very direct connection between Krishanmurtian ideas and what one sees in *Schoolscapes*. In terms of cinematographic praxis, *Schoolscapes* is quite unlike the other two films in the Rishi Valley trilogy, let alone the Doon School films. Its 77-minute duration is made up of precisely forty shots, the great majority of which are between one and five minutes long. These have mostly been taken from a single static position, though there are a few instances of panning, and one example of the use of the zoom. They are also mostly relatively wide-angle shots, though there are a few close-ups, while other shots have clearly been taken on the end of the zoom, with some foreshortening of the image as a result. Many shots are taken from low down, either looking up at the subject, or because the subject is sitting down anyway. Each shot thus constitutes a short scene in itself, and is separated from the neighbouring shot-scenes by fades down and up from black, and with no carrying across of sound from one shot-scene to the next (figure 14.6, bottom).[19]

In making *Schoolscapes* in this way, MacDougall was quite consciously conducting an experiment. The aim of this experiment was to see if it was possible to use the moving image camera to achieve that state of engaged attention that Krishnamurti describes as 'awareness'. In order to carry out the experiment, MacDougall adopted a cinematographic praxis inspired by the Lumière brothers who, in the earliest days of cinema, had managed to excite their audiences simply by producing a series of 'views' of the world, shooting from a single static position and running the film for as long as the stock allowed, which in their case usually meant for less than a minute.[20]

In terms of substantive content, on the other hand, *Schoolscapes* is not dissimilar to the other Rishi Valley films. Each shot-scene provides a vignette of some aspect of life at the school, with particular emphasis on the mundane everyday activities such as getting up, washing and eating, leisure activities and so on, just as one sees in the other films. There are also some scenes of formal instruction, but in music and dance rather than in classrooms. In the only shot of a classroom, one of the shortest in the film, the pupils' desks are empty. There is some casual conversation in some scenes, and one scene in which a boy gives an extended response to an interview question from MacDougall, though this ends before the boy has completed what he has to say. These scenes are the exceptions that prove the more general rule that there is very little dialogue in the film, be it between the subjects themselves or between the film-maker and the subjects.

Some recurrent images show support staff at work, doing such things as washing blankets, sluicing down the school dairy and making chapattis, and there is some narrative development in the progress of these activities, as the film returns to them more than once. Like many of MacDougall's films about schools, this one begins first thing in the morning, with the pupils getting up, and ends with a night-time scene, showing a boy leaving the school by bus, presumably for the vacation. But otherwise there is no strong narrative thread running through the film. Nor is there any form of exterior commentary on the film, be it in the form of narration, or in the form of titles other than the opening titles and the end credits.

*Schoolscapes* is exquisitely executed cinematographically, every shot-scene being carefully and superbly crafted. Whether it is equally successful in enabling one to enter a state of 'awareness', which was MacDougall's original experimental objective, I am less certain, but I leave it to those who are better versed in Krishnamurti's ideas to make a more informed judgement. Where I am more confident is in relation to *Schoolscapes* specifically as an ethnographic film: in that it involves no sustained exploration of the interconnection between practices, ideas and relations, its ethnographicness is much less marked than is the case with MacDougall's other films about Indian schools.

## DAVID MACDOUGALL'S FILMS WITH INDIAN CHILDREN: *GANDHI'S CHILDREN*

Much more substantial as a work of ethnographic cinema in my view is *Gandhi's Children*, a film that David MacDougall shot in 2005 – the same year as he shot *Schoolscapes* – but which was not released until 2008. This film concerns the Prayas Children's Home for Boys, an institution situated at Jahangirpuri on the northern outskirts of New Delhi. This serves as both a shelter for boys who are homeless or displaced, and as a sort of reformatory for boys who have been caught engaged in criminal acts of various kinds, mostly petty theft. At 185 minutes, it is the longest film that MacDougall has made to date, and also, in my view, the strongest of his Indian films, possibly of his entire oeuvre, be it ethnographically, cinematographically or politically. It is also, among his Indian school films, the one that conforms most closely to the classical Observational Cinema praxis.[21]

The film is divided into 12 distinct chapters, mostly between 10 and 20 minutes long, though two or three are somewhat longer, up to 30 minutes. Many of these chapters begin at dawn or end at night, giving the impression that they represent a chronologically ordered sequence of episodes rather than being a series of thematically defined segments, as had been the case with the chapters of *Doon School Chronicles*.

The film as a whole is framed by two particularly striking sequences. It begins with a highly cinematic opening sequence placed around the main titles that sets the tone for the film as whole. This cuts back and forth between the harsh polluted exterior beyond the forbidding fortress that is the home, and the boys still slumbering innocently in their beds, some intertwined in one another's arms. As the boys rise and perform their ablutions, the film keeps returning to the exterior, to show sewage belching from a pumping station adjacent to the home and a bird eating a rat, while on the soundtrack there is an incessant cawing of crows, the grinding of machinery or, within the home, a dispiriting cacophony of sounds echoing around the large and empty central atrium.

Meanwhile, at the other end of the film, there is something approaching a happy ending, as some of the boys are shown leaving to go back to their family homes, clearly in high spirits. But the final images remind us that they are the lucky ones, for we then see a series of other boys looking out wistfully from behind the barred windows of the home and we are reminded that it is a gaol as well as a refuge (figure 14.7).

Within this general framework of chapters, the film proceeds initially by introducing us to daily life in the institution in a largely observational mode. We discover the revolting hygienic conditions in which the boys are obliged to wash and exercise bodily functions; we see them queueing for their meagre rations, which they eat from metal trays on the floor; we see them lined up in their uniforms praying fervently, apparently in a Christian manner, for their own well-being and that of Mother India. We see them playing cricket in the yard, and playing board games and dancing in the dormitory.

We are also introduced to the harsh social relations in the home: older boys direct the younger ones in cleaning out the latrines and slap them about the face for supposed misdemeanours, though we also see moving examples of support and mutual solidarity. Through the voice of one boy, Ritesh, we learn that the boys in the school belong to two groups: *courtwalas*, who have been brought to the home because they have committed criminal offences, and *homewalas*, who are homeless or lost. Ritesh also explains the fagging system, whereby the older boys, who are heads of dormitories, oblige the younger boys to do things for them, such as wash their clothes, which we then see them doing.

We are also shown a group of newly arrived boys being registered by an elegant administrator. As they are questioned about their background, dwarfed by the large office chair in which they are required to sit, often emaciated and in rags, we begin to learn about the variety of circumstances that have led them to end up at the Prayas Home. Some boys are homeless because their parents have died, others have simply been abandoned or have got lost entirely by accident, others have run away from home because they were being beaten. Others had been brought to Delhi by relatives, or have even made their own way there, in order to work for miniscule wages

**14.7** *Gandhi's Children* (2008). Street children and orphans are given food and lodging at the Prayas Home, but it is also a place of imprisonment.

in some sort of cottage industry operation, only for this to be raided and closed down by the police because it contravened child labour laws.

Gradually, however, this observational mode of the film gives way to a more conversational 'talking heads' mode, and individual boys or groups of boys then expand on these life histories. One boy tells how he travelled round the country sleeping on trains, going as far as Mumbai, over 500 miles away. Another group talk about their criminal activities, about how they were caught and often severely beaten by police. However, in contrast to the conversation-interviews of *Doon School Chronicles*, these conversations do not stand outside the temporal horizon of the film, but are sewn directly into it, in the manner of the classical Observational Cinema praxis. That is, they occur only once and seemingly arise within the general chronologically ordered sequence of events as represented in the film.

As with the Rishi Valley films, the centre of gravity of *Gandhi's Children* remains unequivocally with the children. Apart from a few brief exchanges with the Sikh doctor and with one of the administrators, there is no conversational engagement with any adult in the film. Although the Prayas Home website stresses the importance of the education and training that it offers to the boys, there are only a couple of brief classroom scenes, neither at all edifying, and an equally brief and dialogue-free scene of boys in what appears to be some kind of clothes-making training workshop. Nor does education and training crop up in the children's testimonies, except in passing. Throughout the film, the camera remains resolutely at a child's eye level in any social interaction.

All this is very much in accordance with the 'refractory idea' that had impressed itself upon MacDougall as he was shooting the Doon School films many years earlier, namely that 'children might actually write the agenda for adults', and that, as a consequence, one should attend carefully to their view of the world rather than impose adult preconceptions upon them. Echoing the quotation from John Locke that featured at the start of *The Age of Reason*, this film begins with a quotation from M. K. Gandhi that makes a complementary point while also accounting for the title of the film: 'the greatest lessons in life, if we would but stoop and humble ourselves … we would learn from the so-called ignorant children'.

But although there are certainly elements of continuity, *Gandhi's Children* represents, to my mind, both a more engaging and an ethnographically richer film than any of MacDougall's earlier films about Indian children. This is primarily because the young subjects of *Gandhi's Children* have had a direct and challenging experience of life outside the home, which infuses what they have to say with a particular weight. The matter-of-fact and dignified way in which they talk about the most harrowing of experiences outside the home and the sheer resilience that they have shown in surviving them are truly remarkable. So too is their ability to deal with the draconian regime within the home.

By contrast, the children who feature in the Doon and Rishi Valley school films are undoubtedly formidably intelligent and well read, while their perception of human relations and their moral judgements may be much more refined than most adults are generally prepared to acknowledge in children. Yet their thoughts and commentaries rarely stray beyond the narrow world of the school in which they live. If they do talk about what is happening in the world outside, it is mostly in relation to such trivial matters as professional cricket, the English football league or Michael Jackson. This difference is reflected in the sphere of action of the films themselves, which in the earlier films remains entirely restricted to the school grounds. In *Gandhi's Children*, on the other hand, the camera moves outside the gates of the Prayas Home to explore the surrounding streets, as if to emphasise the connection between this exterior world and the interior world of the institution.

Indeed, whereas in the earlier films, the separation of the schools from the outside world is mostly taken entirely for granted and simply not discussed, in *Gandhi's Children* the boundary between inside and outside remains both highly permeable and deeply contested. Although many of the children in the home have been 'rescued' from a life of homelessness, poor diets and exploitation, most of them, the film suggests, would prefer that life to being locked up in the Prayas Home.

The many ambiguities of this situation are encapsulated in a scene early in the film when a large group of boys are brought to the home after the police closed down the embroidery factory where they were working. It transpires that these boys had been recruited and brought to Delhi from poor rural villages in Bihar and Uttar Pradesh. But the boys themselves, who appear to be relatively well-dressed and in reasonably good health, are far from pleased with their 'rescue'. They explain that they kept only a small part of what they earned in the factory as pocket money and the rest was sent back home to their families to enable them to buy food. If they are now obliged to return home themselves, it will be to suffer hunger with the rest of their families. Only if a family is rich, one boy explains, can they afford to keep a child at home. 'If they're poor, how can they educate him?' These boys simply cannot understand why the government is stopping them from working and locking them up in the Prayas Home instead.

*Gandhi's Children* has often been referred to as a 'masterpiece' in reviews and appreciations, though certain features of the film have been subject to some adverse comment. First, there is the sheer length of the film: at over three hours, it will surely not be viewed as often as it deserves, at least not in its entirety. Although every life history dealt with in the film is undoubtedly unique and interesting, it is certainly arguable that the film could have offered the same degree of insight into the general issues raised by the Prayas Home while exploring the circumstances of a smaller number of boys.

Second, and more importantly, some viewers have raised questions about the way in which the film enters into the most intimate personal physical spaces of the boys as they shower and use the squat toilets, not once, but at various different points in the film. While these truly disgusting facilities are evidently a powerful component of the experience of everyday life at the Prayas Home, some critics have asked whether it is acceptable from an ethical perspective to expose the dignity of the subjects of an ethnographic film to such a degree.

However, MacDougall has defended the inclusion of these scenes on the grounds that they featured prominently in the material shot by the five boys participating in the video workshop that he was running at the Prayas Home alongside his own shoot. As he wanted *Gandhi's Children* to be as faithful as possible to their experiences, he did not want to back away from that reality merely on account of his own ethnocentric prejudices or the sensitivities of the eventual audience. He also took particular care not to focus on individuals in those scenes.[22]

Whatever one's views on these last matters, it is surely undeniable that in exploring the many ambiguous and complex issues surrounding the work of the Prayas Home with a combination of sensitivity and great cinematographic skill, *Gandhi's Children* is an ethnographic film of the highest quality that has resonances that reach far beyond the particular situation that it portrays. For not only are we encouraged to reflect upon the circumstances of the children in the Prayas Home, but also more generally about the difficulties and complexities of providing the conditions for a happy and secure childhood in circumstances of extreme social and economic deprivation. For those who might have regretted that such a talented ethnographic film-maker as David MacDougall should spend quite so many years exploring the hermetic world of the most privileged of Indian children, *Gandhi's Children* represents a decisive and welcome return to a topic with broader social and political implications.

Over the course of this chapter, I have sought to show that although there may be many differences between the praxis of the films made by David and Judith MacDougall since they set themselves up as freelance ethnographic film-makers and that of the work that they produced earlier in their careers, there are also strong elements of continuity. Moreover, even when they have deviated from the norms of Observational Cinema as practised in its classical form, it has been more in the nature of a temporary fluctuation or a moment of experimentation rather than a decisive and irreversible change in any particular direction.

Thus, when the MacDougalls made *Photo Wallahs* in the early 1990s, it stood out as an exception within the broader body of their work up to that point in that, rather than being based on a particular social situation and a limited number of principal characters, as all their previous films had been, it consisted of the exploration of a single central idea and featured a large number of different characters, none of whom was significantly more important than any other. But *Photo Wallahs* has – so far – proved to be something of a one-off within their oeuvre, since they have not made any other films that are quite like it. The film that followed, *Tempus de Baristas*, represented by and large a return to the earlier paradigm.

There has been a similar fluctuation in the Indian school films. In the Doon School films, there is recurrent use of formal interviews standing outside the temporal horizon of the films, a practice that would have been considered anathema according to the norms of Observational Cinema in its classical mode. Similarly, in *The Age of Reason*, the relationship between film-maker and subject defines the parameters of the film in a way that is previously unparalleled in the MacDougalls' work. The use of commentary at certain key points is also unusual. These 'deviant' features largely disappear in the Rishi Valley trilogy, but there are other innovations instead, notably in the highly observational, mostly non-participatory *Schoolscapes*, which is almost entirely lacking in the conversational dialogues that had been one of the hallmarks of the MacDougall's work since *To Live with Herds*.

But then *Gandhi's Children*, shot in the same year as *Schoolscapes*, represents a striking return to the classical Observational Cinema mode. It has not, however, been a permanent return, since *Under the Palace Wall*, David MacDougall's most recent work at the time of writing, has more in common with *Schoolscapes*. Released in 2014 and made while David was running a film training workshop in Delwara, Rajasthan, this film is also highly observational and non-dialogical, though there is also a strong element of continuity with his earlier work in that it is narratively structured by an 'as if' chronology, presenting material shot over several weeks as if it were a day in the life of the village, beginning at first light and ending at dusk.

As Colin Young observed in his original manifesto-essay on Observational Cinema, 'any intellectual discipline will outgrow its early enthusiasms and change its methodologies'.[23] This is in effect what David and Judith Mac-Dougall have being doing since the early 1990s. The films made during this period have led to the diversification of the praxis of Observational Cinema, greatly enriching it in the process. Through a process of experimentation and innovation, they have shown that it is not necessary to remain slavishly tied to a particular formula for making ethnographic films. Arguably, the ethnographicness of the films that they produced in this period has also varied, ranging from those that are densely and indisputably ethnographic such as *Gandhi's Children*, to those that are more in the manner of works of cinematographic experimentation, of which the most notable example would be *Schoolscapes*.

But what all these recent films have in common, which they share with the MacDougalls' earlier work, is that irrespective of the particular practical innovations that they may have involved, they have been based, almost without exception, on a period of extended immersive fieldwork, a participatory and collaborative relationship with the subjects, and a high degree of film craft. In all these various respects, they are films that go beyond observation while also being exemplary works of Observational Cinema.

## Notes

1 I am particularly grateful to David MacDougall for his detailed commentaries on two different drafts of this chapter, one in March 2017, the other in August 2018.

2 In 1989 (i.e. after the MacDougalls had left the organisation), the Australian Institute for Aboriginal Studies (AIAS) was renamed the Australian Institute for Aboriginal and Torres Straits Islander Studies (AIATSIS).

3 In addition, David has made a further four films in India that have yet to be released. These are all relatively short, totalling approximately a further 75 minutes.

4 These workshops have so far taken place at six different locations: the Doon School in Dehra Dun, Uttarakhand; a government school in New Delhi; the Prayas Children's Home for Boys, also in New Delhi; the private Rishi Valley School in Andhra Pradesh, a government primary school in the village of Delwara in Rajasthan; and a day school in Ladakh. Regrettably, a discussion of these projects lies beyond the scope of this chapter, but readers are encouraged to consult *The Asia Pacific Journal of Anthropology* 15(2) (2014): 453–79 where scholars from a variety of academic backgrounds comment on the four films produced through the New Delhi government school project. This publication also includes a brief introduction by David MacDougall explaining the general background of the workshops. See also Potts (2015).

5 MacDougall (1992b), 98.

6 See Chapter 11, pp. 329, 336, 339, and Chapter 12, p. 359 for references to Dai Vaughan's work on ethnographic films made for British television. For his writing about editing, see Vaughan (1999).

7 MacDougall (1992b), 99. See the discussion of *The Song of Ceylon* in Chapter 1, pp. 50–2.

8 MacDougall (2001).

9 David MacDougall, personal communication, August 2018. I am grateful to MacDougall for this estimate of his shooting ratio which is based on a thorough revision of his camera logs and is slightly at variance with the previously published figures.

10 MacDougall (2001), 18.

11 In this discussion, I draw on David MacDougall's articles both about the Doon School films (MacDougall 2001, 2006c and 2006d) and about the representation of childhood on film more generally (2006b). See also his most recent accounts (2019), particularly pp. 49–53 and 89–102.

12 MacDougall (2006d), 125.

13 MacDougall acknowledges that his interest in the way in which the subjects of his later Doon School films handled this period of transition in their lives was 'no doubt' related to his own boarding school experience. In an uncharacteristically personal aside, he comments, 'even today when I dream, I almost never dream about living in a family. I am part of a group, often among strangers – a collection of people trying to make a life together' (MacDougall 2006d), 127.

14 Perhaps the most extended example of voice-over narration in MacDougall's oeuvre is in *Link-Up Diary*, one of the last films that the MacDougalls made in Australia, with David working, unusually, on his own. However, in this case, the voice-over is primarily informational, whereas in *The Age of Reason*, it is much more subjective.

15 Notwithstanding the citation of Locke at the beginning of the film, he is not the originator of the phrase borrowed for the title of the film. *The Age of Reason* was originally the title given to a series of pamphlets published around the beginning of the nineteenth century by the English and early American political activist, Thomas Paine.

16 MacDougall (2006d), 141.

17 Of the four other films that MacDougall shot at the Rishi Valley School, only one has so far been formally released: this is *Arnav at Six*, shot in 2008 and released in 2012. The others are *Motion and Emotion* and *Of Kites and Filming* both shot in 2004, and *Mohnish Sings*, shot in 2008 (David MacDougall, personal communication, March 2017).

18 See Anna Grimshaw's discussion of Krishnamurti's concept of 'awareness' in Grimshaw and Hockings (2011), 394–5. She also draws attention to the striking similarities between Krishnamurti's ideas and MacDougall's discussion of the act of looking in the introductory chapter of his book, *The Corporeal Image* (MacDougall 2006a), 7–8.

19 MacDougall had first attempted to shoot a film consisting of a series of long takes, with one shot per scene, as far back as 1988–89, the period when he was making *Photo Wallahs* in Mussorie with Judith MacDougall. Although the film was never completed, it still exists in the form of an edited 16 mm workprint (David MacDougall, personal communication, August 2018).

20 See Chapter 2, pp. 79–81.

21 MacDougall has recently published a powerful account of his experience of making this film (2019), pp. 53–60.

22 Personal communication, August 2018. MacDougall adds that, in general, in the film as a whole, he felt that he had treated the boys with respect and was confident that they themselves would have regarded the exclusion of the scenes in question as an entirely unwarranted misrepresentation of their situation. He also quotes directly from a letter that he had received from one of the most prominent subjects: 'It was brave of you to bring the reality before everyone. I do not understand why people get offended. I think seeing is not more disgusting than actually living in such conditions for many years continuously.' See also MacDougall's discussion of this specific point in his recent book (2019), p. 58.

23 Young (1993), 113.

# 15

# Negative capability and the flux of life: films of the Sensory Ethnography Lab

S INCE its establishment in 2006, the Sensory Ethnography Lab at the University of Harvard (henceforth the SEL) has been responsible for an impressive series of innovative and technically accomplished films, a number of which have vaulted the frontiers of academia and been widely distributed through festivals and even general cinema release, mostly to critical acclaim in the mass media. At the same time, these films have contributed to a lively debate within academia about the very nature of ethnographic film-making and, indeed, of ethnography more generally. Furthermore, their work is constantly evolving and diversifying, making any generalisation perilous. As with this book as a whole, the time frame of this chapter pertains only up until 2015, and their most recent work will most probably require some further refinement of the arguments and analyses presented here. But with these caveats, certain general characteristics can be discerned. One thing is certainly clear: although the films of the SEL have been described as 'observational', and with good reason, they are very different in terms of their underlying praxis to the films of Observational Cinema.[1]

The first part of this chapter is concerned with the general ideas and influences that inform the praxis of the SEL and with the films that first established its reputation, which were made through the joint endeavours of Lucien Castaing-Taylor, Ilisa Barbash and Ernst Karel. In the latter part, I consider some more recent works, including the films made by those who might be called the 'second wave' of SEL film-makers, that is, those who were involved at some point in the media training courses that have been offered through the departments of Anthropology and of Visual and Environmental Studies at Harvard since 2006. These film-makers include Véréna Paravel, John Paul 'J. P.' Sniadecki and Stephanie Spray.

As I describe, the film-making praxis of the SEL has been moving progressively away from a conception of ethnography that is in tune with the one on which this book is based. While this movement has not been without its twists and turns, and some doubling back, there can be no doubt about the general direction of travel.

FOUNDATIONS AND INFLUENCES

The SEL was initially set up at Harvard as a collaborative venture between the Department of Anthropology and the Department of Visual and Environmental Studies. On the home page of its website, it describes itself as 'an experimental laboratory that promotes innovative combinations of aesthetics and ethnography'. In addition to film, it is also involved in the production of still photography, sound recordings and installations, though in this chapter I shall be concerned exclusively with the SEL's film productions.

The founding director of the SEL was Lucien Castaing-Taylor and he continues to act as its director to this day. Castaing-Taylor, who is British, studied anthropology as an undergraduate at the University of Cambridge and later joined the doctoral programme at the University of California, Berkeley. As a film-maker, his initial training was on the documentary film production course offered by Center for Visual Anthropology at the University of Southern California (USC). Although a number of others have made major and very important contributions to the work of the SEL, Castaing-Taylor has played the predominant role in determining its overall orientation, both by personal example as a film-maker, and also as a teacher on the various postgraduate media training programmes offered at Harvard. In many ways, the SEL could be seen as the institutional embodiment of an intellectual and creative agenda that Castaing-Taylor first laid out in embryonic form as far back as a series of publications that appeared in the 1990s, some years before he arrived at Harvard.[2]

In addition to his position at the SEL, Castaing-Taylor has also been the Director (later joined as co-Director by the film-maker and historian of science, Peter L. Galison) and previously the Associate Director, of the Film Study Center, since 2002. This body was first set up in 1957 to support the production of non-fiction films, initially under the wing of Harvard's Peabody Museum of Archaeology and Ethnology, though in 1964, it transferred to the Carpenter Center for Visual Arts. Although the Film Study Center is now independent of the Carpenter Center, the two bodies continue to collaborate. The first film to be produced through the Film Study Center was John Marshall's work, *The Hunters* (1957), while the first director was Robert Gardner, who continued in this position for forty years, until 1997. His films, *Dead Birds* (1963) and *Forest of Bliss* (1985) were also produced with the assistance of the Center.[3] Today, as described on its website, the Center aims to support a broad range of audiovisual creative practice, 'from the ethnographic to the experimental', with a continuing emphasis on non-fiction films but now also including other media and installations. The Center has supported the production of many of the best-known SEL works, as well as works by independent non-fiction film-makers associated with Harvard in one way or another.[4]

Another important influence on the praxis of the SEL has been Ernst Karel, a sonic ethnographer and sound artist who holds a PhD in anthropology from the University of Chicago. Until 2017, Karel held the post of manager of the SEL, while simultaneously being the assistant director of the Film Study Center and a teacher on the practical media training programmes. As well as producing his own acoustic works, which have ranged from sonic ethnographies to more abstract compositional works, Karel has contributed to almost all the major films produced by the SEL, be it as sound recordist, sound editor or sound designer, or some combination of all three roles. In conjunction with the high standards of cinematography that generally characterise SEL films, their distinctively sensorial quality can in large part be attributed to the complex and layered soundtracks created for them by Karel. Indeed, as the screen studies scholar, Scott MacDonald has observed, Karel's 'contributions to this body of work would be difficult to overestimate'.[5]

Although the film-makers associated with the SEL have mostly come from anthropology or social science backgrounds themselves, through the Film Study Center, as well as through the Harvard Film Archive, located in the Carpenter Center, they have been engaged in an active dialogue with film-makers from a range of very different backgrounds.[6] As a result, the SEL film-making praxis has been much influenced by non-fiction film-making approaches lying well outside conventional ethnographic film traditions. Among the film-makers whose work has been particularly influential, Castaing-Taylor himself identifies Jana Sevcikova, Pedro Costa, Sergei Dvortesvoy and Artavazd Peleyshan.[7]

Another important influence appears to have been films in a tradition of North American avant-garde formalist film-making, sometimes referred to as 'structural' film-making, as represented, for example, by the work of Peter Hutton, James Benning and Sharon Lockhart, all of whom have been visitors to Harvard over the years. Of the film-makers working in this tradition, the one who seems to have had the closest ties is Lockhart, who has not only shown her work regularly at the Film Study Center and the Film Archive, but has also worked directly with students enrolled on the media training programmes on a practical project. In addition, a number of her films have been produced with the assistance of the Film Study Center, or Studio7Arts, the production company that Robert Gardner set up towards the end of his life. Certainly, once one is familiar with Lockhart's work, it becomes much easier to appreciate what at least some SEL film-makers have been aiming to achieve.

Lockhart's films are typically constructed around a series of prolonged shots taken from a single static position (normally of at least five minutes, often much longer). The soundtracks usually consist simply of synch sounds: although these may include dialogue, it is rarely comprehensible. Most of her films show people apparently going about their business regardless of the camera, though in fact their movements have often been carefully prepared and even choreographed by Lockhart, so that, in effect, their action on screen is more in the nature of a performance than an example of their normal everyday behaviour. A number of her films have been shot in exotic locations and she usually undertakes a period of research prior to shooting. Probably for these reasons, her work has been described on occasion, both by herself and by art film commentators, as 'ethnographic', though when judged by the criteria for the definition of that term proposed in this book, their ethnographicness is, at best, limited.[8]

SEL film-makers have also been influenced by certain philosophical ideas, which are signalled by a number of key terms that crop up regularly in their writings and interviews. Particularly important are the allusions to 'aesthetics', as in the mission statement on the SEL website cited above. This is a reference, not to anything exclusively to do with fine arts, as one might think, but rather to the use of this term by the American pragmatist philosopher John Dewey to refer to any form of experiential engagement with the world that effects a transition from a state of disorder to a state of harmony. As such, it is applicable to everyday technical processes and relationships with the environment, as well as to all manner of art forms, from the most elitist to the most popular.

Also prominent in SEL discourse are references to the 'flux of life', 'life-worlds', 'lived experience', 'the magnitude of human existence' and other similar phrases, all of which are allusions to the ideas of philosophers in the phenomenological tradition, particularly Martin Heidegger and Maurice Merleau-Ponty. Another author alluded to in SEL commentaries is the post-structuralist Jean-François Lyotard, notably in relation to his analysis of the way in which discursive modes of representation seek to control the more unruly but fuller figurative modes. Regardless of their precise intellectual origin, however, all these allusions are usually invoked by SEL film-makers for the same general purpose, namely, to assert the importance of corporeal experience as a mode of human engagement with the world, and thereby to underwrite the relative neglect of discursive language in SEL films in favour of more sensorial material.

Whether these philosophical thinkers were all quite so convinced of the limits of language as a means of mediating human relationships with the world as some SEL film-makers appear to believe is debatable: after all, Heidegger famously observed that 'Language is the House of Being. In its house, man dwells.'[9] However, it is not my concern here to contest the validity of these philosophical ideas, nor their application to ethnographic film-making, but rather to identify in pragmatic operational terms the nature of SEL film-making praxis.

In this regard, one can draw a number of instructive parallels between the work of the SEL film-makers and their institutional forebear, Robert Gardner. The most significant of these concerns the role of dialogue. As with Gardner's work, there is typically little emphasis on dialogue in SEL films. In some of their films, there is a limited amount of dialogue between subjects, while in others, there is a similarly limited amount of dialogue between subjects and film-makers. But there is nothing like the pronounced emphasis on 'conversation' such as one finds in Observational Cinema.[10]

This relative lack of interest in dialogue is related to another point of comparison between the praxes of Gardner and the SEL, namely the degree to which they are participatory and reflexive. As Gardner readily acknowledged, although he was concerned to provide an accurate account of the life-worlds that he presented in his films, he was more interested in what those worlds meant to him, philosophically or artistically, than in what they meant to the people who actually lived them. As a corollary, one rarely hears the subjects' voices in his films, nor do we ever hear his own voice enquiring about their views of the world, or exploring how their practices might relate to their general cultural ideas or their networks of social relationships. In SEL films, while we do sometimes get to hear the film-makers' voices in dialogue with the subjects, the content of these dialogues is often rather trivial and related to the immediate circumstances of filming itself rather than to the making of connections between what the film is showing the subjects doing and more general features of their worldview or social and political circumstances. On the whole then, SEL films are not very much more reflexive and participatory than those of Gardner.

This lack of emphasis on verbal exchange is not, however, associated with a lack of interest among SEL film-makers in sound more generally. On the contrary, SEL films usually feature soundtracks that have been most intensively fashioned, often by Ernst Karel. Here one may draw a direct parallel between the vital role that Karel has played in the making of SEL films and the similarly important role that the sound editor Michel Chalufour played in many of Gardner's major films. Where there is a difference is in the editing of the picture track. In general, SEL film-makers do not make use of dense metaphorical associations between adjacent shots or sequences to communicate their meanings, certainly not to anything like the degree to which Gardner deployed these associations in *Forest of Bliss*, as described at length in Chapter 9.

One can also draw a more personal comparison between Gardner and Castaing-Taylor. Having once been enthusiastic advocates for the use of film within the discipline of anthropology, both subsequently became disillusioned with the academic world. In recent interviews, Castaing-Taylor has taken to describing himself as a 'recovering anthropologist', who still might preface his work as a film-maker on a particular project with a period of first-hand familiarisation, in the manner of classical participant-observation fieldwork, but who otherwise actively seeks to remain as ignorant as possible of the subject matter, for fear of 'polluting' his own apperceptions with any previous literature or previous way of dealing with the subject.[11]

Castaing-Taylor also now regularly disclaims, with admirable candour, any interest in clarifying or explaining, or indeed 'saying' anything, since for him, this would involve an unacceptable reduction of the inherent ambiguity of the world. Instead, he suggests that the SEL, as a collective endeavour, should be more invested in what the early-nineteenth-century Romantic poet, John Keats called 'negative capability', that is, the capacity to be 'in uncertainties, Mysteries, doubts without any irritable reaching after fact and reason'. But while it would certainly be inspiring to feel that one's work is based on the same principles as that of William Shakespeare – cited by Keats in the same passage as the supreme exponent of 'negative capability' – it is difficult to see how this frank disclaimer of any interest in fact or reason is compatible with the general project of ethnography as this is understood by most of its contemporary academic practitioners.

## BEYOND ACADEMIA: *SWEETGRASS* AS THE PIONEER WORK OF THE SEL

The film that first drew attention to the work of the SEL beyond the realms of academia, and in spectacular fashion, was *Sweetgrass*, a feature-length film about the life of a group of sheep herders working for a small family business in Big Timber, a small town in southern Montana, just north of Yellowstone Park. This film was co-directed by Ilisa Barbash and Castaing-Taylor. Although it was not released until 2009, the main bulk of the shooting took place between 2001 and 2003 when the film-makers were still teaching anthropology at the University of Colorado Boulder. During this period, both spent prolonged periods of fieldwork in Big Timber.[12]

In total, they shot around 200 hours of footage, which were reduced to no more than 101 minutes in the final film (i.e. involving a cutting ratio of 120:1, which even in the video era is really exraordinarily high). In addition, accompanying the DVD version, at least as released in the UK, there are ten short Bonus Films, totalling around 55 minutes, which provide an interesting complement to the main film. Starting in 2007, eight further films were produced for display as an installation under the collective title, *Sheep Rushes*: six of these films offer more extended versions of material included in the main film, but two are unique to the installation. With a total running time of almost 80 minutes, these eight films also complement the main film but are interesting in their own right, and I shall therefore discuss them in a separate section.

In terms of its general narrative shape, *Sweetgrass* is based on a conventional 'as if' chronology: material shot over two or three years was reordered in the edit suite to suggest a chronology of a number of consecutive months within a single year, running from late winter through to the autumn.

15.1 *Sweetgrass* (2009). Left, Pat Connolly complains to his mother by mobile phone about life on the high plains. Right, at the end of the trail, John Ahern moves on to an uncertain future.

The film begins with a pre-title sequence of establishment shots of the landscape dusted with snow. This is followed by the title inserted in among various extended shots of the sheep, before the film plunges abruptly into the noisy and claustrophobic confines of a shearing trailer. Here, one is immediately struck by the deft but seemingly uncaring way in which the shearers handle the animals, as if they were mere objects on a production line, which, in a sense, they are – this is a business after all. Spring then follows and the sheep herders are shown being equally brusque in their handling of new-born lambs.

Around twenty-five minutes into the film, the tone changes decisively as a vast flock of three thousand sheep is driven along the main street of Big Timber and up into the high plains of the nearby Absaroka-Beartooth mountain range, where they will spend the summer. Here, amid the stunning natural beauty of the peaks and a stream of Western movie tropes, the film comes to revolve around two male characters with very contrasting attitudes to the animals, as we discover through the radio microphones that they are wearing. The older of the two, the much-wrinkled John Ahern, sings to the sheep and addresses them as 'my girls', while the other, Pat Connolly, who is deeply disillusioned with life on the trail, more often curses them roundly. After following the day-to-day activities of Ahern and Connolly as they herd the sheep, scare off night-time grizzlies and other predators, and engage in desultory conversations in and around their cook tent, the summer period culminates in a classical crisis scene in which Connolly takes himself up to a high point and uses his mobile phone to unburden himself of all his woes to his mother (figure 15.1, left).

This scene is much commented upon in reviews of the film, since its whining tone clashes almost comically with the epic grandeur of the surroundings, as well as with the trope of the resilient Marlboro Man. The film then moves into valedictory mode as the sheep are herded back down the mountain in clouds of dust to the stockyards at Big Timber. Finally, in

15.2 *Sweetgrass* (2009). Left, a 'bellwether' ewe, the only creature, human or ovine, to look intently down the barrel of the camera. Right, the sheep are herded through the forest on the way to the high plains.

a memorable concluding shot, like a drifter in a Steinbeck novel, we see Ahern as a passenger in a pick-up truck, as sparing as ever with words and pulling on his smoke, on the road again, moving on to some unknown, uncertain destination (figure 15.1, right).

The cinematography on *Sweetgrass*, performed by Castaing-Taylor, is highly accomplished. So too is the sound recording, which involved the use of up to eight radio mikes, attached to animals as well as people. In the end credits, Castaing-Taylor is described merely as the person who 'recorded' the material, but this modest title belies the highly considered visual style that informs the way in which the material has been shot. Most takes are long, often in wide-angle, with close-ups, zooms, even mid-shots being a relative rarity. There are, however, some notable exceptions, including the zoomed-in close-up among the establishing shots of the pre-title sequence of a 'bellwether' ewe, that is, an animal that has been given a bell on account of its tendency to be a leader of the flock. This sheep looks unflinchingly down the barrel of the camera lens, the only subject, human or ovine, to do so in the course of the entire film (figure 15.2, left).

Again with a few exceptions, the material is shot from an unprivileged perspective – one that would be available to someone participating normally in the events portrayed. While some of the wide shots appear to have been taken from a tripod, notably the slow pans across the mountain scenery, most are hand-held, or more strictly speaking harness-held, since throughout the shoot, Castaing-Taylor wore a harness from which he could suspend the camera in order to keep his hands free for assisting the sheep herders or riding his horse. While he was shooting he made it clear to the subjects that he did not wish to engage in conversation, with the result that while there are a number of casual references to him, at no point does a human subject ever directly address or even look at the camera. When he was not shooting, however, Castaing-Taylor reports that he was often involved in animated discussion with his subjects.

Once they had completed the editing, Barbash and Castaing-Taylor took the financially bold decision to copy the film – originally shot on relatively low quality NTSC video – onto 35 mm stock, and in this form they sent it around international festivals. After a slow start, including rejection by many specifically ethnographic film festivals, resounding success at more general major film festivals led to international theatrical distribution and eventually to the garnering of a host of highly enthusiastic reviews from even the most hard-nosed of the US feature film commentariat.[13] Almost all expressed their simultaneous surprise and joy at the discovery that men for all the world like the cowboys of the Old West should still be living at this hour, though, in a heart-rending punctum reserved to an intertitle right at the end of the final credits, it is revealed that after more than a century of operation, the family farm at the heart of the film had closed down in 2004, the year after filming had been completed. In effect, this brought all sheep herding in the Absaroka-Beartooth mountains to an end.

Whether the film is equally successful from a specifically ethnographic point of view, and if so, in what sense, clearly depends crucially on how one defines ethnography itself. In interviews, the film-makers have spoken of their concern to give as much attention to the sheep as to the human subjects in the film, often referring to the long history of human–ovine symbiosis stretching back to the Neolithic era. In cutting the film, they explain, they sought to establish the sheep both as a collectivity and as individuals (as in the form of the bellwether ewe), even before introducing the people, who, for the first twenty minutes of the film are shown communicating only with the sheep (and one or two dogs). On account of this prominence of the sheep, particularly in the early part of the film, some reviewers have suggested that the film should be considered an important contribution to the current interest in multispecies ethnography.

*Sweetgrass* undoubtedly offers a fine and detailed ethnographic description of certain aspects of the life of Montana sheep herders while at the same time affording a strong sense of 'being there' among a sea of sheep and the vastness of the Absaroka-Beartooth mountains (figure 15.2, right). But if one seeks to go beyond merely descriptive ethnographicness, this requires more than just the evocation of 'lived experience', even if it is powerfully and effectively achieved, as in this case. It also requires, as I have argued at various points in this book, the establishment of connections between the practices of 'lived experience' with the ideas and social relations that sustain the 'life-world' that is portrayed on the screen. In *Sweetgrass*, these connections are certainly present but they remain in the background.

However, it is these connections that inform most of what we see on the screen, including the interspecific relationships between human beings and sheep. For, contrary to what some of the film-makers' remarks in interviews seem to imply, what we are witnessing in *Sweetgrass* is not some kind of generic encounter of humanity and sheep that has been going on since prehistory, but rather the operation of a small family business which is, moreover, on the point of economic collapse due to the concatenation of a series of historically specific circumstances, including the general reduction in the consumption of lamb in the USA as a whole and other, more local factors to do with grazing permits in national parks. Arguably, it is this set of circumstances, more than any other, that impacts on the manner in which the characters in the film relate to the practice of sheep herding and, by extension, on the manner in which they relate to the animals.

While Castaing-Taylor was trailing in the mountains, Barbash remained in Big Timber, and shot scenes of life in and around the town, including rodeos, shooting competitions, even political meetings. But when cutting the film, they decided to leave all this material out of the film and focus instead on what one might term the 'front-line' of sheepherding. Clearly, this was an entirely legitimate choice and it certainly seems likely that to have burdened the film with all this additional information would have been to its detriment as a cinematic spectacle. But this decision also limited the complexity of the ethnographic account that the film could offer.

On the other hand, a good sense of the broader context of ideas and relations underpinning the world represented in *Sweetgrass* is offered in the Bonus Films that feature on the DVD as well as in the film-makers' voice-over commentary that is one of the audio options for playback. The Bonus Films cover the other end, so to speak, of a number of the processes that we see in the main film, including the insemination of the ewes, and the marshalling and weighing of sheep before they are sent off to market. More importantly, in following these processes, we are made aware of the importance of family relations to the way in which this sheepherding business is conducted, and in particular of the centrality of Lawrence Allestad, the ranch owner and paterfamilias, and by the film-makers' own account, a man to be reckoned with. In the main film, however, although he appears at various crucial points, he is not identified. Also clearly important are his wife Elaine and various other relatives, including their son Billy, but they too only have anonymous walk-on parts in *Sweetgrass* itself.

It also transpires that the principal characters, Ahern and Connolly, are cousins, while the young teenagers who help drive the sheep up through the forest are Connolly's niece and nephew. Many other people, including women, old men and even children, all seem to be involved in the business of sheepherding at one point or another. We discover that the ethnicity of the Allestads as 'Wegians' (i.e descendants of Norwegian immigrants), is important to them and serves to distinguish them from Connolly and Ahern, their hired hands, who are 'Irish'. The men doing the shearing, on the other hand, belong to neither group, but are a specialist gang who move from farm to farm with their trailer, and come from much further afield, even as far as New Zealand. As time is money for them, they are anxious to despatch the shearing of the lambs as expeditiously as possible, and as they do it all the time they have become highly efficient at this work.

Another aspect that comes across in these additional materials is how many skills are involved the practice of sheepherding. Early on in the main film, a young man – whom we discover from the film-makers' voice-over is Billy Allestad – tells a joke about a man who goes to buy himself a new brain only to discover, to his surprise, that a cowboy brain is much more expensive than that of a lawyer or a banker because, as the punchline has it, 'it has never been used'. The main film itself does little to contradict the old adage that many a true word is spoken in jest; for while we do get a sense of the skilled nature of the sheepherders' practices in the birthing scene in which they are trying to get ewes to adopt motherless lambs, once we are up in the mountains, over the radio microphones we get a great deal of ugly invective from Connolly and many charmingly mumbled cowboy songs from Ahern, but only a limited sense of the skills that the two of them must have had to deploy in managing a vast flock of sheep vulnerable to predators over several months. We see them shooting ineffectively at grizzlies, but it is only from the additional materials that we learn that they are missing the bears on purpose, and shooting only to scare them because, owing to the federal regulations regarding 'wilderness' areas, they would be heavily fined and could even be sent to gaol if they actually killed a bear.

There is also a marked difference in the language used by Connolly and Ahern in the additional materials, compared to their speech in the main film. *In the Cook Tent*, one of the Bonus Films, shows that, on occasion at least, they could be very articulate. After a couple of preliminary shots, this 8-minute film consists of a single shot taken looking in from the front of the tent, with Connolly in the foreground and Ahern beyond. There is an almost identical shot in the main film, obviously taken at the same time, in which both men are silent and impassive, conforming to the Western movie trope of the cowboy as a man of few words. However, in *In the Cook Tent*, they talk in a lively manner about a number of legendary local characters, including Roy Connolly, Pat's grandfather, who was often on the wrong side of the law on account of his predilection for horse-rustling, but who was also both an accomplished and a cunning horseman, who knew how to handle himself at rodeos. This then leads on to a general discussion of horsemanship skills. In contrast to the material presented in the main film, as he tells these stories Connolly often looks across to Castaing-Taylor behind the camera to include him in the discussion through eye contact, even if not verbally.

As *In the Cook Tent* shows, the sheepherders' experience of the 'life-world' presented in *Sweetgrass* consists not just of corporeal practices related to sheepherding but is also heavily invested with other ideas, memories and values that are only accessible to third parties through language. Moreover, these ideas relate not just to social relations, but also to the environment and to animals, a point made obliquely in two other Bonus films, in which Connolly, Billy and Lawrence Allestad, and another man talk, first about elk hunting and then about their relationships with dogs. A multispecies ethnography that does not embrace this intellectual and cultural dimension of the relationship between species can only ever be partial.

Clearly, no ethnographic film can cover everything and *Sweetgrass* does what it does with great conviction, to paraphrase Flaherty's celebrated dictum cited in the Introduction to this part of the book. In a sense, the Bonus Films and the film-makers' voice-over commentary serve something of the same contextualising function as the 'study guide' so piously and routinely called for by proponents of ethnographic film over the years, and so rarely produced in practice. When taken together with the main film, these additional materials certainly greatly increase the complexity of the audiovisual ethnographic account that Barbash and Castaing-Taylor offer of the last days of sheepherding in Montana at the beginning of the twenty-first century.

Even when taken on its own, without the Bonus Films, *Sweetgrass* offers a richly descriptive account of certain aspects of this sheepherding life that can be appreciated in much the same way that one might appreciate *The Hunters* as an account of San hunting practices in the 1950s. It may be that it offers only a partial account, marked by certain selective exclusions. But this does not prevent one from admiring *Sweetgrass* as an extremely well made film that is clearly firmly anchored in the relationship of trust built up by film-makers over the course of their long-term commitment to the community where it was produced.

## ETHNOGRAPHIC FILM AS GALLERY INSTALLATION: *SHEEP RUSHES*

Although *Sweetgrass* was of crucial importance in establishing the reputation of the SEL, perhaps the best indicator of its future direction was not *Sweetgrass* itself, but rather *Sheep Rushes*, the suite of eight much shorter films that were edited from the same body of rushes. These were not intended for screening in a cinema or lecture hall, but rather for presentation in an art gallery in the manner of an installation. The first such presentation occurred in 2007, some two years before the completion of *Sweetgrass*, and involved only three of the films. Subsequent gallery presentations have involved various combinations of the films up to and including all eight of them. In contrast to *Sweetgrass*, Lucien Castaing-Taylor is generally identified as the sole director of *Sheep Rushes*, though Ilisa Barbash continues to be credited as the producer, while Ernst Karel acted as sound editor, as in the longer film.[14]

Apart from the first film, *Hell Roaring Creek*, which is almost twenty minutes in duration, all the films in the *Sheep Rushes* suite are between 5 and 12 minutes long, each offering a vignette of a certain aspect of the sheepherders' life. Again with the exception of *Hell Roaring Creek* as well as one other shorter film, *Bedding Down*, which are unique to *Sheep Rushes*, there is considerable overlap between these installation films and the material that appears in *Sweetgrass*. This overlap is greater in some films than in others, but as a general rule, a given situation is represented at greater length in the *Sheep Rushes* version.

In sharp contrast to *Sweetgrass*, however, though some of the films have a certain internal narrative structure, there is no attempt to insert the films as a group into any sort of overarching narrative arc. In the accompanying textual catalogues, the *Sheep Rushes* films are generally presented in the chronological order in which they were shot, with the shearing and lambing coming after the grazing on the high plains, as they did in reality. But when the films are presented in an art gallery, visitors are not required to view them in any prescribed order. Instead, each individual film is presented on a loop and visitors are free to enter and leave as they please, at any point.

The image track of most of the *Sheep Rushes* films features long takes and minimal editing, legitimating the slightly ironic title in the sense that they approximate – though in fact still remain far from – unedited film rushes. The soundtrack, on the other hand, has been extensively edited by Karel and is rich, multilayered and distributed over five channels. Indeed, Castaing-Taylor has commented that he considers these films to be 'audiovideos', works that are more sound pieces than image pieces. This combination of highly observational camerawork and enhanced soundtracks invites an intense visual and acoustic engagement with the material in order, it would seem, to provoke thoughts that are not confined to the parochial world of Big Timber but are of a rather more general philosophical, even existential order.

This is certainly suggested by *Geworfen*, the alternative title given to the last film in the suite and the main title of which is *Into-the-Jug*. This film, which is 11 minutes long, consists of a series of extended shots showing the birthing of lambs in the 'jugs', the small wooden pens about 5 ft × 5 ft within the lambing shed at the Allestad ranch. With ruthless proximity, the camera shows the lambs being laboriously dragged out of their mothers' bodies and then literally thrown onto the upturned lid of a plastic dustbin along with some other lambs, in a bloody, shapeless pile, still covered in amniotic fluid. There is some banter between the man who is doing the birthing (Lawrence Allestad, as we know from the Bonus Films) and one or more off-screen third parties, but this is not particularly significant. One of these shots appears in the main film, but in being shown here in combination with a number of others on the same subject, and in isolation from any other material, it has much greater impact. The image of the biological process, in combination with the apparent indifference of the sheepherders to the fact that they are dealing with sentient beings, will surely be unsettling for some viewers.

While the hyphens in the main title offer a clue, it is *Geworfen*, the alternative title, which suggests that this film should not be understood merely as a descriptive account of the sheepherders of Big Timber treating their animals with a ruthless pragmatism, but rather that the lambs' experience as shown in the film may also serve as a metaphor for the *human* condition. For *Geworfen* would appear to be a play on words, albeit one that is highly recondite: in the simplest sense, this title consists merely of the past participle of the German verb *werfen*, which literally means to throw or to drop, but is also used to describe the giving of birth by animals; however, *Geworfen* is also a reference to a key concept of Heideggerian philosophy, *Geworfenheit*, usually translated into English as 'thrownness'. This concept encapsulates the Heideggerian idea that human beings are arbitrarily 'thrown' at birth into a Being-in-the-World (just as lambs are thrown, similarly hyphenated, 'Into-the-Jug') that is constrained and paradoxical, primarily because it is finite.

Although I suspect that there is considerable irony at play here, this reading of the transcendent in the ethnographically particular is reminiscent of Robert Gardner's much-cited observation regarding the making of *Dead Birds* – that he was less interested in the Dani themselves than in the opportunity that the making of a film about their warfare afforded for addressing the issue of human mortality, or as he put it, 'how we all, as humans, meet our animal fate'.[15] Similarly, it seems that through *Into-the-Jug* (*Geworfen*), we are being invited to think of how we meet our animal fate when we are born.

But if *Sheep Rushes* is reminiscent in some senses of Gardner's work in terms of its ultimate philosophical objectives, in terms of the practical film-making, this suite of films is more directly reminiscent of the work of the North American 'structural' film-makers. This is particularly true of *Hell Roaring Creek*, which being the first and most substantial film of the suite, is therefore of interest to describe here at some length.

After a simple white-on-black title that disappears after a few seconds, the film begins with a black screen underlain by the intense sound of the water running over stones, gurgling loudly. After what seems like an eternal 45 seconds, the image finally cuts in abruptly to reveal a wide shot taken in the thin light of dawn, from a low, static position, right in the middle of the eponymous creek, with the water rushing towards the camera. Initially, there is nothing to observe other than the water and a screen of conifers with some mountain slopes in the background, nor anything to hear other than the roaring sound of the water. But then there are a few bleats and a sheepherder emerges in the semi-darkness on the right-hand bank, with some sheep and dogs milling about.

This continues for a full five minutes, before the sheepherder finally crosses the stream on foot and after some hesitation, a few sheep follow. This encourages other sheep, until soon there is an almost unbroken stream of sheep crossing the creek from right to left, at right angles to the creek itself. The stream gradually becomes a flood and continues unabated for most of the remaining 15 minutes of the film, as the light gradually increases: the younger sheep leap and skip across, the larger and older ones proceed cautiously, some move in groups, others go it alone. There are two thirty-second breaks in the image – one about a third of the way into the film, the other at about two-thirds. These are the occasion for some minor adjustments in framing and exposure but the sound of the roaring water continues unbroken across both breaks.

The overall effect of *Hell Roaring Creek* is almost unbearably monotonous. This, however, would seem to be precisely the film-maker's intention since the very monotony encourages what Scott MacDonald, in a more general context, has called the 'retraining of perception'.[16] That is, one comes to appreciate, in a way that is not merely factual, and may even be experiential, the vast number of animals involved. Also, within the endlessly repeated crossing of the stream, one comes to attend to the variation within the flock: sheep are proverbially animals that copy one another unthinkingly but here we see each animal apparently crossing in its own distinctive way.

Finally, the meditative reverie into which one has been encouraged to fall is broken as a number of mounted figures bring up the rear of the flock from the right, and also cross the stream. After the last rider leaves the frame on the left, the image of the now empty creek continues for a further 15 seconds before cutting to black. However, the sound of the roaring creek continues unabated under the black screen for a further 25 seconds, returning us metaphorically to the beginning of the film. Indeed, for those watching the film on a loop in a gallery, it would literally return them to the beginning and the crossing would start again.

For Scott MacDonald, *Hell Roaring Creek* represents an 'accomplished instance' of avant-garde film-making in the 'structural' manner. However, Castaing-Taylor himself, referring to *Sheep Rushes* as whole, describes his objectives in more philosophical terms, presenting the installation as an attempt to engage spectatorial attention in 'sheer manifestations of being' which, he believes, can be captured in 'figural' forms of expression, but only if one is prepared to abandon narrative and other discursive, linear modes of representation. In embracing the figural so wholeheartedly and rejecting discourse, *Sheep Rushes* represents a significant departure from narrative-based forms of film-making, including, of course, *Sweetgrass*.[17]

Yet while one might entirely respect Castaing-Taylor's philosophico-artistic aims in producing this installation, this is very different from the project of ethnographic film – if this is conceived of as an attempt to use the medium of film to understand the world from the point of view of the subjects and to explore the connections between ideas, practices and relations that are at play in the construction of their social world. If the practice of ethnography is understood in this latter sense, while one may discern certain ethnographic qualities in some of the other films in the suite, it is difficult to identify anything that is specifically ethnographic about *Hell Roaring Creek*.

In watching this film, we may come to understand something about the behaviour of herded sheep while experiencing vicariously their crossing of the stream in vast numbers. But we learn very little about the human beings in the film or about their relationship to the sheep. In short, however accomplished *Hell Roaring Creek* may be as an example of 'structural' film-making, or however successful it may be in capturing 'sheer manifestations of being', its contribution to ethnography is surely minimal.

## A DETOUR THROUGH THE AMERICAN DREAM: *FOREIGN PARTS*

*Hell Roaring Creek* anticipated the general direction that the praxis underlying SEL films would take in subsequent years. This has involved a progressive movement away from ethnography conceived as a process of dialogical engagement with the subjects and towards the evocation, through a combination of a privileged observational camera and highly elaborated soundtracks, of cinematic experiences that are not anchored in the ideas and relations of the subjects but rather give expression, in Gardnerian fashion, to the artistic or philosophical concerns of the film-makers. But while this may have been the general direction of travel, it has been a movement that has been circuitous, as demonstrated particularly by *Foreign Parts*, an SEL film released in 2011. This is one of the most dialogical of all the major films produced by the SEL prior to 2015, including even *Sweetgrass*.

*Foreign Parts* was shot in a vehicle scrapyard at Willets Point, a rambling agglomeration of car body shops beneath the Line No. 7 subway track in the Queens district of New York City. It has a running time of 80 minutes and was the outcome of collaboration between Véréna Paravel, a French anthropologist who was by then an associate of the SEL, and J. P. Sniadecki, one of the first students to enrol on the SEL's Media Practice programme in 2006. After completing that programme, Sniadecki had gone on to carry out doctoral research about independent documentary production in Beijing and at the same time, to travel widely around China, becoming a prolific maker of non-fiction films in many different parts of the country. These films showed Sniadecki to be a talented cinematographer, with a discerning eye, though their ethnographicness is limited by the fact that they are mostly based on no more than brief acquaintance with the subjects.

The original idea for *Foreign Parts* came from Paravel, who stumbled upon Willets Point when making an earlier film about the various communities connected by the No. 7 subway line. She had been struck by the juxtaposition of dynamism and dereliction, beauty and squalor, the order within apparent chaos of the site, and immediately saw it as an opportunity to make a film about a location that could serve as a microcosm of what she later described as the 'larger narratives in the history of the [United States] – such as post-industrialisation, immigration, political violence, environmental decay, and the breakdown of democracy'.[18] Owing to personal security concerns raised by her working there alone, Lucien Castaing-Taylor suggested that to make the film Paravel should join forces with Sniadecki, whose previous work in China had raised some of the same issues.

Paravel and Sniadecki visited Willets Point over a two-year period 'on and off' in 2008 and 2009, sharing the camera as well as the direction, and working through the various different seasons of the year. After a lengthy period of editing, the film began appearing at festivals in late 2010, and the following year it was released on DVD accompanied by a Bonus Extras feature including eight shorter films. These expand on various issues and situations dealt with in the main film and provide an interesting complement to it.

Ernst Karel again makes a major contribution, laying down a beautifully layered soundtrack in post-production that subtly reconciles the grinding sounds of the scrapyard, the booming of overhead aeroplanes and the almost ever-present strains of Latino music with the speech of the characters, and even some moments of relative tranquility, as when a cock crows one quiet Sunday morning. The cinematography is also generally of a very high standard and features many long observational shots, often exquisitely executed. Much of the material appears to have been shot hand-held, with a notable prevalence of extended tracking shots that follow people walking. But there are also many beautifully composed formal shots that would appear to have been shot from a tripod. Indeed, the tripod itself shows up in the background to quite a number of shots.

Through an engaging mosaic of sequences, *Foreign Parts* certainly offers a strong sense of the general atmosphere of life in Willets Park. However, from a strictly ethnographic perspective, notwithstanding its excellent technical quality, it suffers from a certain lack of focus: the film contains many different threads, but none of them is pursued in any great depth.

As an intertitle explains right at the end of the film, at the time that *Foreign Parts* was shot, there were around 250 small businesses at Willets Point providing employment to some 2,000 people, many of whom were relatively recent migrants to the USA. The migrants who appear in the film are preponderantly Latinos, though it is clear that while some are from the Hispanic Caribbean, others are from Central America and others again from Andean South America. From the Bonus Extras films, we discover that there are also people at Willets Point from Jamaica, some francophone Black Antillians, presumably from Haiti, and people whose accent suggests that they are from Eastern Europe or the Balkans. A man with a South Asian accent appears briefly in the main film, and at somewhat greater length in one of the Bonus films. As far as this migrant population is concerned, the film rarely gets beyond the forecourts of their businesses, either physically or metaphorically, offering little insight into the ideas, dreams and hopes of these migrants, or the family and personal ties that no doubt radiate out from Willets Point far across the world and along which travel remittances, sentiments and desire. A *Jaguar* or *Moi, un Noir* for our times, this film is not.

But to be fair, as the film-makers have explained in interviews, whatever the title might suggest, *Foreign Parts* was not intended to be a film about migrants as such. Certainly, the subjects with whom they primarily engage dialogically are not foreigners, but rather long-term US citizens. They include Julia, a cat-loving middle-aged African American woman who lives in a car, has an issue with alcohol and subsists by panhandling. They also include Joe Ardizzone, a retired 78-year-old who has lived there most of his life, and Luís and Sara, a young couple who also live in a car. In one of the Bonus films, we discover that Luís is originally from Florida, while Sara identifies herself at one point in the main film as 'the only white girl' at Willets Point. Their story provides one of the minor threads within the film, but it is not pursued to any great extent.

Of these English-speaking subjects, only Luís is directly involved in the business of the scrapyard, but we see him at work no more than briefly, seemingly because he spent at least some of the filming period in gaol. More broadly, the social relationships that hold Willets Point together as a working environment are only superficially explored. Although there are many shots of people engaged in work-related activities, there is little sense of this work as a social process, be it as a skilled practice, or as a business with, no doubt, any number of dark sides and 'angles', or as an activity that

15.3 *Foreign Parts* (2011). Left, Road Runner says his prayers as if he were before the Wailing Wall. Right, Joe Ardizzone: 'When the real estate taxes come up ... then all of sudden they know exactly where we live.'

takes places within a given set of interpersonal and interethnic relationships, let alone as part of individual or collective imaginaries.

The only subject involved in the scrapyard business whom the film-makers follow at any significant length is a middle-aged man, nicknamed 'Road Runner', on account of his role directing clients to the businesses where they might be able to get the spares that they need. Early on in the film, Road Runner is visited by two young Hassidic rabbis, who provide him with tefillin so that he can recite his prayers. This he duly does, and in a wonderful scene, with power tools whizzing in the background, he is seen reciting prayers in front of the corrugated iron wall of his workshop, as if it were the Wailing Wall in Jerusalem (figure 15.3, left). Unfortunately, Road Runner soon drops out of the film, though the same two rabbis reappear much later and try to persuade another, older man to strap on the tefillin and say his prayers, assuring him of all the luck that it will bring to his business. However, this second man declines, preferring instead to share a glass of vodka with his visitors. But scenes of this kind that reach into what Ervin Goffman might have called the backstage of the lives of those actively involved in the scrapyard are the exception rather than the rule, both in *Foreign Parts* itself and in the films offered as Bonus Extras.

However, if I understand the film-makers' intentions correctly, as described in their media interviews, even the English-speaking interlocutors are of secondary importance to their project: the main focus of the film was not intended to be particular human subjects as such, but rather the scrapyard itself and the many contradictions inherent to the American Dream that it symbolised.[19] This would explain why the film features so many lengthy observational shots of the physical features of the scrapyard. But while these certainly impart a sensorially rich sense of the place, to expect an audience to read them as an explicit critique of the American Dream seems to me rather optimistic, not least because there must be many places that look and sound like Willets Point all over the world.

There is also a more explicit, locally focused political story threaded through the film, even if most of the time it lies in the background. About a quarter of the way into the film, Sara, the 'white' homeless woman, reveals that all the businesses are going to have to move in order to make way for the redevelopment of the site. Thereafter, the main political argument of the film is carried by Joe Ardizzone, who is totally uncompromising: as he sees it, the city politicians neglect Willets Point except when it comes to taxation; the planners responsible for redevelopment know absolutely nothing; and the whole scheme is merely a ploy for the mayor to reward his wealthy friends. Joe spends much of the film, and also some of the Bonus Extra films, stomping manically around Willets Point shouting these opinions, Canute-like, all seemingly to little effect (figure 15.3, right).

What is interesting from an ethnographic point of view is why Joe's arguments gained such little traction – despite being very well founded, as matters turned out.[20] One of the Bonus Extra films suggest some of the reasons why: many migrants in fact thought that they would be better off relocated to another site, while organising political resistance would have been difficult given that so few people had any legal rights of residence. But these complexities are not explored systematically through the following of political processes or relationships. There is a brief scene of a political meeting that fails to start because of lack of attendance, and another wonderful and veritably Kafkaesque scene of Joe visiting the grand local government offices to try and find what is going on, but to no avail. Later, among the final credits, beneath an intertitle announcing the sale of the site, we hear some voices finally expressing resistance to the process, but these remain anonymous while the circumstances of this resistance, so at odds with what we have seen in the films, remain unexplained.

Certainly *Foreign Parts* has many merits as a descriptive account of the scrapyard and offers some understanding of the lives of the homeless people who found a refuge there. As I commented in relation to *Sweetgrass*, it is impossible for any ethnographic film to cover everything about any given subject. But one cannot help but feel that a greater focus on the ethnography of the migrants' experience, and the economic and political processes surrounding the scrapyard would have afforded the film-makers the opportunity to address more directly the 'larger narratives' about the USA that had struck Paravel so forcefully when she first stumbled upon Willets Point. More generally, for all the ambitious claims by the film-makers to be invested in the 'plenitude of lived experience', 'the sensual weight of lived duration' and even 'the magnitude of human existence', this is a film that is more about surfaces than about what lies beneath. That is, it is more about technical processes, public spaces and the material environment than it is about social relationships, private domains and what is going on inside the hearts and minds of the subjects who once made their living in Willets Point.

## LEVIATHAN AND MANAKAMANA

The progressive, if circuitous, movement of the SEL away from a conception of ethnography of the kind on which this book is based went a decisive step further with the production of two subsequent films, *Leviathan*, released in 2012, and *Manakamana*, released in 2014. In that these two films involve a non-dialogical and arguably objectifying scrutiny of their human subjects, they could even be said to be at odds with much contemporary ethnographic practice. But this has not prevented them from being hailed as masterpieces of 'ethnographic' cinema by reviewers in the mass media and from the world of the visual arts.

The first of these films, *Leviathan*, was jointly directed by Lucien Castaing-Taylor and Véréna Paravel. This film does not appear to have been based on extended ethnographic fieldwork. Rather, it was shot over the course of six expeditions, each of 'up to two weeks', onboard the *Athena*, a trawler working the Grand Banks fishing grounds off the northeast Atlantic coast of the USA. This trawler was operating out of New Bedford, Massachusetts, one of several ports used by nineteenth-century whalers of the kind immortalised in Herman Melville's classic novel, *Moby-Dick*. The title of the film is in part a reference to the eponymous great white whale that is Captain Ahab's nemesis in that work.

However, this is only one of several possible connotations of the title. A quotation from the Book of Job at the beginning of the film (reminiscent of the quotation from W. B. Yeats's poem on the Upanishads at the beginning of *Forest of Bliss*) suggests that the title is also a reference, not to a cetacean monster as such, but rather to some more abstract and fearsome force deep within the sea itself. Meanwhile, in interviews, the film-makers have suggested that the title could also be considered a reference to the trawler, or even a reference to the film itself. On an entirely different note, Thomas Hobbes's celebrated seventeenth-century political tract of the same title has also been invoked.[21]

These multiple connotations of the title – which, moreover, does not actually appear in the film itself until the end credits – are symptomatic of a more general reluctance on the part of the film-makers to tie the film to any particular theme or agenda. Paravel has commented that even they themselves do not know exactly what *Leviathan* is about, while Castaing-Taylor has explained that they were seeking to make a film that did not 'say' anything, but rather offered an experience that would not be reduced in any way by having a meaning attached to it. And indeed, it is entirely possible to appreciate the film simply as an intriguing cinematic interplay of light, colours, shapes, movement and sounds, without worrying overmuch about their referential significance. Considered purely in these terms, it is undoubtedly an astounding tour de force.

In a practical sense, *Leviathan* consists primarily of a series of prolonged shots, mostly in wide-angle, mainly of various different aspects of the technical processes taking place onboard the trawler. Most of the shots were taken with GoPro cameras, which were preferred to HD video cameras on account of the more filmic quality of the images. It was also mostly shot at night using the powerful lights of the trawler for illumination: this, together with the day-glo colours of the equipment and the crew's all-weather overalls, affords the most dazzling visual effects in the exterior shots taken onboard the trawler, while those taken out to sea pick out, in the most remarkable manner, evanescent flashes of surging foam and the ghostly white forms of the flocking seagulls following the boat.

The film-makers have explained that in all but four shots, the cameras were attached to themselves or to the crew, or were suspended from poles that they were holding. Even so, they mostly offer a highly privileged perspective on what is going on, that is, one that would not normally be available to a human participant in the events portrayed. Even the shots taken from GoPro cameras attached to the helmets of the crew offer a perspective that is distortedly frenetic and wide-angle compared to that which would be afforded to a normal human observer standing in the same position.

For the most part, the action roves with ease, in a manner reminiscent of the Vertovian ciné-eye, from the crew hauling in chains or gutting fish, to deck-level shots of fish swilling about in the bilge waters, then out to sea and under the water, before turning upwards to show the seagulls in flight, sometimes as seen from below, sometimes from above. At various points, the camera hangs down the side of the hull and we see a stream of bloodied effluent and fish parts cascading from the deck into the sea, which in turn attract the seagulls who alternately whirl in the air or dive into the water. In the latter part of the film, we look down from the top of the mast and also from the vantage point of a camera situated on a pole in front of the prow, looking down as the trawler surges powerfully through the swell. This dramatic visual account is accompanied by an equally privileged and highly elaborated soundtrack, perhaps more accurately described as composed than edited by Ernst Karel, this time in collaboration with Jacob Ribicoff, a leading feature film sound designer.

There is no narrative to the film, be it chronological, thematic or formal, though the brilliant sound composition lends it a certain rhythmic quality, in the manner of an avant-garde musical work. Apart from a few more

442

15.4 *Leviathan* (2012). Left, the only conventionally well-lit shot of a human being in the entire film is a reflection. Right, many of the most dramatic shots were taken from GoPro cameras dropped over the side of the trawler.

or less incomprehensible shouts and tannoy announcements, there is also almost no dialogue and very little interaction between the human subjects, let alone between film-makers and subjects. There is one conventionally well-lit and naturalistic shot of a member of the crew operating a winch, though even this is only a reflection on a glass window (figure 15.4, left). There is also a shot of a man taking a shower as seen through a steamed-up lens. But otherwise the shots of the crew mostly take the form of close-ups, often in low light, of no more than parts of their bodies as they go about their work. Meanwhile, confused jumbles of dying fish slosh back and forth in the tanks, a seabird struggles to escape from the deck, as all the while chains clank loudly, the motors of the winches grind, gulls cry and the deep unrelenting sea pounds, roars and thunders by turn. The overall impression is of a cacophonous and dystopian world of chaos, tumult and destruction.

As a work of cinematic craft, *Leviathan* has been showered with praise by the mass media reviewers and rightly so. But considered more narrowly as an ethnographic account of life on board the *Athena*, its status is more debatable. It may be 'immersive', as so many of the reviews of the film proclaim, but this is true only in relation to the physical universe that it represents: it certainly does not immerse itself in the social and cultural world of the human subjects.

In the same way that in making *Sweetgrass*, Castaing-Taylor and Ilisa Barbash decided to dispense with the material shot in Big Timber, in making *Leviathan*, Castaing-Taylor and Paravel concluded that the 50 hours of material that they shot on shore in the factories and warehouses of New Bedford, while interesting in itself, would be difficult to reconcile with the very different kind of material shot once out at sea. But while it was probably a good decision not to burden the film with this on-shore material, not only does *Leviathan* make no reference to the social relations that link the trawler to the shore, but it does not offer any account of the social relations of the people onboard either.

*Leviathan* certainly evokes, in a very powerful way, the brutal physical impact of this mode of fishing, both on the crew and the fish stocks. The crew is shown to be exhausted, their arms lacerated by their work. As for the fish, we are offered only too many close-up images of the cruel death that they suffer: a particularly memorable image is of two crewmen holding up a series of ray fish with hooks and then hacking off their wings. However, the film offers us no sense of how the people on board the *Athena* relate to one another, either as a crew or as individuals, what they think of the experience of being at sea or about the sea itself, nor of their sense of their work and how it articulates with the rest of their lives. The film-makers offer us a very strong impression of what it is like to be on board the *Athena*, but do the crew feel the same way? It is impossible to tell. Nor do we get any sense of the skills that the crew bring to their work, which in the case of those who have to steer that ship through stormy conditions at night, such as we see in the film, must be considerable.

In fact, human subjects feature centrally in relatively few shots in the film as a whole: most are primarily concerned with the sea, the fish, the seagulls or the technology. In the last ten minutes of the film, there are no human beings at all. To the extent that they do feature, the crew are mostly presented in a highly objectified form, as tattooed obese bodies or anonymous waterproof-clad beings, engaged in fragmentary mechanical activities, without opinions, identities or beliefs, and almost as mute as the fish species with whom, in an ironic touch, they share equal billing in the final credits. Thus for all its many virtues as a work of cinema, given its almost total neglect of the social and cultural aspects of life on board the *Athena*, it is difficult to see how *Leviathan* could be regarded specifically as an ethnographic film in any strong sense.

As with the other SEL films described above, the DVD of *Leviathan* also features another shorter film, but whereas the Bonus Films of *Sweetgrass* and *Foreign Parts* enrich the ethnographic account offered by the main film, in this case the additional film merely offers a further objectification of the human subjects. This film, entitled *Still Life*, consists of a single unchanging wide-angle shot, unbroken for 29 minutes, which shows the crewmen's galley area as recorded by a seemingly unmanned camera set up at the end of the dining table, with a television set above, out of the field of vision, and a frying pan and a metal casserole on the table itself. There is a similar shot in the main film, in which an exhausted crewman is shown watching a television show for several minutes before he finally falls asleep. In *Still Life*, the camera records this space as three crewmen come in and out, engage in some desultory and largely inaudible conversation, and look up at the television situated above the camera. There are a couple of minutes at each end of the film in which there is no one in the galley at all, and the audience is offered the opportunity to consider the dining table with its frying pan and its casserole standing in isolation.

If *Leviathan* has something in common with Robert Gardner's work in its existential reach and grand cinematic gesture, *Still Life* offers us a work that, in common with *Hell Roaring Creek* before it, lies rather at the interface between cinema and installation, and as such, would probably be most constructively regarded, not as a film of ethnographic ambition, but rather as a work that is in dialogue with 'structural' cinema.

The same is true, I suggest, of *Manakamana*. Certainly, this film has both the formal structure and underlying theoretical rationale that are typical of this genre of cinema. The directors of this film were Stephanie Spray and Pacho Velez, and as with so many SEL films, Ernst Karel carried out the postproduction sound-mix. As a contemporary of J. P. Sniadecki at Harvard, Spray was also among the first students to take the media training courses offered there after the SEL was set up in 2006. For some years prior to enrolling on the course, she had been regularly visiting Nepal, where she had studied the Gandharva, an itinerant caste of traditional musicians. For his part, Velez was a documentary film-maker who had completed an MFA in Los Angeles where he had come into contact with a number of leading 'structural' film-makers, including James Benning and Thom Andersen.[22]

In practical terms, *Manakamana* consists of eleven unbroken takes, each of approximately 10 minutes' duration. Ten of these are of people riding in a cable car in the Nepalese Himalayas, either on their way up to, or on their way back down from a mountain-top temple dedicated to a Hindu goddess from whose name the title of the film is derived. There is also one 10-minute take of some tethered goats making the upward journey, on their way to being offered as a sacrifice to the goddess. Owing to the entirely fortuitous circumstance that the journey time of the cable cars, be it up or down, was slightly less than the 11-minute duration of a standard 400 ft 16 mm magazine, Velez had the idea to shoot the journeys on film rather than on digital video. In order to ensure that all the shots were taken from a common fixed point and that there was no camera movement, the film-makers arranged for a wooden structure to be built on one side of a cable car cabin into which they then inserted their tripod and a 16 mm camera. This was not just any 16 mm camera, however, but rather the very same Aaton 7 LTR that Robert Gardner had used to shoot *Forest of Bliss* and which he had subsequently donated to the Film Study Center at Harvard.

From this position, ranged on one side of the cabin, with Spray taking sound and Velez on camera, they filmed their subjects, numbering variously between one and three people, sitting parallel to themselves, a few feet away on the other side of car. With the camera rock-steady within its wooden structure, the framing, a wide-angle shot of the subjects' upper body, remains constant throughout all eleven takes. Meanwhile, beyond the subjects, the mountain slopes, in slightly soft focus, rush by in the background, in a manner that is weirdly reminiscent of the back projections in the car scenes of Hollywood cinema from the 1930s. On the soundtrack, the regular clattering sound as the car passes the pylons holding up the cables marks the passage of time within each journey in an intriguing metronomic fashion.

The six upward journeys, including the goats' journey, are presented in the first half of the film, one after another, followed by the five downward journeys in the second half. There is no break in the film between the journeys since the film-makers take advantage of the darkness into which the cars arrive at the terminal to cut directly to the start of the next journey, which also begins in the dark. The sound of machinery turning the cars around in preparation for another journey, no doubt carefully mixed by Karel at post-production, enhances the sense of continuity between the takes.[23]

Many of the travellers are elderly and wear traditional local dress, though they are often accompanied by a younger person who appears to be a relative. But one of the upward journeys features three longhaired Nepalese heavy metal rockers while one of the downward trips shows two young women who are clearly not from the local area, one of whom appears to be a North American tourist, the other Asian, possibly Nepali, but who also speaks with a North American accent. In another of the downward journeys, two traditional musicians tune up and play their sarangis, four-stringed instruments played with a bow (though the bows are not actually in shot). Each time a new set of travellers emerges from the darkness constitutes, in effect, a minor but amusing *coup de théâtre* (figure 15.5).

None of the travellers is actually followed all the way to the goddess's temple, though during the two-minute black transition that demarcates the upward from the downward journeys, and which follows immediately after the goats' ascent at the midpoint of the film, there are not only machinery noises, but also the ringing of bells, crowd noises and some goat bleats, signifying, one supposes, that the unfortunate animals have met their allotted fate. Only in one case, that of a couple, seemingly mother and son, the latter carrying a cockerel that pokes its head into shot on the way up, do we see travellers making both upward and downward journeys. The upturned feet of the cockerel that are just visible at the bottom of the screen on their way down suggest that its life too has been offered to the goddess.

The elegant formal simplicity of *Manakamana* belies the great amount of care that went into achieving this effect. The eleven takes of the final film were selected from a total of thirty-six trips in the cable car, filmed over the course of eight weeks spread across two different summers, in 2011 and 2012. Most of the takes derive from the first visit: the second visit was

**15.5** *Manakamana* (2014). Each time a new set of travellers emerges from the darkness works as an amusing *coup de théâtre*.

mainly to shoot 'pick-ups', including the shot of the goats. The temperature inside the cars was often very high, and they were like 'mobile greenhouses' in the summer. Post-production was very lengthy: it took eighteen months to select and order the eleven shots that make up the final film. Initially, the film-makers ordered the film as a series of eighteen sequentially up-and-down journeys, but concluded that in order to focus the audience's attention on the 'small human revelations' happening in front of the camera, the more counterintuitive final structure was necessary.

Within this structure, they located the first spoken words at a classical Hollywood plot point, around twenty-five minutes into the film, with the explicit purpose of bringing about a radical change in the audience's expectations at that point. A similar degree of thought went into the final shot: at one stage, the film-makers intended to end with the sarangi players taking the film home with their music, but then realised that they had a rather more effective 'character arc' in the couple who went up with a live cockerel and came down with a dead one.

However, the 'small human revelations' that, in the film-makers' view, constitute the ethnography of the film are indeed very slight. For the most part, the travellers do or say very little and what they do say is mostly trivial or fragmentary. During the first two upward journeys, one involving an elderly man and a boy whom one presumes to be his grandson (figure 15.5, top left), and the other a woman on her own bearing what appears to be a floral offering to the goddess, not a single word is spoken. Instead the subjects avert their eyes from the camera and stare out of the windows, only occasionally stealing a furtive glance at the film-makers. The third journey is made by the couple carrying a cockerel as an offering to the goddess. Initially, they seem very ill at ease, but eventually they make some desultory comments about how the ride makes their ears pop and also about the countryside below.

By comparison, the three elderly ladies of the fourth ride are positively garrulous. One laments to another – evidently her co-wife – that their husband could not come on account of a twisted ankle and then they too engage in some chitchat about the countryside passing below. The same speaker also relates a legend about Manakamana and although she does not actually address the camera, this appears to be primarily for the benefit of the film-makers since her companions pay very little attention, preferring to look out of the window. No doubt they have heard the story many times before.

Then come the rockers, who chatter on in a superficial way about their lives, their ears popping, and also about the countryside. They have small digital cameras and take pictures of themselves, the countryside, a small kitten that one of them is carrying, indeed everything except the film crew sitting directly in front of them (figure 15.5, top right). Last of the upward travellers are the goats, who are transported in a different sort of car, open to the elements. They say nothing, of course, though they do bleat a great deal at the beginning. Their appearance from out of the darkness of the terminal represents the most humorous *coup de théâtre* of all, though its comedic value is soon tempered by the realisation that formal structure of the film will require one to spend the next ten minutes looking at their backsides.

The ethnographic content of the five downward journeys is no more substantial. They involve, first, a woman with a freshly anointed forehead who comments on the beauty of her souvenir model of the temple (though this is out of shot), then come the North American tourist and her Asian friend (figure 15.5, bottom left), then two local women, probably mother and daughter, who have difficulty eating melting ice cream on a stick, then the traditional musicians (figure 15.5, bottom right). There is much further embarrassed silence and trivial commentary on the countryside below. Finally, the couple with the newly sacrificed cockerel return, their foreheads also freshly anointed. After again sitting in awkward silence for some minutes, apparently engrossed in their own thoughts, the woman comments that their daughter should have come instead of her. But the man reminds her that she was the one 'who was invited'. Then, after some further minor comments about the largely invisible landscape, the film stock runs out just before the car arrives at the terminal, leaving both this final journey and the film as a whole to be completed in sound only.

On its release on the international film festival circuit, *Manakamana* was widely acclaimed as a huge success. Although a number of reviews noted that it provoked walk-outs by audience members frustrated by its silences, the film also generated much positive comment, of diverse kinds. Some reviewers saw the film as a metaphor for human life as a journey suspended on a thread; some extolled the beauty of the landscape and the aura of tranquility within the cable car cabin; others again appreciated the formal parallels between the mechanical movement through time and space of the cabin with the movement through time and space of cinema. Clearly the film 'worked' for many people as an artistic or poetic experience.

Yet although in all these regards *Manakamana* may be magnificent, it is not easily classifiable as an ethnographic film, certainly not as one of any great depth or substance. For, as with a number of SEL films, it remains on the surface of its subject matter from an ethnographic point of view in that it eschews any in-depth exploration of the ideas of its subjects. As an ethnographic film about journeying to a holy site, it is surely a major shortcoming that it offers no insight into the motivations of the travellers. One learns from sources outside the film that the goddess Manakamana grants wishes, indeed that is what her name means. But what wishes do the travellers hope that she will grant? And how does the sacrifice of their animals fit into the relationship between pilgrims and the goddess?

In interviews, the film-makers speak about the practice of sacrifice as if it involved some form of mystical communion with divinity; but on comparative ethnographic grounds, I wonder whether, in fact, the subjects have a very much more pragmatic attitude, seeing it as an entirely rational exchange of a valued animal for the goddess's intervention, to ensure an entirely mundane form of good fortune such as a return to good health or a good crop. But there is no way of telling, for instead of any insight into these matters, we are offered the travellers' mostly banal ruminations on the largely invisible terrain below. These comments are subtitled but, according to a leading specialist on the anthropology of Nepal, the translations are not entirely reliable.[24]

However, arguably the most significant limitation of *Manakamana* considered specifically as an ethnographic film relates to the fact that it entirely obscures the long-standing nature of the relationship between the subjects and Stephanie Spray. From the interviews with the film-makers, it transpires that most of the subjects were very well-known to Spray. The three elderly ladies were her 'adopted Nepali mothers', while other subjects had appeared in her earlier films, notably the two traditional musicians, a man and his nephew. Even the outsiders, the young tourist women, were 'acquaintances'. Nor were these subjects merely travelling in the cable cars by chance when the film-makers happened to be making their film. On the contrary, as suggested by the reference to an invitation in the last journey, in the manner of a Sharon Lockhart film, the subjects appear to have been carefully selected in advance by the film-makers.

In one sense, it is reassuring to discover that this was the case. Clearly, from an ethical point of view, it would have been completely intolerable if the film had been made on the basis of the entrapment of unsuspecting pilgrims who, when innocently getting into the cable car, suddenly found themselves confronted by two foreigners with an intimidating array of film equipment. But at the same time, this information about the lengthy pre-existing relationship between Spray and the subjects makes one realise just how artificial the situation presented in the film actually is. In effect, what this film offers us is a sort of artistic experiment in which selected subjects were placed in front of a fixed camera and then asked over the 10-minute duration of the journey not to make eye contact, let alone speak to a person sitting a few feet away whom they may have known for many years, in some cases for more than a decade. Given these circumstances, it is little wonder that many of the subjects look embarrassed, say little or nothing of any significance, avert their eyes, or simply sit there mutely, apparently lost in their own thoughts.

The film-makers, and indeed some interviewers, detect in the silent non-verbal behaviour of the subjects of *Manakamana* a whole range of 'polarities' between presence and absence, the sacred and the profane, time and space, and so on. But, as I would read it, this behaviour would have had less to do with such transcendent matters than with the abnormal and restrictive conditions under which the film was made. Can we really believe, for example, that a Nepalese grandfather taking his grandson on a trip on a cable car, as in the first take, would say absolutely nothing to him for the entire journey, were it not for the presence of the film-makers and their equipment? The withdrawal of the subjects into themselves had surely nothing to do with religious inspiration, and everything to do with the fact that impassivity was the only means whereby the subjects could protect themselves against the intrusion of the 16 mm camera encased in a wooden structure that was whirring away a couple of feet from their noses.

In short, while the film-makers may have every right to claim that *Manakamana* has integrity as a work of 'structural' cinema, as an ethnographic film its integrity is more debatable. In one of the interviews, Spray remarks that in her films, she aims to 'unsettle presumptions about racial or cultural difference and the inequalities that they perpetuate'. This is an entirely laudable aim and no doubt one that is most sincerely held. However, it is difficult to reconcile this aim with *Manakamana*, which, in its obscuring of the relationship between the film-maker and subjects, and in its offering up of its largely mute subjects to the intense scrutiny of an intrusively close and non-participatory camera, is uncomfortably reminiscent of retrogressive, entirely discredited modes of ethnographic representation.

As with Robert Gardner's oeuvre, probably the most constructive way to approach the recent films produced by the SEL film-makers is to applaud their ambitious cinematic quality and their bold experimentalism, even while recognising that they are on a journey that may have started at the same place, but which has now taken them to somewhere that is far removed from the project on which most contemporary practitioners of ethnography, whatever the medium, are engaged most of the time. 'Negative capability' may produce magnificent works of art, but most ethnographers, for good or for ill, remain committed to 'reaching after fact and reason', however 'irritable' that might be.

Thus while there is much to admire in the films produced by the SEL in terms of the craft that has gone into their making, in my view the more general praxis on which they are based does not offer the best model for the future direction of ethnographic film-making. In the next and final chapter of this book, I will consider a number of films that are based on a more dialogical, participatory praxis and which therefore seem to me to suggest various paths along which ethnographic film-making may develop in the future that are more generally in tune with contemporary ethnographic practice.

## Notes

1 I am very grateful to Lucien Castaing-Taylor for commenting on an almost final draft of this chapter in Febuary 2019 and in so doing, correcting various errors of fact and challenging certain interpretations. We agreed though that on some matters, we would simply have to agree to disagree …

2 These earlier publications of Lucien Castaing-Taylor, then known only as Lucien Taylor, would include Taylor (1996; 1998a; 1998b).

3 See the discussion of *The Hunters* in Chapter 4 for this book, pp. 133–8, and of Robert Gardner's work more generally in Chapter 9.

4 See the Film Study Center website at filmstudycenter.org/about/.

5 MacDonald (2013), 315. See Karel's personal website at ek.klingt.org for a detailed account of his remarkable productivity across a range of different sonic fields.

6 See the Harvard Film Archive site at https://library.harvard.edu/film/general_info.html

7 Personal communication, February 2019.

8 See Sheets (2016) and particularly Lockhart's website at www.lockhartstudio.com.

9 Heidegger (1978), 217.

10 See particularly Chapter 10, pp. 295–8. In commenting on a draft of this chapter in February 2019, Castaing-Taylor pointed out that two of his most recent works with Véréna Paravel, namely, *Sominoloquies* (2017), which is structured around the oneiric monologues of Dion McGregor, a 1960s songwriter living in New York, and *Caniba* (2018), based on the also largely monological testimony of the (in)famous Japanese cannibal, Issei Sagawa, are as he put it, graphically, 'stuffed full of words from nose to tail'. However, these films fall outside the temporal remit of this book and, regrettably, I have not yet had the opportunity to view them. But judging by the trailers and reviews on the Web, neither film would appear to have specifically ethnographic objectives.

11 See Peleg (2017).

12 Unless otherwise indicated, the details given here about the making of *Sweetgrass* are drawn freely either from the film-makers' commentary on the DVD or from the interviews that they have given to Scott MacDonald (2015), 373–93, and Jay Kuehner (see Castaing-Taylor 2016).

13 The film was even spotted by one Facebook follower as an Air France inflight film, which must surely be some kind of 'first' for an ethnographic film produced from within an academic institution.

14 In this discussion of *Sheep Rushes*, I draw particularly on an interview that Castaing-Taylor gave to Scott MacDonald (2015), 393–400.

15 Gardner (1972), 35. See also Chapter 9, p. 262.

16 MacDonald (2013), 324.

17 Compare and contrast MacDonald (2013), 325–6 with MacDonald (2015), 396.

18 See Alvarez (2012).

19 In addition to the textual interview with Alvarez (2012) already cited, see the interview with the film-makers at the Punto de Vista festival in Pamplona, Spain, in November 2011, which is available in two different forms on YouTube.

20 Joe's cynicism proved to be right on the money: after the filming had been completed, the Willets Point site, which until that point had been public land, was sold to a private property developer, who was indeed a friend of the mayor, as well as being a former partner of the notorious Ponzi scheme fraudster Bernie Madoff. For a journalistic account of the shenanigans surrounding the development of Willets Point, see www.heralddeparis.com/hoodwinked-are-the-wilpons-about-to-pull-off-the-ultimate-developers-dream/237510 (last consulted 13 February 2019).

21 In this discussion, I draw particularly on an interview given by the film-makers to Scott MacDonald (2015), 404–10.

22 This discussion of *Manakamana* draws on a number of sources, including Spray's website at www.stephaniespray.com/about/, and interviews with Spray and Velez conducted by Scott MacDonald (2015), 410–17, and by Lucien Castaing-Taylor and Véréna Paravel, the producers of the film. The latter interview formed part of the film press-kit that was available at www.manakamanafilm.com/director-qa, though as of February 2019 this website had apparently expired.

23 Connoiseurs of Jean Rouch's films will be reminded of his two-roll 16 mm fiction *Gare du Nord* (1965) in which the darkness of an elevator shaft is used to make an invisible join between the two 10-minute takes that make up the complete film (Henley 2009, 187–92).

24 David Gellner (2015) detects various minor errors, including, for example, the mistranslation of 'this is like falling from a plane' as 'they probably built it from a plane'.

# 16

# Participatory perspectives

T HE films considered in this final chapter were based on a participatory praxis and involved an extended period of ethnographic fieldwork. They were all made in a cultural environment that differed significantly from the film-maker's own, thereby raising certain questions – some intellectual, others ethical – that are not so starkly posed when film-maker, subjects and audience all inhabit much the same cultural universe. As authored works of cinema, they all go beyond observation in the sense that the relationship between film-maker and subjects, far from being obscured or ignored, is central to the process of production and is inscribed, in varying degrees, in the filmic text itself. In this sense, they might be considered as examples of what Faye Ginsburg has recently termed 'relational documentary'.[1] However, there are also a number of significant differences between them regarding the precise form in which this relationship is conducted and presented stylistically. As such, I offer them here as examples of a range of possible 'ways of doing' that – among many others – may provide the basis for taking ethnographic film-making into the future.

Shot over a twelve-year period between 1996 and 2008, and finally released in 2012, *Tracks Across Sand* is a series of films produced under the direction of the anthropologist Hugh Brody. It traces the historical background, the complex preparatory processes and the aftermath of the land restitution claim that, in 1999, resulted in the ≠Khomani San of the Southern Kalahari in South Africa being awarded formal title to some 65,000 hectares of land in and around the Kgalagadi National Park in the Northern Cape district, close to the frontiers with Namibia and Botswana.[2]

There are seventeen films in the series, of very variable lengths: the shortest is no longer than a minute, the longest is 52 minutes. All of them are distributed on a single DVD of almost four hours duration. Even this is only a fraction of the 135 hours of rushes that was available to Brody when editing, all of which have been stored in an archive where they will be available to future generations. Resonating with the circumstances of many indigenous peoples across the world, the story that *Tracks Across Sand* tells – of loss, restitution, followed by a realisation that the recuperation of land is not a panacea for all the ills suffered by an indigenous people – is one that serves, as an intertitle declares at the end of the introductory film, as 'a story of our times'.

The origins of the ≠Khomani San land restitution project lay in a chance meeting in 1992, at a private game reserve not far from Cape Town, between Roger Chennells, a white South African human rights lawyer and Dawid Kruiper, a San elder, who at that time was scratching out a living selling handicrafts and posing for tourist photographs on the periphery of the game reserve. Kruiper told Chennells the story of his group's eviction from their ancestral lands around the Kgalagadi Park (then still called the Gemsbok National Park), which lay some 500 miles to the north of the place where the two men met. These evictions had mostly occurred in two separate waves, one in the 1930s, and then again later in the 1970s. Chennells realised that the legal instruments introduced by the African National Congress as part of the new post-apartheid constitution, which overturned the discriminatory Native Lands Act of 1913, could provide the vehicle for making a claim for the restitution of the ≠Khomani San lands that did not involve raising questions of aboriginal title, which in a South African context would have been highly problematic. Accordingly, encouraged and supported professionally by Chennells, Kruiper and his family entered a formal claim for restitution in 1994.

In the absence of any written evidence of the ≠Khomani San's prior occupancy, the Kruiper land claim could have been subject to legal challenge. In order to combat this possibility, a cultural mapping programme was initiated in 1996. This was designed to establish, mostly on the basis of interviews with ≠Khomani San elders, not only the material facts of their use of their ancestral lands for subsistence purposes, but also their cultural appropriation of these lands in the form of the naming of landmarks, burial sites, stories of childhood experiences and other indicators of cultural significance. One of those involved in the project was Nigel Crawhall, a sociolinguist working with the South African National Language Project. As Crawhall had studied in Canada, he knew of Brody's work on cultural mapping in connection with the land rights claims of the Canadian Inuit in the 1970s. It was on these grounds, rather than as a film-maker, that Brody was initially invited to take part in the project.

On the *Tracks Across Sand* DVD, the main body of the material is framed by the two longest films: an *Overture* of 30 minutes that provides an overview of the whole process and an *Aftermath* of 52 minutes which considers the general circumstances of the ≠Khomani San in 2008, nine years after they had been awarded the land title. Lying between these two films is a series of much shorter films that cover the cultural mapping process. Following *Aftermath*, there is a sort of epilogue of five short interviews with the non-San involved in the project. The interviewees include Grace Humphries, the director of an NGO that supports the San, Levi Namaseb, a Namibian linguist who participated in the cultural mapping, as well as Chennells, Crawhall and Brody himself. Finally, the DVD offers a gallery of portraits of all the principal protagonists of the films and copies of the geographical maps that arose from the cultural mapping process.

Shortly after he became involved in the project, Brody realised that the process that he had developed with the Inuit would have to be accommodated in order to meet the very different circumstances of the ≠Khomani San. While the Inuit were still living on their lands when Brody worked with them in the 1970s, the ≠Khomani San had been exiled from their ancestral territories for as long as two generations, and were now mostly living in squatter camps in urban or peri-urban locations, scattered across South Africa. Therefore, as well as recording accounts of traditional resource use, Brody and his colleagues also developed what they called 'time-lines' with their San collaborators, that is, accounts of the history of their dispossession, first in the 1930s and then again in the 1970s. These are presented, sometimes supported by archival photographs, in three short films under the general title 'Evictions'.

Another element that took on increasing significance as the cultural mapping proceeded, and which is the subject of two short films on the DVD, was the recovery of N/uu, the original language of the ≠Khomani San (and one of some fourteen distinct languages originally spoken by San populations across southern Africa). Following their eviction from the Southern Kalahari and in the face of intense disdain for their traditional culture on the part of the surrounding population, many ≠Khomani San had abandoned their language and subsequent generations had grown up speaking only Afrikaans: so much so that in 1970, N/uu was officially declared to be extinct. However, the researchers working on the cultural mapping project soon began to discover that a number of elderly people were still able to speak N/uu: by the end of the project, they had discovered some 28 speakers of the language, albeit dispersed over very large distances.

In many instances, it was only when these elderly San spoke N/uu for the purposes of the project that their children or grandchildren became aware that they still could speak it. One of the most moving sequences in the whole of the *Tracks Across Sand* DVD is some amateurish video footage of the occasion when three elderly sisters, all speakers of N/uu, surrounded by marvelling members of their respective families and two equally entranced sociolinguists, identify an audio recording made in the 1930s as being in N/uu and offer a translation. It transpires that the recording concerns a traditional custom practised when a bride-to-be was in seclusion prior to her marriage: this involved setting aside a choice antelope rib which was then roasted when she finally emerged to be married. Inspired by the memory of those distant marriage feasts, the three elderly sisters then break into spontaneous singing and rhythmic clapping.

At various points, San elders express the pious hope that young people will now learn the N/uu language again, though the films make clear that it is very unlikely that this will ever happen in sufficient numbers for N/uu to replace Afrikaans as the lingua franca of the ≠Khomani San. But the recovery of the language served a more general purpose of the cultural mapping project, namely, to instil a sense of pride in a collective identity among families that, since the evictions, had been dispersed and disconnected.

This was a central objective of other aspects of the project too, such as the working out of genealogies, which is the subject of one film, and of the recording of traditional ideas about the use and significance of features of the natural environment of the southern Kalahari, which is a theme that crops up in various forms through a number of the films. In one sequence, a man shows how he reads game animal tracks, in another an elderly woman recounts how ostrich eggs may be used as water carriers, while in a further series of very short films, anecdotes are told about particular trees: at one, an unrequited lover tried to hang himself but was saved by his father, while the branch of another tree served as the back of an imaginary donkey for a group of children (figure 16.1). A particularly moving sequence shows four elderly women scattering sand on what might appear to an outsider to be an unexceptional patch of desert scrub. This, the women reveal, is the burial place of their parents and grandparents. One of them says that she feels great pride to be back, looking again at the place where she buried her mother but from which she had been exiled for many years.

The most challenging film in the series to edit would surely have been *Aftermath*, the longest film and the one that presents ≠Khomani San life nine years after the settlement of the land claim. For, as an intertitle dramatically asserts midway through the film, 'The claim may have brought justice, but it could not ensure well-being.' The cultural mapping films tell a feel-good story, in which it is relatively easy to distinguish the good from the bad. But this is not the case with *Aftermath*, which is heavily laden with ambiguities. For the euphoria of the day when none other than President-elect Thabo Mbeki came in a helicopter to present the title to the San, bringing with him the first, desperately-wished-for rains for many years, was soon to be replaced by tension and discord.

16.1 Cultural mapping in *Tracks Across Sand* (2012). Left, Dawid Kruiper indicates the site of a beehive where his family gathered honey in the 1930s; right, /Una and her sister Keis identify the branch that broke as they swung on it as children.

In effect, the land claim had physically gathered together in the Southern Kalahari a group of people who may have shared historical roots but who were in no sense a community. As a result, there was intense rivalry between different families for control over the resources that the government had made available along with the acknowledgement of the land claim. These resources were frequently squandered, though it was often not clear whether this was due to simple mismanagement or corruption.

Moreover, although the claim had established San rights over a large amount of land, it did little to address the fundamental issue of poverty. The San could now hunt and gather as their ancestors had done, but that was no longer sufficient to ensure a sense of material well-being, particularly for younger people. The isolation of the Southern Kalahari meant that the opportunities to generate a cash income were few and the provision of health and educational services was even more sporadic than it had been in the marginal shanty towns where the San had previously lived. Even drinking water was in short supply.

Although *Aftermath* considers the many positive aspects of the new circumstances of the ≠Khomani San, it does not shy away from the fact that there have also been many social difficulties in the post-claim period. As the San themselves relate, there have been a disturbing number of cases of murder and rape while alcoholism has also been a widespread problem. The film includes a harrowing sequence in a liquor store and interviews two blind-drunk young men, continuing even after an older San man pleads with the film-makers to stop as it would make for bad publicity.

A stern critic might argue that *Aftermath* does not directly confront an issue that emerges strongly in some textual accounts of the ≠Khomani San land claim settlement. These suggest that the ≠Khomani San were caught in the same double-bind as the San of John Marshall's films in Namibia, that is, the fundamental contradiction inherent in the fact that while both the original land claim and the subsequent funding from the government and development aid donors were based on the presumption that the San wished to continue indefinitely with their traditional way of life, the harsh reality was that this was simply no longer viable, economically or socially. The only immediately practical way for the ≠Khomani San to escape from this double-bind was to eke out a meagre income from enacting a pathetic simulacrum of their traditional way of life for tourists, selling handicrafts and giving lessons in animal tracking to outsiders who would never use these skills for real. While some ≠Khomani San, including the original claimant Dawid Kruiper, were prepared to take this route, others wanted to introduce commercial livestock farming onto the land (goats and sheep rather than cattle). But this would not only have threatened the continuation of the hunting and gathering way of life on which the original land claim had been built, but would also have undermined the political authority of Kriuper and his family.[3]

Taken as a whole, *Tracks Across Sand* represents an excellent example of how an inter-related group of films may be used to explore a complex social and historical process in an ethnographic manner. Each of the seventeen films in the collection, regardless of length, has been carefully conceived, shot and edited, and has its own intrinsic narrative. Moreover, the collection as a whole has been structured, with the various different aspects of the land claim presented systematically in a series of films that are self-contained but which circle around the same themes. A number of key sequences recur time and again, in the manner of musical leitmotifs, while almost the entirety of the sequences that make up the opening film of the collection reappear again in later individual films, usually at greater length. It is therefore entirely appropriate that this opening film should have been dubbed *Overture*, even if at first sight this term might strike some viewers as somewhat grandiose.

According to the criteria proposed in this book, one would have no hesitation in qualifying *Tracks Across Sand* as an ethnographic work. Yet, in practical film-making terms, the sequences in the collection that could be described as observational are relatively few: there is a fine observational scene in which a group of San pack up their personal effects on the edge of a small town and head off to the ancestral lands, and there are also a number of observational scenes of children, and even adults, playing in the sand dunes once they arrive. But these are the exceptions that prove the general rule. Instead, 'talking heads' predominate throughout the collection. In this regard, *Tracks Across Sand* is markedly different in stylistic terms to Brody's own highly observational early film, *Eskimos of Pond Inlet: The People's Land*, discussed in Chapter 11. But different circumstances call for different film-making praxes: the Inuit were still living on their lands, while the ≠Khomani San were often recalling a world that no longer existed, even if they hoped, one day, to recreate it.

*Tracks Across Sand* not only contradicts the common assumption that in order to be ethnographic, a film has to be observational but it also gives the lie to the idea that films dominated by the spoken word cannot have a sensorial quality. Not only is the cinematography and soundtrack of these films of an exceptionally high standard, communicating a strong sense of place, but one cannot help but be moved by the eloquence and sheer poetry of the oral testimonies offered by the elderly San interlocutors. Rather than written documents, physical structures or monuments, it is these oral testimonies that communicate the San's continuing deep emotional connection to their ancestral lands, despite two generations of absence.

## PARTICIPATORY FILM-MAKING AS ETHNOFICTION: *TRANSFICTION*

If *Tracks Across Sand* contradicts the idea that in order to be ethnographic, it is necessary for a film to be observational, the next example of participatory film-making represents a challenge to the notion that an ethnographic film necessarily takes the form of a factual documentary.

Of course, this challenge is nothing new, since it was laid down by Jean Rouch as long ago as the 1950s when he began working on a series of films in West Africa that involved an innovative blend of fact and fiction, including such well-known works as *Jaguar* (1957–71) and *Moi, un Noir* (1960). Rouch himself never formulated a systematic methodology for this genre of film-making, which would eventually come to be known as 'ethnofiction' by third parties. (He himself preferred the term 'science fiction', a sort of pun based on the fact that in French, the term 'science' covers not just the natural sciences but also the social sciences, including ethnography.) For present purposes, one could say that the essential defining features of 'ethnofiction' include, first, the anchoring of the film in extended ethnographic field research and second, close collaboration between film-maker and subjects in the performance of a series of spontaneous improvisations, albeit within the framework of a story that is loosely agreed upon beforehand though subject to constant revision as the filming proceeds.[4]

Rouch first developed the ethnofictional format as a way to reach those parts of human experience that neither written texts, nor more conventional documentary film-making were capable of reaching. In line with his abiding interest in Surrealism, the otherwise unreachable realm that Rouch himself sought to access through ethnofiction was his subjects' fantasies, dreams and imaginaries, which he believed would only emerge when the subjects were invited to improvise their everyday lives for a camera. But while this is one way of using the ethnofiction format, it can also be used as a means of representing more mundane aspects of subjects' everyday lives that would otherwise be impossible to show for ethical or logistical reasons.

It is now more than sixty years since Rouch made his first ethnofictions, and in the interim there have been relatively few attempts to emulate his works in this particular genre. I would surmise that this is because the successful production of an ethnofiction requires an unusual combination of skills and circumstances. These include an ethnographic researcher with a developed sense of dramaturgy and the cinematographic skills to match, as well as a group of subjects with whom the researcher has not only developed deep bonds of trust, but who also have at least a performative disposition that allows them to throw themselves with conviction into improvising the roles required for the film.

It was certainly a fortuitous coming together of this set of circumstances that allowed *Transfiction* to be made. This work, which was inspired by a combination of Rouch's ethnofictional practice and the politically oriented applied theatre of the Brazilian dramaturge, Augusto Boal, concerns the life of transgendered people in São Paulo, the largest city in Brazil. It was directed by Johannes Sjöberg, who is Swedish in origin and who is now a member of staff of the Drama department at the University of Manchester. In addition to holding academic qualifications in both dramatic arts and anthropology, Sjöberg has also had considerable acting experience outside a strictly academic environment. At time that he made *Transfiction*, he was a doctoral student in Applied Theatre, though he was also attached to the Social Anthropology department at Manchester. The film was made in the course of some fifteen months of ethnographic field research carried out in 2005–6 with the transgendered community in São Paulo, in particular with those associated with *Os Satyros*, a bohemian theatre in the centre of the city. In the classical Rouchian manner, Sjöberg himself acted as both cameraman and director, while the sound was taken by a local person.[5]

*Transfiction* has a running time of 57 minutes and was first released in 2007. The central narrative is built around two male-to-female transgendered characters: Zilda, who makes a living as a sex worker, and Meg, a hairdresser who works in a beauty salon. These characters were respectively played by Bibi Meirelles and Fabia Mirassos, both of whom were themselves transgendered. There was also a continuity between their real-life professions and those of the characters in the film: Bibi had worked as a transgendered sex worker in the past and was proud of having done so, while Fabia did indeed make a living as a hairdresser. Although Bibi and Fabia were friends in real life, there were also significant differences between them. Most obviously, Bibi was ten years older and whereas Fabia could easily pass herself off as a highly attractive woman, Bibi's feminity was less immediately

16.2 Ethnofiction in *Transfiction* (2007). Fabia Mirassos, left, who plays Meg, and Bibi Meirelles, who plays Zilda, at the salon where Fabia works as a hairdresser, both in the film and in her everyday life.

convincing from a purely visual point of view (figure 16.2). While Bibi's lifestyle was highly unconventional and her material circumstances were precarious, Fabia led a relatively stable life, maintaining an almost bourgeois existence with her husband in their own house in a residential suburb of São Paulo.

Although this contrast is not underlined in the film in an explicit manner, there was also an important difference in the way that they respectively related to their sexuality: both were biologically male, but whereas Bibi had moved on from becoming aware as a teenager that she was a sexually gay man, Fabia had felt from a very early age that she was a female person trapped inside a male body. Despite this difference, both Bibi and Fabia might be referred to by other Brazilians as *travesti*, though there is considerable controversy, both politically and academically, about the precise meaning of this term.[6]

From his own account of the process, it would seem that Sjöberg exercised rather more directorial control than Rouch (or at least more than Rouch generally liked to confess). At the outset, Sjöberg agreed with Bibi and Fabia that the film should not deal with such high-profile and already much discussed issues as police harassment or AIDS, but rather should focus on the impact on the transgendered people of low-key, day-to-day prejudice. Within this general framework, Bibi and Fabia initially had complete freedom to come up with ideas for scenes based on their own personal experiences.

Sjöberg also sometimes asked them to develop scenes that were not based directly on their own lives but which would provide an opportunity to tackle issues or situations that had arisen in the lives of other transgendered people whom he had interviewed for his research.

However, Sjöberg was also concerned that the various scenes should hang together within a beginning–middle–end narrative structure, and as the filming proceeded, the more this tended to restrict the scenes that came to be filmed. Other considerations were more ethical: Sjöberg undertook never to push Bibi and Fabia to act out anything that they did not want to or which they would later come to regret. He also assumed responsibility for ensuring that it was made clear that anything that occurred in the film which was illegal, or which cast the film characters in an unflattering light, was entirely fictional and did not pertain to them in their normal lives outside the film.

Just as Rouch does at the beginning of *La Pyramide humaine*, Sjöberg begins *Transfiction* with a sort of reflexive prelude in which he is shown explaining the nature of the ethnofictional approach to his principal protagonists. The other minor characters and those playing them are then introduced one by one, supported in most cases by a shot of them discussing with Bibi or Fabia how precisely they should handle the scene in which they appear. Some of the people playing the minor roles were friends of Bibi and Fabia from the transgendered community, while others were Sjöberg's friends.

This prelude also includes an important sequence in which the principal protagonists discuss the relationship between themselves in real life and the roles that they play in the film. Bibi says confidently that while Zilda and she are definitely different people, she has no difficulty in playing this character, thereby suggesting that they have at least some elements of experience in common. Fabia's response is more complex: she suggests that she is using the fictional character of Meg as a sort of protection against acknowledging the fact that she and Meg are really one and the same person, and that the painful issues that Meg confronts in the film are also ones that she needs to confront in her own life. This comment reveals that for her, the making of the film represented an opportunity not merely to make known the prejudice encountered by transgendered people in São Paulo, but also to engage in a form of therapy through living out the personal traumas that she had suffered as a child on account of her sexuality.

Despite all this initial reflexivity about the making of the film, the performances are so thoroughly engaging that one soon forgets that the narrative is entirely fictional. The main body of film begins with a scene set in Meg's beauty salon in which she is touching up Zilda's make-up and it is established that they are friends. It then presents a series of scenes from their respective lives. Zilda goes for a stroll in a red-light district, albeit by day, with Hanah, a fellow sex worker, and they discuss in ribald terms how difficult their business is becoming now that they are getting older. Later, we see Zilda applying to rent an apartment and then for a job, unsuccessfully in both cases. In between these two scenes, we even see her in her role as a sex-worker entertaining a client, though the light is switched off and the narrative moves away before any serious action begins.

These scenes of Zilda are intercut with various scenes featuring Meg and her husband, Eduardo, a character played not by her real-life husband, but by Carlos, a neighbour and close friend since childhood. Meg is an altogether more disturbed character than the happy-go-lucky Zilda. She remains troubled by the traumas that she suffered as a child when she was bullied at school on account of her effeminate appearance, an experience to which the film returns several times in the form of flashbacks. In order to film these scenes, Sjöberg returned with Fabia to the same physical locations where she had originally suffered these traumatic experiences, including her former school and the deserted street where she once had to run away from a gang of boys who were threatening to beat her up. At various points, the stories of the two main characters intersect: a third of the way through, Zilda helps Meg to inject her breasts with silicon, and at the end of the film, Zilda returns to the salon to tell Meg the happy ending of her part of the story, namely, that one of her clients, a shy Frenchman, has asked her to go to live with him in Paris. She is then seen setting off for the airport, while Meg is left still worrying about her childhood experiences.

Finally, the film vouchsafes Meg a happy ending too, though one that requires a return to profilmic reality to achieve. From behind the camera, Sjöberg asks her how they should end the film, and Meg, now in her real persona as Fabia, suggests that she should return to her house and give her husband some flowers. This she duly does and then some further reflexive moments wrap the film up: Sjöberg thanks Bibi outside the salon, and then shares a glass of wine with Fabia and Carlos, the person who plays her husband in the film. Finally, as the credits roll, Sjöberg himself is shown in the salon as he is gradually transformed from a rough and bearded hetero man into a gleaming *travesti*, with shiny red lips and a brunette wig.

In and around this central story, *Transfiction* is given a certain aesthetic 'feel' by the authorial strategies that Sjöberg adopted in shooting and editing. Following Rouch's example, Sjöberg shot most of the film as if it were a *cinéma-vérité* documentary, using long unbroken takes whenever possible. However, in order to keep the fantasy elements firmly anchored in the real world of contemporary São Paulo, the ethnofictional story is discreetly punctuated at various points with brief snatches of contingent reality footage entirely unconnected with the central story – establishment shots of crowds on the streets, anonymous passing traffic, prostitutes touting for business at night, a homeless street kid wandering by the side of the road.

Sjöberg supplements these classical 'reality effects' with another kind of effect that is their polar opposite, and which is based on a sort of double bluff. This takes the form of a number of establishing shots of the city in which the camera waves around in an unstable manner, with crash zooms and tilted horizons. By including these shots, which he executed in this way entirely intentionally, Sjöberg's aim was to enhance the general sense of authenticity of the film by imitating the aesthetic of a handheld camera such as one might find in an early *cinéma-vérité* documentary.

In the shot-sequence in which Zilda imagines herself in Paris, the waving around of the camera becomes even more extravagant. Shot in Paris itself, the camera pans up rockily from a couple of blurred tricolor flags to zoom in on the Eiffel Tower before then circling around it and burning out in a burst of sunlight beyond. The aesthetic of this shot is so unrealistic that it could not be mistaken for the work of even the most incompetent of *cinéma-vérité* camerapersons. Rather the idea here is to evoke the dream-like quality of Zilda's fantasy of going Paris.

Once in the edit suite, Sjöberg superimposed on the *cinéma-vérité* visual aesthetic various forms of music that reference the cultural tropes through which the protagonists approached both their real life and their performances, in much the same manner as Rouch superimposed the high-life hit *Jaguar* at various points on his ethnofiction of the same name.[7] Since both Bibi and Fabia had been greatly influenced by Brazilian television soap operas, Sjöberg uses music of the kind associated with these works at all the major transition points between scenes. Music is also used at various points to suggest the place of *travestis* in the Brazilian collective imaginary, which, interestingly, is rather ambiguous: they are seen as the inhabitants of a dangerous and risky world but one that perhaps even the straightest person might be tempted to enter. This is achieved through a number of returns to unstable handheld close-up shots of Claudia Wonder, a well-known *travesti* nightclub singer in a long white wig, bandanna and extravagant lipstick, performing a song with suggestive lyrics:

> *travesti* in my body/*travesti* in your bed ...
> *travesti* of your love/*travesti* of your whip ...

Behind the ironic and light-hearted soap-opera aesthetic style, *Transfiction* offers a number of serious insights into the circumstances of transgendered people in São Paulo. Perhaps the most important of these is that due to everyday prejudices, many transgendered people can find themselves obliged to work in prostitution simply because few other jobs are open to them. But what is particularly valuable about the film specifically as an ethnographic work is that transgendered prostitution is presented in an original and fresh way, as the sex workers themselves see it, that is, not as a sordid and shameful activity, but rather as an entirely normal, even skilful service that can make shy people happy. This may be a controversial point of view, but this is clearly how Zilda/Bibi see her/their metier.

Much the same could be said of Zilda's happy ending: in the real world, the chances of a transgendered sex worker being whisked off to Paris by one of their clients must surely be remote, but in this sequence, in the best traditions of the Rouchian ethnofictional approach, what we are offered is not the description of reality as such, but the acting out of Zilda/Bibi's fantasy life. And that, as Jean Rouch would surely have said, is just as interesting from an ethnographic point of view as a sober account of the facts and figures about transgendered prostitution in São Paulo today.

There were also a number of other advantages to the adoption of an ethnofictional approach in this particular case. Many of the scenes in *Transfiction* would have been impossible to film in a conventional documentary manner, be it for practical or ethical reasons, while the scene in which Zilda injects Meg's breasts with silicon shows what is, in reality, a completely illegal activity. But there is also a more subtle quality to this film that has nothing to do with ethics, logistics or legality as such, but rather with a sort of emotional texture that is only very rarely present in a straightforwardly factual documentary. This applies particularly to the scenes involving the character of Meg and the support that she receives from her on-screen husband in coming to terms with her transgendered identity. It is difficult to imagine that the loving, supportive intimacy of their relationship could be captured on film unless, paradoxically, the characters were not merely ignoring the presence of the cameraperson, as they would be doing in a documentary, but rather were pretending that he was not there at all, as in this ethnofiction.

Although *Transfiction* is manifestly a fiction, I would have no hesitation in classifying it as an ethnographic film on the grounds that it is based on extended prior ethnographic research, communicates very effectively the subjects' point of view and 'the hold that life has' on them, as well as having a great deal to say about the connections between practices, ideas and relations in the broader life-world of transgendered people in São Paulo. It also respects the norms of contemporary ethnographic research ethics in that it involved close collaboration with the subjects at all stages of the production. Although Fabia and Bibi were not present in the edit suite, they approved the final version of the film before it was screened publicly anywhere else. Moreover, if we can accept Sjöberg at his word, both protagonists regarded the making of the film as a positive experience: indeed, a year after the filming was completed, Fabia told him that it was the most effective therapy that she had ever undergone.

## Participatory film-making as dialogue: *Koriam's Law*

Yet another 'way of doing' ethnographic film authorship in a participatory manner involves foregrounding the personal experience of the ethnographer as they take part in the life of the subjects during fieldwork, and using this as the vehicle through which the multiple interconnections between the practices, ideas and relations of the subjects may be explored. There have been a number of interesting examples of films of this kind in recent years, ranging from those in which the ethnographer is a leading character in a film that is directed and technically realised by others, through those in which the ethnographer is both a character and the director but relies on others to carry out the technical roles, to those in which the ethnographer does everything, participating in the action, directing the film, as well as carrying out all the technical roles.

An interesting example of the first case, in which the ethnographer appears as a leading character in a film directed by others, is *Koriam's Law and the Dead who Govern*, released in 2005. This film concerns the ideas and practices of the Kivung Association, a religious and political movement based in and around Pomio, an administrative district on the eastern shore of the island of New Britain, Papua New Guinea. It was based on the long-term fieldwork of the Australian anthropologist Andrew Lattas and was jointly directed by Gary Kildea and Andrea Simon.

This film was originally conceived as part of a US television series on millenarian religious movements. This was produced by Simon, who recruited Kildea to the project on account of his long experience as a cinematographer working in Papua New Guinea. When the television series ran into difficulty, Kildea asked Simon if he could use the 52 hours of rushes to cut a somewhat different kind of film. Simon agreed, and *Koriam's Law*, with a running time of 110 minutes, is the result. Although Simon and Kildea jointly produced and directed this film, it was Kildea who carried out the editing as well as the shooting.[8]

Founded in 1964 by Michael Koriam Urekit, a local leader, the Kivung Association movement is based on the belief, widely held in Melanesia, that material well-being depends on the establishment of good relations with the dead, who are ever-present in everyday life even though they remain invisible. Koriam gave this idea a political edge by proposing that the disparity in wealth between Whites and Melanesians was due to the fact that the former had somehow managed to establish an inside track with the dead and were siphoning off the material wealth offered by the latter for their exclusive use. The aim of the movement, at least as originally formulated, was to develop ritual procedures that would allow its members to establish their own relationship with the dead, bypassing the local Catholic mission, which they saw as being complicit in the Whites' secretive insider dealings with the dead. As a number of subjects explain in the film, in their view any attempt to achieve material well-being through business or other economic development activities is a waste of time: what really matters is getting hold of the esoteric knowledge that is required to persuade the dead to provide this wealth.

*Koriam's Law* is constructed around a series of dialogues between Andrew Lattas and leading members of the Kivung Association movement. But the film is very much more than the record of an academic research project in that it raises a series of questions about postcolonial social and political relations, as well as about the disjunctions between local and global systems of religious belief. Underlying the dialogues between Lattas and his interlocutors, there is a strong, even if mostly unspoken tension, namely, that while Lattas is trying to find out more about the Kivung Association, the Melanesians are trying to unlock the secret of the Whites' special relationship with the dead, all the while believing that Lattas, as a White, must himself hold this secret knowledge but is unwilling to share it with them.

In the early part of the film, these dialogical exchanges are intercut with a series of scenes in which people in the village of Matong are shown practising the ritual procedures that the Kivung Association has developed in order to establish its own direct relationship with the dead. These ritual procedures draw in part on indigenous practices, notably in offering food to the dead as a means of encouraging eventual reciprocity. But they have also been modelled in part on the religious and administrative practices of the Whites: the association members reason that as these procedures have apparently been effective in securing material rewards from the dead for the Whites, they should also work for them. One of the most widespread involves paying money into a glass jar, known as a 'Novena bottle', every time one has committed a sin or other form of moral infraction. At the same time, a paper ledger, referred to as a 'report', is kept of these payments, and when the Novena bottle is full, it is added in with the money and offered to the dead. As Lattas comments, whereas in the past the people of Pomio communicated with the dead through dreams or by becoming possessed, now they do so by means of these 'reports' and donations of money. The money itself is used in part to pay for more food offerings to the dead, while part is donated to the Kivung Association itself (figure 16.3, left).

A particularly telling scene takes place close to the cemetery: we do not see into the cemetery itself, but one of Lattas's interlocutors introduces him to a noticeboard where the names of the dead are listed, as if on a European war memorial. The dead include a certain 'Australia', an anonymous Australian who died of disease during the Second World War. As his relatives never came to collect his remains, the people of Pomio have adopted him as one of their dead, and have been 'feeding' him in the expectation that he will return the favour. Eventually, the Kivung Association people

**16.3** *Koriam's Law and the Dead Who Govern* (2005). Left, the people of Pomio, New Britain, Papua New Guinea, have developed their own ceremony, modelled on Catholic liturgy, in which they offer food and money to the dead. But the Catholic priest, right, urges them to use these resources to help their living children instead.

believe, the dead will be resurrected and the cemetery will be transformed into a modern city, where Whites and Blacks will live in harmony and on equal terms.

About a third of the way into the film, there is something of a change of gear. This begins with the arrival by boat of an itinerant Catholic priest, a European who speaks both English and pidgin with a German accent. He greets the film-makers in a friendly manner and explains that he has come to conduct a Christmas Day mass. Having changed into his full ritual robes from the shorts and baseball cap in which he arrived, the priest first talks to his Melanesian congregation about events that happened in Palestine two millennia ago and then offers them the opportunity to eat the body of a man who lived at that time. In other words, he discusses events described in the Bible and offers them Holy Communion. In the context of the film, however, his words and ritual procedures seem no more well-founded in any rational apperception of the world than the Kivung practices that we have seen immediately beforehand. In his sermon, he then rails against the collection of Novena money for the dead: he urges his congregation to use this money to ensure the health of their children instead (figure 16.3, right). At face value, this might seem like an entirely positive humane proposition, but having been made aware of the Kivung Association's beliefs, we can now understand how his homily might be interpreted as no more than a devious stratagem intended to discourage Pomio people from building the relationships with the dead that are required to unlock material well-being.

The action of the film then moves to the village of Salel, where the headquarters of the Kivung Association are located. Here, we are introduced to an eloquent and seemingly well-educated man who describes himself as a local 'governor' operating in the 'political realm' but who is still guided by the spiritual beliefs of the Kivung Association. The views of the dead are communicated to him by a woman who has been possessed by the spirit of her son, named Jo, who died during a miscarriage, but who is believed to be the spiritual son of one of the founders of the movement. The governor describes Jo as 'a sort of contemporary Melanesian version of Jesus'.

The governor then explains that although some people have attempted to discredit the Association by calling it a 'cargo cult', it does not have anything to do with waiting for cargo, at least not now. Instead, it is focused on securing development aid through the government and indeed has been successful in getting funding for a number of local schools and copra plantations. This section of the film culminates in an elaborate celebration of the thirty-fourth anniversary of the foundation of the Kivung movement, with much speechifying, choral singing and traditional dances. This is attended by members of the national parliament who have flown in especially for the occasion, testifying to the increasing political weight of the Association. It may not be a cargo cult in the classical anthropological sense, but we see that the Association has clearly been very successful in attracting wealth from elsewhere.

Finally, for the last ten minutes, the film returns to Matong and to the dialogue between Andrew Lattas and Peter Avarea, one his principal interlocutors. In a moving passage, Peter, who is disabled, says that he believes that the Kivung Association will prosper, and that in due course of time it will arrange for his legs to be made good again. He adds that although some people will think that he has told Lattas too much, he himself believes that Melanesians should not be afraid to speak out. As the sun is hot, they agree to take a break, and the film concludes with a final valedictory image of the sea, allowing us a calm moment of reflection before the credits break in, dispersing the powerful spell that the film has cast.

It has to be acknowledged that there is a certain stylistic unevenness in this film, which can perhaps be traced to the fact that it had two directors and was originally conceived as a television programme. Moreover, some viewers have felt that the editing is not as effective as it might have been: although the Kivung Association's beliefs and organisational arrangements clearly pose a challenge to European ways of thinking, some critics have suggested that they could nevertheless have been presented in a clearer fashion. But notwithstanding these possible limitations, *Koriam's Law* offers an interesting model of the possibilities that can arise when an ethnographic film-making project is based upon a combination of close collaborative relationships with the subjects achieved through long-term ethnographic fieldwork and cinematographic craft skills of the highest order. The particular strength of the film lies in the fact that, paradoxically, it takes advantage of the materiality of the medium of film to convince the viewer of the reality of the immaterial world of the dead for the subjects of the film. It may be not be possible for an irreligious Western viewer to believe, as the members of the Kivung Association do, that the dead really do govern the lives of the living, but *Koriam's Law* certainly encourages us – to use the turn of phrase coined by Jean Rouch – to believe in their beliefs.

## PARTICIPATORY FILM-MAKING THROUGH LONG-TERM PERSONAL ENGAGEMENT: THE HAMAR TRILOGY AND *DUKA'S DILEMMA*

In the case of *Koriam's Law*, though the ethnographer's long-standing relationship to the subjects provides the main channel through which the subject matter of the film is explored, Andrew Lattas himself did not direct it. Recent years have seen a number of ethnographic films that are similarly reflexive and based on a long-standing relationship with the subjects, but which have also been directed by the ethnographer.

A particularly good example is *Duka's Dilemma*, which was shot in 2001 and released in 2002. This film was directed by the anthropologist Jean Lydall and was based on her close relationship with the Hamar people of southern Ethiopia, whose way of life is based on a combination of cattle herding and millet agriculture. At the time of filming, this relationship reached back some three decades to 1970 when, together with her husband, Ivo Strecker, Lydall first carried out fieldwork with the Hamar. Early on in that fieldwork, in 1971, Lydall and Strecker had advised Robert Gardner on the making of *Rivers of Sand*, but they had been deeply dissatisfied with the result. They took particular exception to what they considered to be the simplistic way in which Gardner had represented Hamar gender relationships as being based on the oppression of 'meek overworked' women by 'vain indolent' men. It was in order to counter Gardner's filmic representation of the Hamar that both Lydall and Strecker later took up film-making themselves.[9]

After working with Strecker on two films for the German television station SWF in 1982–83, Lydall then collaborated with the anthropologically trained director Joanna Head between 1990 and 1994 to make a trilogy of films about the life experiences of Hamar women for the BBC Television series, *Under the Sun*. Although *Duka's Dilemma* is somewhat different from the BBC trilogy in terms of cinematographic praxis, there are many elements of continuity with regard to subject matter. In effect then, *Duka's Dilemma* constitutes the fourth instalment in a quartet of films about Hamar women's lives that interconnect and complement one another at a number of different levels. Certainly, the viewing of *Duka's Dilemma* is greatly enriched by prior

**16.4** The Hamar trilogy, *Under the Sun* strand. In *The Women Who Smile* (1990), left, and *Two Girls Go Hunting* (1991), the focus is on the lives of women. Right, in the third part, *Our Way of Loving* (1994), it also embraces other themes, including the 'leap across the cattle', the male initiation ceremony.

acquaintance with the *Under the Sun* trilogy. I therefore consider it here in that broader context.

In practical terms, the first film in the BBC trilogy, *The Women Who Smile*, was directly inspired by the prior example of Melissa Llewelyn-Davies's films about the Maasai. This was no coincidence since Joanna Head, the director, had started her film-making career in the early 1980s working as a researcher on the *Worlds Apart* series that Llewelyn-Davies co-produced out of BBC Bristol with Chris Curling.[10] As with many of Llewelyn-Davies's Maasai films, *The Women Who Smile* is constructed around a series of intimate conversational interviews with a number of key female interlocutors: an unmarried woman in her 20s still living in her father's house, a recently widowed but still young woman with four small children and, finally, an older woman with eight surviving children (a further ten having died in infancy), who had recently persuaded her husband to take a second wife. Although the second film in the trilogy, *Two Girls Go Hunting*, also remained closely focused on female experience as it followed two girls through the process of getting married (the metaphorical 'hunting' referred to in the title), the third film, *Our Way of Loving*, covered a somewhat broader range of themes, including some scenes of contact with the outside world, a funeral and some tense bridewealth negotiations. It culminated in an extended sequence about the 'leap across the cattle', the rite of passage that young men have to complete before they are allowed to marry (figure 16.4). Throughout all three films, one is very aware of Lydall's presence since we frequently hear her voice in the conversational exchanges with the subjects.

The general picture that emerges from this trilogy of BBC films suggests that while Robert Gardner may have indulged in some ethnographically erroneous symbolic juxtapositions and exaggerated both the shiftlessness

471

of Hamar men and the lack of the agency of Hamar women in managing their lives, he was not entirely wrong in so far as the general tenor of gender relations in their society is concerned. For, as the female interlocutors explain to Lydall with candour and charm, and more with an air of regret than with bitterness, their lives are highly restricted compared to those of men. Whereas a boy is regarded as a 'person' as soon as he is a born, a girl child is regarded as no more than a 'guest' in her own home since she is already thought to 'belong' to her future husband. Having enjoyed certain freedoms as a girl, marriage is a time of sadness for the bride, for not only is she separated from her family and obliged to go and live in the house of a man whom she has never met, nor played any part in choosing, but that house becomes a 'trap' from which there is no escape. Although marriage for a woman may be metaphorically compared to hunting among the Hamar, there is no 'glory song' attached to it, as there is when a young man brings back his first major kill. On the contrary, marriage for a woman entails a great deal of hard labour: looking after children, preparing food, tending livestock, working in the fields, cleaning the house and kraal, and being ever attentive to her husband's beck and call. Only a mature woman, who has many children and some in-married daughters-in-law to help her with the chores, and who, in the ideal case, can persuade her husband to take a second wife to share the burden, can gain a significant measure of relief from this workload.

Most disturbing of all in these testimonies is the recurrent reference to the beatings that husbands seemingly routinely inflict on their wives. Both women and men refer to these beatings as if they were an inevitable fact of life that one is obliged to accept if one is a woman and expected to administer if one is a man. What is particularly unsettling is that these beatings are often spoken about, particularly by the men but even sometimes by women, by subjects who are grinning broadly as they do so. At first, one is inclined to think that this is a sign of embarrassment because the subjects know that Lydall will not approve of the practice. But in the third film of the trilogy, as suggested by the title, *Our Way of Loving*, it becomes evident that if the Hamar show a certain embarrassment in talking about these beatings, it is not on account of the admission of intergender violence, or at least not only so, but also because beatings can be associated with the arousal of erotic passions.

This is certainly suggested by the preliminary rituals associated with the 'leap across the cattle' male initiation ceremony that features in the final extended sequence of *Our Way of Loving*. Prior to the main ceremony, a relative of the initiate, who has himself already been initiated, is expected to arm himself with a fistful of thin switches and to whip any woman that he comes across. In *Rivers of Sand*, Robert Gardner presents this whipping as a symbolic expression of Hamar men's violence against women, suggesting, through editorial juxtapositioning, that there is a parallel between the whipping of women and the treatment meted out to donkeys or cattle.[11] Judging by the way this practice is presented in *Our Way of Loving*, this is entirely misconceived. For those who come to be whipped are not random women whom the initiand's relative just happens to encounter, but rather women and girls who had previously been the initiand's actual or potential lovers but whom he should now foreswear – at least in principle. Immediately prior to his leap across the cattle, these former lovers present themselves to the initiand's relative of their own free will and in an extrovert manner, some blowing horns and others whistles, noisily and actively provoke him into whipping them. Afterwards, they will wear the deep and permanent scars that his whip will make across their backs with pride, as a symbol of the intensity of their love for the initiand. In due course of time, the initiand may give them gifts in exchange for this expression of love for him.

When Jean Lydall came to make *Duka's Dilemma* and was free, as the director, to adopt the practical approach that she most preferred, she chose not to follow the television model used in the films that she had made with Joanna Head, but rather one that was more akin to the approach that David and Judith MacDougall had developed in their work in East Africa in the 1970s.[12]

The most immediate practical consequence of this change of praxis was that rather than being made by a professional television crew, *Duka's Dilemma* was shot by Lydall's daughter, Kaira Strecker, who had trained a camerawoman. Kaira also recorded the sound and later did the editing. As a child, Kaira had spent several years living with her parents while they were engaged in fieldwork among the Hamar, and although by the time of filming her command was a little rusty, she could therefore speak their language. Not only did she know the Hamar, but they knew her: indeed, in the opening sequence Duka, the principal subject, addresses her as 'little sister' and urges her to film well. Kaira brought her 3-year-old son, Tammo, to show to Duka, and we see him at various points in the film, playing with Hamar children. We also see Kaira herself in the final sequence while the family's Land Rover appears in the background of several shots. Such elements of reflexivity, while not entirely ruled out by Joanna Head, were kept to a minimum in the BBC films.

Conversational exchanges between Lydall and the subjects are central to *Duka's Dilemma* just as they had been in the BBC films, but in general they are more informal. These exchanges mostly take place while the subject is engaged in some other activity, a strategy that Head had sought rather to avoid. A more striking difference concerns the voice-over commentary. During the production of the BBC films, Lydall had suggested that she should speak the commentary herself, despite her reservations about the quality of her own voice, so that the voice-over would link up with her voice as it is heard recurrently in conversation with the subjects. But the BBC producers had opted instead to use professional voice-artists with the usual aesthetic effect of distancing and objectifying the subjects, notwithstanding the fact that the voice-artists were all women and, in one case, had what was supposedly an African accent. Their smooth professional voices punctuate the BBC films at regular intervals from beginning to end, whereas in *Duka's Dilemma*, other than the brief commentary spoken in Hamar by Kaira near the beginning of the film, there is no voice-over at all. When contextualising information is necessary, it is delivered through intertitle cards instead.

The eponymous principal subject of *Duka's Dilemma* is a woman whom Lydall had known since she was a child. Indeed, Duka represents a strong thread of continuity running through all four films of the quartet: she was the unmarried woman in *The Women Who Smile*, then one of the two women who get married in *Two Girls Go Hunting*, and she also appears frequently in *Our Way of Loving*, by which time she was a married woman with two small children. As *Duka's Dilemma* opens, some eight years on from the previous film, Duka is in her late 30s and mother to five children. We discover that she is in what could perhaps be more exactly described as a predicament rather than a dilemma (since there does not appear to be much of a choice involved): as she explains in the opening sequence, she had recently been sick for a prolonged period and Sago, her husband, had taken advantage of her indisposition to take a second, much younger wife, Boro, whom he has married surreptitiously 'in the bush'. He has done so much to the disapproval of his mother, Sagonda, a widow, and a lively and feisty character who had also appeared in the earlier films.

The narrative of *Duka's Dilemma* consists, essentially, of following the social processes through which these four characters negotiate the consequences of Boro's sudden and, to Duka, disturbing arrival. Audiences familiar with the earlier films will know that in Hamar society, co-wives are usually strangers to one another at first since they will often have come from different villages, but that, over time, they can be an important source of mutual support in fulfilling their many domestic obligations and, as necessary, standing up to their husbands. Similarly, the relationship between in-married women and their mothers-in-law, who also generally begin as complete strangers to one another, can also become close and mutually supportive.

However, at the beginning of *Duka's Dilemma*, the relationship between Duka and Boro is poor: although Duka seeks to be generous and welcoming, and presents her husband's decision to marry again as a desire to provide her with additional help in looking after the children – indeed even as an arrangement that she herself had decided upon – Duka also sees Boro as a rival (figure 16.5, left). Boro herself is very hostile and bad-tempered, not

16.5 *Duka's Dilemma* (2001). Left, when Duka's husband takes a much younger second wife, Boro, initially she feels threatened. But after she helps Boro through the process of giving birth, right, the two wives become mutually supportive.

only towards Duka, but also towards their common mother-in-law Sagonda, whom she considers, with good reason, to be on Duka's side. Meanwhile, Sago remains aloof from the whole process, contenting himself with shouting instructions at his wives and his mother from outside the family kraal.

Duka herself surmises that the situation is made worse by the fact that Boro has not yet had any children, and that as soon as she does have a child of her own she will be much happier. This comment anticipates a particularly powerful and dynamic scene in which Boro gives birth and during which she is energetically assisted by both Duka and Sagonda, and one or two other women from the village: as women go to live in their husband's village after marriage among the Hamar, Boro's own mother and sisters are far away (figure 16.5, right). This scene is very well and sensitively shot by Kaira but spares little detail, and as such, has been criticised for being far too intrusive. But Lydall has robustly defended the scene on the grounds that on the basis of her long-standing relationship with the Hamar, she was confident that the subjects would find it entirely acceptable to show the process of birthing so explicitly, and moreover, in the film itself, they specifically give Kaira permission to film. What is certainly the case is that Duka's prediction is proved right, and following the birth, Boro becomes much happier with her lot. The relationship between the co-wives becomes mutually supportive, with Duka working in Boro's fields while she is recovering from the birth and even breastfeeding her baby. Later in the film, when Duka gives birth to her own son, Boro provides her with food and drink, while Duka is shown breastfeeding both babies simultaneously.

A secondary theme running through the film concerns the tension between Sagonda and Sago, her son. Sagonda feels that she is given insufficient respect as a widow and deserves to have her own house, built for her by

Sago. She takes advantage of the gathering of male elders for the naming ceremony for Duka's baby (and possibly of the presence of the camera as well) to threaten to take herself off to the local town and 'sell her vagina'. Eventually the matter is resolved by a council of elders, who find for Sagonda, thereby demonstrating that contrary to the general trend, women sometimes can prevail in Hamar society, though usually only if they are senior women. The film then builds to a 'happy ending': Sagonda's house is built by a work-party organised by Sago, while the final sequence consists of a tranquil scene of both Duka and Boro together with Sago and their children, at home in their kraal.

In an epilogue, Kaira appears on screen and asks Duka if there is anything else that she would like to say. Duka replies that she has nothing to add except the hope that Kaira will show the film to the father of her son and to all her friends, and that, as a result, people will understand the Hamar and like them. Whether the film is successful in this last regard is, of course, necessarily moot, but what the film certainly does show is the benefit of a participatory praxis based on a long-term relationship between ethnographer and subjects.

## PARTICIPATORY FILM-MAKING AS 'SENSORY APPRENTICESHIP': *KALANDA*

In the final example considered here, the ethnographer's relationship to the subjects is again the vehicle through which the themes of the film are explored, but in this case the ethnographer not only acted as director of the film but also carried out the principal technical roles as well. A very effective example of this particular mode of participatory praxis is *Descending with Angels*, which was shot, directed and edited by Christian Suhr and released in 2013. This film was based on eighteen months of field research in Aarhuus in Denmark, conducted by Suhr himself, among the Salafi Islamic community of the city and in the local psychiatric hospital. The film compares and contrasts Islamic and secular forms of healing what one might broadly call mental tribulation, which is interpreted as the effects of spirit possession by the Islamic community and as a mental illness by the psychiatrists. However, although this film is very well made, both from a technical and editorial point of view, it has recently been the subject of a book-length commentary by Suhr himself, published in the same series as this one, and this provides a much more informed analysis of the film than anything that I could offer here.[13]

I therefore turn instead to a more recent film, which was released in 2015 when the maker was still a doctoral student at the University of Manchester. Whereas the praxis of Suhr's film is based on relatively conventional observational realism, the ethnographer-film-maker in this case took advantage of recent developments in digital technology to be more aesthetically experimental. In this sense, it constitutes an interesting attempt to combine the 'sensorial' approach of the Harvard Sensory Ethnography Lab with a more participatory praxis.

The ethnographer-film-maker in question was Lorenzo Ferrarini, an Italian, who carried out doctoral fieldwork over the course of two years in the region west of Bobo-Dioulasso, in southwestern Burkina Faso in 2011–12. The principal focus of this research was *donsoya*, a body of esoteric beliefs and practices associated with hunting found in various forms throughout the Mande cultural area of West Africa. In the course of this fieldwork, Ferrarini shot the material for what would eventually become an hour-long documentary, *Kalanda – The Knowledge of the Bush*. This is structured around his own initiation into *donsoya*.[14]

As a body of knowledge, *donsoya* involves not only hunting skills per se, such as an awareness of the habits of potential prey and how to walk through the forest with minimal noise, but also a knowledge of the magical procedures deemed necessary to offer protection to hunters. In order to achieve this protection, a hunter needs to know how to make up the amulets containing sacred texts from the Koran that he will wear while hunting. He also needs to know how to prepare certain powders that he should apply both to his own body and to his gun, as well as to his prey after it has been killed. In addition to this more technical knowledge, Ferrarini also learned more generally about the work of *donso* hunters as diviners and healers, and about their relationships with the musicians who play a remarkable harp-like instrument known locally as *n'goni*.

This knowledge is passed on to Ferrarini in *Kalanda* as a series of lessons from a master-hunter, Adama Sogo Traoré. Sitting beneath a tree in his traditional mud-walled compound, Traoré is framed in mid-shot, attired in various elegant boubous as the film proceeds. Speaking eloquently in Jula, the local trade language, he looks down at Ferrarini who is both literally and metaphorically sitting at his feet behind the camera (figure 16.6, left). The teacher frequently sends Ferrarini off to be instructed by others in certain specific aspects of *donsoya* and we see him out hunting in the bush by day, collecting medicinal plants, visiting a man who washes his gun and another who makes amulets, as well as learning from a musician about the praise songs that he sings to the hunters. The musician also shows Ferrarini the extraordinary shirt that he wears, covered with mirrors, cowrie shells and fetishes in order to protect himself against evil-doers. After each of these episodes, Ferrarini returns to sit at Adama's feet.

Ferrarini refers to his enskilment in *donsoya* as a 'sensory apprenticeship' since the sensory dimension is as important as the linguistic. When sent off by Adama to learn from a younger hunter, Lasseni, Ferrarini does not just

16.6 *Kalanda* (2015). Left, sitting at the feet of the master-hunter, Adama Sogo Traoré, the film-maker is instructed about *donsoya*; right, while learning to hunt, he used an extreme wide-angle lens to emphasise his initial perceptual frustration.

interview him, but accompanies him on a hunt. In shooting the sequence showing this hunt, Ferrarini broke with conventional observational realist norms in order to emphasise certain aspects of this learning experience: thus, for example, he held the camera much lower than level of his eyes, even though this was not strictly realistic, since he wanted to emphasise the sense of scanning meticulously for evidence of small game hiding under the bushes. He also used an extreme wide-angle lens, which makes it difficult for the spectator to focus on any particular detail. In this way, he hoped to communicate the sense of perceptual frustration that he himself felt when first learning to hunt (figure 16.6, right).

Since mastering the acoustic aspects of hunting is particularly important in the process of becoming an initiated *donso* hunter, Ferrarini also put a great deal of thought into the sound design of his film. Although much of the film consists of 'normal' synchronous sound, this was supplemented by the extensive use of wild-tracks. These were often recorded on two cardioid microphones positioned more or less at right angles to one another, sometimes in a single static position in order to record general ambient sound, while at other times they were attached a boom pole and used to capture such things as human steps moving over various different surfaces at different speeds. In the hunting sequence described, Ferrarini supplemented the synchronous ambient sound track with wild-tracks in order to communicate a sense of the process whereby the novice becomes aware of the acoustic environment.

Drawing on previous usages by the ethnographer of boxers in Chicago, Loïc Waquant, and ultimately by the neurophenomenologist Francisco Varela, Ferrarini refers to his praxis in making *Kalanda* as 'enactive'. This 'way of doing' ethnographic film-making, as he presents it, is based on the idea that it is through immersion in the sensory world of the subjects and the first-hand acting out of key aspects of that life that the film-maker achieves ethnographic understanding. Also important, however, is the principle that this immersion should always involve active collaborative relationships with the subjects.

The making of *Kalanda* was collaborative in a number of different regards. In a precise technical sense, inspired by the example of Steven Feld's ground-breaking work among the Kaluli of Papua New Guinea, Ferrarini used sound editing software in the field to work directly with his hunter-instructor Lasseni in order to get a sense of how his recordings sounded to an experienced *donso*. This allowed him to distinguish recordings of a good hunter moving through the bush as compared to his own noisy beginner's movements. This then enabled him to use these sounds in the appropriate way on the soundtrack of his film.

Later, Ferrarini showed all the different chapters of his film to their subjects, not only to receive their feeback about the accuracy or significance of the material, but also to seek their approval to include that material in the final film since much of the knowledge involved was considered to be secret, and not suitable for showing to women or to men who had not been instructed in *donsoya*. Even since it was completed, *Kalanda* has continued to be a collaborative project in the sense that part of the income from sales of the film and associated photographs is systematically returned to the subjects.

An important point, however, is that the collaborative nature of Ferrarini's praxis is sewn into the very structure of the film rather than signalled in an overt manner. Indeed, compared to *Koriam's Law* or even *Duka's Dilemma*, the reflexivity of *Kalanda* is relatively low-key and discreet. We are aware of the ethnographer-film-maker as the initiate sitting at the feet of his teacher, and at one point in the film we see close-ups of parts of Ferrarini's body (feet, arms, back) in a series of static shots that show him washing in a protective medicinal solution. At another point, we see Lasseni watching rushes on Ferrarini's laptop. But until the final shot of the film, we never see more than a part of his body, nor do we hear his voice in voice-over commentary.

At the same time, in its extensive manipulation of sound and image, Ferrarini's praxis in *Kalanda* goes well beyond observation. In addition to the manipulations aimed at communicating the experience of his 'sensory apprenticeship', there are also passages of time-lapse photography, still photographs inserted into the middle of observational shots, and asynchronic-ity, all of which remind the viewer of the limitations of observational realism. *Kalanda* also goes beyond observation in its narrative structure, notably in relation to the principal structuring device of the apprentice sitting at the master's feet, who is then sent off to consult third parties. This device was entirely enacted for the film in the sense that the exchanges between Adama and Ferrarini were filmed *after* all the consultations with third parties. Once he had a rough cut of most these consultations, Ferrarini showed them to Adama and asked him for his comments so that he could link these various scenes together. Ferrarini reports that Adama performed these links 'brilliantly': only occasionally did he have to provoke Adama with questions.

Also beyond observation is the framing of the master–apprentice narrative by the two shots of Ferrarini hunting at night that open and close the film. As the film itself makes clear in a reflexive manner, these shots have been very carefully set up and lit, and, moreover, they are presented in reverse chronological order. In the opening shot, in a carefully placed pool of light in the darkness, we see a close-up of two pairs of hands, one black, holding a recently slaughtered antelope, while the other is white and is scattering powder into the antelope's eyes and wounds. This is a record of Ferrarini's first kill at night – the climax of his instruction in *donsoya*. However, it is not until the final shot of the film that we finally see him emerge from behind his tripod-mounted camera and set off into the darkness, along with his two *donso* companions, in order to make that kill. On the soundtrack, Adama's voice is heard reminding Ferrarini that when one becomes a *donso*, it should be a lifelong commitment, rounding off the film with the classical narrative device of a projection into the future.

If the praxis underlying *Kalanda* goes beyond observation in all these ways, it is also very different from the praxis of the Sensory Ethnography Lab (SEL). Like the SEL film-makers, Ferrarini uses digital technology in imaginative ways in an attempt to evoke sensory aspects of experience. Also like them, he recurs to theorists writing from a phenomenological perspective to provide an endorsement of this aspect of his praxis. But in contrast to at least some SEL film-makers, Ferrarini is not afraid to use language, both verbal and cinematographic, to make connections between ideas, actions and social relations, and his praxis is in general very much more participatory and reflexive. In this sense, he has developed a 'way of doing' ethnographic film-making that draws effectively on a range of different traditions to produce an account that is simultaneously sensory, linguistic and analytical.

What is particularly valuable, in my view, about all the films considered in this final chapter is that they are based in the first instance on a form of committed engagement with the subjects – explicitly political in the case of *Tracks Across Sand*, implicitly political in the case of *Transfiction* and *Koriam's Law*, more moral and personal in the case of *Duka's Dilemma* and *Kalanda*. In a variety of forms, these works offer a range of examples of how the medium of film, deployed in a participatory manner, can be used to develop a rich ethnographic account, structured by an engaging narrative, of the many connections between practices, ideas and relations in the social lives of their subjects. But notwithstanding the strongly collaborative ethos of these works, there is no pretence on the part of their makers that they have somehow been authored by the subjects: in all cases, the creative, intellectual and ethical responsibility for the films remain manifestly with the film-makers.

These films should not be considered models to be emulated in every particular: they are models of possibility rather than models of perfection. Nor should they form the basis for some sort of future orthodoxy. But in going beyond observation in their variously reflexive and participatory praxes, while at the same time remaining clearly authored by their makers, these films reach back to the shared anthropology of Jean Rouch while also suggesting interesting possibilities for 'ways of doing' of ethnographic film in the twenty-first century.

## Notes

1 Ginsburg (2018).
2 I am grateful to Hugh Brody for his comments in December 2018 on the manuscript version of this section of the chapter.
3 See Robbins (2008), 51–76. See also the discussion of John Marshall's later films about the Namibian San in Chapter 6, pp. 188–93.
4 See Henley (2009), 67–100.
5 In this discussion, I draw on Sjöberg's doctoral thesis (2008a), particularly pp. 114–34, and two later articles, Sjöberg (2008b; 2018). I am grateful to Sjöberg himself for his comments on a preliminary version of this section.
6 See Sjöberg (2008a), 74–80.
7 See Henley (2009), 79–81.
8 In a career stretching back to the 1970s, Gary Kildea has been one of the leading exponents of Observational Cinema. See Crawford (2004) and Kildea (2007) for overviews of his work. See also Chapter 10, pp. 306–9.
9 See Chapter 9, pp. 260–1 and Lydall (2008), 37. In writing this section, I have drawn on this article as well as on an earlier article by Lydall (1992). I have also drawn on Lydall and Strecker's jointly signed response to a favourable academic review of Gardner's film (1978).
10 For a detailed discussion of Llewelyn-Davies's films, see Chapter 12, pp. 357–68.
11 See Chapter 9, p. 270.
12 Lydall (2008), 43 ff. See Chapter 5 for a discussion of the MacDougall's East African films. Initially, Lydall had approached the BBC with a proposal, but by 2000, the *Under the Sun* series had come to an end and there was very little interest in commissioning research-based ethnographic films in British television. It was this that led Lydall to initiate the film herself, though in the later stages of production, she received support from the German television station, WDR (Westdeutscher Rundfunk) and the IWF (Institut für den Wissenschaftlichen Film).
13 See Suhr (2019). Suhr was also involved, this time in a co-directorial role, in another good example of participatory film-making based on a long-term relationship between an ethnographer and the subjects. This was *Ngat is Dead*, which was filmed on Baluan, one of the Admiralty Islands, which lie off the northern coast of Papua New Guinea. Released in 2009, this film followed the Dutch anthropologist Ton Otto, the other co-director, as he returned to Baluan, where he had carried out fieldwork over many

years, in order to attend the mortuary ceremonies of a senior man who had adopted him as a son.

14 Ferrarini also made a number of shorter films, as well as producing a substantial portfolio of photographs and audio recordings. For further details see https://lorenzoferrarini.com. In describing the making of *Kalanda*, I draw on Ferrarini's own published account (2017). See also the review of the film by Steven Feld (2016). I am grateful to Ferrarini for his comments on a draft of this section.

# An epilogue
# Return to Kiriwina – the
# ethnographic film-maker
# as author

IF there is a single general conclusion to be drawn from the multitude of examples of ethnographic film-making considered in the course of this book, it is that if one's purpose is to make an ethnographic film that goes beyond the merely descriptive, one should not attempt to eliminate, sidestep, or hide the authorship of that film, nor seek to consign it to others, be it the subjects of the film or the audience. Rather the aim should be to develop modes of film authorship that, while playing to the strengths of film as a medium of communication, also reflect contemporary ideas about the practice of ethnography more generally.

As I have described in this book, for around seventy-five of the 120 or so years during which the moving image camera has been used for ethnographic purposes, its principal value was perceived, certainly in English-speaking academic anthropology, as being related to its capacity to copy the world in a mimetic manner. As such, it was seen as a device for collecting data in an objective fashion that could act as a control on the inevitably more subjective observations made through the human eye alone. Although this view of the moving image camera still surfaces from time to time, it has, by and large, been abandoned. Instead, it has come to be widely valued for its capacity – particularly when used in conjunction with a skilfully recorded soundtrack – to generate accounts of the world that are imbued with a strong sense of 'lived experience'.

In the General Introduction to this book, I suggested that in this capacity to evoke a sense of lived experience, ethnographic film-making offers the possibility of reconnecting with an aspect of human life that Bronislaw Malinowski, the original Ethnographer, sought to describe through his concept of the 'subjective desire of feeling', and which he detected in numerous practices and sentiments of everyday life among the people of the Trobriand Islands. Malinowski considered these 'imponderabilia' to be the 'flesh and blood' of social life and argued that their elicitation was even more important than the description of 'institutions, customs or codes', by which he meant social organisation and culture as systems of abstract ideas. Indeed, he went so far as to suggest that an ethnographic account that failed to include the 'subjective desire of feeling' would 'miss the greatest reward' to be obtained from the study of humankind.

However, notwithstanding this ancestral endorsement, in the last analysis the mere evocation of lived experience through film, however technically sophisticated, however sensorial, is never going to be sufficient to achieve an account of social life that is ethnographic in more than a superficial manner. In the first place, the experience evoked is never going to be very profound: it will always be highly vicarious, only a pale shadow of the experience of the subjects' life as they experience it, and even as experienced by the film-maker in the course of filming. Moreover, it pertains to only two of the five senses, sight and hearing (though if we allow for 'haptic' effects, we might include an element of touch as well). It is a form of experience in which the viewer is unable to make any intervention, nor suffer any consequence. If the evocation of lived experience through film is based on an informed awareness derived from the prolonged immersion of the film-maker in the world of the subjects, then it may certainly possess a certain ethnographic value in a purely descriptive sense. But the understanding that it can offer of that world is only ever going to be limited.

If one wants to go further and offer some insight as to why life is experienced in this way in this particular social situation, then it is necessary to anchor this evocation of experience in some social or cultural context. Or, to continue with Malinowski's corporeal metaphors, one should seek to relate the 'flesh and blood' practices of lived experience to what he called the 'skeleton' of a social group, that is, to its network of social relations, or to its 'spirit', its culturally specific ideas. In ethnographic film-making, the making of these connections often entails recurring to some form of language, be it the metaphorical language of cinematic narrative, or more literal forms of language in the form of verbal discourse by the subjects or by the film-maker themselves. The challenge of ethnographic film-making then is to find a way of authoring films that employ these forms of language without at the same time undermining the unique capacity of the medium of film to impart a sense of lived experience.

It is now just over a century since Malinowski found himself suddenly set down on a beach on Kiriwina, the largest of the Trobriand Islands, as the dinghy that had brought him there sailed away over the horizon. Although the fieldwork method that he developed there over the ensuing years, more by force of circumstance than by design, has since been much criticised, refined and diversified, the central principle on which it was based, namely, the first-hand immersion of the researcher in the life of the community of study over a prolonged period – only later dubbed 'participant-observation' – remains central to the ethnographic method. In a small homage to this anniversary then, let us end the narrative of this book in the most classical of fashions by returning to the beginning of the story – both of this book and of modern anthropology – and taking up Malinowski's famous invitation to imagine ourselves set down on that beach, but with the difference that among the gear with which we are surrounded is a modern digital film-making kit.

Let us imagine too that we have given ourselves the task of using that equipment to make a film about what Malinowski once described as 'perhaps the most difficult and bewildering aspect of Trobriand culture for the investigating sociologist', that is, the Trobriand funeral.[1] There were many things about this event that attracted Malinowski's attention, but one feature that particularly intrigued him was that the extravagance of expressions of grief depended not on personal sentiment but rather on the precise nature of the kinship relationship between the mourner and the deceased. Moreover, the impact of these kinship relations on the practice of mourning was not what one might expect at a funeral in Europe, where it would be reasonable to posit that the closer the relative to the deceased, be it through blood or marriage, the more likely it would be that they would be openly grieving.

On Kiriwina, Malinowski discovered, things were not quite so straight-forward. For when an eminent man died, his wife and children, along with all his relatives through marriage, would mourn ostentatiously, putting on rags for clothes, shaving their heads and 'howling like demons in despair'. In sharp contrast, the man's closest siblings would continue to dress normally, would not shave their hair, and although they might discretely weep, they would not 'parade' their grief.

Part of the reason for this difference, Malinowski claimed, was that in Trobriand society, which was intensely matrilineal, not only a man's wife and his relatives by marriage, but even his own children were regarded as 'mere strangers'. (So extreme was their matrilineal ideology that, as Malinowski famously reported elsewhere, the Trobrianders denied that a father played any role in the physiological reproduction of his children). But, if they really were 'mere strangers', why would they be grieving more openly than the man's closest siblings? This is where Trobriand ideas about sorcery come into play in Malinowski's account: for in a society that attributed most deaths to the work of sorcerers coming from outside, a man's wife and children, being 'mere strangers', would be among the prime suspects for having caused his death. Therefore, whatever their personal sentiments, it was imperative for them to express their grief in a dramatic, overt manner in order to deflect any suspicions of this kind.

How would one go about making a film about the Trobriand funeral that took this cultural context into account? With the aid of modern film-making technology, we could set about evoking a strong experiential sense of what it would be like to be at a Trobriand funeral. With the long takes allowed by modern cameras and the sophisticated soundscapes made possible by digital audio technology, we could impart a subtly textured sense of both the physical space and of its acoustics. Through sensitive editing, we could communicate a sense of the duration of the funeral, its *longueurs* and its intensities, its experiential highs and lows. We could take care not to make this editing too slick, including some incidental, even discordant reality effects that would impart a sense of the ambiguity and flux of social life. By careful attention to narrative devices, we could engage the audience in the progression of the funeral to such a degree that they would have a sense of becoming entirely enfolded within the event themselves.

And yet, however effectively we might have evoked an embodied sense of the funeral in our film, if there were no reference to local ideas about matriliny and sorcery, the reasons why some people were 'howling like demons' and others were remaining stoically reserved would remain obscure. We might have been successful in communicating an experiential sense of the funeral, but it would have been entirely an outsider's sense of this experience, unmarked by the valency that the experience would have had for an insider. But if we wanted to provide the audience with sufficient understanding of the social and cultural context to make the experience of the funeral comprehensible in insider's terms, our aim should be to do so without so burdening the film with verbal explanations that destroyed the sense of 'being there'. The best method for reconciling these seemingly contradictory demands, I suggest, is to make sure, as far as is possible, that the necessary connections between practices, relations and ideas are made without leaving the diegesis, that is, the world created by the film.

One possible strategy would be to lay an explanatory verbal commentary over the images, but that can be quickly dismissed as it would undoubtedly turn the film into a ponderous pedagogical lecture and deprive it entirely of any sensorial quality. Alternatively, we might conduct formal interviews with some of the leading participants and ask them to tell us why some people were grieving more than others. But this too could lead the film to become too heavily dominated by speech.

So, instead, we could decide merely to follow the whole process of the funeral in an observational fashion – before, during and not forgetting afterwards – in the expectation that this would throw up, in the normal ebb and flow of events, in the informal conversations between the participants and in connection with the minor incidents surrounding the funeral, sufficient contextualising detail for the audience to understand why some people grieved more energetically than others. By adopting a participatory praxis, we could bring our key interlocutors into the process of elucidation, conducting with them what were, in effect, interviews as the event unfurled, but presenting them as contingent conversations. Once back in the edit suite, while respecting the chronology of the main constituent events of the funeral, we could move all these incidental events and conversational commentaries around, juxtaposing them as necessary, in order to throw light on the differential expressions of grief.

But as even this might not be sufficient to achieve our goal, we might also need to assist the process further by some discreet textual intertitles, or even, in the last resort, by some restrained lines of voice-over narration. The more it seemed that this narration emerged from within the world represented in the film itself, the better it would suit our purposes. In the ideal case, it would be the voice of a subject, either recorded as the funeral was ongoing, or afterwards, in response to a screening of the film in an edit suite. Failing that, it could be our own voice, particularly if that had been heard in synch on location. By appearing to belong within the world of the film, these voices, although in fact extraneous to that world, would minimise the disruption of the sense of 'being there' at the funeral on Kiriwina.

What we certainly could not do, at least not while still claiming to make a film of any significant ethnographicness, would be simply to show the mourners 'howling' at length without any form of contextualisation, as if the meaning of their grief were somehow self-evident and that the longer and the more sensorially we invited the audience to experience them grieving, the more its significance would become clear.

Rather, in order to make our imaginary ethnographic film about the Trobriand funeral, we would need to draw on all the knowledge and mutual confidence that we had managed to build up with our Trobriand hosts in order to work out with them the most effective way of fashioning an account that, without leaving the diegesis of the film, clarified the multiple connections between what the subjects were doing and what they were thinking, between what they were thinking and what they were feeling, between what they were feeling and the nature of their relationships to other people. In this way, we would then be well-placed to make a complex and textured ethnographic film, one that would go beyond the mere evocation of experience, beyond mere description, beyond observation.

### Note

1   As described in Malinowski (1932b), 126–39.

# Appendix: British television documentaries produced in collaboration with ethnographic researchers

THIS appendix provides a listing of documentaries produced for British television based on ethnographic research in which there was direct collaboration with the ethnographer who had carried out that research. Although I have gone to some lengths to try and ensure that it is comprehensive, I readily acknowledge that there may be some additional cases that I have overlooked.

In most cases, the ethnographers listed were academic anthropologists, though some were postgraduate students at the time. In a minority of cases, they were regional specialists who had no formal anthropological qualifications but who had carried out ethnographic research based on extended participant-observation among the social group who were the subject of the film. I have also included a few cases in which anthropologists with relevant regional expertise advised on films made in the same region, though not actually in the very same communities in which they had previously carried out prolonged ethnographic research.

There was also considerable variation in the degree of involvement of the ethnographer in the actual production, with some having the status almost of co-directors while others did little more than provide information and access in the field to the film-makers. But in the ideal-typical case, the ethnographic researcher was involved in all stages of the production: in the conception of the original project, on location during shooting and also, at least for a short period, during the editing phase.

The films are classified according to the year in which they were broadcast. Sometimes the information on this aspect in the sources is contradictory, so I have had to exercise some discretionary judgement on occasion. In most cases, shooting would have taken place one or even two years before the broadcast date. In all cases, I have used the term 'director' to refer to the principal author of the film, though in television parlance, particularly in the earlier years of this listing, the term 'producer' might well have been used to designate this role.

## Series in the comparative format

### Family of Man – BBC (1969–70)

Seven-part series directed by John Percival

Ethnographic consultants: Roger Ballard (Andheri, Northwest India), Thomas J. Larson (Hambukushu, Okavango Delta, Botswana), Andrew Strathern (Kawelka, Papua New Guinea Highlands).

### Face Values/Other People's Lives – BBC/Royal Anthropological Institute (1978/82)

Originally a seven-part series of one-hour films directed by David Cordingley and broadcast in 1978.

Ethnographic consultants: Jeremy Boissevain (Malta), Patricia Caplan (Mafia Island, Tanzania), Anthony Forge (Bali, Indonesia), Anne Sutherland (California Gypsies), Terence Turner (Kayapó, Central Brazil).

Series consultant: Jean La Fontaine.

Later re-edited and released in 1982 as *Other People's Lives*, a series of ten shorter films aimed at educational audiences, each dedicated to a single topic within a single society. The general series director of this second version was Peter Ramsden, who had been the assistant director of the original series.

## Series in the 'one-by-four' format

| Title | Director | Ethnographer | Group/place |
| --- | --- | --- | --- |

### Disappearing World – Granada Television (1970–93)

★ films made by the *Disappearing World* unit but broadcast under a different title

| Title | Director | Ethnographer | Group/place |
| --- | --- | --- | --- |
| **1970–71** | | | |
| *A Clearing in the Jungle* | Charlie Nairn | Jean-Paul Dumont | Panare, southern Venezuela |
| *The Last of the Cuiva* | Brian Moser | Bernard Arcand | Cuiva, Eastern Llanos, Colombia |
| *Embera: The End of the Road* | Brian Moser | Ariane Deluz | Embera, Chocó, Colombia |
| *War of the Gods* | Brian Moser | Peter Silverwood-Cope | Makú, Vaupés region, Colombia |
| | | Stephen Hugh Jones, | Barasana, Vaupés region, Colombia |
| | | Christine Hugh-Jones | |

**Series in the 'one-by-four' format** (Continued)

| Title | Director | Ethnographer | Group/place |
|---|---|---|---|
| **1972** | | | |
| *The Tuareg* | Charlie Nairn | Jeremy Keenan | Tuareg, Hoggar Mountains, Algeria |
| *The Meo* | Brian Moser | Jacques Lemoine | Meo (Hmong), Laos |
| **1973** | | | |
| *Dervishes of Kurdistan* | Brian Moser | Ali Bulookbashi, André Singer | Kurds, Iran |
| *Kataragama: A God for all Seasons* | Charlie Nairn | Gananath Obeyesekere | Sinhalese, Sri Lanka |
| **1974–75** | | | |
| *The Mursi* | Leslie Woodhead | David Turton | Mursi, Ethiopia |
| *The Mehinacu* | Carlos Pasini | Thomas Gregor | Mehinaku, Upper Xingu, Central Brazil |
| *Masai Women* | Chris Curling | Melissa Llewelyn-Davies | Maasai, Kenya |
| *The Kawelka: Ongka's Big Moka* | Charlie Nairn | Andrew Strathern | Kawelka, Highland Papua New Guinea |
| *The Quechua* | Carlos Pasini | Michael Sallnow | Kamawara, Peruvian Andes |
| *The Sakkudei* | John Sheppard | Reimar Scheffold | Sakkudei, Mentawei Islands, Sumatra |
| *Masai Manhood* | Chris Curling | Melissa Llewelyn-Davies | Maasai, Kenya |
| **1975–76** | | | |
| *Mongolia* | | | |
|   *On the Edge of the Gobi*★ | Brian Moser | Owen Lattimore | Khalka, Mongolia |
|   *The City on the Steppes*★ | Brian Moser | Owen Lattimore | Khalka, Mongolia |
| *The Kirghiz of Afghanistan* | Charlie Nairn | Nazif Shahrani | Kirghiz, Afghanistan |
| *The Shilluk of Southern Sudan* | Chris Curling | Paul Howell, Walter Kunijwok | Shilluk, Sudan |

| | | | |
|---|---|---|---|
| **1977** | | | |
| *The Eskimos of Pond Inlet: The People's Land* | Michael Grigsby | Hugh Brody | Iglulingmuit, Canadian Arctic |
| *Some Women of Marrakesh* | Melissa Llewelyn-Davies | Elizabeth Fernea | Marrakesh, Atlas Mountains, Morocco |
| *Saints and Spirits*★ | Melissa Llewelyn-Davies | Elizabeth Fernea | Marrakesh, Atlas Mountains, Morocco |
| *The Rendille* | Chris Curling | Anders Grum | Rendille, Kenya |
| *Sherpas of Nepal* | Leslie Woodhead | Sherry Ortner | Sherpas, Nepal |
| *Umbanda: The Problem Solver* | Stephen Cross | Peter Fry | São Paulo, Brazil |
| **1979–80** | | | |
| *Khyber*★ | André Singer | Akbar Ahmed, Louis Dupree | Pathans, Pakistan, Afghanistan |
| *Afghan Exodus*★ | André Singer | Akbar Ahmed, Rémy Dor | Pathans, Kirghiz, Hazara, Pakistan |
| *The Pathans* | André Singer | Akbar Ahmed | Pathans, Pakistan |
| **1982** | | | |
| *The Kwegu* | Leslie Woodhead | David Turton | Kwegu, Ethiopia |
| *Witchcraft Among the Azande* | André Singer | John Ryle | Azande, Sudan |
| *Asante Market Women* | Claudia Milne | Charlotte Boaitey | Asante, Ghana |
| **1983** | | | |
| *Inside China* | | | |
| *Living with the Revolution*★ | Leslie Woodhead | Barbara Hazard | Shanghai region, China |
| *The Newest Revolution*★ | Leslie Woodhead | Barbara Hazard | Shanghai region, China |
| *The Kazakhs of China*★ | André Singer | Shirin Akiner | Kazakhs, Xinjiang, China |
| **1985** | | | |
| *In Search of Cool Ground* | | | |
| *The Mursi* (reversion 1974 film) | Leslie Woodhead | David Turton | Mursi, Ethiopia |
| *The Kwegu* (reversion 1982 film) | Leslie Woodhead | David Turton | Kwegu, Ethiopia |
| *The Migrants* | Leslie Woodhead | David Turton | Mursi, Ethiopia |

491

**Series in the 'one-by-four' format** (Continued)

| Title | Director | Ethnographer | Group/place |
|---|---|---|---|
| **1987** | | | |
| *The Basques of Santazi* | Leslie Woodhead | Sandra Ott | Basques, France |
| *The Kayapo* | Michael Beckham | Terence Turner | Kayapó, Central Brazil |
| *The Lau of Malaita* | Leslie Woodhead | Pierre Maranda | Lau, Solomon Islands |
| **1988** | | | |
| *The Whale Hunters of Lamalera, Indonesia* | John Blake | Robert Barnes | Lamaholot, Lembata, Indonesia |
| *Across the Tracks: the Vlach Gypsies in Hungary* | John Blake | Michael Stewart | Vlach Gypsies, Hungary |
| *The Wodaabe* | Leslie Woodhead | Mette Bovin | Wodaabe, Niger |
| **1989** | | | |
| *Kayapo: Out of the Forest* | Michael Beckham | Terence Turner | Kayapó, Central Brazil |
| *The Villagers of Sierra de Gredos* | Peter Carr | William Kavanagh | Central Spain |
| *The Herders of Mongun-Taiga* | John Sheppard | Caroline Humphrey | Tuva, Central Asia |
| **1990** | | | |
| *The Mende* | Bruce Macdonald | Mariane Ferme | Mende, Sierra Leone |
| *The Trobriand Islanders of Papua New Guinea* | David Wason | Annette Weiner | Trobriand Islands, Papua New Guinea |
| *The Kalasha: Rites of Spring* | John Sheppard | Peter Parkes | Kalasha, North West Frontier, Pakistan |
| **1991** | | | |
| *Mursi: The Land is Bad* | Leslie Woodhead | David Turton | Mursi, Ethiopia |
| *Mursi: Nitha* | Leslie Woodhead | David Turton | Mursi, Ethiopia |
| *The Albanians of Rrogam* | David Wason | Berit Backer | Rrogam, Albania |
| *Cakchiquel Maya of San Antonio Palopó* | Bruce Macdonald | Tracy Bachrach Ehlers | Cakchiquel Maya, Guatemala |

| | | | |
|---|---|---|---|
| **1993** | | | |
| *War* | | | |
| *Orphans of Passage* | Bruce Macdonald | Wendy James | Uduk, Sudan |
| *We Are All Neighbours* | Debbie Christie | Tone Bringa | Visjnica, Bosnia |
| *The Longest Struggle* | John Sheppard, Tom Sheahan | Michael Mahda | Karen, Burma |
| ***Frontier – ATV/Central Independent Television (1980–?)*** | | | |
| **1980** | | | |
| *People of the Barrio* | Brian Moser | Caroline Moser | Guayaquil, Ecuador |
| **1985** | | | |
| *A Small Family Business* | Brian Moser | Stephen Hugh-Jones | Vaupés region, Colombia |
| *God Gave Us the Leaf* | Brian Moser | Mauricio Mamani | Altiplano, Bolivia |
| ***Women of the Middle East – Channel 4 (1982)*** | | | |
| *The Veiled Revolution* | Marilyn Gaunt | Elizabeth Fernea | Cairo, Egypt |
| *The Price of Change* | Marilyn Gaunt | Elizabeth Fernea | Cairo, Egypt |
| *Women Under Siege* | Marilyn Gaunt | Elizabeth Fernea | Palestinian refugees, southern Lebanon |
| ***Worlds Apart – BBC Bristol (1982–85)*** | | | |
| **1982** | | | |
| *The South-East Nuba* | Chris Curling | James Faris | Nuba, Sudan |
| *The Panare: Scenes from the Frontier* | Chris Curling | Paul Henley | Panare, southern Venezuela |
| *The Raj Gonds: Reflections in a Peacock Crown* | Chris Curling, Peter Loizos | Michael Yorke | Gonds, South India |
| *The Muria* | Chris Curling | [anon.] | Muria, Central India |
| *A Connemara Family* | Melissa Llewelyn-Davies | Hugh Brody | Connemara, West of Ireland |

**Series in the 'one-by-four' format** (Continued)

| Title | Director | Ethnographer | Group/place |
|---|---|---|---|
| **1984** | | | |
| *The Women's Olamal: The Social Organization of a Maasai Fertility Ceremony* | Melissa Llewelyn-Davies | Melissa Llewelyn-Davies | Maasai, Kenya |
| **1985** | | | |
| *Maasai Diary* | Melissa Llewelyn-Davies | Melissa Llewelyn-Davies | Maasai, Kenya |
| *The Prophet's Village* | | | |
| *Two Ways of Justice* | | | |
| *Two Mothers* | | | |
| *Two Journeys* | | | |
| *Nine Cows And An Ox* | | | |
| ***Under the Sun – BBC Elstree (1989–99)*** | | | |
| **1989** | | | |
| *The Shaman and His Apprentice* | Howard Reid | Graham Townsley | Yaminahua, Peruvian Amazonia |
| **1990** | | | |
| *Feathered Arrows* | Jean-Paul Davidson | Thomas Gregor | Mehinaku, Upper Xingu, Central Brazil |
| *The Women Who Smile* | Joanna Head | Jean Lydall | Hamar, Ethiopia |
| *Left-handed Man of Madagascar* | Jeremy Marre | John Mack | Madagascar |
| *Dust and Ashes* | Michael Yorke | Michael Yorke | Kumbh Mela, Allahabad, North India |

| | | | |
|---|---|---|---|
| **1991** | | | |
| *Two Girls Go Hunting* | Joanna Head | Jean Lydall | Hamar, Ethiopia |
| *Marriage Egyptian Style* | Joanna Head | Reem Saad | Cairo, Eygpt |
| *Eunuchs: India's Third Gender* | Michael Yorke | Michael Yorke | Mumbai, India |
| **1993** | | | |
| *Dreams From The Forest* | Jean-Paul Davidson | Thomas Gregor | Mehinaku, Upper Xingu, Central Brazil |
| **1994** | | | |
| *Our Way of Loving* | Joanna Head | Jean Lydall | Hamar, Ethiopia |
| *Guardians of the Flutes* | Paul Reddish | Gilbert Herdt | Sambia, Highland Papua New Guinea |
| **Nomads – Channel 4 (1991)** | | | |
| *Kenya: Year of the Clouds* | Christopher Hooke | J. Terrence McCabe | Ngisonyoka Turkana, Kenya |
| *Mauritania: The Wealth of Blood* | Ned Johnston | Diana Stone | Nouakchott, Mauritania |
| *Siberia: After the Shaman* | Graham Johnston | Piers Vitebsky | Evenki, Russian Arctic |
| **Fragile Earth – Channel 4 (1982–93)** | | | |
| **1989** | | | |
| *The Goddess and the Computer* | André Singer | Stephen Lansing | Bali, Indonesia |
| **1993** | | | |
| *Survivors of the Rainforest* | Andy Jillings | Jacques Lizot | Yanomami, Venezuelan Amazonia |
| **Fine Cut – BBC Elstree (1990–94)** | | | |
| **1992** | | | |
| *Madame L'Eau* | Jean Rouch | Jean Rouch | Amsterdam and Niger |
| *Forest of Bliss* | Robert Gardner | Akos Östor | Varanasi (Benares), North India |
| *My Crazy Life* | Jean-Pierre Gorin | Dan Marks | Gangs, Los Angeles and Samoa |
| **1993** | | | |
| *Memories and Dreams* | Melissa Llewelyn-Davies | Melissa Llewelyn-Davies | Maasai, Kenya |
| *Tempus de Baristas* | David MacDougall | Paolo Piquereddu | Urzulei, Sardinia |

## Other Series and Feature Documentaries

| Title | Director | Ethnographer | Group/place |
|---|---|---|---|
| **1982** | | | |
| *People of the Islands* (Channel 4) | Hugh Brody | Hugh Brody | Canadian Arctic |
| **1986** | | | |
| *On Indian Land* (Channel 4) | Hugh Brody | Hugh Brody | Gitskan and Wet'suwet'en, Northwest Canada |
| **1989** | | | |
| *The Storyteller* (*Bookmark*, BBC 2) | Jean-Paul Davidson | Emilienne Ireland | Waurá, Upper Xingu, Central Brazil |
| **1990** | | | |
| *Hunters and Bombers* (Channel 4) | Hugh Brody, Nigel Markham | Hugh Brody | Innu, Labrador, Canada |
| *Scenes After A Revolution* (*Everyman*, BBC1) | Melissa Llewelyn-Davies | Michael Stewart | Translyvania and Bucharest, Romania |
| **1992** | | | |
| *Before Columbus* (series, Central Independent Television) | Brian Moser | Stephan Schwartzman | Various Native American groups in North and South America |
| **1994** | | | |
| *What Magdalena Said* (*Everyman*, BBC 1) | Michael Stewart | Michael Stewart | Rom, Czech Republic |
| **1997** | | | |
| *Royal Watchers* (*United Kingdom*, BBC 2) | Paul Henley | Anne Rowbottom | Various locations, UK |
| **1998** | | | |
| *Divorce Iranian Style* (Channel 4) | Kim Longinotto | Ziba Mir-Hosseini | Tehran, Iran |
| **2001** | | | |
| *Runaway* (Channel 4) | Kim Longinotto | Ziba Mir-Hosseini | Tehran, Iran |
| *Fire Will Eat Us* (*True Stories*, Channel 4) | Leslie Woodhead | David Turton | Mursi, Ethiopia |

# Textual references

*Note: all links to on-line materials were tested and found to be working on 13 February 2019.*

Acciaioli, Greg (2004) The consequences of conation: pedagogy and the inductive films of an ethical film-maker. In E. Douglas Lewis, ed., *Timothy Asch and Ethnographic Film*, pp. 123–48. London and New York: Routledge Harwood Anthropology.

Altman, Rick (2006) From lecturer's prop to industrial product: The early history of travel films. In Jeffrey Ruoff, ed., *Virtual Voyages: Cinema and Travel*, pp. 61–76. Durham and London: Duke University Press.

Alvarez, Patricia (2012) Interview with Véréna Paravel and J. P. Sniadecki. *Fieldsights – Visual and New Media Review, Cultural Anthropology Online*, 17 December 2012. www.culanth.org/fieldsights/33-interview-with-verena-paravel-and-j-p-sniadecki.

Amad, Paula (2010) *Counter-Archive: Film, the Everyday, and Albert Kahn's Archives de la Planète*. New York: Columbia University Press.

Anderson, Jane and María Montenegro (2017) Collaborative encounters in digital cultural property. In Jane L. Anderson and Haidy Geismar, eds, *The Routledge Companion to Cultural Property*. Abingdon and New York: Routledge.

Anonymous (1929) Kinematography. *Notes and Queries*. 5th edn, pp. 379–80. Edited for the British Association for the Advancement of Science by a Committee of Section H. London: Royal Anthropological Institute.

Asch, Timothy (1979) Making a film record of the Yanomamo Indians of Southern Venezuela. *Perspectives on Film* 2: 4–9, 44–9. University Park: Pennsylvania State University.

—— (1986) How and why the films were made. In Linda Connor, Patsy Asch and Timothy Asch, *Jero Tapakan: Balinese Healer. An Ethnographic Film Monograph*, pp. 39–53. Cambridge: Cambridge University Press.

—— (1988) Collaboration in ethnographic filmmaking: a personal view. In Jack R. Rollwagen, ed., *Anthropological Filmmaking: Anthropological Perspectives on the Production of Film and Video for General Public Audiences*, pp. 1–29. Abingdon: Harwood Academic Publishers.

Asch, Timothy, John Marshall and Peter Spier (1973) Ethnographic film: structure and function. *Annual Review of Anthropology* 2: 179–85.

Asch, Timothy with Jesús Ignacio Cardozo, Hortensia Caballero and José Bortoli (1991) The story we now want to hear is not ours to tell. Relinquishing control over representation: toward sharing visual communication skills with the Yanomami. *Visual Anthropology* 7(2): 102–6.

Aubert, Michelle and Jean-Claude Seguin (1996) *La Production cinématographique des Frères Lumière*. Éditions Mémoires de cinéma/Librarie du premier siècle du cinéma/CNC.

Aufderheide, Patricia (1995) The Video in the Villages project: video-making with and by Brazilian Indians. *Visual Anthropology Review* 11(2): 83–93.

—— (2008) 'You see the world of the Other and you look at your own': the evolution of the Video in the Villages project. *Journal of Film and Video* 60(2): 26–34.

Baily, John (2017) *War, Exile and the Music of Afghanistan: The Ethnographer's Tale*. SOAS Ethnomusicology Series. London and New York: Ashgate-Routledge.

Balard, Martine (1999) *Dahomey 1930: mission catholique et culte vodoun. L'œuvre de Francis Aupiais (1877–1945), missionaire et ethnographe*. Paris: L'Harmattan.

—— (2007) Les combats du père Aupiais (1877–1945), missionaire et ethnographe du Dahomey pour la reconnaissance africaine. *Histoire et missions chrétiennes* 2(2): 74–93.

Balikci, Asen (1988) Anthropologists and ethnographic filmmaking. In Jack Rollwagen, ed., *Anthropological Filmmaking: Anthropological Perspectives on the Production of Film and Video for General Public Audiences*, pp. 31–45. Abingdon: Harwood Academic Publishers.

—— (1989) Anthropology, film and the Arctic peoples. *Anthropology Today* 5(2): 3–10.

—— (1995) Reconstructing cultures on film. In Paul Hockings, ed., *Principles of Visual Anthropology*, 2nd edn, pp. 181–91. Berlin and New York: Mouton de Gruyter.

Banks, Marcus (1988) The non-transparency of ethnographic film. *Anthropology Today* 4(5): 2–3.

—— (1992) Which films are the ethnographic films? In Peter Crawford and David Turton, eds, *Film as Ethnography*, pp. 116–30. Manchester and New York: Manchester University Press.

—— (1994) Television and anthropology: an unhappy marriage? *Visual Anthropology* 7(1): 21–45.

Banks, Marcus and David Zeitlyn (2015) *Visual Methods in Social Research*, 2nd edn. London: Sage Publishing.

Barbash, Ilisa (2007) Out of words: a conversation with Robert Gardner. In Ilisa Barbash and Lucien Taylor, eds, *The Cinema of Robert Gardner*, pp. 93–118. Oxford: Berg.

Barley, Nigel (1989) *Native Land*. Viking Penguin.

Barnouw, Erik (1983) *Documentary: A History of the Non-fiction Film*. Revised edn. Oxford: Oxford University Press.

Bateson, Gregory and Margaret Mead (1942) *Balinese Character: A Photographic Analysis*. New York: New York Academy of Sciences.

Batty, Philip (2013) 'Primitive Blacks face White man's laws': the 1932 anthropological expedition to Mt. Liebig, Central Australia. In Joshua A. Bell, Alison K. Brown, and Robert J. Gordon, eds, *Recreating First Contact: Expeditions, Anthropology, and Popular Culture*, pp. 197–214. Washington DC: Smithsonian Institution Scholarly Press.

Baxter, P. T. W. (1977) The Rendille. *RAIN* 20: 7–9.

Bazin, André (2005) *What is Cinema?* Essays selected and translated by Hugh Gray, vol. 1. Berkeley, Los Angeles, London: University of California Press.

Beausoleil, Jeanne, ed. (1996) *Pour une reconnaissance africaine, Dahomey 1930; Des images au service d'une idée*. Boulogne: Musée Albert-Kahn.

Beidelman, Thomas O. (1992) Millenium. *Cultural Anthropology* 7(4): 508–15.

Bell, Joshua A., Alison K. Brown and Robert J. Gordon (2013) Appendix – Films, Technology, and Institutional Histories. In Joshua A. Bell, Alison K. Brown, and Robert J. Gordon, eds, *Recreating First Contact: Expeditions, Anthropology, and Popular Culture*, pp. 241–52. Washington DC: Smithsonian Institution Scholarly Press.

Benthall, Jonathan (2014) Fail better? Reflections on *Face Values* and *Millenium*. *Anthropology Today* 30(2): 25.

Berner, Margit (2006) From 'prisoners of war' to proof of paternity: racial anthropologists and the meaning of 'Others' in Austria. In Marius Turda and Paul Weindling, eds, *'Blood and Homeland': Eugenics and Racial Nationalism in Central and Southeast Europe 1900–1940*, pp. 41–53. Budapest: Central European University Press.

Berthe, Jamie (2018) Au-delà des critique entomologiques: Rouch et le cinéma africain, un autre point de vue. In Rina Sherman, ed., *Dans le sillage de Jean Rouch: Témoinages et essais*, pp. 127–42. Paris: Éditions de la Maison des sciences de l'homme.

Biella, Peter, Napoleon A. Chagnon and Gary Seaman, eds (1997) *Yanomamö Interactive: The Ax Fight*. CD-ROM. Case Studies in Cultural Anthropology Multimedia Series. Harcourt Brace College Publishers.

Bishop, John (2007) Life by myth: the development of ethnographic filming in the work of John Marshall. In Beate Engelbrecht, ed., *Memories of the Origins of Visual Anthropology*, pp. 87–94. Frankfurt: Peter Lang.

Bloom, Peter J. (2006) Trans-Saharan Automotive Cinema. Citroën-, Renault-, and Peugeot-sponsored Documentary Interwar Crossing Films. In Jeffrey Ruoff, ed., *Virtual Voyages: Cinema and Travel*, pp. 139–56. Durham and London: Duke University Press.

—— (2008) *French Colonial Documentaries: Mythologies of Humanitarianism*. Minneapolis: University of Minnesota Press.

Blue, James (1996) Jean Rouch: interviewed by James Blue. In Kevin Macdonald and Mark Cousins, eds, *Imagining Reality: The Faber Book of Documentary*, pp. 268–70. London and Boston: Faber & Faber. Originally published in *Film Comment* 2(2), Spring 1964.

Bradburd, Daniel (2013) *Grass* before *Kong* – 'Natives' in the films of Merian Cooper and Ernest Schoedsack. In Joshua A. Bell, Alison K. Brown and Robert J. Gordon, eds, *Recreating First Contact: Expeditions, Anthropology, and Popular Culture*, pp. 55–71. Washington DC: Smithsonian Institution Scholarly Press.

Bringa, Tone (1995) *Being Muslim the Bosnian Way: Identity and Community in a Central Bosnian Village*. Princeton: Princeton University Press.

Brody, Hugh (1975) *The People's Land: Eskimos and Whites in the Eastern Arctic*. Harmondsworth: Penguin.

—— (1977) Seeming to be real: *Disappearing World* and the film in Pond Inlet. *Cambridge Anthropology. Special Issue Ethnographic Film*, pp. 22–31.

Brown, Liz (1978) The two worlds of Marrakech. *Screen* 19(2): 85–118.

Browne, Colin (2014) Unmasking the Documentary: Notes on the Anxiety of Edward Curtis. In Brad Evans and Aaron Glass, eds, *Return to the Land of the Head Hunters: Edward S. Curtis, the Kwakwaka'wka, and the Making of Modern Cinema*, pp. 167–89. Seattle: University of Washington Press and the Bill Holm Center, Burke Museum.

Bruzzi, Stella (2000) *New Documentary: A Critical Introduction*. London and New York: Routledge.

Bryson, Ian (2002) *Bringing to Light: A History of Ethnographic Filmmaking at the Australian Institute of Aboriginal and Torres Strait Islander Studies*. Canberra: Aboriginal Studies Press.

—— (2007) Visual anthropology: the AIATSIS contribution. In Beate Englebrecht, ed., *Memories of the Origins of Ethnographic Film*, pp. 295–305. Frankfurt am Main: Peter Lang.

Bugos, Paul, Jr, Stephan Carter and Timothy Asch (1975) *The Ax Fight: Film Notes*. Cambridge, Mass.: Documentary Educational Resources.

Caiuby, Novaes, Sylvia, Eduardo da Cunha and Paul Henley (2017) The first documentary? Luiz Thomaz Reis, the Rondon Commission and the making of *Rituais e Festas Boróro* (1917) *Visual Anthropology* 30(1): 105–46.

Caplan, Patricia (1993) Review of *We Are All Neighbours. Anthropology Today* 9(6): 20–2.

—— (2005) In search of the exotic: a discussion of the BBC2 series *Tribe. Anthropology Today* 21(2): 3–7.

—— (2013) An anthropologist among the filmmakers. A cautionary tale: Part 1. The politics of production. *Anthropology Today* 29(6): 23–6.

—— (2014) An anthropologist among the filmmakers. A cautionary tale: Part 2. The politics of circulation. *Anthropology Today* 30(1): 15–19.

Castaing-Taylor, Lucien (2016) Sweetgrass: 'Baaaaaah. Bleeeeeet'. From an introductory text and interview with Jay Kuehner at Vancouver International Film Festival, 2009. In Rupert Cox, Andrew Irving and Christopher Wright, eds, *Beyond Text?: Critical Practices and Sensory Anthropology*, pp. 148–55. Manchester: Manchester University Press.

Castro, Teresa (2008) Les *Archives de la Planète* et les rythmes de l'Histoire. *1895. Mille huit cent quatre-vingt-quize* 54: 56–81.

Chagnon, Napoleon (1997) *Yanomamö*, 5th edn. Harcourt Brace College Publishers.

Chalfen, Richard (1992) Picturing culture through indigenous imagery: a telling story. In Peter Crawford and David Turton, eds, *Film as Ethnography*, pp. 222–41. Manchester: Manchester University Press.

—— (2007) The Worth/Adair Navajo experiment – Unanticipated results and reactions. In Beate Englebrecht, ed., *Memories of the Origins of Ethnographic Film*, pp. 165–75. Frankfurt am Main: Peter Lang.

Chopra, Radikha (1989) Robert Gardner's *Forest of Bliss:* a review. *Society of Visual Anthropology Newsletter* 5(1): 2–3.

Clifford, James (1988a) Power and dialogue in ethnography: Marcel Griaule's initiation. In James Clifford, *The Predicament of Culture: Twentieth Century Ethnography, Literature and Art*, pp. 55–91. Cambridge, Mass.: Harvard University Press.

—— (1988b) On ethnographic surrealism. In James Clifford, *The Predicament of Culture: Twentieth Century Ethnography, Literature and Art*, pp. 117–51. Cambridge, Mass.: Harvard University Press.

—— (1991) Documents: a decomposition. *Visual Anthropology Review* 71: 62–83.

Clifford, James and George Marcus, eds (1986) *Writing Culture: The Poetics and Politics of Ethnography*. Berkeley: University of California Press.

Colleyn, Jean-Paul (2005) Jean Rouch: an anthropologist ahead of his time. *American Anthropologist* 107(1): 112–15.

Connor, Linda H., Patsy Asch and Timothy Asch (1986) *Jero Tapakan: Balinese Healer.* An ethnographic film monograph. Cambridge: Cambridge University Press.

Connor, Linda H. and Patsy Asch (2004) Subjects, images, voices: representation of gender in the films of Tim Asch. In E. Douglas Lewis, ed., *Timothy Asch and Ethnographic Film*, pp. 163–84. London and New York: Routledge Harwood Anthropology.

Crawford, Peter (1992) *Grass:* the visual narrativity of pastoral nomadism. In Peter Crawford and Jan Ketil Simonsen, eds, *Ethnographic Film Aesthetics and Narrative Traditions*, pp. 121–38. Aarhus: Intervention Press.

—— (2004) Respect the moment! A retrospective of the cinematographic work of Gary Kildea. In Pille Runnel, ed., *Tartu visuaalse kultuuri päevad*, pp. 75–91. Estonian National Museum. Also at www.slideshare.net/Antropologiavisualuff/ respect-the-moment-gary-kildea-27229077.

Curtis, Edward S. (1915) *In the Land of the Head Hunters*. Indian Life and Lore Series. World Book Company (reprinted in 1992).

de Brigard, Emilie (1995) The history of ethnographic film. In Paul Hockings, ed., *Principles of Visual Anthropology*, 2nd edn, pp. 13–43. Berlin and New York: Mouton de Gruyter.

de Bromhead, Antoinette (2014) *A Film-maker's Odyssey: Adventures in Film and Anthropology*. Højbjerg: Intervention Press.

de Heusch, Luc (2007) The prehistory of ethnographic film. In Beate Engelbrecht, ed., *Memories of the Origins of Visual Anthropology*, pp. 15–22. Frankfurt: Peter Lang.

de Pastre, Béatrice with Philippe Costantini (2017) *Jean Rouch, l'Homme-Cinéma: Découvrir les films de Jean Rouch*. Paris: CNC/Bnf/Somogy.

De Rosa, Francesca (2018) Arquivos colonais e representações da *alteridade* nos documentários do Estado Novo. In Jorge Seabra, ed., *Cinemas en português. Moçambique: Auto e Heteroperceções*, pp. 101–16. Imprensa da Universidade de Coimbra.

Deger, Jennifer (2006) *Shimmering Screens: Making Media in an Aboriginal Community*. Minneapolis: University of Minneapolis Press.

Deveson, Philippa with Ian Dunlop (2012) The ethnographic filmmaking of Ian Dunlop in a decade of change. In Natasha Fijn, ed., *Perspectives on Ethnographic Film*. Special edition of Humanities Research, vol. XVIII, no. 1, pp. 47–78.

Douglas, Mary (1975) If the Dogon ... In Mary Douglas, *Implicit Meanings: Essays in Anthropology*, 124–41. London and Boston: Routledge & Kegan Paul.

—— (1995) Réflexions sur le renard pâle et deux anthropologies: à propos du surréalisme et de l'anthropologie française. In Christopher W. Thompson, ed., *L'Autre et le Sacré: surréalisme, cinéma, ethnologie*, pp. 199–218. Paris: L'Harmattan.

Dunlop, Ian (1979) Ethnographic film-making in Australia: the first seventy years (1898–1968). *Aboriginal History* 3(1–2): 111–19 (reprinted in 1983 in *Studies in Visual Communication* 9(1): 11–18).

—— (2003) Background notes for *Peoples of the Australian Western Desert* and *Desert People*. shop.nfsa.gov.au/people-of-the-australian-western-desert.

Durington, Matthew and Jay Ruby (2011) Ethnographic film. In Marcus Banks and Jay Ruby, eds, *Made to Be Seen: Perspectives on the History of Visual Anthropology*, pp. 190–208. Chicago and London: University of Chicago Press.

Durosay, Daniel (1993) Introduction. In Marc Allégret, *Carnets du Congo: voyage avec André Gide*, 2nd edn, pp. 11–57. Paris: CNRS.

Eaton, Michael, ed. (1979) *Anthropology, Reality, Cinema: The Films of Jean Rouch*. London: British Film Institute.

Elder, Sarah (1995) Collaborative filmmaking: an open space for making meaning, a moral ground for ethnographic film. *Visual Anthropology Review* 11(2): 94–101.

Evans, Brad (1998) Catherine Russell's recovery of the *Head-Hunters*. *Visual Anthropology* 11(3): 221–42.

—— (2014) Indian movies and the vernacular of modernism. In Brad Evans and Aaron Glass, eds, *Return to the Land of the Head Hunters: Edward S. Curtis, the Kwakwaka'wka, and the Making of Modern Cinema*, pp. 190–211. Seattle: University of Washington Press and the Bill Holm Center, Burke Museum.

Evans, Brad and Aaron Glass, eds (2014) *Return to the Land of the Head Hunters: Edward S. Curtis, the Kwakwaka'wka, and the Making of Modern Cinema*. Seattle: University of Washington Press and the Bill Holm Center, Burke Museum.

Faris, James (1992) Anthropological transparency: film, representation and politics. In Peter Crawford and David Turton, eds, *Film as Ethnography*, pp. 171–82. Manchester: Manchester University Press.

Fausto, Carlos (2011) No registro da cultura: o cheiro do branco e o cinema dos índios. In Ana de Carvalho, Ernesto de Carvalho and Vincent Carelli, eds, *Vídeo nas Aldeias – 25 anos*, pp. 160–8. Livraria Cultura. See also www.videonasaldeias.org.br/2009/biblioteca.php?c=30.

Feld, Steven (2016) Film Review – *Kalanda: The Knowledge of the Bush*. *Visual Anthropology Review* 32(1): 84–5.

Fernea, Elizabeth Warnock (1998) *In Search of Islamic Feminism: One Woman's Global Journey*. New York: Anchor Books.

Ferrarini, Lorenzo (2017) Enactive Filmmaking: Rethinking Ethnographic Cinema in the First Person. *Visual Anthropology Review* 33(2): 130–40.

Feuchtwang, Stephan (1983) The Kazakhs of China. *RAIN* 57: 10.

Fieschi, Jean-André and André Téchiné (1967) Jean Rouch: 'Jaguar'. *Cahiers du Cinéma* 195: 17–20.

Flaherty, Robert (1996) Robert Flaherty Talking. In Kevin Macdonald and Mark Cousins, eds, *Imagining Reality: The Faber Book of Documentary*, pp. 36–43. London and Boston: Faber & Faber. Originally published in 1950.

Flaherty, Robert in collaboration with Frances Hubbard Flaherty (1924) *My Eskimo Friends: 'Nanook of the North'*. London: Heinemann.

Flores, Carlos (2007) Sharing anthropology: collaborative video experiences among Maya film-makers in post-war Guatemala. In Sarah Pink, ed., *Visual Interventions: Applied Visual Anthropology*, pp. 209–24. New York and Oxford: Berghahn.

Forman, Denis (1985) International Festival of Ethnographic Film: Opening speech, 24 September. *Anthropology Today* 1(6): 2–4.

Fox, James (1977) *Harvest of the Palm: Ecological Change in Eastern Indonesia*. Cambridge, Mass.: Harvard University Press.

—— (2004) Efforts and events in a long collaboration: working with Tim Asch on ethnographic films on Roti in eastern Indonesia. In E. Douglas Lewis, ed., *Timothy Asch and Ethnographic Film*, pp. 83–96. London and New York: Routledge Harwood Anthropology.

Fuhrmann, Wolfgang (2007) First contact: the beginning of ethnographic filmmaking in Germany, 1900–1930. *History of Anthropology Newsletter* 34(1): 3–9.

—— (2013) Ethnographic film practices in silent German cinema. In Joshua A. Bell, Alison K. Brown, and Robert J. Gordon, eds, *Recreating First Contact: Expeditions, Anthropology, and Popular Culture*, pp. 41–54. Washington DC: Smithsonian Institution Scholarly Press.

—— (2015) *Imperial Projections: Screening the German Colonies*. Oxford and New York: Berghahn Press.

Fulchignoni, Enrico (2003) Jean Rouch with Enrico Fulchignoni: ciné-anthropology. In Steven Feld, ed., *Ciné-Ethnography*, pp. 147–87. Minneapolis and London: University of Minnesota Press. Originally published in French in 1981.

Gabriel, Teshome H. (1982) *Third Cinema in the Third World: The Aesthetics of Liberation.* Ann Arbor, Mich.: UMI Research Press.

Gardner, Robert (1972) On the making of *Dead Birds*. In Karl Heider and Robert Gardner, *The Dani of West Irian: An Ethnographic Companion to the Film* Dead Birds. New York: MSS Modular Publications Inc.

—— (2006) *The Impulse to Preserve: Reflections of a Filmmaker.* New York: Other Press LLC.

—— (2010) Kalahari journal. In Charles Warren, ed., *Just Representations: Robert Gardner*, pp. 2–30. Cambridge, Mass.: Studio7Arts and Peabody Museum Press.

Gardner, Robert and Ákos Östör (2001) *Making* Forest of Bliss: *Intention, Circumstance and Chance in Non-fiction Film*. Cambridge, Mass. and London: Harvard Film Archive.

Gauthier, Lionel and Laurent Pellé (2000) *Jean Rouch: Récits photographiques*. Paris: Éditions Muséum national d'Histoire naturelle – Musée de l'Homme.

Geertz, Clifford (1988) *Works and Lives: The Anthropologist as Author.* Stanford: Stanford University Press.

Gellner, David N. (2015) How not to make a documentary: A personal view of the movie 'Manakamana'. www.academia.edu/10110376/How_Not_to_Make_a_Documentary_A_Personal_View_of_the_Movie_Manakamana.

Georgakas, Dan, Udayan Gupta and Judy Janda (2003) The politics of visual anthropology. In Steven Feld, ed., *Ciné-Ethnography*, pp. 210–25. Minneapolis and London: University of Minnesota Press.

Gidley, Mick (1982) From the Hopi Snake Dance to the 'The Ten Commandments': Edward S. Curtis as filmmaker. *Studies in Visual Communication* 8(3): 70–9.

—— (2014) Edward Curtis and *In the Land of the Head Hunters*. Four Contexts. In Brad Evans and Aaron Glass, eds, *Return to the Land of the Head Hunters: Edward S. Curtis, the Kwakwaka'wka, and the Making of Modern Cinema*, pp. 42–60. Seattle: University of Washington Press and the Bill Holm Center, Burke Museum.

Ginsburg, Faye (1991) Indigenous media: Faustian contract or global village? *Cultural Anthropology* 6(1): 92–112.

—— (1994) Culture/media. A(mild) polemic. *Anthropology Today* 10(2): 5–15.

—— (1995a) Mediating culture: indigenous media, ethnographic film, and the production of identity. In Leslie Devereaux and Roger Hillman, eds, *Fields of Vision: Essays in Film Studies, Visual Anthropology, and Photography*, pp. 256–91. Berkeley, Los Angeles and London: University of California Press.

—— (1995b) The parallax effect: the impact of aboriginal media on ethnographic film. *Visual Anthropology Review* 11(2): 64–76.

—— (1997) Comment on 'Televisualist Anthropology' by James F. Weiner. *Current Anthropology* 38(2): 213–16.

—— (2011) Native intelligence: a short history of debates on indigenous media and ethnographic film. In Marcus Banks and Jay Ruby, eds, *Made to be Seen: Perspectives on the History of Visual Anthropology*, pp. 234–55. Chicago and London: University of Chicago Press.

—— (2018) Decolonizing documentary on-screen and off: sensory ethnography and the aesthetics of accountability. *Film Quarterly* 72(1): 39–49.

Gitlin, Daniella (2012) To experience *Song of Ceylon*. *Senses of Cinema* 62. sensesofcinema.com/2012/feature-articles/to-experience-song-of-ceylon/.

Glass, Aaron (2014) The Kwakwaka'wka Business of Showing: Tradition Meets Modernity on the Silver Screen and the World Stage. In Brad Evans and Aaron Glass, eds, *Return to the Land of the Head Hunters: Edward S. Curtis, the Kwakwaka'wka, and the Making of Modern Cinema*, pp. 315–57. Seattle: University of Washington Press and the Bill Holm Center, Burke Museum.

Glass, Aaron and Brad Evans (2014) Introduction. Edward Curtis meets the Kwakwaka'wka: Cultural Encounter and Indigenous Agency *In the Land of the Head Hunters*. In Brad Evans and Aaron Glass, eds, *Return to the Land of the Head Hunters: Edward S. Curtis, the Kwakwaka'wka, and the Making of Modern Cinema*, pp. 3–39. Seattle: University of Washington Press and the Bill Holm Center, Burke Museum.

Gluckman, Max (1958) *Analysis of a social situation in modern Zululand*. Rhodes-Livingstone Papers no. 28. Originally published in 1940.

Gonzalez, Nancie L. (1993) An argument about a film. In Jay Ruby, ed., *The Cinema of John Marshall*, pp. 179–93. Abingdon: Harwood Academic Publishers.

Gordon, Robert J. (2003) Introduction: *A Kalahari Family*. *Visual Anthropology Review* 19(1–2): 102–13.

Gordon, Robert J. and Stuart S. Douglas (2000) *The Bushman Myth: The Making of a Namibian Underclass*. Boulder: Westview Press.

Gordon, Robert J., Alison K. Brown and Joshua A. Bell (2013) Expeditions, their films and histories: an introduction. In Joshua A. Bell, Alison K. Brown and Robert J. Gordon, eds, *Recreating First Contact: Expeditions, Anthropology, and Popular Culture*, pp. 1–30. Washington DC: Smithsonian Institution Scholarly Press.

Gregor, Thomas A. and Daniel R. Gross (2004) Guilt by association: the culture of accusation and the American Anthropological Association's investigation of *Darkness in El Dorado*. *American Anthropologist* 106(4): 687–98.

Griaule, Marcel (1957) *Méthode de l'ethnographie*. Paris: Presses Universitaires de France.

Griffiths, Alison (2002) *Wondrous Difference: Cinema, Anthropology and Turn-of-the-Century Culture*. New York: Columbia University Press.

Grimshaw, Anna (1995) *Conversations with Anthropological Film-makers: Melissa Llewelyn-Davies*. Prickly Pear Press, no. 8. Also available at www.thememorybank.co.uk/pricklypear/8.pdf.

—— (2001) *The Ethnographer's Eye: Ways of Seeing in Anthropology*. Cambridge: Cambridge University Press.

Grimshaw, Anna and Paul Hockings (2011) Two recent films from David MacDougall. *Visual Anthropology* 24(4): 391–9.

Grimshaw, Anna and Nikos Papastergiadis (1995) *Conversations with Anthropological Film-makers: David MacDougall*. Prickly Pear Press, no. 9. Also available at www.thememorybank.co.uk/pricklypear/9.pdf.

Grimshaw, Anna and Amanda Ravetz (2009) *Observational Cinema: Anthropology, Film, and the Exploration of Social Life*. Bloomington: Indiana University Press.

Guldin, Jere (2014) *In The Land of the Head Hunters*: Reconstruction, not restoration. In Brad Evans and Aaron Glass, eds, *Return to the Land of the Head Hunters: Edward S. Curtis, the Kwakwaka'wka, and the Making of Modern Cinema*, pp. 260–8. Seattle: University of Washington Press and the Bill Holm Center, Burke Museum.

Guynn, William (1998) The art of national projection. Basil Wright's *Song of Ceylon*. In Barry Keith Grant and Jeannette Sloniowski, eds, *Documenting the Documentary*, pp. 83–98. Detroit: Wayne State University Press.

Haddon, Alfred (1901) *Head-hunters: Black, White and Brown*. London: Methuen.

Haffner, Pierre (1996) Les avis de cinq cinéastes d'Afrique noire. In René Prédal, ed., *Jean Rouch ou le ciné-plaisir*. Special edition of *CinémAction*, vol. 81, pp. 89–103. Éditions Corlet. First published in 1982.

Harper, Douglas, ed. (1994) Cape Breton 1952: The photographic vision of Timothy Asch. *Visual Sociology* 9 (2).

— (2004) An ethnographic gaze: scenes in the anthropological life of Timothy Asch. In E. Douglas Lewis, ed., *Timothy Asch and Ethnographic Film*, pp. 17–56. London and New York: Routledge Harwood Anthropology.

Heidegger, Martin (1978) Letter on humanism. In David F. Krell, ed., *Martin Heidegger: Basic Writings*, pp. 213–65. London: Routledge. Originally published in 1947.

Heider, Karl (1976) *Ethnographic Film*. Austin: University of Texas Press.

— (2007) Gardner's first shots: vectored landscapes. In Ilisa Barbash and Lucien Taylor, eds, *The Cinema of Robert Gardner*, pp. 79–92. Oxford: Berg.

Hempel, Paul (2009) Theodor Koch-Grünberg and visual anthropology in early twentieth-century German anthropology. In Christopher Morton and Elizabeth Edwards, eds, *Photography, Anthropology and History: Expanding the Frame*, pp. 193–219. Ashgate.

Henley, Paul (2009) *The Adventure of the Real: Jean Rouch and the Craft of Ethnographic Cinema*. Chicago and London: University of Chicago Press.

— (2013a) From documentation to representation: recovering the films of Margaret Mead and Gregory Bateson. *Visual Anthropology* 26(2): 75–108.

— (2013b) Thick inscription and the unwitting witness: reading the films of Alfred Haddon and Baldwin Spencer. *Visual Anthropology* 26(5): 383–429.

— (2017) Avant Jean Rouch: le cinéma 'ethnographique' français tourné en Afrique subsaharienne. *Journal des africanistes* 87(1/2): 34–62.

— (2018) The authoring of Observational Cinema: conversations with Colin Young. *Visual Anthropology* 31(3): 193–235.

— (2020) *L'Aventure du réel: Jean Rouch et la pratique du cinéma ethnographique*. Trans. Joëlle Hauzeur. Presses universitaires de Rennes.

Hercus, Luise (1980) How we danced the Mudlunga. *Aboriginal History* 4(1): 4–31.

Hinkson, Melinda (2008) New media projects at Yuendumu: towards a history and analysis of intercultural engagement. In Luke Taylor et al., eds, *The Power of Knowledge, the Resonance of Tradition*, pp. 157–68. Canberra: Australian Institute of Aboriginal and Torres Strait Islander Studies.

Hockings, Paul (1988) Gone with the Gael: Filming an Irish village. In Jack Rollwagen, ed., *Anthropological Filmmaking: Anthropological Perspectives on the Production of Film and Video for General Public Audiences*, pp. 143–59. Abingdon: Harwood Academic Publishers.

Holm, Bill (2014) Foreword. In Brad Evans and Aaron Glass, eds, *Return to the Land of the Head Hunters: Edward S. Curtis, the Kwakwaka'wka, and the Making of Modern Cinema*, pp. xii–xvii. Seattle: University of Washington Press and the Bill Holm Center, Burke Museum.

Holm, Bill and George Irving Quimby (1980) *Edward S. Curtis in the Land of the War Canoes: A Pioneer Cinematographer in the Pacific Northwest*. Thomas Burke Memorial Washing State Museum Monograph no. 2. Seattle and London: University of Washington Press.

Homiak, John P. (1990a) Melville J. Herskovits: motor behavior and the imaging of Afro-American Culture. *Visual Anthropology* 3(1): 11–29.

— (1990b) The anthropological visualization of Haiti: reflections on the films of Melville Herskovits and Maya Deren. *Commission on Visual Anthropology Review*, Spring 1990: 13–21.

— (2003) *A Kalahari Family*: some thoughts on reflexivity, voice and social location. *Visual Anthropology Review* 19(1–2): 128–34.

— (2013) Foreword. In Joshua A. Bell, Alison K. Brown and Robert J. Gordon, eds, *Recreating First Contact: Expeditions, Anthropology, and Popular Culture*, pp. v–xii. Washington DC: Smithsonian Institution Scholarly Press.

Homiak, John P. and Keyan G. Tomaselli (1999) Structured absences: shot logs on the Marshall family expeditionary films, 1950–1958. *Visual Anthropology* 12(2–3): 289–338.

Hughes-Freeland, Felicia (2006) Tribes and tribulations: a response to Pat Caplan. *Anthropology Today* 22(2): 22–3.

Ichioka, Yasuko (1995) Ethnographic filmmaking for Japanese television. In Paul Hockings, ed., *Principles of Visual Anthropology*, 2nd edn, pp. 441–56. Berlin and New York: Mouton de Gruyter.

Jacknis, Ira (1987) The picturesque and the scientific: Franz Boas' plan for anthropological filmmaking. *Visual Anthropology* 1(1): 59–64.

Jamin, Jean (1991) Anxious science: ethnography as a devil's dictionary. *Visual Anthropology Review* 7(1): 84–91.

Jenkins, Alan (1986) Disappearing World goes to China: a production study of anthropological films. *Anthropology Today* 2(3): 6–13.

Jensen, Gordon D. and Luh Ketut Suryani (1992) *The Balinese People: A Reinvestigation of Character*. Singapore and Oxford: Oxford University Press.

Jolly, Éric (2014) *Démasquer la société dogon. Sahara-Soudan, janvier–avril 1935*. Les Carnets de Bérose, no. 4. Série Missions, enquêtes et terrains – Années 1930. Lahic/Ministère de la Culture et de la Communication. www.berose.fr/IMG/pdf/carnet_be_rose_4.pdf.

—— (2017) Cinéma ethnographique. In *À la naissance de l'ethnologie française. Les missions ethnographiques en Afrique subsaharienne (1928–1939)*. naissanceethnologie.fr/exhibits/show/cinema.

Jordan, Pierre-L. (1992) *Cinéma: Premier Contact – Premier Regard*. Marseille: Musées de Marseille/Images en Manoeuvres Editions.

Kildea, Gary (2007) Interview of Gary Kildea. www.dspace.cam.ac.uk/handle/1810/183663.

Kildea, Gary and Margaret Willson (1986) Interpreting ethnographic film: an exchange about *Celso and Cora. Anthropology Today* 2(4): 15–17.

King, Eleanor M. (1993) Fieldwork in Brazil: Petrullo's visit to the Yawalpiti. *Expedition* 35(3): 34–43. Available at www.penn.museum/documents/publications/expedition/PDFs/35-3/Fieldwork.pdf.

Knight, John (1993) Making a tribal difference in the modern world. *Anthropology Today* 9(1): 22–4.

Kuklick, Henrika (2013) Afterword. In Joshua A. Bell, Alison K. Brown and Robert J. Gordon, eds, *Recreating First Contact: Expeditions, Anthropology, and Popular Culture*, pp. 231–9. Washington DC: Smithsonian Institution Scholarly Press.

Laracy, Hugh (2013) Patrick O'Reilly (1900–1988): Bibliographer of the Pacific. In Hugh Laracy, *Watriama and Co.: Further Pacific Portraits*, pp. 257–65. Canberra: ANU Press.

Lawson, Mark (1993) An original of the species. *Independent* (10 February 1993). www.independent.co.uk/arts-entertainment/television-1472093.html.

Leprohon, Pierre (1945) *L'Exotisme et le Cinéma: les 'chasseurs d'images' a la conquête du monde* … Paris: Éditions Susse.

Lewis, E. Douglas (1988) *People of the Source. The Social and Ceremonial Order of Tana Wai Brama on Flores*. Verhandelingen van het Instituut voor Taal-, Land- en Volkenkunde no. 135. Dordrecht, Holland and Providence, Rhode Island: Foris Publications.

—— (2004a) Introduction. Timothy Asch in America and Australia. In E. Douglas Lewis, ed., *Timothy Asch and Ethnographic Film*, pp. 1–16. London and New York: Routledge Harwood Anthropology.

—— (2004b) From event to ethnography: film-making and ethnographic research in Tana 'Ai, Flores, eastern Indonesia. In E. Douglas Lewis, ed., *Timothy Asch and Ethnographic Film*, pp. 97–122. London and New York: Routledge Harwood Anthropology.

—— (2004c) Person, event, and the location of the cinematic subject in Timothy Asch's films on Indonesia. In E. Douglas Lewis, ed., *Timothy Asch and Ethnographic Film*, pp. 263–82. London and New York: Routledge Harwood Anthropology.

Lindstrom, Lamont (2013) On safari with Martin and Osa Johnson. In Joshua A. Bell, Alison K. Brown and Robert J. Gordon, eds, *Recreating First Contact: Expeditions, Anthropology, and Popular Culture*, pp. 147–61. Washington DC: Smithsonian Institution Scholarly Press.

Llewelyn-Davies, Melissa (1978) Two contexts of solidarity among pastoral Maasai women. In Patricia Caplan and Janet Burja, eds, *Women United, Women Divided*, pp. 206–37. London and Bloomington: Tavistock.

—— (1981) Women, warriors, and patriarchs. In Sherry B. Ortner and Harriet Whitehead, eds, *Sexual Meanings: The Cultural Construction of Gender and Sexuality*, pp. 330–58. Cambridge and New York: Cambridge University Press.

Loizos, Peter (1980) Granada Television's *Disappearing World* series: an appraisal. *American Anthropologist* 82(3): 573–94.

—— (1993) *Innovation in Ethnographic Film: From Innocence to Self-consciousness 1955–1985.* Manchester: Manchester University Press.

—— (1995) Robert Gardner's *Rivers of Sand:* toward a reappraisal. In Leslie Devereaux and Roger Hillman, eds, *Fields of Vision: Essays in Film studies, Visual Anthropology, and Photography*, pp. 311–25. Berkeley, Los Angeles, London: University of California Press.

Lutkehaus, Nancy C. (2004) Man, a course of study: situating Tim Asch's pedagogy and ethnographic films. In E. Douglas Lewis, ed., *Timothy Asch and Ethnographic Film*, pp. 57–73. London and New York: Routledge Harwood Anthropology.

Lydall, Jean (1992) Filming *The Women Who Smile*. In Peter Ian Crawford and Jan Ketil Simonsen, eds, *Ethnographic Film Aesthetics and Narrative Traditions*, pp. 141–58. Aarhus: Intervention Press.

—— (2008) Intimacy, Integrity, and Indulgence in Anthropological Film. *Journal of Film and Video* 60(2): 35–49.

Lydall, Jean and Ivo Strecker (1978) A critique of Lionel Bender's review of *Rivers of Sand*. *American Anthropologist* 80(4): 945–6.

MacDonald, Scott (2013) *American Ethnographic Film and Personal Documentary: The Cambridge Turn.* Berkeley, Los Angeles, London: University of California Press.

—— (2015) *Avant-Doc: Intersections of Documentary and Avant-Garde Cinema.* Oxford University Press.

MacDougall, David (1992a) Complicities of style. In Peter Ian Crawford and David Turton, eds, *Film as Ethnography*, pp. 90–8. Manchester: Manchester University Press. Also published in *Transcultural Cinema*, pp. 140–9, Princeton: Princeton University Press, 1998.

—— (1992b) *Photo Wallahs*: an encounter with photography. *Visual Anthropology* 8(2): 96–100.

—— (1995a) Beyond observational cinema. In Paul Hockings, ed., *Principles of Visual Anthropology*, 2nd edn, pp. 115–32. Berlin and New York: Mouton de Gruyter.

—— (1995b) The subjective voice in ethnographic film. In Leslie Devereaux and Roger Hillman, eds, *Fields of Vision: Essays in Film Studies, Visual Anthropology, and Photography*, pp. 217–55. Berkeley, Los Angeles, London: University of California Press.

—— (1997) The visual in anthropology. In Marcus Banks and Howard Morphy, eds, *Rethinking Visual Anthropology*, pp. 276–95. New Haven and London: Yale University Press.

—— (1998a) *Transcultural Cinema*. Edited and with an introduction by Lucien Taylor. Princeton: Princeton University Press.

—— (1998b) Visual anthropology and the ways of knowing. In David MacDougall, *Transcultural Cinema*, pp. 61–92. Princeton: Princeton University Press. Originally published in 1995.

—— (1998c) Whose story is it? In David MacDougall, *Transcultural Cinema*, pp. 150–64. Princeton: Princeton University Press. Originally published in 1991.

—— (1998d) Subtitling ethnographic films. In David MacDougall, *Transcultural Cinema*, pp. 165–76. Princeton: Princeton University Press. Originally published in 1995.

—— (1998e) Unprivileged camera style. In David MacDougall, *Transcultural Cinema*, pp. 199–208. Princeton: Princeton University Press. Originally published in 1982.

—— (1998f) When less is less. In David MacDougall, *Transcultural Cinema*, pp. 209–23. Princeton: Princeton University Press. Originally published in 1992.

—— (2001) Renewing ethnographic film. Is digital video changing the genre? *Anthropology Today* 17(3): 15–21.

—— (2006a) Introduction: meaning and being. In *The Corporeal Image: Film, Ethnography, and the Senses*, pp. 1–9. Princeton: Princeton University Press.

—— (2006b) Films of childhood. In *The Corporeal Image: Film, Ethnography, and the Senses*, pp. 67–93. Princeton: Princeton University Press.

—— (2006c) Social aesthetics and the Doon School. In *The Corporeal Image: Film, Ethnography, and the Senses*, pp. 94–119. Princeton: Princeton University Press.

—— (2006d) Doon School reconsidered. In *The Corporeal Image: Film, Ethnography, and the Senses*, pp. 120–44. Princeton: Princeton University Press.

—— (2007) Colin Young, ethnographic film and the film culture of the 1960s. In Beate Englebrecht, ed., *Memories of the Origins of Ethnographic Film*, pp. 123–31. Frankfurt am Main: Peter Lang.

—— (2019) *The Looking Machine: Essays on Cinema, Anthropology and Documentary Filmmaking*. Manchester: Manchester University Press.

MacFarlane, Alan (2007) Interview of David MacDougall. Available at www.youtube.com/watch?v=4oyjVMfebsM.

—— (2010) Early Ethnographic Film in Britain: A Reflection on the Work of Christoph von Fürer Heimendorf. *Visual Anthropology* 23(5): 375–97.

Malinowski, Bronislaw (1932a) *Argonauts of the Western Pacific: An Account of Native Enterprise and Adventure in the Archipelagos of Melanesian New Guinea*. 2nd impression. London: Routledge & Kegan Paul. First published in 1922.

—— (1932b) *The Sexual Life of Savages in North-Western Melanesia: An Ethnographic Account of Courtship, Marriage, and Family Life Among the Natives of the Trobriand Islands, British New Guinea*, 3rd edn. London: Routledge & Kegan Paul. First published in 1929.

Mamber, Stephen (1974) *Cinema Verité in America: Studies in Uncontrolled Documentary*. Cambridge, Mass. and London: MIT Press.

Marcus, Alan (2006) *Nanook of the North* as primal drama. *Visual Anthropology* 19(3–4): 201–22.

Marcus, George E. and Dick Cushman (1982) Ethnographies as texts. *Annual Review of Anthropology* 11: 25–69.

Marshall, John (1993) Filming and learning. In Jay Ruby, ed., *The Cinema of John Marshall*, pp. 1–133. Abingdon: Harwood Academic Publishers.

Marshall Thomas, Elizabeth (1959) *The Harmless People*. Harmondsworth: Penguin.

Martinez, Wilton (1995) The challenges of a pioneer: Tim Asch, Otherness, and film reception. *Visual Anthropology Review* 11(1): 53–82.

Martins, Luciana (2007) Illusions of power: vision, technology and the geographical exploration of the Amazon, 1924–1925. *Journal of Latin American Cultural Studies* 16(3): 285–307.

—— (2012) Geographical exploration and the elusive mapping of Amazonia. *The Geographical Review* 102(2): 225–44.

Mattei Muller, Marie-Claude (2007) *Lengua y Cultura Yanomami. Diccionario ilustrado Yanomami-Español/ Español-Yanomami*. Caracas: UNESCO.

McCarty, Mark (1995) McCarty's Law and How to Break It. In Paul Hockings, ed., *Principles of Visual Anthropology*, 2nd edn, pp. 69–75. Berlin and New York: Mouton de Gruyter.

McLuhan, Marshall and Quentin Fiore (1967) *The Medium is the Massage: An Inventory of Effects*. New York: Random House.

Mead, Margaret (1995) Visual anthropology in a discipline of words. In Paul Hockings, ed., *Principles of Visual Anthropology*, 2nd edn, pp. 3–10. Berlin and New York: Mouton de Gruyter.

Mead, Margaret and Gregory Bateson (1977) Margaret Mead and Gregory Bateson on the use of the camera in anthropology. *Studies in the Anthropology of Visual Communication* 4(2): 78–80.

Michaels, Eric (1986) *Aboriginal Invention of Television: Central Australia 1982–1986*. Canberra: Australian Institute of Aboriginal Studies.

Miller, Cynthia (2007) Ethnographic documentary filmmakers Sarah Elder and Leonard Kamerling: an interview. *Post Script* 27 (1). www.questia.com/read/1G1–176371864/ethnographic-documentary-filmmakers-sarah-elder-and.

Mir-Hosseini, Ziba (2002) Negotiating the politics of gender in Iran: an ethnography of a documentary. In Richard Tapper, ed., *The New Iranian Cinema*, pp. 167–99. London: I. B. Tauris.

Morin, Edgar (2003) Chronicle of a film. In Steven Feld, ed. and trans., *Ciné-Ethnography*. Minneapolis and London: University of Minnesota Press, pp. 229–65. Originally published in French in 1962.

Morphy, Howard (1984) *Journey to the Crocodile's Nest: An Accompanying Monograph to the Film* Madarrpa Funeral at Gurka'wuy. Afterword by Ian Dunlop. Canberra: Australian Institute of Aboriginal Studies.

—— (1994) The interpretation of ritual: reflections from film on anthropological practice. *Man* (NS) 29(1): 117–46.

—— (2007) The aesthetics of communication and the communication of cultural aesthetics: a perspective on Ian Dunlop's films of Aboriginal Australia. In Beate Englebrecht, ed., *Memories of the Origins of Ethnographic Film*, pp. 321–40. Frankfurt am Main: Peter Lang.

—— (2012) Becoming a visual anthropologist. In Natasha Fijn, ed., *Perspectives on Ethnographic Film*. Special edition of Humanities Research, vol. XVIII, no. 1, pp. 15–46.

Morris, Alan G. (1987) The reflections of the collector: San and Khoi skeletons in museum collections. *The South African Archaeology Bulletin* 42(1): 12–22.

Morris, Rosalind C. (1994) *New Worlds from Fragments: Film, Ethnography, and the Representation of Northwest Coast Cultures.* Boulder and Oxford: Westview Press.

Mortimer, Lorraine (2019) *Roger Sandall's Films and Contemporary Anthropology: Explorations in the Aesthetic, the Existential, and the Possible.* Bloomington: Indiana University Press.

Moser, Brian (1988) Foreword. In André Singer with Leslie Woodhead, *Disappearing World: Television and Anthropology*, pp. 9–14. London: Boxtree in association with Granada Television.

Moser, Brian and Donald Tayler (1963) Tribes of the Piraparaná. *The Geographical Journal* 129(4): 437–49.

Muenala, Yauri (2018) *Kikinkunawan: visualidades comunes. La autorepresentación en la práctica audiovisual de realizadores otovalos kichua.* Quito: Abya-Yala.

Murray Levine, Alison (2005) Film and colonial memory: *La Croisière noire* 1924–2004. In Alec G. Hargreaves, ed., *Memory, Empire, and Postcolonialism: Legacies of French Colonialism*, pp. 81–97. Lexington Books, Rowman & Littlefield.

—— (2010) *Framing the Nation: Documentary Film in Interwar France.* New York and London: Continuum.

Myers, Fred R. (1988) From ethnography to metaphor: recent films from David and Judith MacDougall. *Cultural Anthropology* 3(2): 205–20.

—— (1993) *Djungguwan at Gurka'wuy* by Ian Dunlop. Film Review. *American Anthropologist* 95(1): 250–2.

Naficy, Hamid (2006) Ethnographic and expedition films about nomadic tribes – the case of *Grass* (1925). In Jeffrey Ruoff, ed., *Virtual Voyages: Cinema and Travel*, pp. 117–38. Durham and London: Duke University Press.

Nichols, Bill (2004) What really happened: a reassessment of *The Ax Fight*. In E. Douglas Lewis, ed., *Timothy Asch and Ethnographic Film*, pp. 229–37. London and New York: Routledge Harwood Anthropology.

O'Reilly, Patrick (1970) Le 'documentaire' ethnographique en Océanie. In Jean Rouch and Monique Salzmann, eds, *Premier catalogue sélectif international de films ethnographiques sur la région du Pacifique*, pp. 281–305. Paris: UNESCO.

Oppitz, Michael (1988) A day in the city of death. 'Forest of Bliss' (by Robert Gardner) – a film review. *Anthropos* 83: 210–12.

Östör, Ákos (1994) *Forest of Bliss:* Film and Anthropology. *East-West Film Journal* 8(2): 70–104.

Oswalt, Wendell H. (2008) *This Land Was Theirs: A Study of Native North Americans*, 9th edn. Oxford: Oxford University Press.

Parry, Jonathan (1988) Comment on Robert Gardner's 'Forest of Bliss'. *Society for Visual Anthropology Newsletter* 4(2): 4–7.

Peleg, Hila (2017) We are somatic creatures: Hila Peleg in conversation with Rosalind Nashashibi, Véréna Paravel and Lucien Castaing-Taylor, and Ben Russell. *South Magazine* no. 9/*documenta* 14, no. 4. www.documenta14.de/en/south/25216_we_are_somatic_creatures_hila_peleg_in_conversation_with_rosalind_nashashibi_ve_re_na_paravel_and_lucien_castaing_taylor_and_ben_russell.

Pequet, Luc, ed. (2017) *Jean Rouch: ethnologue et cinéaste*. Special edition of the *Journal des africanistes*, vol. 87(1–2). Paris: Société des africanistes.

Peterson, Leighton C. (2013) Reclaiming Diné film: visual sovereignty and the return of *Navajo Film Themselves*. *Visual Anthropology Review* 29(1): 29–41.

Petrič, Vlada (1987) *Constructivism in Film: The Man with the Movie Camera, A Cinematic Analysis*. Cambridge: Cambridge University Press.

Piault, Colette (2007a) Forbidden speech/controlled speech: some observations on the role of the word in Rouch's films. *Visual Anthropology Review* 23(1): 38–42. Originally published in French in 1996.

—— (2007b) Speech-dominated or dominating?: an interview with Jean Rouch. *Visual Anthropology Review* 23(1): 43–53. Originally published in French in 1996.

Piault, Marc-Henri (2000) *Anthropologie et cinéma: passage à l'image, passage par l'image*. Paris: Éditions Nathan.

Pink, Sarah (2011) Digital visual anthropology: potentials and challenges. In Marcus Banks and Jay Ruby, eds, *Made to be Seen: Perspectives on the History of Visual Anthropology*, pp. 209–33. Chicago and London: University of Chicago Press.

Potts, Rowena (2015) A conversation with David MacDougall: Reflections on the childhood and modernity workshop films. *Visual Anthropology Review* 31(2): 190–200.

Prins, Harald E. L. and John Bishop (2001–2) Edmund Carpenter: explorations in media anthropology. *Visual Anthropology Review* 17(2): 110–40.

Quinn, Frederick (1980) Beti society in the nineteenth century. *Africa* 50(3): 293–304.

Rassool, Ciraj (2015) Re-storing the skeletons of empire: return, reburial and rehumanisation in Southern Africa. *Journal of Southern African Studies* 41(3): 653–70.

Richardson, Michael (1990) Report on RAI questionnaire. *Anthropology Today* 6(1): 11–12.

Robbins, Steven L. (2008) *From Revolution to Rights in South Africa: Social Movements, NGOs and Popular Politics after Apartheid*. James Curry and University of KwaZulu-Natal Press.

Rondon, Cândido Mariano da Silva, ed. (1946) *Índios do Brasil–do Centro, Noroeste e Sul do Mato Grosso*. vol. 1. Conselho Nacional de Proteção aos Índios, Ministério de Agricultura. Rio de Janeiro. Available online via the Museo do Índio, Rio de Janeiro, at www.docvirt.com/docreader.net/DocReader.aspx?bib=museudoindio&pagfis=.

Rony, Fatimah Tobing (1996) *The Third Eye: Race, Cinema and Ethnographic Spectacle*. Durham and London: Duke University Press.

Rotha, Paul with Basil Wright (1980) Nanook and the North. *Studies in Visual Communication* 6(2): 33–60.

Rouch, Jean (1955) À propos de films ethnographiques. *Positif* 14–15: 145–9.

—— (1956) Migrations au Ghana (Gold Coast): Enquête 1953–1955. *Journal de la Société des Africanistes* 26: 33–196.

—— ed. (1967a) *Premier catalogue sélectif international de films ethnographiques sur l'Afrique noire*. Paris: UNESCO. Available at unesdoc.unesco.org/ark:/48223/pf0000003622.

—— (1967b) Situation et tendances du cinéma en Afrique. In Jean Rouch, ed., *Premier catalogue sélectif international de films ethnographiques sur l'Afrique noire*, pp. 374–408. Paris: UNESCO.

—— (1968) Le film ethnographique. In Jean Poirier, ed., *Encyclopédie de la Pléiade: ethnologie générale*, pp. 429–71. Paris: Gallimard.

—— (1989) *La religion et la magie songhay*, 2nd edn. Bruxelles: Éditions de la Université de Bruxelles.

—— (1995a) The camera and man. In Paul Hockings, ed., *Principles of Visual Anthropology*, 2nd edn, pp. 79–98. Berlin and New York: Mouton de Gruyter.

—— (1995b) Our totemic ancestors and crazed masters. In Paul Hockings, ed., *Principles of Visual Anthropology*, 2nd edn, pp. 217–32. Berlin and New York: Mouton de Gruyter.

—— (1995c) L'autre et le sacré: jeu sacré, jeu politique. In Christopher W. Thompson, ed., *L'Autre et le Sacré: surréalisme, cinéma, ethnologie*, pp. 407–31. Paris: L'Harmattan.

—— (2003a) On the vicissitudes of the self: the possessed dancer, the magician, the sorcerer, the filmmaker, and the ethnographer. In Steven Feld, ed., *Ciné-Ethnography*, pp. 87–101. Minneapolis and London: University of Minnesota Press. Originally published in French in 1971.

—— (2003b) The mad fox and the pale master. In Steven Feld, ed., *Ciné-Ethnography*, pp. 102–26. Minneapolis and London: University of Minnesota Press. Translated from a text originally published in 1978.

—— (2009) Essai sur les avatars de la personne du possédée, du magicien, du corcier, du cinéaste et de l'ethnographe. In Jean-Paul Colleyn, ed., *Jean Rouch: cinéma et anthropologie*, pp. 141–53. Cahiers du Cinéma/essais. Paris: INA (Institut national de l'audiovisuel). Originally published in 1975.

Rouch, Jean and Monique Salzmann, eds (1970) *Premier catalogue sélectif international de films ethnographiques sur la région du Pacifique*. UNESCO: Paris. Available at unesdoc.unesco.org/images/0000/000031/003117fb.pdf.

Rowbottom, Anne (2002a) Subject positions and 'real royalists': monarchy and vernacular civil religion. In Nigel Rapport, ed., *British Subjects: An Anthropology of Britain*, pp. 31–48. Oxford: Berg.

—— (2000b) Following the Queen: the place of the Royal Family in the context of Royal visits and civil religion. *Sociological Research Online* 7(2). www.socresonline.org.uk/7/2/rowbottom.html.

Ruby, Jay (1975) Is an ethnographic film a filmic ethnography? *Studies in the Anthropology of Visual Communication* 2(2): 104–11. Also available at astro.temple.edu/%7Eruby/ruby/is.html.

—— (1980) Franz Boas and early camera study of behavior. *Kinesics Report* 3(1): 6–11, 16. Also available at astro.temple.edu/~ruby/ruby/boas.html.

—— (1995a) Out of synch: the cinema of Tim Asch. *Visual Anthropology Review* 11(1): 19–35.

—— (1995b) The moral burden of authorship in ethnographic. *Visual Anthropology Review* 11(2): 77–82.

—— (2000) *Picturing Culture: Explorations of Film and Anthropology*. Chicago and London: University of Chicago Press.

Ruoff, Jeff (2002) Around the world in eighty minutes: the travel lecture film. *Visual Anthropology* 15(1): 91–114.

Russell, Catherine (1999) *Experimental Ethnography: The Work of Film in the Age of Video*. Durham and London: Duke University Press.

Sandall, Roger (1972) Observation and identity. *Sight and Sound* 41(4): 192–6.

—— (1975) Ethnographic film documentaries. In Paul Hockings, ed., *Principles of Visual Anthropology*, 1st edn, pp. 125–32. Berlin and New York: Mouton de Gruyter.

Sariskova, Oksana (2017) *Screening Soviet Nationalities. Kulturfilms from the Far North to Central Asia*. London and New York: I. B. Tauris.

Saunders, Dave (2007) *Direct Cinema: Observational Documentary and the Politics of the Sixties*. London and New York: Wallflower Press.

Schiwy, Freya (2009) *Indianizing Film: Decolonization, the Andes and the Question of Technology*. Rutgers University Press.

Schrire, Carmel (2003) The conciliators: Bushmania and the nightmare of survival. *Visual Anthropology Review* 19(2–3): 160–5.

Schüller, Dietrich (1987) *Buschmann spricht in den Phonographen* – Film von Rudolf Pöch, 1908. *Wissenschaftlichen Film*(Wien) nos 36/37: 133–9.

Serceau, Daniel (1996) Entretien avec Pierre Braunberger. In René Prédal, ed., *Jean Rouch ou le ciné-plaisir*. Special issue of *CinémAction*, vol. 81, pp. 170–1. Condé-sur-Noireau: Éditions Corlet-Télérama. Originally published in 1982 in René Prédal, ed., *Jean Rouch, un griot gaulois*. Special issue of *CinémAction*, vol. 17, pp. 158–60. Paris: L'Harmattan.

Seton, Marie (1971) Basil Wright's *Song of Ceylon*. In Lewis Jacobs, ed., *The Documentary Tradition*, pp. 101–4. W. W. Norton. Originally published in the journal *Film Art* in 1935.

Sheets, Hilarie M. (2016) An artist explores the lives of girls labeled difficult. *New York Times* (16 May 2016, Art and Design section). www.nytimes.com/2016/05/22/arts/design/an-artist-explores-the-lives-of-girls-labeled-difficult.html.

Sherman, Rina, ed. (2018) *Dans le sillage de Jean Rouch: Témoinages et essais.* Éditions de la Maison des sciences de l'homme.

Sillitoe, Paul (2003) Time to be professional? *Anthropology Today* 19(1): 1–2.

Singer, André (1992) Anthropology in broadcasting. In Peter Crawford and David Turton, eds, *Film as Ethnography*, pp. 264–73. Manchester: Manchester University Press.

—— (2006) Tribes and tribulations: a response to Hughes-Freeland. *Anthropology Today* 22(3): 24–5.

Singer, André with Steven Seidenberg (1992) Televising culture: the representations of anthropology in British broadcasting. *Visual Anthropology Review* 8(1): 122–5.

Sjöberg, Johannes (2008a) Ethnofiction: genre hybridity in theory and practice-based research. PhD manuscript. School of Arts Histories and Cultures, University of Manchester.

—— (2008b) Ethnofiction: drama as a creative research practice in ethnographic film. *Journal of Media Practice* 9(3): 229–42.

—— (2018) Une sorte de pyschodrame: l'art dramatique comme méthode ethnographique dans les films de Jean Rouch. In Rina Sherman, ed., *Dans le sillage de Jean Rouch: Témoinages et essais*, pp. 195–208. Paris: Éditions de la Maison des sciences de l'homme.

Staal, J. F. 'Frits' (1989) Anthropologists against death. *Society for Visual Anthropology Newsletter* 5(1): 14, 19.

Starr, Cecile (1996) *Song of Ceylon.* An interview with Basil Wright. In Kevin MacDonald and Mark Cousins, eds, *Imagining Reality: The Faber Book of Documentary*, pp. 102–11. London: Faber & Faber. Originally published in *Film-Maker's Newsletter* 9(1) in November 1975.

Stoller, Paul (1992) *The Cinematic Griot: The Ethnography of Jean Rouch.* Chicago and London: University of Chicago Press.

Strathern, Andrew (1977) Making 'Ongka's Big Moka'. *Cambridge Anthropology. Special Issue Ethnographic Film*, pp. 32–46.

Strathern, Marilyn (1997) Comment on 'Televisualist Anthropology' by James F. Weiner. *Current Anthropology* 38(2): 224–6.

Strecker, Ivo (1988) Filming among the Hamar. *Visual Anthropology* 1(3): 369–78.

Suhr, Christian (2019) *Descending with Angels. Islamic Exorcism and Psychiatry: A Film Monograph.* Manchester: Manchester University Press.

Sutherland, Anne, ed. (1978) *Face Values: Some Anthropological Themes.* British Broadcasting Corporation.

Sutton, Mark Q. (2017) *An Introduction to Native North America*, 5th edn. Abingdon: Routledge.

Taylor, Lucien (1996) Iconophobia: how anthropology lost it at the movies. *Transition* 69: 64–88.

—— (1998a) Introduction. In David MacDougall, *Transcultural Cinema*, pp. 3–21. Princeton: Princeton University Press.

—— (1998b) 'Visual Anthropology Is Dead, Long Live Visual Anthropology!' *American Anthropologist* 100(2): 534–7.

—— (2003) A life on the edge of film and anthropology. In Steven Feld, ed., *Ciné-Ethnography*, pp. 129–46. Minneapolis and London: University of Minnesota Press. Originally published in 1991 in *Visual Anthropology Review* 7(1): 92–102.

Tedlock, Barbara (1983) Zuni Sacred Theater. *American Indian Quarterly* 7(3): 93–110.

Thompson, Christopher (1995) De Buñuel à Rouch: les surréalistes devant le documentaire et le film ethnographique. In Christopher W. Thompson, ed., *L'Autre et le Sacré: surréalisme, cinéma, ethnologie*, pp. 263–81. Paris: L'Harmattan.

Tierney, Patrick (2000) *Darkness in El Dorado: How Scientists and Journalists Devastated the Amazon.* New York and London: W. W. Norton.

Tomaselli, Keyan G. and John P. Homiak (1999) Powering popular conceptions: the !Kung in the Marshall family expedition films of the 1950s. *Visual Anthropology* 12(2–3): 153–84.

Torresan, Angela (2011) *Round Trip*: Filming a Return Home. *Visual Anthropology Review* 27(2): 119–30.

Turin, Mark (2003) An Interview with Asen Balikci. Available at www.sms.cam.ac.uk/media/1111527.

Turner, Terence (1990) Visual media, cultural politics, and anthropological practice: some implications of recent uses of film and video among the Kayapo of Brazil. *Commission on Visual Anthropology Review*, Spring 1990: 8–13.

—— (1991a) Representing, resisting, rethinking: historical transformations of Kayapo and anthropological consciousness. In George W. Stocking, ed., *Colonial Situations: Essays on the Contextualization of Ethnographic Knowledge. History of Anthropology*, vol. 7, pp. 285–313. Madison: University of Wisconsin Press.

—— (1991b) The social dynamics of video media in an indigenous society: the cultural meaning and the personal politics of video-making in Kayapo communities. *Visual Anthropology Review* 7(2): 68–76.

—— (1992a) Defiant images: the Kayapo appropriation of video. *Anthropology Today* 8(6): 5–16.

—— (1992b) The Kayapo on television: an anthropological viewing. *Visual Anthropology Review* 8(1): 107–12.

—— (1995) Representation, collaboration and mediation in contemporary ethnographic and indigenous media. *Visual Anthropology Review* 11(2): 102–6.

—— (1997) Comment on 'Televisualist Anthropology' by James F. Weiner. *Current Anthropology* 38(2): 226–9.

—— (2002) Representation, politics, and cultural imagination in indigenous video: general points and Kayapo examples. In Faye D. Ginsburg, Lila Abu Lughod and Brian Larkin, eds, *Media Worlds: Anthropology on New Terrain*, pp. 75–89. Berkeley and Los Angeles: University of California Press

Turton, David (1988) Looking for a cool place: the Mursi, 1890s to 1980s. In Douglas Johnson and David Anderson, eds, *The Ecology of Survival: Case Studies from Northeast African History*, pp. 261–82. Boulder and London: Westview Press and Lester Crook Academic Publishing.

—— (1992a) Anthropology on television: what next? In Peter Crawford and David Turton, eds, *Film as Ethnography*, pp. 283–99. Manchester: Manchester University Press.

—— (1992b) How to make a speech in Mursi. In Peter Crawford and Jan Ketil Simonsen, eds, *Ethnographic Film Aesthetics and Narrative Traditions*, pp. 159–75. Aarhus: Intervention Press.

Van Vuuren, Lauren (2013) 'The Africa I Know': film and the making of 'Bushmen' in Laurens van der Post's *Lost World of Kalahari* (1956). In Joshua A. Bell, Alison K. Brown, and Robert J. Gordon, eds, *Recreating First Contact: Expeditions, Anthropology, and Popular Culture*, pp. 215–30. Washington DC: Smithsonian Institution Scholarly Press.

Vaughan, Dai (1999) *For Documentary: Twelve Essays*. Berkeley, Los Angeles, London: University of California Press.

Wanono, Nadine (1987) *Ciné-rituel de femmes dogon*. Paris: Éditions du CNRS.

—— (2006) From spatial analysis to virtual wonder. In Metje Postma and Peter Ian Crawford, eds, *Reflecting Visual Ethnography: Using the Camera in Anthropological Research*, pp. 252–69. Højbjerg and Leiden: Intervention Press and CNWS Publications.

Weinberger, Eliot (1994) The camera people. In Lucien Taylor, ed., *Visualizing Theory: Selected Essay from V.A.R. 1990–1994*, pp. 3–26. New York and London: Routledge.

Weiner, James (1997) Televisualist anthropology: representation, aesthetics, politics. *Current Anthropology* 38(2): 197–235.

Wenger, Tisa (2009) *We Have A Religion: The 1920s Pueblo Dance Controversy and American Religious Freedom*. University of North Carolina Press.

Werbner, Richard (1984) The Manchester School in South–Central Africa. *Annual Review of Anthropology* 13: 157–85.

Werner, François (2015) The Archives of the Planet: the life and works of Albert Kahn. *Visual Anthropology* 28(5): 438–50.

Wiessner, Polly (2003) Owners of the future? Calories, cash, casualties and self-sufficiency in the Nyae Nyae area between 1996 and 2003. *Visual Anthropology Review* 19(1–2): 149–59.

Wilmsen, Edwin N. (1999) Knowledge as the source of progress: the Marshall family testament to the 'Bushmen'. *Visual Anthropology* 12(2–3): 213–65.

—— (2003) A Kalahari family named Marshall: "I want a record, not a movie". *Visual Anthropology Review* 19(1–2): 114–27.

Wilson, Pamela and Michelle Stewart, eds (2008) *Global Indigenous Media: Cultures, Poetics, and Politics*. Durham and London: Duke University Press.

Winston, Brian (1995) *Claiming the Real: The Documentary Film Revisited*. London: British Film Institute.

—— (2000) *Lies, Damn Lies and Documentaries*. London: British Film Institute.

—— (2013) Life as narrativised. In Brian Winston, ed., *The Documentary Film Book*, pp. 89–97. Palgrave/Macmillan on behalf of the British Film Institute.

Woodhead, Leslie (2006) Making 'The Mursi'. www.mursi.org/documents-and-texts/published-articles/woodhead-leslie.

Worth, Sol and John Adair (1972) *Through Navajo Eyes: An Exploration in Film Communication and Anthropology*. Bloomington: Indiana University Press.

Wortham, Erica Cusi (2013) *Indigenous Media in Mexico: Culture, Community, and the State*. Durham and London: Duke University Press.

Wright, Terence (1992) Television narrative and ethnographic film. In Peter Crawford and David Turton, eds, *Film as Ethnography*, pp. 274–82. Manchester: Manchester University Press.

Yellen, John (1984) The integration of hunting into prehistoric hunting and gathering economies. In M. Hall and G. Avery, eds, *Frontiers: Southern African Archaeology Today*, pp. 53–64. Cambridge: Cambridge University Press.

Young, Colin (1982a) MacDougall conversations. *RAIN* 50: 5–8.

—— (1982b) Vérité – the true story. *Edinburgh International Television Festival Programme* no. 7, pp. 58–65.

—— (1995) Observational cinema. In Paul Hockings, ed., *Principles of Visual Anthropology*, 2nd edn, pp. 99–113. Berlin and New York: Mouton de Gruyter.

Young, Colin with Edmund Carpenter (1966) Films made by Americans in the Pacific which have any anthropological or ethnographic significance. See unesdoc.unesco.org/images/0014/001437/143776eb.pdf.

Zamorano Villareal, Gabriela (2017) *Indigenous Media and Political Imaginaries in Contemporary Bolivia*. Lincoln: University of Nebraska Press.

Zhang, Zhongyun, ed. (n.d.) *The Eye of the Villager: Yunnan and Vietnam Community-based Visual Education and Communication*. Yunnan Academy of Social Sciences.

513

# Selected film references

THIS filmography is not intended to be a systematic catalogue, but merely a listing of the films that are referred to at some length in this book. The listing is alphabetically by title, but disregarding definite and indefinite articles if these form part of the title (i.e. 'The', 'A', 'An' or foreign language equivalents). When foreign films have an established name in English, I use that by preference and give the original name in parentheses, if known, for example, *Chronicle of a Summer* (*Chronique d'un été*). When foreign films do not have an established name in English, I may offer a translation in parentheses. If the title is one proposed by the original production entity, it is indicated in italics, for example, *Pour la suite du monde (For The Ones To Come)*. If the translation is my own, it is not in italics, for example, *Rituais e Festas Borôro* (Bororo Rituals and Festivals).

The entries should not be regarded as definitive. Many of the details in the sources are contradictory: some sources date films from the year of production, others from year of release. In this listing, I have aimed to give the year of release, but release dates may vary from one country to another, or a film may have been released several times in slightly different forms. There is often a contradiction between the year indicated on the film itself and the year given in accompanying literature or on the DVD case. In this instance, I have generally preferred the year given on the film. Running times and even titles may also vary for a range of different reasons. In many instances, I have made a judgement as to which source of information is most likely to be correct, but I certainly cannot guarantee to have always got it right.

Nor are the entries comprehensive. In general, I list only the director(s) of the film, though when there has been a consultant anthropologist and I know their name, I include them as well, indicated by the abbreviaton 'Anth.:'. Where I know the film to have been part of a series of some kind, or a television 'strand' (a recurrent series of series, continuing over several years) I list that too. All the films should be presumed to be in colour, unless it is indicated that they are monochrome by the abbreviation 'b&w' (i.e. black and white). Similarly, all films should be assumed to have sound unless indicated to the contrary.

Often the entity responsible for the production is not clear from the sources, nor from the film itself: here too, I have often made what is only a partially informed judgement as to the entity principally responsible. When a film is distributed by an agency that I know to be different from the production entity, I include that as well, indicated by the abbreviation 'Dist.'. A given film may be distributed by more than one agency but in most instances, I give only the one best known to me or most likely to be accessible to readers of this book. Many early films can be accessed through my own website, *The Silent Time Machine*, at www.silenttimemachine.net.

A number of production or distribution agencies recur frequently in the listing, and I refer to them by the following acronyms or abbreviations:

AIAS/AIATSIS – Australian Institute of Aboriginal Studies, which in 1989 became the Australian Institute of Aboriginal and Torres Strait Islander Studies.

ANU – Department of Anthropology, Research School of Pacific Studies, Australian National University, Canberra.

BFI – the national British Film Institute, which distributes films both online and in the form of DVDs. One can access the BFI archives at www.bfi. org.uk/archive-collections.

CNC (Centre national du cinéma) – this includes the French national film archive which holds a large collection of early films of ethnographic interest, many of which have been digitised. The online catalogue can be consulted via www.cnc-aff.fr/internet_cnc/Home.aspx?Menu=MNU_ ACCUEIL.

CNRS Images – the audiovisual department of the French national research institute, the Centre National de Recherches Scientifiques. See http:// videotheque.cnrs.fr/ for a complete listing of ethnographic films available online or in the form of DVDs.

DER – Documentary Educational Resources, based in Watertown, on the outskirts of Boston, Massachusetts, USA. Founded by ethnographic film-makers John Marshall and Timothy Asch in 1968. For a comprehensive listing of films distributed by DER, see www.der.org. Many of their films are also distributed through the online streaming platform, Kanopy, at www.kanopy.com.

Penn Museum – this is the abbreviated name of the University of Pennsylvania Museum of Archaeology and Anthropology. This museum offers a substantial archive of films of ethnographic interest online, most of which it produced itself. See https://archive.org/details/UPMAA_films&tab=collection.

NFB/ONF – National Film Board/Office National du Film, Canada. Many of their films are now available online at www.nfb.ca or through the Kanopy on-line streaming platform at www.kanopy.com.

RAI (UK) – Royal Anthropological Institute, based in London, UK (not to be confused with RAI – Radiotelevisione italiana, the Italian state broadcasting company). For a comprehensive listing of films distributed by the Royal Anthropological Institute, see www.rai.org.uk/film.

*Across the Tracks: the Vlach Gypsies in Hungary.* John Blake. 1988. 52 min. Anth.: Michael Stewart. *Disappearing World* strand. Granada Television. Dist.: RAI (UK).

*Age of Reason, The.* David MacDougall. 2004. 86 min. Doon School Quintet, no. 5. Centre for Cross-Cultural Research, ANU. Dist.: RAI (UK).

*Altar of Fire.* Robert Gardner and J.F.Staal. 1976. 45 min. Film Study Center, Harvard University. Dist.: DER.

*American Family, An.* Craig Gilbert. 1973. 720 min. A television series in 12 parts. PBS Television.

*Argument About A Marriage, An.* John Marshall. 1969. 18 min. The !Kung series. Center for Documentary Anthropology (later DER). Dist.: DER.

*Ark, The.* Molly Dineen. 1993. 240 min. Television series in 4 parts. BBC Television. Dist.: BFI.

*Art of Regret, The.* Judith MacDougall and Kathy Zhang. 2007. 60 min. Centre for Cross-Cultural Research, ANU. Dist.: RAI (UK).

*At Patantja Claypan.* Ian Dunlop. 1967. 55 min. b&w. Australian Commonwealth Film Unit for the Australian Institute of Aboriginal Studies. Dist.: Film Australia.

*At the Time of Whaling.* Sarah Elder and Leonard Kammerling. 1974. 38 min. Alaska Native Heritage Film Project, Alaska University Museum. Dist.: DER.

*At the Winter Sea Ice Camp.* Robert Young. 1967. 137 mins (in four parts). Anth.: Asen Balikci. The Netsilik Eskimo series. Education Development Center and NFB/ONF. Dist.: NFB/ONF via www.nfb.ca/subjects/inuit/netsilik. Also via www.kanopy.com.

*Au pays des Dogons* (In the Land of the Dogons). Marcel Griaule. 1941. 11 min. b&w. Société des Films Sirius. Dist.: Éditions Montparnasse in the DVD collection, *Jean Rouch: une aventure africaine,* 2010.

*Au pays des mages noirs* (In the Land of the Black Wizards). Jean Rouch, Pierre Ponty and Jean Sauvy. 1947. 13 min. b&w. Actualités françaises. Dist.: Kinofilm.

*Awareness.* David and Judith MacDougall. 2010. 67 min. Rishi Valley trilogy, no. 3. Centre for Cross-Cultural Research, ANU. Dist.: RAI (UK).

*Ax Fight, The.* Timothy Asch and Napoleon Chagnon. 1975. 30 min. Pennsylvania State University. Dist.: DER.

*Baka: People of the Rainforest.* Phil Agland. 1987. 104 min. DJA River Films for Channel 4 Television.

*Baka: A Cry from the Rainforest.* Phil Agland. 2013. 89 min. River Films for Channel 4 Television.

*Balinese Family, A.* Gregory Bateson and Margaret Mead. 1951. 20 min. b&w. Character Formation in Different Cultures series.

*Balinese Trance Seance, A.* Timothy Asch and Patsy Asch. 1980. 30 min. Anth.: Linda Connor. ANU. Dist.: DER and RAI (UK).

*Basques of Santazi, The.* Leslie Woodhead. 1987. 52 min. Anth.: Sandra Ott. *Disappearing World* strand. Granada Television. Dist.: RAI (UK).

*Bataille sur le grand fleuve* (Battle on the Big River). Jean Rouch. 1952. 33 min. IFAN/ CNC/ Musée de l'Homme. Dist.: Éditions Montparnasse.

*Bathing Babies in Three Cultures.* Gregory Bateson and Margaret Mead. 1954. 12 min. b&w. Character Formation in Different Cultures series.

*Before Columbus.* Brian Moser. 1993. 153 min. Anth.: Stephan Schwartzman. Television series in 3 parts. Central Television.

*Beyond the Clouds.* Phil Agland. 1994. 336 min. Television series in 7 parts. River Films for Channel 4.

*Bitter Roots: The Ends of a Kalahari Myth.* Adrian Strong. 2010. 71 min. Anth.: Claire Ritchie. Dist.: DER.

*Blunden Harbor.* Robert Gardner with William Heick. 1951. 22 min. b&w. Dist.: DER.

*Bougainville.* Patrick O'Reilly. 1935/early 1970s. 70/37 min. b&w. Dist.: CNRS online videothèque.

*Buffalo Dance.* W.K-L. Dickson and William Heise. 1894. 15 sec. b&w. silent. Edison Manufacturing Co. Dist.: Library of Congress, Washington online film collection.

*Buschmann Spricht in den Phonographen (A Bushmann Speaks into the Phonograph).* Rudolf Pöch. 1908/1984. 56 sec. b&w. Viewable at www.youtube.com/watch?v=a2bdPlcrMX4.

*Caught in a Web.* Toni de Bromhead. 1986. 156 min. Television series in 3 parts. Channel 4 Television.

*Celebration of Origins, A.* Timothy Asch and Patsy Asch. 1993. Anth.: E. Douglas Lewis. ANU. Dist.: DER.

*Celso and Cora: A Manila Story.* Gary Kildea. 1983. 104 min. Australian Film Commission and Nippon-AV. Dist.: RAI (UK).

*Chester Grimes.* David Hancock and Herb di Gioia. 1972. 50 min. The Vermont Center for Cultural Studies Inc.

*Childhood Rivalry.* Gregory Bateson and Margaret Mead. 1954. 16 min. b&w. Character Formation in Different Cultures series.

*Chronicle of a Summer (Chronique d'un été).* Jean Rouch and Edgar Morin. 1961. 90 min. b&w. Argos films. Dist.: Éditions Montparnasse (original French version); Criterion (subtitled English version).

*Cimetières dans la falaise* (Cemeteries in the Cliff Face). Jean Rouch. 20 min. Anth.: Marcel Griaule and Germaine Dieterlen. IFAN/CNC/Musée de l'Homme. Dist.: Éditions Montparnasse.

*City on the Steppes, The.* Brian Moser. 1975. 52 min. *Mongolia* series. Granada Television. Dist.: RAI (UK).

*Clearing in the Jungle, A.* Charlie Nairn. 1970. 38 min. Anth.: Jean-Paul Dumont. *Disappearing World* strand. Granada Television. Dist.: RAI (UK).

*Conversations with Dundiwuy.* Ian Dunlop. 1995. 50 min. Film Australia. Dist.: RAI (UK).

*Corumbiara.* Vincent Carelli. 2009. 117 min. Video in the Villages.

*Croisière noire, La.* Léon Poirier. 1926. 52 min. b&w. Société anonyme André Citroën.

*Cuyagua – Devil Dancers.* Paul Henley with Georges Drion. 1986. 52 min. National Film and Television School and Royal Anthropological Institute. Re-edited and re-mastered in 2011, 41 min. Dist.: RAI (UK).

*Cuyagua – The Saint with Two Faces.* Paul Henley with Georges Drion. 1987. 56 min. National Film and Television School and Royal Anthropological Institute. Re-edited and re-mastered in 2011, 43 min. Dist.: RAI (UK).

*Dama d'Ambara, Le* (The Dama of Ambara). Jean Rouch and Germaine Dieterlen. 1980. 62 min. Comité du film ethnographique. Dist.: CNRS Images.

*Dances of the Kwakiutl.* Robert Gardner with William Heick. 1951. 9 min. Dist.: DER.

*Danse indienne* (Indian Dance). Gabriel Veyre. 1898. 50 sec. (?). b&w. silent. Lumière Frères.

*Dead Birds.* Robert Gardner. 1964. 83 min. Film Study Center, Harvard University. Dist.: DER.

*Deep Hearts.* Robert Gardner. 1979. 49 min. Film Study Center, Harvard University. Dist.: DER.

*Delhi: Die Grosse Stadt in Vorderindien* (Delhi: Great Capital of India). Unknown director. 1909. 4 min. stencil-coloured. silent. Pathé Frères. Dist.: BFI online collection.

*Dervishes of Kurdistan.* Brian Moser. 1973. 52 min. *Disappearing World* strand. Granada Television. Dist.: RAI (UK).

*Descending with Angels.* Christian Suhr. 2013. 74 min. Persona Films. Dist.: DER.

*Desert People.* Ian Dunlop. 1967. 49 min. b&w. Australian Commonwealth Film Unit for the Australian Institute of Aboriginal Studies. Dist.: Film Australia.

*Diary of a Maasai Village.* Melissa Llewelyn-Davies. 1985. 220 min. In five parts. BBC Bristol. Dist.: DER.

*Dinner Party, The.* Paul Watson. 1997. 50 min. Channel 4 Television.

*Divorce Iranian Style.* Kim Longinotto. 1998. 80 min. Anth.: Ziba Mir-Hosseini. Channel 4 Television.

*Diya.* Judith MacDougall. 2001. 55 min. Dist.: RAI (UK).

*Djungguwan at Gurka'wuy.* Ian Dunlop. 1989. 233 min. Anth.: Howard Morphy. Australian Commonwealth Film Unit. Dist.: Film Australia.

*Doon School Chronicles*. David MacDougall. 2000. 140 min. Doon School Quintet, no. 1. Centre for Cross-Cultural Research, ANU. Dist.: RAI.

*Dreams from the Forest*. Jean-Paul Davidson. 1990. 50 min. Anth.: Thomas Gregor. *Under the Sun* strand. BBC Television.

*Duka's Dilemma. A Visit to Hamar, Southern Ethiopia*. Jean Lydall and Kaira Strecker. 2001. 87 min. IWF Knowledge and Media. Dist.: DER.

*Dust and Ashes*. Michael Yorke. 1989. 50 min. *Under the Sun* strand. BBC Television.

*Duwayne Masure*. Herb di Gioia and David Hancock. 40 min. b&w. University of California Los Angeles, Motion Pictures Division. MFA Thesis Film.

*Elephant Boy*. Robert J. Flaherty and Zoltan Korda. 1937. 85 min. b&w. London Films/ United Artists.

*Eskimo, The: Fight for Life*. Robert Young. 1970. 50 min. Anth.: Asen Balikci. Education Development Center. Dist.: Memorial University Newfoundland Distance Learning and Teaching Support. http://collections.mun.ca/cdm4/item_viewer.php?CISOROOT=/ extension&CISOPTR=2974

*Eskimos of Pond Inlet: The People's Land*. Michael Grigsby. 1977. 52 min. Anth.: Hugh Brody. *Disappearing World* strand. Granada Television. Dist.: RAI (UK).

*Eu já virei espirito* (I Have Already Become A Spirit). Carlos Fausto and Takumã Kuikuru. 2013. 18 min. Video in the Villages.

*Eux et Moi (Them and Me)*. Stéphane Breton. 2001. 63 min. Les Films d'Ici for Arte (France).

*Face Values*. David Cordingley. 1978. 365 min. Anth.: Jeremy Boissevain, Patricia Caplan, Anthony Forge, Jean La Fontaine, Anne Sutherland, Terence Turner. Television series in 7 parts. BBC Television.

*Factory, The*. Paul Watson. 1995. 250 min. Television series in 5 parts. Granada Television for Channel 4.

*Familiar Places*. David MacDougall. 1980. 50 min. AIAS. Dist.: RAI (UK).

*Family, The*. Paul Watson. 1974. 360 min. A television series in 12 parts. BBC.

*Family of Man*. John Percival. 1969–70. 350 min. Anth.: Roger Ballard, Thomas Larson and Andrew Strathern. A television series in 7 parts. BBC.

*Feast, The*. Timothy Asch and Napoleon Chagnon. 1970. 29 min. Pennsylvania State University. Dist.: DER.

*Feathered Arrows*. Jean-Paul Davidson. 1990. 50 min. Anth.: Thomas Gregor. *Under the Sun* strand. BBC Television.

*Fire Will Eat Us*. Leslie Woodhead. 2001. 75 min. Anth.: David Turton. Granada Television for Channel 4.

*First Days in the Life of a New Guinea Baby*. Gregory Bateson and Margaret Mead. 1952. 15 min. b&w. Character Formation in Different Cultures series.

*Fishing at the Stone Weir, Parts 1 & 2*. Douglas Wilkinson and Quentin Brown. 1967. Anth.: Asen Balikci. 57 min. NFB/ONF.

*Fishing Party, The*. Paul Watson. 1986. 40 min. BBC Television.

*Foreign Parts*. Véréna Paravel and John Paul Sniadecki. 2010. 80 min. Sensory Ethnography Lab, University of Harvard.

*Forest of Bliss*. Robert Gardner. 1985. 89 min. Anth.: Åkos Östör. Film Study Center, Harvard University.

*Forest People (Lesnye liudi)*. Alexander Litvinov. 1928. 45 min. b&w. silent. Sovkino.

*From the Ikpeng Children to the World*. Natuyu Yuwipo Txicão, Karané Txicão and Kumaré Txicão. 2002. 35 min. Video in the Villages. Dist.: DER.

*Gaea Girls*. Kim Longinotto and Jano Williams. 2000. 106 min. Channel 4 Television.

*Gandhi's Children*. David MacDougall. 2008. 185 min. Centre for Cross-Cultural Research, Australian National University. Dist.: RAI (UK).

*God Gave Us the Leaf*. Brian Moser. 1985. 53 min. Anth.: Mauricio Mamani. *Frontier* series. ATV.

*Good-bye Old Man*. David MacDougall. 1977. 70 min. AIAS. Dist.: RAI (UK).

*Grass – A Nation's Battle for Life*. Merian C. Cooper and Ernest B. Schoedsack. 1925. 71 min. b&w. silent. Paramount/Famous Players Lasky. Dist.: Milestone Films.

*Group of Women, A.* John Marshall. 1961. 5 min. The !Kung series. Center for Documentary Anthropology (later DER).

*Guardians of the Flutes: the secrets of male initiation.* Paul Reddish. 1994. 50 min. Anth.: Gilbert Herdt. *Under the Sun* strand. BBC Television.

*Heart of the Angel, The.* Molly Dineen. 1989. 40 min. BBC Television.

*HMS Brilliant.* Chris Terrill. 1995. 300 min. Television series in 6 parts. BBC Television.

*Hopi Indians of the Southwest and Snake Dance of the 9th Day.* Unknown director. 1925. 17 min. b&w. silent. American Museum of Natural History.

*House-Opening, The.* Judith MacDougall. 1980. 45 min. AIAS. Dist.: RAI (UK).

*Hunters, The.* John Marshall. 1957. 72 min. The !Kung series. Film Study Center, Harvard University. Dist.: DER.

*Hyperwomen, The.* Leonardo Sette, Carlos Fausto. 2011. 80 min. Video in the Villages.

*Iauaretê – Waterfall of the Jaguars.* Vincent Carelli. 2006. 48 min. Video in the Villages.

*Ika Hands.* Robert Gardner. 1988. 58 min. Film Study Center, University of Harvard. Dist.: DER.

*Imbalu: Ritual of Manhood of the Gisu of Uganda.* Richard Hawkins and Suzette Heald. 1988. 69 min. University of California Los Angeles, Ethnographic Film Program. Dist.: RAI (UK).

*Imbé Gikegii* (Scent of the Pequi Fruit). Takumã and Maricá Kuikuro. 2006. 36 min. Video in the Villages.

*In Search of a Bororo Mr. Right.* Flavia Kremer. 2019. 30 min. University of Manchester, Brazilian Ministry of Culture.

*In the Land of the Head Hunters: A Drama of Primitive Life on the Shores of the North Pacific.* Edward S. Curtis. 1914. Originally approx 90 min. b&w (colour tinted). Re-released in a substantially re-edited 47-minute form 1973 as *In the Land of the War Canoes* by Bill Holm and George Quimby. Released for a third time in 2008, under the original title and closer to the original editorial structure, by Milestone Films in a 66-min. version supervised by Brad Evans and Aaron Glass.

*Jaguar.* Jean Rouch. 1971. 92 min. Les Films de la Pléiade. Dist.: Éditions Montparnasse.

*Jero on Jero: A Balinese Trance Seance Observed.* Timothy Asch and Patsy Asch. 17 min. Anth.: Linda Connor. ANU. Dist.: DER.

*Jero Tapakan: Stories from the Life of a Balinese Healer.* Timothy Asch and Patsy Asch. 1983. 26 min. Anth.: Linda Connor. ANU. Dist.: DER.

*Joking Relationship, A.* John Marshall. 1962. 13 min. The !Kung series. Center for Documentary Anthropology (later DER).

*Kalahari Family, A.* John Marshall. 2002. 330 min. Television series in 5 parts. Dist.: DER.

*Kalanda- The Knowledge of the Bush.* Lorenzo Ferrarini. 2015. 62 min. Dist.: lorenzoferrarini.com.

*Karam in Jaipur.* David MacDougall. 2001. 54 min. Doon School Quintet, no. 3. Centre for Cross-Cultural Research, ANU. Dist.: RAI (UK).

*Karba's First Years.* Gregory Bateson and Margaret Mead. 1952. 20 min. b&w. Character Formation in Different Cultures series.

*Kataragama – A God for All Seasons.* Charlie Nairn. 1973. 52 min. Anth.: Gananath Obeyesekere. *Disappearing World* strand. Granada Television. Dist.: RAI (UK).

*Kazakhs, The.* André Singer. 1983. 52 min. Anth.: Shirin Akiner. *Inside China* series. Granada Television. Dist.: RAI (UK).

*Kenya Boran.* David MacDougall and James Blue. 1974. Parts I and II. 33 min. each part. Anth.: Paul Baxter. Faces of Change series. American Universities Field Staff. Dist.: DER.

*Kirghiz of Afghanistan, The.* (1975). Charlie Nairn. 1975. 52 min. Anth.: M. Nazif Shahrani. *Disappearing World* strand. Granada Television. Dist.: RAI (UK).

*Koriam's Law and the Dead who Govern.* Gary Kildea and Andrea Simon. 2005. 110 min. Anth.: Andrew Lattas. Research School of Pacific and Asian Studies, ANU and Arcadia Pictures, New York. Dist.: RAI (UK).

*Kula – Argonauts of the Western Pacific.* Yasuko Ichioka. 1971. 66 min. Our Wonderful World series. Nippon A–V.

*Kwakiutl of British Columbia, The: a Documentary by Franz Boas.* Franz Boas and Bill Holm. 1930/1972. 48 min. b&w. Footage shot by Boas in 1930 and re-edited by Holm in 1972. Burke Museum, University of Washington, Seattle.

*Kwegu, The.* Leslie Woodhead. 1982. 52 min. Anth.: David Turton. *Disappearing World* strand. Rebroadcast in 1985 as part of the *In Search of Cool Ground* trilogy. Granada Television.

*Land of the Long Day.* Douglas Wilkinson. 1952. 38 min. NFB/ONF.

*Land is Bad, The.* Leslie Woodhead. 1991. 52 min. Anth.: David Turton. *Disappearing World* strand. Granada Television. Dist.: RAI (UK).

*Land Without Bread (Las Hurdes – Tierra sin pan).* Luis Buñuel. 1933. 30 min. b&w.

*Last of the Cuiva, The.* Brian Moser. 1971. 65 min. Anth.: Bernard Arcand. *Disappearing World* strand. Granada Television. Dist.: RAI (UK).

*Leap Across the Cattle, The: an initiation rite of the Hamar, southern Ethiopia.* Ivo Strecker. 1979. 46 min. IWF.

*Learning to Dance in Bali.* Gregory Bateson and Margaret Mead. 1978. 10 min. b&w.

*Left-handed Man of Madagascar, The.* Jeremy Marre. 1990. 50 min. Anth.: John Mack. *Under the Sun* strand. BBC Television.

*Leviathan.* Véréna Paravel and Lucien Taylor. 2012. 87 min. Sensory Ethnography Lab, University of Harvard.

*Life Apart, A.* Michael Grigsby. 1973. 65 min. Granada Television.

*Link-Up Diary.* David MacDougall. 1987. 86 min. AIAS. Dist.: RAI (UK).

*Living with the Revolution.* Leslie Woodhead. 1983. 52 min. Anth.: Barbara Hazard. *Inside China* series. Granada Television. Dist.: RAI (UK).

*Lorang's Way: A Turkana Man.* David and Judith MacDougall. 1979. 69 min. *Turkana Conversations* series, no. 1. Rice University Media Center. Dist.: RAI (UK).

*Louisiana Story.* Robert Flaherty. 1948. 78 min. b&w. Standard Oil.

*Loved by a Maori Chieftess.* Gaston Méliès. 1913. 34 min. b&w. Star Film.

*Madame l'eau.* Jean Rouch. 1992. 103/120/135 min. (various versions). NF1/SODAPERAGA/BBC.

*Madarrpa Funeral at Gurka'wuy.* Ian Dunlop. 1979. 88 min. Anth.: Howard Morphy. Film Australia. Dist.: RAI (UK).

*Magical Death.* Napoleon Chagnon. 1973. 29 min. Pennsylvania State University. Dist.: DER.

*Maîtres fous, Les* (The Mad Masters). Jean Rouch. 1955. 29 min. Les Films de la Pléiade. Dist.: Éditions Montparnasse.

*Man of Aran.* Robert Flaherty. 1934. 77 min. b&w. Gainsborough Pictures.

*Manakamana.* Stephanie Spray and Pacho Velez. 2014. 111 min. Sensory Ethnography Lab, University of Harvard.

*Marathon.* Robert Gardner and Joyce Chopra. 1965. 28 min. Film Study Center, Harvard.

*Martírio.* Vincent Carelli. Co-directed by Ernest de Carvalho and Tita (Tatiana Soares de Almeida). 2016. 162 min. Papo Amarelo and Video in the Villages.

*Masai Manhood.* Chris Curling. 1975. 52 min. Anth.: Melissa Llewelyn-Davies. *Disappearing World* strand. Granada Television. Dist.: RAI (UK).

*Masai Women.* Chris Curling. 1974. 52 min. Anth.: Melissa Llewelyn-Davies. *Disappearing World* strand. Granada Television. Dist.: RAI (UK).

*Matto Grosso, the Great Brazilian Wilderness.* John Clarke, Floyd Crosby and David Newell. 1932. 48 min. b&w. Dist.: Penn Museum.

*Medium Is the Masseuse, The: A Balinese Massage with Jero Tapakan.* Timothy Asch and Patsy Asch. 1983. 30 min. Anth.: Linda Connor. ANU. Dist.: DER.

*Meeting the Ancestors (A Arca dos Zo'é).* Vincent Carelli. 1993. 22 min. Anth.: Dominique Gallois. Video in the Villages. Dist.: DER.

*Mehinaku, The.* Carlos Pasini. 1974. 52 min. Anth.: Thomas Gregor. *Disappearing World* strand. Granada Television. Dist.: RAI (UK).

*Memories and Dreams.* Melissa Llewelyn-Davies. 1993. 90 min. *Fine Cut* television strand. BBC Television.

*Men Bathing.* John Marshall. 1973. 14 min. !Kung series. DER.

*Migrants, The.* Leslie Woodhead. 1985. 52 min. Anth.: David Turton. *In Search of Cool Ground* trilogy, *Disappearing World* strand. Granada Television. Dist.: RAI (UK).

*Millenium: Tribal Wisdom and the Modern World.* Adrian Malone. 1992. 600 min. Anth.: David Maybury-Lewis. Television series in 10 parts. Adrian Malone Productions.

*Moana: A Romance of the Golden Age.* Robert Flaherty. 1926. 85 min. Famous Players-Lasky Corporation.

*Moi, un Noir* (Me, a Black Man). Jean Rouch. 1960. 73 min. Les Films de la Pléiade. Dist.: Éditions Montparnasse.

*Mursi, The.* Leslie Woodhead. 1974. 52 min. Anth.: David Turton. *Disappearing World* strand. Rebroadcast in 1985 as part of the *In Search of Cool Ground* trilogy. Granada Television. Dist.: RAI (UK).

*N/um Tchai: the Ceremonial Dance of the !Kung Bushmen.* John Marshall. 1969. 20 min. b&w. The !Kung series. Center for Documentary Anthropology (later DER).

*N!ai: the story of a !Kung woman.* John Marshall and Adrienne Miesmer. 1980. 58 min. The !Kung series. DER.

*Naim and Jabar.* Herb di Gioia and David Hancock. 1974. 50 min. Faces of Change series. Dist.: DER.

*Nanook of the North.* Robert Flaherty. 1922. 65 min. Revillon Frères.

*Native Land.* Tim Raynor. 1989. Anth.: Nigel Barley. Television series in 6 parts. Channel 4 Television.

*Navajo Film Themselves.* Mike Anderson, Mary Jane Tsosie, Maxine Tsosie, Susie Benally, John Nelson, Alfred Clah, Alta Kahn. 1966. 125 min. b&w. Silent. Series of 7 films. University of Pennsylvania. Dist.: Penn Museum.

*Nawi.* David and Judith MacDougall. 1970. 20 min. University of California Los Angeles, Ethnographic Film Program. Dist.: RAI (UK).

*New Boys, The.* David MacDougall. 2003. 100 min. Doon School Quintet, no. 4 . Centre for Cross-Cultural Research, ANU. Dist.: RAI (UK).

*Newest Revolution, The.* Leslie Woodhead. 1983. 52 min. Anth.: Barbara Hazard. *Inside China* series. Granada Television. Dist.: RAI (UK).

*Ngat is Dead: Studying Mortuary Traditions.* Christian Suhr and Ton Otto. 2009. 59 min. Moesgaard Film. Dist.: RAI (UK).

*Nguné Elü* (The Day the Moon Menstruated). Takumã and Maricá Kuikuro. 2004. 28 min. Video in the Villages.

*Nine Forsaken Fragments.* Robert Gardner. 2009. 50 min. Studio7Arts.

*Nitha.* Leslie Woodhead. 1991. 52 min. Anth.: David Turton. *Disappearing World* strand. Granada Television. Dist.: RAI (UK).

*Nomads.* Various directors. 1991. Television series of 4 parts. Malone Gill for Channel 4 Television.

*Nuer, The.* Hilary Harris and George Breidenbach, with the assistance of Robert Gardner. 1971. 73 min. Film Study Center, Harvard University. Dist.: DER.

*On the Edge of the Gobi.* Brian Moser. 1975. 52 min. *Mongolia* series. Granada Television. Dist.: RAI (UK).

*On the Spring Ice.* Sarah Elder and Leonard Kamerling. 1975. 45 min. Alaska Native Heritage Film Project, Alaska University Museum. Dist.: DER.

*Ongka's Big Moka.* Charlie Nairn. 1974. 52 min. Anth.: Andrew Strathern. *Disappearing World* strand. Granada Television. Dist.: RAI (UK).

*Our Way of Loving.* Joanna Head and Jean Lydall. 1994. 50 min. *Under the Sun* strand. BBC Television.

*Panare, The: Scenes from the Frontier.* Chris Curling. 1982. 55 min. Anth.: Paul Henley. *Worlds Apart* strand. BBC Television (Bristol). Dist.: RAI (UK).

*People of the Australian Western Desert.* Ian Dunlop. 1967. 314 min. b&w. A series in 19 parts. Australian Commonwealth Film Unit for the Australian Institute of Aboriginal Studies. Dist.: Film Australia.

*People of the Barrio.* Brian Moser. 1980. 52 min. Anth.: Caroline Moser. ATV Television.

*People of the Islands.* Hugh Brody. 1982. 80 min. Channel 4 Television.

*Peter and Jane Flint.* David Hancock and Herb di Gioia. 1975. 120 min. The Vermont Center for Cultural Studies Inc.

*Peter Murray.* David Hancock and Herb di Gioia. 1975. 50 min. The Vermont Center for Cultural Studies Inc.

*Photo Wallahs: An Encounter with Photography in Mussoorie, a North Indian Hill Station.* David and Judith MacDougall. 1991. 59 min. Oxnard Film Production. Dist.: RAI (UK).

*Piraparaná.* Brian Moser and Donald Tayler. 1965. 27 min. Derrick Knight and Partners.

*Pirinop, My First Contact (Pirinop, Meu Primeiro Contato).* Mari Corrêa, Kumaré Txicão and Karané Txicão. 2007. 83 min. Video in the Villages.

*Planète Baruya.* Ian Dunlop. 1976. 202 min. Anth.: Maurice Godelier. Commonwealth Film Unit/CNRS/FR3. Dist.: CNRS Images.

*Police.* Charles Stewart and Roger Graeff. 1982. 405 min. Television series in 9 parts. BBC Bristol.

*Pour la suite du monde* (For the Ones to Come). Michel Brault and Pierre Perrault. 1962. 105 min. b&w. NFB/ONF.

*Primitive Peoples of the Matto Grosso: 'Bororo'* and *Primitive Peoples of the Matto Grosso: 'Xingu'.* Ted Nemeth and Vincent Petrullo. 1941. 18 min. and 16 min. b&w. Dist.: Penn Museum website.

*Pyramide humaine, La* (The Human Pyramid). Jean Rouch. 1961. 88 min. Les Films de la Pléiade. Dist.: Éditions Montparnasse.

*Reclaiming the Forest.* Paul Henley with Georges Drion. 1985. 39 min. National Film and Television School and Royal Anthropological Institute. Dist.: RAI (UK).

*Releasing the Spirits: A Village Cremation in Bali.* Patsy Asch, Timothy Asch and Linda Connor. 1991. 41 min. ANU. Dist.: DER.

*Rendille, The.* Chris Curling. 1977. 52 min. Anth.: Anders Grum. *Disappearing World* strand. Granada Television.

*Returning Home: Revival of a Bosnian Village.* Tone Bringa and Peter Loizos. 2001. 48 min. Dist.: Nordic Anthropological Film Association.

*Rêve plus fort que la mort, Le* (The Dream more Powerful than Death). Jean Rouch and Bernard Surugue. 2002. 88 min. AMIP, IRD, CNRS Images, CNC, CFE, Clea Productions. Dist.: CNRS Images.

*Rituais e Festas Borôro* (Bororo Rituals and Festivals). Luiz Thomaz Reis. 1917. 20 min. b&w. Conselho Nacional de Proteção aos Índios. Dist.: Museo do Índio on-line archive.

*Rivers of Sand.* Robert Gardner. 1974. 83 min. Film Study Center, Harvard University. Dist.: DER.

*Runaway.* Kim Longinotto. 2001. 87 min. Anth.: Ziba Mir-Hosseini. Channel 4 Television.

*Saints and Spirits: Religious Expression in Morocco.* Melissa Llewelyn-Davies and Elizabeth Fernea. 1979. 26 min. Center for Middle Eastern Studies, University of Texas and Granada Television. Dist.: Icarus Films.

*Salma.* Kim Longinotto. 2013. 90 min. Channel 4 Television.

*SchoolScapes: Scenes from a School in South India.* David MacDougall. 2007. 77 min. Rishi Valley trilogy, no. 2. Centre for Cross-Cultural Research, ANU and Fieldwork Films. Dist.: Berkeley Media (US) and RAI (UK).

*Secrets of the Tribe.* José Padilha. 2010. 98 min. Avenue B/ Zazen Productions. Dist.: DER.

*Shalako Ceremonial.* Owen Cattell. 1923. 29 min. b&w. Silent. American Museum of Natural History.

*Shaman and His Apprentice, The.* Howard Reid. 1989. 50 min. Anth.: Graham Townsley. *Under the Sun* strand. BBC Television.

*Shanghai Vice.* Phil Agland. 1999. 336 min. Television series in 7 parts. River Films for Channel 4 Television.

*Sheep Rushes.* Lucien Castaing-Taylor. 2007. 80 min. A series of 8 installation films. Sensory Ethnography Lab, University of Harvard.

*Sigui synthèse (1967–1973). L'invention de la parole et de la mort* (Sigui synthesis, 1967–73 – the Invention of Speech and of Death). Jean Rouch and Germaine Dieterlin. 1981. 120 min. Comité du Film Ethnographique, Musée de l'Homme. Dist.: Éditions Montparnasse.
*Sisters in Law.* Kim Longinotto and Florence Ayisi. 2005. 105 min. Channel 4 Television.
*Sioux Ghost Dance.* W. K.-L. Dickson and William Heise. 1894. 21 sec. b&w. silent. Edison Manufacturing Co. Dist.: Library of Congress, Washington on-line film collection.
*Sixth Part of the World, A.* Dziga Vertov. 1926. 73 min. b&w. silent. Sovkino. Dist.: Austrian Film Museum, DVD no. 53.
*Small Family Business, A.* Brian Moser. 1985. 53 min. Anth.: Stephen Hugh Jones. *Frontier* television series. ATV.
*Soho Stories.* Chris Terrill. 1996. 480 min. Television series in 12 parts. BBC Television.
*Some Alien Creatures.* David MacDougall. 2005. 74 min. Rishi Valley trilogy, no. 1. Centre for Cross-Cultural Research, ANU. Dist.: RAI (UK).
*Some Women of Marrakech.* Melissa Llewelyn-Davies. 1977. 52 min. Anth.: Elizabeth Fernea. Anth.: Melissa Llewelyn-Davies. *Disappearing World* strand. Granada Television. Dist.: RAI (UK).
*Song of Ceylon, The.* Basil Wright. 1934. 38 min. b&w. GPO Film Unit. Dist.: BFI Screenonline.
*Sons of Haji Omar.* Asen Balikci, Timothy Asch and Patsy Asch. 1978. 58 min. NFB/ONF. Dist.: DER.
*Sons of Shiva.* Robert Gardner and Ákos Östör. 1985. 29 min. *Pleasing God* series. Harvard Film Study Center. Dist.: DER.
*Sous les masques noirs* (Beneath the Black African Masks). Marcel Griaule. 1941. 9 min. b&w. Société des Films Sirius. Dist.: Éditions Montparnasse in the DVD collection, *Jean Rouch: une aventure africaine*, 2010.
*Spear and Sword, The: A Ceremonial Payment of Bridewealth. The Island of Roti, Eastern Indonesia.* Timothy Asch and Patsy Asch. 1988. 22 min. Anth.: James Fox. ANU. Dist.: DER.
*Sso: rite indigène des Etons et des Manguisas.* Maurice Bertaut and René Bugniet. 1935. 56 min. b&w. Haut Commissariat de la République française au Cameroun.
*Storyteller, The.* Jean-Paul Davidson. 1990. 50 min. Anth.: Emilienne Ireland. *Bookmark* strand. BBC Television.
*Strangers Abroad.* André Singer. 1986. 312 min. Television series in 6 parts. Central Television.
*Strangeways.* Rex Bloomstein. 1980. Television series in 8 parts. BBC Television.
*Sunny and the Dark Horse.* David and Judith MacDougall. 1986. 85 min. AIAS. Dist.: RAI (UK).
*Survivors of the Rainforest.* Andy Jillings. 1994. 52 min. Anth.: Jacques Lizot. *Fragile Earth* strand. CSI Films for Channel 4 Television.
*Sylvania Waters.* Paul Watson. 1992. 360 min. Television series in 12 parts. BBC Television.
*Sweetgrass.* Ilisa Barbash and Lucien Castaing-Taylor. 2009. 105 min. University of Colorado at Boulder and University of Harvard. Dist.: www.cinemaguild.com
*Takeover.* David and Judith MacDougall. 1979. 88 min. AIAS. Dist.: RAI (UK).
*Tambours d'avant, Les: Tourou et Bitti* (The Drums of Yesteryear: Tourou and Bitti). Jean Rouch. 1972. 12 min. Comité du Film Ethnographique. Dist.: Éditions Montparnasse.
*Tempus de Baristas.* David MacDougall. 1993. 100 min. Istituto Superiore Regionale Etnografico (Nuoro). Dist.: RAI (UK).
*Through These Eyes.* Charles Laird. 2004. 55 min. NFB/ONF. See www.nfb.ca/film/through_these_eyes.
*Titicut Follies.* Wiseman, Frederick with John Marshall. 1967. 84 min. b&w. Zipporah Films.
*To Get That Country.* David MacDougall. 1978. 70 min. AIAS. Dist.: RAI (UK).
*To Live with Herds.* David MacDougall. 1972. 70 min. b&w. University of California Los Angeles, Ethnographic Film Program/ Rice University Media Center. Dist.: RAI (UK).
*Towards Baruya Manhood.* Ian Dunlop. 1972. 465 min. In 9 parts. Anth.: Maurice Godelier. Commonwealth Film Unit. Dist.: RAI (UK).
*Tracks Across Sand. The ≠Khomani San of the Southern Kalahari. The story of a land claim.* Hugh Brody. 228 min. A collection of 17 films. Comic Relief, Open Channels, University of the Fraser Valley. Dist.: www.facetofacemedica.ca.

*Trance and Dance in Bali.* Gregory Bateson and Margaret Mead. 1952. 22 min. b&w. Character Formation in Different Cultures series. Dist.: Library of Congress on-line video collection.

*Transfiction.* Johannes Sjöberg. 2007. 57 min. Centre for Screen Studies, University of Manchester. Dist.: RAI (UK).

*Trobriand Cricket: An Ingenious Response to Colonialism.* Gary Kildea and Jerry W. Leach. 1976. Cambridge Museum of Archaeology and Ethnology and others. 52 min. Dist.: RAI (UK).

*Two Girls Go Hunting.* Joanna Head and Jean Lydall. 1991. 50 min. *Under the Sun* strand. BBC Television.

*Uksuum Cauyai – The Drums of Winter.* Sarah Elder and Leonard Kamerling. 1988. 90 min. Alaska Native Heritage Film Project, Alaska University Museum. Dist.: DER.

*Under the Men's Tree.* David and Judith MacDougall. 1973. 15 min. b&w. University of California Los Angeles, Ethnographic Film Program. Dist.: RAI (UK).

*Under the Palace Wall.* David MacDougall. 2014. 53 min. Research School of the Humanities, ANU and Fieldwork Films. Dist.: RAI (UK).

*Village, The.* Mark McCarty and Paul Hockings. 1968. 70 min. b&w. University of Califonia Los Angeles, Ethnographic Film Program. Dist.: DER.

*Voyage au Congo.* André Gide and Marc Allégret. 1927. 113 min. b&w. silent. Pierre Braunberger. Dist.: Icarus Films, see icarusfilms.com/if-voy.

*Waiting for Harry.* Kim McKenzie. 1982. 57 min. AIAS. Dist.: RAI (UK).

*War of the Gods.* Brian Moser. 1971. 65 min. Anth.: Peter Silverwood-Cope, Christine and Stephen Hugh-Jones. *Disappearing World* strand. Granada Television. Dist.: RAI (UK).

*Water of Words, The: A Cultural Ecology of an Eastern Indonesian Island.* Timothy Asch and Patsy Asch. 1983. 30 min. Anth.. James Fox. ANU. Dist.: DER.

*We are All Neighbours.* Debbie Christie. 1993. 52 min. Anth.: Tone Bringa. *Disappearing World* strand. Granada Television. Dist.: RAI (UK).

*Wedding Camels, The: A Turkana Marriage.* David and Judith MacDougall. 1977. 108 min. *Turkana Conversations* series, no. 3. Rice University Media Center. Dist.: RAI (UK).

*Wife Among Wives, A.* David and Judith MacDougall. 1981. 67 min. *Turkana Conversations* series, no. 2. Rice University Media Center. Dist.: RAI (UK).

*With Morning Hearts.* David MacDougall. 110 min. 2001. Doon School Quintet, no. 2. Centre for Cross-Cultural Research, ANU. Dist.: RAI (UK).

*Women Who Smile, The.* Joanna Head and Jean Lydall. 1990. 50 min. *Under the Sun* strand. BBC Television.

*Women's Olamal, The: the organisation of a Maasai fertility ceremony.* Melissa Llewelyn-Davies. 1984. 113 min. *Worlds Apart* strand. BBC Television, Bristol.

*Yenendi: les hommes qui font la pluie* (Yenendi – the Rainmakers). Jean Rouch. 1952. 25 min. IFAN/CNC/Musée de l'Homme. Dist.: CNRS Images.

# Index

Note:

- Page numbers in bold indicate passages in which the person or topic listed is the subject of extended discussion.
- Films are normally listed by title under the director's name, when the latter is known, or failing that, under the name of the production company. Readers unsure of a director's name should consult the selected filmography on pp. 514–24. Films that do not appear in that filmography are listed in this index directly under the title but are then cross-referenced to the director or the production company.
- Texts are listed under the name of the author.
- 'n.' after a page reference indicates the number of a note on that page.